Lecture Notes
in Business Information Processing   11

Series Editors

Wil van der Aalst
Eindhoven Technical University, The Netherlands
John Mylopoulos
University of Trento, Italy
Norman M. Sadeh
Carnegie Mellon University, Pittsburgh, PA, USA
Michael J. Shaw
University of Illinois, Urbana-Champaign, IL, USA
Clemens Szyperski
Microsoft Research, Redmond, WA, USA

Richard F. Paige   Bertrand Meyer (Eds.)

Objects, Components, Models and Patterns

46th International Conference, TOOLS EUROPE 2008
Zurich, Switzerland, June 30–July 4, 2008
Proceedings

 Springer

Volume Editors

Richard F. Paige
University of York
Department of Computer Science, York, UK
E-mail: paige@cs.york.ac.uk

Bertrand Meyer
ETH Zurich
Department of Computer Science, Zurich, Switzerland
E-mail: Bertrand.Meyer@inf.ethz.ch

Library of Congress Control Number: 2008929604

ACM Computing Classification (1998): D.2, H.1, K.6

ISSN   1865-1348
ISBN   978-3-540-69823-4 Springer Berlin Heidelberg New York

Springer is a part of Springer Science+Business Media

springer.com

© Springer-Verlag Berlin Heidelberg 2008

Typesetting: Camera-ready by author, data conversion by Scientific Publishing Services, Chennai, India
Printed on acid-free paper   SPIN: 12282777   06/3180   5 4 3 2 1 0

Preface

The TOOLS conference series started in 1989 and, over the following 15 years, held 45 sessions: TOOLS EUROPE, TOOLS USA, TOOLS PACIFIC, TOOLS CHINA and TOOLS EASTERN EUROPE. TOOLS played a major role in the spread of object-oriented and component technologies; many seminal software concepts now taken for granted were first discussed at TOOLS, taking advantage of the informal, application-oriented, technically intense and marketing-free atmosphere of the conference. Invited speakers have included countless luminaries of science and industry.

After an interruption of four years, TOOLS started again in June 2007, hosted by ETH Zurich with great success. TOOLS has broadened its scope beyond the original topics of object technology and component-based development to encompass all modern, practical approaches to software development. In doing so, it kept with the traditional TOOLS spirit of technical excellence, focus on practicality, combination of theory and applications, and reliance on the best experts from academia and industry.

The 2008 edition of the conference was again held at ETH Zurich, and continued to reflect TOOLS's fundamental tradition. This year, TOOLS was co-located with two other distinct-but-related conferences: the International Conference on Model Transformation (ICMT), with a strong focus on model-driven engineering and, in particular, model transformation technology and theory; and the International Conference on Software Engineering for Offshore and Outsourced Development (SEAFOOD). This co-location, combined with three excellent workshops (on Web 2.0 Pattern Mining, Business Support and MDA, and FAMIX and Moose in Software Engineering) and five tutorials, gave the TOOLS week an unparalleled program of practical and theoretical talks, and a fantastic opportunity for researchers and practitioners in software development to network.

The TOOLS week of conferences was further distinguished by a number of excellent keynote speakers: Michael Brodie (Verizon), John Mylopoulos (University of Trento and the University of Toronto), Erik Meijer (Microsoft), and the ICMT keynote speaker Krzysztof Czarnecki (University of Waterloo). These speakers reflect the TOOLS themes of practicality, combination of theory and application, and substantial expertise.

This volume includes the 21 fully refereed and revised papers accepted by the TOOLS Program Committee. The committee received 58 submissions, a total slightly lower than the previous TOOLS conference, but offset by the submissions received by the co-located events. All told, submission to all three conferences held in the TOOLS week totalled 149, and the overall acceptance rate at these three conferences was 33%.

The 46th TOOLS conference was the result of the hard work of many hundreds of people, including the Program Committee and additional reviewers who worked hard – and to somewhat unrealistic deadlines! – to select papers, offer feedback and advice, and to ensure that the technical quality that TOOLS is known for was upheld. The Organizing Committee worked hard to schedule all the events (a complicated undertaking in itself!) We would like to thank everyone for their invaluable contributions.

June 2008   Richard Paige

Organization

TOOLS EUROPE 2008 was organized by the Chair of Software Engineering, ETH Zurich, Switzerland.

Executive Committee

Conference Chair	Bertrand Meyer (ETH Zurich, Switzerland)
Program Chair	Richard Paige (University of York, UK)
Publicity Chairs	Laurence Tratt (University of Bournemouth, UK)
	Philippe Lahire (Université de Nice Sophia-Antipolis, France)
Workshop Chairs	Stéphane Ducasse (INRIA Lille, France)
	Alexandre Bergel (INRIA Lille, France)
Tutorial Chairs	Phil Brooke (University of Teesside, UK)
	Manuel Oriol (ETH Zurich, Switzerland)
Organizing Committee	Claudia Günthart, Manuel Oriol, Marco Piccioni

Program Committee

Patrick Albert
Uwe Assmann
Balbir Barn
Michael Barnett
Claude Baudoin
Bernhard Beckert
Jean Bézivin
Jean-Pierre Briot
Phil Brooke
Marsha Chechik
Dave Clarke
Bernard Coulette
Jin Song Dong
Gregor Engels
Patrick Eugster
José Fiadeiro
Judit Nyekyne Gaizler
Benoît Garbinato
Carlo Ghezzi
Martin Glinz

Martin Gogolla
Jeff Gray
Pedro Guerreiro
Alan Hartman
Valerie Issarny
Gerti Kappel
Joseph Kiniry
Ivan Kurtev
Philippe Lahire
Ralf Lämmel
Mingshu Li
Tiziana Margaria
Erik Meijer
Peter Müller
David Naumann
Oscar Nierstrasz
Manuel Oriol
Jonathan Ostroff
Alfonso Pierantonio
Awais Rashid

Nicolas Rouquette
Anthony Savidis
Doug Schmidt
Bran Selic
Anatoly Shalyto
Jim Steel

Dave Thomas
Laurence Tratt
T.H. Tse
Antonio Vallecillo
Amiram Yehudai
Andreas Zeller

Additional Reviewers

Hakim Belhaouari
Thorsten Bormer
Sebastian Cech
Chunqing Chen
Fabian Christ
Antonio Cicchetti
Duc-Hanh Dang
Fintan Fairmichael
Alexander Foerster
Christoph Gladisch
Orla Greevy
Radu Grigore
Baris Güldali
Florian Heidenreich
Mikolas Janota
Horst Kargl
Andrei Kirshin
Vladimir Klebanov

Dimitrios Kolovos
Hervé Leblanc
Thomas Ledoux
Adrian Lienhard
Hermann Pehl
Nadia Polikarpova
Lukas Renggli
Jose E. Rivera
Louis Rose
Julia Rubin
Davide Di Ruscio
David Röthlisberger
Bruno Silvestre
Arndt Von Staa
Jun Sun
Faraz Ahmadi Torshizi
Manuel Wimmer
Steffen Zschaler

Table of Contents

The End of the Computing Era: Hephaestus Meets the Olympians
(Abstract) 1
    Michael L. Brodie

Modeling of Component Environment in Presence of Callbacks and
Autonomous Activities 2
    Pavel Parizek and Frantisek Plasil

Efficient Model Checking of Networked Applications 22
    *Cyrille Artho, Watcharin Leungwattanakit, Masami Hagiya, and
    Yoshinori Tanabe*

Controlling Accessibility in Agile Projects with the Access Modifier
Modifier 41
    Philipp Bouillon, Eric Großkinsky, and Friedrich Steimann

Towards Raising the Failure of Unit Tests to the Level of
Compiler-Reported Errors 60
    Friedrich Steimann, Thomas Eichstädt-Engelen, and Martin Schaaf

Virtual Machine Support for Stateful Aspects 80
    Yuri Phink and Amiram Yehudai

Guarded Program Transformations Using JTL 100
    Tal Cohen, Joseph (Yossi) Gil, and Itay Maman

A Multiparadigm Study of Crosscutting Modularity in Design
Patterns 121
    *Martin Kuhlemann, Sven Apel, Marko Rosenmüller, and
    Roberto Lopez-Herrejon*

Representing and Operating with Model Differences 141
    José E. Rivera and Antonio Vallecillo

Optimizing Dynamic Class Composition in a Statically Typed
Language 161
    Anders Bach Nielsen and Erik Ernst

Ownership, Uniqueness, and Immutability 178
    *Johan Östlund, Tobias Wrigstad, Dave Clarke, and
    Beatrice Åkerblom*

Object Incompleteness and Dynamic Composition in Java-Like
Languages 198
    Lorenzo Bettini, Viviana Bono, and Betti Venneri

The Meta in Meta-object Architectures 218
      Marcus Denker, Mathieu Suen, and Stéphane Ducasse

An AsmL Semantics for Dynamic Structures and Run Time
Schedulability in UML-RT 238
      Stefan Leue, Alin Ştefănescu, and Wei Wei

Component Reassembling and State Transfer in MADCAR-Based
Self-adaptive Software 258
      Guillaume Grondin, Noury Bouraqadi, and Laurent Vercouter

A Comparison of State-Based Modelling Tools for Model Validation 278
      Emine G. Aydal, Mark Utting, and Jim Woodcock

MontiCore: Modular Development of Textual Domain Specific
Languages 297
      Holger Krahn, Bernhard Rumpe, and Steven Völkel

Proof-Transforming Compilation of Eiffel Programs 316
      Martin Nordio, Peter Müller, and Bertrand Meyer

Engineering Associations: From Models to Code and Back through
Semantics 336
      Zinovy Diskin, Steve Easterbrook, and Juergen Dingel

On the Efficiency of Design Patterns Implemented in C# 3.0 356
      Judith Bishop and R. Nigel Horspool

A Framework for Model Transformation By-Example: Concepts and
Tool Support 372
      Michael Strommer and Manuel Wimmer

Web Applications Design and Development with WebML and
WebRatio 5.0 392
      *Roberto Acerbis, Aldo Bongio, Marco Brambilla, Stefano Butti,
      Stefano Ceri, and Piero Fraternali*

Author Index 413

The End of the Computing Era: Hephaestus Meets the Olympians

Michael L. Brodie

Chief Scientist, Verizon Communications, USA
michael.brodie@verizon.com

Abstract. Our Digital World is becoming increasingly real (and *vice versa*), is being extended to include the physical world, and is growing in size, scope, and significance apparently on its own trajectory. The elimination of the ancient boundaries of time, space, location, and organizational structure appear to be unleashing social and other forces that threaten to disrupt real and automated systems replacing them with organically evolving digital ecosystems. Yet at the threshold of these amazing changes do we have the tools to understand, design, or harness these changes for safety, improvement, innovation, and economic growth?

In ancient times, Hephaestus, the Greek god of technology, devised cunning machines with which to right transgressions only to find that his machines aggravated problems that were beyond his understanding.

This talk will briefly review the amazing growth of the Web and of our increasingly digital world as indicators of two fundamental shifts. We will first look at the End of the Computing Era and the emergence of the Problem Solving Era in which the problem owners attempt to solve problems with increasing realism and complexity aided by technology – not *vice versa*. Second, we will examine the emergence of a fundamentally more flexible, adaptive, and dynamic computing, Computer Science 2.0, and how it might serve the next generation of problem solving with its pillars of semantic technologies, service-oriented computing, and the semantic web.

R.F. Paige and B. Meyer (Eds.): TOOLS EUROPE 2008, LNBIP 11, p. 1, 2008.
© Springer-Verlag Berlin Heidelberg 2008

Modeling of Component Environment in Presence of Callbacks and Autonomous Activities

Pavel Parizek[1] and Frantisek Plasil[1,2]

[1] Charles University in Prague, Faculty of Mathematics and Physics,
Department of Software Engineering, Distributed Systems Research Group
{parizek,plasil}@dsrg.mff.cuni.cz
http://dsrg.mff.cuni.cz
[2] Academy of Sciences of the Czech Republic,
Institute of Computer Science

Abstract. A popular approach to compositional verification of component-based applications is based on the assume-guarantee paradigm, where an assumption models behavior of an environment for each component. Real-life component applications often involve complex interaction patterns like callbacks and autonomous activities, which have to be considered by the model of environment's behavior. In general, such patterns can be properly modeled only by a formalism that (i) supports independent atomic events for method invocation and return from a method and (ii) allows to specify explicit interleaving of events on component's provided and required interfaces - the formalism of behavior protocols satisfies these requirements. This paper attempts to answer the question whether the model involving only events on provided interfaces (calling protocol) could be valid under certain constraints on component behavior. The key contribution are the constraints on interleaving of events related to callbacks and autonomous activities, which are expressed via syntactical patterns, and evaluation of the proposed constraints on real-life component applications.

Keywords: Assume-guarantee reasoning, behavior protocols, modeling of environment behavior, callbacks, autonomous activities.

1 Introduction

Modern software systems are often developed via composition of independent components with well-defined interfaces and (formal) behavior specification of some sort. When reliability of a software system built from components is a critical issue, formal verification such as program model checking becomes a necessity. Since model checking of the whole complex ("real-life") system at a time is prone to state explosion, compositional methods have to be used. A basic idea of compositional model checking [6] is the checking of (local) properties of isolated components and inferring (global) properties of the whole system

R.F. Paige and B. Meyer (Eds.): TOOLS EUROPE 2008, LNBIP 11, pp. 2–21, 2008.
© Springer-Verlag Berlin Heidelberg 2008

from the local properties. This way, state explosion is partially addressed, since a single isolated component typically triggers a smaller state space compared to the whole system.

A popular approach to compositional model checking of component applications is based on the assume-guarantee paradigm [18]: For each component subject to checking, an assumption is stated on the behavior of the component's environment (e.g. the rest of a particular component application); similarly, the "guarantee" are the properties to hold if the component works properly in the assumed environment (e.g. absence of concurrency errors and compliance with behavior specification). Thus, a successful model checking of the component against the properties under the specific assumption guarantees the component to work properly when put into an environment modeled by the assumption.

Specific to program model checkers such as Java PathFinder (JPF) [21] is that they check only complete programs (featuring main()). Thus checking of an isolated component (its implementation, i.e. for instance of its Java code) is not directly possible ([17], [10]), since also its environment has to be provided in the form of a program (code). Thus, program model checking of a primitive component is associated with the *problem of missing environment* [14]. A typical solution to it in case of JPF is to construct an "artificial" environment (Java code) from an assumption formed as a behavior model as in [14][20], where the behavior model is based on LTS defined either directly [10], or in the formalism of behavior protocols [19]. Then, JPF is applied to the complete program composed of the component and environment.

In general, real-life component applications feature circular dependencies among components involving complex interaction schemes. Nevertheless, for the purpose of program model checking of an isolated component, these schemes have to be abstracted down to interaction patterns between the component and its environment pairs. Based on non-trivial case studies [1][8], we have identified the following four patterns of interaction between a component C and its environment E to be the most typical ones (*C-E patterns*):

a) *synchronous callback* (Fig. 1a), executed in the same thread as the call that triggered the callback;

b) *asynchronous callback* (Fig. 1b), executed in a different thread than the trigger call;

c) *autonomous activity* (Fig. 1c) on a required interface, which is performed by an inner thread of the component;

d)*synchronous reaction* (Fig. 1d) to a call on a component's provided interface.

In Fig. 1, each of the sequence diagrams contains activation boxes representing threads (T1 and T2) running in the component and environment in a particular moment of time. More specifically, in Fig. 1a, m denotes a method called on the component by the environment, and t denotes the trigger (invoked in m) of the callback b; note that all calls are performed by the same thread (T1). As to Fig. 1b, the only difference is that the callback b is asynchronous, i.e. it is performed by a different thread (T2) than the trigger t. In case of Fig. 1c, the

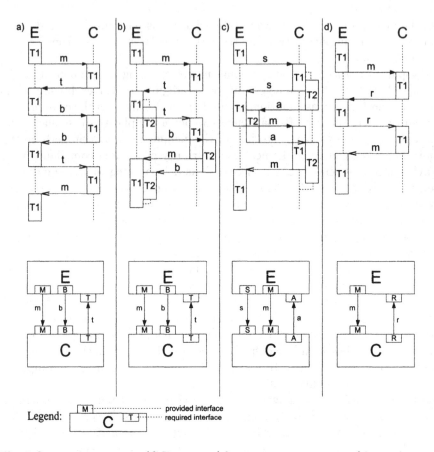

Fig. 1. Interaction patterns (C-E patterns) between a component and its environment

method s called on the component by the environment (in thread T1) starts an autonomous activity performed by an inner thread (T2), which calls the method a of the environment. The latter overlaps with the call of m issued by the environment. Finally, in Fig. 1d, r denotes a synchronous reaction to the call of the method m issued by the environment (both performed in the same thread).

These sequence diagrams clearly show that proper modeling of these C-E patterns via a specific formalism is possible only if the formalism allows to explicitly model the interleaving of method invocations and returns from methods on C's provided and required interfaces. Specifically, a method call as whole cannot be modeled as an atomic event (like in [10]); instead, independent constructs for method invocation (*invocation event*), return from a method (*return event*) and method execution (*method body*) have to be supported by the formalism. We say that a model of environment's behavior is *valid* if it precisely describes all occurrences of the C-E patterns in the interaction between a component and its environment.

The formalism of behavior protocols [19], developed in our group, supports independent invocation and return events on C's provided and required interfaces (details in Sect. 2) and therefore allows to model all the C-E patterns properly. In our former work, we introduced two specific approaches to modeling of environment's behavior: *inverted frame protocol* [14] and *context protocol* [15]. Both of them are generic, i.e. not limited to any particular communication pattern between E and C, and valid. The key difference between these two is that the inverted frame protocol models E that exercises C in all ways it was designed for (*maximal-calling environment*), while the context protocol models the actual use of C in the given context of a component-based application (*context environment*). Specifically, the context protocol may be simpler than the inverted frame protocol, e.g. in terms of level of parallelism (i.e. the assumption on environment behavior is weaker), if the particular application uses only a subset of C's functionality.

Unfortunately, the actual JPF model checking of a component combined with an environment determined by any of these two modeling approaches is prone to state explosion, in particular for two reasons:

(1) Java code of E is complex, since it has to ensure proper interleaving of the events on C's provided interfaces triggered by E with the events on C's required interfaces triggered by C itself. Technically, since there is no direct language support for expressing acceptance of a method call depending upon calling history in Java, the interleaving has to be enforced indirectly, e.g. via synchronization tools (`wait`, `notify`) and state variables.

(2) As to the context environment, its construction is also prone to state explosion, since the context protocol is derived from behavior specifications of the other components in a particular component application via an algorithm similar to the one employed in behavior compliance model checking [11]. In [15] we presented a syntactical algorithm for derivation of a context protocol, which has a low time and space complexity; however, it does not support autonomous activities and does not handle cycles in architecture (and thus callbacks) properly in general.

The issues (1) and (2) are particularly pressuring when C is designed to handle a high level of parallel activities (threads). Then, this has to be reflected in E to exercise C accordingly. To alleviate the state explosion problem associated with these issues we proposed in [16] a simplified approach to modeling environment behavior: *calling protocol*. Roughly speaking, a calling protocol models precisely only the events on C's provided interfaces, i.e. it models only the calls issued by E, under the assumption that the calls issued by C are accepted by E at any time (and in parallel) - this is an overapproximation of the desired behavior of E. Thus the Java code of E is simple, since it does not have to ensure proper interleaving of the events on C's provided and required interfaces. On the other hand, capturing this interleaving is necessary for an appropriate modeling of the C-E patterns in general, and thus for validity of a calling protocol-based model of environment's behavior. An open question is whether there are constraints on behavior of C under which the calling protocol-based approach could provide a valid model of E.

1.1   Goals and Structure of the Paper

The goal of this paper is to answer the question whether the calling protocol-based approach can provide a valid model of environment behavior in the context of the C-E patterns, if, in the component's behavior specification, certain constraints are imposed on the sequencing and interleaving of the C-E events with other events on the component interfaces.

The structure of the paper is as follows. Sect. 2 provides an overview of the formalism of behavior protocols and its use for modeling of environment behavior. Sect. 3 presents the key contribution of the paper - an answer to the question of validity of the calling protocol-based approach under certain constraints on component behavior and an algorithm for automated construction of a valid calling protocol-based model of environment's behavior. Sect. 4 shows experimental results and the rest contains evaluation, related work and a conclusion.

2   Behavior Protocols

The formalism of behavior protocols - a simple process algebra - was introduced in [19] as a means of modeling behavior of software components in terms of traces of atomic events on the components' external interfaces. Specifically, a *frame protocol* FP_C of a component C is an expression that defines C's behavior as a set $L(FP_C)$ of finite traces of atomic events on its provided and required interfaces.

Syntactically, a behavior protocol reminds a regular expression over an alphabet of atomic events of the form <prefix><interface>.<method><suffix>. Here, the prefix ? denotes acceptance, while ! denotes emit; likewise, the suffix ↑ denotes a method invocation and ↓ denotes a return from a method. Thus, four types of atomic events are supported: !i.m↑ denotes emitting of a call to method m on interface i, ?i.m↑ acceptance of the call, !i.m↓ emitting of return from the method, and, finally, ?i.m↓ denotes acceptance of the return. Several useful shortcuts are also defined: !i.m{P} stands for !i.m↑ ; P ; ?i.m↓ (*method call*), and ?i.m{P} stands for ?i.m↑ ; P ; !i.m↑ (*method acceptance*). Both in !i.m{P} and ?i.m{P}, a protocol P models a *method body* (possibly empty). As for operators, behavior protocols support the standard regular expression operators (sequence (;), alternative (+), and repetition (*)); moreover, there are two operators for parallel composition: (1) Operator |, which generates all the interleavings of the event traces defined by its operands; the events do not communicate, nor synchronize. It is used to express parallel activities in the frame protocol of C. (2) Operator ∇_S ("consent"), producing also all interleavings of the event traces defined by its operands, where, however, the neighboring events from S (with "opposite" prefix) are complementary - they synchronize and are forced to communicate (producing internal action τ similar to CCS and CSP). An example of such complementary events would be the pair !I.m↑ and ?I.m↑. This operator is used to produce the composed behavior of cooperating components, while S comprises all the events on the component's bindings. Moreover,

Table 1. Frame protocols of C in Fig. 1

a) synchronous callback: $FP_{Ca} = \text{?M.m } \{!T.t\{?B.b\}\}$
b) asynchronous callback: $FP_{Cb} = \text{?M.m}\uparrow; !T.t\uparrow; ?T.t\downarrow; ?B.b\uparrow; !M.m\downarrow; !B.b\downarrow$
c) autonomous activity: $FP_{Cc} = \text{?S.s}; !A.a\uparrow; ?M.m\uparrow; ?A.a\downarrow; !M.m\downarrow$
d) synchronous reaction: $FP_{Cd} = \text{?M.m } \{!R.r\}$

it also indicates communication errors (deadlock and "bad activity" - there is no complementary event to $!I.m\uparrow$ in a trace, i.e. a call cannot be answered).

Using behavior protocols, a quite complex behavior can be modeled - see, e.g., [1] for a behavior model of a real-life component application. Advantageously, it is possible to model the explicit interleaving of events on both the provided and required interfaces of a component in its frame protocol. Specifically, the frame protocol of C in Fig. 1 in the alternatives a) - d) would take the form as in Tab. 1.

2.1   Modeling Environment via Behavior Protocols

Consider again the missing environment problem and the setting on Fig. 1. Obviously, the environment of an isolated component C can be considered as another component E bound to C. Thus the model of E's behavior can be a frame protocol of E. Since a required interface is always bound to a matching provided interface, the former issuing calls and the latter accepting calls, the corresponding events in both frame protocols ought to be complementary. For example, the frame protocols of E in Fig. 1 in alternatives a) - d) would have the form as in Tab. 2.

Table 2. Frame protocols of E in Fig. 1

a) $FP_{Ea} = !M.m \{?T.t\{!B.b\}\}$
b) $FP_{Eb} = !M.m\uparrow; ?T.t\uparrow; !T.t\downarrow; !B.b\uparrow; ?M.m\downarrow; ?B.b\downarrow$
c) $FP_{Ec} = !S.s; ?A.a\uparrow; !M.m\uparrow; !A.a\downarrow; ?M.m\downarrow$
d) $FP_{Ed} = !M.m \{?R.r\}$

Obviously, an event issued by E (such as $!M.m\uparrow$) has to be accepted by C (such as $?M.m\uparrow$) at the right moment and vice versa. As an aside, this (behavior compliance [19]) can be formally verified by parallel composition via consent, $FP_E \nabla_S FP_C$, which should not indicate any communication error; for $FP_{Eb} \nabla_S FP_{Cb}$ this is obviously true, since FP_{Eb} was created by simply replacing all ? by ! and vice versa - FP_{Eb} is the *inverted frame protocol* (FP_{Cb}^{-1}) of C_b. Because of that and since here S comprises all events on the interfaces M, T and B, the consent operator produces traces composed of τ only.

In general, any protocol FP_E for which $FP_E \nabla_S FP_C$ does not yield any composition error is called *environment protocol* of C, further denoted as EP_C. In Sect. 1, we proposed three specific techniques to construct C's environment protocol: (i) inverted frame protocol (EP_C^{inv}), (ii) context protocol (EP_C^{ctx}) and (iii) calling protocol (EP_C^{call}). Event though these techniques aim at "decent" exercising of C, an environment protocol may be very simple, designed to help check a specific property. Assume for instance that the interface M of C in Fig. 1 features also a method x and $FP'_{Ca} = $?M.m {!T.t{?B.b}} + ?M.x. Then, $EP'_{Ca} = $!M.x would be an environment protocol since $EP'_{Ca} \nabla_S FP'_{Ca}$ does not yield any composition error.

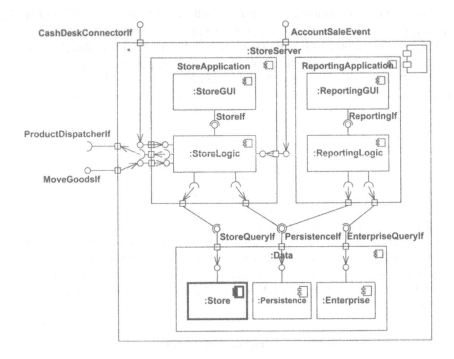

Fig. 2. Architecture of the StoreServer component

Nevertheless, the three techniques (i) - (iii) are much more of practical importance; below, they are illustrated on a part of the component architecture created in our group for the solution to the CoCoME assignment [8] (Fig. 2); the solution was based on the Fractal component model [3] and behavior protocols. Here we focus especially on the Store component, the functionality of which is not fully used by StoreApplication that accesses Store indirectly via Data. Specifically, the actual use of Store employs only a subset of the traces allowed by its frame protocol FP_{Store} (Fig. 3a); for example, FP_{Store} states that it is possible to call any method of the StoreQueryIf interface at most four times in parallel; however, assume that the queryProductById and queryStockItem methods on this interface are (indirectly) called three times in parallel by StoreApplication and the other methods are called only twice in parallel, or not at all in parallel. Therefore, the context protocol EP_{Store}^{ctx} (Fig. 3c) of Store is much simpler in terms of level of parallelism than its inverted frame protocol EP_{Store}^{inv} (Fig. 3b).

Since the `Store` component has no required interface, its calling protocol EP_{Store}^{call} is equal to its context protocol, thus being obviously a valid model of the `Store`'s environment behavior in this special case.

In summary, the basic idea of the techniques (i)-(iii) for construction of a model of C's environment (E) behavior is as follows:

Re (i) The inverted frame protocol EP_C^{inv} of a component C is constructed directly from the component's frame protocol FP_C by replacing all the prefixes ? by ! and vice versa.

a) $FP_{Store} = ($
```
    ?StoreQueryIf.queryProductById +
    ?StoreQueryIf.queryStockItem +
    # calls of other methods on StoreQueryIf follow
)*
|
# the fragment above repeated three more times
```

b) $EP_{Store}^{inv} = ($
```
    !StoreQueryIf.queryProductById +
    !StoreQueryIf.queryStockItem +
    # calls of other methods on StoreQueryIf follow
)*
|
# the fragment above repeated three more times
```

c) $EP_{Store}^{ctx} = ($ `!StoreQueryIf.queryStockItem* ; ... )*`
```
|
(
    !StoreQueryIf.queryProductById*
    +
    !StoreQueryIf.queryStockItem*
)*
|
!StoreQueryIf.queryProductById*
|
(
    ... ;
    (
        ( !StoreQueryIf.queryProductById*; ... )
        +
        ( ... ; !StoreQueryIf.queryStockItem* )
        +
        ...
    )
)*
```

Fig. 3. a) A fragment of the frame protocol of `Store`; b) a fragment of the inverted frame protocol of `Store`; c) a fragment of the context protocol of `Store`

Re (ii) The component's context protocol EP_C^{ctx} is derived via consent composition of the frame protocols of all the other components bound to C at the same level of nesting and the context protocol (or inverted frame protocol) of the C's parent component (if there is one).

Re (iii) The calling protocol can be derived in two ways: either via syntactical omitting of events on required interfaces from the inverted frame protocol or context protocol, or directly from the frame protocols of all the components in an architecture (including the one subject to checking) via a syntactical algorithm described in Sect. 3.2. In both cases, events on C's required interfaces, i.e. calls of E from C, are modeled implicitly in such a way that they are allowed to happen at any time and in parallel with any other event on any C's interface; technically, the environment protocol based on a calling protocol takes the form

$$EP_C^{call} = \texttt{<calling protocol>} \mid \texttt{?m1*} \mid \ldots \mid \texttt{?m1*} \mid \qquad \text{(E1)}$$
$$\mid \texttt{?m2*} \mid \ldots \mid \texttt{?mN*}$$

where $\texttt{m1}, \ldots, \texttt{mN}$ represent methods of the component's required interfaces (obviously several instances of the same method can be accepted in parallel; nevertheless, the number $\texttt{N}$ and the number of appearances of each $\texttt{?mi*}$ have to be finite). Such EP_C^{call} is compliant with FP_C (assuming that compliance holds for frame protocols of all components in the application, which C belongs to), i.e. there are no communication errors, for the following reasons: (a) an environment modeled by EP_C^{call} calls C only in a way allowed by FP_C, since EP_C^{call} is derived from the frame protocols of the components cooperating with C at the same level of nesting (assuming their behavior is compliant); (b) an environment modeled by EP_C^{call} can accept any call from C at any time and in parallel with any other event on a C's interface (both provided and required).

3   Calling Protocol vs. Callbacks and Autonomous Activities

As indicated at the end of Sect. 1, an environment protocol based on a calling protocol (EP_C^{call}) is an imprecise model (overapproximation) of E's behavior in general, since it models in detail only the events on the C's provided interfaces and assumes a generic acceptance of calls on the required interfaces. Therefore, specifically, it is not possible to model detailed interleaving of events on these interfaces, which is necessary for proper modeling of callbacks and autonomous activities.

In this section, we propose certain syntactical constraints on C's frame protocol FP_C to ensure that no other events than those related to synchronous reactions, triggers of callbacks, and autonomous activities take place on the required interfaces of C; also, we answer the question whether EP_C^{call} can be a valid model of E's behavior if these constraints are satisfied.

The key idea is to express the constraints on FP_C via the following syntactical schemes (for simplicity, names of interfaces are omitted in event identifications):

(A) To express synchronous callbacks (and synchronous reactions) correctly, the constraint is that in FP_C the events corresponding to a particular callback **b** and a trigger **t** for **b** have to be nested according to the scheme

$$FP_C = \alpha_1 \; op_1 \; ?m\{ \; \alpha_2 \; op_2 \; !t\{?b\} \; op_3 \; \alpha_3 \} \; op_4 \; \alpha_4 \qquad (A1)$$

where α_i may involve only synchronous reactions (C-E pattern (d)) and arbitrary behavior protocol operators except consent (∇), and op_i is either the sequence operator (;) or the alternative operator (+). Specifically, the frame protocol $FP'_C = \alpha_1 op_1 \; ?m \; ; \; \alpha_2 \; ; \; !t \; ; \; \alpha_3 \; ; \; ?b \; op_2 \alpha_4$, which would be the only option when using the LTS-based approach of [10], violates the constraint. An example of a frame protocol that satisfies the constraint is

$$FP'_{Ca} = ?m1\{!r1\} \; ; \; ?m2\{!t\{?b\} \; + \; !r2\} \; ; \; ?m3\{!r3\} \qquad (EX\text{-}A1)$$

(B) To express asynchronous callbacks (and (A)) correctly, the constraint on FP_C is that it is necessary to use parallel composition of the events corresponding to a particular callback **b** with other events, including the trigger **t** of **b**, according to the scheme

$$FP_C = \beta_1 \; op_1 \; ?m\!\uparrow \; ; \; \beta_2 \; ; \; !t\!\uparrow \; ; \; ((?t\!\downarrow \; ; \; \beta_3 \; ; \; !m\!\downarrow \; op_2 \; \beta_4) \; | \; ?b) \quad (B1)$$

where β_i is composed of behavior protocols satisfying the constraint A connected via arbitrary behavior protocol operators except the consent (∇), and op_i is again either ; or +. Specifically, a violation of the constraint would be to use explicit sequencing of events like in $?m\!\uparrow \; ; \; !t\!\uparrow \; ; \; ?t\!\downarrow \; ; \; ?b\!\uparrow \; ; \; !m\!\downarrow \; ; \; !b\!\downarrow$ (Tab. 1b), since an asynchronous callback runs in a different thread than the trigger and therefore unpredictable thread scheduling has to be considered. An example of a frame protocol that satisfies the constraint is

$$FP'_{Cb} = ?m1 \; ; \; ?m2\!\uparrow \; ; \; !t\!\uparrow \; ; \; ((?t\!\downarrow \; ; \; !m2\!\downarrow \; ; \; ?m3\{!r3\}) \; | \; ?b) \quad (EX\text{-}B1)$$

(C) To express autonomous activities on required interfaces (and (B)) correctly, the constraint is that it is also necessary to use parallel composition (as in (B)), since such activities are performed by C's inner threads and thus non-deterministic scheduling of the threads has to be considered. Specifically, the events corresponding to a particular autonomous activity **a** have to be composed via the and-parallel operator with other events that can occur after the start of the inner thread (in method **s**). Thus, when involving autonomous activities, FP_C has to comply with the scheme

$$FP_C = \gamma_1 \; op_1 \; ?s\!\uparrow \; ; \; ((!s\!\downarrow \; ; \; \gamma_2) \; | \; !a) \qquad (C1)$$

where γ_i is composed of behavior protocols satisfying the constraint B connected via arbitrary behavior protocol operators except the consent (∇). For example, the frame protocol $FP'_C = \gamma_1 op_1 \; ?s \; ; \; \gamma_2 \; ; \; !a\!\uparrow \; ; \; \gamma_3 \; ; \; ?a\!\downarrow \; ; \; \gamma_4$ is not valid, since the events for the autonomous activity **a** are not allowed to happen before the call to **s** returns (i.e. before $!s\!\downarrow$ occurs). An example of a frame protocol that satisfies the constraint is

$$FP'_{Cc} = \text{?m1} \ ; \ \text{?s↑} \ ; \ ((\text{!s↓} \ ; \ (\text{?m2} + \text{?m3}\{\text{!r3}\})) \ | \ \text{!a}) \qquad \text{(EX-C1)}$$

In summary, to satisfy the constraints, a frame protocol has to be constructed in a hierarchical manner, with synchronous reactions and synchronous callbacks (compliant to the constraint A) lower than asynchronous callbacks (compliant to B), and with autonomous activities (compliant to C) at the top.

3.1   Calling & Trigger Protocol

An important question is whether from a FP_C (and frame protocols of other components at the same level of nesting as C) satisfying the constraints A, B, and C an EP_C^{call} can be derived such that it would be a valid model of behavior of C's environment; i.e., whether it suffices to model precisely only the interleaving of events on C's provided interfaces when callbacks and autonomous activities are considered. To answer this question, it is sufficient to consider the possible meanings of an event on a required interface in the frame protocol FP_C satisfying the constraints; such an event can be:

(1) A synchronous reaction r to a call on a provided interface, when r is not a trigger of a callback.

(2) An autonomous activity a on a required interface, when a is not a trigger of a callback.

(3) A trigger t of a callback b (either synchronous or asynchronous).

In cases (1) and (2), it is appropriate to model r, resp. a, implicitly (as in E1), since it has no relationship with any event on C's provided interfaces. On the other hand, a trigger t of a callback b (case 3) cannot be modeled implicitly, since b can be executed by E only after C invokes t - if t were modeled implicitly, then E could execute b even before t was invoked by the component.

Therefore, the answer to the question of sufficiency of the constraints is that the environment protocol based on a calling protocol (EP_C^{call}) is not a valid model of E's behavior if the interaction between C and E involves callbacks, since triggers of callbacks are modeled implicitly in EP_C^{call} - precise interleaving of a callback and its trigger has to be preserved in a valid model of E's behavior.

As a solution to this problem, we propose to define the environment protocol of a component C on the basis of a *calling & trigger protocol* that models a precise interleaving of the events on C's provided interfaces (including callbacks) and triggers of callbacks. In principle, the environment protocol takes the form

$$EP_C^{trig} = \text{<calling \& trigger protocol>} \ | \ \text{?m1*} \ | \ ... \ | \qquad \text{(E2)}$$
$$| \ \text{?m1*} \ | \ \text{?m2*} \ | \ ... \ | \ \text{?mN*}$$

where m1, ..., mN are all the methods of the C's required interfaces except triggers of callbacks. Compliance of EP_C^{trig} with FP_C holds for similar reasons like in case of EP_C^{call} (end of Sect. 2.1) - note that although an environment modeled by EP_C^{trig} can accept triggers of callbacks from a component C only at particular moments of time, C will not invoke any trigger at an inappropriate time, since frame protocols of C and components cooperating with C at the same level of nesting are assumed to be compliant.

An environment protocol based on a calling & trigger protocol for (A1) has to comply with the scheme

$$EP_C^{trig} = (\alpha_{1\_prov}^{-1} \; op_1 \; !\texttt{m}\{\alpha_{2\_prov}^{-1} \; op_2 \; ?\texttt{t}\{!\texttt{b}\} \; op_3 \; \alpha_{3\_prov}^{-1}\} \; op_4 \tag{A2}$$
$$op_4 \; \alpha_{4\_prov}^{-1}) \; | \; \alpha_{1\_req}^{-1} \; | \; \dots \; | \; \alpha_{4\_req}^{-1}$$

where $\alpha_{i\_prov}^{-1}$ denotes the events on provided interfaces from α_i^{-1} and $\alpha_{i\_req}^{-1}$ denotes the events on required interfaces from α_i^{-1} (α_i^{-1} contains the events from α_i with ? replaced by ! and vice versa). For illustration, the proper environment protocol for (EX-A1) is $EP_{Ca}^{trig'} = (!\texttt{m1} \; ; \; !\texttt{m2}\{?\texttt{t}\{!\texttt{b}\}\} \; ; \; !\texttt{m3}) \; | \; ?\texttt{r1} \; | \; ?\texttt{r2} \; | \; ?\texttt{r3}$.

Similarly, an environment protocol for (B1) has to comply with the scheme

$$EP_C^{trig} = (\beta_{1\_prov}^{-1} \; op_1 \; !\texttt{m}{\uparrow} \; ; \; \beta_{2\_prov}^{-1} \; ; \; ?\texttt{t}{\uparrow} \; ; \; ((!\texttt{t}{\downarrow} \; ; \; \beta_{3\_prov}^{-1} \; ; \tag{B2}$$
$$; \; ?\texttt{m}{\downarrow} \; op_2 \; \beta_{4\_prov}^{-1}) \; | \; !\texttt{b})) \; | \; \beta_{1\_req}^{-1} \; | \; \dots \; | \; \beta_{4\_req}^{-1},$$

while an environment protocol for (C1) has to comply with the scheme

$$EP_C^{trig} = ((\gamma_{1\_prov}^{-1} \; op_1 \; !\texttt{s} \; ; \; \gamma_{2\_prov}^{-1}) \; | \; ?\texttt{a}) \; | \; \gamma_{1\_req}^{-1} \; | \; \gamma_{2\_req}^{-1}. \tag{C2}$$

The proper environment protocol for (EX-B1) is $EP_{Cb}^{trig'} = (!\texttt{m1} \; ; \; !\texttt{m2}{\uparrow}$; ?\texttt{t}{\uparrow} \; ; \; ((!\texttt{t}{\downarrow} \; ; \; ?\texttt{m2}{\downarrow} \; ; \; !\texttt{m3}) \; | \; !\texttt{b})) \; | \; ?\texttt{r3}$, while the proper environment protocol for (EX-C1) is $EP_{Cc}^{trig'} = (!\texttt{m1} \; ; \; !\texttt{s}{\uparrow} \; ; \; ((?\texttt{s}{\downarrow} \; ; \; (!\texttt{m2} + !\texttt{m3})) \; | \; !\texttt{a})) \; | \; ?\texttt{r3}$.

3.2 Construction of Calling and Trigger Protocol

The algorithm for construction of a calling & trigger protocol (CTP) is based on the syntactical algorithm for derivation of a context protocol that was presented in [15] - the main difference is the newly added support for callbacks and autonomous activities. Only the basic idea is described here, i.e. technical details are omitted.

In general, the algorithm accepts frame protocols of all components (primitive and composite) in the given application and bindings between the components as an input, and its output are $CTPs$ for all primitive components in the application. The frame protocols have to be augmented with identification of events that correspond to triggers for callbacks and autonomous activities.

The algorithm works in a recursive way: when executed on a specific composite component C, it computes CTP_{Ci} for each of its sub-components $C_1, \dots, C_N$, and then applies itself recursively on each C_i.

More specifically, the following steps have to be performed to compute the calling & trigger protocol CTP_{Ck} of C_k, a sub-component of C:

1) A directed graph G of bindings between C and the sub-components of C is constructed and then pruned to form a sub-graph G_{Ck} that contains only the paths involving C_k. The sub-graph G_{Ck} contains a node N_C corresponding to C and a node N_{Ci} for each sub-component C_i of C; in particular, it contains a node N_{Ck} for C_k.

2) An intermediate version IP_{Ck} of CTP_{Ck} is constructed via a syntactical expansion of method call shortcuts during traversal of G_{Ck} in a DFS manner. The traversal consists of two phases - (i) processing synchronous reactions and autonomous activities on required interfaces, and (ii) processing callbacks. Technically, the first phase starts at N_C with CTP_C of C (inverted frame protocol is used for the top-level composite component) and ends when all the edges on all paths between N_C and N_{Ck} are processed (cycles are ignored in this phase); the second phase starts at C_k and processes all cycles involving C_k. When processing a specific edge E_{lm}, which connects nodes N_{Cl} and N_{Cm} (for C_l and C_m), in the first phase, the current version IP_{Ck}^{lm} (computed prior to processing of E_{lm}) of IP_{Ck} is expanded in the following way: assuming that a required interface R_l of C_l is bound to a provided interface P_m of C_m, each method call shortcut on R_l in IP_{Ck}^{lm} is expanded to the corresponding method body defined in the frame protocol of C_m.

For example, if IP_{Ck}^{lm} contains "...; !R1.m1 ; !R1.m2 ;..." and the frame protocol of C_m contains "...; ?Pm.m1{prot1} ; ?Pm.m2{prot2 + prot3} ; ...", the result of one step of expansion has the form "...; prot1 ; (prot2 + prot3) ;...".

3) CTP_{Ck} is derived from IP_{Ck} by dropping (i) all the events related to other sub-components of C and (ii) all events on the required interfaces of C_k with the exception of triggers for callbacks, which have to be preserved.

In general, these three steps have to be performed for each sub-component of each composite component in the given component application in order to get a calling & trigger protocol for each primitive component.

4   Tools and Experiments

In order to show the benefits of use of the calling & trigger protocol-based approach instead of a context protocol or an inverted frame protocol, we have implemented construction of a context protocol (via consent composition) and a calling & trigger protocol (Sect. 3.2), and performed several experiments.

Our implementation of construction of a calling & trigger protocol and a context protocol does not depend on a specific component system, i.e. it can be used with any component system that supports formal behavior specification

Table 3. Results for the Store component

	Inverted frame protocol-based EP	Context protocol-based EP	Calling & trigger protocol-based EP
Time to compute EP	0 s	3 s	0.1 s
Total time (EP + JPF)	n/a	1102 s	1095 s
Total memory	> 2048 MB	762 MB	748 MB

via behavior protocols (currently SOFA [4] and Fractal [1]). Moreover, the automated environment generator for JPF (EnvGen for JPF) [13] is available in both SOFA and Fractal versions, and thus we provide a complete JPF-based toolset for checking Java implementation of isolated SOFA or Fractal primitive components against the following properties: obeying of a frame protocol by the component's Java code [17] and all the properties supported by JPF out of the box (e.g. deadlocks and assertion violations).

Table 4. Results for the `ValidityChecker` component

	Inverted frame protocol-based EP	Context protocol-based EP	Calling & trigger protocol-based EP
Time to compute EP	0 s	2 s	0.5 s
Total time (EP + JPF)	n/a	n/a	485 s
Total memory	> 2048 MB	> 2048 MB	412 MB

We have performed several experiments on the `Store` component (Sect. 2.1) and the `ValidityChecker` component, which forms a part of the demo component application developed in the CRE project [1] - frame protocol, context protocol and calling & trigger protocol of `ValidityChecker` are in the appendix. For each experiment, we measured the following characteristics: time needed to compute a particular environment protocol, total time (computation of EP and JPF checking) and total memory; the value "> 2048 MB" for total memory means that JPF run out of available memory (2 GB) - total time is set to "n/a" in such a case.

Results of experiments (in Tab. 3 and Tab. 4) show that (i) construction of a calling & trigger protocol takes less time and memory than construction of a context protocol for these two components and (ii) total time and memory of environment's behavior model construction, environment generation and checking with JPF (against obeying of a frame protocol, deadlocks and race conditions) are the lowest if the calling & trigger protocol-based approach is used. Time needed to compute EP^{ctx} of both `Store` and `ValidityChecker` is also quite low, since frame protocols of other components bound to them (in the particular applications) do not involve very high level of parallelism and thus state explosion did not occur. The main result is that the whole process of environment construction and, above all, JPF checking has a lower time and space complexity for calling & trigger protocol than if the other approaches are used.

5   Evaluation and Related Work

In general, our experiments confirm that although EP_C^{trig} for a component C specifies an "additional" parallelism (a parallel operator for each method of the C's required interfaces), the size of the JPF state space in checking C with an environment modeled by EP_C^{trig} is not increased (i.e. state explosion does not occur because of that), since the "additional" parallelism is not reflected in the environment's Java code explicitly via additional threads - the environment only has to be prepared to accept the call of any method from C (except triggers of callbacks) at any time and in parallel with other activities. On the contrary, modeling environment by EP_C^{trig} has the benefit of low time and space complexity (i) of construction of the model with respect to use of EP_C^{ctx}, and (ii) of JPF checking of component's Java code with respect to the use of EP_C^{inv}.

There are many other approaches to modeling behavior of software components and their environment that can be used to perform compositional verification of component-based applications (e.g. [9], [10], [5] and [12]); in particular, [9] and [10] do so on the basis of the assume-guarantee paradigm. However, to our knowledge, none of them supports independent constructs for the following atomic events explicitly in the modeling language: acceptance of a method invocation (?i.m↑ in behavior protocols), emitting a method invocation (!i.m↑), acceptance of a return from a method (?i.m↓), and emitting a return from a method (!i.m↓). Process algebra-based approaches ([9], [5]) typically support input (acceptance) and output (emit) actions explicitly in the modeling language, while transition systems-based approaches (e.g. [10] and [12]) support general events. In any case, it is possible to distinguish the events via usage of different names (e.g. event names m1_invoke, resp. m1_return, for invocation of m1, resp. for return from the method); however, an automated composition checking may fail even for compliant behavior specifications in such a case, since the developer of each of them can choose a different naming scheme (e.g. m1_invoke versus m1↑). We believe that a formalism for modeling component behavior should support all the four types of atomic events, since:

(a) independent constructs for method invocation and return from a method are necessary for proper modeling of callbacks and autonomous activities, and

(b) independent input and output actions are necessary for compliance checking, i.e. for checking the absence of communication errors between components.

Program model checking of open systems (isolated software components, device drivers, etc) typically involves construction of an "artificial" environment - an open system subject to checking and its environment then form a closed system (a complete program). The environment typically has the form of a program, as in our approach [14] and in [10], where the environment is defined in Java, or in SLAM/SDV [2], where the model of the windows kernel (environment for device drivers) is defined in the C language. In general, each approach to model checking of open software systems involves a custom tool or algorithm for construction of the environment, since each program model checker features a unique combination of API and input modeling language (i.e. different combination than the other program model checkers).

As for automated construction of the model of environment's behavior, one recent approach [7] is based on the L^* algorithm for incremental learning of regular languages. The basic idea of this approach is to iteratively refine an initial assumption about behavior of the environment for a component subject to checking. At each step of the iteration, model checking is used to check whether the component satisfies the property, and if not, the assumption is modified according to the counterexample. The iteration terminates when the component satisfies the given property in the environment modeled by the assumption. An advantage of our approach over [7] is lower time and memory complexity, since use of model checking is not needed for construction of EP^{trig}.

6   Conclusion

In our former work, we introduced two specific approaches to modeling of environment's behavior: inverted frame protocol and context protocol. However, JPF checking of a component with the environment determined by any of these modeling approaches is prone to state explosion for the following reasons: (i) Java code of the environment is complex, since it has to ensure proper interleaving of invocation and return events on the component's provided and required interfaces, (ii) for the context protocol, the algorithm for its construction involves model checking, while for the inverted frame protocol, the environment involves high level of parallelism. To address the problem of state explosion, in [16] we proposed to use a model of environment's behavior based on the calling protocol. Since the calling protocol-based approach models precisely only the events on component's provided interfaces, it does not allow to express C-E patterns properly in general (it is an overapproximation of the desired behavior).

Therefore, in this paper we proposed a slightly modified idea - calling & trigger protocol, which models precise interleaving of events on provided interfaces and triggers of callbacks, and the "other events" models implicitly, similar to [16] with no threat of state explosion. The key idea is to impose certain constraints on the frame protocol of a component in terms of interleaving of C-E events with other events and to express the constraints via syntactical patterns the frame protocol has to follow, and then, if the constrains are satisfied, derive in an automated way the calling & trigger protocol. The experiments confirm that the idea is viable.

As a future work, we plan to create a tool for automated recognition of those component frame protocols that do not satisfy the constraints and to integrate it into the SOFA runtime environment.

Acknowledgments. This work was partially supported by the Grant Agency of the Czech Republic (project number 201/06/0770).

References

1. Adamek, J., Bures, T., Jezek, P., Kofron, J., Mencl, V., Parizek, P., Plasil, F.:
   Component Reliability Extensions for Fractal Component Model (2006),
   http://kraken.cs.cas.cz/ft/public/public_index.phtml

2. Ball, T., Bounimova, E., Cook, B., Levin, V., Lichtenberg, J., McGarvey, C., Ondrusek, B., Rajamani, S.K., Ustuner, A.: Thorough Static Analysis of Device Drivers. In: Proceedings of EuroSys 2006. ACM Press (2006)

3. Bruneton, E., Coupaye, T., Leclercq, M., Quema, V., Stefani, J.B.: The FRACTAL component model and its support in Java. Softw. Pract. Exper. 36(11-12) (2006)

4. Bures, T., Hnetynka, P., Plasil, F.: SOFA 2.0: Balancing Advanced Features in a Hierarchical Component Model. In: Proceedings of SERA 2006. IEEE CS (2006)

5. Brim, L., Cerna, I., Varekova, P., Zimmerova, B.: Component-interaction Automata as a Verification-oriented Component-based System Specification. In: Proceedings of SAVCBS 2005. ACM Press (2005)

6. Clarke, E.M., Long, D.E., McMillan, K.L.: Compositional Model Checking. In: Proceedings of LICS 1989. IEEE CS (1989)

7. Cobleigh, J.M., Giannakopoulou, D., Pasareanu, C.S.: Learning Assumptions for Compositional Verification. In: Garavel, H., Hatcliff, J. (eds.) TACAS 2003. LNCS, vol. 2619. Springer, Heidelberg (2003)

8. CoCoME, http://agrausch.informatik.uni-kl.de/CoCoME

9. de Alfaro, L., Henzinger, T.A.: Interface Automata. In: Proceedings of 8th European Software Engineering Conference. ACM Press (2001)

10. Giannakopoulou, D., Pasareanu, C.S., Cobleigh, J.M.: Assume-guarantee Verification of Source Code with Design-Level Assumptions. In: Proceedings of 26th International Conference on Software Engineering (ICSE) (2004)

11. Mach, M., Plasil, F., Kofron, J.: Behavior Protocol Verification: Fighting State Explosion. International Journal of Computer and Information Science 6 (2005)

12. Ostroff, J.: Composition and Refinement of Discrete Real-Time Systems. ACM Transactions on Software Engineering and Methodology 8(1) (1999)

13. Parizek, P.: Environment Generator for Java PathFinder, http://dsrg.mff.cuni.cz/projects/envgen

14. Parizek, P., Plasil, F.: Specification and Generation of Environment for Model Checking of Software Components. In: Proceedings of FESCA 2006. ENTCS, vol. 176(2) (2006)

15. Parizek, P., Plasil, F.: Modeling Environment for Component Model Checking from Hierarchical Architecture. In: Proceedings of FACS 2006, ENTCS, vol. 182 (2006)

16. Parizek, P., Plasil, F.: Partial Verification of Software Components: Heuristics for Environment Construction. In: Proc. of 33rd EUROMICRO SEAA. IEEE CS (2007)

17. Parizek, P., Plasil, F., Kofron, J.: Model Checking of Software Components: Combining Java PathFinder and Behavior Protocol Model Checker. In: Proceedings of SEW 2006. IEEE CS (2006)

18. Pasareanu, C.S., Dwyer, M., Huth, M.: Assume-guarantee model checking of software: A comparative case study. In: Dams, D.R., Gerth, R., Leue, S., Massink, M. (eds.) SPIN 1999. LNCS. vol. 1680. Springer, Heidelberg (1999)

19. Plasil, F., Visnovsky, S.: Behavior Protocols for Software Components. IEEE Transactions on Software Engineering 28(11) (2002)

20. Tkachuk, O., Dwyer, M.B., Pasareanu, C.S.: Automated Environment Generation for Software Model Checking. In: Proceedings of ASE 2003, IEEE CS (2003)

21. Visser, W., Havelund, K., Brat, G., Park, S., Lerda, F.: Model Checking Programs. Automated Software Engineering Journal 10(2) (2003)

Appendix

$FP_{ValidityChecker} =$

```
(
  ?IToken.SetEvidence
  |
  ?IToken.SetValidity
  |
  (
    ?IToken.SetAccountCredentials {
      !ICustomCallback.SetAccountCredentials
    }
    +
    NULL
  )
)
;
?ILifetimeController.Start^ ; !ITimer.SetTimeout^
;
(
  (
    ?Timer.SetTimeout$ ; !ILifetimeController.Start$
    ;
    (
      ?IToken.InvalidateAndSave {
        !ITimer.CancelTimeouts;
        (!ICustomCallback.InvalidatingToken + NULL);
        !ITokenCallback.TokenInvalidated
      }*
      |
      ?IToken.InvalidateAndSave {
        !ITimer.CancelTimeouts;
        (!ICustomCallback.InvalidatingToken + NULL);
        !ITokenCallback.TokenInvalidated
      }*
    )
  )
  |
  ?ITimerCallback.Timeout {
    (!ICustomCallback.InvalidatingToken + NULL);
    !ITokenCallback.TokenInvalidated
  }*
)
```

$EP^{inv}_{ValidityChecker} = EP^{ctx}_{ValidityChecker} =$

```
(
  !IToken.SetEvidence
  |
  !IToken.SetValidity
  |
  (
    !IToken.SetAccountCredentials {
      ?ICustomCallback.SetAccountCredentials
    }
    +
    NULL
  )
)
;
!ILifetimeController.Start^ ; ?ITimer.SetTimeout^
;
(
  (
    !Timer.SetTimeout$ ; ?ILifetimeController.Start$
    ;
    (
      !IToken.InvalidateAndSave {
        ?ITimer.CancelTimeouts;
        (?ICustomCallback.InvalidatingToken + NULL);
        ?ITokenCallback.TokenInvalidated
      }*
      |
      !IToken.InvalidateAndSave {
        ?ITimer.CancelTimeouts;
        (?ICustomCallback.InvalidatingToken + NULL);
        ?ITokenCallback.TokenInvalidated
      }*
    )
  )
  |
  !ITimerCallback.Timeout {
    (?ICustomCallback.InvalidatingToken + NULL);
    ?ITokenCallback.TokenInvalidated
  }*
)
```

$$EP^{trig}_{ValidityChecker} =$$

```
(
  (
    !IToken.SetEvidence
```

```
    |
    !IToken.SetValidity
    |
    (
      !IToken.SetAccountCredentials
      +
      NULL
    )
  )
  ;
  !ILifetimeController.Start^ ; ?ITimer.SetTimeout^
  ;
  (
    (
      !Timer.SetTimeout$ ; ?ILifetimeController.Start$
      ;
      (
        !IToken.InvalidateAndSave*
        |
        !IToken.InvalidateAndSave*
      )
    )
    |
    !ITimerCallback.Timeout*
  )
)
|
?ICustomCallback.SetAccountCredentials*
|
?ITimer.CancelTimeouts*
|
?ITimer.CancelTimeouts*
|
?ICustomCallback.InvalidatingToken*
|
?ICustomCallback.InvalidatingToken*
|
?ICustomCallback.InvalidatingToken*
|
?ITokenCallback.TokenInvalidated*
|
?ITokenCallback.TokenInvalidated*
|
?ITokenCallback.TokenInvalidated*
```

Efficient Model Checking of Networked Applications

Cyrille Artho[1], Watcharin Leungwattanakit[2], Masami Hagiya[2],
and Yoshinori Tanabe[3]

[1] Research Center for Information Security (RCIS), AIST, Tokyo, Japan
c.artho@aist.go.jp
[2] University of Tokyo, Tokyo, Japan
watcharin,hagiya@is.s.u-tokyo.ac.jp
[3] Research Center for Verification and Semantics (CVS), AIST, Tokyo, Japan
tanabe.yoshinori@aist.go.jp

Abstract. Most applications today communicate with other processes over a network. Such applications are often multi-threaded. The non-determinism in the thread and communication schedules makes it desirable to model check such applications. When model checking such a networked application, a simple state space exploration scheme is not applicable, as the process being model checked would repeat communication operations when revisiting a given state after backtracking. We propose a solution that encapsulates such operations in a caching layer that is capable of hiding redundant communication operations from the environment. This approach is both more portable and more scalable than other approaches, as only a single process executes inside the model checker.

Keywords: Software model checking, network communication, software testing, caching.

1 Introduction

Networked software is complex. It is often implemented as a concurrent program, using threads [21] to handle multiple active communication channels. This introduces two dimensions of non-determinism: Both the thread schedule of the software, and the order in which incoming requests or messages arrive, cannot be controlled by the application. In software testing, a given test execution only covers one particular instance of all possible schedules. For exhaustive analysis, it is desirable to model check software, to ensure that no schedules cause a failure.

Model checking explores, as far as computational resources allow, the entire behavior of a system under test by investigating each reachable system state [9], accounting for non-determinism in external inputs, such as thread schedules. Recently, model checking has been applied directly to software [2,5,7,10,12,13,23]. However, conventional software model checking techniques are not applicable to networked programs. The problem is that state space exploration involves backtracking. After backtracking, the model checker will again execute certain parts of the program (and thus certain input/output operations). However, external processes, which are not under the control of the model checker, cannot be kept in synchronization with backtracking. Backtracking would result in repeated communication operations, causing direct communication between the application being model checked and external processes to fail.

R.F. Paige and B. Meyer (Eds.): TOOLS EUROPE 2008, LNBIP 11, pp. 22–40, 2008.

Our work proposes a solution to this problem. It covers all input/output (I/O) operations on streams and is applicable when I/O operations always produce the same data stream, regardless of the non-determinism of the schedule. While our solution is implemented for Java programs, the ideas are applicable to any software model checker or programming language supporting TCP-based networking [22]. A large number of programs uses TCP-based communication and is amenable to such verification. Previous work introduced the idea of caching I/O communication traces for model checking [4]. This paper extends that work and contributes the following achievements:

1. We show the necessity of matching requests to responses and introduce a solution for this problem. We also amend problems arising with more complex protocols that were not solved in the initial solution [4].
2. We introduce a full implementation of the caching approach, which is capable of model checking complex networked Java applications such as an HTTP server. Its performance is orders of magnitudes faster than previous work based on centralization of applications [1,19].

This paper is organized as follows: An intuition for our algorithm is given in Section 2, while Section 3 formalizes our algorithm. The implementation is of our approach is described in Section 4, and experiments are given in Section 5. Section 6 describes related work. Section 7 concludes this paper, and future work is outlined in Section 8.

2 Intuition of the Caching Algorithm

2.1 Software Model Checking

Model checking of a multi-threaded program analyzes all non-deterministic decisions in a program. Non-determinism includes all possible interleavings between threads that can be generated by the thread scheduler or through possible delays in incoming communication. Alternative schedules are explored by storing the current program state in a *milestone*, and backtracking to such a milestone, running the program again from that state under a different schedule.

Figure 1 shows an example to illustrate the problem occurring with communication operations. The program consists of two threads, which print out their thread name. Consider all possible schedules for this simple program. When both threads are started, either T1 or T2 may execute first, depending on the schedule. In testing, only one of these two outcomes will actually occur; in model checking, both outcomes are explored.

Figure 2 illustrates the state space exploration of this simple program when executing it in a software model checker. Boxes depict the set of threads that can be scheduled for

Thread 1	Thread 2

`void run() {`
`    print "[T1]";`
`}`
	`void run() {`
	`    print "[T2]";`
	`}`

Fig. 1. Example program to illustrate backtracking in a software model checker

execution. Transitions are shown by arrows and labeled with the output generated in that transition. After thread initialization, the scheduler has to make a choice of which thread to run first. As both choices should be explored, the model checker saves the complete program state at this point in a milestone. Assume the state space exploration then picks T_1. After its message is printed, only T_2 remains. After execution of T_2, both threads have finished, terminating the program. The model checker subsequently backtracks to a previously stored program state. After backtracking, the model checker explores the other possible schedule. The operations of T_1 and T_2 are executed again, in reverse order.

This simple example shows how the same operations are repeated after backtracking. As long as repeated operations target the program heap, their effect is usually consistent, as the entire program state is restored from a milestone. Therefore, repeated operations have the same effect on the restored memory as the original ones, as long as all components affected are captured by milestones. In this example, printing to the screen was repeated. While the state of the console cannot be backtracked by the model checker, this redundant output is usually ignored. However, input/output operations that affect other processes cannot be treated in this direct way.

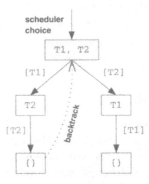

Fig. 2. State space exploration for the example program

2.2   Handling Redundant Actions After Backtracking

Effects of input/output (I/O) operations cannot be captured in milestones, as the *environment* of the system outside the current process is affected. When model checking an application that is part of a distributed system using multiple processes, external processes are not backtracked during model checking. Thus, two problems arise:

1. The application will re-send data after backtracking. This will interfere with the correct functionality of external processes.
2. After backtracking, the application will expect external input again. However, an external process does not re-send previously transmitted data.

One possible solution to this problem is to lift the power of a model checker from process level to operating system (OS) level. This way, any I/O operation is under control of the model checker [17]. However, this approach suffers from scalability problems, as the combination of multiple processes yields a very large state space. The same scalability problem arises if one transforms several processes into a single process by a technique called *centralization* [19]. With a model for TCP, networked applications can be model checked, but the approach does not scale to large systems [1,3].

Stub-based approaches replace external processes with a simplified representation [6,8,11,16]. In such work, external processes are not executed, and the stub returns a (previously known) result mimicking the behavior of the real implementation.

Our approach differs in that it only executes a single process inside the model checker, and runs all the other applications externally in their real implementation. Figure 3 depicts the overall architecture of the system. Let "system under test" (SUT) denote the application executing inside the model checker. Execution of the SUT is therefore subject to backtracking. Redundant externally visible operations, such as input/output, have to be hidden from external processes. External processes are called *peers* and can implement either client or server functionality, as defined in [22]. In our solution, a special cache layer intercepts any network traffic. This cache layer represents the state of communication between the SUT and external processes at different points in time. After backtracking to an earlier program state, data previously received by the SUT is replayed by the cache when requested again. Data previously sent by the SUT is not sent again over the network; instead, it is compared to the data contained in the cache. The underlying assumption is that communication between processes is independent of the thread schedule. Therefore, the order in which I/O operations occur must be consistent for all possible thread interleavings. If this were not the case, behavior of the communication resource would be undefined. Whenever communication proceeds beyond previously cached information, new data is both physically transmitted over the network and also added to the cache.

As an example, a simple program involving two threads is given in Figure 4. Each thread first writes a message to its own (unique) communication channel and then reads from it. Both communication channels interact with external processes (or with the same external process using two independent connections). Both threads run concurrently, so any interleaving of their operations is possible. Their combined state space is explored inside the model checker, as shown on the left side of Figure 5. In that figure, write and read operations are abbreviated by w_i and r_i, respectively, with i denoting the thread ID. As can be clearly seen, execution of all possible interleavings results in multiple backtracking operations, and each communication operation is repeated several times. However, in a given execution trace, each operation only occurs once. Operations within each thread are totally ordered, resulting in a partial order on I/O

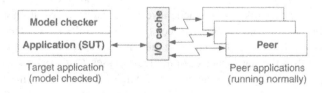

Fig. 3. Cache layer architecture

Thread 1	Thread 2
| ```
void run() {
    conn1.write("1");
    r1 = conn1.read();
}
``` | ```
void run() {
    conn2.write("2");
    r2 = conn2.read();
}
``` |

Fig. 4. Example program communicating with peer processes

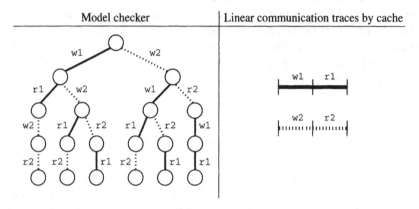

| Model checker | Linear communication traces by cache |

Fig. 5. State space exploration inside the model checker (left) and communication traces stored by the cache layer (right)

operations across all threads. Our cache layer takes advantage of this. The cache keeps track of I/O operations during the entire state space exploration and maintains a linearization of each communication trace. Each communication trace reflects the (total) order of messages within each communication channel. Identical physical communication operations of each execution trace are executed only once. The results of these operations is cached in a linear communication trace, as shown on the right side of Figure 5.

In our approach, all processes involved are executed; however, only a single process runs inside the model checker. Our approach therefore combines the (relative) scalability of running a single (usually multi-threaded [21]) process inside the model checker with the benefit of finding implementation errors when analyzing real applications. Indeed, peer processes may even run on external hosts and require features such as database access that a given model checker cannot support. As our approach only exhaustively searches the state space of *one* process at a time, it has to be applied once to each application: Each process is run once in the model checker, with its peers as external processes. Thanks to our cache layer, external processes do not have to be backtracked. In essence, our cache produces the same results as a perfect stub. The scalability improvement comes from the fact that the state space of one process is exponentially smaller than the state space of multiple processes. Our work differs from stub generation [6] in that we generate the corresponding data on the fly, without requiring a previous execution, and that we can handle peer processes running on other hosts or platforms. For a more detailed comparison, see Section 6.

2.3   Extension to More Complex Protocols

So far, the design described is sufficient for simple protocols consisting of one (atomic) request and response [4]. However, keeping track of data stream positions is not sufficient for protocols where several requests and responses are interleaved, and for requests that consist of multiple parts. For example, in HTTP, a GET request consists of two lines, one line containing a URL, and another empty line to mark a complete request.

As an example that will also serve to test the performance of the approach, we take a simple protocol where the server returns the nth character of the alphabet requested. A request consists of a number between 1 and 26, and a newline character (\n). Assume that a client running this protocol is model checked, and the server runs as a peer application (see Figure 6). The client consists of a request thread, sending the request in two steps to the server, and a response thread, which reads the (atomic) response when available.

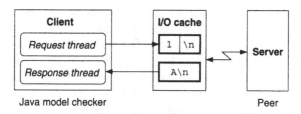

Fig. 6. A multi-threaded client requiring the cache to match requests to responses

Assume that in the first schedule, the model checker executes both request steps before the response is read. Both parts of the communication are then cached by the cache layer as described above. Now, the model checker tries a different schedule and backtracks to the state after the first half of the request, and executes the response thread. Clearly, the response should not (yet) be returned by the cache layer! Correctness of the cache layer can therefore only be ensured by polling the server after each request, in order to verify if a matching response exists for a complete request.

Previous work has implemented the basic I/O cache idea [4], but the design and implementation had several flaws.[1] This paper presents the first complete, fully working implementation, which has successfully been applied to complex software such as a concurrent HTTP server.

3   Formalization of the Caching Algorithm

A *request* is a message sent (written) to the peer, and a *response* is a message received (read) from the it. Our approach depends on two key assumptions:

---

[1] In the original design, communication channels were not always correctly assigned to threads. Furthermore, non-atomic messages could not be handled at all. Finally, the requirement to cache close operations as originally proposed [4] is redundant and can be dropped.

1. Deterministic peer responses: For each request sequence, there exists a corresponding unique response sequence.
2. Consistent application behavior: For each thread and each socket, the same requests are issued regardless of the thread schedule.

These assumptions allow for model checking a system when only one execution of peer processes is observed. Based on these two assumptions, we define our execution semantics of the state space exploration of input/output operations, which also verifies the second assumption.[2] The following definitions assume an assignment operator := as in computer programs, allowing for updates of variables and functions.

3.1 Stream Abstraction

A *data stream* s is a finite sequence of messages m: $s = \langle m_0, \ldots, m_{|s|-1} \rangle$. A *stream pointer* $sp_s = i$ refers to a particular index i in the message sequence of a given data stream s. A *communication trace* $t = \langle req, resp, \text{limit} \rangle$ consists of two data streams, a request stream *req* and a response stream *resp*, and a function $\text{limit}(sp_{req}) : sp_{resp}$. This function takes a request pointer and returns its corresponding response pointer.

Programs operate on a set T of communication traces t (which correspond to streams or sockets in a given programming language). One communication trace is associated to each socket. We augment the normal program state consisting of a global heap and several threads that each carry their own program counter and stack, by a pair of stream pointers $\langle sp_{req}, sp_{resp} \rangle$ for each communication trace t. This *extended program state* is managed by the model checker and subject to backtracking. Definitions below assume that stream pointers are changed by backtracking, while data in T remains unchanged.

In our approach, all communication traces have to be consistent with the first seen communication trace: In any possible program execution, there has to be one unique trace $\hat{t}$ such that for all thread schedules, $t = \hat{t}$ when the program terminates normally.[3] Consistency is checked by verifying message data of repeated requests against previously cached request data.

3.2 Execution Semantics

Model checking of a program using I/O is performed as follows: When progressing beyond previously cached messages, all operations are directly executed, using the functionality provided by the standard library. The result of that library function, using the correct set of parameters, will be denoted by lib_xy(...), where xy represents the original library function. Any error codes returned by library function will also be returned by our model. Our library model treats errors as if they occurred deterministically, e. g. as a result of invalid parameters. As our approach requires a deterministic response, nondeterministic errors arising from communication failures of the underlying network cannot be covered. For brevity, we omit error handling here.[4]

---

[2] As responses are cached, the first assumption cannot be verified at run-time. However, inconsistent peer behavior is detected if the peer itself is model checked in a separate analysis run.

[3] We omit treatment of input/output errors here. In such cases, program behavior diverges.

[4] Approaches that backtrack all processes involved, such as centralization, can inject communication failures into the simulation, but suffer from poor scalability [3].

Without loss of generality, we assume that each message has size 1. Multiple messages from a client may be required in order to elicit a server response. Conversely, at a given state, a response may consist of multiple messages of size 1. Operations always work on a given trace t, which is omitted in the following definitions for brevity.

Helper function `pollResponse` (see Algorithm 1) serves to check whether a given request produces a response from the peer. Responses are checked for and cached proactively, in order to correctly treat programs where responses are processed by an independent thread. Whenever a program reads from the same connection later on, cached response data will be used to determine the size of the response, i. e., the limit of the incoming message. Function `pollResponse` checks if data is available on the physical connection, and stores that data. It also updates function limit, which denotes the extent of the response received. This function is always defined up to the position where a request has been cached, i. e., up to $|req| - 1$.

Function `write` behaves in two possible ways, as shown in Algorithm 2: if previously recorded communication data extends beyond the current position, then current data is compared to previously written data. If no cached data exists at the current position, data is physically sent to the peer, and the peer is polled for a response. Reading data returns previously cached data, if a corresponding response had been cached by `pollResponse` after the last message was sent. If no data is available, function `read` blocks (see Algorithm 3).

When opening a connection (through `connect` or `accept` on the client and server side, respectively), the library function normally returns a socket object *sock* representing as a handle to that connection. As the behaviors of `connect` and `accept` are very similar, we will subsume both functions with `open` in this discussion. Our model library returns the same socket, but also maintains a communication trace object t for each socket. Subsequent communication via *sock* is cached in t . When backtracking to a point before the creation of *sock* (and t), *sock* is discarded, but t is merely marked as unused, such that re-execution of function `open` will retrieve the previously seen communication trace. Algorithm 4 summarizes this functionality. (Our implementation requires a consistent order in which sockets are created by different threads; relaxation of this criterion is subject to future work.) Closing a socket marks a communication trace t as unused, which allows it to be used again after backtracking, as shown in Algorithm 5.

3.3   Example Execution Scenario

Figure 7 shows an example state space exploration of the alphabet client described in Section 2. The first column depicts state space exploration, with the current state shown in black. The state of trace t and function limit in the current state are shown in the next two columns. In the protocol used by this example, newline characters that complete a request or response have been omitted for simplicity. The example client uses only one connection, so there exists only a single trace t. Trace t is illustrated as a two-row table with a request record (top), response record (bottom), and stream pointers pointing to a particular position in each data stream. Note that in this example, no data is returned after a connection is made; this results in an initial entry $0 \rightarrow 0$ for limit.

Algorithm 1. Function `pollResponse`. n is the size of the request.

$i := \text{limit}(sp_{req})$ (limit at current position)
while (data is available) do
    $resp_i := \text{lib\_read}(\ldots)$
    increment i
$\text{limit}(sp_{req} + n) := i$ (limit at new position)

Algorithm 2. Function `write`; d is the payload to be written.

$i := sp_{req}$
if $i < |req|$ then (check against cached data)
    abort if $req_i \neq d$
else (physically write new data and cache it)
    call `lib_write`$(\ldots)$
    $req_i := d$
    call `pollResponse`$(n = 1)$
increment sp_{req}

Algorithm 3. Function `read`.

$i := sp_{resp}$
if $i = \text{limit}(sp_{req})$ then (no data available)
    suspend current thread until data available
    call `pollResponse`$(n = 0)$
increment sp_{resp}
return $resp_i$ (cached data)

Algorithm 4. Function `open`.

---

create new socket object *sock*
if unused communication trace t_{old} available then
    $t := t_{old}$
else
    open new physical connection for *sock*
    $t :=$ new communication trace
mark t as used
bind t to *sock* (subsequent operations on s will access communication trace t)
call `pollResponse`$(n = 0)$ (certain protocols return data without requiring a request)

Algorithm 5. Function `close`, operating on socket *sock* and its trace t.

$i = sp_{req}$
if $i < |req|$ then (premature close)
    abort
if $i = |req|$ then
    if physical connection for *sock* is open, close it
    mark t as unused

State space exploration	Trace t	limit	Remarks
send "1" ⓪ ●	0 1 2 ↓ [1] [A] ↑	$0 \rightarrow 0$ $1 \rightarrow 1$	After an initial request "1", function `pollReponse` records server response "A". If the reader thread were scheduled now, it could read that response.
send "1" ⓪ send "2" ① ●	0 1 2 ↓ [1][2] [A][B] ↑	$0 \rightarrow 0$ $1 \rightarrow 1$ $2 \rightarrow 2$	A second request results in another response and another update of limit. If the reader thread were to access responses now, it would advance sp_{resp} twice, until the limit at the current request position (2) is reached.
send "1" ⓪ send "2" ① receive "A" ② ③	0 1 2 ↓ [1][2] [A][B] ↑	$0 \rightarrow 0$ $1 \rightarrow 1$ $2 \rightarrow 2$	After backtracking to the state after the first request, sp_{req} is backtracked to 1. The reader thread is scheduled, and accesses response data. The persistent mapping in limit ensures that only the first response is returned by the cache.

Fig. 7. An example demonstrating the interaction between sp_{req}, sp_{resp}, and limit

3.4 Limitations of Our Approach

Any program whose written messages fulfill the consistency criteria defined above can be model checked successfully using our approach. However, there are classes of programs that are normally considered to be valid, for which our criteria are too strict. This includes software that logs events to a file or network connection. For this discussion it is assumed that logging occurs by using methods open, write, and close. Assume further that actions of each thread can be interleaved with actions of other threads, which include logging.

If log entries of individual threads depend only on thread-local data, they are independent of each other. In such a case, different correct interleavings of log entries can occur without violating program correctness. If log data is sent over a single shared communication channel, occurrence of different message interleavings violates the criterion saying that written data at a specific position must be equal for all thread interleavings. Such programs can therefore not be model checked with our approach, unless some messages are exempted from the consistency check.

On a more general level, applications where communication depends on the global application state are not applicable to our approach. For instance, a chat server where the server sends a message back to all clients currently connected will violate our consistency criterion. In such a server, one connection is maintained per client. As the order in which incoming messages are processed differs between schedules, several interleavings of incoming messages are possible. As a consequence of this, the sequence of outgoing message varies as well across different schedules. The resulting inconsistency prevents our approach from being applicable. Applications where communication varies across schedules can still be model checked with our approach by abstraction over messages data, utilizing the same sequence of messages for each thread. In the

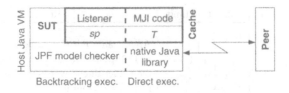

Fig. 8. The implementation architecture

chat server case, all messages are replaced by a string constant to allow our approach to proceed.

A large number of programs fulfills our requirement of deterministic communication traces. This includes any service-oriented architecture where several clients are served concurrently, but independently. Programs that violate the given invariant can still be model checked by using application centralization [1,3]. Centralization can also cope with slow responses, which occur when the network is slow or a response requires extensive computation on the peer.

In the caching approach, polling assumes that a response is ready shortly after a request has been sent. In our implementation, a short delay is induced in the SUT to wait for the response. Still, it cannot be guaranteed that a response is always received when logically possible. This shortcoming could only be overcome by inspection of the server, to determine whether a request has been fully processed. This could be implemented by code instrumentation in all peer systems, and is subject to future work.

4   Implementation

The I/O cache implements the Java library API for network I/O [15]. It fully controls messages exchanged between the system under test (SUT) in the model checker and external processes. Implementation details depend on the model checker and the way it allows access to internal events. We chose Java PathFinder (JPF) [23], a system to verify executable Java bytecode programs, as our model checker. It was chosen because it is openly available and features a stable API for extending model checker actions.

JPF is an execution framework for software verification purposes. Its latest version supports user extensions via two extension mechanisms, *listeners* and the *Model Java Interface*. During the execution of JPF, its internal state changes after each executed instruction. A listener subscribes to certain internal events, such as instruction execution or backtracking. It is notified by the JPF when such an event happens. The listener uses this information to verify application properties or customize search patterns. In our work, the listener notifies the cache layer when a state transition takes place.

The Model Java Interface (MJI) separates the Java virtual machine (VM) of JPF from the underlying Java VM of the host computer system, called *host VM*. The difference between JPF and host VM involves the backtracking function of the JPF. When an instruction is executed by the host VM, no backtracking occurs. An instruction executed by JPF is model checked with specified properties and subject to backtracking.

The architecture is summarized by Figure 8. The dashed vertical line shows which part of the cache code (shown by a solid box) execute within JPF, and which part execute directly on the host Java VM. In Java, the network library is implemented in package *java.net*. Key classes include *Socket*, *InetAddress* and *InetSocketAddress*. These classes contain native methods that physically communicate over the network. For these methods, backtracking is not possible. However, JPF allows users to replace standard library classes with user-defined classes. This extension is implemented through the MJI mechanism by creating two classes, called *model class* and *native peer* class, for each replaced standard class.

When the SUT is model checked by JPF, user-defined classes are executed instead of the standard library code. The native peer class, however, is still executed on the host JVM. Note that the model class can propagate methods where backtracking is not needed to the corresponding native peer class. User-defined classes can also utilize the MJI mechanism in order to avoid backtracking. By replacing the original Socket class with our customized version, communication between the SUT and its environment is redirected to the cache layer. The cache layer returns input and output communication channels to the client and behaves like the real peer.

5   Experiments

For evaluation of our approach, we conducted a number of experiments. To facilitate automation, these experiments were performed on a single computer. In principle, peer applications could also be run on a different host when using our I/O caching approach. While this may be necessary to model check software working together with third-party clients or services, having all processes under our control greatly facilitated the setup.

For model checking, startup of the SUT and the remote application have to be synchronized. Otherwise, the client may attempt to contact the server before it is ready. Premature client startup can be avoided in two ways:

1. Extra control code could be added to the client, ensuring that the server is ready. For instance, the client could retry a communication attempt in the event of failure.
2. Starting the client is delayed after starting the server. This allows the server to initialize itself and be ready for communication.

The second approach may start the client prematurely, if the delay is too small. In practice, it has the advantage that the SUT does not have to be modified, and proved to work quite well. If the client is started too early, this can be seen immediately from the client log. Restarting the client later therefore fixes this issue. Automation of this could be achieved by using operating system utilities such as `trace`, `strace`, or `truss` [14], to supervise system calls.

The Java PathFinder model checker [23], version 4 revision 353, was used for our experiment. This version features great performance improvements over version 3. Unfortunately, revision 354 introduced a new bug that prevented us from running the centralized test applications on newer revisions.[5]

---

[5] While we have reported that bug more than a year ago, we were unable to produce a small test case that reproduces it. The large size and run-time of the test producing a failure has made it impossible to determine the exact location of the problem.

Table 1. Example applications used

Application	Description
Daytime client	Returns the current time (RFC 867).
Jget client, version 0.4.1	Multi-threaded, multi-connection HTTP client.
Web server (for Jget)	Multi-threaded, multi-connection HTTP server.
Alphabet client/server	Returns the nth character of the alphabet.
Chat server	Sends messages of one client to all clients.

5.1 Example Applications

Table 1 gives an overview of the examples used as benchmarks. The *daytime client* connects to a server, which sends a fixed string back to the client.[6] While the server is single-threaded, the client launches concurrent requests. In this case, the client is more complex than the sequential server, and was the focus of model checking.

Jget [18] is a multi-threaded download client, which issues a number of concurrent partial download requests in addition to the main request. Depending on which task finishes first, Jget either uses the entire file downloaded by the main thread, or it assembles the file from the pieces returned by the partial downloads. Essentially, the worker threads are in a (controlled) race condition against the main thread. This creates the challenge of ensuring that the complete file is received when the program shuts down. In order to allow for the necessary concurrency and partial downloads, we augmented an existing example web server [20] with ability to serve parts of a file. The resulting system proved too complex for model checking with JPF, so it was abstracted to a slightly simpler system. The abstract system has all strings of HTTP reduced to very short literals, eliminating the necessity of string parsing.

The *alphabet client* generates two threads per connection: a producer and a consumer thread. They communicate with the *alphabet server*. The server expects a string containing a number, terminated by a newline character, and returns the corresponding character of the alphabet. In this case, both the client and the server are multi-threaded, and were model checked.

The chat server, described in more detail in [1], sends the input of one client back to all clients, including the one that sent the input. The original chat client transmits its ID at the beginning of each message. This ID causes a mismatch in the cached server input when the order of server worker threads is reversed after backtracking. Therefore, the client ID was stripped from the transmitted messages when using our cache approach. (Code that builds a compound string using that ID was left in the system to maintain the same complexity for comparison purposes.)

5.2 Results

All experiments were run on an Intel Core 2 Duo Mac 2.33 GHz with 2 GB of RAM, running Mac OS 10.4.11. JPF was given 1 GB of memory, a limit that was never

---

[6] For the purpose of model checking, the "date" used was hard-coded in the replacement class for `java.util.Date`.

Table 2. Results of our experiments. The table lists the applications with the number of connections or threads used first. The "scale" parameter refers to the number of messages per connection in the alphabet server, and the number of concurrent connections accepted in the chat server case. Results using the centralization approach are compared to analyzing the client and the server side separately, using our I/O caching approach.

Appl.	# conn./ threads	Scale param.	Centralization Time [mm:ss]	States new	revisited	I/O caching approach — Client Time [mm:ss]	States new	revisited	Server Time [mm:ss]	States new	revisited
daytime	2	n/a	0:57	33123	71608	0:01	204	229	Server implementation		
	3		55:39	715941	4726181	0:03	2140	3983	is not concurrent.		
	4		>2 h			0:38	25744	67638			
	5					10:16	356122	1216424			
	6					>2 h					
Jget	2	n/a	>2 h			0:50	31015	50640	0:14	7636	14250
alphabet	2	1	112:24	JPF error		0:04	3631	8711	0:02	102	96
		2	>2 h			0:11	11386	27978	0:02	226	214
		3				0:25	27211	67871	0:03	394	372
		4				0:50	54246	136362	0:03	610	574
		5				1:28	96253	243045	0:03	874	820
	3	1	>2 h			4:42	226646	904025	0:03	1072	2069
		2				30:14	1383304	5764677	0:06	4011	7587
		3				138:38	5017624	21325338	0:10	9347	17347
		4				>2 h			0:18	17947	32951
		5							0:28	30579	55755
	4	1	>2 h			>2 h			0:16	12014	65646
		2							1:16	70308	200088
		3							3:39	208228	579576
		4							8:26	483812	1331400
		5							16:31	967092	2643048
	5	1	>2 h			>2 h			3:14	134700	537111
		2							26:06	1185717	4516299
		3							97:46	4407369	16449707
		4							>2 h		
	6	1	>2 h			>2 h			42:25	1487902	7432964
		2							>2 h		
	7	1	>2 h			>2 h			>2 h		
chat	2	1	2:12	50284	143439	Client implementation			0:03	112	81
		2	77:08	714830	2668937	is not concurrent.			0:08	4100	4935
	3	1	89:28	1819345	6786956				0:03	112	81
		2	>2 h						0:08	4100	4935
		3							3:52	115036	221174
	4	1	>2 h						0:03	112	81
		2							0:08	4100	4935
		3							3:56	115036	221174
		4							>2 h		

exhausted, and a time limit of two hours. The standard properties used by JPF were verified: We checked against deadlocks, uncaught exceptions, and assertion violations. The original version of Jget (0.4.1) included a few initial bugs in the calculation of ranges, and an inefficient design that relied on busy-waiting. These initial flaws were fixed prior to further analysis. When model checking the final abstracted version of Jget, we found that Jget erroneously reported an incomplete download, even though the entire file was received. Furthermore, the abstract version of the web server may exhibit a (handled) null pointer exception due to sloppy error handling in our own extension for download ranges. Investigation of the problems in Jget (whether due to a bug in the original application or in the abstraction) remains subject to future work; therefore, we did not investigate other settings for Jget.

No program contained a critical error that would have terminated the state space search by JPF and resulted in an error message. JPF therefore investigated the full state space, allowing a comparison of the size of both models. Where possible, we compared the results of our approach to model checking all the clients and the server processes using centralization [1]. Note that in our new caching approach, the client and server are analyzed separately, while in centralization, they are analyzed together. Our approach therefore requires at least two model checker runs, but allows for analyzing much larger programs, as the state space explosion of combined processes is avoided. However, our approach sacrifices analysis of all possible combinations of client/server behaviors for efficiency. This is most obvious for the Jget/web server pair, where only one possible schedule on the client side is exhibited when model checking the server.

Table 2 shows the results of all our experiments. The daytime server and the chat client do not exhibit any concurrency; therefore, an analysis by JPF was not necessary, as it would not reveal any results that cannot be obtained by ordinary testing. The table is divided into three parts: A description of the test case, and the results of the centralization and caching approaches. The test setup includes the name of the application, the number of connections or threads used, and a scale parameter for the last two cases. For the alphabet server, the number of messages per connection was varied. For the chat server, limiting the number of concurrently accepted clients was another way to curb the state space.

The second and third part of the table show the results for the two different approaches. The I/O caching approach is analyzing the client and server separately, with the peer process(es) running outside the model checker. As the peer processes consume next to no resources compared to the model checker, only the time spent in the model checker is shown. For completed runs, the number of program states analyzed by the model checker is shown as well. "New" states refer to distinct program states; "revisited" states refer to redundant states that resulted in backtracking.

Finally, we have also verified that the I/O caching approach finds synchronization problems present in faulty versions of the chat server that were investigated in earlier work [1]. These errors can be found if two or more clients are present. With both I/O caching and centralization, JPF immediately finds a schedule exhibiting a data race. However, the I/O cache allows for more in-depth analysis of the revised chat server, where the absence of faults can be confirmed for up to three clients with our new approach.

5.3 Summary

Our experiments in Table 2 show that model checking with our I/O caching approach is orders of magnitudes faster than model checking using centralization. Our new approach is capable of analyzing interesting and complex system such as concurrent client/server implementations with up to at least three concurrent connections. The fact that concurrency problems can be ruled out at that scale gives good confidence that they are also absent for a larger number of connections, even though no formal proof for this exists. We therefore think that our approach constitutes a very important breakthrough in scalability for model checking networked software.

The reason for this improved scalability is that our approach executes only a single process inside the model checker, analyzing all interleavings of its threads. This avoids analysis of the product of all state spaces of all processes. When analyzing a complete system consisting of multiple processes, each process should be analyzed in turn in the model checker using our cache, with other processes running as peers. The resulting complexity of all analysis runs will correspond to the sum of the state spaces of each process. This is vastly smaller than the product thereof. Our caching approach inherently cannot analyze all possible schedules of peer processes, making it less sound than aggregation-based approaches such as centralization [1]. However, this sacrifice allows scalability to systems that were previously out of reach, making it more useful in practice.

6 Related Work

Software model checkers [2,5,7,10,12,13,23] store the full program state (or differences to a previously stored state) for backtracking. They are typically implemented as explicit-state model checkers. Milestone creation and backtracking operations occur many times during state space exploration. This causes operations to be executed several times when a set of schedules is explored. Such exploration does not treat communication behavior accurately, as described in the introduction.

One solution is to model I/O operations as as stubs. In this approach, communication operations are modeled by shared memory, semaphores, and channels. Peer processes are included in the resulting system [8,16] or modeled by a (possibly abstracted) environment process or stub [5,7,11]. Abstraction in the environment ensures scalability but can lead to false positives requiring refinement of the model. In most tools, stubs for communication operations and environment processes are provided manually, at a level of abstraction suitable to the problem at hand [8,11,16]. The process of generating the optimal abstraction can be automated but is of course still constrained by computational resources [5,7]. Our approach is fully automated, requiring no abstraction. However, applicability relies on the equality of communication traces between schedules, a property that is checked at run-time.

A general solution to model checking multiple communicating processes is to lift the power of a model checker to operating system (OS) level. This way, the effect of I/O operations are visible inside the model checker. An existing system that indeed stores and restores full OS states is based on user-mode Linux [17]. That model checker uses the GNU debugger to store states and intercept system calls. The effects of system calls are modeled by hand, but applications can be model checked together without modifying the application code. In that approach, the combined state space of all processes is explored. Our approach analyzes a single process at a time inside a model checker, while running other processes normally. Our approach is therefore more scalable but requires programs to fulfill certain restrictions. On the technical side, OS-level model checkers intercept communication at device level, where the network device itself is wrapped. We intercept communication at library call level.

External processes could be backtracked in tandem with the system under test, for instance, by restarting them [8,13]. In existing implementations, one central scheduler controls and backtracks several processes, effectively implementing a multi-process model checker [13,16]. Like all approaches controlling multiple processes inside the model checker, it incurs a massive state space explosion.

In an alternative approach, multiple processes are analyzed in a single-process model checker after applying program transformation. *Centralization* transforms multiple processes into threads, creating a single-process application [19]. This allows several processes to run in the same model checker, but does not solve the problem of modeling inter-process communication (input/output). Recent work modeled network communication in the centralized model where all processes are executed inside the model checker [1,3]. Communication and backtracking of centralized processes all occur in a single model checker. Other work has implemented this approach in a similar way, but sacrificed full automation in favor of manual instrumentation of communication operations [6]. That tool has another mode in which it can run, allowing for replacing peer processes with stubs. In this approach, a program that just repeats previously observed communication contents is used as peer. Recent work has gone into automating this process by a tool that captures communication in a corresponding stub program [6]. When using stubs from a previous recorded communication, the assumptions mentioned in Section 3 also have to hold. In contrast to stub usage, our approach eliminates the need for an intermediary stub program. Our approach records communication and replays it on the fly, in one module. Furthermore, it even allows model checking of applications where external processes are not running on a platform that the model checkers supports.

Our approach curbs state space explosion by only running a single process inside the model checker. It builds on previous work [4] that introduced the idea of I/O caching. Previous work has several shortcomings and flaws that prevented the idea from working on realistic examples. First, it did not always correctly associate sockets to traces, and traces to threads. Second, it lacked the crucial idea of proactive response caching. Because of this, the implementation showed problems on more complex examples. Our work is the first one to complete to formalization and implementation of the I/O caching idea [4] proposed earlier.

7   Conclusions

When model checking communicating programs, processes outside the model checker are affected by communication but not subject to backtracking. Executing different branches of a non-deterministic decision is not applicable to external communication. With traditional approaches for model checking software, input/output operations had to be subsumed by stubs, or multiple processes had to be executed inside the model checker. The former is difficult to automate, while the latter suffers from scalability problems.

We defined special caching semantics for stream-based I/O, which includes network communication. This generates the corresponding behavior of a stub on the fly, during model checking. If program behavior is independent of the execution schedule, such a program can be model checked using our cache layer semantics. Unlike most previous work, we can handle implementations using standard network libraries without any manual intervention, while eliminating some scalability issues of some related approaches. We also have a fully working and very scalable implementation of our algorithm for the Java PathFinder model checker, and we could successfully model check several complex applications where multiple clients interact with in parallel with a server.

8 Future Work

Future work includes possible relaxations of the completeness criteria defined, regarding the order of I/O operations and socket creations. Specifically, certain interleaved write actions on the same communication channel should be allowed, such as log entries.

Current work focuses on model checking applications communicating by TCP. This protocol is reliable in the sense that message order is preserved, and messages are not lost. However, we think that the main concept can be modified and be applied to I/O failures, where communication is interrupted. This would also make it possible to model check applications communicating by lightweight but unreliable protocols such as the User Datagram Protocol (UDP). We will also work on the issue of slow responses, by implementing a tool that instruments the peer application in order to signal readiness for new requests to the model checker. Finally, it remains to be seen how far our approach, which has so far been tried on service-oriented client-server systems, is applicable to peer-to-peer systems or multicast protocols.

References

1. Artho, C., Garoche, P.: Accurate centralization for applying model checking on networked applications. In: Proc. 21st Intl. Conf. on Automated Software Engineering (ASE 2006), Tokyo, Japan, pp. 177–188. IEEE Computer Society (2006)
2. Artho, C., Schuppan, V., Biere, A., Eugster, P., Baur, M., Zweimüller, B.: JNuke: Efficient Dynamic Analysis for Java. In: Alur, R., Peled, D.A. (eds.) CAV 2004. LNCS, vol. 3114, pp. 462–465. Springer, Heidelberg (2004)
3. Artho, C., Sommer, C., Honiden, S.: Model checking networked programs in the presence of transmission failures. In: Proc. 1st Joint IEEE/IFIP Symposium on Theoretical Aspects of Software Engineering (TASE 2007), Shanghai, China, pp. 219–228. IEEE Computer Society (2007)
4. Artho, C., Zweimüller, B., Biere, A., Shibayama, E., Honiden, S.: Efficient model checking of applications with input/output. In: Moreno Díaz, R., Pichler, F., Quesada Arencibia, A. (eds.) EUROCAST 2007. LNCS, vol. 4739, pp. 515–522. Springer, Heidelberg (2007)
5. Ball, T., Podelski, A., Rajamani, S.: Boolean and Cartesian Abstractions for Model Checking C Programs. In: Margaria, T., Yi, W. (eds.) TACAS 2001. LNCS, vol. 2031, pp. 268–285. Springer, Heidelberg (2001)
6. Barlas, E., Bultan, T.: Netstub: a framework for verification of distributed Java applications. In: Proc. 22nd Intl. Conf. on Automated Software Engineering (ASE 2007), Atlanta, USA, pp. 24–33. ACM (2007)
7. Chaki, S., Clarke, E., Groce, A., Jha, S., Veith, H.: Modular verification of software components in C. IEEE Transactions on Software Engineering 30(6), 388–402 (2004)

8. Chandra, S., Godefroid, P., Palm, C.: Software model checking in practice: an industrial case study. In: Proc. 24th Intl. Conf. on Software Engineering (ICSE 2002), pp. 431–441. ACM Press, New York (2002)

9. Clarke, E., Grumberg, O., Peled, D.: Model checking. MIT Press, Cambridge (1999)

10. Corbett, J., Dwyer, M., Hatcliff, J., Pasareanu, C.: Bandera: Extracting finite-state models from Java source code. In: Proc. 22nd Intl. Conf. on Software Engineering (ICSE 2000), Limerick, Ireland, pp. 439–448. ACM Press (2000)

11. Dingel, J.: Computer-assisted assume/guarantee reasoning with VeriSoft. In: Proc. 25th Intl. Conf. on Software Engineering (ICSE 2003), Washington, USA, pp. 138–148. IEEE Computer Society (2003)

12. Dwyer, M., Hatcliff, J., Hoosier, M.: Building your own software model checker using the Bogor extensible model checking framework. In: Etessami, K., Rajamani, S.K. (eds.) CAV 2005. LNCS, vol. 3576, pp. 148–152. Springer, Heidelberg (2005)

13. Godefroid, P.: Model checking for programming languages using VeriSoft. In: Proc. 24th ACM Symposium on Principles of Programming Languages (POPL 1997), Paris, France, pp. 174–186. ACM Press (1997)

14. Goldberg, I., Wagner, D., Thomas, R., Brewer, E.: A secure environment for untrusted helper applications. In: Proc. 6th Usenix Security Symposium (SSYM 1996), San Jose, USA, pp. 1–13. USENIX Association (1996)

15. Gosling, J., Joy, B., Steele, G., Bracha, G.: The Java Language Specification, 3rd edn. Addison-Wesley (2005)

16. Musuvathi, M., Park, D., Chou, A., Engler, D., Dill, D.: CMC: a pragmatic approach to model checking real code. SIGOPS Oper. Syst. Rev. 36(SI), 75–88 (2002)

17. Nakagawa, Y., Potter, R., Yamamoto, M., Hagiya, M., Kato, K.: In: Proc. Workshop on Dependable Software: Tools and Methods, Yokohama, Japan, pp. 215–220 (2005)

18. Paredes, S.: Jget (2006), http://www.cec.uchile.cl/~sparedes/jget/

19. Stoller, S., Liu, Y.: Transformations for model checking distributed Java programs. In: Dwyer, M.B. (ed.) SPIN 2001. LNCS, vol. 2057, pp. 192–199. Springer, Heidelberg (2001)

20. Sun Microsystems, Santa Clara, USA. A simple, multi-threaded HTTP server (2008), http://www.java.sun.com/developer/technicalArticles/Networking/Webserver/

21. Tanenbaum, A.: Modern operating systems. Prentice-Hall (1992)

22. Tanenbaum, A.: Computer Networks. Prentice-Hall (2002)

23. Visser, W., Havelund, K., Brat, G., Park, S., Lerda, F.: Model checking programs. Automated Software Engineering Journal 10(2), 203–232 (2003)

Controlling Accessibility in Agile Projects with the Access Modifier Modifier

Philipp Bouillon[1], Eric Großkinsky[2], and Friedrich Steimann[3]

[1] Tensegrity Software GmbH
Im Mediapark 6a
D-50670 Köln
Philipp.Bouillon@tensegrity.de
[2] LG Programmiersysteme
Fernuniversität in Hagen
D-58084 Hagen
egrosskinsky@online.de
[3] LG Programmiersysteme
Fernuniversität in Hagen
D-58084 Hagen
steimann@acm.org

Abstract. Access modifiers like public and private let the programmer control the accessibility of class members. Restricted accessibility supports encapsulation, i.e., the hiding of implementation details behind the interface of a class. However, what is an implementation detail and what makes the interface of a class is often subject to change: especially in an agile setting (with absence of an upfront design dictating accessibility levels), the interface of a class evolves much like its implementation, settling only towards the finalization of a project. However, while insufficient accessibility is reported by the compiler, excessive accessibility is not, the effect being that massively refactored programs usually end up with larger interfaces than necessary. With our ACCESS MODIFIER MODIFIER tool, we allow programmers to increase and keep accessibility at higher levels during the development phase, and reduce it only once the required access has stabilized. Fixed design decisions (such as a published API) can be designated by corresponding annotations, making them immune to changes through our tool. Evaluating the ACCESS MODIFIER MODIFIER on a number of internal packages taken from the JAVA open source community, we found that accessibility was excessive in 32% of cases on average.

Keywords: Design, Encapsulation, Agile software development, Refactoring, Tool support.

1 Introduction

In languages like JAVA supporting information hiding [19] through access modifiers such as private and public, any attempt to reference an insufficiently accessible class member results in a compile-time error [9]. By contrast, excessive accessibility does not — instead, it is often tacitly assumed that higher than required accessibility, or

R.F. Paige and B. Meyer (Eds.): TOOLS EUROPE 2008, LNBIP 11, pp. 41–59, 2008.

even accessibility without any access from within the program, is granted intention-ally, i.e., that it reflects the designed interface (or API) of a class. However, in pro-gramming practice, in agile settings especially, the design of interfaces changes as part of the refactoring of code, and changes to accessibility are driven by what is nec-essary rather than what is superfluous, usually leading to the phenomenon that high levels of accessibility that are no longer needed are nevertheless maintained. While this may seem an inexcusable lack of discipline, we conjecture that it is also due to a lack of information: the maintainer of a class is not necessarily aware of all its clients and the access they require, so that reducing accessibility is a trial and error process. What would be needed instead is some kind of warning indicating where accessibility is unnecessarily high.

In JAVA, access modifiers do not only control accessibility of program elements, they also contribute to the semantics of a program. In particular, accessibility has an effect on dynamic binding and also on static method resolution under overloading and hiding [9]. Seemingly innocuous changes of access modifiers may therefore silently change the meaning of a program, so that tools preventing such unintended changes should be highly welcome.

To address these problems, we have devised a new tool, called ACCESS MODIFIER MODIFIER (AMM), that helps the programmer control the accessibility of class mem-bers. We have implemented this tool as a plug-in to the ECLIPSE Java Development Tools (JDT), and evaluated it by automatically applying it to several internal packages of large and well-known projects. The tool and a brief guide to its use are available for download at http://www.fernuni-hagen.de/ps/prjs/AMM2/.

The contribution of this paper is fourfold:

1. We define the notions of sufficient and excessive accessibility of class members.
2. We investigate the conditions under which excessive accessibility levels can be changed without changing program semantics.
3. We describe the implementation of a tool that helps control the accessibility of class members.
4. We present empirical evidence that our tool support for accessibility changes, re-ductions especially, is useful in practice.

The remainder of this paper is organized as follows. In Section 2, we take a quick look at how programmers set accessibility of class members in practice, and derive from their behaviour desirable tool support. In the sections that follow, we address our four contribution listed above. We conclude by discussing our approach and by com-paring it to related work.

2 Motivation

In JAVA, accessibility levels of class members control the interfaces of classes and packages. As long as the design has not stabilized, these interfaces are subject to change. Changes may require an increase in accessibility, or may allow a decrease; in the first case, action by the developer is mandatory (otherwise the program will not compile), in the second, it is optional. In both cases, the changes are initiated by add-ing or removing dependencies in some remote place (different class or package) and therefore require the parallel editing of two source code locations (files), disrupting the work flow in an untoward way.

Under these conditions, programmers usually experience a certain tension between the goals "ease of coding" and "achieving maximum encapsulation". The poles of this tension are succinctly described by the following, opposing approaches:

1. *Create Publicly Privatize Later.* This is the liberal approach pursued by developers striving for maximum flexibility during development: all methods of a class are inherited to its subclasses and can be accessed freely by other classes. While this design may be viewed as needlessly bloating the interface of a class, it saves the developers from anticipating adequate accessibility levels. At the same time, public accessibility facilitates unit testing which, depending on the testing framework used, requires public access to the methods under test. On the other hand, without additional API documentation it leaves users of the so-designed classes ignorant of which methods they can rely on (the stable, or published [6] interface) and which are subject to change without notice. Privatizing members later is possible, but difficult (see below); in particular, care must be taken that this does not change program semantics (see Section 4).

2. *Create Privately Publish Later.* This is the cautious approach pursued by programmers caring about information hiding, acknowledging the fact that "it's easy to widen accessibility, but more difficult to reduce the accessibility of a feature in working code." [2] It leaves no doubt concerning the required accessibility of a member: if it is higher than private, then this is so because it is actually needed, not because someone speculated that it might be needed in the future [2]. However, even these developers must face the fact that as the design changes, a member may be left with excessive accessibility, and the resulting problem is the same as that for the first approach. Also, when it turns out that the accessibility must be increased, they cannot be sure that this change does not affect program semantics.

Both approaches are extreme and in programming practice, a mixture of both will likely occur. However, each approach is representative of one practical programming problem that we would like to address with our AMM:

1. For creating publicly and privatizing later, an indication that informs the developer of member declarations whose accessibility level is higher than required by design during and in particular at the end of development would be helpful. This accessibility should be reducible to the minimum required level using a corresponding micro-refactoring offered to the programmer (in ECLIPSE in the guise of a so-called Quick Fix). In doing so, the tool should be aware of whether the reduction is at all possible without changing program semantics. It should also be able to accept that a given member is part of the API, so that accessibility should not be reduced, or only criticized as being too high.

2. For creating privately and publishing later, when access to a member with insufficient accessibility is needed, the developer should be allowed to increase its accessibility without having to switch to its declaration site. This is already possible in ECLIPSE, although only via the detour of using the inaccessible member, thus forcing a compile-time error which can then be removed via the offered Quick Fix increasing accessibility as required. However, it would be more convenient were the developer allowed to inspect the hidden members and select from those (in the

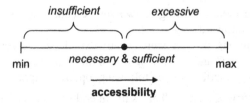

Fig. 1. A class member's accessibility status is either *insufficient*, or *necessary and sufficient*, or *excessive*. While accessibility must be sufficient for a program to compile, excessive levels of accessibility are accepted. In absence of an API (i.e., for closed, monolithic programs), the necessary and sufficient accessibility level (depicted by the dot) of each program element is uniquely determined by the program and can be derived by means of a whole-program analysis.

same manner so-called Content Assist works for accessible members), having the selected member's accessibility adapted before using it.[1] Again, the AMM tool should guarantee that this does not change program semantics, this time by not offering members whose accessibility level must be maintained.

The privatization functionality described above can also be useful when a project has been tested and is now to be released, so that the test suites are removed, allowing accessibility of methods previously required to be public solely for the sake of testing to be reduced. For this purpose, an automated execution of all suggested accessibility reductions is desirable.

3   Sufficient and Excessive Accessibility

Before elaborating on how the above goals can be achieved, an analysis of the problem is necessary. For this, we begin with a definition of the terms of sufficient and excessive accessibility.

Sufficient (or its converse, *insufficient*) and *necessary* (or its converse, *excessive*) accessibility are determined by the access control rules of the language, and by the mutual use dependencies of program elements organized in modules. JAVA has four accessibility levels named *public*, *protected*, *default* (deriving form the fact that it has no corresponding access modifier keyword; also called *package local*), and *private*, and two module constructs (module in the sense that something can be hidden inside it), namely *class* and *package*. Dependency is divided into *uses* (or *call*) dependency and *inheritance* (subclassing). Public accessibility of the members of a class lets them being depended upon by any other class, protected by all its subclasses and any class in the same package, default by any class in the same package, and private only by the owning class. These simple rules suffice to detect access violations, i.e., attempts to access class members declared to be out of reach (i.e., *inaccessible*, sometimes also be referred to as invisible, although this term is defined differently in the JAVA language

---

[1] To whom this appears as sabotaging the very purpose of modularization (or information hiding [19]), be reminded that the strategy is "create privately, publish later". In agile development, corresponding design changes are a matter of fact. Cf. Section 7.

specification [9]). If no access violations occur, the accessibility of all members is *sufficient*. It may however be *excessive*, namely when it is sufficient, but higher than necessary, so that accessibility of members can be reduced without becoming insufficient.[2] Figure 1 illustrates the situation.

To distinguish sufficient and excessive accessibility (defined by use) from the accessibility expressed by access modifiers (public etc., defined by declaration), we refer to the former as *status* and to the latter as *level* of accessibility (but omit this distinction if it is not clear from the context). The status of accessibility is a property of the level of accessibility and as such (indirectly) a property of a class member, even though insufficient accessibility is usually ascribed to concrete uses of a class member and not to the class member itself. Because in JAVA, the clients of a class member are not known to that member or its owning class (this is different, e.g., for EIFFEL, which has a dedicated export [17]), all accessibility states must be determined globally, i.e., by an analysis of the whole program.[3] There is however an important difference between the accessibility states *sufficient* and *excessive* with respect to the development process, i.e., with respect to adding and removing dependencies on class members during development:

- When adding a new or removing an existing dependency, (preservation of) *sufficient* accessibility can always be checked locally, i.e., solely by determining the position of the calling or subclassing class relative to the class depended upon in the package structure and in the class hierarchy.
- By contrast, *non-excessive* accessibility is harder to maintain. In particular, it cannot be checked locally: as shown in Figure 2, adding or removing a dependency may or may not affect the excessiveness of accessibility, and which is actually the case is not determined by the now using, or no longer using, class alone.

It is important to understand that accessibility *status* is determined by the actual use of (or dependency on) class members in a project, while accessibility *level* determines their actual usability. This inversion of relationship is reflected in the implementation of our AMM tool, which needs to set up inverse data structures (see Section 5).

3.1 Accessibility Status and APIs

Things are less clear-cut when projects are analysed that are designed for use by others or open for extension (such as libraries or frameworks). In such projects, necessary and sufficient accessibility levels are not only determined by the actual (present) dependencies, but also by the *designed interface* to the external world, which is often referred to as the *Application Programming Interface* (API). Members of the API may

---

[2] In mathematical logic, a condition can be *necessary* (i.e., not *excessive*), but not *sufficient*. We do not consider this case here — a program with insufficient accessibility is incorrect (does not compile) and therefore outside the scope of this paper.

[3] Note that compilers commonly do not perform whole program analyses, but check sufficiency of accessibility per use. Insufficient accessibility is then marked as an error of the use site (attempted access violation) and not of the inaccessible class member. This reflects the viewpoint that the language should enforce information hiding. The scope of this paper is however slightly different.

```
package same;
class Called {
  private void m() {…} // insufficient accessibility
  public void n() {…}  // sufficient and excessive accessibility
  public void p() {…}  // necessary and sufficient accessibility
}

package same;
class Caller {
    …
    Called o = …
    o.m(); // compile-time error
    o.n(); // OK
    o.p(); // OK
    …
}

package other;
import same.Called;
class Caller {
    …
    Called o = …
    o.p(); // OK
    …
}
```

Fig. 2. Insufficient, necessary and sufficient, and excessive accessibility of members of a serving class, determined by two client classes, one in the same, one in another package. When adding access to n() in other.Caller, it is not decidable locally whether its status of accessibility changes from *excessive* to *necessary and sufficient* (it does, actually). Vice versa, when removing access to p(), it is unclear whether status of p() changes from *necessary and sufficient* to *excessive* (it does again). Note that insufficient accessibility is usually marked at the call site (through a corresponding compile-time error), while excessive accessibility can only be ascribed to the called (or, rather, not called) site (cf. Footnote 3).

be required to be declared public even if not being accessed from within the project itself, or protected even without the existence of project-internal subclasses. In these cases, accessibility of a class member is excessive only if the member is not part of the API, even if there is no actual dependency *within* the project requiring the given accessibility.

Unfortunately, JAVA has no linguistic means to express what is part of the API — the meaning of public or protected accessibility is unspecific in that use of the corresponding access modifiers cannot distinguish internally required from externally required accessibility [6]. It follows that if the API is not otherwise formally documented (e.g., through javadoc tags), it is impossible to decide mechanically whether a member's accessibility is excessive. To make up for JAVA's inability to distinguish API form internally required accessibility levels, some development teams have adopted the Eclipse Naming Conventions to designate packages whose public and protected methods are supposed to be *not* part of the API:

All packages that are part of the platform implementation but contain no API that should be exposed to ISVs [Independent Software Vendors] are considered internal implementation packages. All implementation packages should be flagged as internal, with the tag occurring just after the major package name. ISVs will be told that all packages marked internal are out of bounds. (A simple text search for ".internal." detects suspicious reference in source files; likewise, "/internal/" is suspicious in .class files). [4]

and also:

Packages with [the .internal] prefix are implementation packages for use within the given module. Types and fields that are accessible within these packages MUST NOT be used outside the module itself. Some runtime environments may enforce this reduced accessibility scope. [8]

Instead of marking packages as internal, we will introduce an annotation that tags class members as being part of the API, so that our tool never classifies their accessibility as excessive. However, we will make use of the "internal" naming convention in the evaluation of our approach (Section 6).

3.2 Accessibility Status and Subtyping

Subtyping dictates that accessibility of methods overridden in subtypes must not be lower than that in their supertypes (so that the cancellation of members by making them inaccessible is made impossible). While this is required by the principle of substitutability [16], it tends to get in the way when subclassing is done primarily for the sake of inheritance; often, then, many inherited class members are unneeded, so that their accessibility is factually excessive (and required only by the possibility of substitution, which may never take place). In this case, replacing inheritance with forwarding or delegation [12] is indicated.

However, it is possible that the necessary accessibility of a member overridden in a subclass is higher than that in its superclass. This is for instance the case when a client of the subclass requires public access, whereas for the superclass protected access suffices. When this additional client is moved to the same package as the subclass, the accessibility can be lowered to protected. If the accessibility required from the member in the superclass is then changed to default, the accessibility of both can be reduced simultaneously to this level.

Things are reversed when an increase of accessibility for a superclass's method is required. If its subclasses override the method with same (former) accessibility level, the increase in the superclass is not allowed unless the subclasses are changed with it. In these cases, increasing visibility of the whole hierarchy may be indicated.

Note that in JAVA, the same rules apply to static methods, for which hiding replaces overriding [9, § 8.4.8]: the access modifier of a hiding method must provide at least as much access as the hidden method, or a compile-time error occurs.

3.3 Interface Implementation

JAVA has a special type construct, named *interface*, whose members are implicitly public. Interfaces can be subtyped by classes, in which case the class must implement all methods declared by the interface. As with subclassing and overriding, visibility of implemented methods must not be reduced — in this case, it must remain public.

Things are slightly complicated by the fact that interface implementation introduces the possibility of multiple subtyping, i.e., that a class can have more than one

```
class A {
    public void m() {...}
}

interface I {
    void m();
}

class B extends A implements I {
    ...
}
```

Fig. 3. Indirect accessibility constraint imposed by a subclass implementing an interface

direct supertype (a superclass and one or more interfaces). This leads to the constellation shown in Figure 3, in which visibility of m in A cannot be reduced, but not because A implements I, but because a subclass of it does.

3.4 Anonymous Subclasses

JAVA allows anonymous subclasses which can override methods just like ordinary subclasses. Their existence therefore has to be considered when searching for excessiveness of accessibility, and also when checking for a possible increase of accessibility in a superclass (see Section 3.2). A somewhat unexpected constraint results from anonymous subclasses *not* overriding methods: upon occurrence of the expression

```
new C(){}.m()
```

in a program, accessibility of m() in C cannot be reduced beyond what is required by the (location of the) expression.

4 Accessibility and Program Semantics

Access modifiers not only control the accessibility of class members by their clients, they also play a role when selecting from a number of competing member definitions. When the members are methods, this selection process is called binding. JAVA distinguishes static and dynamic binding; each will be considered separately.

4.1 Dynamic Binding: Overriding with Open Recursion

As discussed in Section 3.2, the accessibility of overriding and overridden methods depends on each other in that the accessibility of the overriding method in the subclass must be at least that of the overridden method in the superclass. One might be led to believe that accessibility of the methods can be changed freely as long as this constraint is satisfied. However, this is not the case.

Subclassing comes with an interesting twist to uses-dependency: while methods defined in the superclass can be called from the subclass and its clients, they can also call methods defined in the subclass, namely via overriding and open recursion [20] (the mechanism behind the TEMPLATE METHOD pattern [7]). For overriding, the overridden method must be declared at least default if the subclass, the superclass and all intermediate classes are in the same package, and at least protected otherwise.

```
class Super {
    public void m() {
        n();
    }

    public void n() {// private possible, but changes semantics
        System.out.println("Super.n");
    }
}
class Sub extends Super {
    public void n() {
        System.out.println("Sub.n");
    }
}
class Client {
    public static void main(String[] args) {
        Sub o = new Sub();
        o.m();
    }
}
```

Fig. 4. Overriding and open recursion prohibiting reduction of accessibility: if accessibility of n() in Super is reduced to private, the overridden version is Sub is no longer called

Now consider the code from Figure 4. It satisfies the condition that accessibility of n() is no less in Sub than it is in Super. Changing accessibility of n() in Super to private does not violate this condition. However, it changes program semantics: executed on an instance of class Sub, m() now calls n() in Super instead of in Sub — the dynamic binding has silently been removed. Vice versa, assuming that n() had been declared private in Super in the first place, increasing its accessibility to default, protected or public would also change semantics, this time by introducing a dynamic binding that was previously absent. In JAVA, access modifiers do not only decide over whether a program is correct (in that it respects the declared interfaces and thus information hiding), they also have an effect on program semantics.

With JAVA 5, this problem has partly been fixed by introducing the @Override annotation, which issues a compile-time error if a so-tagged method does not actually override. So if in Figure 4, n() in Sub were tagged with @Override, accessibility of n() in Super could not be lowered to the degree that it is no longer overridden (here private). The problem would have been completely fixed if the JAVA 5 compiler had required all overriding methods to be so tagged: in this case, increasing accessibility of n() in Super from private to some higher level would reject the definition of n() in Sub as lacking the @Override annotation. Note that C# has a required keyword override for overriding methods, which fully solves the problem; for JAVA, the ECLIPSE JDT offer a compiler switch whose selection makes the @Override annotation mandatory for overriding methods. In absence of either, an additional constraint for changing accessibility of methods is that it must not introduce or remove a dynamic binding.[4]

---

[4] Unlike in [12], we do not check here for actual occurrence of open recursion, but only for presence of overriding. This makes the required analysis significantly simpler.

```
class Super {…}

class Sub extends Super {…}

class Server {

    public void m(Super o) {
        System.out.println("m(Super)");
    }

    public void m(Sub o) {// private possible, but changes semantics
        System.out.println("m(Sub)");
    }
}
class Client {
    void callMSub() {
        Sub o = new Sub();
        Server s = new Server();
        s.m(o);
    }
}
```

Fig. 5. Overloading prohibiting adjustment of accessibility: if accessibility of m(Sub) is reduced to private, m(Super) is called instead

4.2 Static Binding: Overloading and the Most Specific Method

A second problem that is related to subtyping, but does not involve dynamic binding, occurs when determining the most specific method in a set of overloaded method declarations. In JAVA, when a method call matches several of a set of overloaded methods (i.e., methods available for the same class or interface with identical name and arity, but different parameter types), the most specific one is chosen ([9], § 15.12.2). If this most specific method is made inaccessible by reducing its accessibility, no compile-time error will result if a uniquely determined, less specific one can be linked instead. However, this static binding to a different method also changes the semantics of the program; Figure 5 gives an example of the problem.

The problem is somewhat worsened by the fact that as of JAVA 5, primitive and their wrapper types are mutually assignment compatible. The details of the resulting problems are discussed in [10]. Issues around variable parameter numbers (a new feature of JAVA 5) are not considered, neither here nor in [10].

A rather unexpected problem may occur when an up cast is used to disambiguate an otherwise ambiguous method call. If accessibility of the method that causes the ambiguity is reduced, the type cast becomes unnecessary, which may lead to a compile-time warning, or even error, with certain compilers.

5 The Access Modifier Modifier Tool

To make the support described in Section 2 under the conditions of Sections 3 and 4 available to the programmer, we have implemented the AMM as a plug-in to ECLIPSE's JAVA Development Tools (JDT). The plug-in implements the JDT's builder extension point and is activated whenever the JDT have performed their own build.

The AMM integrates seamlessly with the JDT's standard user interface in that it

- adds a new type of warning equipped with two possible Quick Fixes (one for reducing accessibility, one for introducing an @API annotation) and in that it
- extends the existing Content Assist with the possibility to show as yet inaccessible members, associating an automatic increase of accessibility with their selection.

However, despite the possibility to reuse the user interface, the actual implementation of the tool meant considerable work from scratch. The reasons for this must be sought among the following.

When a class is compiled by the JDT, the compiler checks all references to other classes' members for their accessibility. If a member is inaccessible from the class, the corresponding reference (not the member declaration!) is marked as illegal. This can be done in a local manner, i.e., without considering other than the referencing and the referenced class (plus perhaps its superclasses). Sufficient accessibility of a referenced member (as its accessibility status; cf. Section 3) can be deduced from a compiling program, i.e., from a program that contains no illegal references to that member. Also, upon change of a reference (by adding, removing, or moving it to a different location) sufficiency of accessibility of a class member can be updated based on the change alone, irrespective of all other references: higher demands will lead to an error), while lower demands leave sufficiency untouched.

Things are quite different for the accessibility status taken care of by the AMM, namely excessive accessibility. From a legal reference to another class's member, or even from the fact that all references are legal with respect to the accessibility rules of JAVA, it cannot be deduced whether accessibility status is necessary and sufficient, or excessive (cf. Figure 1). Even worse, when a reference is added, removed, or moved to a different location, the change's effect on accessibility status is unpredictable without knowing the requirements of all other references. The AMM tool therefore requires significant additional data structures.

5.1 Full Build

For a full build, the AMM traverses the abstract syntax tree (AST) of all open projects in the workspace that depend on the project for which accessibility is to be controlled (and for which the full build has been triggered), and collects all calls to methods of this project. The set of methods can be further restricted by setting a corresponding package filter; such a restriction, for instance to internal packages (cf. Section 3.1), is often useful and has in fact been exploited in our evaluation of the AMM (Section 6). The call dependencies collected in this manner are stored in two hash tables, one — named *Callees* — keeping the set of methods called by each method, the other — named *Callers* — the set of types from which each method is called. The necessary and sufficient accessibility level can then be computed for each method as the maximum accessibility level required from the types stored in *Callers*, subject to the restrictions discussed in Sections 3 and 4, which are checked as described in [10]. After the build has completed and the computed warnings have been issued and the corresponding markers have been set (see Figure 6), the hash tables are stored on disk for later use by incremental builds.

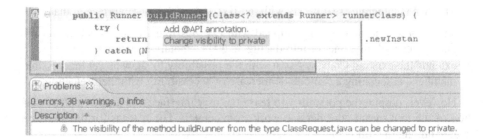

Fig. 6. Warning issued by the AMM tool, and quick fixes offered

5.2 Incremental Build

An incremental build is triggered by a change in one compilation unit (CU). The JDT notify the AMM builder of this change, who can then commence its action.

In a first step, the AMM builder updates the callees (as stored in *Callee*) of all methods contained in the changed CU (including added and deleted methods), and also the calling types of each newly called or no longer called method (as stored in *Callers*). In the second step, it visits all updated callee methods determined in the first step. Each of these methods is looked up in *Callers* to compute the new necessary and sufficient accessibility (again as the maximum of the accessibility levels as required by each calling type). The AMM builder then proceeds checking the preconditions for changeability of accessibility as described above, and updates warnings and markers correspondingly.

5.3 Reducing Accessibility or Adding an @API Annotation

The warnings computed by the AMM tool are displayed in the JDT's problem view, as shown in Figure 6. Corresponding Quick Fixes allow the reduction of visibility without opening the editor of the class hosting the member in question, or alternatively the insertion of an @API annotation. A second Quick Fix offered in the Problems view reduces accessibility according to all selected warnings at once (not shown).

5.4 Increasing Accessibility

Increasing accessibility with the AMM tool is integrated into the JDT's Content Assist, by providing a plug-in for the corresponding extension point. This plug-in adds to the standard Content Assist a page containing the members currently inaccessible from the object reference on which it is invoked. Upon selection of the desired member, the required increase of accessibility is checked against the preconditions listed in Sections 3 and 4 and, if satisfied, the increase is performed. The selected member is then automatically inserted in the code (the standard behaviour of Content Assist).

Table 1. Projects used for evaluating our AMM tool (size is number of compilation units)

PROJECT	FULL NAME AND VERSION	SIZE	SOURCE	ANALYZED PACKAGES
JUNIT	version 4.4	226	junit.org	.internal*
SVNKIT	version 1.1.4	687	svnkit.com	org.smatesoft.svn.core.internal.*
ECLIPSE	JDT core[§] version 3.3.1.1	1132	eclipse.org	.jdt.internal.*
HARMONY	Apache Harmony JDK version 5.0	6765	harmony.apache.org	*.internal* w/o *.test* and *.nls

[§] Size includes all JDT projects of Eclipse; accessibility reductions have been computed for the org.eclipse.jdt.core project only.

6   Evaluation

Designed to improve the consistency of source code, our AMM tool is not of the breed that is indispensable for the on-time delivery of correct programs. In order for it to be used, the imposed costs have to be carefully weighed against the expected benefits. The following evaluation should provide a basis for such a trade-off.

6.1   Usefulness

We have evaluated the usefulness of our AMM tool by applying it to internal packages of several open source JAVA programs. Programs were selected based on the existence of packages clearly designated as internal[5] and on the fact that the packages and their enclosing projects were extensively covered by JUNIT tests. We collected the numbers of possible reductions in accessibility indicated by the AMM tool, and checked unchanged semantics of the packages and their dependents by executing the unit tests after all suggested changes had been performed. The selected packages and size of containing programs are listed in Table 1; the results of the evaluation are given in Table 2.

Overall, the relatively high numbers of possible reductions came as a surprise: although we had hoped that our evaluation would demonstrate the usefulness of the AMM tool, we did not expect unnecessary openness of internal packages to be that high. On average, 32% of all access modifiers of methods in internal packages were higher than required by their use of other packages. In particular, the relatively high number of unnecessary public accessibilities (70% of all excessive accessibilities) appears troubling.

There are various possible explanations for this. One is that access to classes hosting the members in question is limited, eliminating the need for individual class member access restriction. Another explanation is that internal packages have been designed with future internal extensions in mind, so that members are intentionally made accessible to other internal or non-internal project packages without already being used by these. One indication for this is the relatively high number of protected members that could have been declared private; for instance, these make up for 41%

---

[5] This turned out to be very selective — only few projects actually do this.

Table 2. Results of the evaluation (see text)

| PROJECT | MEMBERS OF INTERNAL PACKAGES | CHANGES FROM TO | | | | | | TOTAL | GAIN |
| | | public | | | protected | | default | | |
		protected	default	private	default	private	private		
JUNIT	131	2	8	9	1	15	4	37	28%
SVNKIT	3555	11	731	219	214	60	2	1237	35%
ECLIPSE	12780	431	1764	631	800	462	161	4249	33%
HARMONY	1805	25	199	67	12	9	17	330	18%
total	18271	470	2703	931	1027	546	184	5853	32%

of all possible reductions in the internal packages of JUNIT. If this is actually the case, and if the authors insist on offering this internal interface to future extensions, introduction of a corresponding annotation would be in place (but see Section 7 for a discussion why we believe this is not necessary). A third explanation is that the internal naming conventions described in Section 3.1 are not strictly adhered to. One indication for this is that we found "external API" comments for methods in the internal packages of ECLIPSE's JDT. The last explanation is that developers have been uncertain about the accessibility status of their class members, and left accessibility on a level "that worked"; this is where our AMM tool steps in.

The findings delivered by our AMM tool are not without systematic errors. First, since its program analysis does not cover reflection, it is unable to detect and consider reflective calls. In the case of JUNIT this introduced two erroneous accessibility reductions (both from public to default). Generally, since JUNIT calls the methods representing test cases reflectively, test packages should be excluded from accessibility reductions. Note that this could be achieved automatically if the AMM treated the @Test annotations of JUNIT 4 like @API annotations and so left test cases untouched.[6]

Second, possible reductions of groups of methods (a method and its overridings; cf. Section 3.2) are not determined: if a method declared public that can be reduced to protected or default is overridden, the overriding methods with accessibility levels enforced by subtyping are not at the same time marked as reducible (because with the superclass's accessibility as is, they cannot). However, as soon as the accessibility of the overridden method is reduced, the overriding methods will be marked by the AMM as reducible. The so-induced reducibilities are immediately detected by the incremental build process; they have been included in the numbers of Table 2.

Last but not least, the JUNIT test coverage we required introduced a certain systematic error, since it may be the case that members have been made accessible only for the sake of testing, not because they are part of the designed API (cf. Section 2). However, this error does not enhance our results — rather, without the unit tests the overall sufficient accessibility could be even lower than what we are presenting here.[7]

---

[6] A similar problem occurred during testing the correctness of the AMM tool on the JDT core: its test methods call some of the tested methods reflectively, which is not discovered by the program analysis, thus causing failures. We therefore supplemented correctness tests of our implementation using unit tests from other projects without such problems (but which did not have packages designated as internal, which is why they were not included in our study).

[7] On the other hand, in absence of @API annotations, unit tests may be considered as simulating use by other clients.

Table 3. Spatial and temporal requirements of our AMM tool

PROJECT	NO OF CALLERS[$]	SPACE (MB)		TIME (SEC)[*]
		MAX	RESIDUAL[§]	FULL AMM BUILD
JUNIT	45	167	0.45	4.5
SVNKIT	1735	231	4.83	100
ECLIPSE	5225	349	53.3	1,978
HARMONY	125	493	34.3	2,720

[$] number of entries in the *Callers* hash table (see Section 5)
[§] as stored on disk
[*] obtained on a contemporary PC with dual core CPU rated at 3 GHz

6.2 Cost

Checking for excessive accessibility is not free, and if it is too expensive (in terms of time or memory required), it will likely be of no real use. We have therefore measured the requirements of our AMM tool; the results are compiled in Table 3. Note that memory demands must be divided into what is needed for the actual analysis and what is needed (as bookkeeping, or caching) for incremental builds; we have therefore determined the maximum memory requirement during a full build and the residual (after the build completed) separately. The maximum memory requirements for incremental builds during their computation are always lower than those for the full build. We did not attempt to measure incremental build time systematically, but our experiments showed that it is tolerable in most cases.

Clearly, time and space requirements of our current implementation for full builds are considerable (and unacceptable for large projects such as HARMONY). While we expect that a lot can be gained from optimization (which we have not attempted so far), it is also clear that a lot of overhead is imposed by ECLIPSE's builder interface, which required us to use explicit searches for types and methods, both imposing heavy performance penalties. Integrating the AMM into ECLIPSE's native JAVA build process (so that it has access to the resolved parse tree) should speed it up considerably.

The long time required for a full build of HARMONY (especially when considering the comparatively small number of callers) must be ascribed to the collection and analysis of uses of the class Object and other frequently extended classes (HARMONY is a reimplementation of SUN's JDK): numbers of overridings of methods of these classes are literally in the thousands, so that precondition checking (which involves a detection of overriding) using the JDT's search facilities (cf. above) takes its toll.

7 Discussion

For the first version of our AMM tool (described in detail in [10]), we assumed a much more process-oriented viewpoint and designed a system in which accessibility levels could be changed collaboratively. According to this viewpoint, a developer could "open" a class (i.e., all its members) for maximum accessibility, use the members as desired, and later "close" it to the original accessibility levels. Openings and closures could be stacked, and all changes were stored in annotations parameterized with the author and time of action. This documented changed interface designs automatically, and always allowed a rollback to the original design. By contrast, the current version of the AMM tool does not record the accessibility levels it overrides, so that in case a change in design is changed back, the original accessibility levels (and the resulting interfaces) are unknown. However, assuming that accessibility was at the lowest possible level (interfaces were minimal) prior to the first design change, this is no problem, since the original level follows from the original design: reverting to the original design lets the AMM tool compute the original accessibility levels (unless @API annotations have been added or removed).

When we first devised the new AMM tool, we called the @API annotation @Sic (Latin for "so", meaning "so intended"). Technically the same, @Sic was more neutral with respect to intent, i.e., its only expressed purpose was that the so tagged access modifier should not be changed by the AMM. Therefore, @Sic could also rightfully be used for designating internal interfaces, in particular for members whose accessibility is higher than currently required by the project itself *or* its API, to indicate that the project has been prepared for *internal* extension (for instance in future releases; cf. the discussion of our findings in the case of JUNIT in Section 6.1). However, we maintain that this would taint the annotation with problems it is trying to avoid: as design changes, @Sic annotations must be added and removed, and if the latter is forgotten, accessibility will become excessive again.[8]

7.1 Related Work

Although clearly a practical problem, dealing with accessibility seems to have attracted not much attention from the scientific community. One of the few exceptions we are aware of is the work by Ardourel and Huchard [1], whose notion of access graphs helps with finding fitting access levels on a more general, language-independent level. Based on these access graphs, the authors offer various tools for extracting, displaying, analysing, and editing access information, and also for generating the access modifiers for programs in a specific language. However, the functionality of our AMM tool seems to have not been implemented.

Deriving necessary and sufficient accessibility from a program is related to, but sufficiently different from, type inference [11, 18, 24]. In fact, languages like JAVA mix type and accessibility information: while a type usually restricts the possible values of typed expressions and with it the operations that can be performed on them (or, rather, on the objects they deliver), accessibility restricts the set of possible operations (but not the values!) depending on where the expression occurs relative to the definition of the type. Thus, objects of the same type, or even the same object, may appear to have different capabilities depending on by whom they are referenced, even if the type of the reference is the same. This is orthogonal to access control through differently typed references (polymorphism): in JAVA, this would likely occur through context-specific interfaces [21, 23].

---

[8] One could argue that the same is true for the @API annotation; however, external interfaces are more prominent than internal ones and thus also more carefully maintained. In particular, the @API annotation can be used for other purposes as well, for instance for the generation of documentation. If by all means desired, an @II annotation could be added to designate internal interfaces.

Our work must not be confused with that on *access rights analysis* as for instance performed by Larry Koved and co-workers [14, 15]. In JAVA, access rights (which are a different concept than access control [9]) are granted by existence of permission objects, instances of subclasses of the special class **Permission**. The required access rights cannot be checked statically, but must be computed using an analysis of control and data flow. Irrespective of all differences, adequately setting access rights suffers from the same problem of finding out what is necessary and sufficient: while insufficient access rights can be identified during testing (there is no static checking of access rights), there is no guarantee that these satisfy the *principle of least privilege.* Koved et al. have solved the problem using a context-sensitive, flow-sensitive interprocedural data flow analysis; as it turns out, their precision is much higher than can be made use of by the JAVA security system with its relatively coarse granularity. However, none of the results can be transferred to our approach, since JAVA's access control is static, ignoring all data flow.

The AMM can be viewed as a refactoring tool with built-in smell detector [5]. While the refactoring itself is trivial, smell detection and checking of preconditions (i.e., excluding occasions in which changing accessibility would change program semantics) is not; in particular, both require efficient implementations for the tool to be usable.

In response to strong criticism of the aspect-oriented programming community's disrespect of traditional interfaces and modularization (see e.g. [22] for an overview), it has been suggested that aspect-related interfaces are computed only once the system has been composed [13]. In a way, our AMM tool is capable of doing precisely this for traditional (i.e., non-aspect related) module (class) interfaces: if the *Create Publicly, Privatize Later* (Section 2) approach is pursued, the project can start with no interfaces at all, and the AMM can compute them once the project is completed. However, this approach is only feasible if there is no a priori design, especially if there is no need for a design that allows distribution of modules to different teams so that these can work independently. The latter was of course Parnas's original motivation behind the conception of information hiding and modularity [19] — in fact, he makes no secret of his opinion that language designers misunderstood what modularity is all about [3]. Leaving internal control of accessibility to our AMM tool and using @API annotations for the published interfaces separates language issues from the designers' intent.

7.2 Future Work

There are several things we did not consider in this paper and the current implementation of the AMM. First and most importantly, we did not consider field members, even though their accessibility states are interesting for the very same reasons as those of methods. This decision was driven by our more general interest in interfaced-based programming [21, 23], and the fact that interfaces do not publish field members. However, consideration of field access should pose no theoretical problems, although it means considerable extra work (due to different rules for accessibility under inheritance).

Second, accessibility of classes could also be controlled through the AMM. Again, we did not pursue this, which saved us from having to deal with a certain combinatorial complexity: if all members of a class drop below certain accessibility, and if there exist no references to the class itself requiring higher accessibility, would it make more sense to lower the accessibility of the class instead of that of its members?

Last but not least, it is tempting to try and re-implement the AMM using a constraint satisfaction framework such as the ones described in [11, 24]. Besides being a theoretical challenge (how does necessary and sufficient accessibility relate to an inferred type?), it should be interesting to see if constraint solution strategies exist that outperform our conventional implementation described in Section 5.

8 Conclusion

Evidence we have collected suggests that even in well-designed JAVA projects, accessibility of class members often exceeds what is required by the access rules of the language, or dictated by the API of the projects. Convinced that finding out and setting the minimum required access level of a class member is a real problem for the programmer, we have devised a tool that does this completely automatically. The tool is based on a whole-program analysis which it performs and maintains as part of the project build process, thereby allowing complete and omniscient control of accessibility. The costs associated with this tool, at least as it is currently implemented, are non-negligible.

References

1. Ardourel, G., Huchard, M.: Access graphs: Another view on static access control for a better understanding and use. Journal of Object Technology 1(5), 95–116 (2002)
2. Create Privately Publish Later, http://c2.com/ppr/wiki/JavaIdioms/CreatePrivatelyPublishLater.html
3. Devanbu, P.T., Balzer, B., Batory, D.S., Kiczales, G., Launchbury, J., Parnas, D.L., Tarr, P.L.: Modularity in the new millenium: A panel summary. In: ICSE, pp. 723–724 (2003)
4. Eclipse Naming Conventions, http://wiki.eclipse.org/Naming_Conventions#Internal_Implementation_Packages
5. M Fowler Refactoring: Improving the Design of Existing Code. Addison-Wesley (1999)
6. Fowler, M.: Public versus published interfaces. IEEE Software 19(2), 18–19 (2002)
7. Gamma, E., Helm, R., Johnson, R.: J Vlissides Design Patterns – Elements of Reusable Software. Addison-Wesley (1995)
8. Package Naming Conventions Used in the Apache Harmony Class Library, http://harmony.apache.org/subcomponents/classlibrary/pkgnaming.html
9. Gosling, J., Joy, B., Steele, G., Bracha, G.: The Java Language Specification, http://java.sun.com/docs/books/jls/
10. Großkinsky, E.: Access Modifier Modifier: Ein Werkzeug zur Einstellung der Sichtbarkeit in Java-Programmen (Master-Arbeit, Lehrgebiet Programmiersysteme, Fernuniversität in Hagen (2007)
11. Kegel, H.: Constraint-basierte Typinferenz für Java 5 (Diplomarbeit, Fakultät für Mathematik und Informatik, Fernuniversität in Hagen 2007)
12. Kegel, H., Steimann, F.: Systematically refactoring inheritance to delegation in Java. In: ICSE (2008)
13. Kiczales, G., Mezini, M.: Aspect-oriented programming and modular reasoning. In: ICSE, pp. 49–58 (2005)

14. Koved, L., Pistoia, M., Kershenbaum, A.: Access rights analysis for Java. In: OOPSLA, pp. 359–372 (2002)
15. Leeman, G., Kershenbaum, A., Koved, L., Reimer, D.: Detecting unwanted synchronization in Java programs. In: Conf. on Software Engineering and Applications, pp. 122–132 (2004)
16. Liskov, B., Wing, J.M.: A behavioral notion of subtyping. ACM Trans. Program. Lang. Syst. 16(6), 1811–1841 (1994)
17. Meyer, B.: Object-Oriented Software Construction, 2nd edn. Prentice Hall International (1997)
18. Palsberg, J., Schwartzbach, M.I.: Object-oriented type inference. In: Proc. of OOPSLA, pp. 146–161 (1991)
19. Parnas, D.L.: On the criteria to be used in decomposing systems into modules. Commun. ACM 15(12), 1053–1058 (1972)
20. BC Pierce Types and Programming Languages. MIT Press (2002)
21. Steimann, F., Mayer, P.: Patterns of interface-based programming. Journal of Object Technology 4(5), 75–94 (2005)
22. Steimann, F.: The paradoxical success of aspect-oriented programming. In: OOPSLA, pp. 481–497 (2006)
23. Steimann, F.: The Infer Type refactoring and its use for interface-based programming. Journal of Object Technology 6(2), 67–89 (2007)
24. Tip, F.: Refactoring using type constraints. In: Riis Nielson, H., Filé, G. (eds.) SAS 2007. LNCS, vol. 4634, pp. 1–17. Springer, Heidelberg (2007)

Towards Raising the Failure of Unit Tests to the Level of Compiler-Reported Errors

Friedrich Steimann[1], Thomas Eichstädt-Engelen[2], and Martin Schaaf[3]

[1] LG Programmiersysteme
Fernuniversität in Hagen
D-58084 Hagen
steimann@acm.org
[2] LG Programmiersysteme
Fernuniversität in Hagen
D-58084 Hagen
te@eichstaedt.net
[3] 101tec.com
Mansfelder Straße 13
D-06108 Halle
Martin.Schaaf@feu.de

Abstract. Running unit tests suites with contemporary tools such as JUNIT can show the presence of bugs, but not their locations. This is different from checking a program with a compiler, which always points the programmer to the most likely causes of the errors it detects. We argue that there is enough information in test suites and the programs under test to exclude many locations in the source as reasons for the failure of test cases, and further to rank the remaining locations according to derived evidence of their faultiness. We present a framework for the management of fault locators whose error diagnoses are based on data about a program and its test cases, especially as collected during test runs, and demonstrate that it is capable of performing reasonably well using a couple of simple fault locators in different evaluation scenarios.

Keywords: Regression testing, Debugging, Fault localization.

1 Introduction

Continuous testing [7, 23, 24] is a big step forward towards making the detection of logical errors part of the edit/compile/run cycle: whenever a resource has been edited and saved, it is not only checked by the compiler for absence of syntactic and semantic (i.e., type) errors, but also — by running all relevant unit tests — for absence of certain logical errors. However, presently a failed unit test is presented to the programmer as just that — in particular, no indication is given of where the error is located in the source code. By contrast, the compiler names not only the syntactic or semantic rule violated by an incorrect program, it also tries to point the programmer to the place in the source code where the error occurred. Would not the same be desirable for logical errors detected by failed unit tests?

R.F. Paige and B. Meyer (Eds.): TOOLS EUROPE 2008, LNBIP 11, pp. 60–79, 2008.

A first simple approach to solving this problem explicitly links each test case to one or more methods under test (MUTs). Whenever a test case fails, the reason for the failure must be sought among the designated MUTs. Using JAVA and JUNIT, test cases (which are implemented as methods in JUNIT) can be linked to MUTs via a corresponding method annotation. An integrated development environment (IDE) such as ECLIPSE can then be extended to link failed unit tests directly with potential error locations in the source code.

In our own prior work, we have implemented this approach as a plug-in to ECLIPSE, named EZUNIT [4, 19]. It supports the programmer with creating and maintaining @MUT annotations by performing a static call graph analysis of test methods, producing all candidate MUTs. A filter can be set to exclude calls to libraries (such as the JDK) or other parts of a project known or assumed to be correct, minimizing the set of potential MUTs to select from; the annotations themselves can be used for quick navigation between a test and its MUTs and vice versa. Whenever a unit test fails, the corresponding MUTs are marked by a red T in the gutter of the editor, and a corresponding hint is shown in ECLIPSE's Problem view [4, 19]. The programmer can thus navigate directly to potential fault locations in the source code, much like (s)he can for compiler-reported errors. However, the setting up and maintenance of @MUT annotations is tedious and error-prone.

In this paper, we describe how we advanced our work on logical error spotting (hereafter referred to as *fault localization*) by automatically narrowing down the set of possible fault locations using information that is present in the program and its tests. In particular, we

- present a framework that can incorporate arbitrary a priori fault predictors (such as program metrics) into its reasoning,
- show how information obtained from the execution of unit test suites can be used to compute a posteriori possibilities of fault locations, and
- demonstrate how making precise control flow information available can increase the accuracy of fault localization.

Especially for the utilization of precise control flow information, which is usually expensive — if not impossible — to obtain, we exploit a characteristic property of JUNIT test cases, namely that their traces do not change unless either a called method or a test case itself is changed. This allows us to record the trace of a test run once (using an available program tracing tool) and keep it until invalidated by a change of source code. That this is worth its effort, and more generally that our approach to fault localization is feasible, is shown by a systematic evaluation which is also presented.

The remainder of this paper is organized as follows. First, we describe the problem we are trying to solve, arguing why we believe that it is indeed a relevant problem. In Section 3 we present a number of fault locating strategies we have implemented and tested our framework with. In Section 4 we show the results of a systematic evaluation of the fault locators, which uses historical bugs found in archives of open source code bases, error seeding to inject faults in correct programs, and practical experience of professional programmers. Section 5 describes the architecture of EZUNIT as an ECLIPSE plugin, and how it offers extension points for additional fault locators. Other fault locators we considered, but did not implement, are presented in Section 6; a discussion with related work concludes our presentation.

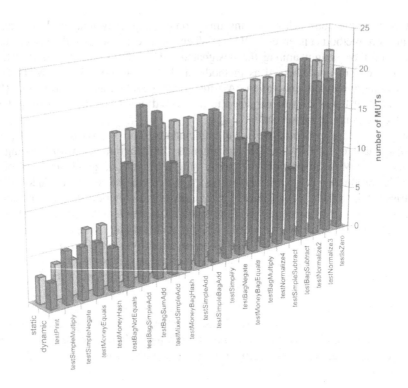

Fig. 1. Number of methods called by each unit test of JUNIT's Money example, as derived from tracing (dynamic, front row) and a program analysis (static, rear row). Both direct and indirect calls are counted. See Section 5.1 for an explanation of the differences.

2 Problem

When first presenting our approach to practitioners, we heard objections of the kind "when I see a failed unit test, I know exactly where to look for the error". While this may be true in certain situations (for instance when only few changes were made since the last successful run of a test suite), we doubted the general validity of the claim and measured the number of methods called in the course of the execution of test runs. Figure 1 shows the number of methods called by each test case of a simple test suite (the Money example from the JUNIT distribution). Considering that the test cases contained in MoneyTest are examples for beginners, the common assumption that test cases are usually so simple that there is no doubt concerning the reason for a failure is clearly relativized.

In a way, the problem of blame assignment for failed unit tests is like the problem of medical diagnosis (or any kind of diagnosis for that matter): a single or a set of symptoms must be mapped to possible diagnoses, where the only causal knowledge available is the mapping of diagnoses to symptoms. Transferred to testing: a single or a set of failed unit tests must be mapped to possible fault locations, where the faults and their locations cause the unit tests to fail. Unfortunately, this causality (as a mapping) is only seldom injective.

EZUNIT can be viewed as attempting such a diagnosis. However, its first version accommodated only for binary answers: a method is either included as a possible reason for failure, or it is not. With no other information given, the developer has to look at a whole (and unordered) set of locations in order to find and fix an error. For instance, as suggested by Figure 1 the number of methods to be considered (if no filters or specific @MUT annotations are set) is 15.6 (static) and 13.1 (dynamic) on average.

Fortunately, there is more information in a program and its test cases, so that heuristics can be developed that rate one fault location as more likely than another. For example, complexity measures can be used to assign a priori probabilities of faultiness to methods; information from past test runs, error reports, and error fixes can be collected and evaluated using statistical methods; and so forth. In order to exploit such information, the binary fault localization framework of EZUNIT must be extended to collect graded evidence, to combine individual results (as delivered by different fault locators in use) by appropriate operators, and to present its suggestions to the developer in adequate form.

3 Fault Locators

With the term *fault locator* we mean an algorithm that computes the possibility of a piece of source code containing a logical error. We use the term *possibility* here in an informal sense as a measure of uncertainty distinct from probability. In particular, we do not require the computed possibilities for exclusive alternatives to add up to 1, as probability theory dictates — indeed, it is entirely feasible that several mutually exclusive fault locations have a possibility of 1, meaning that it is completely possible for either to host the error. However, just like a probability of 0, a possibility of 0 definitely rules out fault locations, and higher possibility values are indicative of stronger support for a fault location in the available data. Thus our possibilities could be interpreted as possibilities in the sense of possibility theory [9]; yet, we have no pretensions of being formal here.

Fault locators always have a granularity associated with them [15, 26]. Generally, granularity levels can range from the whole program to a single expression; yet the extremes are rather useless in most practical settings — knowing that there is an error in the program helps only little with finding it, and having hundreds of statements with non-zero possibilities of being fault locations (which is what is to be expected with most location strategies currently available) is not helpful either. For EZUNIT, we constrain ourselves to defining fault locators that compute possibilities for whole methods rather than single statements or lines in the source code. Besides saving the developer from being flooded with uncontrollable amounts of data, this allows us to utilize certain information that can be assigned to whole methods, but not to single statements.

Clearly, only methods that are actually called by a unit test can contribute to its success or failure.[1] If non-execution of a method was the reason for the failure of a test, then this must be ascribed to an executed method (including the test case itself) whose fault it was that the method did not get called. On the other hand, if non-execution of a method was the reason for the success of a test (because it was faulty

---

[1] In JAVA, code can exist outside of methods, for instance in variable initializers. We consider this code as part of the constructors of the class, which are called for test object creation.

and should have been called, but was not), then there is no way to detect this (unless the uncalled method was listed in the test's @MUT annotation as described in the Introduction; however, we do not pursue this fault detection strategy, which was detailed in [4, 19], here).

One might deduce from this that only methods actually called by a failed unit test, and thus only failed unit tests, need be analyzed. However, as will be seen, some fault locators exploit the information that certain unit tests have passed, and which methods were called by these tests.

The evaluators we have devised and experimented with can be divided into two categories. The first category relies on prior possibilities, i.e., on evidence that is independent of the outcome of testing and of the fact whether a method was called by a test case that failed. The second category assumes no prior possibilities of faultiness, but instead collects information from the actual successes and failures of a test run.

3.1 Fault Locators Based on Prior Knowledge

Assuming that some methods of a program are more error-prone than others, there is a prior possibility of faultiness. This prior possibility can be a derived property of a method (for instance its complexity) or it can be ascribed by extraneous factors, such as its author's confidence in its correctness, or the number of fixes it already needed. Note that in our setting it makes little sense to asses a priori possibility of error freeness by determining test coverage: since tests can fail (and indeed our aim is to exploit the information gained from failed tests), we will not count good test coverage as an a priori sign of freeness from faults.

For the evaluation presented in Section 4 , we have used two simple complexity measures of methods: lines of code (LOC) and McCabe's cyclomatic complexity (CC), which measures the number of linearly-independent paths through a method (basically by counting the number of branches and loops, adding 1) [18]. To map these complexity measures to possibility values, we have normalized LOC by the longest method in the program, and bounded and normalized CC with 10. Note that this way, every method of a program is a possible fault location (i.e., its a priori possibility is greater than 0), but the possibility of simple methods (such as setters and getters) is rather low. Any other complexity measure could also have been used (and indeed such has been done by others; see Section 7), but since our primary focus is on exploiting information obtained from the execution of unit tests, and more generally on the presentation of EZUNIT as a framework that can combine any prior knowledge with evidence obtained ex post, LOC and CC should be seen as placeholders only.

3.2 Fault Locators Based on Posterior Knowledge

The prior possibility of a fault location is relativized by posterior information available after a test suite has been run: the possibility of being the reason for a failure of methods that were not called by a test case that failed drops to zero. Apart from this, with no other information given the ranking of possible fault locations as suggested by the computed prior possibilities remains unchanged; in particular, of all methods contributing to failed tests, the one with the highest prior possibility of being the reason for failure is also the one with the highest posterior possibility.

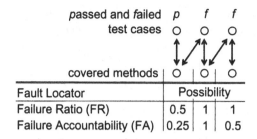

Fig. 2. A posteriori possibility measures taking number of passed and failed tests into account

However, running a test suite does not only rule out methods from having contributed to possible failures, it also provides its own graded evidence for methods as fault locations, which can be interpreted as independent posterior possibility (i.e., one that is *not* derived from prior possibility). The argumentation goes as follows.

As suggested by Figure 1, a test case usually calls several methods, and each method is called by several test cases. Methods that are called exclusively by test cases that pass cannot be held accountable for failures in the test suite, so that their possibility can be set to 0 (see above). At the opposite extreme, for a method that is called exclusively by failed test cases, there is no posterior evidence against its faultiness, so that the possibility can be set to 1. For all other cases, the possibility is a value between 0 and 1, for instance as calculated by the ratio of participations in failed test cases to the total number of participations in test cases. We call the corresponding measure *failure ratio* (FR) and define it formally as follows:

Let T be the set of test cases in a test suite, and M be the set of methods called by this suite. We then define a function $c: T \to \wp(M)$ (where is $\wp(.)$ stands for the powerset) such that $c(t)$ computes the set of MUTs for a $t \in T$, and say that test case t covers the methods in $c(t)$. We further define a pair of functions $p: M \to \wp(T)$ and $f: M \to \wp(T)$ such that $p(m)$ computes the set of passed test cases from T that cover m, i.e.,

$$p(m) = \{t \in T \mid m \in c(t) \land passed(t)\}$$

and $f(m)$ computes the set of failed test cases accordingly. The FR value for a method $m \in M$ is then defined as

$$FR(m) = \frac{\left| f(m) \right|}{\left| f(m) \right| + \left| p(m) \right|}$$

As can be seen from Figure 2, FR is insensitive to the absolute number of failed tests that a MUT presumed as faulty can explain. In particular, it ranks a method that is called by all failed test cases and none that passed the same as one that is called by only one failed test case, where there are more test cases that failed. We have therefore devised a second fault locator that takes the contribution to total failures into account. This fault locator, which we call *failure accountability* (FA), is defined as

$$FA(m) = FR(m) \frac{|f(m)|}{\left| \bigcup_{m' \in M} f(m') \right|}$$

It yields a value of 1 for a method m if and only if all test cases covering m and no other test cases fail. Observe how FA ranks a method covered by one passed and one failed test below one covered by one failed test only, and both below one covered by all failed tests (Figure 2).

The computation of posterior possibilities as described above depends critically on the availability of information which methods have been called. As discussed in more detail in Section 5.1, the methods called in the course of a test run can be determined by a control flow analysis performed at compile time, or by tracing the program. As will be seen, the preciser the information is, the better is the expected result.

4   Evaluation

We have evaluated EZUNIT in a number of ways:

1. For archived versions of programs known to have bugs undetected by their accompanying test suites, we have applied EZUNIT using test suites from successor versions of the programs which made sure that the bugs had been fixed, and recorded how well each fault locator was able to spot the bugs.
2. We have used error seeding to inject errors into programs extensively covered by unit tests, and recorded how well each fault locator was able to spot the errors.
3. We have used EZUNIT in a commercial software development setting and observed its precision and usability.

For each kind of evaluation, we ranked the possible fault locations according to their possibility values as computed by EZUNIT separately for each of the four fault locators described above. Assuming that faultiness of n MUTs with same possibility values is equally distributed, we computed their rank (relative to their predecessors) as $(n + 1)/2$ so that the rank always represents the *expected* number of method lookups required until the fault is found.

4.1   Evaluation Based on Flawed Historical Releases

Prior to JUNIT 3.8, its Money example had a small bug: when comparing two money bags with unequal currencies for equality, a null pointer exception was raised. JUNIT 3.8 added a test case testBagNotEquals() unveiling the error, and fixed it. Incidentally (and contrary to the claims mentioned in Section 2), the location of the actual error was less than obvious from the failed test case: in class MoneyBag, method

```
private boolean contains(Money aMoney) {
    Money m= findMoney(aMoney.currency());
    return m.amount() == aMoney.amount();
}
```

Table 1. Number of locations to search before fault is found (halves are due to same possibility, and thus equal ranking, of several methods). Possib. locat. counts the methods called by test cases that failed (thus being fault locations to be taken into consideration given the test suite).

PROJECT	FAULT LOCATION (METHOD)	NO. OF TESTS		POSSIB. LOCAT.		RANK (EXPECTED NECESSARY LOOKUPS)							
						LOC		CC		FR		FA	
		p	f	stat	dyn	stat	dyn	stat	dyn	stat	dyn	stat	dyn
JUNIT 3.7 Money	contains	21	1	23	13	8½	4½	8½	4½	1½	2½	1½	2½
JUNIT 4.3	format	294	4	8	5	2	2	1	1	6½	2	6½	2
BEANUTILS 1.6	copyProperty	338	6	196	29	2½	1	1	3½	8	3	2	1
before	soundex	62	9	14	14	2	2	2½	2½	4	5	2	2
after 1st fix		68	3	15	9	2	1	2	1	12½	7	12½	6½
after 2nd fix		70	1	9	9	1	1	1	1	6½	6½	6½	6½
before	getMapping-Code	62	9	14	14	7	7	7½	6½	4	5	2	2
after 1st fix		68	3	15	9	5	3	4½	3	12½	7	12½	6½
after 2nd fix		70	1	9	9	3	3	3	3	6½	6½	6½	6½
before	setMax-Length	62	9	14	14	11½	11½	11½	11½	4	5	6	7
after 1st fix		68	3	15	9	12	6½	12	6½	1	1	1	1
after 2nd fix		70	1	9	9	6½	6½	6½	6½	1	1	1	1
before	decode-Base64	62	9	14	14	1	1	1	1	13½	13	11½	14
after 1st fix		68	3	15	9	1	1	1	1	8½	5	6½	5
after 2nd fix		70	1	9	9	–	–	–	–	–	–	–	–
before	discard-Whitespace	62	9	14	14	3	3	7½	6½	13½	14	11½	14
after 1st fix		68	3	15	9	3	3	7½	6½	8½	4	6½	3½
after 2nd fix		70	1	9	9	–	–	–	–	–	–	–	–

(Left vertical label: APACHE COMMMONS CODEC 1.1)

lacked a test for m being not null, but this method is only one out of 14 methods invoked by the test case (cf. Figure 1).

Running the test suite of MoneyTest from JUNIT 3.8 on the flawed implementation of the Money example from JUNIT 3.7, the fault locators based on a priori possibility presented in Section 3 (LOC and CC) perform rather poorly (see Table 1, first row). Indeed, as it turns out the problem of the method was that it was too short and its cyclomatic complexity too low: in JUNIT 3.8, the flaw was fixed by inserting

```
if (m == null) return false;
```

in the method body. By contrast, the fault locators based on posterior information (passed and failed tests cases) ranked the flawed method highly.

In another example, a flaw was detected in JUNIT 4.3 in the method static String format(String, Object, Object) of class org.junit.Assert: the contained lines

```
String expectedString= expected.toString();
String actualString= actual.toString();
```

cause a null pointer exception whenever expected or actual are null. JUNIT 4.3.1 had this fixed by writing

```
String expectedString= String.valueOf(expected);
String actualString= String.valueOf(actual);
```

instead. The fault is covered by four new test cases, which all fail when executed on JUNIT 4.3. Copying these test cases to the test suite of JUNIT 4.3 and running it with

EzUNIT produced the result shown in the second row of Table 1: the culprit method was ranked 1st, 2nd and 6½th out of 8 statically and 1st and 2nd out of 5 dynamically. Note that the performances of FR and FA are poor in the static case because format is included in the static call graph of several passing test cases even though it is factually not called by these cases, which has a lowering effect on FR and FA (cf. Section 3.2).

In a third example, APACHE's BeanUtils 1.6.1 fixed a bug of its predecessor, version 1.6, in method copyProperty(Object, String, Object) from class BeanUtils (problem and fix are complex and not detailed here). Running the test suites of version 1.6.1 on the source code of version 1.6 with JUNIT produces three errors and three failures; running them with EzUNIT ranks copyProperty highly among the large number of possible fault locations (see Table 1). The perfect hit of FA is due to the fact that copyProperty is the only method whose faultiness can explain all failed tests (i.e., that was called by all failed test cases). Again, this result is diluted by static call graph computation, which includes methods not called.

All previous examples have in common that they contain only a single bug, which is unveiled by one or more test cases designed to detect this one bug. To see how our approach performs when there are more bugs we resort to a final example.

The APACHE Commons Codec 1.2 fixed the following list of bugs of its predecessor, version 1.1 [2]: [2]

1. Modified Base64 to remedy non-compliance with RFC 2045. Non-Base64 characters were not being discarded during the decoding.
2. Soundex: The HW rule is not applied; hyphens and apostrophes are not ignored.
3. Soundex.setMaxLength causes bugs and is not needed.

   The bugs manifest themselves as follows:

1. Class binary.Base64 in version 1.1 contained the method

   ```
   public static byte[] decodeBase64(byte[] base64Data) {
       // RFC 2045 suggests line wrapping at (no more than) 76
       // characters -- we may have embedded whitespace.
       base64Data = discardWhitespace(base64Data);
       ...
   ```

   which was replaced by

   ```
   public static byte[] decodeBase64(byte[] base64Data) {
       // RFC 2045 requires that we discard ALL non-Base64 characters
       base64Data = discardNonBase64(base64Data);
       ...
   ```

   in version 1.2. The flaw is covered by two new test cases in class Base64Test
2. Fixing this bug required substantial changes to methods getMappingCode and soundex in class Soundex, including the introduction of several new methods. The fix is covered by six new test cases in class SoundexTest.
3. The loop conditional count < maxLength in method String soundex(String) of class Soundex erroneously used the maximum length, which was later corrected to count

---

[2] There are in fact two more [2], but one appears to be not one of version 1.1 (which did not include the methods said to be fixed), and the other (use of a number literal instead of a variable) was not unveiled by any of the added test cases.

< out.length. It is questionable whether being able to call setMaxLength with a parameter value unequal to out.length was the flaw, or if the method soundex itself was flawed (cf. the bug description above).

After first running the test suite of Commons Codec 1.1 extended with the relevant tests of version 1.2, 9 failed tests are reported (see Table 1). Since overall, soundex is ranked highest (it is in fact involved in 7 of the failed test cases, leading to a high FA), we assume that the developer finds bug 2 from the above list first. Note that fixing it involves changes to soundex and getMappingCode, the latter also being ranked highly — in fact, both and a third method have identical posterior possibilities so that the expected number of lookups until the bug is found is calculated as 2.

Rerunning the test suite after the bug has been fixed produces the ranking labelled with "after 1st fix". Since the posterior possibilities based rank of setMaxLength has changed to 1, we assume that the developer inspects this method next. However, setMaxLength is a plain setter that is obviously correct. Therefore, we assume that the developer proceeds with the other possible fault locations and detects the bug in decodeBase64 (bug 1 from the above list). Note that the bug might have been considered as being one of discardWhiteSpace (whose call from decodeBase64 was replaced by one of a new method discardNonBase64; see above); this is also on the list, but overall ranked lower. Also note that soundex and getMappingCode still appear on the lists, despite the previous bug fix.

After having fixed the second problem, the test suite is rerun again, leading to the rows labelled with "after 2nd fix". As can be seen, decodeBase64 and discardWhiteSpace have now been ruled out as possible fault locations, and while setMaxLength has remained in front, the ranks of soundex and getMappingCode have increased. This is indeed where the final bug (bug 3) is located.

Overall, using tracing to detect the MUTs (and thus the possible failure locations) leads to visibly better results than static call graph analysis. The few cases in which it does not are due to the calling of library methods whose source code was unavailable for program analysis. This is typically the case for assertEquals and related methods from the JUNIT framework, which are called from tests cases and which invoke the equals method which is often overridden in classes under test, but whose invocation remains undetectable for the program analysis (due to the unavailability of the source code of assertEquals; cf. Section 5.1).

4.2 Evaluation Based on Error Seeding

Evidence collected from our above described experiments is somewhat anecdotal in character, and it is unclear whether and how it generalizes. To increase belief in the feasibility of our approach, a more systematic evaluation is needed. Such an evaluation is generally difficult; however, in our special case it can be obtained by a relatively simple mechanism, namely by injecting errors into otherwise correct programs and seeing whether EZUNIT can locate them accurately.

Table 2. The nine code changes performed by JESTER, as used for our evaluation

#	BOTH WAYS		#	FROM	TO
1., 2.	==	!=	7.	if (…)	if (true || …)
3., 4.	false	true	8.	if (…)	if (false && …)
5., 6.	++	--	9.	<number>	<number + 1>

To do this, we have integrated the error seeding algorithm of JESTER [12, 17] into the evaluation part of EzUNIT. JESTER's approach is to systematically alter JAVA programs in such a way that their syntax remains intact, but their logic likely changes. If such a change does not cause a test failure, JESTER suggests that a unit test be added that detects the changed (and thus presumably flawed) logic.

Contrary to JESTER's focus, we are not interested in changes that pass the test suites, but only in those that cause tests to fail. Knowing which changes JESTER performed, we can thus evaluate our fault locators for their ability to spot the error inducing method (which must always be the one changed by JESTER if all unit tests passed successfully prior to the change). If the test suite passes in spite of a change performed by JESTER, the change is of no use for our evaluation purposes; it must be undone and the next one tried.

We have implemented this evaluation procedure as part of EzUNIT so that it runs completely automatically. The procedure is sketched as follows:

1. Check whether the test suite passes initially.
2. Until all possible errors have been injected:
3. Inject a single error into a known method.
4. Run the test suite using EzUNIT and its implemented fault locators.
5. If the test suite fails:
6. For each fault locator, determine and record the position of the changed method in its diagnosis (rank as described above).
7. Undo the change.

The changes JESTER is capable of performing are listed in Table 2. Note that the set of manipulations is rather limited — basically, Boolean expressions are changed (affecting control flow), integer increment and decrement are swapped, and numbers are incremented by 1. More complex code manipulations, especially of objects, would be desirable, but such changes are tricky, and since code manipulation is not an essential part of our work, only of its evaluation, we did not pursue this further. One problem of JESTER's manipulation is that it can introduce infinite loops, so that all unit tests had to be equipped with timeouts (a new feature of JUNIT 4). Infinite recursion can also be introduced (and cannot be caught by timeouts, since its causes stack overflows very quickly); however, during our experiments this never happened.

Applied to the Money example from the JUNIT distribution, the evaluation produced the results shown in Table 3. As can be seen, trace-based FA performs better than any other fault locator: in more than half of all cases, the flawed method is expected to be found among the first two suggestions and on average, the injected error is expected to be found in the 3.4^{th} method. A more comprehensive evaluation drawing from the projects listed in Table 4 produced the results shown in Figure 3: according to this evaluation, dynamic FA ranked the flawed method first in 60% of all cases, and in a total of 76%, no more than two lookups need be expected.

The impressive performance of dynamically determined FA should not be overrated. It is mostly due to the fact that in our special evaluation scenario, there is always precisely one flawed method in the program (so that this method must account for all failed test cases), and that FA degrades all methods whose assumed faultiness does not explain all test case failures (see Section 3.2). Only if the flawed method, m, participates in more successful test cases than a competitor, m', (so that $FR(m)$, which

Table 3. Evaluation results using error seeding for the Money example from the JUNIT distribution. Each row counts the number of hits at the corresponding ranks.

RANK	STATIC (CALL GRAPH)				DYNAMIC (TRACE)			
	LOC	CC	FR	FA	LOC	CC	FR	FA
1–1½	3	7	4	4	5	5	7	14
2–2½	7	3	0	1	0	4	1	3
3–3½	0	2	0	0	4	3	4	4
4–4½	3	3	1	0	3	2	2	0
5–5½	2	3	0	0	0	6	2	1
6–6½	3	0	0	0	4	1	0	1
7–7½	0	0	1	6	4	0	1	2
8–8½	0	0	0	0	1	2	1	0
9–25	4	4	16	11	6	4	9	2
average	5.8	5.4	11.5	10.5	6.9	5.7	6.6	3.4

is one factor of FA(m), is lower than FR(m')), it can be the case that FA does not rank m highest.[3] It follows that a definition of FA that ignores FR would perform better, but only as long as there is only one error in the program.[4]

The better than expected performance of the fault locators based on a priori possibilities (LOC and CC) is due to an inherent bias of our evaluation procedure: given the complexity metrics (Section 3.1) and code changes performed by JESTER (Table 2), longer methods and in particular those with more if statements (i.e., methods that are more complex by definition) are likely to be changed more frequently and thus are more often the sources of (injected) faults. Since the more complex methods inherently lead the lists of possible fault locations derived from the complexity-based fault locators, the hit rate of these locators must be expected to be higher than a random selection. This is particularly true for CC: every if statement not only increases it by 1, it also leads to at least two code changes that are almost certainly errors (change 7 and 8 from Table 2, and often also change 1 or 2). Assuming that programmers tend to make more errors the longer or the more complex a method is, the bias may reflect a natural condition; yet, the first example of Section 4.1 suggests that this is not generally the case.

4.3 Evaluation in Practice

Using EZUNIT in routine software development, we found that it was most helpful when used by the author of the tests and the methods being tested. This is somewhat disappointing, since the goal of EZUNIT is to point the programmer to so few possible error locations that intimate knowledge of test cases or MUTs would not be necessary to find and fix the bug. And yet, without having a least basic understanding of tests and their MUTs, spotting the bug within a method marked as a possible fault location was found to be difficult. Our developers then tried to understand the test by analysing the test case and methods it calls from the bottom up (and this without the

---

[3] Example: Given 2 failed test cases, if m' is called by 1 test case, which fails, and m is called by 5 test cases, of which 2 fail, FA(m') is computed as 0.5, compared to 0.4 for FA(m).

[4] Note that it still would not be perfect since there can be several methods with identical FA value.

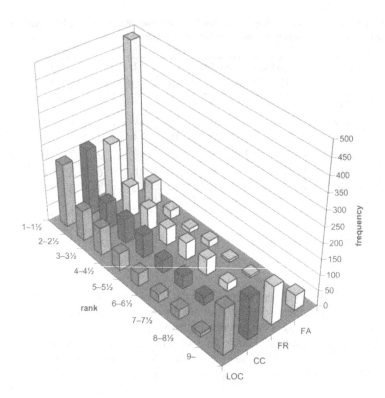

Fig. 3. Hit rates of the fault locators of Section 3 based on tracing, applied to the projects of Table 4 (excluding MATH and JUNIT)

information provided by EZUNIT); and in this effort to understand the case, the bug was usually found. Surely, the tracing information cached by EZUNIT could be used to replay a failed test case without setting break points and executing the program in the debugger, but we did not explore this possibility further.

Also, EZUNIT proved of limited practical value when the test suites were run immediately after a MUT that was known to have passed all tests previously had been changed (continuous testing): as long as the developer remembered correctly what he had done, he went back to the changes immediately rather than seek assistance from the suggestions offered by EZUNIT. If he forgot, the recently changed locations in the source code could be brought to his attention by other means (see Section 7); yet again, we did not pursue this further.

Things were different, however, when a test written by a developer failed some time after work on the tested functionality had been finished (regression testing): in these cases, the developer usually had an idea of where to look for the fault (given his understanding of the tests and the program), but often found that this idea was misleading. The list of ranked fault locations was then helpful for choosing the next location to look at (recall that, as mentioned in Section 2, developers are often unaware of the exact methods invoked by a test case); in fact, we found that the cases in which the bug was not among the top ranked possible fault locations were rather rare.

Table 4. Performance data for JUNIT, EZUNIT with static call graph analysis, and EZUNIT with tracing; both for full and incremental tracing; times in seconds

| PROJECT | NO. OF TEST CASES | AVG. NO. OF MUTS | | JUNIT | EZUNIT | | | |
| | | stat | dyn | | full trace | | incremental | |
					stat	dyn	stat	dyn
JUNIT Money	22	16	13	0.09	13	4	7.1	4.0
JUNIT	308	38	9	1.02	541	35	36.9	26.3
BEANUTILS	336	62	9	1.48	1363	11	210	4.5
CODEC	191	11	6	0.72	127	107	6.7	34.0
MAIL	75	12	10	0.01	58	11	4.7	14.0
MATH	1022	39	10	35	12018	5604	282	485

5 Architecture of EZUNIT

EZUNIT is implemented as a plugin to the ECLIPSE Java Development Tools (JDT) that itself offers points for extension. If tracing is to be used to determine the exact set of methods called by each test case, it requires the Test and Performance Tools Platform (TPTP) [10], which offers an API for tracing programs from within the IDE, to be installed. For the evaluation of the tracing information and its presentation in the UI, EZUNIT implements its own test run listener (the standard way of extending the JUNIT framework). EZUNIT adds possible fault locations to the Problems view of ECLIPSE (in which the compiler-reported errors are shown) and sets corresponding gutter markers [4, 19]; the current version also comes with its own view, which presents the detailed diagnosis (including the values of all fault locators) to the user.

5.1 Call Graph Computation

Inheriting from its predecessor, EZUNIT can perform a static call graph analysis of test cases. For this, it constructs and traverses the method call graph, taking overriding of methods and dynamic binding into account. On its traversal through the graph, EZUNIT applies filtering expressions provided by the user to exclude library and other methods from being considered as potential fault locations. Note that since libraries may call user-defined methods through dynamic binding (via so-called hook methods), static analysis cannot stop once it enters a library. Yet, if the source code of libraries is unavailable, such calls must remain undetected.[5] Another deficiency of static analysis is that it cannot detect reflective method calls.

Since static call graph analysis is imprecise (it usually contains methods that are never called) and also incomplete (because of reflection, and also because it requires the availability of source code), replacing it with a dynamic call graph analysis seems worthwhile. However, analysis of dynamic control flow is usually computationally expensive. And yet, in the special case of unit testing things are extremely simplified: since each test run sets up precisely the same fixture and executes only methods whose behaviour does not depend on random (including user input) or extraneous

---

[5] This explains why the number of called methods counted during tracing may surpass that computed through program analysis; cf. Figure 1.

state[6], every run has exactly the same trace, so that dynamic control flow analysis becomes trivial. In fact, unless the test cases or the MUTs are changed, caching the trace of a single test run is sufficient. The cache of a test case is invalidated by each of the following events:

1. The test method is changed.
2. The body of one of the MUTs of the test method is changed.
3. The signature of one of the MUTs of the test method is changed, or the MUT is overridden by a new method, or an overloading of the method is added.
4. A MUT of the test method is deleted.

The latter two events take the possibility of a change of method binding into account. Note that the information which methods have changed is also the basis of continuous testing [7, 23, 24] and certain debugging techniques [8, 30], and in fact we have exploited this information for fault location itself [11]; however, we do not pursue these approaches here.

To get an impression of the computational overhead induced by tracing, in comparison to that induced by static control flow analysis and to plain JUNIT, we have measured the execution time required for a number of test suites. The results are presented in Table 4. All times were obtained on a contemporary PC with an Intel Centrino Duo T5600 processor run at 1.83GHz, with 2 GB of RAM. The incremental times were obtained after random changes to the MUTs had been made and represent averages (explaining why the ratio of *static* to *dynamic* does not follow that of the full traces).

To our surprise, dynamic tracing does not generally perform worse than static call graph computation — quite the contrary, in most cases it performs significantly better. This is due to the rather slow implementation of call graph analysis, which builds on ECLIPSE JDT's search facilities for finding the methods called. Also, overriding and dynamic binding of methods lead to significant branching in the static call graphs, since all possible method bindings need to be considered. That this is indeed a problem can be seen from the significantly larger number of MUTs statically derived for JUNIT and BeanUtils, when compared to the actual, dynamically determined MUTs. In fact, it turned out that dynamic tracing is slower only when the MUTs contain loops or (mutually) recursive calls; this is particularly the case in the MATH project.

Compared to the test suite execution times required by JUNIT, EZUNIT is slow. In fact, the time required for a full trace (the first run of a test suite) can become so long that it makes running unit tests an overnight job. On the other hand, the incremental build times seem acceptable in all cases so that, once a full trace has been obtained, work should not be hindered unduly.

5.2   Adding New Fault Locators

EZUNIT is an extension to ECLIPSE that itself offers an interface for extension. This interface (an extension point in ECLIPSE terminology) is used by the Fault Locator Manager to invoke the fault locators plugged in.

New fault locators that are implemented as plug-ins for the extension point must implement an interface that declares methods through which the Fault Locator

---

[6] Mutual independence of test cases and independence of their order of execution is a general requirement of unit testing.

Manager can feed the plug-ins with the tracing and other useful data (including the failed and successful tests cases, as well as comprehensive information about the execution of methods as collected by the profiling of TPTP). The plug-in must then compute its possibility values for each MUT and store it in a map that can be queried by the Manager. The EzUNIT framework turns these possibility values into a ranking and presents them to the developer.

In our current implementation, EzUNIT combines the possibilities obtained by each fault locator into a single aggregate value. Initially, this value is the unweighted average of the possibility values delivered by each locator. However, the user can vote for a locator by selecting it in the view, which increases its weight. This can be seen as a first implementation of a simple learning strategy (see Section 6).

6 Other Possible Fault Locators

There are various ways to improve the specificity of fault location, some more, some less obvious. The following list is not exhaustive.

Fault Location Based on Dynamic Object Flow Analysis. The most obvious, but also perhaps the most difficult, extension to our framework is an analysis of dynamic object flow. Since test failures are usually triggered by the failure of an **assert*** method in which a found parameter is compared with an expected one, a backward analysis of where the unexpectedly found parameter comes from would be extremely helpful to locate the error. However, available techniques for such an analysis, such as dynamic program slicing [1, 16], prove difficult in practice [29] (cf. Section 7). Nevertheless, we expect the greatest potential for narrowing error sources to come from such analyses.

Fault Location Based on Violated Program Assertions. Design by contract guards method calls with preconditions and method returns with postconditions. Blame assignment under design by contract is simple: if the precondition is violated, it is the caller's fault; if the postcondition is violated, it is the fault of the called.

Design by contract combines well with unit testing [5, 21]. Rather than waiting for a method to be called during the normal course of a program, test cases can force it to execute. The postcondition of a method under test may replace the test oracle (delivering the expected result), but then, postconditions are usually less specific, and having an independent oracle can help debug postconditions (in case a result is classified as false by a unit test, but passed the postcondition of the method under test, it may be that the postcondition is not sensitive enough).

More important in our context is the simple fact that the failure of a precondition narrows potential culprits to the methods executed before the call, and that of a postcondition to the methods executed inside the called method (including itself). Assuming that all pre- and postconditions in a program are correct, EzUNIT can be extended to catch failed assertions and exploit the stack trace or, if dynamic tracing is switched on, the trace to exclude the methods that cannot have contributed to the violation.

Fault Location Based on Subjective Prior Assessment. As mentioned in Section 3.1, prior possibility measures such as complexity can be complemented by a subjective estimation, or confidence, of the error-proneness of a method. This can be added to MUTs using a corresponding annotation, which can be treated just like a derived prior possibility.

Fault Location Based on Learned Combinations of Fault Locators. In this paper, we have evaluated our fault locators separately. However, EzUNIT currently implements one ad hoc aggregation of their individual votes (see Section 5.2). Indeed, it could be assumed that the best approaches are those that mix a number of different approaches, sometimes in other than obvious ways. It is therefore conceivable to apply machine learning strategies to find a combination of different (and differently weighted) locators that yields better results than any individual one (but see [20] for why this may be of limited value). This could replace for the simple feedback loop currently implemented in EzUNIT, which allows the programmer to mark the locator that actually caused the error, making the selection and combination of locators adapt to the specifics of the programmer or the project being worked on.

7 Related Work

There is a significant amount of work in the literature on predicting presence and locations of errors in programs based on a priori knowledge, such as program metrics (e.g., [3, 20]). While fault predictions of this kind are useful to direct verification and testing efforts (especially in settings in which resources for these activities are limited [3, 13, 20]), as we have argued they can also be used in combination with concrete knowledge of the presence of specific faults, to track down their locations ex post.

A posterior possibility indicator much related to ours has been suggested and evaluated in [14]. It uses the fraction of failed test cases that executed a statement (note the finer granularity) and that of passed test cases to compute a measure similar to our FR. This measure is coded as colour of the statement (varying from red for 1 to green for 0) and complemented by brightness as a measure of belief in (or evidence for) the correctness of the colour, computed as the maximum of the two above fractions. By contrast, we have used the fraction of failed test cases that executed a method as an integral part of FA, to account for the explanatory power of a single potential fault for the total set of failed test cases. Adding the fault locator suggested in [14] to EzUNIT would require an extension to a second dimension, the support (or credibility) visualized as brightness; however, this makes ranking, and thus a quantitative comparison of performance, difficult. Also, we would have to change granularity from method to statement level, invalidating our a priori possibility based fault locators.

As an enhancement of JUNIT, our approach is somewhat related to David Saff's work on continuous testing [23, 24]. Continuous testing pursues the idea that test execution, like compilation, can be performed incrementally and in the background. Whenever a developer changes something and triggers a (successful) compilation, all tests whose outcome is possibly affected by that change are automatically rerun. Thus, like our own work Saff's raises unit testing to the level of syntactic and semantic (type) checking, yet it does so in an *orthogonal dimension*: continuous testing is about *when tests are executed*, our work is about *how the results are interpreted and presented*. It should be interesting to see whether and how the two approaches can be combined into one, particularly since the mutual dependency of testing and program units under test is common to both of them.

Both approaches can profit from change impact analysis, which can identify the set of tests whose execution behaviour may have changed due to a (set of) change(s) to a software system. CHIANTI [22] is such a change impact analysis tool that is also able to identify the set of (atomic) changes that affect a failed test case. CHIANTI uses static analysis in combination with dynamic or static call graphs. JUNIT/CIA [27] is an extension to CHIANTI that not only identifies the affecting changes for a failing test case, but also classifies them according to their likelihood of failure induction (green, yellow, and red). However, it always requires a previous successful test run and a change history, which we do not.

Delta debugging [30] is a general debugging technique that works by bisecting an input (source code, program input, or program state) recursively until the error is isolated. One particular variant of delta debugging (named DDCHANGE [8]) compares the last version of a program that passed all unit tests with one whose changes relative to this version make unit tests fail. In its current implementation, it makes no prior assumptions about where the error might be located (which is theoretically not a big problem because bisection has logarithmic complexity). However, despite this huge theoretical advantage delta debugging as currently implemented is rather slow (and the ECLIPSE plug-ins currently available resisted integration in our framework).

In another instantiation of delta debugging, Cleve and Zeller have used differences in program states of a passing and failed runs of a program to track down error locations in space and time [6]. They do so by first identifying variables that are carriers of erroneous state and then identifying the state transitions through which this state came about. Their approach has been shown to yield better results than any other technique of fault localization known thus far, but its technical demands (monitoring the execution state of programs) are heavy.

It has been shown that dynamic program slicing [1, 16] can help discover faults [28], but the computational effort is enormous. We have not yet investigated the possible performance gains (reduction of complexity) made possible by the special setting of unit testing, but expect that it will make it more tractable.

8 Conclusion

While unit testing automates the detection of errors, their localization is currently still mostly an intellectual act. By providing a framework that allows the integration of arbitrary a priori indicators of fault location with information derived from monitoring the success and failure of JUNIT test suites, we have laid the technical groundwork for a symptom-to-diagnosis mapping for logical programming errors that is tightly embedded in the edit/compile/run-cycle. We have evaluated the feasibility of our approach by providing four sample fault locators and measuring how well these were able to localize errors in three different evaluation settings. The results are promising and warrant continuation of our work.

Acknowledgements

The authors are indebted to Philip Bouillon for his contributions to earlier versions of EZUNIT, and to Jens Krinke for his pointers to and discussions with related work.

References

1. Agrawal, H., Horgan, J.R.: Dynamic program slicing. In: Proceedings of the ACM SIGPLAN 1990 Conference on Programming Language Design and Implementation, pp. 246–256 (1990)
2. Apache Commons Codec, http://commons.apache.org/codec/changes-report.html
3. Basili, V.R., Briand, L.C., Melo, W.L.: A validation of object-oriented design metrics as quality indicators. IEEE Trans. Software Eng. 22(10), 751–761 (1996)
4. Bouillon, P., Krinke, J., Meyer, N., Steimann, F.: EzUnit: A framework for associating failed unit tests with potential programming errors. In: Concas, G., Damiani, E., Scotto, M., Succi, G. (eds.) XP 2007. LNCS, vol. 4536, Springer, Heidelberg (2007)
5. Cheon, Y., Leavens, G.T.: A simple and practical approach to unit testing: The JML and JUnit way. In: Magnusson, B. (ed.) ECOOP 2002. LNCS, vol. 2374, pp. 231–255. Springer, Heidelberg (2002)
6. Cleve, H., Zeller, A.: Locating causes of program failures. In: Inverardi, P., Jazayeri, M. (eds.) ICSE 2005. LNCS, vol. 4309, pp. 342–351. Springer, Heidelberg (2006)
7. Continuous Testing, http://groups.csail.mit.edu/pag/continuoustesting/
8. DDChange, http://ddchange.martin-burger.de/
9. Dubois, D., Prade, H.: Possibility theory, probability theory and multiple-valued logics: a clarification. Annals of Mathematics and Artificial Intelligence 32, 1–4, 35–66 (2001)
10. Eclipse Test & Performance Tools Platform Project, http://www.eclipse.org/tptp/
11. Eichstädt-Engelen, T.: Integration von Tracing in ein Framework zur Verknüpfung von gescheiterten Unit-Tests mit Fehlerquellen (Bachelor-Arbeit, Fernuniversität in Hagen, 2008)
12. Harold, E.R.: Test your tests with Jester, http://www.ibm.com/developerworks/java/library/j-jester/
13. Hassan, A.E., Holt, R.C.: The top ten list: Dynamic fault prediction. In: ICSM, pp. 263–272 (2005)
14. Jones, J.A., Harrold, M.J., Stasko, J.T.: Visualization of test information to assist fault localization. In: ICSE, pp. 467–477 (2002)
15. Kim, S., Zimmermann, T., Whitehead Jr., E.J., Zeller, A.: Predicting faults from cached history. In: ICSE, pp. 489–498 (2007)
16. Korel, B., Laski, J.: Dynamic program slicing. Information Processing Letters 29(3), 155–163 (1998)
17. Lever, S.: Eclipse platform integration of Jester — The JUnit test tester. In: Baumeister, H., Marchesi, M., Holcombe, M. (eds.) XP 2005. LNCS, vol. 3556, pp. 325–326. Springer, Heidelberg (2005)
18. McCabe, T.J.: A complexity measure. IEEE TSE 2(4), 308–320 (1976)
19. Meyer, N.: Ein Eclipse-Framework zur Markierung von logischen Fehlern im Quellcode (Master-Arbeit, Fernuniversität in Hagen, 2007)

20. Nagappan, N., Ball, T., Zeller, A.: Mining metrics to predict component failures. In: ICSE, pp. 452–461 (2006)
21. Parasoft Corp Using Design by Contract to Automate Java Software and Component Testing Technical Paper (Parasoft, 2002)
22. Ren, X., Shah, F., Tip, F., Ryder, B.G., Chesley, O.: Chianti: A tool for change impact analysis of Java programs. In: OOPSLA, pp. 432–448 (2004)
23. Saff, D., Ernst, M.D.: Reducing wasted development time via continuous testing. In: ISSRE 2003, 14th International Symposium on Software Reliability Engineering, pp. 281–292 (2003)
24. Saff, D., Ernst, M.D.: An experimental evaluation of continuous testing during development. In: ISSTA 2004, International Symposium on Software Testing and Analysis, pp. 76–85 (2004)
25. Schaaf, M.: Integration und Evaluation von Verfahren zur Bestimmung wahrscheinlicher Ur-sachen des Scheiterns von Unit-Tests in Eclipse (Bachelor-Arbeit, Fernuniv Hagen, 2008)
26. Schröter, A., Zimmermann, T., Zeller, A.: Predicting component failures at design time. In: ISESE, pp. 18–27 (2006)
27. Störzer, M., Ryder, B.G., Ren, X., Tip, F.: Finding failure-inducing changes in Java programs using change classification. In: SIGSOFT 2006/FSE-14, pp. 57–68 (2006)
28. Zhang, X., Gupta, N., Gupta, R.: A study of effectiveness of dynamic slicing in locating real faults. Empirical Software Engineering 12(2), 143–160 (2007)
29. Zhang, X., Gupta, R., Zhang, Y.: Cost and precision tradeoffs of dynamic slicing algorithms. ACM TOPLAS 27(4), 631–661 (2005)
30. Zeller, A.: Yesterday, my program worked. Today, it does not. Why? In: ESEC / SIGSOFT FSE, pp. 253–267 (1999)

Virtual Machine Support for Stateful Aspects

Yuri Phink and Amiram Yehudai

School of Computer Science, Tel Aviv University, Tel Aviv, Israel
yphink@gmail.com, amiramy@post.tau.ac.il

Abstract. State Machines are very useful for modeling behavior of reactive systems. Stateful aspects have been proposed as a way to declara-
tively attach advice to transitions in a State Machine, so that the State
Machine structure is seen in the implementation. Vanderperren et al.
proposed an extension of the JAsCo Aspect-Oriented Programming Language for stateful aspects. This work proposes a low-overhead stateful
aspects mechanism with the same semantics as JAsCo's, built as an extension of Steamloom, a VM-supported AOP solution. The interface of
our mechanism is similar to the aspect interface provided by Steamloom,
with minimal augmentation. We provide detailed overhead analysis that
highlights the advantages of our implementation.

Keywords: Stateful Aspects, VM support for AOP, Aspect Oriented
Programming.

1 Introduction

One of the most popular implementations of AOP is AspectJ [15,23]. This language introduces a concept of an *aspect*, which is quite similar to the regular
class from the structural point of view. An aspect contains the definitions of
pointcuts, which specify those places in the application flow, named *join points*,
where behavior is to be changed, by executing an *advice*, a specific code segment
which may also be defined in the aspect. The process of combining the code of
the aspects with that of the regular Java classes is called *weaving*.

Some AOP implementations introduce aspect's dynamic nature by means of
Dynamic Aspect Deployment as well as *Dynamic Applicability Conditions*. Dynamic aspect deployment means that an AOP platform is able to (un)deploy
aspects during run-time, meaning that the application should not be restarted
in order to take effect. Several platforms, e.g. JAsCo [26], AspectWerkz [6,20,24]
and PROSE [16,28] support dynamic aspect deployment as part of its interface
and infrastructure.

A dynamic applicability condition is used when the advice is to be executed
only if a certain programmer defined condition, that can be verified only at application run-time, is satisfied. Examples of such conditions are AspectJ *cflow*
and *target* pointcuts. Also, there are AOP approaches like CaesarJ [25] which
implement a sort of dynamic aspect deployment actually through dynamic applicability condition mechanism. The aspect deployment is performed as the

R.F. Paige and B. Meyer (Eds.): TOOLS EUROPE 2008, LNBIP 11, pp. 80–99, 2008.
© Springer-Verlag Berlin Heidelberg 2008

application starts (statically), but the aspect is indicated to be applicable once it is explicitly deployed.

Following the idea of dynamic applicability condition a new aspect structure named *stateful aspect* [10] was proposed, which is intended for describing the aspect applicability conditions in terms of a sequence or protocol of run-time events. Some motivation for the stateful aspect research is provided by JAsCo stateful aspects paper [19]:

> Explicit protocols are nevertheless frequently encountered in a wide range of fields such as Component-Based Software Development [22,13], data communications [18] and business processes [2]. We therefore believe that protocols are valid targets for aspect application, and argue that it is desirable to support them in the pointcut language itself; delegating the actual control-mechanism implementation to the weaver.

To the best of our knowledge there are two main implementations of stateful aspects available today. It is stateful aspect extension of JAsCo AOP [19] and tracematches extension of abc [1,4]. While the work on tracematches provide an interesting reference mainly for compile-time weaving implementations, JAsCo AOP implements runtime weaving.

Moreover, JAsCo AOP implementation provides a subsystem that can weave in and out advice in run-time as the state of the stateful aspect changes. Precisely, each transition from one state to another results in weaving out advice that are attached to the former state and weaving in the advice that are attached to the new state.

Still there is an alternative approach for stateful aspect runtime deployment which is weaving all the advice during aspect initialization. In this approach an applicability test is inserted before the advice call, to check that the current state matches the state associated with the advice. This strategy is also implemented in JAsCo AOP infrastructure, by providing the Java Annotation "WeaveAll" in the aspect definition. We will use the name *WeaveAll Strategy* throughout this paper to indicate this behavior.

The decision which of the two approaches to use is application dependent, because there is a performance tradeoff. Runtime weaving of advice is a very expensive operation in comparison to the overhead of the applicability test described above. Roughly speaking, if a stateful aspect state changes frequently in runtime, the preferred strategy would be weaving in all the advice of this aspect with the corresponding applicability tests. This way no weaving will occur when the state of this aspect changes.

AOP has proved to be a very useful tool for software development, but its usefulness depends on low overhead AOP implementations. Stateful aspects are applicable in many systems that express reactive behavior [9], therefore it is important to have an efficient implementation for them. The goal of our work is to provide an implementation of stateful aspects that minimizes the overhead of the WeaveAll strategy.

Most AOP implementations which support dynamic weaving rely on standard Java Virtual machines, hence they establish their infrastructure at the application level. Abc tracematches extension [1] is the example for such an infrastructure which is discussed in this paper. Nevertheless, there are few implementations of AOP support that maintain their mechanism at the level of virtual machine. One of them is Steamloom [5], which is an AOP extension of IBM Jikes Research Virtual Machine [27]. Steamloom presents, among others, two advantages over other known systems: separation of AOP infrastructure and the application, which results in a more friendly solution to the programmer; byte-code level weaving implemented in the VM which usually results in minimal AOP infrastructure overhead.

This paper presents Steamloom SA, a low overhead stateful aspect mechanism implementing WeaveAll strategy, which is built as an extension of Steamloom and thus utilizes the advantages of VM level support. We start by showing, in Section 2, examples of stateful aspects. Section 3 presents Steamloom SA interface. Section 4 deals with some implementation issues of our stateful aspect mechanism. Section 5 is the evaluation of the presented implementation including performance analysis and discussion. Section 6 presents related work and we end up with conclusions in Section 7.

2   Stateful Aspects Examples

Most AOP approaches do not support describing the aspect applicability conditions in terms of a sequence or protocol of run-time events. These conditions should, therefore, be implemented at the application level of the aspect definition. For example, it is likely that the aspect definition will contain an object shared between the advice invocations. This way all the stateful conditions (state test) and corresponding transitions (state change) are performed against the shared object as part of the advice invocation procedure, see Listing 1. In this AspectJ example the shared object is "shouldLog". However, we would like to conceal the stateful aspect infrastructure from the programmer and let him use stateful aspect interface instead. The example of such an interface is illustrated in Listing 2. The "stateful" keyword indicates a structure of DFA states and transitions so that later it will be used in advice definition. To define a DFA as a core stateful aspect mechanism we used similar structure and syntax to the one used in JAsCo [19]: an advice can be attached to a transition; the transition is defined by the equality sentence such that to the left of the equal sign the name of the transition is given and to the right its operativity is defined. Observe that in this notation states do not have names. Instead, a state is identified by the set of transitions out of it. The initial DFA state is identified by the first transition definition in the "stateful" block. The "stateful" block in the Listing 2 determines the following DFA:

- "t1" is the only transition from the initial state. Its condition is "logIn()" pointcut.
- When "t1" transition is performed, the DFA is moved to the next state. Two transitions are available from this state : "t2" and "t3", with conditions "execute(p)" and "logOut()" correspondingly.

– When "t2" transition is performed the DFA remains in this state.
– When "t3" transition is performed the DFA is moved to the initial state.

The DFA from the example described above is illustrated in Figure 1.

Observe that the examples from Listing 1 and Listing 2 define the same stateful aspect logic. Clearly, the example with the stateful aspect interface is a more readable version than the one with the application-implemented stateful aspect.

```
aspect StatefulLogging {
    boolean shouldLog = false;

    pointcut logIn (): call (void
       Application.logIn (Parameters userParms ));
    pointcut logOut (): call (void
       Application.logOut (Parameters userParms ));
    pointcut execute (Parameters p):
       call (public *.*(Parameters) && args (p));

    before (): logIn () {
        shouldLog = true;
    }

    before (): logOut () {
        shouldLog = false;
    }

    before (Parameters p): execute (p) {
        if (shouldLog)
        {
            System.out.println ("Username⌴is⌴" + p.user +
                "⌴function⌴is⌴" + thisJoinPoint.getSignature ());
        }
    }
}
```

Listing 1. AspectJ example of application-implemented stateful aspect. This is a simple Logging stateful aspect example.

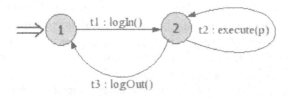

Fig. 1. A DFA for the stateful aspect example of Listing 2

```
aspect StatefulLoggingAlternative {

    pointcut logIn (): call (void
        Application . logIn (Parameters userParms ));
    pointcut logOut (): call (void
        Application . logOut (Parameters userParms ));
    pointcut execute (Parameters p):
        call (public *.*(Parameters ) && args (p ));

    stateful (t1)   // t1 - initial transition
    {
        t1 = logIn () -> t2 || t3 ;
        t2 (Parameters p) = execute (p) -> t2 || t3 ;
        t3 = logOut () -> t1 ;
    }

    before (Parameters p): t2 (p) {
        System . out . println ("Username‿is‿" + p . user +
            "‿function‿is‿" + thisJoinPoint . getSignature ());
    }
}
```

Listing 2. An example of possible AspectJ extension for stateful aspects (JAsCo style)

3   Steamloom SA Interface

Currently, Steamloom's aspect interface is quite cumbersome because its authors' goal has not been the creation of the most convenient aspect definition interface but rather solid AOP execution platform. The same holds for the Steamloom SA interface presented in this paper. We have not pretended to build a user-friendly interface, however it is clear that this interface can be wrapped by a preprocessor which takes JAsCo like stateful aspect definitions and transforms them into the interface of Steamloom SA. Moreover, it is possible to build a visual tool based on the interface described below so that stateful aspects will be shown graphically, i.e. state machine diagrams. This way stateful aspect development becomes even more handy.

A regular Steamloom aspect definition example is shown in Listing 3, and Listing 4 presents the stateful aspect of Listing 2 (whose DFA was shown in Figure 1) as a Steamloom SA interface example. Steamloom interface and Steamloom SA interface are both partially based on Java Reflection classes. The advice method used in aspect definition is declared as an instance of the class "Method". The advice themselves take two parameters: the advice method and the advice class instance. A Pointcut is declared through the interface provided by Steamloom. Finally, "Aspect" ("StatefulAspect") class instance is initialized and all the previously defined advice and pointcuts are provided to this instance as the parameters to its corresponding functions. Then the aspect is deployed by calling the "deploy()" function. A detailed explanation of the Steamloom interface can be found in M. Haupt's Doctoral Dissertation [14].

```
// Advice method receives one parameter of type Parameters
Method m1 = TestAdvice.class.getDeclaredMethod("advice1" ,
    new Class[] {Parameters.class});
Method m2 = TestAdvice.class.getDeclaredMethod("advice2" ,
    null);

TestAdvice adviceClass = new TestAdvice();
BeforeAdvice adB1 = new BeforeAdvice (m1, adviceClass);

// The first parameter of the called function
// should be passed to the advice method
adB1.appendArg(1);

AfterAdvice adA2 = new AfterAdvice (m2, adviceClass);

PointcutDesignator p1 = SimpleParser.getPointcut(
    "call(void_TestClass.test1(Parameters))");
PointcutDesignator p2 =
    SimpleParser.getPointcut("call(void_TestClass.test2())");

Aspect a = new Aspect();

// Association of an advice with a pointcut
a.associate ( adB1 , p1 );
a.associate ( adA2 , p2 );

a.deploy ();
```

Listing 3. Example of Steamloom aspect interface usage

These examples differ amongst them mainly due to the addition of *transition* term. In the original Steamloom's aspect definition an advice is attached to the pointcut, whereas in Steamloom SA we define possible state transitions by "addTransition()" function first and only then we attach the advice to the transition we have previously defined.

This newly introduced function receives three parameters: source state ID, target state ID and a pointcut. The ID of the starting state of stateful aspect is always 1. New states are defined once they are given as a parameters to the function.

The return value of "addTransition()" is an integer that represents an ID of the created transition. It is later used in association of an advice with the transition using "associate()" function.

```
// Advice method receives one parameter of
// type Parameters
Method m1 = TestAdvice.class.getDeclaredMethod("adviceMethod",
        new Class[] {Parameters.class});

TestAdvice adviceClass = new TestAdvice();

PointcutDesignator p1 = SimpleParser.getPointcut(
    "call(void_Application.logIn(Parameters))");
PointcutDesignator p2 = SimpleParser.getPointcut(
    "call(void_Application.logOut(Parameters))");
PointcutDesignator p3 = SimpleParser.getPointcut(
    "call(public_*.*(Parameters))");

AfterAdvice ad = new AfterAdvice(m1, adviceClass);

// The first parameter of the called function
// should be passed to the advice method
ad.appendArg(1);

// max number of states = 2
StatefulAspect a = new StatefulAspect(2);

int tid1 = a.addTransition(1,2,p1);
int tid2 = a.addTransition(2,1,p2);
int tid3 = a.addTransition(2,2,p3);

// Association of an advice with a transition
a.associate(ad,tid3);

a.deploy();
```

Listing 4. Example of Steamloom SA interface usage

4 Steamloom SA Implementation

As has been mentioned in the introduction, one of Steamloom's substantial advantages is its byte-code level weaving. The core idea of stateful aspect implementation in Steamloom is to weave in the minimal byte-code sequence in all transition pointcuts together with the advice invocation, if any attached. This sequence should perform all the relevant stateful operations which mainly include a *state test* - whether the current state is the same as the source state of this transition, and a *state change* - movement to the destination state.

4.1 Stateful Aspect Semantics

Prior to the implementation part the semantics of stateful aspect mechanism had been defined. It is intended to be identical to JAsCo stateful aspect semantics, meaning that it conforms with the semantics of the formal stateful aspects framework proposed by Douence et al. [10]. The following basic operational semantics were recognized in JAsCo:

1. The state test and state change are performed only before the join point, i.e. these tests are prepended to Before Advice.
2. Only one state change of the same stateful aspect can occur in one join point.
3. The After Advice attached to the transition of the stateful aspect is executed only if the corresponding Before Advice state test has been successful.

The last rule matches with the semantic of a runtime condition evaluation in Steamloom, called *residue*. Any dynamic properties that should be evaluated prior to the After Advice execution are actually tested before the join point shadow (excluding method execution pointcut). Considering that the state test procedure is a dynamic property that should be tested with a corresponding residue, Steamloom SA implementation preserves the above scheme used in Steamloom. For example, attachment of an After Advice to the pointcut "call (**void** x()) && **this**(A)" in Steamloom causes the insertion of the residue that tests whether the current object can be assigned to "A" before the call to the function "**void** x()". The same holds for the state test procedure implemented in Steamloom SA.

4.2 Deployment Procedure

Steamloom design declares a basic unit – *AspectUnit* which defines a pointcut and an associated advice, and is used to construct an aspect. In Steamloom, an aspect is defined as a list of associated pointcuts and advice represented by the AspectUnit structure. Deployment of an Aspect, therefore, refers to the deployment of all the AspectUnits stored within it.

As illustrated in the interface of Steamloom SA, there is a difference in the advice association between regular aspects and stateful aspects. However, the only thing that is actually different is the interface. The implementation keeps the original design of AspectUnit as the association of the pointcut and the advice. The notion of the transition stays only at the interface level, i.e. "StatefulAspect" class level. Actual (un)deployment is performed on the AspectUnit that represents the advice and the pointcut of the associated transition. The deployment procedure iterates through the list of transitions and performs AspectUnits deployment strictly in the following order:

1. If a Before Advice is attached to the transition then the new AspectUnit is created using this advice and the transition's pointcut. Otherwise, the new AspectUnit with the association of dummy Before Advice and the transition's pointcut is created. The created AspectUnit is then deployed.
2. If an After Advice is attached to the transition then the new AspectUnit is created using this advice and the transition's pointcut. The created AspectUnit is then deployed.

Note that the dummy Before Advice is necessary, because even in the absence of an explicitly attached Before Advice, we need to weave in the code that performs state test and state change as part of the stateful aspect mechanism.

The order of AspectUnits deployment presented above is mandatory because of the relationship between Before and After Advice in the same join point. Since After Advice's execution depends on the state test procedure of the Before Advice in the same join point, this Before Advice should be deployed first.

Stateful aspect undeployment is implemented in the intuitive way, similar to the deployment itself. The main loop iterates through AspectUnits of each transition and undeploys them in the reversed order: first the AspectUnit that holds After Advice and then the AspectUnit that holds Before Advice are undeployed. However, stateful aspect undeployment has an advantage over the regular aspect undeployment in Steamloom. Steamloom's current version provides no means of atomicity when the aspect is undeployed. In other words, it is possible that only some of the AspectUnits that constitute the aspect will be undeployed while others are still active and the application is running. Such situation will not occur in stateful aspects of Steamloom SA, since the first operation that is performed by the undeployment procedure is setting the current state of stateful aspect to zero. This operation ensures that no AspectUnits of this stateful aspect are applicable, since state test procedure from now on will always fail. This is relevant until all the AspectUnits of the given stateful aspect are undeployed. When the undeployment process is finished, no state test is done since there is no footprint left of the undeployed aspect in the application.

4.3 Stateful Shared Object

Through the basic model of state test and state change code weaving, the need for some sort of inter-advice shared object that stores the current state can be identified. In the same way as the Advice Instance management was implemented in Steamloom, the problem of shared object management was solved. The Advice Instance management core solution was the extension of a Type Information Block with an array reference, AIT - Advice Instance Table. This array was designed to contain the object instances that held advice methods. Since the index of the array was known at compile time, the advice method invocation performed nearly as regular method invocation. The TIB modification led to the creation of the new byte-code instruction, *aaitpush*. This instruction gets an index and pushes the value (object) from the position identified by the given index in AIT to the stack. This suffices to invoke an advice method call immediately after.

Inter-advice shared object management is implemented using the same technique, since a class level deployment is a general case of a deployment for stateful aspects also. The TIB is extended by an additional array reference, SAT - Stateful Aspect Table. Each entry in the SAT is designed to hold an object that in its turn holds an integer variable. This variable identifies the transitions that are available from the current state of the specific stateful aspect (it can be said that this variable identifies the current state). The integer is built up of 32 bits, which limits stateful aspects to at most 32 transitions, because each bit is associated with a transition in our implementation.

The design above has two benefits:

1. The new construct has the same characteristics as Advice Instance management, including the performance issues, because an index within SAT becomes known during compile time too.
2. The integer value that identifies the current state is taken out of the object that is stored in SAT. This allows for the state test procedure to be implemented by a lightweight operation - logical AND.

Thus, new byte-code instruction, *asatpush*, had to be added in order to take out a SAT reference from the TIB and push the object at a given index to the stack. It is implemented almost identically to aaitpush instruction.

4.4 Woven Code Details

The result of an aspect deployment in Steamloom is the method's altered Java byte-code which is later compiled by JIT compiler [3] once the need for this method execution arises during an application execution. The altered Java byte-code has two additional blocks of instructions that are added: one before the join point, and one after the join point. Before Advice which is weaved in exactly before the join point plays crucial role for the stateful aspect mechanism in Steamloom SA. The newly presented instruction, asatpush, appears as part of a Before Advice instruction block. An After Advice instruction block exists only if the programmer has explicitly added an After Advice to the transition.

The technical details of these instruction blocks may be found in the first author's MSc thesis [17].

5 Evaluation

The main purpose of this work is to propose a low overhead stateful aspect mechanism. This section presents the performance data to substantiate our claim. In this section we present an in-depth performance comparison and discussion between JAsCo and Steamloom SA. Earlier we have mentioned the abc team work on tracematches that provides similar capabilities, though using compile-time weaving. Nevertheless it is still interesting to measure the overhead of their implementation. Therefore the same benchmarks that are used in this analysis are applied also on the tracematches extension of AspectBench Compiler and the results are presented. The third implementation of stateful aspects that is measured and presented in this section is application-implemented stateful aspects. It is implemented using Steamloom existing aspect interface.

5.1 Performance Criteria

Several run-time configurations are used to measure the overhead of each of the systems: Steamloom SA, JAsCo and abc. The measurements are accumulated using JavaGrande benchmark framework [8]. This framework provides three types of Java performance assessment mechanisms, while in this work only the first type (Section 1, as named in [8]), *micro-measurements*, are used. The original benchmark implements measurements of all basic Java operations like different types of method calls, exception handling etc. The benchmark's output is the executed operation's throughput, i.e. how many operations of this type are executed per second.

Only the method call's benchmark (out of the available set of operations) is used in order to measure stateful aspect implementation overhead. Listing 5 presents the simple algorithm of this benchmark.

In this work we are interested in focusing on operations' overhead rather then operations' throughput. It simplifies understanding of the results and the comparison between them. This is achieved by reversing the result (throughput) we get and scaling it to the units of nanoseconds. For example, if the operation's throughput is 30,000 (ops/sec) then its operation's overhead is equal to $\frac{1}{30,000} 10^9 \approx 33,333$ (nanoseconds).

```
// N                  : number of operations executed
//                       in one measurement iteration
// MAX_OPERATIONS     : the operations number threshold
//                       in a measurement cycle
// THRESHOLD          : time threshold in a measurement cycle
JGFrun()
{
    count=0;time=0;
    tools.addTimer("MethodCall");
    tools.startTimer("MethodCall");

    while (count < MAX_OPERATIONS && time < THRESHOLD)
    {
        for (int i=0; i<N; i++)
            <Method Call Operation>;

        tools.stopTimer("MethodCall");
        time = tools.readTimer("MethodCall");
        tools.addOpsToTimer("MethodCall",N);

        count += N; N = N*2;
    }

    print(tools.perfTimer("MethodCall"));    // ops/time
}
```

Listing 5. JavaGrande benchmark algorithm for method call throughput measurement

Following is the list of configurations of method call operations used in performance assessment. This list covers all the possible overhead measurements of stateful aspect mechanism. Note that the abbreviations in parantheses are used to identify each configuration in Figure 2 and Figure 4.

no stateful aspect (No SA) Unaffected method call.

state test only (ST only) Method call is a join point of stateful aspect transition, but state test procedure fails, i.e. no transition is done.

state test and change (ST&C) Method call is a join point of stateful aspect transition without any advice method call, i.e. state test and change procedure is executed successfully.

state test and change and BA call (ST&C BA) Method call is a join point of stateful aspect transition with Before Advice method call.

state test and change and AA call (ST&C AA) Method call is a join point of stateful aspect transition with After Advice method call.

Each configuration was implemented in the same manner in Steamloom SA, JAsCo and abc using its own interface correspondingly. It is worth noting that JAsCo was configured to perform using WeaveAll strategy.

In addition, some configurations were implemented in Steamloom aspect interface because we wanted to compare between the infrastructure overhead of application-implemented stateful aspect and Steamloom SA stateful aspect. Generally, there is a difficulty in performance comparison between AOP platform-supported and application-implemented stateful aspect. Application-implemented stateful aspects are always adapted to specific application needs. In this case different tests executed by AOP platform-supported stateful aspects may be avoided in the concrete application. Note that there are different architectural issues which are taken into consideration in a generic implementation (AOP platform-supported) of stateful aspects. These should be mapped out in order to provide at least partial generic implementation of application-implemented stateful aspects so that the comparison will still be relevant:

- Advice of the same stateful aspect instance can belong to different classes. It would be rather different in application-implemented stateful aspects since the advice of the same stateful aspect must share information, like *current state*.
- Not every application that needs a stateful aspect is multi-threaded. Since Steamloom SA implementation is thread-safe, its performance is degraded when compared to application-implemented stateful aspect that does not use any synchronization mechanism.
- AOP platform-supported stateful aspect implementation avoids more than one state change in one join point. The treatment of this issue involves an additional code in Steamloom SA and probably would not be needed at all in most application-implemented stateful aspects.

When the design of a general solution for stateful aspects was formulated, the sample prototype of partially generic application-developed implementation of stateful aspect was written (see Listing 6). This application-implemented stateful aspect was utilized by the regular Steamloom aspect interface to perform the most accurate measurements. The methods "advice1()" and "advice2()" are used as Before Advice methods in order to comply with stateful aspect semantics.

Listing 6 serves an example of a simple stateful aspect with two states and two transitions, one in each direction. This implementation is partially generic because it fulfills 2 out of 3 generic solution requirements: the first one (advice instances from multiple classes) can be considered as covered since the addition of another advice method class variable to this StatefulAspect class can be done obviously and used by, for example, "advice2()" method; the second one (Thread safe *state test and change* procedure) is fulfilled by a "<**synchronized**>" block when a state is checked and changed. However, there is no treatment of multiple state change in one join point problem. This requirement was not addressed for two reasons:

- The problem this requirement solves occurs rarely.
- An attempt to solve this problem by using an additional code results in performance deterioration because awareness of join point information is needed inside the advice methods, which is only provided by an expensive context reification procedure.

```java
public class StatefulAspect {
    int state =1;
    AdviceMethodsClass t = new AdviceMethodsClass ();

    public void advice1 () {
        boolean executeAdvice = false;
        synchronized (this) {
            if (state == 1) {
                state = 2; executeAdvice = true;
            }
        }
        if (executeAdvice)
            t. method1 ();
    }

    public void advice2 () {
        boolean executeAdvice = false;
        synchronized (this) {
            if (state == 2) {
                state = 1; executeAdvice = true;
            }
        }
        if (executeAdvice)
            t. method2 ();
    }
}
```

Listing 6. Application-implemented stateful aspect example in Java

Nevertheless, it can be interesting to examine the relation between infrastructure overhead of this and AOP platform-supported solution. Note that the configuration which contains After Advice method call was not implemented by the application-implemented stateful aspect. Semantics require that After Advice method should be able to determine whether Before Advice method of the current join point have successfully executed *state check and change* procedure. However, it is possible only if instantiation granularity control (for instance, *perAll* instantiation control keyword in JAsCo) is supported by AOP platform, but it is not the case with Steamloom. The *perAll* JAsCo's keyword enables the creation of different aspect instances per each join point, which allows information sharing between Before and After advice of the same aspect in a specific join point.

In addition to the measured configurations presented above, two other cases were evaluated for JAsCo AOP platform only. The requirements for these configurations measurements and their results are elaborated in the next section.

Note that we do not supply any performance comparison between the VM implementation of asatpush operation and the Java code that simulates the same logic. The performance analysis of a similar byte-code operation was already presented in the dissertation of Haupt [14].

5.2   Results and Analysis

The performance data collection is done in the following environment: Steamloom 2.3.1 version (based on 2.3.1 version of Jikes RVM) and JAsCo 0.8.7 on standard VM for Java 1.6. The abc tracematches benchmarks were executed on Jikes RVM 2.9.2 since there were some technical difficulties running it on the older version of Jikes (2.3.1). The executing machine details are: Intel Pentium D CPU 3.40 Ghz, 2GB RAM, Linux OS version 2.6.22 Fedora Core 6.

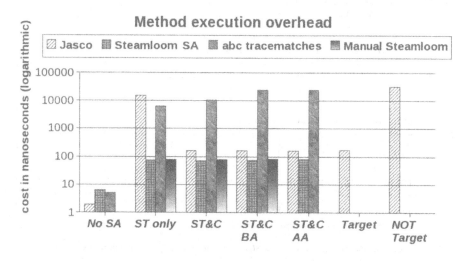

Fig. 2. Performance measurement results

The resulting chart is illustrated in Figure 2. The chart presents a logarithmic scale of the values that represent matching operation's overhead (operation's cost), which computation was described in the previous section . *Steamloom SA* bars indicate the data collected on Steamloom SA and *Manual Steamloom* bars relate to the application-implemented stateful aspect example presented in the previous section.

First we observe that the unaffected method call overhead of Steamloom is quite higher then JAsCo's, which is actually method call overhead of standard VM for Java 1.6. This comparison is used to validate whether we need to perform some normalization to the data gathered. However, because all other values in the chart are significantly larger then that of unaffected method call in each of the two AOP platforms, we decided to leave the original data as is without normalization since it will not change anything significantly.

JAsCo Implementation Details

Looking at the resulting chart the reader can notice that JAsCo has a serious performance downgrade at join points where no transition is done. This downgrade is the result of JAsCo specific implementation. To explain it we first introduce the difference between JAsCo and Steamloom SA design.

```
<automata state = 1>
if this joinpont matches p1
     then move to state 3;

<automata state = 2>
if this joinpont matches p1
     then move to state 3;
if this joinpont matches p2
     then move to state 4;
```

Listing 7. JAsCo's *state test and change* implementation

```
<this join point matches p1>
if current state = 1
     then move to state 3;
if current state = 2
     then move to state 3;

<this join point matches p2>
if current state = 2
     then move to state 4;
```

Listing 8. Steamloom SA's *state test and change* implementation

JAsCo uses JPLIS (Java Programming Language Instrumentation Services) to weave in the modified method in run-time with the corresponding calls to Before and/or After advice. This way the original method is called between these advice method calls. Prior to any advice method call there are different tests performed to decide whether the advice is applicable. Some of these tests are related to stateful aspect mechanism, i.e. the state test and change procedure. The state test and change procedure in JAsCo is implemented in a different manner. States and transitions are defined as objects. All the transitions that are possible from the state are stored as part of the state object data. When the state test and change procedure is entered, the search for a suitable transition from the current state is performed. The successful finding is defined by the match of transition's pointcut and the current join point. Once such transition is found (at least one), the current state of the stateful aspect is changed and the indication of success is returned to the modified application's method in order to execute the attached advice, if any.

The illustration of the implementation differences between JAsCo and Steamloom SA follows.

We show the pseudo Java code of the state test and change procedure for the stateful aspect represented by the DFA of Figure 3, as executed in JAsCo and in Steamloom SA, in Listing 7 and Listing 8 respectively. The condition in angle brackets indicates the beginning of the code's block that is executed if the condition is implicitly true.

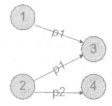

Fig. 3. DFA that contains 4 states and 3 transitions.

Finding the transition whose pointcut matches the current join point in JAsCo is a relatively expensive operation. Therefore, under some circumstances, JAsCo caches successful matches in the current join point so that repeatable searches are avoided. However, if such transition is not found, no caching is performed. The performance overhead of unsuccessful state change (state test only) is therefore very high compared to other state test and change configurations presented in Figure 2. Note also that the transition caching described above is not applied to every successful match. There are several pointcut designators that , if included in a pointcut, disable the caching facility because their evaluated value may change during application execution at the same join point. The ultimate example for such a pointcut designator is *cflow*. In addition, *not* pointcut designator, if included in the pointcut, also disables caching in the current JAsCo implementation. For this reason we have added to the performance comparison chart presented above two additional configurations which were measured only for JAsCo: a pointcut that contains *target* designator and a pointcut with *not target* designator. It is presented to reemphasize the significant influence of "un-cachable" pointcuts on performance.

Observe that even cachable pointcuts in JAsCo (all other measurements) have doubled overhead compared to the corresponding configurations in our

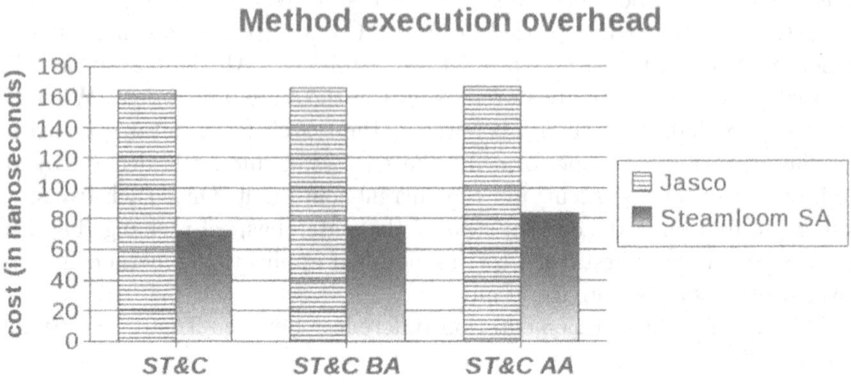

Method execution overhead

Fig. 4. Performance measurement results for cachable pointcuts

implementation. Figure 4 illustrates the original cost comparison of those operations which exploit JAsCo caching facility. These results highlight the advantages
of VM supported stateful aspect solution.

Application-Implemented Stateful Aspects
Some configurations of application-implemented stateful aspect were compared
with Steamloom SA. Each configuration is an adapted version of the code presented in the Listing 6. The overhead of application-implemented stateful aspect
and the overhead of Steamloom SA are nearly identical. This emphasizes the
advantage of VM supported stateful aspect solution which is fully generic in
contrast to the partially generic solution of application-implemented stateful aspect. Needless to say that application-implemented stateful aspect eliminates a
clear separation between AOP infrastructure and application code, therefore it
is certainly less preferred.

Abc Tracematches
The first benchmark (No stateful aspect) provides the information about the
overhead of the infrastructure before any aspect was applied. In this case it is
actually the overhead of calling a method in Jikes RVM 2.9.2. Once an aspect
oriented activity takes place (all the following benchmarks) the overhead of a
method execution is increased significantly due to the heavy AOP infrastructure at the application level. The results evidence the insight that any AOP
infrastructure including stateful aspects provided at the application level has its
drawback in performance. This drawback, as we presented, can be effectively
removed if the stateful aspect mechanism is moved to the VM level.

6   Related Work

Hitherto, the stateful aspect concept have been employed only by a small number of AOP approaches due to its rather young research. The first stateful aspect formal model was proposed by Douence et al. [10,12] with the proof of

concept implementation described in [11]. Also, Walker et al. introduce *declarative event patterns* (DEPs) [21] as a means to specify protocols as patterns of multiple events, which offers "stateful aspect"like supporting approach. These researches were done prior to the implementation of JAsCo stateful aspects extension, therefore a short survey about them can be found in the "Related work" section of [19]. Another stateful aspect implementation provided by abc tracematches extension [1,4] is quite interesting especially because of the optimized implementation of free variables matching. It provides the programmer with the implicit mechanism of "correct" free variable matching, which often makes the development significantly easier. However, the performance of the basic stateful aspect mechanism is far from being optimal, mainly because of the application level AOP infrastructure. Also, this solution, like AspectJ, does not support runtime weaving, which can be identified as a necessary requirement in many systems.

As far as we know, our work is the only one that aims at better performance regarding a pure stateful aspect mechanism. The approaches that were discussed above, though, make different contributions to stateful aspect research, like higher level of declarative expressibility, smart aspect conflict resolution, optimal free variables matching and etc.

7   Conclusion

This paper presents Steamloom SA, an implementation of stateful aspects mechanism working on the VM level. The contributions of this work are the following:

- The implementation presented here introduces very low overhead in comparison with stateful aspect implementation in JAsCo and abc tracematches.
- It supports the same semantics for stateful aspects implemented in JAsCo.
- Run-time deployment and undeployment of stateful aspect is possible. The undeployment is performed atomically.
- Steamloom SA's infrastructure overhead is almost equal to the overhead of the partially generic application-implemented stateful aspect proposed in this paper.
- Steamloom SA inherits from Steamloom the separation of AOP infrastructure from the application code.

Our implementation is aimed at introducing the performance gain of VM-supported stateful aspects, therefore not all the features presented in JAsCo solution, like "isApplicable()" and automatic undeployment, are implemented here. Also, our solution does not support Around Advice as part of stateful aspect because of the fact that treatment of Around Advice is quite different than that of other advice in Steamloom specific implementation. We believe that it is enough to show the advantages of VM-supported stateful aspects solution using other types of advice (Before Advice, After Advice) because, in general, the same implementation design can be utilized for Around Advice in stateful aspect.

Future research can elaborate the idea of implementing *Jumping Aspects* [7] mechanism efficiently in VM level. When this implementation becomes available, Steamloom SA can be enhanced with an Adaptive Optimization System for stateful aspects, which like AOS in Jikes RVM [27], chooses dynamically what kind of weaving strategy should be applied for the specific aspect. The original AOS in Jikes RVM is used for deciding when a method should be compiled with an optimized compiler. Similarly, as we have mentioned in the introduction there is a tradeoff between dynamic advice (un)deployment as the state of stateful aspect changes and the WeaveAll Strategy. AOS for stateful aspects should involve statistical analysis of application runtime and, based on that analysis, decide which advice of the stateful aspect should be weaved in unconditionally, while others will be weaved in only upon the approach of the corresponding state.

In addition, it is quite interesting to investigate the possibility to provide a highly optimized VM-level implementation of free variables matching mechanism, similar to the one presented in abc tracematches extension. This issue is also open for the future research.

Acknowledgements. We would like to thank Michael Haupt for his great help with Steamloom architecture and Christoph Bockisch for the provision of BAT sources. We wish to thanks the anonymous reviewers of a previous version for comments that helped us to improve the paper.

References

1. Allan, C., Augustinov, P., Christensen, A.S., Hendren, L., Kuzins, S., Lhoták, O., de Moor, O., Sereni, D., Sittampalam, G., Tibble, J.: Adding Trace Matching with Free Variables to AspectJ. J. SIGPLAN Not 40, 345–364 (2005)
2. Andrews, T., Curbera, F., et al.: Business Process Execution Language for Web Services Specification (2003),
   http://www.ibm.com/developerworks/library/ws-bpel/
3. Arnold, M., Fink, S., Grove, D., Hind, M., Sweeney, P.F.: Adaptive Optimization in the Jalapeño JVM. In: 15th ACM SIGPLAN Conference on Object-Oriented Programming, Systems, Languages & Applications (Addendum), pp. 125–126. ACM Press, New York (2000)
4. Avgustinov, P., Tibble, J., de Moor, O.: Making trace monitors feasible. J. SIGPLAN Not 42, 589–608 (2007)
5. Bockisch, C., Haupt, M., Mezini, M., Ostermann, K.: Virtual machine support for dynamic join points. In: 3rd International Conference on Aspect-Oriented Software Development, pp. 83–92. ACM Press, New York (2004)
6. Bonér ,J.: AspectWerkz - Dynamic AOP for Java (2003),
   http://codehaus.org/~jboner/papers/aosd2004_aspectwerkz.pdf
7. Brichau, J., de Meuter, W., de Volder, K.: Jumping Aspects. In: Workshop on Aspects and Dimensions of Concerns (2000)
8. Bull, J.M., Smith, L.A., Westhead, M.D., Henty, D.S., Davey, R.A.: A Benchmark Suite for High Performance Java. J. Concurrency: Practice and Experience 12, 375–388 (2000)

9. Cottenier, T., van den Berg, A., Elrad, T.: Stateful aspects: the case for aspect-oriented modeling. In: 10th international workshop on Aspect-oriented modeling, pp. 7–14. ACM Press, New York (2007)
10. Douence, R., Fradet, P., Südholt, M.: A framework for the detection and resolution of aspect interactions. In: 1st ACM SIGPLAN/SIGSOFT Conference on Generative Programming and Component Engineering, pp. 173–188. Springer, London (2002)
11. Douence, R., Fradet, P., Südholt, M.: Trace-based Aspects. In: Aspect-Oriented Software Development, pp. 201–218. Addison Wesley (2004)
12. Douence, R., Fradet, P., Südholt, M.: Composition, Reuse and Interaction Analysis of Stateful Aspects. In: 3th International Conference on Aspect-Oriented Software Development, pp. 141–150. ACM, New York (2004)
13. Farías, A., Südholt, M.: On components with explicit protocols satisfying a notion of correctness by construction. In: Distributed Objects and Applications, pp. 995–1012. Springer, London (2002)
14. Haupt, M.: Virtual Machine Support for Aspect-Oriented Programming Languages. Doctoral Dissertation (2006)
15. Kiczales, G., Hilsdale, E., Hugunin, J., Kersten, M., Palm, J., Griswold, W.G.: An overview of AspectJ. In: 15th European Conference on Object-Oriented Programming, pp. 327–353. Springer, London (2001)
16. Nicoara, A., Alonso, G.: Dynamic AOP with PROSE. In: CAiSE Workshops, FEUP Edições, Porto, pp. 125–138 (2005)
17. Phink, Y.: Virtual Machine Support for Stateful Aspects. M.Sc. Thesis, Tel-Aviv University (in preparation, 2008)
18. Tanenbaum, A.S.: Computer Networks, 4th edn. Prentice Hall Professional Technical Reference (2002)
19. Vanderperren, W., Suvee, D., Cibran, M.A., De Fraine, B.: Stateful Aspects in JAsCo. In: Gschwind, T., Aßmann, U., Nierstrasz, O. (eds.) SC 2005. LNCS, vol. 3628, pp. 167–181. Springer, Heidelberg (2005)
20. Vasseur, A.: Dynamic AOP and Runtime Weaving for Java - How does AspectWerkz Address It? (2004), http://aspectwerkz.codehaus.org/downloads/papers/aosd2004-daw-aspectwerkz.pdf
21. Walker, R.J., Viggers, K.: Implementing Protocols via Declarative Event Patterns. J. SIGSOFT Soft. Eng. Notes 29, 159–169 (2004)
22. Yellin, D., Strom, R.: Protocol Specifications and Component Adaptors. J. ACM Trans. Program. Lang. Syst. 19, 292–333 (1997)
23. AspectJ, http://www.eclipse.org/aspectj
24. AspectWerkz, http://aspectwerkz.codehaus.org
25. CaesarJ, http://caesarj.org
26. JAsCo, http://ssel.vub.ac.be/jasco
27. The Jikes Research Virtual Machine, http://jikesrvm.sourceforge.net
28. PROSE, http://prose.ethz.ch

Guarded Program Transformations Using JTL

Tal Cohen[1,*], Joseph (Yossi) Gil[2], and Itay Maman[2]

[1] Google Haifa Engineering Center
[2] Department of Computer Science, Technion—Israel Institute of Technology
talcohen@google.com, {yogi,imaman}@cs.technion.ac.il

Abstract. There is a growing research interest in employing the logic paradigm for making *queries* on software in general, and OOP software in particular. We describes a side-effect-free technique of using the paradigm for the general task of *program transformation*. Our technique offers a variety of applications, such as implementing generic structures (without erasure) in JAVA, a Lint-like program checker, and more. By allowing the transformation target to be a different language than the source (*program translation*), we show how the language can be employed for tasks like the generation of database schemas or XML DTDs that match JAVA classes.

The technique is an extension of JTL (Java Tools Language, [12]), which is a high-level abstraction over DATALOG. We discuss the JTL-to-DATALOG compilation process, and how the program transformation extension can be added to JTL without deviating from the logic paradigm, and specifically without introducing side-effects to logic programs.

Keywords: Declarative Programming, Program Transformations.

1 Introduction

The logic paradigm is attracting increasing attention in the software engineering community, e.g., CodeQuest [20] and JQuery [22] and even dating back to the work of Minsky [29] and law governed systems [30]. The aspect-orientation school is also showing a growing interest in this paradigm, with work on aspect-oriented logic meta programming [15], the ALPHA system [31], Carma [7], LOGICAJ [33], the work of Gybels and Kellens [19] and more.

Our own work in this area, JTL (the Java Tools Language) [12, 13, 11], is a logic-paradigm language designed for the purpose of making queries over the static structure of JAVA programs. JTL's design took a special effort to adapt the logic to the task at hand, and to provide a Query-By-Example [38] flavor to queries.

Much (though not all) of this previous art is characterized by use of the logic paradigm for *querying* code, rather than code generation. (Exceptions include TYRUBA and LOGICAJ, which concentrate in code weaving—a kind of transformation.)

This paper describes a technique of using the paradigm for the *production of output*. The technique is demonstrated through a JTL language extension, which hinges on

---

* Work done while the author was at the Technion.

R.F. Paige and B. Meyer (Eds.): TOOLS EUROPE 2008, LNBIP 11, pp. 100–120, 2008.

associating each predicate with a "baggage" string variable (or more generally, an array of such variables). This variable can be interpreted as the query's output, or *result*.

There are clear and simple rules for computing the result of compound predicates from the results of their components. Chief to this extension is the introduction of *tautology predicates*; a tautology is a predicate which always holds for all settings of the arguments, but returns a string result describing the parameters.

Specifically, the JTL primitive- and library-predicates were redesigned so that each predicate returns a string which is the JAVA code fragment that best describes this string. Thus, predicate `final` returns the string "final" and the pattern `final abstract` returns the string "final abstract". Moreover, many tautologies, such as `visibility` (returning either of "public", "protected", "private" or the empty string, depending on the argument's visibility) were added to the library.

Complementing tautologies is a construct that allows the JTL program to *discard* the result of a JTL expression (that is: the result will not appear in the result of the enclosing expression). This allow a JTL predicates to be conceptually divided into two components: the *guard* [16], which describes the pre-requisites for the transformation, and the *transformer*, which is the clockwork behind the production of output for the matched code.

The result of a query evaluation can then be used for many purposes. We describe here the following applications of this extension:

1. *Program Transformation.* Perhaps the most obvious application of the string result is to generate JAVA code. e.g., it is straightforward to write a small JTL program that, given an interface, generates a class boilerplate that implements this interface, including method bodies to be refined by a programmer. Many other refactoring tasks are readily implemented as JTL transformations. Further, one can use JTL to implement mixins [5] in JAVA, or even genericity (which does not suffer from the restrictions due to erasure semantics and is as powerful as MIXGEN and NEXTGEN [2]).

2. *Translation.* The literature [37, 35] distinguishes between *rephrasing* transformations (such as the refactoring steps discussed above) and *translating* transformations. Examples for translation include using JTL to generate SQL code that defines a database scheme corresponding to a given JAVA class. In the same fashion, it is possible to generate an XML datatype definition out of a class structure.

   Some other translation applications which JTL can handle include a Lint-like tool detecting coding convention violations and potential bugs ("code smells"), and a documentation tool which may elicit a JavaDoc skeleton out of class signatures.

3. *Using JTL as a limited AOP Language.* The relationship between program transformation and aspects is a fascinating subject [18, 25, 15, 17, 26]. The community is aware of this relationship ever since the original introduction of AOP [23], which stated that "*some transformations are aspectual in nature*".

   We give examples showing that JTL can be used to produce JAVA code that augments the original code, or even replaces it entirely, and that this code production supports aspect orientation. While in some senses, the code is not as elegant as in "pure" aspect-oriented programming languages, JTL does introduce discipline into program transformations, including the definition of pointcuts to which advice are applied. And because the pointcuts themselves are defined in JTL's powerful query language, we find that this toy AOP language has some capabilities that are unmatched even by ASPECTJ.[1]

In a sense, these abilities are not surprising: software that can generate textual output can, in principle, generate programs in any desired programming language. One of the important factors that make our approach better for this task is that the production of output is an *implicit* part of the pattern matching process. Programmer intervention is required only where the defaults are not appropriate.

Contributions. The power of a purely declarative system for querying a codebase is generally acknowledged (e.g., [20, 12]). This paper shows how this power can be extended to the output generation domain. Since any transformation program must provide an orderly selection of transformed elements, there is a great advantage in using the same language for both tasks. Novel aspects and contributions of this work include:

1. *Declarative Non-Intrusive High-Level String Generation.* We demonstrate the power of a *declarative* specification of string output generation, directed by the process of pattern matching. Towards this end we introduce specific high-level mechanisms such as list and set iterations, *tautologies*, multiple output streams, and more. These additions do not break the semantics of existing JTL code.
2. *Simplification of the Output Validation Process.* The process of program transformation is in fact a kind of software composition. It is therefore paramount to offer a way that will validate the output of a program transformation tool ahead of time. As explained in §6, the clean, logic paradigm based output generation should contribute to output validation.
3. *Representing transformations using* DATALOG. We show how JTL's high-level queries can be compiled into pure DATALOG, including the generation of string output. This is achieved without resorting to artifacts such as side-effects, which are alien to logic programming.

We note that this version of JTL does not deal yet with statements which may appear in method bodies. This is not an inherent limitation: We can almost technically generalize our results (as hinted in [12]), and use our underlying relational model to express recursive statement structure and more generally any AST. There is of course an engineering challenge in doing that without blowing up the underlying library.

Outline. The remainder of this paper is organized as follows: We start with a short introduction to JTL (§2), and proceed with a description of the new mechanisms for producing output (§3). §4 demonstrates some applications of the new language capabilities. In §5 we show how these mechanisms affect the JTL-to-DATALOG compilation process. The output validation problem is briefly discussed in §6. Finally, §7 presents related work and concludes.

---

[1] See [12] for a discussion of JTL's pointcut-expression capabilities.

2   A Brief Overview of JTL

This section overviews the JTL core, at a level sufficient for reading the examples given in this paper. Readers familiar with the language may skip this section; readers looking for a more detailed description are referred to previous works describing the language [12,11], and the JTL web-site at www.cs.technion.ac.il/jtl.

Simple predicates. Just like other languages in the logic paradigm, the basic constructs of JTL are *predicates*, also called *patterns*. Many (but not all) JTL primitives are JAVA keywords; each such keyword matches precisely those program elements which are declared by it. *Conjunction* is denoted with a space or a comma, *disjunction* is denoted by a vertical bar, and *negation* by an exclamation mark; operator precedence is the usual, while square brackets may be used to override precedence. For example, the expression `[public | protected] !static int` matches non-`static` class members (both fields and methods) of type `int` that are either `public` or `protected`.

Predicate definitions are used to name expressions. For example,

```
instance := !static;
service := public instance method;
```

names the `instance` and `service` predicates, which can now be used just like primitive predicates in composing expressions.[2]

Unary predicates (such as those above) operate on a single implicit parameter, the *subject*, which is denoted # (similar to the JAVA keyword `this`). JTL also supports binary (and higher-arity) predicates, which accept an explicit *argument* (or arguments) in addition to the implicit subject. For example, the binary primitive predicate `declares[M]` holds if # is a class or interface which declares the member M. Similarly, `extends[S]` holds if s is the superclass of #.

As in DATALOG, variables always begin with an upper-case letter, whereas predicate names must begin in lower-case. JTL allows using any number of the special characters +, * and ' in the suffix of identifiers; the standard JTL library thus defines `extends+` as the transitive closure of `extends` and `extends*` as the reflexive version of `extends+`. The underscore symbol ("_") represents an unnamed variable; it is useful if we do not care about a certain position in the relation that a predicate matches.

Developers can define their own binary predicates; e.g., given

```
interfaceof[C] := C.class C.implements[#];
```

the term `I.interfaceof[T]` holds if T is a class that implements interface I. The above can be re-written more concisely using several syntactic aids: the *subject-chaining* operator, "&"; dropping the square brackets, which are optional in binary predicates; and omitting the optional dot. The result is: `interfaceof C := C class & implements #;`

This allows for readable, English-like predicates. Yet because the arity of predicates is fixed (even for overloaded versions), no syntactic ambiguity arises.

JTL employs variable binding similar to that of DATALOG. The `common` predicate in the following example holds if # and T have a common super-interface:

```
common T := implements X, T implements X;
```

---

[2] Predicates `instance` and `service` are in fact part of JTL's rich standard library.

JTL's Kind System. The examples seen so far can be readily rewritten in DATALOG, possibly with the aid of auxiliary predicates. One may accuse JTL for being syntactic sugar for DATALOG. A more fair description is that JTL offers higher level abstractions on top of core DATALOG, and is compiled to DATALOG, just as EIFFEL is compiled to C. One such abstraction is a type system.

Types in JTL are called *kinds*. JTL basic kinds include TYPE (the kind of JAVA classes and interfaces), MEMBER (class members), STRING (a simple string value), PACKAGE and more. Compound kinds are lists, including MEMBERS (a list of MEMBERS), STRINGS, etc. See §5.3 for a discussion of the implementation of lists in JTL.

Iteration Constructs. The loop control structure of imperative programming languages is almost always translated to recursive predicate definitions involving multiple rules in logic programming. JTL's *quantifiers* are a higher level-abstraction, which allows a more concise and clear expression of such situations. Quantifiers are conditions over sets, e.g., a *universal* quantifier checks that all members of a set satisfy a given predicate.

Set Quantifiers. The following predicate, for example, checks that *all* interfaces that the subject class implements are public:

```
all_interfaces_public := implements: { all public; };
```

The computation here involves two stages: (a) generating a set, and (b) applying a quantified condition to the entire set. The ":" character that follows the binary predicate implements turns this predicate into a *generator*, which returns the set of all xs such that the expression #.implements[X] holds. Quantifier application is then carried out inside the curly brackets. Specifically, all public is a *set condition* which checks that predicate public holds for all members of this set.

In a sense, the curly brackets are a looping construct iterating over the elements of the generated set. The current element of the iteration serves as the subject of the quantified condition. The internal curly brackets scope hides the subject variable of the external scope; therefore, the condition public from the previous example will be evaluated against each of the values in the generated set.

JTL's quantifiers include: has (alias exists), all, no, one, many, and empty (which is equivalent to all false). A condition without a quantifier is understood as an existential quantifier. If the curly brackets contain no quantifiers, empty; is assumed. If a curly brackets scope has no preceding generator, then the default members: is inferred.

Argument Predicates and List Quantifiers. The list of arguments to a method can be examined by an *argument list predicate*. The most simple argument list is the empty list, which matches methods and constructors that accept no arguments. An asterisk is an arguments list predicate which matches a sequence of zero or more types. Thus, the standard-library predicate invocable := (*); matches members which may take any number of arguments, i.e., constructors and methods, but not fields.

Another example of list quantification is (int,*,int), which means that the first and last elements are of type int, and any number of parameters may occur in between.

Other Predicates. *Name predicates*, such as 'finalize', are enclosed in single quotes, and are matched against a class or member's name. Standard JAVA regular expressions can be used, except that the wildcard character is denoted by a question mark rather than a dot, so 'set?*' matches all members whose name begins with "set".

To match the type of a class member, use *type predicates*, which are regular expression enclosed between forward slashes; e.g., predicate /java.util.?*/ method matches all methods with a return type from the java.util package (or its sub-packages).

The underscore is a special type predicate which matches any type. Hence, the expression public _ (_, int, *) matches public methods that accept an int as their second argument, and return any type (but not constructors, which have no return type).

Type predicates can also be used as literals of kind MEMBER, i.e., as actual parameters to predicates—as in interface extends /Serializable/, which matches any interface that extends the standard Serializable interface.

Additional signature predicates exist for testing the throws list of a method or constructor, and the annotations attached to any language element.

3   JTL Extensions for Program Transformation

In a nutshell, JTL is a simply typed high level language in the logic paradigm, whose underlying model is that of DATALOG augmented with well founded negation, but without function symbols. That is to say that JTL (unlike PROLOG) uses variable *binding*, rather than *unification*, and predicates' parameters, just like other variables, are atomic. Abstraction mechanisms over plain DATALOG offered by JTL include features such as set and list predicates, cascades and scoped definitions. The language is object-oriented in the (limited) sense that every predicate has an implicit receiver. Primitive types in JTL include STRING, MEMBER (representing e.g., methods and fields) and TYPE (representing e.g., classes and interfaces); there are no compound types.

The observation that enabled the support of transformations is that a predicate in the logic paradigm can include variables to be used for output, their value being set as part of the standard process of evaluating the predicate. This is also true for JTL predicates. Because JTL supports string variables (the STRING kind), it is possible to harness such output-only variables for the generation of string output. To do so, all one needs to do is introduce an additional parameter of this kind to every relevant predicate, and appropriate terms in the predicate's body to bind the value of this variable as part of the pattern-matching process. However, the process of managing this "baggage" variable is tiresome and error prone.

This section describes a JTL language extension which automatically manages this baggage information. §4 will give a number of detailed applications of the mechanism, ranging from program transformation tools to an AOP language.

The principle behind the extension is simple: every JTL predicate implicitly carries with it an unbounded array of baggage anonymous STRING variables, which are computed by the predicate. These variables are output only—an invocation of a predicate cannot specify an initial value for any of them. The compilation process translates into DATALOG only baggage which is actually used. Thus, plain JTL queries, as well as their DATALOG equivalent, are not changed, since no baggage variables are used.

In most output-producing applications, only the first baggage variable, called the *standard output* or just the *output* of the predicate, is used. The output parameter is sometimes called the "returned value" in the context of program transformation.

The description begins (§3.1) with the assumption that there is indeed only one such baggage; the subsequent §3.2 explains how multiple baggage variables are managed. §3.3 shows how escaping inside string literals can be used for producing more expressive output. The most important feature of baggage processing—the iterative production of output with quantifiers—is the subject of §3.4.

3.1   Simple Baggage Management

The essence of the baggage extension is that the output of a compound predicate is constructed by default from its component predicates. Since the initial purpose of our extension was the production of JAVA code, the library was so designed that the output of JTL predicates that are also JAVA keywords (e.g., `synchronized`) return their own name on a successful match. Other primitive predicates (e.g., `method`) return an empty string. Type and name patterns return the matching type or name. The fundamental principle is that whenever possible, any predicate returns the text of a JAVA code fragment that can be used for specifying the match.

The returned value of the conjunction of two predicates is the concatenation of the components. By default, this concatenation trims white spaces on both ends of the concatenated components, and then injects a single space between these. Disjunction of two predicates returns the string returned by the first predicate that is satisfied. Thus, for example, the predicate `public static [int | long]` field `'old?*'` can be applied to some field called `oldValue`, in which case it will generate an output such as "public static int oldValue".

String literals are valid predicates in JTL, except that they always succeed. They return in the output their own value. By using strings, predicates can generate output which is different from echoing their building blocks. For example, the pattern `class '?*' "extends Number"` generates, when applied to class `Complex`, the output "class Complex extends Number". The string literal in the pattern does not present any requirement to the tested program element, and the string result need not be an echo of that element. The pattern above, for example, will successfully match class `String`, which does *not* extend `Number`.

String literals are just one example of what we call *tautologies*: predicates which hold for any value of their parameters. Tautologies are used solely for producing output. The most simple tautology is the predicate `nothing`, which returns the empty string, i.e., `nothing := ""`;. With the language extension, the JTL library was extended with many such tautologies, e.g., `visibility` mentioned above in §1, or `multiplicity`, defined as `static | nothing`.

Other tautologies in the library include `modifiers`, returning the string of all modifiers used in the definition of a JAVA code element; `signature`, returning the type, name, and parameters of methods, or just the type and name of fields; `header`, including the modifiers and signature; the (primitive) `torso`, returning the body (without the head and embracing curly brackets) of a method or a class; and `preliminaries`, returning the package declaration of a class, etc. Tautology `declaration`, whose baggage is the full definition of a program element, is useful for the exact replication of the matched element. We have (for classes and methods, but not for fields)

```
declaration := preliminaries header "{" torso "}";
```

The following demonstrates how tautology `header` and several other auxiliary tautologies are defined:

```
header := modifiers declarator '?*' parents;                          (1)
modifiers := concreteness strictness visibility ...;
concreteness := abstract | final | nothing;
strictness := strictfp | nothing;
...

declarator := class | interface | enum | @interface;
parents := superclass optional_interfaces;
superclass := extends T ![T is Object] | nothing;
...
```

(The declaration of `optional_interfaces` is shown below, in §3.4.) The actual definitions are a bit more involved, since they have to account for annotations and generic parameters, and must have overloaded versions for elements of kind **MEMBER**.

The negation operator, !, discards any output generated by the expression it negates. For example, `!static` will generate an empty string when successfully matched. Thus `multiplicity` can be also defined as **static | !static**.

Finally, if a JTL main query returns several answers, then the output of the whole program is obtained by concatenating the outputs of each result, but the order is unspecified. Thus, if a JTL query matches all methods called by a given method, then the order by which these methods are generated is unspecified, and hence the concatenation of the string results can be in any order. In most cases however, JTL programs are written to produce a single output, or be applied in a setting where only one output makes sense.

3.2 Multiple Baggage

It is sometimes desirable to suppress the output of one or more constituents of a pattern, even if they are not negated. This can be done by prepending the percent character, %, to the expression. For example, the predicate

```
%public %static %final _ '?*';                                        (2)
```

will match any public static final element, but print only its type and name, without the modifiers that were tested for. Predicate (2) can also be written using square brackets:

```
%[public static final] _ '?*';                                        (3)
```

The suppression syntax is in fact one facet of a more complex mechanism, which allows predicates to generate multiple string results, directed to different *output streams*. By default, any string output becomes part of string result 1, which is normally mapped to the standard output stream (stdout in Unix jargon). Also defined are string result 0, which discards its own content (/dev/null), and string result 2, the standard error stream (stderr).

To direct an expression's string output to a specific string result, prepend a percent sign and the desired string result's number to the expression. A percent sign with no number, as used above in (2) and (3), defaults to %0, i.e., a discarded string result.

For example, consider the following predicate:

```
testClassName := %2[ class '[a-z]?*' "begins with a lowercase letter." ];
```

If matched by a class, it will send output to string result 2, i.e., the standard error stream; possible output can be "class badlyNamed begins with a lowercase letter". If, however, the expression is not matched (in this case, because the class does not begin with a lowercase letter), no output is generated.

By using disjunction, we can present an alternative output for those classes that do not match the expression; for example:

$$
\begin{aligned}
\texttt{testClassName := \%2[class '[a-z]?*' "begins with a lowercase letter."]} \\
\texttt{| [class '?*' "is properly named."];}
\end{aligned} \tag{4}
$$

Because it is not directed to any specific stream, the string result of the second part of the predicate is directed to the standard output. As explained below in §5.4, the disjunction operator's output is evaluated in a non-commutative manner, so that its right-hand operand can generate output only if its left-hand one yielded false. Thus, predicate (4) will generate exactly one of two possible messages, to one of two possible output streams, when applied to a class. The query testClassName[x] is a tautology for classes, matching any class x; its *output*, however, depends on x's name.

A configuration file binds any string result generated by a JTL program to specific destinations (such as files). Multiple output streams can be used in a single translation job. However, to process a large codebase with multiple classes, there is no need to define an output stream per input file; rather, Ant-like tools can be used to run JTL once per input file.

JTL also includes mechanisms for redirecting the string result generated by a subexpression into a different string result in the calling expression, or even to bind string results to variables. The syntax $\%n > m\ p$ will redirect the string result of predicate p in output stream n into output stream m of the caller. For example, the expression

```
[%2>1 p1] | "failed"                                        (5)
```

will yield the string result that p1 sends to output stream 2, in output stream 1. If p1 fails, (5) will generate the output failed. However, if p1 succeeds without generating any output in stream 2 (e.g., it generates no output at all, or output to other streams only) then (5) will generate no output. To bind string results to a variable, the syntax $\%n > V\ p$ can be used, binding the output of predicate p in output stream n to variable V of the caller. Thus, writing %2>Error refactor will assign the output stream 2 of predicate refactor to variable Error. Redirection into a variable is only permitted if the variable is output-only—that is, if no other assignments into it occur in the product. To determine whether a variable is output-only, we rely on JTL's pre-analysis stage [10] designed to decide whether a query result is bounded (e.g., returning all class ancestors), or unbounded in the sense that it depends of whole program information (e.g., returning all class's descendants). A by-product of this analysis tells decides whether a variable is output only.

If necessary, file redirection can also be achieved from within JTL just as in the AWK programming language. E.g.,%2>"/tmp/err.log" refactor will redirect the standard error result of refactor to the file named /tmp/err.log. It is also possible to redirect output into a file whose name is computed at runtime, as explained at the conclusion of the following §3.3.

Admittedly, redirection syntax degrades from the language elegance, but it is expected to be used rather rarely.

3.3 String Literals

Baggage programming often uses string literal tautologies. Escaping in these for special characters is just as within JAVA string literals. For example, "\n" can be used to generate a newline character. An easier way to generate multi-line strings, however, is by enclosing them in \[... \], which can span multiple lines.

When output is generated, a padding space is normally added between every pair of strings. However, if a plus sign is added directly in front of (following) a string literal, no padding space will be added before (after) that string. For example, the predicate **class** "New"+ ′?*′ will generate the output "class NewList" when applied to the class List.

The character # has a special meaning inside JTL strings; it can be used to output the value of variables as part of the string. For example, the predicate

$$\text{\textbf{class} "ChildOf"+ [′?*′ \textbf{is} T] "extends \#T"} \qquad (6)$$

will yield "class ChildOfInteger extends Integer" when applied to Integer. The first appearance of T in predicate (6) captures the name of the current class into the variable; its second appearance, inside the string, outputs its value.

When applied to JAVA types, a name pattern returns (as a string value) the short name of a class, whereas a type pattern returns the fully-qualified class name. We can therefore write (6) as **class** "ChildOf"+ ′?*′ "extends" _ to obtain "class ChildOfInteger extends java.lang.Integer".

The sharp character itself can be generated using a backslash, i.e., "\#". To output the value of # (the current receiver) in a string, just write "#". For example, the following binary tautology, when applied to an element of kind **MEMBER**, outputs the name of that element with the parameter prepended to it: prepend[Prefix] := "#Prefix"+"#";.

In case of ambiguity, the identifier following # can be enclosed in square brackets. More generally, # followed by square brackets can be used to access not only variables, but also output of other JTL expressions.[3] For example, the following tautology returns a renamed declaration of a JAVA method or field:

```
rename[Prefix] := modifiers _ prepend[Prefix] [
    method (*) throwsList "{ #[torso] }"
  | field "= #[torso];"
];
```

3.4 Baggage Management in Quantifiers

In the rename predicate example above, the term (*) outputs the list of all parameters of a method. Set and list quantifiers generate output like any other compound predicates. Different quantifiers used inside the generated scope generate output differently. In particular, **one** will generate the output of the set or list member that was successfully matched; **many** and **all** will generate the output of every successfully matched member; and **no** generates no output. The extension introduces one additional quantifier, which

---

[3] Note that using JTL expressions inside a string literal may mean that the literal is not a tautology, e.g., "#[public|private]" is not a tautology.

is a tautology: writing **optional** p; in a quantification context prints the output of p, but only if p is matched.

For example, the following predicate will generate a list of all fields and methods in a class that were named in violation of the JAVA coding convention:

```
badlyNamedClassMembers := %class %{
    [field|method] '[A-Z]?*' "is badly named.";          (7)
%}
```

By default, the opening and closing characters (`(` or `{`) print themselves; their output can be suppressed (or redirected) by prepending a % to each character, as above.

Two (pseudo) quantifiers, **first** and **last**, are in charge of producing output at the beginning or the end of the quantification process. The separator between the output for each matched member (as generated by the different quantifiers) is a newline character in set quantifiers, or a comma in the case of list quantifiers. This can be changed using another pseudo-quantifier, **between**. The tautology optional_interfaces used in the above definition of header (1) requires precisely this mechanism:

```
optional_interfaces := implements: %{
    first "implements";
    exists _;   -- and names of all super interfaces
    between ",";   -- separated by a comma
    last nothing;   -- and no ending text
%}
| nothing;
```

Since we use the **exists** quantifier, the entire predicate in the curly bracket fails if the class implements no interfaces—in which case the "**first**" string "implements" is not printed; if this is the case, then the | **nothing** at the end of the definition ensures that the predicate remains a tautology, printing nothing if need be.

4   Transformation Examples

This section shows how JTL's baggage can be used for various tasks of program transformation. The description ignores the details of input and output management; the implicit assumption is that the transformation is governed by a build-configuration tool, which directs the output to a dedicated directory, orchestrates the compilation of the resulting source files, etc. This makes it possible to apply a JTL program in certain cases to replace an existing class, and in others, to add code to an existing software base.

4.1   Using JTL in an IDE and for Refactoring

We have previously described [12] the JTL Eclipse plug-in, and how it can be used to detect programming errors and potential bugs. It should be obvious that baggage output makes it possible for JTL to not only detect such problems, but also provide useful error and warning messages. Pattern (7) in the previous section shows an example.

JTL can also be put to use in refactoring services supplied by the IDE.[4] The following pattern extracts the public protocol of a given class, generating an **interface** that the class may then implement:

---

[4] We note, however, that some refactoring steps exceed JTL's expressive power.

```
elicit_interface := %class  -- Guard: applicable to classes only
  modifiers "interface" prepend["P_"]  -- Produce header
  {  -- iterate over all members
    optional %public !static method header ";" ;
  };
```

We see in this example the recurring JTL programming idiom of having a *guard* [16] which checks for the applicability of the transformation rule, and a *transformer* which is a tautology. (Note that by convention, the output of guards is suppressed, using the percent character.) The interface is generated by simply printing the header declaration of all public, non-static methods.

The converse IDE task is also not difficult. Given an interface, the following JTL code shows how, as done in Eclipse, a prototype implementation is generated:

```
defVal := %boolean "false" | %primitive "0" | %void nothing | "null";
gen_class := %interface  -- Guard: applicable to interfaces only
    modifiers "class" prepend["C_"] "implements #" {
        header \[ {
            return #[defVal];
        } \]
    };
```

The above also demonstrates how JTL can be used much like output-directed languages such as PHP and ASP: output is defined by a multi-line string literal, into which, at selected points, results of evaluation are injected. Here, the value of the tautology defVal is used to generate a proper default returned value.

4.2 JTL as a Lightweight AOP Language

With its built-in mechanism for iterating over class members, and generate JAVA source code as output, it is possible to use JTL as a quick-and-dirty AOP language. The following JTL predicate is in fact an "aspect" which generates a new version of its class parameter. This new version is enriched with a simple logging mechanism, attached to all public methods by means of a simple "before" advice.

```
1  loggingAspect := %class header declares: {
2    targetMethod := public !abstract method;  -- pointcut definition
3    %targetMethod header \[ {
4          System.out.println("Entering method #");
5          #[torso]
6        } \]
7    | declaration;
8  }
```

The local predicate targetMethod defines the kinds of methods which may be subjected to aspect application—in other words, it is a guard serving as a pointcut definition. The condition in the existential quantifier is a tautology; therefore, output will be generated for every element in the set. The first branch in the tautology, its guard (line 3), is the term %targetMethod.

If the member is matched against the guard, the method's header is printed, followed by a *modified* version of the method body. If, however, the member does not match the targetMethod pointcut, the disjunction alternative declaration will be used—i.e., class members that are not concrete public methods will be copied unchanged.

Having seen the basic building blocks used for applying aspects using JTL, we can now try to improve our logging aspect. For example, we can change the logging aspect so that it prints the actual arguments as well, in addition to the invoked method's name. To do so, we define the following tautology:

```
actualsAsString := %(
    first \["(" + \]; last \[ + ")" \]; between \[ + "," + \];
    argName;   -- at least one; iterate as needed
%)
| "()";   -- no arguments
```

Given a method signature with arguments list $(type_1\ name_1,\ \ldots\ type_n\ name_n)$, this predicate will generate the output "(" + $name_1$ + "," + ... + $name_n$ + ")", which is exactly what we need to print the actual parameter values.

The logging aspect can now employ actualsAsString to provide a more detailed log output; the code generated will be specific per method to which the advice is applied. Note that implementing an equivalent aspect with ASPECTJ requires the usage of run-time reflection in order to iterate over each actual parameter in a method-independent manner.

JTL AOP can be used to define not only **before**, but also **around, after returning** or **after throwing** advice, by renaming the original method and creating a new version which embeds a call to the original.

The following section discusses additional uses for JTL, outside of AOP, that can be reached by replacing, augmenting, or subclassing existing classes.

4.3   Templates, Mixins and Generics

Since JTL can generate code based on a given JAVA type (or list of types), it can be used to implement generic types. The singleton pattern below is a simple example: it is a generic that generates a SINGLETON class from a given base class. Given class, e.g., Connection, this predicate will generate a new class, SingletonConnection, with the regular singleton interface:

```
1   singleton := "public" class "Singleton"+ '?*', %[# is T] {
2       %[public constructor ()]
3       | %2 "#T has no public zero-args constructor.";
4       last \[
5           private #T() { } // No public constructor
6           private static #T instance = null;
7           public static #T getInstance() {
8               if (instance == null) instance = new #T();
9               return instance;
10          }
11      \];
12  }
```

This seemingly trivial example cannot be implemented using JAVA's generics, because those rely on erasure [6]. It takes the power of NEXTGEN, with it's first-class genericity, to define such a generic type.

The JTL pattern is also superior to the C++ template approach, because the requirements presented by the class (its *concept* of the parameter) are expressed explicitly. The lack of concept specification mechanism is an acknowledged limitation of the C++ template mechanism [34]. With the JTL example above, in case the provided type argument does not include an appropriate constructor (i.e., does not match the concept), a straightforward error message is printed to `stderr` (line 3). This will be appreciated by anyone who had to cope with the error messages generated by C++ templates.

Because the generic parameter does not undergo erasure, JTL can also be used to define mixins [5]. Here is an example that implements the classic mixin `Undo` [3]:

```
undoMixin := "public" class [# is T]
                "Undoable#T extends #T" {
    %[!private void setName(String)]
      | %2 "#T has no matching setName method.";
    %[!private String getName()]
      | %2 "#T has no matching getName method.";
    all ![!private undo()]
      | %2 "Conflict with existing undo method.";

    last \[
        private String oldName;
        public void undo() { setName(oldName); }
        public void setName(String name) {
            oldName = getName();
            super.setName(name);
        }
    \];
}
```

Here, too, the pattern explicitly specifies its expectations from the type argument—including not only a list of those members that must be included, but also a list of members that must *not* be included (to prevent accidental overriding [3]).

4.4 Non-JAVA Output

There is nothing inherent in JTL that forces the generated output to be JAVA source code. Indeed, some of the most innovative uses generate non-JAVA textual output by applying JTL programs to JAVA code. This section presents a few such examples.

A classic nonfunctional concern used in aspect-oriented systems is persistence, i.e., updating a class so that it can store instances of itself in a relational database, or load instances from it. In most modern systems (such as JAVA EE v5), the mapping between classes and tables is defined using annotations. For example, here are two classes, mapped to different tables, with a foreign key relationship between them:

```
@Table class Account {
  @Id @Column long id; // Primary key
  @Column float balance;
  @ForeignKey @Column(name="OWNER_ID") Person owner;
}

@Table(name="OWNER") class Person {
  @Id @Column long id;
  @NotNull @Column String firstName;
  @NotNull @Column String lastName;
}
```

In this simplified example, the annotation @Table marks a class as persistent, i.e., mapped to a database table. If the name element is not specified, the table name defaults to the class name. Similarly, the annotation @Column marks a persisted field; the column name defaults to the field's name, unless the name element is used to specify otherwise. The special annotation @Id is used to mark the primary-key column.

Given classes annotated in such a manner, we can use the generateDDL JTL program to generate SQL DDL (Data Definition Language) statements, which can then be used to create a matching database schema:

```
generateDDL := %class "CREATE TABLE " tableName %{
  first "("; last ")"; between ",";
  %[ @Column field ] => %sqlType
    | %2 ["Unsupported field type, field" '?*'];
  columnName sqlType sqlConstraints;
%}

sqlType := %String "VARCHAR" | %integral "INTEGER" | %real "FLOAT" | %Date "DATE" |
  %boolean "ENUM('Y','N')" | %BigDecimal "DECIMAL(32,2)" | foreignKey;

sqlConstraints := [ %@NotNull "NOT NULL" | nothing ]
  [ %@Id "PRIMARY KEY" | nothing ]
  [ %@Unique "UNIQUE" | nothing ];

foreignKey := %[ field, _ is FK ]    --target table/class is the field's own type
  "FOREIGN KEY REFERENCES" FK.tableName;

tableName := [ %@Table(name=TName:STRING) "#TName" ]
  | [ %@Table() '?*' ]    --Default table name = class name
  | %2 "Class is not mapped to DB table.";

columnName := [ %@Column(value=CName:STRING) "#CName" ]
  | [ %@Column() '?*' ];    --Default column name = field name
```

Using the first, last, and between directives, this query generates a comma-separated list of items, one per field in the class, enclosed in parenthesis. The program also includes error checking, e.g., to detect fields with no matching SQL column type.

When applied to the two classes presented above, generateDDL creates the following output (pretty-printed here for easier reading):

```
CREATE TABLE Account (id INTEGER PRIMARY KEY,
  balance FLOAT,
  OWNER_ID FOREIGN KEY REFERENCES OWNER);
CREATE TABLE OWNER (id INTEGER PRIMARY KEY,
  firstName VARCHAR NOT NULL,
  lastName VARCHAR NOT NULL);
```

In much the same way, JTL can be used to generate an XML Schema or DTD specification, describing an XML file format that matches the structure of a given class.

5   Implementation Issues

This section describes how the baggage extension affects the JTL-to-DATALOG compilation process (some familiarity with DATALOG [1] is assumed) and related implementation considerations. §5.1 begins the discussion by explaining first how plain JTL is compiled to DATALOG. Then, §5.2 explains how the computation of baggage is incorporated into the process. §5.3 deals with the rather intricate issue of processing lists. Finally, §5.4 explains how the implementation of disjunction is commutative for all arguments except for baggage, and justifies this design decision.

5.1   Translating JTL into Datalog

JTL provides high-level abstraction on top of a DATALOG core. We will now briefly illustrate how JTL source code can be translated into DATALOG. The examples presented here only serve to highlight the fundamentals of the JTL to DATALOG mapping;

the full details of the translation algorithm are beyond the scope of this paper. Some of the optimization techniques and algorithms used, e.g., to prevent the generation of non-terminating programs, including correctness proofs, are included in a paper by one of the current authors and others [10].

The first translation step is that of the subject variable: the subject variable in JTL is translated into a standard DATALOG variable which prepends all other actual arguments. For example, the JTL expression p1 := **abstract**, **extends** X, X **abstract**; is equivalent to this DATALOG expression:

```
p1(This) :- abstract(This), extends(This,X), abstract(X).
```

Disjunctive expression are not as simple since DATALOG requires the introduction of a new rule for each branch of a disjunctive expression. Thus, p2 := **public** [**interface** | **class**]; is translated into:

```
p2(This) :- public(This), aux(This).
aux(This) :- interface(This).
aux(This) :- class(This).
```

The following predicate poses a greater challenge:

```
p3[T] := public extends T [T abstract | interface];
```

Here, the parameter T appears in the **extends** invocation and also on the left-hand side of the disjunction, but not on the right-hand side. The translation into DATALOG requires the use of a special EDB predicate, always(X), which holds for every possible x value:

```
p3(This) :- public(This), extends(This,T), aux(This,T).
aux(This,T) :- interface(This), always(T).
aux(This,T) :- abstract(T), always(This).
```

The translation of quantifiers relies on the natural semantics of DATALOG, where every predicate invocation induces an implicit existential quantifier. For example,
p4 := **class** members: { **abstract**; };
Is equivalent to this DATALOG definition:

```
p4(This) :- class(This), members(This,M), abstract(M).
```

By using negation, we can express the universal quantifier in terms of the existential one, the negative quantifier in terms of the universal one, etc.

5.2 Calculating String Results

The output mechanism does not require the introduction of any side-effects to JTL. Rather, when compiling JTL predicates to DATALOG, we have that the string output is presented as an additional "hidden", or implicit parameter to DATALOG queries. This parameter is used for output only. For example, the JTL predicate pa := **public abstract**; compiles to DATALOG as:

```
pa(This,Result) :- public(This,Result1),
   abstract(This,Result2),
   concatenate(Result1,Result2,Result).
```

Thus, Result is the "baggage" implicit parameter that gave this mechanism its name.

Multiple output streams (§3.2) mandate the use of multiple baggage variables. The "redirection" of output from one stream to another involves changing the order in which the baggage variables are passed from one DATALOG predicate to another; redirection to a variable (the $n>V$ syntax) implies binding the JTL variable V to a baggage parameter.

5.3 List Processing

Many previous applications of the logic paradigm for processing software employed PROLOG rather than DATALOG. CodeQuest [20] pioneered the use of DATALOG (with stratified negation) for this task. Although PROLOG is more expressive than DATALOG because it allows function symbols in terms, it is less prone to automatic reasoning, such as deciding termination. JTL is unique in that it is DATALOG-like, but assumes an underlying infinite database; as shown by Ramakrishnan et al. [32], the move to a database with infinite relations (represented by the Extensional Database, or EDB) makes it possible to capture some of the expressive power of function symbols (such as list processing) in DATALOG.

Lists in JTL are represented using the kinds TYPES (a list of TYPE elements), STRINGS, etc. List processing is done using the EDB predicates head_is, tail_is, and nil, each of which has an overloaded version per list kind. L.head_is$[H]$ holds if H is the first item of list L; L_1.tail_is$[L_2]$ holds if L_2 equals L_1 sans the head; and L.nil holds if L is empty. Given this trio of EDB predicates, it is mundane to define predicates such as concat for list concatenation (see [32, ex. 7]), and others.

We can now explain how, e.g., argument list predicates are evaluated, using args, a primitive binary predicate. M.args$[L_T]$ holds if M is a method and L_T (of kind TYPES) is its list or argument types. One may use args to write arbitrary recursive predicates for any desired iterative processing of the list of arguments of a method; list queries build on top of this ability. A list quantification pattern, such as

```
args: (many abstract,int,exist final)
```

is evaluated in two steps: (a) list generation; and (b) application of the quantified conditions to the list—this is achieved by searching for a disjoint partitioning of the list into sublists that satisfy the quantifiers. In this example, we search for L_T such that #.args$[L_T]$ holds, and then apply the three quantifiers to it. The predicate holds if there are sublists L_1, L_2, and L_3, such that L_T is the concatenation of the three, and it holds that there is more than one abstract type in L_1; L_2 has precisely one element, which matches int; and there is at least one final type in L_3.

With list queries, there is no default quantifier; instead, a predicate expecting a list parameter is considered a quantifier, and a predicate expecting a *list element* parameter is the quantifier requiring that the respective sublist has exactly one element matching this pattern. The default generator for list queries is args: (compared with members: for set queries).

Now, the argument list pattern () (matching functions with no arguments) is shorthand for args:(empty), while pattern (*) is shorthand for args:(all true). Similarly, the argument list pattern (_,String,*) is shorthand for the more explicit pattern args:(one true,String,all true).

5.4 Non-commutativity of the Disjunction Operator

The extension requires that for disjunction, output will be generated only for the first matched branch. To this end, each branch of the disjunction is considered true only if all previous branches are false; i.e., a pattern such as p_or_a := **public** | **abstract**; is compiled to:

```
p_or_a(This,Result) :- public(This,Result).
p_or_a(This,Result) :- !public(This,_), abstract(This,Result).
```

Note that the operation remains commutative with regard to the question of which program elements match it; the pattern **abstract** | **public** will match exactly the same set of elements. Commutativity is compromised only with regard to the string output, where it is undesired.

To better appreciate this design choice consider predicate add_equals, which unconditionally adds an equals() method to its implicit class argument. Then, there is a straightforward implementation of tautology fix_equals which only adds this method it is not present:

```
fix_equals := has_equals declaration | add_equals;
```

(We assume a standard implementation of the obvious predicate has_equals.) However, this implementation will fail if baggage is computed commutatively. The remedy is in the more verbose version

```
fix_equals := has_equals declaration | !has_equals add_equals;
```

More generally, it was our experience that in the case of alteration between several alternatives only one output is meaningful. Our decision then saves the overhead of manual insertion of code (which is quadratically increasing in size) to ensure mutual exclusion of these alternatives. Conversely, if several alternatives are satisfied, we found no way of combining their output commutatively.

6 Output Validation

A limitation of using JTL for transformations is that it is not "type safe", in the sense that there is no assurance that all possible outputs are valid programs in the target language.[5] However, code generated by a JTL program is never executed directly; it must first be compiled by the target language's compiler. Thus, the lack of output type safety in JTL will never manifest itself at runtime.

In ASPECTJ, type safety (in the sense above) is achieved by minimizing the expressiveness of its output language: complex situations, e.g., iteration over parameters of advised methods, are deferred to runtime and are actually implemented by reflection-based JAVA code. Thus, while ASPECTJ weaves valid JAVA bytecode, this code can actually fail at runtime due to type-safety issues. Conversely, in JTL, a similar effect is achieved by writing a predicate that iterates over the parameters of a method and generates advised code as its result (see example in §4.2). The generated code still has to undergo the standard JAVA compilation, thereby ensuring that it is well-typed, and it cannot fail at runtime for type-safety reasons (unless of course the author chooses to generate code that uses reflection).

---

[5] A recent work that aims for this goal is MorphJ [21].

Formally proving that a given JTL program produces only valid output in its target language is more complex, although it might be possible. Even proving that a plain procedural program produces correct SQL is known to be difficult [27, 9] and, in its most general form, undecidable. Yet the nature of string production in JTL is such that it is governed by a context-free grammar (CFG); that is, every JTL predicate also serves as a CFG of all possible results it may produce. For example, the predicate

[`public` | `protected`] `static` has two possible outputs, public static or protected static.

The problem if CFG inclusion is known to be undecidable in the general case. Still, the fact that JTL programs are CFGs can be used to generate the required formal proof in some cases. Minamide and Tozawa [28] show that it is possible (and practical) to check, for any given grammar G, whether $G \subseteq G_{\mathrm{XML}}$ (the grammer of XML), and further, given a fixed XML Data Type Definition D, the problem of whether $G \subseteq G_D$ is also decidable. Minamide and Tozawa use this result for checking if a given PHP program produces correct XHTML (a specific XML DTD), but they rely on converting the imperative statements of PHP into a grammar specification. This conversion is approximate by nature; in contrast no such approximation is needed with JTL, and one can automatically check, for any given JTL program p and any given DTD D, whether the output of p conforms to D. The problem is more difficult, however, for target languages such of SQL or JAVA.

7   Related Work and Discussion

The work on program transformations is predated to at least D. E. Knuth's call for "program-manipulation systems" in his famous "Structured programming with go to statements" paper [24]. Shortly afterwards, Balzer, Goldman and Wile [4] presented the concept of *transformational implementation*, where an abstract program specification is converted into an optimized, concrete program by successive transformations.

By convention, transformations in JTL have two components: *guards* (similar to a "pointcut" in the AOP terminology), which are logical predicates for deciding the applicability of a *transformer* (similar to "advices"), which is a tautology predicate in charge of output production. Examples in this paper show that JTL is an expressive tool for such output production—the transformation, or the process of aspect application, is syntax directed, much like syntax-directed code generation in compiler technology.

JTL can be categorized using Wijngaarden and Visser's taxonomy of transformation systems [35] as a *local-input, local-output, source-driven, single-stage* system.

This work shows how a certain extent of aspect weaving can be presented as rephrasing transformations. This perspective was presented earlier by Fradet and Südholt [18], whose work focused on "aspects which can be described as static, source-to-source program transformations". It was in fact one of the earliest attempts to answer the question, "what exactly *are* aspects?". Unlike JTL, the framework presented by Fradet and Südholt utilizes AST-based transformations, thereby offering a richer set of possible join-points, enabling the manipulation of method internals.

Lämmel [25] also represents aspects as program transformations, whereas the developers of LOGICAJ [33] go as far as claiming that "[t]he feature set of ASPECTJ can be completely mapped to a set of conditional program transformations".[6] LOGICAJ uses

---

[6] http://roots.iai.uni-bonn.de/research/tailor/aop

program transformations as a foundation for AOP, and in particular for extending standard AOP with generic aspects. More recently, Lopez-Herrejon et al. [26] developed an algebraic model that relates aspects to program transformations.

The ELIDE system for Explicit Programming [8] defines *modifiers* that are placed, somewhat like annotations, in JAVA code; programs associated with these modifiers can then change the JAVA code in various ways, including the generation of new methods and classes or the insertion of code before/after methods. By using queries that match standard Java annotations, JTL transformations can be used to a similar effect.

Unlike JTL, ELIDE handlers use JAVA-like code to modify the base JAVA code; yet similarly to JTL, ELIDE's code can include multi-line strings (enclosed in %{ ... }%) and has an "escape" syntax for quoting variables inside such strings.

The Stratego system [36] is a generic term rewriting tool. As such it is useful in a wider range of applications. By focusing on the domain of Java programs, JTL sports a nicer and more intuitive syntax, thus making it more user friendly.

JTL is not the first system to use logic-based program transformation for weaving aspects. Indeed, De Volder and D'Hondt's [15] coin the term *aspect-oriented logic meta programming* (AOLMP) to describe logic programs that reason about aspect declarations. The system they present is based on TYRUBA [14], a simplified variant of PROLOG with special devices for manipulating JAVA code. Whereas JTL presents an open-ended and untamed system, De Volder and D'Hondt's system presents a very orderly alternative, where output is generated using quoted code blocks.

We therefore find that, compared to other AOP-by-transformation systems, JTL is limited in the kind of transformations it can apply for weaving aspects, and the level of reasoning about aspects that it provides—which is why we view it as a "quick-and-dirty" AOP language. The windfall, however, is that program transformation in JTL is not limited to AOP alone, as evident from some of the examples provided in this paper—the generation of stub classes from interfaces, the generation of SQL DDL to match classes, the definition of generic classes, etc.

Acknowledgments. We thank Andrew Black for his meticulous review and insightful comments.

References

1. Ajtai, M., Gurevich, Y.: Datalog vs. First-Order Logic. In: FOCS 1989 (1989)
2. Allen, E., Bannet, J., Cartwright, R.: A first-class approach to genericity. In: OOPSLA 2003 (2003)
3. Ancona, D., Lagorio, G., Zucca, E.: Jam—designing a Java extension with mixins. ACM Trans. Prog. Lang. Syst. 25(5), 641–712 (2003)
4. Balzer, R., Goldman, N.M., Wile, D.S.: On the transformational implementation approach to programming. In: ICSE 1976 (1976)
5. Bracha, G., Cook, W.R.: Mixin-based inheritance. In: OOPSLA 1990(1990)
6. Bracha, G., Odersky, M., Stoutamire, D., Wadler, P.: Making the future safe for the past: Adding genericity to the Java programming language. In: OOPSLA 1998 (1998)
7. Brichau, J., Kellens, A., Gybels, K., Mens, K., Hirschfeld, R., D'Hondt, T.: Application-specific models and pointcuts using a logic meta language. In: ESUG 2006 (2006)
8. Bryant, A., et al.: Explicit programming. In: AOSD 2002 (2002)
9. Christensen, A.S., Møller, A., Schwartzbach, M.I.: Precise analysis of string expressions. In: Cousot, R. (ed.) SAS 2003. LNCS, vol. 2694. Springer, Heidelberg (2003)

10. Cohen, S., Gil, J.Y., Zarivach, E.: Datalog programs over infinite databases, revisited. In: Arenas, M., Schwartzbach, M.I. (eds.) DBPL 2007. LNCS, vol. 4797. Springer, Heidelberg (2007)
11. Cohen, T.: Applying Aspect-Oriented Software Development to Middleware Frameworks. PhD thesis, The Technion — Israel Institute of Technology (2007)
12. Cohen, T., Gil, J.Y., Maman, I.: JTL—the Java Tools Language. In: OOPSLA 2006 (2006)
13. Cohen, T., Gil, J.Y., Maman, I.: JTL and the annoying subtleties of precise μ-pattern definitions. Int. Workshop on Design Pattern Detection for Rev. Eng. (2006)
14. De Volder, K.: Type-Oriented Logic Meta Programming. PhD thesis, Vrije Universiteit Brussel (1998)
15. De Volder, K., D'Hondt, T.: Aspect-oriented logic meta programming. In: Int. Conf. on Reflection (1999)
16. Dijkstra, E.W.: Guarded commands, non-determinancy and a calculus for the derivation of programs. In: Bauer, F.L., Samelson, K. (eds.) Lang. Hierarchies and Interfaces (1975)
17. Filman, R.E., Havelund, K.: Realizing aspects by transforming for events. In: ASE 2002 (2002)
18. Fradet, P., Südholt, M.: An aspect language for robust programming. In: Guerraoui, R. (ed.) ECOOP 1999. LNCS, vol. 1628. Springer, Heidelberg (1999)
19. Gybels, K., Kellens, A.: An experiment in using inductive logic programming to uncover pointcuts. In: European Interactive Workshop on Aspects in Software (2004)
20. Hajiyev, E., Verbaere, M., de Moor, O.: CodeQuest. In: Thomas, D. (ed.) ECOOP 2006. LNCS, vol. 4067, Springer, Heidelberg (2006)
21. Huang, S.S., Smaragdakis, Y.: Class Morphing: Expressive and Safe Static Reflection. In: PLDI 2008 (2008)
22. Janzen, D., De Volder, K.: Navigating and querying code without getting lost. In: AOSD 2003 (2003)
23. Kiczales, G., et al.: Aspect-Oriented Programming. In: Aksit, M., Matsuoka, S. (eds.) ECOOP 1997. LNCS, vol. 1241. Springer, Heidelberg (1997)
24. Knuth, D.E.: Structured programming with goto statements. ACM Comp. Surv. 6(4) (1974)
25. Lammel, R.: Declarative aspect-oriented programming. In: Partial Evaluation and Semantic-Based Program Manipulation (1999)
26. Lopez-Herrejon, R., et al.: A disciplined approach to aspect composition. In: PEPM 2006 (2006)
27. Meijer, E., Beckman, B., Bierman, G.: LINQ. In: SIGMOD 2006 (2006)
28. Minamide, Y., Tozawa, A.: XML validation for context free grammars. In: Kobayashi, N. (ed.) APLAS 2006. LNCS, vol. 4279. Springer, Heidelberg (2006)
29. Minsky, N.: Towards alias-free pointers. In: Cointe, P. (ed.) ECOOP 1996. LNCS, vol. 1098. Springer, Heidelberg (1996)
30. Minsky, N., Leichter, J.: Law-governed Linda as a coord.model. In: Ciancarini, P., Nierstrasz, O., Yonezawa, A. (eds.) ECOOP-WS 1994. LNCS, vol. 924, pp. 125–146. Springer, Heidelberg (1995)
31. Ostermann, K., et al.: Expressive pointcuts for increased modularity. In: Black, A.P. (ed.) ECOOP 2005. LNCS, vol. 3586. Springer, Heidelberg (2005)
32. Ramakrishnan, R., et al.: Safety of recursive Horn clauses with infinite relations. In: PODS 1987 (1987)
33. Rho, T., et al.: LogicAJ (2006),
    http://roots.iai.uni-bonn.de/research/logicaj/
34. Stroustrup, B., Reis, G.D.: Concepts—design choices for template argument checking. ISO/IEC JTC1/SC22/WG21 no. 1522 (2003)
35. van Wijngaarden, J., Visser, E.: Program transformation mechanics. Technical Report UU-CS-2003-048, Utrecht University (2003)
36. Visser, E.: Stratego. Rewriting Techniques and Applications (2001)
37. Visser, E.: A survey of strategies in program transformation systems. ENTCS 57 (2001)
38. Zloof, M.M.: Query By Example. In: Proc. of the Nat. Comp. Conf. (1975)

A Multiparadigm Study of Crosscutting Modularity in Design Patterns

Martin Kuhlemann[1], Sven Apel[2], Marko Rosenmüller[1], and Roberto Lopez-Herrejon[3]

[1] School of Computer Science, University of Magdeburg
{mkuhlema,rosenmue}@ovgu.de
[2] Department of Informatics and Mathematics, University of Passau
apel@uni-passau.de
[3] Computing Laboratory, University of Oxford
rlopez@comlab.ox.ac.uk

Abstract. Design patterns provide solutions to recurring design problems in object-oriented programming. Design patterns typically crosscut class boundaries so previous work aimed at improving modularity of their implementations. A series of recent studies has focused on aspect-oriented programming while other crosscutting techniques such as collaboration-based designs have remained unexplored. In this paper, we address this limitation by presenting a qualitative case study based on the Gang-of-Four design patterns comparing and contrasting mechanisms of representative languages of collaboration-based designs (Jak) and aspect-oriented programming (AspectJ). Our work yields guidelines for using both paradigms when implementing design patterns exploiting their relative strengths.

Keywords: Aspect-oriented programming, collaboration-based design, design patterns, crosscutting modularity.

1 Introduction

Design patterns are customizable and reusable solutions for recurring problems in object-oriented applications [15]. The implementation of patterns commonly involves or *crosscuts* multiple classes and interfaces that play different roles in a pattern. The crosscutting nature of design patterns has attracted the attention of *aspect-oriented programming (AOP)* advocates who conduct research on techniques and tools to modularize *crosscutting concerns* [25] for the development of customizable software [43, 31, 26]. A core tenet of AOP is that crosscutting concerns, when poorly modularized, lead to code *tangling* (a module contains code of multiple concerns) and *scattering* (the implementation of a concern is spread across multiple modules) [25].

Several studies highlight the relative advantages of AOP over traditional *object-oriented programming (OOP)* for implementing design patterns [22,13,16, 17]. However, AOP is not the only technology capable of modularizing crosscutting concerns. Research on *collaboration-based designs (CBD)* predates AOP [36,

R.F. Paige and B. Meyer (Eds.): TOOLS EUROPE 2008, LNBIP 11, pp. 121–140, 2008.
© Springer-Verlag Berlin Heidelberg 2008

```
 1  public class Point {
 2    public int pos;
 3    public void resetPos(){
 4      this.pos = 0;
 5    }
 6    public void click(){
 7      Locker.lock();
 8      this.resetPos();
 9      Locker.unLock();
10    }
11  }
```

```
12  public aspect ObserverAspect {
13    protected pointcut observedCalls():
14      call(* Point.*(..));
15    before():observedCalls(){
16      System.out.println();
17    }
18    public HashMap Point.obs;
19    public HashMap Point.getObs(){
20      return obs;
21    }
22    declare parents: Point implements
23      SubjectInterface;
24  }
```

Fig. 1. AspectJ concepts used in the case study

8,41] and embraces multiple technologies that extend OOP to attain goals similar to those of AOP [6]. In CBD, a class is divided into code units that modularize the roles played by that class. Collaborations in CBD modularize roles of different classes that collaborate to perform a task.

In this paper, we compare and contrast AspectJ[1] and Jak[2] implementations of the 23 *Gang-of-Four (GoF)* design patterns [15]; AspectJ is an AOP language extension for Java [25] and Jak is a CBD language extension for Java [7]. Both languages are representatives of their paradigms and have been used in several studies, e.g., [6, 22, 16, 17, 13, 26]. For our qualitative comparison, we devise two basic modularity criteria: cohesion and reusability. We measure their relative support in the AspectJ and Jak pattern implementations. Subsequently, we optimize the implementations with respect to each of the two criteria and repeat this evaluation. Based on *all* implementations (initial and optimized), we analyze AspectJ's and Jak's crosscutting mechanisms and offer guidelines for choosing aspects or collaborations in concrete contexts. We show that both criteria cannot fully be met simultaneously using one of either paradigms; our study reveals individual strengths of both approaches and outlines ways for their combination.

2 Background

In the following, we describe the basics of AspectJ and Jak, the categories used for our evaluation, and the criteria analyzed in the AspectJ and Jak implementations.

2.1 Language Mechanisms Used in the Case Study

AspectJ. The key abstraction mechanism of AspectJ is an aspect [24, 28]. An aspect is a class-like entity that includes pointcuts and pieces of advice. Pointcuts select join points (well-defined events during program execution) from a join point model of a base application. Advice is code executed at these join points.

---

[1] http://www.eclipse.org/aspectj/

[2] http://www.cs.utexas.edu/users/schwartz/

Advice may be bound to *abstract* pointcuts that do not select join points directly but get overridden in inheriting aspects to select join points.

Figure 1 depicts a pointcut (Line 13) and a piece of advice (Lines 14-16) that extend all calls to methods of class *Point*. Intertype declarations introduce new methods or fields into existing classes and declare errors statically if user-defined constraints are violated. In Lines 17-20 of Figure 1, *ObserverAspect* introduces the field *obs* and the method *getObs* into

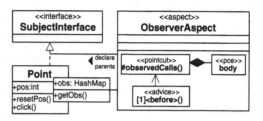

Fig. 2. Graphical notation of an aspect

class *Point*. Aspects can declare a class to implement interfaces or to extend a superclass with *declare parents* clauses. In Line 21, the aspect declares the class *Point* to implement the interface *SubjectInterface*.

```
 1  public class Point {
 2    public int pos;
 3    public void resetPos(){
 4      this.pos = 0;
 5    }
 6    public void click(){
 7      Locker.lock();
 8      this.resetPos();
 9      Locker.unlock();
10    }
11  }
```

```
12  refines class Point implements
      SubjectInterface {
13    public void resetPos(){
14      System.out.println();
15      Super.resetPos();
16    }
17    public HashMap obs;
18    public HashMap getObs(){
19      return obs;
20    }
21  }
```

(a) Collaboration: *Base*   (b) Collaboration: *Observer*

Fig. 3. Jak concepts used in the case study

Figure 2 depicts *ObserverAspect* of Figure 1 in an extended UML notation.[3]

Jak. A *collaboration* is a set of objects (hence the crosscutting) and a protocol that determines how the objects interact. The part of an object that enforces or implements the protocol in a collaboration is called a *role* [37,41]. Collaborations can be implemented using several

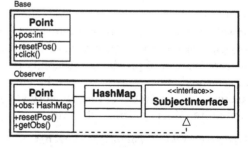

Fig. 4. Graphical notation of collaborations

techniques, like inheritance, encapsulation, or polymorphism. Layers are abstractions for collaborations in Jak and superimpose standard classes with *mixin*

---

[3] To the best of our knowledge, there is no commonly agreed UML notation for aspects [21,18,38]. For this paper, we use the one of Han et al. [21].

Table 1. Pattern categories

Category Name	Design Patterns
No General Accessible Interfaces for Classes	Chain of Responsibility, Command, Composite, Mediator, Observer
Aspects as Object Factories	Flyweight, Iterator, Memento, Prototype, Singleton
Language Constructs	Adapter, Decorator, Proxy, Strategy, Visitor
Multiple Inheritance	Abstract Factory, Bridge, Builder, Factory Method, Template Method
Scattered Code Modularized	Interpreter, State
No Benefit From AspectJ Implementation	Facade

classes [9] that can add new fields and methods to the superimposed class. In Figure 3, the Jak collaboration *Observer* (Fig. 3b) contains a mixin class *Point* which adds a field *obs* (Line 17) and a method *getObs* (Lines 18-20) to the class *Point* of the collaboration *Base* (Fig. 3a).

In Jak, *method refinements* extend methods via overriding, similar to method overriding in Java subclasses. In Figure 3, the collaboration *Base* (Fig. 3a) contains a class *Point*. Method *resetPos* of *Point* of the collaboration *Observer* (Fig. 3b) refines method *resetPos* of class *Point* of the collaboration *Base* by overriding. This overriding method calls the overridden refined method using *Super* (Fig. 3b, Line 15) and adds further statements (Line 14). Figure 4 depicts the collaborations *Base* and *Observer*.[4]

2.2   Categories of Design Patterns

Hannemann et al. [22] defined six categories of design patterns based on the benefits of AspectJ implementations compared to their Java counterparts (see Tab. 1). We use their categories to focus our analysis. The categories consider crosscutting support and allow us to highlight differences between AspectJ and Jak.

No General Accessible Interfaces for Classes. The patterns of this category do not have an interface accessible from clients. Clients that use a class or a set of classes are neither affected nor aware of whether a design pattern of this category is applied or not. Consequently, the interfaces of these patterns mainly structure the code instead of providing reusability of code. That is, these patterns can be implemented entirely with aspects, in which roles are bound to classes through pointcuts. The patterns in this category are Chain Of Responsibility, Command, Composite, Mediator, and Observer.

Aspects as Object Factories. The patterns of this category control access to objects. Factory methods provide access for clients on an aspect instance (using *aspectOf*) or on a class whose methods are advised or introduced by an aspect. That is, an aspect may advise an object-creating method and provide object instances based on the parameters passed to the extended method. Note that

---

[4] We are not aware of a commonly agreed UML notation for collaborations. In this paper, we use the notation of [6, 4, 5].

patterns in this category define only one role. The patterns in this category are Flyweight, Iterator, Memento, Prototype, and Singleton.

Language Constructs. The patterns of this category replace OO constructs by AO language constructs, e.g., methods by inter-type declarations or advice. Thereby, AO implementations sometimes do not completely provide the same capabilities as the OO counterparts. For example, the AO implementation of Decorator cannot be applied dynamically to the decorated object like the OO counterpart [22]. However, implementing patterns with AO language constructs sometimes simplifies the design [11,12]. The patterns in this category are Adapter, Decorator, Proxy, Strategy, and Visitor.

Multiple Inheritance. In the pattern implementations of this category, aspects detach implementations from abstract classes which become interfaces. The pattern-related interfaces are assigned to classes and are extended by the aspects. This results in a limited form of multiple inheritance [22]. The developer can assign different role implementations to a single class by replacing the abstract classes by interfaces that can be extended by aspects. The patterns in this category are Abstract Factory, Bridge, Builder, Factory Method, and Template Method.

Scattered Code Modularized. This category includes patterns that scatter code across different classes in their OO implementation. This code can be modularized using AspectJ, effectively decoupling the set of classes from the communication protocol of the patterns. The patterns in this category are Interpreter and State.

No Benefit from AspectJ Implementation. Patterns in this category do not differ in their OO and AO implementations. The only pattern in this category is Facade.

2.3   Evaluation Criteria

For our case study, we use two criteria that are common in software-engineering, reusability and cohesion, and adapt their definition to our analysis of crosscutting modularity.

Reusability. *Reusability* allows to use a piece of software in a context different than that it has been developed for [10,1]. A reusable piece of software must provide benefits when reused but also must include as less design decisions as possible, because the decisions can conflict with decisions made in the new context [10,40,33].

Design patterns define reusable designs but do not provide reusable implementations [15,34,11]. To attain code reuse, each pattern ideally is implemented by (1) an abstract piece of code that is common to all implementations of the pattern across different applications and (2) application-specific binding code [22,20] – this way, even concerns different from design patterns should be implemented [23]. Both conceptual parts of a pattern implementation offer possibilities for reuse, as we explain next.

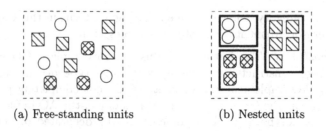

(a) Free-standing units   (b) Nested units

Fig. 5. Different modularizations of one application

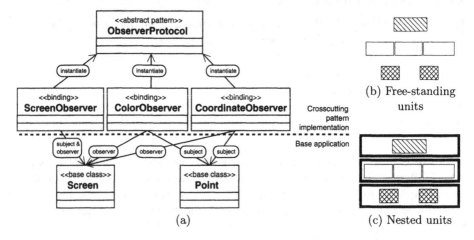

(a)

(b) Free-standing units

(c) Nested units

Fig. 6. Principle Observer implementation and two modularizations

(1) Abstract-Pattern-Reusability is the capability of reusing an abstract design pattern implementation across different applications (Inter-Application-Reusability), that do not share code otherwise. A pattern implementation can only be reused across applications if its implementation is decoupled from other parts of a software. That is, the pattern implementation cannot be reused if it includes application-specific code or if it depends on the application by reference.

(2) Binding-Reusability is the capability of reusing application-specific binding code across different variants of a single application (Intra-Application-Reusability), i.e., across software products that do share a common base. Binding code cannot be reused if a role of a pattern shall be bound to different classes in different variants but all roles of that pattern are bound within one closed code unit[5] [33, 23]. Open code units can be adapted and allow independent reuse of their nested parts.

---

[5] A closed code unit exhibits a well-defined stable description while open units are adaptable [33]. An open code unit is available for extensions or manipulations; a closed unit solely can be used as it is without any adaptation. Please note that this notion of open code units should not be confused with open modules of Aldrich [3] that expose join points explicitly.

In Figure 5, we show two designs, in which code units are depicted with shapes (circle, square, or rounded quare). The *free-standing* units of Figure 5a are reusable because every unit may be reused independently of other units (e.g., other circles). The *nested* units of Figure 5b (e.g., circles) can only be reused independently if the surrounding composite units grouping them are not closed. That is, nesting code units may effect their reusability.

In Figure 6a, we depict the Observer design pattern in UML notation that consists of an abstract pattern implementation (top), binding units (middle), and base application units (bottom); in Figures 6b and 6c, we show different modularizations of this implementation with free-standing code units (Fig. 6b) and nested code units (Fig. 6c). Striped boxes represent abstract code units, white boxes represent binding units, and cross hatch boxes represent base application units. For optimal reuse, every binding code unit, e.g., *ScreenObserver*, and every abstract pattern code unit, e.g., *ObserverProtocol*, should be reusable independently. This is possible if these units are free-standing (cf. Fig. 6b). In case the units are nested (cf. Fig. 6c), they can only be reused if the surrounding composite code unit is open. If the composite units of Figure 6c are closed, their nested code units cannot be reused independently.

Cohesion. *Cohesion* is the grouping of a set of programming constructs that implement a specific task into a single modular unit and referring to the collective group using a name [31].[6] A cohesive code unit implements a specific task completely and, thus, is valuable when being reused [10, 40]. Low cohesive structures of code units increase the complexity of an application [39, 30, 29] because they contain an unstructured set of unrelated units. Hence, semantically related code units cannot be referenced by name in a low-cohesive structure because they are not grouped.

The structure of free-standing code units of Figure 5a is not cohesive because units of different kinds and concerns (depicted by different shapes) are intermixed and sets of semantically related code units cannot be referenced by name. The composite units of Figure 5b are cohesive because every one of these units in turn composes different code units of one concern (here: different atomic code units, e.g., all circles) and, thus, implements this concern completely – every composite unit can be referred to by name.

Figures 6b and 6c show different modularization approaches (with free-standing code units and with nested code units) for the Observer pattern of Figure 6a. Based on our definition of cohesion, nested modularization (as in Fig. 6c) is more cohesive than free-standing modularization (as in Fig. 6b) because it separates unrelated code units (binding, abstract, and base units) and groups semantically related units (e.g., different binding units). Moreover, through nesting, sets of related code units (e.g., all binding units of that pattern or all crosscutting units) can be referenced by name.

---

[6] We use this extended definition of cohesion to highlight the need for module names. This is important especially for modularizing crosscutting concerns because these are designed and coded separately from the classes they crosscut [26].

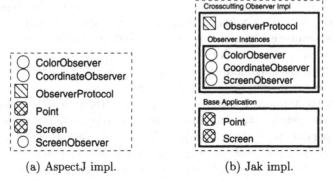

(a) AspectJ impl.   (b) Jak impl.

Fig. 7. AspectJ and Jak implementation of Observer

3   Case Study

In our case study, we reimplemented the AspectJ pattern implementations of Hannemann et al. in Jak.[7] To transform AspectJ to Jak implementations, we used the guidelines presented in [27]. We now discuss the implementations of all 23 GoF design patterns with respect to our two criteria (reusability and cohesion) and our six categories. Firstly, we analyze the initial AspectJ and Jak implementations and then we discuss the implementations optimized towards reuse and cohesion. Due to space limitations, we focus our discussion on representative patterns in each category.

3.1   Initial Implementations

No General Accessible Interfaces for Classes

Cohesion: AspectJ and Jak implementations differ in cohesion.
Binding-reusability: Jak binding implementations are more reusable than AspectJ binding implementations.
Abstract-pattern-reusability: Abstract pattern implementations using AspectJ are more reusable than their Jak counterparts.

Patterns in this category do not need an interface for clients, i.e., they can be implemented abstract and bound to an application in AspectJ. Jak does not provide a mechanism to bind implementations to arbitrary methods directly like abstract pointcuts, but the Jak pattern implementations have been bound to the base code using method refinements. Method refinements are very application-specific in contrast to abstract pointcut bindings, which reduces support for abstract-pattern-reusability for all Jak implementations. However, Jak refinements of bindings can be reused across variants of the application because the composite collaborations that surround the bindings are open code units.

---

[7] See: http://wwwiti.cs.uni-magdeburg.de/~mkuhlema/patternsCBD/

Typical for this category is the Observer implementation. In AspectJ, Observer is implemented in one abstract pattern aspect[8] and three binding aspects[9] that crosscut the classes and bind all pattern roles. The abstract pattern aspect and bindings are not grouped but located among classes they crosscut, that is, the aspects lack cohesion. Each binding aspect binds all pattern roles together which does not allow to vary individual bindings of a class to a pattern role, e.g., *Subject*.

Observer implemented with Jak (Fig. 7b) exhibits high cohesion because the set of base classes is grouped in one composite and named collaboration and the crosscutting and extending concern of the pattern is implemented cohesively in one other collaboration. In that composite collaboration, the whole pattern implementation is aggregated and can be referred to by name (here: *CrosscuttingObserverImpl*). Moreover, the nested collaborations can be reused independently of each other. Binding collaborations like *ColorObserver* are further decomposed (not depicted for brevity) where the nested bindings allow to configure the binding of single pattern roles, e.g., *Subject*.

Using abstract pointcuts in the AspectJ implementation, an abstract pattern implementation can be bound to different applications. Jak extension mechanisms depend on names and types of the base application; thus, they do not allow to detach an abstract implementation of the pattern as easy as AspectJ.

Aspects as Object Factories

Cohesion: AspectJ implementations are less cohesive than their Jak counterparts.
Binding-reusability: Binding code of the AspectJ and Jak implementations in this category is largely equally reusable.
Abstract-pattern-reusability: The AspectJ pattern implementations promote reuse of abstract pattern implementations compared to the Jak implementations.

In this category, the abstract aspects act as hashmap containers to reference objects that they instantiate and control based on intercepted runtime events. Intercepting runtime events can be performed more flexibly with pointcuts and advice in AspectJ than with method refinements in Jak. That is, advice in AspectJ can wrap methods and method calls (and other) which is more fine-grained than the events extensible with Jak, where Jak only allows to wrap methods. Due to missing abstract binding mechanisms in Jak, abstract pattern implementations (here: the hashmap containers) are moved into the binding collaborations – this increases cohesion because only one named pattern module is left but decreases abstract-pattern-reusability in Jak implementations.

The representative pattern of this category is Singleton. Its AspectJ implementation includes an abstract implementation that creates and controls (using a hashmap) singleton objects. A free-standing aspect binds the Singleton role to a specific class and wraps methods and calls that instantiate this class using pointcut and advice; the wrapper code manipulates the abstract implementation's hashmap. The extended classes are not separated from the implementation

---

[8] The abstract aspect is a hashmap container with nested role interfaces.

[9] Each binding aspect extends the abstract aspect and binds both role interfaces *Subject* and *Observer* to the classes of the base implementation.

of the Singleton pattern and the pattern implementing aspects are not aggregated. In the Jak counterpart, the whole pattern implementation of Singleton is aggregated in a single composite collaboration and separated from the set of pattern-unrelated and extended classes, i.e., collaborations are cohesive. However, using the Jak binding mechanism, i.e., method refinements, we can solely extend whole object-creating methods but nothing else, such as constructors or method calls. Method refinements can be reused independently (good binding-reusability) but the role they implement is closely bound to the extended base class (bad abstract-pattern-reusability). The abstract pointcut mechanism of AspectJ is applied to implement the Singleton role abstractly – this implementation is bound afterward to base classes, that is, implementing Singleton abstract is more difficult with Jak than with AspectJ concepts.

Language Constructs

Cohesion, binding-reusability, abstract-pattern-reusability: The AspectJ implementations in this category differ in all criteria from their Jak counterparts.

Patterns in this category deal with redirecting method calls by wrapping existing methods and introducing new ones. Wrapping and introducing methods can be performed in AspectJ as well as in Jak. However, the code that wraps a method has to be assigned one-to-one in Jak while AspectJ allows to wrap different methods with one piece of advice. Due to this weak dependency, AspectJ implementations outperform their Jak counterparts with regard to abstract-pattern-reusability. Due to the close relationship between base classes and collaborations, both were structured cohesively without loosing more reusability; the free-standing (and mostly unrelated) code units of the AspectJ counterparts are less cohesive.

The Proxy implementation with AspectJ uses pointcuts and advice to shield an object by redirecting methods called on it. To shield different methods of an object independently, different free-standing binding aspects shield that object. These binding aspects are ungrouped, which decreases cohesion. The method calls to the shielded object are redirected within an abstract implementation and each binding aspect in essence declares which methods to redirect. In the Jak implementation, abstract pattern implementation and bindings also exist but the overall pattern implementation, i.e., different binding collaborations (each shields a method) together with the abstract role implementation, is aggregated within one collaboration; the extended base implementation of classes is aggregated in another collaboration. Thus, in Jak, both sets, the crosscutting pattern collaborations and the extended base classes, can be referred to by name – this is typical for high cohesion. In Jak as in AspectJ, the nested binding collaborations and the free-standing binding aspects can be reused in different variants of the software. However, due to completely grouping the pattern implementation in composite collaborations in Jak, there is no reusable abstract pattern implementation like in the AspectJ counterpart.

Multiple Inheritance

Cohesion: Jak implementations are more cohesive than the AspectJ counterparts.
Binding- and abstract-pattern-reusability: AspectJ and Jak implementations are equivalent.

Patterns in this category deal with method insertions into classes – for the sake of reuse often realized with multiple inheritance. Both languages, AspectJ and Jak, allow to introduce methods into classes. This way, both languages obey strong bindings of extensions toward the extended class; thus, abstract pattern implementations are tangled with bindings for all patterns in this category. Consequently, no bindings or abstract pattern implementations can be reused independently in the AspectJ or Jak implementations – AspectJ and Jak are equivalent with regard to reuse.

The aspect of Template Method introduces an algorithm method into a class whose subclasses implement the algorithm steps. The aspect that implements the crosscutting pattern Template Method is not separated from the crosscut classes, i.e., different extended pattern-unrelated classes are not grouped but free-standing among crosscutting pattern aspects, this structure of free-standing code units lacks cohesion. In Jak, the set of basic classes and the set of exchangeable Jak extensions are grouped; however, members of these groups can be reused as easily across variants of the software as free-standing aspects in AspectJ. Abstract pattern implementations cannot be separated and reused because introducing the algorithm method into a class binds respective aspects and collaborations closely to this class.

Scattered Code Modularized

Cohesion and binding-reusability: The AspectJ implementations differ in cohesion and binding-reusability from
the Jak implementations.
Abstract-pattern-reusability: All AspectJ and Jak counterparts are equivalent for abstract-pattern-reuse
because no abstract pattern implementation is separated.

Patterns in this category include different roles, in this case different methods, that have to be introduced into classes. These introductions result in a strong binding of the pattern code in AspectJ and Jak, i.e., code that is not abstract and cannot be reused across applications.

In contrast to the Jak implementation of Interpreter, the AspectJ version does not group and separate crosscutting pattern aspects from the set of pattern-unrelated classes thus are not cohesive. All roles of the Interpreter pattern are bound to classes by one closed aspect or by one open and adaptable collaboration, i.e., bindings for different Interpreter roles can be adapted and thus reused across variants more easily in Jak than in AspectJ. Roles are assigned to classes by extending the classes with methods – this prevents abstract pattern implementations in AspectJ and Jak.

No Benefit from AspectJ Implementation

Cohesion, binding-reusability, abstract-pattern-reusability: The AspectJ and Jak implementations of Facade, the
only pattern in this category, are equivalent with re-
gard to the criteria.

Table 2. Results of evaluating initial and optimized implementations

Patterns by Categories / Comparison	Chain of Responsibility	Command	Composite	Mediator	Observer	Flyweight	Iterator	Memento	Prototype	Singleton	Adapter	Decorator	Proxy	Strategy	Visitor	Abstract Factory	Bridge	Builder	Factory Method	Template Method	Interpreter	State	Facade
a) initial AspectJ/initial Jak																							
Cohesion	●	◐	◐	●	●	●	●	●	●	●	◐	●	●	●	◐	●	●	●	●	●	●	●	◐
Binding-Reusability	●	●	●	●	●	●	◐	◐	●	◐	◐	◐	◐	●	●	◐	◐	◐	◐	◐	●	◐	◐
Abstract-Pattern-Reusability	O	O	O	O	O	O	◐	O	O	O	◐	◐	O	O	O	◐	◐	◐	◐	◐	◐	◐	◐
b) cohesive AspectJ/initial Jak																							
Cohesion	◐'	O'	O'	◐'	◐'	◐'	●	◐'	◐'	◐'	◐	◐'	◐'	◐'	◐	●	●	●	◐'	◐'	●	●	◐
Binding-Reusability	●	●	●	●	●	●	◐	◐●	●	◐	◐	●'	●'	●	●	◐	◐	◐	●'	◐	●	◐	◐
Abstract-Pattern-Reusability	◐'	◐'	◐'	◐'	◐'	◐'	◐	◐'	◐'	◐'	◐	◐	◐'	◐'	◐'	◐	◐	◐	◐	◐	◐	◐	◐
c) initial AspectJ/reusable Jak																							
Cohesion	◐'	◐	◐	◐'	●	◐'	●	◐'	◐'	●	◐	●	●	●	◐'	●	●	●	●	●	●	●	◐
Binding-Reusability	●	●	●	●	●	●	◐	◐	●	◐	◐	◐	◐	●	●	◐	◐	◐	◐	◐	●	◐	◐
Abstract-Pattern-Reusability	◐'	◐'	◐'	◐'	◐'	◐'	◐	◐	◐'	◐'	O	◐	◐	O	◐'	◐'	◐	◐	◐	◐	◐	◐	◐

O: AspectJ impl. outperforms Jak impl.; ●: Jak impl. outperforms AspectJ impl.;
◐: both impl. are equal; primed result: changed through optimization

The AspectJ version of Facade uses error-declaration mechanisms that do not affect reuse or cohesion. Both implementations, AspectJ and Jak, do not differ in their structure.

Summary

In Table 2a, we summarize our results. The initial implementations exhibit high cohesion for Jak collaborations and low cohesion for AspectJ aspects. This is because aspects should be reused across applications and therefore must be free-standing. Extensions in Jak are typically bound to an application and thus abstract pattern implementations are often integrated and aggregated with bindings which hampers abstract-pattern-reuse but improves cohesion.

3.2   Optimized Implementations

Interestingly, reusability and cohesion are not satisfied simultaneously in any implementation. Nearly all AspectJ implementations lack cohesion and the majority of Jak implementations lack abstract-pattern-reusability compared to their respective counterparts (cf. Tab. 2a). Trying to eliminate the possibility of this result being a consequence of the legacy initial implementations, we decided to develop a new version of the patterns aiming to improve the lacking property identified. That is, we improved the AspectJ implementations with regard to cohesion and improved the Jak implementations with regard to abstract-pattern-reusability.

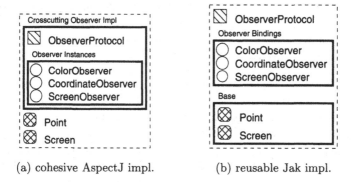

(a) cohesive AspectJ impl.   (b) reusable Jak impl.

Fig. 8. Optimized modularizations of Observer

Cohesion-Optimal AspectJ Implementations. We improved the AspectJ implementations toward cohesion by nesting aspects. For example, to maximize cohesion for Observer, we aggregated the abstract pattern aspect and all binding aspects inside a single composite aspect.[10] The composite aspect encloses related classes and aspects and can be referred to by name. By nesting abstract pattern and binding aspects within composite aspects we improved cohesion in the AspectJ implementations of Chain Of Responsibility, Command, Composite, Decorator, Factory Method, Flyweight, Mediator, Memento, Observer, Prototype, Proxy, Singleton, Strategy, and Template Method. For these patterns, the new implementations became at least equivalent with respect to cohesion compared to their Jak counterparts. In the case of Command and Composite, the new AspectJ implementations even outperform their Jak counterparts because both patterns need redefinitions of existing class declarations (only additions to classes but no changes are possible in Jak).

However, we have observed that all but three cohesion-optimized AspectJ implementations exhibit reduced abstract-pattern-reusability and become equivalent to their Jak counterparts in this respect.[11] The reason for reduced reusability is that composing aspects results in a composite aspect that is closed, i.e., the abstract pattern implementation gets tangled with its bindings and cannot be reused independently. AspectJ implementations cannot be optimized for cohesion without reducing their abstract-pattern-reusability and vice versa. Some of the AspectJ solutions (patterns Decorator, Flyweight, Memento, and Proxy) additionally led to a reduced support for binding-reusability after being optimized for cohesion.[12]

For example, we improved Observer by composing the free-standing aspects (cf. Fig. 7a); thus, we created the structure of Figure 8a with nested aspects.

---

[10] Different nesting techniques of AspectJ, like packages, are possible but are considered inappropriate for aspects [6] because packages are already used as abstractions of (non-crosscutting) classes and cannot be composed.

[11] Decorator, Factory Method, and Template Method already were equivalent here before.

[12] Many of them already lacked binding-reusability before (cf. Tab. 2a).

Now, the AspectJ code structure exhibits high cohesion and is as cohesive as the Jak counterpart. Unfortunately, in this code structure nested aspects cannot be reused independently because their surrounding composite aspects are closed. Consequently, reusability decreases.

Reuse-Optimal Jak Implementations. We have improved abstract-pattern-reusability of Jak implementations by separating abstract pattern implementations from the binding code and from the pattern-unrelated classes into free-standing collaborations. We detached abstract implementations for Command, Chain Of Responsibility, Composite, Flyweight, Mediator, Memento, Observer, Prototype, Strategy, and Visitor. Of these patterns, Chain Of Responsibility, Flyweight, Mediator, Memento, Prototype, and Strategy now exhibit less cohesion and are equivalent to their AspectJ counterparts in this respect. The cohesion of Command, Composite, and Visitor remain equivalent as before, while the Jak Observer remains more cohesive than the AspectJ counterpart. The reuse-optimized Jak Observer implementation remains more cohesive because it still groups (in an open collaboration) binding collaborations, that are free-standing aspects in the AspectJ code. Notably, patterns Proxy and Singleton could not be improved to become as reusable as their AspectJ counterpart. Abstract implementations of these patterns require advanced binding mechanisms such as call-advice or abstract pointcuts unavailable in Jak.

For example, consider Observer where in the initial Jak implementation (cf. Fig. 7b) all pattern collaborations (abstract implementation and binding collaborations) are grouped in a composite collaboration and the extended base classes are grouped within another composite collaboration. After optimizing for reuse, the abstract pattern implementation is extracted from the composite pattern collaboration into a free-standing collaboration and can be reused (see Fig. 8b).

We summarize both comparisons in Table 2 (parts b and c). Firstly, we compare the cohesion-optimized AspectJ versions with the initial Jak implementations (Tab. 2b). Secondly, we compare the reuse-optimized Jak versions with the initial AspectJ implementations (Tab. 2c). We highlight the evaluation results of those patterns with a prime whose evaluation changed due to optimizing.

4   Consequences, Insights, and Guidelines

Consequences and Insights. Using Jak, we were able to build cohesive pattern implementations that obey binding-reusability similar to AspectJ counterparts but not abstract-pattern-reusability. In neither technique it is possible to implement cohesive software that separated abstract pattern implementations.

We have optimized AspectJ and Jak implementations with respect to reusability and cohesion. We observed that when AspectJ implementations are optimized to allow reuse they loose cohesion and vice versa. Thus, an AspectJ developer has to decide between reusability and cohesion uncompromisingly. AspectJ implementations are scattered across free-standing aspects if abstract pattern implementations or binding aspects are to be reused independently. Large composite aspects obey cohesion but are closed and thus their nested aspects cannot be reused independently. For Jak, we observed that with a proper cohesion we could also optimize reusability to some extend (namely binding-reusability). However, neither Jak nor AspectJ implementations are cohesive when they are to be reused across applications (abstract-pattern-reusability). A reason for that might be that AspectJ mechanisms are designed to maximize reuse of abstract (pattern) and application-specific (binding) aspects while scattering and free-standing aspects are accepted for adaptability. Jak provides two options, (1) software can be implemented cohesively including (binding) collaborations that are reusable within an application or (2) the software's collaborations can be implemented in a more reusable manner without cohesion even (everything is scattered in free-standing collaborations).

Guidelines. In summary, we suggest to implement patterns of the categories *Multiple Inheritance* and *Scattered Code Modularized* with Jak instead of AspectJ because all (even all optimized) according Jak pattern implementations outperform their AspectJ counterparts. We do not recommend any particular technique for the pattern of category *No Benefit From AspectJ Implementation* (pattern Facade) because all AspectJ and Jak implementations are pairwise equivalent for both criteria. Pattern implementations in the remaining categories are very diverse with regard to the criteria such that no general guidelines are discernable. To implement each design pattern in a software with the paradigm we proposed, we suggest multi-paradigm approaches, like Caesar or Aspectual Feature Modules [35,6]. In order to choose the best implementation technique for the classes of patterns, the developer has to decide on a per pattern basis or has to balance certain desired criteria of the software to build. For example, if the developer mainly aims at cohesion he/she should implement design patterns with Jak instead of AspectJ for all categories, except *No General Accessible Interface* and *No Benefit From AspectJ Implementation*.

In the case of reusability within applications, i.e., across variants of one application, we favor Jak to implement patterns of the categories *No Accessible Interfaces for Classes* and *Aspects as Object Factories* because all Jak implementations in these categories allow better reuse of bindings (except patterns Iterator and Singleton whose implementations are equivalent). Pattern implementations of the remaining categories are equivalent for binding-reusability.

To build libraries and abstract components that should be reused across applications, AspectJ should be preferred over Jak. The reason is that only AspectJ's abstract pointcut declarations allow to bind abstract pattern implementations to arbitrary base programs. Furthermore, some patterns require sophisticated AspectJ mechanisms not available in Jak to implement reusable abstract implementations, e.g., method call extensions. Jak extensions rely on names in base code more than AspectJ extensions – a fact that hampers abstract pattern implementation. In the categories *No General Accessible Interfaces for Classes* and *Aspects as Object Factories*, all AspectJ implementations but one (pattern Iterator) are suited better for abstract-pattern-reuse than their Jak counterparts; the AspectJ Iterator implementation is as reusable as its Jak counterpart.

Since AspectJ and Jak provide common mechanisms of either AOP and CBD, we argue that our results hold for most AOP and CBD languages.

Threats to Validity. In this study, we made some assumptions. We took the pattern implementations of Hannemann et al. as a base because they are well documented and commonly referred. Our insights and guidelines might differ if other languages of AOP and CBD are evaluated; but, we observed that AspectJ and Jak are most widely used as representatives for AOP and CBD. For criteria different than cohesion and reusability our guidelines cannot say anything – however, cohesion and reusability strongly impact other criteria (maintainability, extensibility, etc.). We did not weight our criteria because we assume each to be equivalently important for evolving and reusing software. Other initial implementations of GoF patterns may fit our criteria better, but therefore we optimized the implementations toward the evaluated criteria.

5   Related Work

Different studies compared OOP and AOP by means of the GoF design patterns. Hannemann et al. defined criteria of well-formed software designs (locality, reusability, composition transparency, and (un)pluggability) to evaluate different design pattern implementations using AspectJ [22]. Garcia et al. evaluated AOP concepts quantitatively on the basis of cohesion and coupling criteria using a case study of design patterns [16]. Gélinas et al. compared AO and OO design patterns with respect to cohesion [17]. Our qualitative study focused on comparing AOP and CBD languages and found that both paradigms provide crosscutting support but exhibit specific strengths with respect to the criteria reusability and cohesion.

We used a definition of cohesion similar to the definition of locality of Hannemann et al. Their work is primarily focused on detaching the pattern code into aspects to enhance cohesion of the pattern. We additionally analyze the cohesion of bindings. In contrast to the notion of cohesion of Garcia et al., we do not limit our focus on pairs of method and advice that access the same field but also attend dependencies between code units based on inheritance or method calls. We have used different criteria than Gélinas et al. because their cohesion criterion is hardly usable to contrast refinements with (abstract) pointcut mechanisms and nested with free-standing code units.

Our definition of reusability roughly corresponds to composition transparency of Hannemann et al. In contrast, we do not only focus on the reusability of the classes that are assigned to a pattern but also on the reusability of binding units across different variants of one software.

Apel et al. performed a qualitative case study on AOP and CBD [6]. They used AOP and CBD to cope with *different* kinds of problems, e.g., the problem of homogeneous crosscutting was tackled using AOP and heterogeneous crosscutting was tackled using CBD concepts. This study neither uses design patterns nor is focused on the duality of AOP and CBD concepts, i.e., they used both,

AOP and CBD concepts, within the same application and evaluated when they used which technique within that application. We evaluate AOP and CBD languages using related programs implemented in mature AOP and CBD languages twice, once in AspectJ and once in Jak. Consequently, we are able to evaluate different implementations based on common criteria.

Meyer et al. focused on the transformation of the GoF design patterns into reusable components [34]. They used language concepts that are specific to the Eiffel programming language, e.g., genericity, contracts, tuples, and agents to implement pattern components. We focus on AOP and CBD to improve design pattern implementations. AOP and CBD are programming techniques not bound to a single programming language as Eiffel but can be applied to different programming languages, like Java and C++, and – in theory – to arbitrary software units [9, 36].

We also have considered category systems for design patterns by Gamma et al. [15], Garcia et al. [16], and others [19,44,14,2] but found them inappropriate for our study. Gamma et al. defined categories of design patterns based on the purpose a design pattern serves and on the scope, i.e., whether the pattern deals with objects or classes. Garcia et al. gave a new categorization system based on every criterion they analyzed in their case study, i.e., every category is associated with one single criterion. Other researchers categorized patterns based on the pattern's adequacy to be a language construct, on the predominant relationship (relationship: one pattern *uses* another pattern), or categorized different patterns than the GoF. We have also applied these categories to analyze our evaluation results but find them too diverse and consequently not meaningful to derive commonalities and significant guidelines for using AspectJ and Jak. For example, Gamma et al. assigned eleven patterns to a category (behavioral patterns) but according pattern implementations in our study were too diverse for cohesion and reuse and did not allow significant results. Furthermore, other researcher's categories overlap, which hampers reasoning about language properties and programming guidelines.

Several researchers introduced further design patterns than the GoF patterns, also for other programming paradigms [14, 42, 44, 28, 32]. All these researchers (including Gamma et al.) aimed at increased flexibility and reuse. We focused on patterns of Gamma et al. because they comprise the best-known patterns for OOP and are domain independent [2].

6   Conclusions

Several researchers observed a lack of modularity in object-oriented design pattern implementations and improved the pattern implementations using AspectJ. We followed this line of research and reimplemented their aspect-oriented design pattern implementations with collaboration-based concepts using the Jak language because Jak also provides crosscutting support needed for modularizing design patterns but both approaches show different mechanisms to support crosscutting.

We have used cohesion and reusability as the qualitative criteria to compare and contrast the AspectJ and Jak design pattern implementations. Based on this evaluation, we have inferred guidelines for implementing design patterns. They apply for initial AspectJ and Jak implementations as well as for implementations that are optimized for cohesion or reuse. We further have shown that AspectJ and Jak are complementary and the developer has to balance desired aims of cohesion and reuse. Concepts of AspectJ and Jak on their own do not suffice in structuring software appropriately. But, we propose to use AspectJ and Jak concepts adequately depending on categories of design patterns, possibly resulting in mixed implementations. This can be achieved by using existing multi-paradigm approaches that combine AspectJ and Jak or similar languages. Finally, our results of comparing AspectJ and Jak can be easily mapped to other AOP and CBD languages.

As further work we target on analyzing and evaluating overlapping design pattern implementations. For that, we modularize design patterns in a large-sized framework. This also addresses the limitation of this work that the evaluated case studies of design patterns are rather small.

Acknowledgments

We thank Jan Hannemann and Gregor Kiczales for their AspectJ pattern implementations which have been the basis of this case study. We thank Christian Kästner for helpful discussions and comments on earlier drafts of this paper. Martin Kuhlemann is supported and partially funded by the *DAAD Doktorandenstipendium* (No. D/07/45661).

References

1. Abadi, M., Cardelli, L.: A Theory of Objects. Springer, New York (1996)
2. Agerbo, E., Cornils, A.: How to Preserve the Benefits of Design Patterns. SIGPLAN Not. 33(10), 134–143 (1998)
3. Aldrich, J.: Open Modules: Modular Reasoning About Advice. In: Black, A.P. (ed.) ECOOP 2005. LNCS, vol. 3586, pp. 144–168. Springer, Heidelberg (2005)
4. Apel, S., Kästner, C., Trujillo, S.: On the Necessity of Empirical Studies in the Assessment of Modularization Mechanisms for Crosscutting Concerns. In: Workshop on Assessment of Contemporary Modularization Techniques, p. 161 (2007)
5. Apel, S., Kästner, C., Leich, T., Saake, G.: Aspect Refinement - Unifying AOP and Stepwise Refinement. JOT 6(9), 13–33 (2007)
6. Apel, S., Leich, T., Saake, G.: Aspectual Feature Modules. IEEE TSE 34(2), 162–180 (2008)
7. Batory, D., Liu, J., Sarvela, J.N.: Refinements and Multi-Dimensional Separation of Concerns. In: FSE, pp. 48–57 (2003)
8. Batory, D., O'Malley, S.: The Design and Implementation of Hierarchical Software Systems with Reusable Components. ACM TOSEM 1(4), 355–398 (1992)
9. Batory, D., Sarvela, J.N., Rauschmayer, A.: Scaling Step-Wise Refinement. IEEE TSE 30(6), 355–371 (2004)

10. Biggerstaff, T.J.: A Perspective of Generative Reuse. Annals of Software Engineering 5, 169–226 (1998)
11. Bosch, J.: Design Patterns as Language Constructs. JOOP 11(2), 18–32 (1998)
12. Bryant, A., Catton, A., De Volder, K., Murphy, G.C.: Explicit Programming. In: AOSD, pp. 10–18 (2002)
13. Cacho, N., Sant'Anna, C., Figueiredo, E., Garcia, A., Batista, T., Lucena, C.: Composing Design Patterns: A Scalability Study of Aspect-Oriented Programming. In: AOSD, pp. 109–121 (2006)
14. Coplien, J.O., Schmidt, D.C. (eds.): PLoPD. ACM Press/Addison-Wesley Publishing Co. (1995)
15. Gamma, E., Helm, R., Johnson, R., Vlissides, J.: Design Patterns: Elements of Reusable Object-Oriented Software. Addison-Wesley (1995)
16. Garcia, A., Sant'Anna, C., Figueiredo, E., Kulesza, U., Lucena, C., A.: Modularizing Design Patterns with Aspects: A Quantitative Study. In: AOSD, pp. 3–14 (2005)
17. Gélinas, J.-F., Badri, M., Badri, L.: A Cohesion Measure for Aspects. JOT 5(7), 75–95 (2006)
18. Georg, G., France, R.B.: UML Aspect Specification Using Role Models. In: OOIS, pp. 186–191 (2002)
19. Gil, J., Lorenz, D.H.: Design Patterns vs. Language Design. In: Workshop on Object-Oriented Technology, pp. 108–111 (1998)
20. Hachani, O., Bardou, D.: On Aspect-Oriented Technology and Object-Oriented Design Patterns. In: Workshop on Analysis of Aspect-Oriented Software (2003)
21. Han, Y., Kniesel, G., Cremers, A.B.: Towards Visual AspectJ by a Meta Model and Modeling Notation. In: Workshop on Aspect-Oriented Modeling (2005)
22. Hannemann, J., Kiczales, G.: Design Pattern Implementation in Java and AspectJ. In: OOPSLA, pp. 161–173 (2002)
23. Hölzle, U.: Integrating Independently-Developed Components in Object-Oriented Languages. In: Nierstrasz, O. (ed.) ECOOP 1993. LNCS, vol. 707, pp. 36–56. Springer, Heidelberg (1993)
24. Kiczales, G., Hilsdale, E., Hugunin, J., Kersten, M., Palm, J., Griswold, W.G.: An Overview of AspectJ. In: Knudsen, J.L. (ed.) ECOOP 2001. LNCS, vol. 2072, pp. 327–353. Springer, Heidelberg (2001)
25. Kiczales, G., Lamping, J., Mendhekar, A., Maeda, C., Lopes, C.V., Loingtier, J.-M., Irwin, J.: Aspect-Oriented Programming. In: Aksit, M., Matsuoka, S. (eds.) ECOOP 1997. LNCS, vol. 1241, pp. 220–242. Springer, Heidelberg (1997)
26. Klaeren, H., Pulvermueller, E., Rashid, A., Speck, A.: Aspect Composition Applying the Design by Contract Principle. In: GCSE, pp. 57–69 (2001)
27. Kuhlemann, M., Rosenmüller, M., Apel, S., Leich, T.: On the Duality of Aspect-Oriented and Feature-Oriented Design Patterns. In: Workshop on Aspects, Components, and Patterns for Infrastructure Software, p. 5 (2007)
28. Laddad, R.: AspectJ in Action: Practical Aspect-Oriented Programming. Manning Publications Co. (2003)
29. Lieberherr, K.: Controlling the Complexity of Software Designs. In: ICSE, pp. 2–11 (2004)
30. Liskov, B.: Data Abstraction and Hierarchy. In: OOPSLA, pp. 17–34 (1987)
31. Lopez-Herrejon, R., Batory, D., Cook, W.R.: Evaluating Support for Features in Advanced Modularization Technologies. In: Black, A.P. (ed.) ECOOP 2005. LNCS, vol. 3586, pp. 169–194. Springer, Heidelberg (2005)
32. Lorenz, D.H.: Visitor Beans: An Aspect-Oriented Pattern. In: Workshop on Object-Oriented Technology, pp. 431–432 (1998)

33. Meyer, B.: Object-Oriented Software Construction, 2nd edn. Prentice Hall PTR (1997)
34. Meyer, B., Arnout, K.: Componentization: The Visitor Example. IEEE Computer 39(7), 23–30 (2006)
35. Mezini, M., Ostermann, K.: Conquering Aspects with Caesar. In: AOSD, pp. 90–99 (2003)
36. Reenskaug, T., Anderson, E., Berre, A., Hurlen, A., Landmark, A., Lehne, O., Nordhagen, E., Ness-Ulseth, E., Oftedal, G., Skaar, A., Stenslet, P.: OORASS: Seamless Support for the Creation and Maintenance of Object-Oriented Systems. JOOP 5(6), 27–41 (1992)
37. Smaragdakis, Y., Batory, D.: Mixin Layers: An Object-Oriented Implementation Technique for Refinements and Collaboration-Based Designs. ACM TOSEM 11(2), 215–255 (2002)
38. Stein, D., Hanenberg, S., Unland, R.: A UML-based Aspect-Oriented Design Notation for AspectJ. In: AOSD, pp. 106–112 (2002)
39. Stevens, W.P., Myers, G.J., Constantine, L.L.: Structured Design. IBM Syst. J. 13(2), 115–139 (1974)
40. Tarr, P., Ossher, H., Harrison, W., Sutton Jr., S.M.: N Degrees of Separation: Multi-Dimensional Separation of Concerns. In: ICSE, pp. 107–119 (1999)
41. VanHilst, M., Notkin, D.: Using Role Components in Implement Collaboration-based Designs. In: OOPSLA, pp. 359–369 (1996)
42. Woolf, B.: Null Object. In: PLoPD, pp. 5–18 (1997)
43. Zhang, C., Jacobsen, H.-A.: Quantifying Aspects in Middleware Platforms. In: AOSD, pp. 130–139 (2003)
44. Zimmer, W.: Relationships Between Design Patterns. In: PLoPD, pp. 345–364 (1995)

Representing and Operating with Model Differences

José E. Rivera and Antonio Vallecillo

Dept. Lenguajes y Ciencias de la Computación
ETS Ingeniería Informática
Universidad de Málaga, Spain
{rivera,av}@lcc.uma.es

Abstract. Models and metamodels play a cornerstone role in Model-Driven Software Development (MDSD). Models conform to metamodels, which usually specify domain-specific languages that allow to represent the various facets of a system in terms of models. This paper discusses the problem of calculating differences between models conforming to arbitrary metamodels, something essential in any MDSD environment for dealing with the management of changes and evolution of software models. We present a metamodel for representing the differences as models, too, following the MDSD "everything is a model" principle. The *Difference Metamodel*, together with the difference and other related operations (do, undo and composition) presented here have been specified in Maude and integrated in an Eclipse-developed environment.

Keywords: Model-driven software development, model difference, model comparison, model evolution, Maude, object matching.

1 Introduction

Model-Driven Software Development (MDSD) is becoming a widely accepted approach for developing complex distributed applications. MDSD advocates the use of models as the key artifacts in all phases of development, from system specification and analysis, to design and implementation. Each model usually addresses one concern, independently from the rest of the issues involved in the construction of the system.

Domain-Specific Modeling (DSM) is a way of designing and developing systems that involves the systematic use of Domain Specific Languages (DSLs) to represent the various facets of a system, in terms of models. Such languages tend to support higher-level abstractions than general-purpose modeling languages, and are closer to the problem domain than to the implementation domain. Thus, a DSL follows the domain abstractions and semantics, allowing modelers to perceive themselves as working directly with domain concepts. Furthermore, the rules of the domain can be included into the language as constraints, disallowing the specification of illegal or incorrect models. The abstract syntax of a DSL is usually described by a metamodel.

So far, most of the efforts have been focused on the definition of models, metamodels and transformations between them. Nowadays, other operations such as

R.F. Paige and B. Meyer (Eds.): TOOLS EUROPE 2008, LNBIP 11, pp. 141–160, 2008.

model subtyping [1], type inference [2] and model difference [3] are becoming increasingly important, too, in order to provide full support to Model-driven Engineering practices.

In particular, model difference is an essential operation in several software development processes [4], including version and change management, software evolution, model/data integration, etc. At the moment, techniques for visualizing and representing model differences are mainly based on edit scripts and coloring techniques [5,6,7]. However, these approaches do not produce models as results of their calculations, and therefore cannot be fully integrated with other MDSD processes. Furthermore, most of them do not fulfill other interesting properties required in MDSD environments, such as composability [8]. Other techniques based on text, data structure or models also exist but are usually restricted to a specific metamodel (namely UML) [5,9,10]. In this paper we present an approach to compare models which conform to arbitrary metamodels. For this purpose we have defined a *Difference Metamodel* so that differences are represented as models, too, that conform to such a metamodel. We have also defined a set of operations on models and on differences that provide support for the calculation of differences, their application and composition. The *Difference Metamodel* and those difference operations have been specified in Maude using the formal notation proposed in [2] to represent models and metamodels, and integrated in our Eclipse developed environment called **Maudeling** [11].

There are several reasons that moved us to formalize our definitions and specifications in Maude. Firstly, in this way we can provide precise definitions of the concepts and operations, at a high level of abstraction, and independently from the particularities of any implementation programming language (such as Java, Python, etc.). Secondly, having formal descriptions also allows the analysis of the specifications produced. Finally, the fact that Maude specifications are executable (with comparable performance to most commercial programming languages) has permitted us to count on efficient implementations of the concepts and operations described here, which are correct by construction.

The structure of this document is as follows. First, Sections 2 and 3 provide a brief introduction to Maude, and how models and metamodels can be represented in Maude, respectively. Section 4 presents our definition and specification of the model difference operation, and the *Difference Metamodel* in which the results are expressed. Section 5 introduces some other difference related operations, their specification in Maude, and the supporting tool. Section 6 compares our work with other related proposals. Finally, Section 7 draws some conclusions and outlines some future research activities.

2 Rewriting Logic and Maude

2.1 Introduction to Maude

Maude [12,13] is a high-level language and a high-performance interpreter and compiler in the OBJ algebraic specification family. It supports membership-equational logic and rewriting logic specification and programming of systems.

Thus, Maude integrates an equational style of functional programming with rewriting logic computation. Because of its efficient rewriting engine, able to execute more than 3 million rewriting steps per second on standard PCs, and because of its metalanguage capabilities, Maude turns out to be an excellent tool to create executable environments for various logics, models of computation, theorem provers, or even programming languages. In addition, Maude has been successfully used in software engineering tools and several applications [14]. We informally describe in this section those Maude's features necessary for understanding the paper; the interested reader is referred to its manual [13] for more details.

Rewriting logic is a logic of change that can naturally deal with state and with highly nondeterministic concurrent computations. A distributed system is axiomatized in rewriting logic by an equational theory describing its set of *states* and a collection of rewrite rules. Maude's underlying equational logic is membership-equational logic, a Horn logic whose atomic sentences are equalities $t = t'$ and *membership assertions* of the form $t : S$, stating that a term t has sort S.

Computation in a functional module is accomplished by using the equations as simplification rules from left to right until a canonical form is found. Some equations, like those expressing the commutativity of binary operators, are not terminating but nonetheless they are supported by means of *operator attributes*, so that Maude performs simplification modulo the equational theories provided by such attributes, which can be associativity (`assoc`), commutativity (`comm`), identity (`id`), and idempotence (`idem`).

While functional modules specify membership-equational theories, rewrite theories are specified by *system modules*. A system module may have the same declarations of a functional module plus rules of the form $t \rightarrow t'$, where t and t' are terms. These rules specify the dynamics of a system in rewriting logic. They describe the local, concurrent transitions possible in the system, i.e., when a part of the system state fits the pattern t then it can change to a new local state fitting pattern t'. The guards of conditional rules act as blocking pre-conditions, in the sense that a conditional rule can only be fired if the condition is satisfied.

2.2   Object-Oriented Specifications: Full Maude

In Maude, concurrent object-oriented systems are specified by object-oriented modules in which classes and subclasses are declared. A class is declared with the syntax `class` $C \mid a_1 : S_1, \ldots, a_n : S_n$, where C is the name of the class, a_i are attribute identifiers, and S_i are the sorts of the corresponding attributes. Objects of a class C are then record-like structures of the form $< O : C \mid a_1 : v_1, \ldots, a_n : v_n >$, where O is the name of the object, and v_i are the current values of its attributes. Objects can interact in a number of different ways, including message passing. Messages are declared in Maude in `msg` clauses, in which the syntax and arguments of the messages are defined.

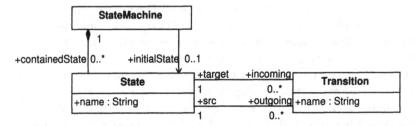

Fig. 1. Simple State Machine Metamodel

In a concurrent object-oriented system, the concurrent state, which is called a *configuration*, has the structure of a multiset made up of objects and messages that evolves by concurrent rewriting using rules that describe the effects of the communication events of objects and messages. The predefined sort Configuration represents configurations of Maude objects and messages, with none as empty configuration and the empty syntax operator _ _ as union of configurations.

Class inheritance is directly supported by Maude's order-sorted type structure. A subclass declaration C < C', indicating that C is a subclass of C', is a particular case of a subsort declaration C < C', by which all attributes, messages, and rules of the superclasses, as well as the newly defined attributes, messages and rules of the subclass characterize its structure and behavior. This corresponds to the traditional notion of subtyping: A is a subtype of B if every <X> that satisfies A also satisfies B. Multiple inheritance is also supported in Maude [12,15].

3   Formalizing Models and Metamodels with Maude

There are several notations to represent models and metamodels, from textual to graphical. In [2] we presented a proposal based on the use of Maude, which not only was expressive enough for these purposes, but also offered good tool support for reasoning about models. In particular, we showed how some basic operations on models, such as model subtyping, type inference, and metric evaluation, can be easily specified in Maude, and made available in development environments such as Eclipse. This section presents just a brief summary of that proposal.

In Maude, models are represented by configurations of objects. Nodes are represented by Maude objects. Nodes may have attributes, that are represented by Maude objects' attributes. Edges are represented by Maude objects' attributes, too, each one representing the reference to the target node of the edge.

Then, metamodels are represented by Maude object-oriented modules. They contain the specification of the Maude classes to which the Maude objects (that represent the corresponding models nodes) belong. In this way, models conform to metamodels by construction.

To illustrate this approach, the following piece of Maude specifications describe a Simple State Machine metamodel (depicted in Fig. 1) as a Maude module.

```
(omod SimpleStateMachines is
    protecting STRING .
    class State |
        name : String,
        stateMachine : Oid,
        incoming : Set{Oid},
        outgoing : Set{Oid} .
    class StateMachine |
        containedStates : Set{Oid},
        initialState : Maybe{Oid} .
    class Transition |
        name : String,
        target : Oid,
        src : Oid .
endom)
```

Metaclasses correspond to Maude classes. Meta-attributes are represented as Maude attributes. Meta-references are represented as attributes too, by means of sets of Maude object identifiers. Depending on the multiplicity, we can use: a single identifier (if the multiplicity is 1); a Maybe{Oid} which is either an identifier or a null value, for representing a [0-1] multiplicity; a Set{Oid} for multiplicity [*]; or a List{Oid} in case the references are ordered.

The instances of such classes will represent models that conform to the example metamodel. For instance, the following configuration of Maude objects shows a possible state machine model that conforms to the SimpleStateMachines metamodel:

```
< 'SM : StateMachine | initialState : 'ST1,
    containedStates : ('ST1, 'ST2) >
< 'ST1 : State | name : "St1", stateMachine : 'SM,
    outgoing : 'TR, incoming : empty >
< 'ST2 : State | name : "St2", stateMachine : 'SM,
    incoming : 'TR, outgoing : empty >
< 'TR : Transition | name : "Tr", src : 'ST1, target : 'ST2 >   .
```

It represents a simple state machine with two states, named St1 and St2, and one transition (Tr) between them. St1 is the initial state of the state machine.

The validity of the objects in a configuration is checked by the Maude type system. In addition, other metamodel properties, such as the valid types of the object referenced, or the valid opposite of a reference (to represent bidirectional relationships), are expressed in Maude in terms of membership axioms. Thus, membership axioms will define the well-formedness rules that any valid model should conform to: a configuration is valid if it is made of valid objects, with valid attributes and references. The well-formedness rules of the simple state machines metamodel can be found in [2].

For those users familiar with the Ecore terminology, there is no need to define the metamodel initially in Maude: ATL (Atlas Transformation Language) model transformations have been defined from Ecore to Maude specifications.

Finally, note that since metamodels are models too, they can also be represented by configurations of objects. The classes of such objects will be the ones specified in the metametamodels, for example, the classes that define the MOF or Ecore metamodels. In this way, metamodels can be handled in the same way as models are, i.e., operations defined over models can be applied to metamodels as well.

4   Model Difference

Having described how models and metamodels can be represented in Maude, this section introduces a model difference definition and its specification in Maude. Thus, both a metamodel to represent model differences and operations to calculate and operate with them are presented.

4.1   Representation: The Difference Metamodel

Our first requirement is that the results of a model difference operation can be expressed as a model, so they can be fully integrated into other MDSD processes. Since models conform to metamodels, we have to define a *Difference Metamodel* with the elements that a difference may contain, and the relationships between them. Furthermore, the *Difference Metamodel* should be general enough to be independent of the metamodel of the source models.

Taking into account these characteristics, we have developed the *Difference Metamodel*, which is depicted in Fig. 2. A difference model will contain all the changes from a *subtrahend* model to a *minuend* model. As usual, we can distinguish three different kinds of changes: element addition, element deletion and element modification. Thus, every element of a difference model (`DiffElement`) will belong to `ModifiedElement` metaclass, `DeletedElement` metaclass or `AddedElement` metaclass, depending on whether the element has been added, deleted or modified, respectively. Elements which do not suffer from any changes, will not be reflected in the difference model.

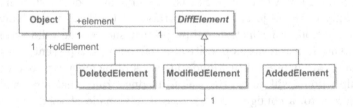

Fig. 2. Difference Metamodel

Every difference element `DiffElement` will have a reference (`element`) to the element that has suffered the change. In case of element modification (`ModifiedElement`), the difference element will refer to both the element of the minuend model (after the modification, `element`), and the element of the subtrahend model (before the modification, `oldElement`).

Modified, deleted and added elements from both operand models are added to the difference model too, so that it is self-contained [8], i.e., the difference model will contain all the changes, not relying on external sources of information (such as the operand models). These elements can belong to any metaclass, since model difference can be applied to models conforming to arbitrary metamodels. Thus we introduce the `Object` metaclass (similar to *EObject* in Ecore) to represent such arbitrary metaclasses.

The *Difference Metamodel* can be specified in Maude as follows:

```
(omod ModelDiff is
  class Object .
  class DiffElement | element : Oid .
  class AddedElement .
  class DeletedElement .
  class ModifiedElement | oldElement : Oid .
  subclasses AddedElement DeletedElement ModifiedElement < DiffElement .
endom)
```

As a matter of fact, class *Object* would not need to be explicitly specified in Maude, because class `Cid` (class identifier) is defined in Maude for this purpose [15]. However, we have defined it for understandability reasons.

4.2   Specification of the Difference Operation

Given a minuend model M_m and a subtrahend model M_s, both conforming to some metamodels (not necessary the same, as we shall later see), the result of applying the model difference operation to them is another model M_d conforming to the *Difference Metamodel* presented above, in such a way that `modelDiff(`M_m, M_s`)` = M_d.

The global comparison process is generally admitted as being composed of two main parts: matching and differencing. The latter makes use of the former to decide whether an element in the minuend model is the *same* (although possibly modified) as another in the subtrahend model. Decomposing the difference operation in these two parts allows the reuse of both algorithms in different applications, such as model *patching* [8]. Thus, we will firstly show how elements are matched, and secondly how the the difference is computed using this information.

Matching Elements. Matching two models M_1 and M_2 conforming to some metamodels (not necessary the same) means finding different objects from both models that represent the same element. The result of applying the match operation to M_1 and M_2 is a match model M_M conforming to the *Match Metamodel*, depicted in Fig. 3.

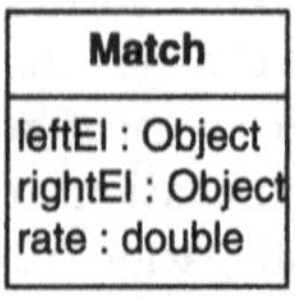

Match
leftEl : Object
rightEl : Object
rate : double

Fig. 3. Match Metamodel

Match model elements (of class `Match`) symbolize links between two objects that represent the same element. Thus, a match model element will refer to both objects (`leftEl` and `rightEl`) and will `rate` their similarity (expressed in terms of a ratio between zero and one).

Matching objects using persistent identifiers. Since Maude objects have persistent identifiers, checking whether two objects represent the same element can be easily done by comparing their identifiers. If their identifiers are the same, the two objects can be said to represent the same element; otherwise, the two objects represent different elements.

Given variables O, O1 and O2 of sort Oid; C1 and C2 of sort Cid; ATTS1 and ATTS2 of sort `AttributeSet`; and CONF1 and CONF2 of sort `Configuration`, the match operation can be specified in Maude as follows:

```
subsort MatchModel < Configuration .
op match : Configuration Configuration -> MatchModel .
eq match(< O : C1 | ATTS1 > CONF1, < O : C2 | ATTS2 > CONF2)
   = < O : Match | leftEl : O, rightEl : O, rate : 1.0 >
     match(CONF1, CONF2) .
eq match(CONF1, CONF2) = none [owise] .
```

For every object of M_1 with the same identifier as another object of M_2, a *match object* that relates them is added to the resulting model. Since [owise] equations are only executed if no other equation holds, when no objects with the same identifier are found (Maude provides configuration matching and reorganization facilities) no more information is added to the match model.

Matching objects using structural similarities. Using persistent universal identifiers makes the matching process simple and robust. However, counting on this kind of identifiers is not always possible: if the two models to compare conform to different metamodels, or have evolved independently, there is little chance that an element being the "same" in the two models has the same identifier. In addition, when comparing models not originally specified in Maude but, e.g., in MOF or Ecore, we cannot assume that the model transformations from MOF or Ecore to Maude will assign the same identifier to two different objects that represent the same element.

A more sophisticated matching algorithm is thus needed. This kind of matching algorithm should compare two elements by their structural similarities. There are several structural matching algorithms described in the literature that can be used, e.g. [16,17]. One of the advantages of using Maude is that this kind of algorithms are usually very easy to specify (compared to those specified in, e.g., Java) thanks to the configuration matching and reorganization facilities that Maude provides.

In this paper we present the structural matching algorithm used in our **Maudeling** framework [11]. The algorithm starts by comparing every object of a model with every object of the other one. Comparing two objects means comparing their metaclasses and structural features to obtain a final joint `rate`. This match rate will represent the similarity between the two compared objects, which are said to *potentially match* when the rate is greater than a given threshold (Th). At the end of the process, a sieve is applied to all potential matches in order to pair only those objects that together obtain the biggest rate, taking into account that a specific object can only belong to one match relationship.

Class and structural features match rates are obtained in the following way:

- Two metaclasses match if they are the same, or there exists an inheritance relation between them.

$$classRate(C_1, C_2) = \begin{cases} 1.0 & \text{if } C_1 = C_2 \\ 0.9 & \text{if } isSubtype(C_1, C_2) \text{ or } isSubtype(C_2, C_1) \\ 0.0 & \text{otherwise} \end{cases}$$

- Structural features are compared, and given a weight, depending on its type. To obtain the final structural features rate, every attribute rate and weight are jointly considered: $sfRate((S_1, S_2, ..S_n), (R_1, R_2, ..R_n)) = w_1 * rate(S_1, R_1) + w_2 * rate(S_2, R_2) + ... + w_n * rate(S_n, R_n)$.
  If a structural feature's upper cardinality is greater than 1 (i.e., if its value is a collection), the average rate is calculated. If a structural feature is defined only in one of the objects, a penalty is applied to the final $sfRate$.

  - Boolean attributes and enumerations match (with $rate = 1.0$) if they have the same value (otherwise $rate = 0.0$).
  - String attribute values distances are calculated using the Levenshtein algorithm [18]. The Levenshtein distance is the minimum number of operations (insertion, deletion, or substitution of a single character) needed to transform one string into another. Depending on the resulting distance, a different rate is given.

$$nameRate(S_1, S_2) = \begin{cases} 1.0 & \text{if } levenshteinDist(S_1, S_2) = 0 \\ 0.9 & \text{if } levenshteinDist(S_1, S_2) = 1 \\ 0.5 & \text{if } levenshteinDist(S_1, S_2) = 2 \\ 0.1 & \text{if } levenshteinDist(S_1, S_2) = 3 \\ 0.0 & \text{otherwise} \end{cases}$$

  - Numerical attribute values match rate is computed with a relative distance function $(1 - \frac{|N_1 - N_2|}{|N_1 + N_2|}$ limited to $[0..1])$
  - References are matched recursively, i.e., objects referenced are compared using the same match operation but without taking into account their own references (to avoid cycles).

Once the class and structural features match rates are calculated, the final joint **rate** is obtained as follows:

$$finalRate = w_c * classRate + w_{sf} * sfRate + w_n * nameRate$$

where $finalRate, classRate, nameRate, sfRate \in [0..1]$, and the weights that we have initially considered are $w_c = 0.5, w_{sf} = 0.25, w_n = 0.0$. The threshold value we normally use is $Th = 0.66$, although the weights and threshold are of course user-defined and easily configurable.

It is worth noting that the weights and threshold values specified above do not allow elements to potentially match if their metaclasses are not related. In addition, a *nameRate* has been included in the equation. In many kinds of models the attribute **name** is considered as an identifier. By including this rate we allow elements of this kind of models to be better matched (assigning the attribute **name** a bigger weight than any other structural feature). For instance, setting the name weight to $w_n = 0.25$, will make objects with the same class and same name to always potentially match. Attribute **name** values are compared in the same way as string values, i.e., using the Levenshtein distance.

If the name rate is omitted (i.e., it is not considered in the computations: $w_n = 0.0$), potential matches are harder: structural features should be more strongly related because no identifier is provided. In all cases, i.e., either using the name as an identifier or not, renamed elements can be detected (objects with different name can potentially match).

Contrary to other approaches (e.g., [16]) in which a model is seen as a tree (levels are determined by the containment relationship), and only objects at the same level are compared, our approach compares every object independently of its depth in the tree. This decision implies more comparisons, but also brings along interesting advantages: (a) moved elements through different levels can be detected; and (b) failing to identify a match does not condition other potential matches below in the tree hierarchy. For example, refactoring is a common technique used for making models evolve. One usual refactorization step is to add packages to improve the grouping structure of the model. This is the kind of change that affects the containment tree, and that can be missed by those approaches that compare elements only at the same level of the tree.

Specifying the Calculation of Differences. As previously mentioned, the model difference operation makes use of the match model in order to decide whether one element in the minuend model is the *same* (although possibly modified) as another in the subtrahend model. Thus, in the global comparison process the match model is calculated before the differencing part starts:

```
subsort DiffModel < Configuration .
op modelDiff : Configuration Configuration -> DiffModel .
op modelDiff : Configuration Configuration MatchModel -> DiffModel .
eq modelDiff(CONF1, CONF2) =
   modelDiff(CONF1, CONF2, match(CONF1,CONF2)) .
```

In order to specify the behavior of the differencing part, we have identified four different situations that may happen when calculating a model difference operation on an element: (1) the element appears in both models (minuend and subtrahend) and has not been modified; (2) the element appears in both models but has been modified; (3) the element only appears in the minuend model; (4) the element only appears in the subtrahend model.

The following four Maude equations specify the modelDiff operation in each case. In all of them we will use the following variables: O, O1 and O2 of sort Oid; C, C1 and C2 of sortCid; ATTS, ATTS1 and ATTS2 of sort AttributeSet; and CONF, CONF1, CONF2 and MATCHM of sort Configuration.

In the first case, we have to check whether two objects (one belonging to the minuend model, the other belonging to the subtrahend model) match, i.e., they represent the same element, and belong to the same class and have the same attribute values (remember that in Maude both object attributes and references are expressed by Maude attributes). If this situation occurs, we have found an element that has not been modified, and therefore no evidence of the element is stored in the difference model:

```
ceq modelDiff(< O1 : C | ATTS > CONF1> < O2 : C | ATTS > CONF2, MATCHM)
  = modelDiff(CONF1, CONF2, MATCHM)
  if match(O1, O2, MATCHM) .
```

The match operation checks whether the corresponding match object that relates O1 and O2 exists in the match model.

```
op match : Oid Oid Configuration -> Bool .
eq match(O1, O2, < O : Match | leftEl : O1, rightEL : O2, ATTS > CONF)
  = true .
eq match(O1, O2, CONF) = false [owise] .
```

In the second case, two objects represent the same element, but the element has been modified, i.e., the two objects match, but either they belong to different classes (Maude allows the dynamic reclassification of objects), or their attributes have different values. In this case, we create an object instance of class ModifiedElement with references to both the object of the subtrahend model (before the modification, oldelement) and the object of the minuend model (after the modification, element). Both operand models' objects are added to the difference model, but only with the relevant attributes, i.e., those that have different values in both objects (storing both values, the old one and the new one), or those that are specified in one object but not in the other (corresponding to deleted attributes if the attributes are specified in objects of the subtrahend model, or corresponding to added attributes if they are specified in objects of the minuend model). The identifiers of the two added objects are modified (with newId and oldId operations) to distinguish them, since Maude objects should have unique identifiers in the same Maude configuration.

Modifications to object identifiers are performed in such a way that it would be possible to "undo" them to get the original identifiers (with originalId operation, defined in next section).

```
ceq modelDiff( < O1 : C1 | ATTS1 > CONF1,
                  < O2 : C2 | ATTS2 > CONF2, MATCHM)
  = < newModId(O1) : ModifiedElement |
      element : newId(O1), oldElement : oldId(O2) >
    < newId(O1) : C1 | attsDiff(ATTS1,ATTS2) >
    < oldId(O2) : C2 | attsDiff(ATTS2,ATTS1) >
    modelDiff(CONF1,CONF2,MATCHM)
  if match(O1, O2, MATCHM) /\ (not(ATTS1 == ATTS2) or not(C1 == C2)) .
```

Note that every element modification is treated in the same way, i.e., meta-class ModifiedElement is used for all kinds of feasible modifications: from a modification in a String attribute value to a change in the order of elements in collections. This decision was made for the sake of simplicity although, of course, the *Difference Metamodel* could be easily extended to explicitly distinguish between different kinds of element modifications, if required.

In the third and fourth cases, one element in one of the models does not match any other element of the other model. If the object only appears in the minuend model, the element has been added; otherwise (i.e., the object only appears in the subtrahend model) the element has been deleted. Thus, we just have to create an object AddedElement (or DeletedElement, respectively), with a reference to the element in question which will be also added to the difference model (modifying its identifier as previously described):

```
eq modelDiff( < O1 : C1 | ATTS1 > CONF1, CONF2, MATCHM )
  = < newAddId(O1) : AddedElement | element : newId(O1) >
    < newId(O1) : C1 | ATTS1 >
    modelDiff(CONF1, CONF2, MATCHM) [owise] .

eq modelDiff( CONF1, < O2 : C2 | ATTS2 > CONF2, MATCHM )
  = < newDelId(O2) : DeletedElement | element : oldId(O2) >
    < oldId(O2) : C2 | ATTS2 >
    modelDiff(CONF1, CONF2, MATCHM) [owise] .
```

Finally, the reader should notice the existence of a final fifth case in case both the minuend and subtrahend models are empty. The result of the modelDiff operation will be an empty difference model, as expected:

```
eq modelDiff( none, none, MATCHMODEL ) = none .
```

4.3   An Example

For illustration purposes, let us introduce a simple example to show how the model difference works, and the results that it obtains. Given the state machine model presented in Section 3, suppose that we add a transition in the opposite direction to the existing one, i.e., a new transition Tr2 from state St2 to state St1. As a result, the following model is obtained:

```
< 'SM : StateMachine | initialState : 'ST1 ,
  containedStates : ('ST1, 'ST2) >
< 'ST1 : State | name : "St1", stateMachine : 'SM,
  outgoing : 'TR, incoming : 'TR2 >
< 'ST2 : State | name : "St2", stateMachine : 'SM,
  outgoing : 'TR2, incoming : 'TR2 >
< 'TR : Transition | name : "Tr", src : 'ST1 , target : 'ST2 >
< 'TR2 : Transition | name : "Tr2", src : 'ST2 , target : 'ST1 >
```

Note that states St1 and St2 are also modified since they have a reference to the incoming and outgoing transitions.

Now, if we take the modified model as the minuend model, and the initial model as the subtrahend model, the result of applying the difference operation is a model (shown below) that conforms to the *Difference Metamodel*:

```
< 'ST1@MOD : ModifiedElement | element : 'ST1@NEW,
  oldElement : 'ST1@OLD>
< 'ST1@NEW : State | incoming : 'TR2 >
< 'ST1@OLD : State | incoming : empty >
< 'ST2@MOD : ModifiedElement | element : 'ST2@NEW,
  oldElement : 'ST2@OLD >
< 'ST2@NEW : State | outgoing : 'TR2 >
< 'ST2@OLD : State | outgoing : empty >
< 'TR2@ADD : AddedElement | element : 'TR2@NEW >
< 'TR2@NEW : Transition | name : "Tr2", src : 'ST2, target : 'ST1 >
```

As we can see, both added transition and states reference modifications are represented in the difference model. Elements were matched as expected, since their name and class were not modified (with $w_n = 0.25$).

An interesting property of this difference operation is that it can be applied to minuend and subtrahend models conforming to different metamodels. Thus, in some situations in which models and metamodels are evolving at the same time, models can be compared as well. Every element (and attribute value) is handled in the same way, no matter whether its metaclass (or any of its meta-attributes) is only defined in the metamodel of one of the (subtrahend or minuend) models.

5   Further Operations

Model difference is probably the main operation for dealing with model evolution and for handling model versions, but it is not the only one required to achieve such processes. There are other related operations that need to be considered too, such as those that do and undo the changes, compose several differences, etc. For instance, operations do and undo will allow us to obtain the minuend model from the subtrahend model, and viceversa, respectively.

In fact, one of the current limitations of other proposals that implement model comparison and difference (e.g. [7]) is that their results cannot be effectively composed, and that these additional operations are hard to define. In our approach, given the way in which the differences have been represented (as models), and the `modelDiff` operation has been specified (as an operation on models), they become natural and easy to define.

5.1 The "do" Operation

Given a model M_s conforming to an arbitrary metamodel MM and a difference model M_d (conforming to the *Difference Metamodel*), the result of applying operation do to them is another model M_m so that: $do(M_s, M_d) = M_m$ and $modelDiff(M_m, M_s) = M_d$.

Operation do applies to a model all the changes specified in a difference model. Basically, it adds to the model all elements referred to by `AddedElements` of the difference model; deletes from the model all elements referred to by `DeletedElements` of the difference model; and modifies those elements of the model which are referred to by `ModifiedElements`.

In Maude, this operation can be specified in terms of three equations (described below) that correspond, respectively, to the addition, deletion and modification of elements. A fourth equation is also included to deal with the empty difference:

```
vars MODEL CONF : Configuration .
vars O O2 OLDO NEWO : Oid .
vars C NEWC OLDC : Cid .
vars ATTS OLDATTS NEWATTS : AttributeSet .

op do : Configuration DiffModel -> Configuration .
eq do(MODEL, < O : AddedElement | element : NEWO >
              < NEWO : NEWC | NEWATTS > CONF)
  = < originalId(NEWO) : NEWC | NEWATTS > do(MODEL, CONF) .
ceq do(< O : C | ATTS > MODEL,
        < O2 : DeletedElement | element : OLDO >
        < OLDO : OLDC | OLDATTS > CONF)
  = do(MODEL, CONF)
  if O = originalId(OLDO) .
ceq do(< O : C | ATTS > MODEL,
        < O2 : ModifiedElement | element : NEWO, oldElement : OLDO >
        < NEWO : NEWC | NEWATTS > < OLDO : OLDC | OLDATTS > CONF)
  = < originalId(NEWO) : NEWC |
        (excludingAll(ATTS,OLDATTS), NEWATTS)) > do(MODEL, CONF)
  if O = originalId(OLDO) .
eq do(MODEL, none) = MODEL .
```

Operation `originalId` recovers the original identifier of the object that was modified, i.e., reverts the changes done by operations `newId` or `oldId` in the model difference. Operation `excludingAll` (used in the third equation), deletes from a Maude attribute set `ATTS` all attributes that have the same name of a given attribute in the `OLDATTS` set. Since `OLDATTS` just contains the attributes that have to be deleted or that were modified, what we are doing here is removing from `ATTS` these elements just to add the `NEWATTS` set later. The `NEWATTS` set contains all the attributes to be added, and the new values of the modified attributes, so that the elements are properly built.

Note that a matching between both models (M_s and M_d) is not needed, because operation do is supposed to be applied to the original model of the difference, and original object identifiers can be recovered from the difference model.

The resulting model M_m will usually conform to the same metamodel MM of M_s, although since model difference can be applied to models conforming to different metamodels, in general we can just affirm that the resulting model M_m will conform to a metamodel which is a *subtype* [1] of the metamodel MM of the original subtrahend M_m.

5.2   The "undo" Operation

Given a model M_m conforming to a metamodel MM and a difference model M_d (conforming to the *Difference Metamodel*), the result of applying operation undo to them is another model M_m so that: undo(M_m,M_d) = M_s and modelDiff(M_m,M_s) = M_d. As well as in operation do, the resulting model M_s will usually conform to the same metamodel MM of M_m (if this was true when the difference was done).

This operation reverts all the changes specified in a difference model. Basically, it adds to the model all elements referred to by DeletedElements of the difference model; deletes from the model all elements referred to by AddedElements of the difference model; and modifies those elements of the model that are referred to by ModifiedElements (but in the opposite way of operation do). Undo equations are not shown here because they are analogous to the do equations.

Operation undo can be considered as the inverse operation of do. Thus, undo(do(M_s, M_d), M_d) = M_s, and do(undo(M_m, M_d), M_d) = M_m. This is always true because of the definition of both operations: do(M_s, M_d) = M_m, and undo(M_m, M_d) = M_s.

5.3   Sequential Composition of Differences

Another important operation provides the sequential composition of differences. In general, each *difference model* represents the changes in a model from one version to the next, i.e., a *delta* (Δ). The diffComp operation specifies the composition of deltas, so that individual deltas can be combined into a single one.

This operation is very useful, for instance, to "optimize" the process of applying successive modifications to the same model, which might introduce complementary changes. For example, if one element is added in one delta and then deleted in another, the composed delta does not need to store both changes. In this way, this operation not only composes delta but also eliminates unnecessary changes and provides more compact model differences, hence improving efficiency.

The following Maude equations are a fragment of the diffComp operation specification. The first equation corresponds to the composition of an addition and a deletion of the same element. In this case, as mentioned before, there will be no evidence of the element in the resulting difference model. The second equation corresponds to the composition of an addition and a modification of the same element. Thus, both an `AddedElement` that refers to the element with its attributes properly modified, and the element itself, will be included in the resulting difference model.

```
ceq diffComp(< O1 : AddedElement | element : NEWO >
                 < NEWO : NEWC | NEWATTS > CONF1,
                 < O2 : DeletedElement | element : OLDO >
                 < OLDO : OLDC | OLDATTS > CONF2)
   = diffComp(CONF1, CONF2)
   if originalId(OLDO) == originalId(NEWO) .

ceq diffComp(< O1 : AddedElement | element : NEWO >
                 < NEWO : NEWC | NEWATTS > CONF1,
                 < O2 : ModifiedElement | element : NEWO2,
                   oldElement : OLDO >
                 < OLDO : OLDC | OLDATTS >
                 < NEWO2 : NEWC2 | NEWATTS2 > CONF2)
   = < O1 : AddedElement | element : NEWO2 >
     < NEWO2 : NEWC2 | excludingAll(NEWATTS, NEWATTS2), NEWATTS2 >
     diffComp(CONF1, CONF2)
   if originalId(NEWO) == originalId(OLDO) .
   ...
eq diffComp(CONF1, CONF2) = CONF1 CONF2 [owise] .
```

When no correspondences are found between the two difference models, i.e., there are no several `DiffElement` that refers to the same element, all the remaining elements (`DiffElements`) from both models are just copied (as specified by the last equation).

5.4 Tool Support

We have developed an Eclipse plug-in, called **Maudeling** [11], which is available for download [19]. This plug-in provides the implementation of all the difference operations specified here.

One of the main advantages of Maude is the possibility of using its execution environment, able to provide efficient implementations of the specifications. In fact, Maude's execution capabilities are comparable in performance and resource consumption to most commercial programming languages' environments. Thus we can efficiently execute the specifications of all the model operations described above.

Internally, ATL is used to automatically transform the Ecore models into their corresponding Maude representations, and then execute the operations in the Maude environment, so that the user does not need to deal with the Maude encoding of models and metamodels.

6   Related Work

There are several works that address the problems of comparing models and calculating their differences. Firstly, we have the works that describe how to compute the difference of models that conform to one specific metamodel, usually UML [5,9,10]. Their specificity and strong dependence on the elements and structure of the given metamodel hinders their generalization as metamodel-independent approaches that can be used with models that conform to arbitrary metamodels.

Secondly, there are several techniques that allow to solve this problem using edit scripts, which are based on representing the modifications as sequences of atomic actions specifying how the initial model is procedurally modified. These approaches are more general and powerful, and have been traditionally used for calculating and representing differences in several contexts. However, edit scripts are intrinsically not declarative, lengthy and very fine-grained, suitable for internal representations but quite ineffective to be adopted for documenting changes in MDSD environments, and difficult to compose. Furthermore, the results of their calculations are not expressed as a model conforming to a specific metamodel, and therefore can not be processed by standard modeling platforms (cf. [20]).

Other works, such as [20], [17] and [16], are closer to ours. In [20], a metamodel-independent approach to difference representation is presented, but with the particularity that the *Difference Metamodel* is not fixed, but created in each case as an extension of the operands' metamodel. This approach is agnostic of calculation method, so it does not introduce any model difference operation, and also requires a complex model transformation process to create the specific Difference Metamodel and to calculate the differences. Matching is based on name comparison; the proposal assumes that this specific attribute always exists and is called **name**. This may hinder its application in some contexts, such as for instance those in which metamodels are defined in languages different to English.

The work described in [17] introduces an algorithm for calculating and representing model differences in a metamodel-independent manner, but the result is not compact (it contains more information than required) and it is more oriented towards graphically representing and visualizing the differences.

Thirdly, EMFCompare [16] is a new interesting approach that uses complex and sophisticated algorithms to compute the structural matching between model elements. However, this proposal makes heavy use of the hierarchical tree for matching the elements, restricting the comparisons to elements in the same level. As discussed in Section 4.2, this restriction may not be effective in some cases, including those in which the changes affect the tree structure (something common in several model refactoring operations). Furthermore, difference models are not self-contained in EMFCompare, and therefore the minuend and subtrahend models are required in order to operate with the differences.

Finally, none of these approaches currently provide good support for composing the deltas and implementing further operations on them.

7   Conclusions

This paper discusses the problem of calculating differences between models conforming to arbitrary metamodels. Differences are represented as models that conform to the *Difference Metamodel*. In this way, the proposal has been devised to comply to the "everything is a model" principle.

The *Difference Metamodel*, and difference and related operations (do, undo and composition) have been specified in Maude and integrated in our Eclipse-developed environment Maudeling [2]. These operations can be applied to models not initially specified in Maude since ATL transformations have been defined from other kinds of representations, such as KM3 or Ecore.

There are several lines of research in which we are currently engaged, or that we plan to address in the near future.

Firstly, we are working on reverse transformations, i.e., transformations from Maude to Ecore model specifications, in order to make Maude completely transparent to the user and allow other tools to use the results produced by Maude.

Secondly, future work will address the problem of conflict detection and resolution in case of concurrent modification of models in distributed collaborative environments, in which parallel composition of differences can be applied to a model (or to parts of it).

Thirdly, we are working on improving the matching algorithm, with more complex heuristics and more customizable parameters, allowing users to assign weights to particular structural features depending on the specificities of their metamodels. In this sense, many of the powerful matching algorithms being developed within the EMFCompare project can also be easily adopted by our proposal, given the powerful specification possibilities of Maude. Counting on a formal supporting framework may bring along interesting benefits, such as proving the correctness of the algorithms, or reasoning about them, something at which Maude is particularly strong.

Finally, we are also working on making all our model operations available via Web services. In this way, users can simply send the appropriate SOAP messages with the (URLs of the) Ecore models to be compared, and get the resulting Ecore model with the difference. These difference models can be provided as operands of do, undo and modelDiff operations, also supported as Web Services. Our goal is to contribute to a Web-based distributed *Model Service Bus*, supporting a set of common services and operations on models that can be used for achieving distributed mega-programming in an effective way.

Acknowledgements. The authors would like to thank Francisco Durán for his help with the Maude system, and also to the anonymous referees for their insightful comments and very constructive suggestions. This work has been supported by Spanish Research Project TIN2005-09405-C02-01.

References

1. Steel, J., Jézéquel, J.M.: Model typing for improving reuse in model-driven engineering. In: Briand, L.C., Williams, C. (eds.) MoDELS 2005. LNCS, vol. 3713, pp. 84–96. Springer, Heidelberg (2005)
2. Romero, J.R., Rivera, J.E., Durán, F., Vallecillo, A.: Formal and tool support for model driven engineering with Maude. Journal of Object Technology 6, 187–207 (2007)
3. Bernstein, P.: Applying model management to classical metadata problems. In: Proc. of Innovative Database Research, pp. 209–220 (2003)
4. Cicchetti, A., di Ruscio, D., Pierantonio, A.: A domain-specific modeling language for model differences. Technical report, Università di L' Aquila (2006)
5. Alanen, M., Porres, I.: Difference and union of models. In: Stevens, P., Whittle, J., Booch, G. (eds.) UML 2003. LNCS, vol. 2863, pp. 2–17. Springer, Heidelberg (2003)
6. Mens, T.: A state-of-the-art survey on software merging. IEEE Trans. Softw. Eng. 28, 449–462 (2002)
7. Ohst, D., Welle, M., Kelter, U.: Differences between versions of UML diagrams. In: Proc. of ESEC/FSE-11: Proceedings of the 9th European software engineering conference, pp. 227–236. ACM Press, Helsinki, Finland (2003)
8. Brun, C., Pierantonio, A.: Model differences in the eclipse modeling framework. Upgrade, Special Issue on Model-Driven Software Development IX (2008)
9. Ohst, D., Welle, M., Kelter, U.: Difference tools for analysis and design documents. In: ICSM 2003: Proceedings of the International Conference on Software Maintenance, p. 13. IEEE Computer Society, Washington (2003)
10. Xing, Z., Stroulia, E.: Umldiff: an algorithm for object-oriented design differencing. In: ASE 2005: Proceedings of the 20th IEEE/ACM international Conference on Automated software engineering, pp. 54–65. ACM Press (2005)
11. Rivera, J.E., Durán, F., Vallecillo, A., Romero, J.R.: Maudeling: Herramienta de gestión de modelos usando Maude. In: JISBD 2007: Actas de XII Jornadas de Ingeniería del Software y Bases de Datos, Zaragoza, Spain (2007)
12. Clavel, M., Durán, F., Eker, S., Lincoln, P., Martí-Oliet, N., Meseguer, J., Quesada, J.: Maude: specification and programming in rewriting logic. Theoretical Computer Science 285, 187–243 (2002)
13. Clavel, M., Durán, F., Eker, S., Lincoln, P., Martí-Oliet, N., Meseguer, J., Talcott, C.: Maude 2.0 Manual (2003), http://maude.cs.uiuc.edu
14. Martí-Oliet, N., Meseguer, J.: Rewriting logic: roadmap and bibliography. Theoretical Computer Science 285, 121–154 (2002)
15. Clavel, M., Durán, F., Eker, S., Lincoln, P., Martí-Oliet, N., Meseguer, J., Talcott, C.: All About Maude - A High-Performance Logical Framework. LNCS, vol. 4350. Springer, Heidelberg (2007)
16. Toulmé, A.: The EMF compare utility (2007), http://www.eclipse.org/modeling/emft/
17. Lin, Y., Gray, J., Jouault, F.: DSMDiff: A differentiation tool for domain-specific models. European Journal of Information Systems 16, 349–361 (2007)

18. Levenshtein, V.I.: Binary codes capable of correcting deletions, insertions, and reversals. Soviet Physics Doklady 10, 707–710 (1966)
19. Rivera, J.E.: Maudeling (2008),
    http://atenea.lcc.uma.es/index.php/Portada/Resources/Maudeling
20. Cicchetti, A., di Ruscio, D., Pierantonio, A.: A metamodel independent approach to difference representation. Journal of Object Technology 6, 165–185 (2007)

Optimizing Dynamic Class Composition in a Statically Typed Language

Anders Bach Nielsen and Erik Ernst

Dept. of Computer Science, University of Aarhus, Denmark
{abachn,eernst}@daimi.au.dk

Abstract. In statically typed languages the set of classes and similar classifiers is commonly fully determined at compile time. Complete classifier representations can then be loaded at run-time, e.g., from a an executable file or a class file. However, some typing constructs—such as virtual classes—enable a type safe treatment of classifiers and their associated types and instances, even in the case where classifiers are created dynamically. This opens the opportunity to make dynamic class computations available as an integrated part of the language semantics. The language gbeta is an example where this is achieved based on mixins and linearization. In this paper we focus on the virtual machine related challenges of supporting dynamic class composition. In particular we present some core algorithms used for creating new classes, as well as some performance enhancements in these algorithms.

Keywords: Virtual Machines, Dynamic Class Composition, Virtual Classes, Mixins, Linearization, gbeta.

1 Introduction

In this paper we focus on the virtual machine related challenges of dynamic creation of classifiers in a statically typed language. Since the related language concepts are not main-stream we will give some context in this introduction, and then proceed to the detailed concepts and algorithms in later sections.

Classifiers such as classes and interfaces are intimately connected to type analysis, and hence statically typed languages commonly require every classifier to be known at compile-time. The compiler creates a complete specification of each classifier, for instance in the shape of a class file, and it may then be used in the static analysis and compilation of other classifiers, as well as for linking into an executable file or loading into a run-time environment. In order to use classes that are not statically known—if possible at all—it must be done using reflection or similar mechanisms that by-pass the type analysis entirely.

Some language constructs, however, enable type safe treatment of dynamically created classifiers and their instances. A notion of existential types [19] is needed in order to describe (partially) unknown types, and a simple notion of dependent types [3,1] is needed in order to maintain the identity of such unknown types outside restricted

R.F. Paige and B. Meyer (Eds.): TOOLS EUROPE 2008, LNBIP 11, pp. 161–177, 2008.

scopes, such as a single open statement. An example of a language concept that satisfies these requirements is virtual classes [16], in particular the generalized version of virtual classes that is associated with family polymorphism [11,21,18] and realized in the language gbeta [9,13].

In this language, dynamic creation of classes is an integrated part of the language design. Classes are first-class values in the language semantics, equipped with computation rules whereby existing classes may be composed dynamically to yield new classes. The concepts that enable this reconciliation of dynamism and static analysis are mixins [5], linearization [7,10], and structural type equivalence with granularity at the level of mixins.

In brief, dynamic class creation—and the associated integration with static typing—is achieved by making the operation of composing mixins available at run-time. Existing classes may then be composed by extracting their mixins and recomposing them into a new class at run-time. In essence, the extra flexibility is achieved by allowing new compositions of mixins, and the static analyzability is maintained by analyzing in terms of mixins, which are not created dynamically. As a consequence, the dynamic semantics represented by a virtual machine must be able to maintain explicit representations of mixins and to compose classes by linearization at run-time. In this paper we present the basic machinery needed in order to do this.

The approach could be applied to other object-oriented languages by adding support for dynamic class creation based on mixin composition. In statically typed languages it is useful because it reconciles static type checking with dynamic class composition. In dynamically typed languages such as Smalltalk [14] or SELF [22], these features might seem redundant because unrestricted modification and recompilation of classes is already available at run-time. However, the combination of flexibility and predictability offered by virtual classes may still be attractive even in the dynamically typed world, as illustrated by the fact that the language Newspeak [4] includes a kind of virtual classes.

However, it is difficult to support these concepts in a virtual machine without paying for it in terms of performance, in time or in space. Well-known techniques may be applied in the statically known cases, but in this paper we focus entirely on the dynamic scenario and discuss only data-structures and algorithms that are capable of working on dynamically created classes.

The main contribution of this work is the design and implementation of the virtual machine that supports the basic mechanisms and algorithms needed to perform the kind of dynamic class composition described above, and some improvements to these algorithms. The most intriguing insight achieved is that dynamic class composition runs at a speed which is comparable to creation of statically compiled classes, and hence dynamic class computation may by used as a standard operation rather than a very expensive exceptional case. The rest of this paper is structured as follows. Section 2 introduces the informal semantics and the concept of class composition. Section 3 shows the actual implementation of the linearization algorithms and presents two improvements. Section 4 shows benchmarks of the virtual machine running the linearization algorithm with and without improvements. Section 5 presents related and future work, and section 6 concludes.

2   Informal Semantics

In this section we present the basic structure and relationships of classes, mixins, and objects that is needed in order to support dynamic class composition, as well as the basic class composition algorithm itself.

2.1   The Basic Classifier Entity Structure

We should note that our actual implementation builds on more general concepts than classes and mixins. The concrete language which is executed by the virtual machine is gbeta [9,13,12], which is a generalization of the language BETA [17]. BETA unifies classes and methods (and several other concepts) into a single abstraction mechanism, the *pattern*, and this unification greatly enhances the expressive power and flexibility. The language gbeta is also based on this unified notion of a pattern, and this concept was generalized significantly in gbeta, compared to BETA. However, it is certainly possible to use a pattern as a class, that is just one out of several different ways to use it. Hence, in this paper we consider only this special case, and we use the main-stream terminology and talk about 'classes' where we could actually have said 'patterns'. Similarly, when we talk about 'mixins' we refer to entities that are capable of being composed in order to create classes, but they are in fact a generalized version of mixins that may also be used in the construction of methods and several other kinds of entities.

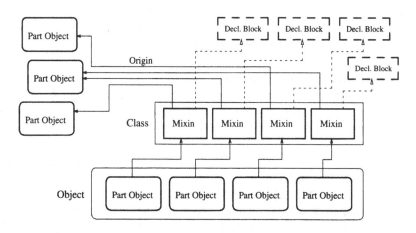

Fig. 1. Class and Object Structure

Figure 1 shows the basic entities needed in order to support gbeta style dynamic class composition. These basic entities are described in the following two paragraphs, and thereafter illustrated by an example.

Programs contain *declaration blocks*, similar to class bodies in many languages, i.e., source code fragments enclosed by braces containing a list of declarations. Such a declaration block defines the features (instance variables, methods, and nested classes) of a mixin. However, in addition to the feature list a mixin has access to a run-time context—similar to an instance of an inner class in the Java language, which contains a reference to its enclosing object. Hence, a *mixin* is a pair of references, one leading to a run-time representation of a declaration block, and the other leading to the context, which is known as the *origin* of the mixin. The context of a mixin is a *part object*. A part object is an instance of a mixin, i.e., a run-time entity which represents a part of an object that offers features corresponding to the declarations given in the declaration block of the mixin.

Finally, mixins and part objects are organized into larger entities: A *class* is a list of distinct mixins, and an *object* is a list of part objects. When creating an object $o = [p_1 \ldots p_k]$ as an instance of a given class $C = [m_1 \ldots m_k]$, the part objects and the mixins match up in the sense that p_i is an instance of m_i for all $i \in 1 \ldots k$. Similarly, the nesting structure in the source code is mirrored by the origin structure among run-time entities, as illustrated in Fig. 2: If a part object p_1 is an instance of a mixin $m_1 = (B_1, p_2)$ with enclosing part object p_2 whose mixin is $m_2 = (B_2, p_3)$, then the declaration block of the former, B_1, is textually directly nested inside B_2.

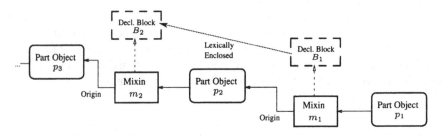

Fig. 2. Relation between Declaration Block in Nested Classes

Since every part object has a mixin that has an enclosing part object, it seems that the nesting structure is infinite. However, the chain ends at a *predefined* part object, which ultimately contains all other entities. It is a compile-time error to try to access the mixin or enclosing part object of the predefined part object.

```
class Company: 1{
    class Employee: 2{ int salary; }
    class Manager: Employee 3{ int bonus; }
}
```

Fig. 3. Class and object example

Figure 3 shows a simple gbeta class Company that contains two nested classes Employee and Manager, which serves as an example to illustrate the concepts of mixin, part object, etc. Note that it is written in a Java-like syntax rather than actual gbeta syntax, for main-stream readability. Also note that the example does not contain methods, because methods are actually the same kind of entities as classes in gbeta.

As illustrated in Fig. 4, an instance c of the class Company then contains one part object, p_c, which is an instance of a mixin, m_c, whose associated declaration block is the one marked by a superscript '1' in the Fig. 3; we will use B to denote the declaration blocks, with the indicated number as a subscript, so this declaration block would be B_1. All mixins of the two nested classes have p_c as their enclosing part object. The class Employee has a single mixin with declaration block B_2, and Manager inherits that mixin and adds another one with declaration block B_3. All in all, Employee is the single mixin class $[(B_2, p_c)]$ and Manager is the class $[(B_3, p_c), (B_2, p_c)]$, of two mixins. A part object which is an instance of (B_2, p_c) would contain storage for the instance variable salary, and similarly an instance of (B_3, p_c) would have storage for bonus. Hence, an instance of Manager would have the two instance variables salary and bonus, as expected.

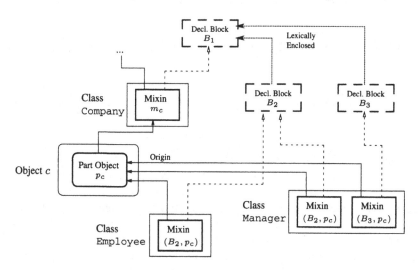

Fig. 4. Structure corresponding to Fig. 3

In general, mixins in the same class need not have the same enclosing part object, and they need not even be part of the same object, that is just the case in the example in Fig. 3 because it is so simple.

Obviously this setup is more complex than the standard object model known from main-stream languages, but in the next section we will describe how it allows for novel features, in particular run-time composition of classes.

2.2 Class Composition

The universe of run-time entities described in the previous section is very flexible, and in particular it directly supports run-time construction of new classes.

Seemingly, dynamic class construction simply amounts to taking some mixins from anywhere and collecting them into a list of mixins, which is the new class. However, in order to ensure type safe execution semantics, class construction must be restricted more than that. Dynamic class *creation* is thus restricted to dynamic class *composition*, which is an operation whereby two mixin lists (i.e., classes) are merged to one mixin list (class).

```
fun linearize [] ys = ys
  | linearize xs [] = xs
  | linearize (xxs as x::xs) (yys as y::ys) =
    if x=y then y::(linearize xs ys)
    else if not (contains y xs)
         then y::(linearize xxs ys)
    else if not (contains x ys)
         then x::(linearize xs yys)
    else y::(linearize (remove y xxs) ys)
and contains x [] = false
  | contains x (y::ys) =
    if x=y then true else contains x ys
and remove _ [] = []
  | remove y (x::xs) =
    if x=y then remove y xs
    else x::(remove y xs)
```

Fig. 5. The linearization algorithm

The algorithm which is used to merge the two lists is presented in Fig. 5 as a small function, `linearize`, in Standard ML. It uses the two auxiliary functions `contains` and `remove` that check for list membership and remove an element from a list. In short, the algorithm transfers the mixins to the result one by one by taking the first element from the right-hand operand if it does not occur in the left-hand operand, otherwise it tries vice-versa, and if that also fails it deletes the left-hand occurrence and continues. Note that ordinary single inheritance comes out as a special case where an existing class (list of mixins) is extended with one new mixin (which is in fact a 'cons' operation on the list). Also note that the algorithm simply implements a set union operation when the order of the mixins in the class is ignored. Types are based on sets of mixins, so this provides class composition with several nice typing properties including commutativity and associativity. However, in this paper we focus on classes rather than the types of classes, and from this point of view the ordering of mixins is significant because it may affect the behavior of objects at runtime.

Historically, the gbeta linearization algorithm was first presented in [10]. This algorithm turned out to be equivalent to a special case of the algorithm known as C3 [2], which was proposed for use in Dylan. C3 operates on inheritance graphs, but the gbeta algorithm works on the special case of two lists, which makes it much simpler. Later [13] the gbeta linearization algorithm was modified into its current form which always succeeds—other linearization algorithms terminate with an inconsistency error for some inheritance hierarchies. This is the algorithm which is shown in Fig. 5, and the generalization happened by including the last **else** clause in `linearize`, which resolves the conflict that makes other linearization algorithms fail. Linearization failure may be

```
1   Class& linearize(Class& clsa, Class& clsb) {
2
3       int i = 0;
4       int asize = clsa.getSize();
5       int j = 0;
6       int bsize = clsb.getSize();
7       int k = 0;
8       Class& tmpcls = *(new Class(asize + bsize + 2));
9       while (i < asize && j < bsize) {
10          if ( clsa.getMixin(i) == clsb.getMixin(j) ) {
11              tmpcls.setMixin( clsb.getMixin(j), k);
12              i++; j++; k++;
13          } else if ( ! classContainsMixin(clsa, i,
14                                        clsb.getMixin(j)) ) {
15              tmpcls.setMixin( clsb.getMixin(j), k);
16              j++; k++;
17          } else if ( ! classContainsMixin(clsb, j,
18                                        clsa.getMixin(i)) ) {
19              tmpcls.setMixin( clsa.getMixin(i), k);
20              i++; k++;
21          } else {
22              clsa = removeMixinFromClass(clsa, i,
23                            mixinPosInClass(clsa, i,
24                                        clsb.getMixin(j)));
25              i = 0;
26              asize = clsa.getSize();
27              tmpcls.setMixin( clsb.getMixin(j), k);
28              j++; k++;
29          }
30      }
31      while (i < asize) {
32          tmpcls.setMixin( clsa.getMixin(i), k);
33          i++; k++;
34      }
35      while (j < bsize) {
36          tmpcls.setMixin( clsb.getMixin(j), k);
37          j++; k++;
38      }
39      Class& rescls = *(new Class(k));
40      for (i = 0; i < rescls.getSize(); i++) {
41          rescls.setMixin( tmpcls.getMixin(i), i);
42      }
43      return rescls;
44  }
```

Fig. 6. The linearization algorithm for dynamically combining two classes

acceptable when it occurs during a programming session because there is a programmer who can solve the problem, but for a dynamic feature it is essential to strive for a robust semantics that does not raise errors at run-time. On top of that, this tie-breaker rule affords programmers a more fine-grained control over the combination of classes and their behavior.

3   The Virtual Machine Realization of the Semantics

The virtual machine is implemented in C++, and Fig. 6 shows the linearization algorithm in the virtual machine that corresponds to the algorithm shown in Fig. 5. It has been simplified compared to the actual implementation by using new expressions rather than allocating entities in the heap, and in a few other ways that do not affect the complexity or the essentials of what it does.

The algorithm explicitly refers to the class `Class` which implements the representation of a class; this is in fact an array of pairs of pointers, each pair corresponding to a mixin. It refers to these mixins by means of methods such as `getMixin` and `setMixin`, but note that since mixins are not objects but just pairs of values the manipulation of mixins is fast.

Similarly to the algorithm in Fig. 5 some subtasks have been factored out of the main algorithm, namely the functions `classContainsMixin`, `mixinPosInClass`, and `removeMixinFromClass`, shown in Fig. 7. They are used to check whether a mixin occurs in a given class, to find its position in a class, and to create a new class which is a copy of the argument class, except that all mixins up to the argument `floor` and the mixin at position `mixinpos` are skipped—i.e., it is a copy that deletes a prefix and a specific mixin from its argument.

It is easy to see that the worst-case complexity of the linearization algorithm is $O(n \cdot m)$ where n and m are the numbers of mixins in the first and second argument, respectively, and that the auxilary functions in Fig. 7 are all linear in the number of mixins in the input class.

3.1   Improving the Linearization Algorithm

This section presents two improvements of the linearization algorithm from the previous section. As mentioned, the algorithm merges two classes to one, but since a class is a list of mixins, this amounts to mapping two lists to one list. Both improvements are based on using a simpler algorithm when the arguments satisfy certain requirements. The first improvement applies when there is a subclass relationship among the arguments, and the second improvement can be used when one of the two arguments consists of only one mixin.

Utilizing the Subclass Relationship. The first improvement is used when the linearization algorithm in Fig. 6 is applied to two classes where one is a subclass of the other. This case is important because it arises whenever family polymorphism [11] is used to express feature composition; more information about this can be found in various papers about family polymorphism including [8,18,20].

```
1  bool classContainsMixin(Class& cls, int pos,
2                                         Mixin m) {
3     for (int i = pos; i < cls.getSize(); i++) {
4        if ( cls.getMixin(i) == m )
5           return true;
6     }
7     return false;
8  }

1  int mixinPosInClass(Class& cls, int pos, Mixin m) {
2     for (int i = pos; i < cls.getSize(); i++) {
3        if ( cls.getMixin(i) == m )
4           return i;
5     }
6     return -1;
7  }

1  Class& removeMixinFromClass(Class& cls, int floor,
                                     int mixinpos) {
2     assert( floor >= 0 && mixinpos >= floor);
3     Class& newcls = *(new Class(cls.getSize() - floor));
4     int i;
5     int j = 0;
6     for (i = floor; i < mixinpos; i++) {
7        newcls.setMixin( cls.getMixin(i), j);
8        j++;
9     }
10    for (i = mixinpos+1; i < cls.getSize(); i++) {
11       newcls.setMixin( cls.getMixin(i), j);
12       j++;
13    }
14    return newcls;
15 }
```

Fig. 7. Auxilary functions for testing if a mixin is in a class, get the index of a mixin in a class and remove a mixin from a class

The subclass relationship is defined as follows: Class C' is a subclass of class C if the list of mixins in C' is a super list of the list of mixins in C, i.e., if C can be created by deleting some of the elements in C'.

Assume that the class B is a subclass of A. As the following discussion shows, the linearization of A and B would result in B.

Let $A = [m_1 \ldots m_n]$, then $B = [m'_1 \ldots m'_k]$ where $k \geq n$ and there is an increasing sequence i_j such that $m_j = m'_{i_j}$ for $j \in 1 \ldots n$.

Considering the presentation of the algorithm in Fig. 5, there are four cases: (1) $m_1 = m'_1$, (2) m'_1 does not occur in A, (3) the previous case does not apply, and m_1 does not occur in B, and (4) case 1 does not apply but m'_1 does occur in A and m_1 does

```
1   int subSuperClassCheck(Class& clsa, Class& clsb) {
2     Class& sub;  Class& super;  int answer;
3     if (clsa.getSize() >= clsb.getSize()) {
4       sub = clsa; super = clsb;
5       answer = -1;
6     } else {
7       sub = clsb; super = clsa;
8       answer = 1;
9     }
10    int i = 0;
11    int subsize = sub.getSize();
12    int j = 0;
13    int supersize = super.getSize();
14    while (i < subsize && j < supersize) {
15      if (sub.getMixin(i) == super.getMixin(j)) {
16        i++; j++;
17      } else {
18        i++;
19      }
20    }
21    if (j >= supersize) {
22      return answer;
23    } else {
24      return 0;
25    }
26  }
```

Fig. 8. Algorithm for Determining the Subclass Relationship between two Classes

occur in B. Because of the subclass relationship we know that (3) and (4) cannot occur, and in the cases (1) and (2) we choose the first mixin from B. Since the arguments to the recursive call are again in the same subclass relationship, the algorithm simply returns B.

This shows clearly that we only add mixins from class B to the resulting class. The example above shows that by creating an algorithm that determines if there is a subclass relationship between two arguments we can improve the linearization algorithm. An implementation of such an algorithm is shown in Fig. 8. The worst case running time of this algorithm is $O(n)$ where n is the length of the longest argument.

The Improved Linearization Algorithm. As described above the linearization of two classes with a subclass relationship will always result in the subclass. Performing the linearization, with the algorithm from Fig. 6, will give a worst case running time of $O(m \cdot n)$ even though we know that the result is the subclass. With the function from Fig. 8 we can improve the linearization algorithm.

The improvement to the linearization algorithm is highlighted in Fig. 9. This addition improves the worst case running time, when merging two classes with a subclass relationship, from $O(m \cdot n)$ to $O(n)$, where n is the longest of the two arguments.

```
1    Class& linearize(Class& clsa, Class& clsb) {
2.1    int d = subSuperClassCheck(clsa, clsb);
2.2    if (d < 0) {
2.3      return clsa;
2.4    } else if (d > 0) {
2.5      return clsb;
2.6    }
3      int i = 0;
4      int asize = clsa.getSize() - 1;
5      int j = 0;
6      int bsize = clsb.getSize() - 1;
7      int k = 0;
8      ...
```

Fig. 9. Linearization Algorithm with Subclass Check

Adding One Extra Mixin. The second improvement comes from merging two classes where one of the classes consists of only one mixin. This is a very common situation in real programs. Adding one mixin to a class is easy, syntactically lightweight and it comes very natural. It is very often seen in the context of virtual classes where a class is further bound by one mixin in each level of the hierarchy. Looking at this case of linearization a class $A = [m_1, \ldots, m_n]$, where $n \geq 1$, with a class $C = [m]$. We get one of two results:

1. If class A already contains m, then the result of the linearization would be A.
2. If class A does not contain m, the resulting class would be constructed by adding the mixin m to A.

These two scenarios are relatively simple. The situation is easy to detect and an algorithm solving this has a linear time complexity in the number of mixins in A.

Considering the presentation of the algorithm in Fig. 5, the execution of the four cases are highly dependent on the arguments. Let us assume class $A = [m_1 \ldots m_n]$, and class $C_1 = [m]$ so that $m \neq m_i$ for all $i \in 1 \ldots n$. We also assume class $C_2 = [m_k]$ for some $k \in 1 \ldots n$.

In the table below, we have summed up the worst case running times of the four interesting combinations of arguments A, C_1 and C_2 for the linearization algorithm from Fig. 6.

$linearize(C_1, A)$	$O(n)$
$linearize(A, C_1)$	$O(n)$
$linearize(C_2, A)$	$O(n)$
$linearize(A, C_2)$	$O(n^2)$

The most interesting combination of arguments to the linearization algorithm is $linearize(A, C_2)$. This combination of arguments has a worst case running time of $O(n^2)$: Assume that $m_k = m_n$. Executing the algorithm from Fig. 6 with the arguments A and C_2 runs in two phases. The first phase is the $n - 1$ iterations of the main loop.

```
1   Class& linearize(Class& clsa, Class& clsb) {
2.1     Class& cls;   Mixin c;   int conc;
2.2     if (clsa.getSize() == 1 ||
2.3         clsb.getSize() == 1) {
2.4       if (clsa.getSize() == 1) {
2.5         c = clsa.getMixin(0);
2.6         cls = clsb; conc = 1;
2.7       } else {
2.8         c = clsb.getMixin(0);
2.9         cls = clsa; conc = 0;
2.10      }
2.11      if (classContainsMixin(cls, 0, c)) {
2.12        return cls;
2.13      } else {
2.14        if (conc == 0)
2.15          return cls.prepend(c);
2.16        else
2.17          return cls.append(c);
2.18      }
2.19    }
3     int i = 0;
4     int asize = clsa.getSize() - 1;
5     int j = 0;
6     int bsize = clsb.getSize() - 1;
7     int k = 0;
8     ...
```

Fig. 10. Linearization algorithm with efficient handling of classes with length one

It searches through class A just to find that m_k is contained in A. It then searches class C_2 with the most specific mixin m_j in A, to find that it is not contained in C_2, and so it adds m_j to the result. The second phase is the last iteration where the mixins m_k and m_n are compared. By assumption they are equal, so this shared value is included in the result. This is a very tedious way to build class A. Looking at the number of instructions needed to perform this computation we get the arithmetic series $n + (n-1) + (n-2) + \ldots + 1$, which is equal to $\frac{1}{2}n(n-1)$ and hence the worst case running time is $O(n^2)$ for merging two classes where one of the classes consists of only one mixin.

The Improved Linearization Algorithm. With the example presented above we want to improve the linearization algorithm from Fig. 6. We want to improve it in a way that we can always guarantee a $O(n)$ time complexity for all arguments. Especially with the same arguments used in the previous section.

The addition is shown in detail in Fig. 10. In short, we test if one of the arguments has only one mixin. If this is the case, we test if this mixin is already contained in the large class. If this is also the case, we know the answer and return the large class. If this is not the case we either append or prepend the mixin to the large class depending on the order of the arguments.

This addition to the linearization algorithm gives us the desired worst case running time of $O(n)$.

4   Benchmarks

We have created six different microbenchmarks that are targeted at both the general linearization cases and the more specific cases. The basic structure of all the six benchmarks are the same. We start a timer, run the desired linearization 200.000 times and stop the timer again. The output time is measured in milliseconds. We run each benchmark 10 times and calculate the average time usage. All six benchmarks are executed under three different circumstances. The first set of benchmarks are run with the original linearization algorithm from Fig. 6. The second set of benchmarks are run with the optimized linearization algorithm including both improvements presented. The last set of benchmarks are compiled, so the compiler performs as many linearizations as possible at compile time and generates a *static class descriptor* for each linearization performed. A static class descriptor mirrors the content of a class, as described in section 2.1, except for the origin part objects. For each mixin the pointer to the origin part object needs to be calculated based on the current context.

1. Linearizes two unrelated classes of each 10 mixins.
2. Linearizes two unrelated classes of each 20 mixins.
3. Linearizes a large class of 20 mixins with an unrelated class of just one mixin.
4. Linearizes a class of one mixin with an unrelated class of 20 mixins.
5. This benchmark uses the optimization based on classes with just one mixin, and it linearizes a large class of 20 mixins with a class of one mixin that is already present in the large class.
6. This benchmark uses the optimization based on the subclass test, and it linearizes a large class of 20 mixins with a superclass of 12 mixins.

All the results are shown in Fig. 11. The results of benchmarks 1 and 2 are as expected. We expect that it is a very uncommon case to merge two large classes of unrelated mixins. The usual case is to extend a class by one mixin at the time. The improvements presented in section 3.1 have no effect on large classes of unrelated mixins. The increase in execution time of the optimized version is quite small. In numbers, benchmark 2 is an increase of 24 msec over 200.000 consecutive linearizations. The last bar in both benchmarks 1 and 2 indicate that it is faster to build the class based on static information instead of performing the merge dynamically.

In benchmarks 3 and 4 we linearize a large class with a class containing only one mixin. In the optimized version this results in appending or prepending a single mixin, respectively. In the unoptimized linearization prepending a mixin was more expensive than appending a mixin. With the optimizations they now have the same execution time, giving a 9% and 18% speedup respectively. We expect these two to be the most common cases in normal programs, because single declaration blocks occur very frequently. These benchmarks indicate clearly that building the class from static information is not always the best choice. In both benchmarks the optimized algorithm is clearly faster.

In benchmark 5 the optimized version gave a speedup of 55%. This was because there was no need to do a linearization. The linear sweep of the longer class revealed

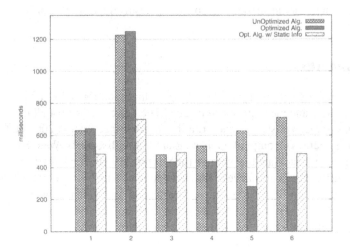

Fig. 11. Benchmarks of the unoptimized and optimized version of the linearization algorithm

that the one mixin of the other class was already present and the longer class would therefore be the result.

Benchmark 6 was just a linearization of two large classes for the unoptimized version of the algorithm. The optimized version detected that one class was a superclass of the other and that the result therefore was the subclass. This optimization gave a speedup of 51%.

Both benchmark 5 and 6 show that creating classes from static class descriptors really depend on the length of the resulting class. In both cases the dynamic merge using the optimized linearization algorithm outperforms the static information created by the compiler. Note, however, that we expect future work to bring performance improvements in the creation of classes from static class descriptors, so the balance may change again.

5   Related and Future Work

Our dynamic class composition is not to be confused with the approach taken in dynamically typed languages such as SELF [22], Smalltalk [14]. In a running Smalltalk image, for instance, it is possible to compile new classes and even to modify and recompile existing classes, in which case all existing instances will be updated accordingly. Existing code may or may not be consistent with the new kinds of objects, but the choice of dynamic typing implies that this problem rests with the programmer who must use ad-hoc analysis and conventions to avoid run-time failure—and this is a delicate balance to which programmers using dynamically typed languages have already dedicated themselves. In a statically typed language, such pervasive inconsistencies at run-time are obviously unacceptable; but our dynamic class composition mechanism is also radically different.

In our design, classes are values, i.e., they are immutable, and class composition is an operation that returns a new value (a new class) without changing the operands (the classes that are being composed). Hence, the need to update all existing instances of a class which has been modified never arises. The reason why it is possible to deal safely with instances of a dynamically created class is that this new class consists of mixins, and class composition does not invalidate the typing properties of each mixin. Hence, code which is compiled to operate on an object with a given set S of mixins will operate type correctly on any object whose mixins form a superset S' of S, no matter whether or not the class with mixins S' was created dynamically.

Considering statically typed languages, we are not aware of any other language than gbeta which offers a similar flexibility in the dynamic creation of classes. However, there are many issues related to the layout and structure of run-time entities which emerge in a less radical form in other statically typed languages. For instance, the C++ object layout uses virtual base pointers to enable navigation when a fixed offset to a data member cannot be used, and similar techniques have been invented for other variants of multiple inheritance. Several results improve on the space and time costs of these challenges citePughW90,EckelG00,ZibinG03. It would be very interesting if these techniques could be transferred to the dynamic setting described in this paper.

Compared to earlier work on gbeta and on virtual classes, in particular [10,11,8,13], this is the first paper that describes support for dynamic class composition in a virtual machine where performance is in focus. There is no support for dynamic creation of classes in [13], and the virtual machine which was implemented and developed in connection with [10,11,8] and similar papers was focused entirely on achieving the correct run-time semantics.

With respect to future work, one obvious improvement to class composition can be found by looking at *inline caches* for methods in SELF or Smalltalk. Smalltalk introduced *lookup caches* [6], and later in SELF added *inline caches* [15] to speed up the methods calls. With inspiration from these techniques we will look into creating caches of dynamically composed classes. This concept of *class caching* brings along some interesting challenges: Where in the virtual machine should this cache reside? How do we create an efficient hashing algorithm where the input is two classes? And how do we handle this cache during garbage collection? We believe that this concept of class caching will further improve the linearization algorithm and make it even more attractive for use in virtual machines.

6   Conclusion

In this paper we have presented the core algorithms used by a virtual machine to compose classes dynamically, as well as some improvements on these algorithms and performance measurements documenting the improvement. The virtual machine described in this paper is not a standard Java or .NET virtual machine, and in particular it supports first-class mixins and linearization at run-time. This makes it possible to reconcile dynamic class composition and static type checking based on virtual classes as provided in the language gbeta. The virtual machine performs dynamic class composition at a speed comparable to creating classes from static class descriptors. This is an intriguing result, because it makes dynamic class composition a realistic alternative to the static approach, rather than an expensive special case. However, it might still be possible to optimize the static case. It would be possible to have similar features in other object-oriented languages, given that the basic concepts and mechanisms were added to their run-time semantics and type systems. This paper demonstrates that is it possible to go down this path.

Acknowledgements. We would like to thank the anonymous reviewers for valuable feedback and suggestions.

References

1. Augustsson, L.: Cayenne - a language with dependent types. In: ICFP, pp. 239–250 (1998)
2. Barrett, K., Cassels, B., Haahr, P., Moon, D.A., Playford, K., Withington, P.T.: A monotonic superclass linearization for dylan. In: Conference on Object-Oriented, pp. 69–82 (1996)
3. Betarte, G.: Dependent Record Types and Algebraic Structures in Type Theory. Phd thesis, Dept. of Computing Science, Chalmers Univ. of Technology and Univ. of Göteborg (1998)
4. Bracha, G.: Executable grammars in newspeak. Electron. Notes Theor. Comput. Sci. 193, 3–18 (2007)
5. Bracha, G., Cook, W.: Mixin-based inheritance. In: Proceedings OOPSLA/ECOOP 1990, ACM SIGPLAN Notices, vol. 25(10), pp. 303–311 (October 1990)
6. Deutsch, L.P., Schiffman, A.M.: Efficient implementation of the Smalltalk-80 system. In: Conference Record of the Eleventh Annual ACM Symposium on Principles of Programming Languages, Salt Lake City, Utah, pp. 297–302 (1984)
7. Ducournau, R., Habib, M., Mugnier, M.L., Huchard, M.: Proposal for a Monotonic Multiple Inheritance Linearization. In: ACM SIGPLAN Notices, Oregon, USA, vol. 29(10), pp. 164–175 (October 1994)
8. Ernst, E.: Higher-order hierarchies. In: Cardelli, L. (ed.) ECOOP 2003. LNCS, vol. 2743, pp. 303–329. Springer, Heidelberg (2003)
9. Ernst, E.: gbeta – a Language with Virtual Attributes, Block Structure, and Propagating, Dynamic Inheritance. PhD thesis, Department of Computer Science, University of Aarhus, Århus, Denmark (1999)
10. Ernst, E.: Propagating class and method combination. In: Guerraoui, R. (ed.) ECOOP 1999. LNCS, vol. 1628. Springer, Heidelberg (1999)
11. Ernst, E.: Family polymorphism. In: Knudsen, J.L. (ed.) ECOOP 2001. LNCS, vol. 2072, pp. 303–326. Springer, Heidelberg (2001)
12. Ernst, E.: Reconciling virtual classes with genericity. In: Lightfoot, D.E., Szyperski, C.A. (eds.) JMLC 2006. LNCS, vol. 4228, pp. 57–72. Springer, Heidelberg (2006)
13. Ernst, E., Ostermann, K., Cook, W.R.: A virtual class calculus. In: POPL 2006: Conference record of the 33rd ACM SIGPLAN-SIGACT symposium on Principles of programming languages, pp. 270–282. ACM Press, New York (2006)
14. Goldberg, A., Robson, D.: Smalltalk–80: The Language. Addison-Wesley, Reading (1989)
15. Hlzle, U., Chambers, C., Ungar, D.: Optimizing dynamically-typed object-oriented languages with polymorphic inline caches (1991)
16. Madsen, O.L., Møller-Pedersen, B.: Virtual classes: A powerful mechanism in object-oriented programming. In: Proceedings OOPSLA 1989, ACM SIGPLAN Notices, vol. 24(10), pp. 397–406 (October 1989)

17. Madsen, O.L., Nygaard, K., Møller-Pedersen, B.: Object-Oriented Programming in The Beta Programming Language. Addison-Wesley (1993)
18. Mezini, M., Ostermann, K.: Conquering aspects with caesar. In: AOSD 2003: Proceedings of the 2nd international conference on Aspect-oriented software development, pp. 90–99. ACM Press, New York (2003)
19. Mitchell, J.C., Plotkin, G.D.: Abstract types have existential types. In: Conference Record of the Twelfth Annual ACM Symposium on Principles of Programming Languages, pp. 37–51. ACM (January 1985)
20. Nystrom, N., Qi, X., Myers, A.C.: J&: nested intersection for scalable software composition. In: OOPSLA 2006: Proceedings of the 21st annual ACM SIGPLAN conference on Object-oriented programming systems, languages, and applications, pp. 21–36. ACM, New York (2006)
21. Odersky, M., Cremet, V., Röckl, C., Zenger, M.: A nominal theory of objects with dependent types. In: Cardelli, L. (ed.) ECOOP 2003. LNCS, vol. 2743, pp. 201–224. Springer, Heidelberg (2003)
22. Ungar, D., Smith, R.B.: Self: The power of simplicity. In: Proceedings OOPSLA 1987, Orlando, FL, pp. 227–242 (October 1987)

Appendix

The Raw Benchmark Data. In the table below we present the execution times (in milliseconds) of all benchmarks. All these benchmarks where run with a pre-allocated heap large enough to cope with the entire execution of the test and no garbage collection was therefore needed. The platform used in these benchmarks was a Intel Centrino Core Duo T2500 2.0 Ghz machine with 1 Gb RAM running Gentoo Linux.

	Unoptimized Alg.	Optimized Alg.	Opt. Alg. w/ Static Info
1	631.1	643.3	483.8
2	1225.6	1249.8	699.1
3	480.4	434.2	493.2
4	533.5	435.8	493.6
5	628.1	280.4	483.9
6	709.9	341.1	484.5

Ownership, Uniqueness, and Immutability

Johan Östlund[1], Tobias Wrigstad[1], Dave Clarke[2], and Beatrice Åkerblom[3]

[1] Purdue University, West Lafayette, Indiana, USA
[2] CWI, Amsterdam, The Netherlands
[3] Stockholm University, Stockholm, Sweden

Abstract. Programming in an object-oriented language demands a fine balance between flexibility and control. At one level, objects need to interact freely to achieve our implementation goals. At a higher level, architectural constraints that ensure the system can be understood by new developers and can evolve as requirements change must be met. To resolve this tension, researchers have developed type systems expressing ownership and behavioural restrictions such as immutability. This work reports on our consolidation of the resulting discoveries into a single programming language. Our language, Joe$_3$, imposes little additional syntactic overhead, yet can encode powerful patterns such as fractional permissions and the reference modes of Flexible Alias Protection.

1 Introduction

Recent years have seen a number of proposals put forward to add more structure to object-oriented programming languages, for example, via ownership types [11] or to increase the amount of control over objects by limiting how they can be accessed by other objects, via notions such as read-only or immutability. Ownership types captures and enforces object nesting statically in the program code by parameterising types over the enclosing objects. Read-only references prevent mutation and have been used in proposals to strengthen object encapsulation and manage aliasing either on its own (e.g., [19,27]) or as parts of other proposals (e.g., [26,18,24]). An immutable object can be thought of as an object to which only read-only references exist. Immutable objects help avoid aliasing problems and data races in multi-threaded programs [4,17], and also enhance program understanding, as read-only or immutable annotations are verified to hold at compile-time [29]. According to Zibin et al. [32], immutability (including read-only references) can be used for modelling, verification, compile- and run-time optimisations, refactoring, test input generation, regression oracle creation, invariant detection, specification mining and program comprehension.

Immutability spans the following spectrum: *Class immutability* ensures that all instances of a class are immutable, for example, Java's String class; *object immutability* ensures that some instances of a class are immutable, though other instances may remain mutable; and *read-only*—or *reference immutability*—prevents modifications of an object via certain references, without precluding the co-existence of normal and read-only references to the same object.

R.F. Paige and B. Meyer (Eds.): TOOLS EUROPE 2008, LNBIP 11, pp. 178–197, 2008.
© Springer-Verlag Berlin Heidelberg 2008

Contributions. The programming language, Joe₃, proposed in this paper offers ownership and externally unique references (the only external reference into an aggregate) to control the alias structure of object graphs, and lightweight effects and a mode system to encode various notions of immutability. It is a relatively straightforward extension[1] of Clarke and Wrigstad's *external uniqueness* proposal (Joline) [13,30], and the syntactic overhead due to additional annotations is surprisingly small given the expressiveness of the language. Not only can we encode the three forms of immutability mentioned above, but we can encode something akin to the *arg* mode from Flexible Alias Protection [26], which allows aggregates to safely rely on immutable parts of external objects, Fractional Permissions [6], which allows an object to mediate between being unaliased and mutable and aliased and immutable, and the context-based immutability of Universes [24], all the while preserving the owners-as-dominators encapsulation invariant of ownership types which guarantees that all accesses to an object's internals go via its interface. Furthermore, as our system is based on ownership types, we can distinguish between outgoing aliases to external, non-representation objects and aliases to internal objects and allow modification of the former (but not the latter) through a read-only reference.

Our system is closest in spirit to SafeJava [4], but we allow access modes on all owner parameters of a class, read-only references and an interplay between borrowing and immutable objects that can encode fractional permissions.

The Status of Read-Only in the Literature. Boyland [7] criticises existing proposals for handling read-only references on the following points:

1. Read-only arguments can be silently captured when passed to methods;
2. A read-only annotation cannot express whether
   (a) the referenced *object* is immutable, so the reference can be safely stored;
   (b) a read-only reference is unique and thus effectively immutable;
   (c) mutable aliases of a read-only reference can exist, implying that the referenced object should be cloned before used, to prevent it being modified underfoot resulting in *observational exposure*, which occurs when changes to state are observed through a read-only reference.

Joe₃ addresses all of these problems. First, Joe₃ supports owner-polymorphic methods, which can express that a method does not capture one or all of its arguments. Second, we decorate owners with modes that govern how the objects owned by that owner will be treated in a context. Together with auxiliary constructs inherited from Joline, the modes can express immutability both in terms of 2.a) and 2.b), and read-only which permits the existence of mutable aliases (2.c). Moreover, Joe₃ supports fractional permissions [6]—converting a mutable unique reference into several immutable references for a certain context. This allows safe representation exposure without the risk for observational exposure.

Joe₃ allows class, object and reference immutability. Unique references, borrowing and owner-polymorphic methods allow us to simulate fractional permissions and staged, external initialisation of immutable objects through auxiliary

---

[1] For brevity, we omit inheritance. Our Joe₃ compiler however supports it.

methods. As we base modification rights on owners (in the spirit of Joe$_1$'s [10] effects system), we achieve what we call *context-based* immutability, which is essentially the same kind of read-only found the Universes system [24], a simple ownership system enforcing deep encapsulation modulo read-only references.

Joe$_3$ allows both read-only references and true immutables in the same language. This provides the safety desired by Boyland, but also allows coding patterns which do rely on observing changes in an object.

Outline. Section 2 introduces the Joe$_3$ language through a set of motivating examples. Section 3 gives a brief formal account of Joe$_3$. Section 4 outlines a few simple but important extensions—immutable classes and Greenhouse and Boyland-style regions [16], describes how they further enhance the system and discusses how to encode the modes of Flexible Alias Protection [26]. Section 5 surveys related work not covered in the previous. Section 6 concludes.

2   Meet Joe$_3$

In this section we describe Joe$_3$ using some motivating examples. A more detailed introduction is given in Section 3. Joe$_3$ is a class-based, object-oriented programming language with deep ownership, owner-polymorphic methods, ownership transfer through external uniqueness, an effects system, and a simple mode system decorating owners with permissions to control how an object may be modified. Beyond the carefully designed combination of features, the annotation of owners with modes is the main novelty in Joe$_3$. The modes indicate that a reference may be read or written (+), only read (-), or immutable (*). Read and immutable annotations on an owner in the class header represent a promise that the code in the class body will not change objects owned by that owner. The key to preserving and respecting immutability and read-only in Joe$_3$ is a simple effects system, expressed through owners, inspired by Clarke and Drossopoulou's Joe$_1$ [10]. Classes and objects have the rights to read or modify objects belonging to certain owners; only a minor extension to the type system of Clarke and Wrigstad's Joline [13,30] is required to ensure this statically.

The syntax of Joe$_3$ (Figure 5) should be understandable to a reader with insight into ownership types and Java-like languages. Classes are parameterised with owners related to each other by an inside/outside nesting relation. Class headers have this form:

class List<data **outside owner**> { ... }

Each class has at least two owner parameters, this and owner, which represent the representation of the current object and the representation of the owner of the current object, respectively. In the example above, the List class has an additional permission to reference objects owned by data, which is nested outside owner. Types are formed by instantiating the owner parameters. For example, the *type* this:List<owner> denotes an object belonging to the representation of the current this and has the right to reference objects owned by owner. There are two nesting relations between owners: inside and outside. They each exist in two forms: one reflexive (inside/outside) and one non-reflexive (strictlyinside/strictlyoutside). Going back to our list example, a type this:List<this> denotes a list object belonging to the current representation (first this), storing objects of the current representation (second this).

Apart from ownership types, the key ingredients in Joe₃ are the following:

- unique types (written unique:Object[2]), a special *borrowing* construct for temporarily treating a unique type non-uniquely, and *owner casts* for converting unique references permanently into normal references.
- modes on owners—mutable '+', read-only '-', and immutable '*'. These appear on formal owner parameters of classes and methods, though not on types.
- an effects revocation clause on methods that states which owners will not be modified in a method. An object's default set of rights is derived from the modes on the owner parameters in the class declaration.

2.1 Motivating Examples

A Mutable List with Readonly Content. Figure 1 shows parts of an implementation of a list class. The owner parameter data is decorated with the mode read-only (denoted '-'), indicating that the list will never cause write effects to objects owned by data. The owner of the list is called owner and is implicitly declared. The method getFirst() is annotated with revoke owner, which means that the method will not modify the list or its transitive state. This means the same as if owner- and this- would have appeared in the class head. This allows the method to be called from objects where the list owner is read-only.

This list class can be instantiated in four different ways, depending on the access rights to the owners in the type held by the current context:

- both the list and its data objects are immutable, which only allows getFirst() to be invoked, and its resulting object is immutable;
- both are mutable, which imposes no additional restrictions;
- the list is mutable but the data objects are not, which imposes no additional restrictions, getFirst() returns a read-only reference; and
- the data objects are mutable, but the list not, which only allows getFirst() to be invoked, and the resulting object is mutable.

The last form is interesting and relies on the fact that we can specify, thanks to ownership types, that the data objects are not part of the representation of the list. Most existing proposals for read-only references (*e.g.*, Islands [18], JAC [19], ModeJava [27], Javari [29], and IGJ [32]) cannot express this constraint in a satisfactory way, as these proposals cannot distinguish between an object's outside and inside.

---

[2] Sometimes we use unique[p]:Object where the owner p acts as a bound for ownership transfer. Uniqueness is *external* [13] meaning we permit *internal* aliases to the unique object.

Context-Based Read-Only. As shown in Figure 2, different clients of the list can have different views of the same list at the same time. The class Reader does not have permission to mutate the list, but has no restrictions on mutating the list elements. Dually, the Writer class can mutate the list but not its elements.

As owner modes only reflect what a class is allowed to do to objects with a certain owner, Writer can add data objects to the list that are read-only to itself and the list, but writable by Example and Reader. This is a powerful and flexible idea. For example, Example can pass the list to Writer to filter out certain objects in the list. Writer can then consume or change the list, or copy its contents to another list, *but not modify them.* Writer can then return the list to Example, without Example losing its right to modify the objects obtained from the returned list. This is similar to the context-based read-only in Universes-based systems [24,23]. In contrast, however, we do not allow representation exposure via read-only references.

```
class Link<data- strictlyoutside owner> {
  data:Object obj = null;
  owner:Link<data> next = null;
}

class List<data- strictlyoutside owner> {
  this:Link<data> first = null;
  void addFirst(data:Object obj) {
    this:Link<data> tmp = new this:Link<data>();
    tmp.obj = obj;
    tmp.next = this.first;
    this.first = tmp;
  }
  void filter(data:Object obj) {
    this:Link<data> tmp = this.first;
    if (tmp == null) return;
    while (tmp.next != null)
      if (tmp.next.obj == obj)
        tmp.next = tmp.next.next;
      else
        tmp = tmp.next;
    if (this.first != null && this.first.obj == obj)
      this.first = this.first.next;
  }
  data:Object getFirst() revoke owner {
    return this.first.obj;
  }
}
```

Fig. 1. Fragment of a list class. As the data owner parameter is declared read-only (via '-') in the class header, no method in List may modify an object owned by data. Observe that the syntactic overhead is minimal for an ownership types system.

```
class Writer<o+ outside owner, data- strictlyoutside o> {
  void mutateList(o:List<data> list) {
    list.addFirst(new data:Object());
  }
}
class Reader<o- outside owner, data+ strictlyoutside o> {
  void mutateElements(o:List<data> list) {
    list.elementAt(0).mutate();
  }
}
class Example {
  void example() {
    this:List<world> list = new this:List<world>();
    this:Writer<this, world> w = new this:Writer<this, world>();
    this:Reader<this, world> r = new this:Reader<this, world>();
    w.mutateList(list);
    r.mutateElements(list);
  }
}
```

Fig. 2. Different views of the same list can exist at the same time. r can modify the elements of list but not the list itself, w can modify the list object, but not the list's contents, and instances of Example can modify both the list and its contents.

Borrowing Blocks and Owner-polymorphic Methods. Before moving on to the last two examples, we need to introduce borrowing blocks and owner-polymorphic methods [12,30,9], which make it easier to program using unique references and ownership. (The interaction between unique references, borrowing, and owner-polymorphic methods has been studied thoroughly by Clarke and Wrigstad [13,30].) A borrowing block has the following syntax:

$$\text{borrow } \textit{lval} \text{ as } \alpha\, x \text{ in } \{ \, s \, \}$$

The borrowing operation destructively reads a unique reference from an l-value *lval* to a non-unique, stack-local variable x for the scope of the block s. The block also introduces a fresh stack-local block-scoped owner that becomes the new owner of the borrowed value. Every type of every variable or field that stores an alias to the borrowed value must have this owner in its type. As the fresh owner is introduced on the stack, the only way to export it is by passing the owner around as an *owner parameter* (see below). If exported, the owner is still confined to the stack and as all method calls in the borrowing block must have returned when the block exits, the exported permission is invalidated so no residual aliasing can exist. Thus, when the borrowing block exits, the borrowed value can be reinstated and is once again unique.

An owner-polymorphic method is simply a method which takes owners as parameters. The methods m1 and m2 in Client in Figure 3 are examples of such. Owner-polymorphic methods can be seen as accepting stack-local permissions to reference (and possibly mutate) objects that it otherwise may not be allowed to

```
class Client {
  <p* inside world> void m1(p:Object obj) {
    obj.mutate(); // Error
    obj.toString(); // Ok
    // assign to field is not possible
  }
  <p- inside world> void m2(p:Object obj) {
    obj.mutate(); // Error
    obj.toString(); // Ok
  }
}
class Fractional<o+ outside owner> {
  unique[this]:Object obj = new this:Object();
  void example(o:Client c) {
    borrow obj as p*:tmp in { // **
      c.m1(tmp); // ***
      c.m2(tmp); // ****
    }
  }
}
```

Fig. 3. Fractional permissions using borrowing and unique references

reference. Owner parameters ($p*$ and $p-$ in the methods in Figure 3) of owner-polymorphic methods are not in the scope at the class level. Thus, method arguments with such a parameter in its type cannot be captured within the method body (it is *borrowed* [5]).

Immutability. The example in Figure 2 shows that a read-only reference to an object does not preclude the existence of mutable references to the same object elsewhere in the system. This allows observational exposure—for good and evil. The immutability annotation '$*$' imposes all the restrictions a read-only type has, but it also guarantees that no aliases with write permission exist in the system. Our simple way of creating an immutable object is to move a *unique* reference into a variable with immutable type, just as in SafeJava [4]. This allows us to encode fractional permissions using our borrowing construct and do staged construction of immutables.

Fractional Permissions. The example in Figure 3 shows an implementation of Fractional Permissions. We can use Joline's borrowing construct to *temporarily* move a mutable unique reference into an immutable variable (line $**$), freely alias the reference (while preserving read-only) (lines $***$ and $****$), and then implicitly move the reference back into the unique variable again and make it mutable. This is essentially Boyland's Fractional Permissions [6]. As stated above, both the owner-polymorphic methods and the borrowing block guarantee not to capture the reference. A borrowed reference can be aliased any number of times in any context to which it has been exported, without the need to keep track of "split permissions" [6] as we know for sure that all permissions to alias

```
class Client<p* outside owner, data+ strictlyoutside p> {
  void method() {
    this:Factory<p, data> f = new this:Factory<p, data>();
    p:List<data> immutable = f.createList();
  }
}
class Factory<p* inside world, data+ strictlyoutside p> {
  p:List<data> createList() {
    unique[p]:List<data> list = new p:List<data>();
    borrow list as temp+ l in { // 2nd stage of construct.
      l.add(new data:Object());
    }
    return list--; // unique reference returned
  }
}
```

Fig. 4. Staged construction of an immutable list

the pointer are invalidated when the borrowing block exits. The price of this convenience is that the conversion from mutable to immutable and back again must be done in the same place.

Interestingly, m1 and m2 are equally safe to call from example. Both methods have revoked their right to cause write effects to objects owned by p, indicated by the * and - annotations on p, respectively. The difference between the two methods is that the first method knows that obj will not change under foot (making it safe to, for example, use obj as a key in a hash table), whereas the second method cannot make such an assumption.

Initialisation of Immutable Objects. Immutable objects need to be mutated in their construction phase. Unless caution is taken the constructor might leak a reference to this (by passing this to a method) or mutate other immutable objects of the same class. The standard solution to this problem in related proposals is to limit the construction phase to the constructor [29,32,17]. Continuing initialisation by calling auxiliary methods *after* the constructor returns is simply not possible. Joe[3], on the other hand, permits *staged construction*, as we demonstrate in Figure 4. In this example a client uses a factory to create an immutable list. The factory creates a unique list and populates it. The list is then destructively read and returned to the caller as an immutable.

Annotating owners at the level of references rather than types is a trade-off. Rather than permitting distinctions to be made using modes on a per reference basis, we admit only per class granularity. Some potential expressiveness is lost, though the effects revocation clauses regain some expressiveness that per reference modes would give. Another virtue of using per class rather than per reference modes is that we avoid some covariance problems found in other proposals (see related work), as what you can do with a reference depends on the context and is not a property of the reference. Furthermore, our proposal

$$
\begin{array}{lcll}
P & ::= & \overline{C} & \text{(program)} \\
C & ::= & \texttt{class } c\langle \overline{\alpha\,\mathsf{R}\,p} \rangle \,\{\ \overline{fd}\ \overline{md}\ \} & \text{(class)} \\
fd & ::= & t\,f := e; & \text{(field)} \\
md & ::= & \langle \overline{\alpha\,\mathsf{R}\,p} \rangle\,t\,m(\overline{t\,x})\,\texttt{revoke}\,E\,\{\ s;\texttt{return } e\ \} & \text{(method)} \\
e & ::= & lval \mid lval\text{--} \mid e.m(\overline{e}) \mid \texttt{new}\,p\,c\langle\sigma\rangle \mid \texttt{null} & \text{(expression)} \\
s & ::= & lval := e \mid t\,x := e \mid s;s \mid e \mid \texttt{borrow}\,lval\,\texttt{as}\,\alpha\,x\,\texttt{in}\,\{\,s\,\} & \text{(statement)} \\
lval & ::= & x \mid e.f & \text{(l-value)} \\
\mathsf{R} & ::= & \prec^{*} \mid \succ^{*} \mid \prec^{+} \mid \succ^{+} & \text{(nesting relation)} \\
t & ::= & p\,c\langle\overline{p}\rangle \mid \texttt{unique}_{p}\,c\langle\overline{p}\rangle & \text{(type)} \\
E & ::= & \epsilon \mid E,p & \text{(write right revocation clause)} \\
\Gamma & ::= & \epsilon \mid \Gamma,x:t \mid \Gamma,\alpha\,\mathsf{R}\,p & \text{(environment)} \\
\sigma & ::= & \overline{\alpha \mapsto p} & \text{(owner substitution)} \\
\alpha & ::= & p\text{-} \mid p\text{+} \mid p\star & \text{(owner param.)}
\end{array}
$$

Fig. 5. Abstract syntax of Joe$_3$. In the code examples, owner nesting relations (R) are written as inside ($\prec^{*}$), or strictly-inside ($\prec^{+}$), etc. for clarity.

is statically checkable in a modular fashion and no run-time representation of modes or owners is required.

3 A Formal Definition of Joe$_3$

In this section, we formally present the static semantics of Joe$_3$.

3.1 Joe$_3$'s Static Semantics

Joe$_3$'s type system is a simplification of Joline's [13,30] extended with effects and modes on owners. To simplify the formal account, we omit inheritance and constructors. Both are straightforward, and are supported by our Joe$_3$ compiler. Furthermore, following Joline, we rely on destructive reads to preserve uniqueness and require that ownership transfer is performed using an explicit operation.

Figure 5 shows Joe$_3$'s syntax. c, m, f, x are metavariables ranging over names of uniquely named classes, methods, fields and local variables, respectively. Types have the syntax $p\,c\langle\overline{p}\rangle$ and we use q and p for owner names. We sometimes write $p\,c\langle\sigma\rangle$ for some type where σ is a map from the names of the owner parameters in the declaration of a class c to the actual owners used in the type. In code, a type's owner is connected to the class name with a ':'.

Unique types have the syntax $\texttt{unique}_{p}\,c\langle\overline{p}\rangle$. The keyword unique specifies that the owner of an object is really the field or variable that contains the only (external) reference to it in the system.

In systems with ownership types, an owner is a permission to reference objects with that owner. Classes, such as the canonical list example, can be parameterised with owners to enable them to be given permission to access external objects. For example, the list class has an owner parameter for the (external) data objects of the list. In Joe$_3$ the owner parameters of a class or owner-polymorphic method also carry information about what effects *the current context may cause on* the objects having the owner in question. For example, if $p-$ (p is read-only) appears in some context c, this means that c may reference objects owned by p, but not modify them directly. We refer to the part of an owner that controls its modification rights as the *mode*.

In contrast with related effect systems (*e.g.*, [16,10]), we use effect annotations on methods to show what is *not* affected by the method—essentially *temporarily revoking* rights. For example, getFirst() in the list in Figure 1 does not modify the list object and is thus declared using a revoke clause:

```
data:Object getFirst() revoke owner { ... }
```

This will force the method body to type-check in an environment where owner (and this) are read-only.

Notation. Given σ—a map from annotated owner parameters to actual owners— let σ^p mean $\sigma \uplus \{\text{owner+} \mapsto p\}$. For the type this:List<owner>, $\sigma = \{\text{owner+} \mapsto \text{this}, \text{data-} \mapsto \text{owner}\}$. We write $\sigma(p\,c\langle\overline{p}\rangle)$ to mean $\sigma(p)\,c\langle\sigma(\overline{p})\rangle$. For simplicity, we sometimes disregard modes and allow $\sigma(p)$. Also, σ° denotes a mode preserving variant of σ s.t. if $q+ \mapsto p \in \sigma$, then $q+ \mapsto p+$ in σ°.

Let $\mathsf{md}(\alpha)$ and $\mathsf{nm}(\alpha)$ return the mode and owner name of α, respectively. For example, if $\alpha = p+$, then $\mathsf{md}(\alpha) = +$ and $\mathsf{nm}(\alpha) = p$.

CT is a class table computed from a program P. It maps class names to type information for fields and methods in the class body. $\mathsf{CT}(c)(f) = t$ means that field f in class c has type t. $\mathsf{CT}(c)(m) = \forall \overline{\alpha\,R\,q}.\overline{t} \to t; E$ means that method m in class c have formal owner-parameters declared $\overline{\alpha\,R\,q}$, formal parameter types $\overline{t}$, return type t and set of revoked rights E. $E \setminus E'$ denotes set difference.

Predicate isunique(t) is true iff t is a unique type. owner(t) returns the owner of a type, and owners(t) returns the owner names used in a type or a method type. Thus, owner($p\,c\langle\overline{p}\rangle) = p$ and owners($p\,c\langle\overline{p}\rangle) = \{p\} \cup \overline{p}$.

E_c denotes the set of owners to which class c has *write* permission. For example, the list class in Figure 1 has $E_{\text{List}} = \{\text{owner}\}$, whereas the writer class in Figure 2 has $E_{\text{Writer}} = \{\text{owner}, \text{o}\}$. E_c is defined thus:

$$E_c = \begin{cases} \{p \mid p+ \in \overline{\alpha}\} \cup \{\text{owner}\} & \text{if class } c\langle\overline{\alpha\,R\_}\rangle \{ \_ \} \in P \\ \bot & \text{otherwise} \end{cases}$$

Good Class. A class is well-formed if all its owner parameters are outside owner. This ensures that a class can only be given permission to reference external objects and is key to preserving the owners-as-dominators property of deep ownership systems [9]. The environment Γ is constructed from the owners in the class header, their nesting relations and modes, plus owner+ and this+ giving an object the right to modify itself. Thus, class-wide read/write permissions are encoded in Γ, and must be respected by field declarations and methods.

$$(\text{CLASS})$$
$$\frac{\begin{array}{c} \Gamma = \text{owner+} \prec^* \text{world}, \text{this+} \prec^+ \text{owner}, \overline{\alpha\,R\,p}, \text{this}:t \\ t = \text{owner}\,c\langle\overline{\mathsf{nm}(\alpha)}\rangle \quad \Gamma \vdash \text{owner+} \prec^* \overline{\mathsf{nm}(\alpha)} \quad \Gamma \vdash \overline{fd} \quad \Gamma \vdash \overline{md} \end{array}}{\vdash \text{class } c\langle\overline{\alpha\,R\,p}\rangle \{ \overline{fd\ md} \}}$$

Good Field, Good Method. The function $\Gamma \operatorname{rev} E$ is a key player in our system—it revokes the write rights mentioned in E, by converting them to read rights in Γ. It also makes sure that this is not writable whenever owner is not. For ex., given $E = \{p\}$, if $\Gamma \operatorname{rev} E \vdash s; \Gamma'$, s cannot write to objects owned by p.

$$\epsilon \operatorname{rev} E = \epsilon \qquad\qquad\qquad p\text{-} \operatorname{rev} E = p\text{-}$$
$$(\Gamma, x : t) \operatorname{rev} E = (\Gamma \operatorname{rev} E), x : t \qquad p\text{+} \operatorname{rev} E = p\text{-},\ \text{if } p \in E \text{ else } p\text{+}$$
$$(\Gamma, \alpha \operatorname{R} p) \operatorname{rev} E = (\Gamma \operatorname{rev} E), (\alpha \operatorname{R} p \operatorname{rev} E) \qquad \text{this+} \operatorname{rev} E = \text{this-},\ \text{if } \mathbf{owner} \in E \text{ else this+}$$
$$(\alpha \operatorname{R} p) \operatorname{rev} E = (\alpha \operatorname{rev} E) \operatorname{R} p \qquad\qquad p\text{\textasteriskcentered} \operatorname{rev} E = p\text{\textasteriskcentered}$$

$$\text{(FIELD)} \qquad\qquad\qquad\qquad \text{(METHOD)}$$
$$\frac{\Gamma \vdash e : t}{\Gamma \vdash t\, f := e} \qquad \frac{\Gamma' = \Gamma, \overline{\alpha \operatorname{R} p} \quad \Gamma' \vdash E \quad (\Gamma' \operatorname{rev} E), \overline{x : t} \vdash s; \Gamma'' \quad \Gamma'' \vdash e : t}{\Gamma \vdash \langle \overline{\alpha \operatorname{R} p} \rangle\, t\, m(\overline{t\, x})\, \mathbf{revoke}\, E\, \{\ s; \mathbf{return}\ e\ \}}$$

A field declaration is well-formed if its initialising expression has the appropriate type. The rules for good method is more complex: any additional owner parameters in the method header are added to Γ, with modes and nesting, and the effect clause must be valid: can only revoke rights that you own.

Expressions. The expression rules extend Joline's semantics with permissions.

$$\text{(EXPR-LVAL)} \qquad\qquad\qquad \text{(EXPR-LVAL-DREAD)}$$
$$\frac{\Gamma \vdash_{\mathsf{lv}} lval : t \quad \neg \mathsf{isunique}(t)}{\Gamma \vdash lval : t} \qquad \frac{\Gamma \vdash_{\mathsf{lv}} lval : t \quad \mathsf{isunique}(t) \quad lval \equiv e.f \Rightarrow \Gamma \vdash e : p\,c\langle \sigma \rangle \wedge \Gamma \vdash p\text{+}\ perm}{\Gamma \vdash lval\text{--} : t}$$

Destructively reading a field in an object owned by some owner p requires that p+ is in the environment.

$$\text{(EXPR-VAR)} \qquad\qquad\qquad\qquad \text{(EXPR-FIELD)}$$
$$\frac{x : t \in \Gamma}{\Gamma \vdash_{\mathsf{lv}} x : t} \qquad \frac{\Gamma \vdash e : p\,c\langle \sigma \rangle \quad \mathsf{CT}(c)(f) = t \quad \mathbf{this} \in \mathsf{owners}(t) \Rightarrow e \equiv \mathbf{this}}{\Gamma \vdash_{\mathsf{lv}} e.f : \sigma^p(t)}$$

Judgements of the form $\Gamma \vdash_{\mathsf{lv}} lval : t$ deal with l-values.

In Joline, owner arguments to owner-polymorphic methods must be passed in explicitly. Here, we assume an inference algorithm exists to bind the names of the owner parameters to the actual arguments, σ_a below, at the call site.

$$\text{(EXPR-INVOKE)}$$
$$\frac{\begin{array}{c} \Gamma \vdash e : p\,c\langle \sigma \rangle \quad \mathsf{CT}(c)(m) = \forall \overline{\alpha \operatorname{R} p}.\overline{t} \to t; E \quad \sigma' = \sigma^p \uplus \sigma_a \\ \Gamma \vdash \sigma'(\overline{\alpha \operatorname{R} p}) \quad \Gamma \vdash \sigma'^\circ(\overline{\alpha})\ perm \quad \Gamma \vdash \overline{e} : \sigma'(\overline{t}) \quad \Gamma \vdash \sigma'(t) \\ \Gamma \vdash \sigma'(E_c \backslash E) \quad \mathbf{this} \in \mathsf{owners}(\mathsf{CT}(c)(m)) \Rightarrow e \equiv \mathbf{this} \end{array}}{\Gamma \vdash e.m(\overline{e}) : t}$$

By the first clause of (EXPR-INVOKE), method invocations are not allowed on unique types. The third clause creates a substitution from the type of the receiver

(σ^p) and the implicit mapping from owner parameter to actual owner (σ_a). $\Gamma \vdash \sigma'^\circ(\overline{\alpha})$ *perm* makes sure that owner parameters that are writable and immutable are instantiated with writable or immutable owners respectively. Clauses six and seven ensure that the argument expressions have the correct types and that the return type is valid. Clause eight checks that the method's effects are valid in in the current context, and clause nine makes sure that any method with this in its type (return types, argument types or owners in the owner parameters declaration) can only be invoked with this as receiver—this is the standard static visibility constraint of ownership types [11].

$$
\frac{(\text{EXPR-NULL})}{\Gamma \vdash \texttt{null} : t} \qquad \frac{(\text{EXPR-NEW})}{\Gamma \vdash \texttt{new } p\,c\langle\overline{p}\rangle : \texttt{unique}_p\,c\langle\overline{p}\rangle}
$$

By (EXPR-NEW), object creation results in unique objects. (Without constructors, it is obviously the case that the returned reference is unique—see Wrigstad's dissertation [30] for an explanation why adding constructors is not a problem.)

Good Statements

$$
\frac{(\text{STAT-LOCAL-ASGN})}{\begin{array}{c} x \neq \texttt{this} \\ x : t \in \Gamma \quad \Gamma \vdash e : t \\ \hline \Gamma \vdash x := e; \Gamma \end{array}} \qquad \frac{(\text{STAT-FIELD-ASGN})}{\begin{array}{c} \Gamma \vdash e : p\,c\langle\sigma\rangle \quad \mathsf{CT}(c)(f) = t \quad \Gamma \vdash e' : \sigma^p(t) \\ \Gamma \vdash p+ \; perm \quad \texttt{this} \in \mathsf{owners}(t) \Rightarrow e \equiv \texttt{this} \\ \hline \Gamma \vdash e.f := e'; \Gamma \end{array}}
$$

Assigning to a field requires write permission to the object containing the field.

$$
\frac{(\text{STAT-BORROW})}{\begin{array}{c} \textit{lval} \equiv e.f \Rightarrow \Gamma \vdash e : q\,c'\langle\_\rangle \wedge \Gamma \vdash q+ \; perm \\ \Gamma \vdash \textit{lval} : \texttt{unique}_p\,c\langle\sigma\rangle \quad \Gamma, \alpha \prec^+ p, x : \mathsf{nm}(\alpha)\,c\langle\sigma\rangle \vdash s; \Gamma \\ \hline \Gamma \vdash \texttt{borrow } \textit{lval} \texttt{ as } \alpha\,x \texttt{ in } \{\ s\ \}; \Gamma \end{array}}
$$

In our system, unique references must be borrowed before they can be used as receivers of method calls or field accesses. The borrowing operation moves the unique object from the source l-value to a stack-local variable temporarily and introduces a fresh owner ordered strictly inside the unique object's movement bound. The new owner is annotated with a read/write permission which must be respected by the body of the borrowing block. As the owner of the borrowed unique goes out of scope when the borrowing block exits, all fields or variables with types that can refer to the borrowed object become inaccessible. Thus, the borrowed value can be reinstated and is once again unique. As borrowing temporarily nullifies the borrowed l-value, the same requirements as (EXPR-DREAD) applies with respect to modifying the owner of the l-value.

$$
\frac{(\text{STAT-SEQUENCE})}{\begin{array}{c} \Gamma \vdash s; \Gamma' \quad \Gamma' \vdash s'; \Gamma'' \\ \hline \Gamma \vdash s; s'; \Gamma'' \end{array}} \qquad \frac{(\text{STAT-DECL})}{\begin{array}{c} \Gamma \vdash e : t \quad x \notin \mathrm{dom}(\Gamma) \\ \hline \Gamma \vdash t\,x := e; \Gamma, x : t \end{array}}
$$

Good Effects Clause revokes write permissions from the current environment.

$$\text{(GOOD-EFFECT)}$$
$$\frac{\forall p \in E.\ \Gamma \vdash p\text{+}\ perm}{\Gamma \vdash E}$$

Good Environment. The rules for good environment require that owner variables are related to some owner already present in the environment or world, and that added variable bindings have types that are well-formed, as usual.

$$\text{(GOOD-EMPTY)} \qquad\qquad \text{(GOOD-R)} \qquad\qquad\qquad\qquad \text{(GOOD-VARTYPE)}$$
$$\frac{}{\epsilon \vdash \diamond} \qquad \frac{\Gamma \vdash q \quad p \notin \operatorname{dom}(\Gamma) \quad \dagger \in \{+,-,\ast\}}{\Gamma, p\dagger\,\mathsf{R}\,q \vdash \diamond} \qquad \frac{\Gamma \vdash t \quad x \notin \operatorname{dom}(\Gamma)}{\Gamma, x : t \vdash \diamond}$$

Good Permissions and Good Owner. By (WORLD), world is a good owner and is always writable. By (GOOD-α), a permission is good if it is in the environment. By (GOOD-p-), a read mode of objects owned by some owner p is good if p with any permission is a good permission—write or immutable implies read.

$$\text{(WORLD)} \qquad \text{(GOOD-}\alpha\text{)} \qquad\qquad \text{(GOOD-}p\text{-)} \qquad\qquad \text{(GOOD-OWNER)}$$
$$\frac{\Gamma \vdash \diamond}{\Gamma \vdash \mathsf{world}\text{+}\ perm} \quad \frac{\Gamma \vdash \diamond \quad \alpha \in \operatorname{dom}(\Gamma)}{\Gamma \vdash \alpha\ perm} \quad \frac{\Gamma \vdash p\dagger\ perm \quad \dagger \in \{+,\ast\}}{\Gamma \vdash p\text{-}\ perm} \quad \frac{\Gamma \vdash \alpha\ perm}{\Gamma \vdash \mathsf{nm}(\alpha)}$$

Good Nesting. Judgements $\Gamma \vdash p \prec^\ast q$ and $\Gamma \vdash p \prec^+ q$ are the reflexive transitive closure and the transitive closure, respectively, of the relation generated from each $\alpha\,\mathsf{R}\,p \in \Gamma$, where $\mathsf{R}, \mathsf{R}^{-1} \in \{\prec^\ast, \prec^+\}$, combined with $p \prec^\ast \mathsf{world}$ for all p.

Good Type. This rule checks that the owner parameters of the type satisfy the ordering declared in the class header, and that all the permissions are valid in the present context. In addition, if an owner parameter in the class header was declared with the mode immutable, then the owner that instantiates the parameter in the type must also be immutable. Without this requirement, one could pass non-immutable objects where immutable objects are expected. On the other hand, we allow parameters with read to be instantiated with write and *vice versa*. In the latter case, only methods that do not have write effects on the owners in question may be invoked on a receiver with the type in point.

$$\text{(TYPE)}$$
$$\frac{q\ast \in \overline{\alpha} \Rightarrow \sigma^\circ(q\ast) = p\ast,\ \text{for some } p}{\quad\text{class } c\langle \overline{\alpha\,\mathsf{R}\,p}\rangle\ \{\ \dots\ \} \in P \quad \Gamma \vdash \sigma^p(\overline{\alpha\,\mathsf{R}\,p}) \quad \Gamma \vdash \sigma^{p\circ}(\overline{\alpha})\ perm \quad}{\Gamma \vdash p\,c\langle\sigma\rangle}$$

$$\text{(UNIQUE-TYPE)} \qquad\qquad\qquad \text{(EXPR-LOSE-UNIQUENESS)}$$
$$\frac{\Gamma \vdash p\,c\langle\sigma\rangle}{\Gamma \vdash \mathsf{unique}_p\,c\langle\sigma\rangle} \qquad \frac{\Gamma \vdash e : \mathsf{unique}_q\,c\langle\sigma\rangle \quad \Gamma \vdash p \prec^\ast q}{\Gamma \vdash (p)\ e : p\,c\langle\sigma\rangle}$$

By (UNIQUE-TYPE), a unique type is well-formed if a non-unique type with the movement bound as owner is well-formed. To simplify the formal account, we chose to make loss of uniqueness explicit using a cast-like operation in (EXPR-LOSE-UNIQUENESS). Allowing it to be implicit via subtyping and subsumption would require a destructive read to be inserted. The (EXPR-LVAL) rules ensure that the e is really free, not simply unique.

3.2 Potentially Identical Owners with Different Modes

The list class in Figure 1 requires that the owner of its data objects is strictly outside the owner of the list itself. This allows for a clearer separation of the objects on the heap: for example, the list cannot contain itself. The downside of defining the list class in this fashion is that it becomes impossible to store representation objects in a list that is also part of the representation. To allow that, the list class head must not use *strictly* outside:

class List< data- **outside owner** > { ... }

The less constraining nesting however leads to another problem: data and owner may be instantiated with the same owners. As data is read-only and owner is mutable, at face value, this might seem like a problem.

We choose to allow this situation as the context where the type appears might not care, or might have additional information to determine that the actual owners of data and the list do not overlap. If no such information is available, we could simply issue a warning. Of course, it is always possible to define different lists with different list heads for the two situations.

For immutables, this is actually a non-problem. The only way an immutable owner can be introduced into the system is through borrowing (or regions, see Section 4.1) where the immutable owner is ordered strictly inside any other known owner. As (TYPE) requires that write and immutable owner parameters are instantiated with owners that are write and immutable (respectively) in the context where the type appears, a situation where $p+$ and $q*$ could refer to the same owner is impossible. As (TYPE) allows a read owner parameter to be instantiated with any mode, it is possible to have overlapping $p-$ and $q*$ in a context if a read owner was instantiated by an immutable at some point. Since objects owned by read owners will not be mutated, immutability holds.

3.3 Invariants and Meta Theory

Due to space restriction, our formalisation of Joe_3 does not include a dynamic semantics, which makes formal invariants difficult to state. However, the formal description of Joe_3 is a small extension of Joline [30] and as modes have no run-time semantics, adapting the soundness results and encapsulation and uniqueness invariants of Joline is relatively straightforward. Here we state our invariants informally and defer their formal definitions and proof to future work:

For immutables, the invariant Joe_3 enforces is that an object referenced by an immutable reference cannot change as a result of evaluating any statement.

For read-only references, Joe_3 guarantees that evaluating a statement can only result in changes to a read-only referenced object if there existed a mutable alias to the object reachable by the statement.

The important encapsulation properties of Joline that carry over to Joe$_3$ are owners-as-dominators, which says that accesses to an object's internals must go via it's interface and external-uniqueness-as-dominating-edges which says that any path from a root to a unique object's internals must go via the unique reference to the object.

3.4 Joe$_3$ Compiler

We have implemented Joe$_3$ as an extension of our Joline compiler, using the Polyglot compiler framework. The compiler has been tested on moderately sized programs with promising results. Future work will involve further evaluation using larger programs.

4 Extensions and Encodings

4.1 Object-Based Regions and Method-Scoped Regions

To increase the precision of effects, we introduce explicitly declared regions, both at object-level and within method bodies. For simplicity, these are excluded from the formal account of the system. Object-based regions are similar to the regions of Greenhouse and Boyland [16] and the domains of Aldrich and Chambers [1], but we enable an ordering between them. Our method-scoped region construct is essentially the same as *scoped regions* in Joline [30], which is an object-oriented variant of classical regions [22,28], adapted to ownership types.

Object-based regions. As discussed in Section 3.2, defining the list class without the use of *strictly* outside places the burden of determining whether data objects are modified by changes to the list on the client of the list. This is because the list cannot distinguish itself from its data objects, as they might have the same owner. As the (static) list owner and data owner are the same, modifications to the list are indistinguishable from modification to its contents.

To tackle this problem and make our system more expressive, we extend Joe$_3$ with regions that introduce a new owner nested strictly inside an owner in the scope. Thus, a class' representation is divided into multiple, disjoint parts (except for nested regions), and an object owned by one region cannot be referenced by another. The syntax for regions is region α { e }. For example:

```
class Example {
  this:Object datum;
  region inner+ strictlyinside this { inner:List<this> list; }
  void method() { list.add(datum); }
}
```

Objects inside the region can be given permission to reference representation objects, but not vice versa (*e.g.*, this is not inside inner). Thus, rep objects outside a region cannot reference objects in the region, so effects on objects outside a region cannot propagate to objects inside it. Above, changes to datum cannot change list, as there are no references from datum to the list.

Method-scoped regions. The *scoped regions* construct in Joline [30] can be added to Joe₃ to enable the construction of method-scoped regions, which introduces a new owner for a temporary scope within some method body. Scoped regions allow the creation of stack-local objects which can be mutated regardless of what other rights exist in the context, even when this is read-only or immutable. Such objects act as local scratch space without requiring that the effects propagate outwards. This pattern occurred frequently in the implementation of the Joline compiler. Our compiler supports method-scoped regions thusly:

```
<d- inside world> void method(d:Something arg) revoke this {
  region temp+ strictlyinside this { ... }
}
```

4.2 Encoding Modes from Flexible Alias Protection

In work [26] that led to the invention of Ownership Types, Noble, Vitek and Potter suggested a set of modes on references to manage the effects of aliasing in object-oriented systems. The modes were *rep, free, var, arg* and *val*. In this section, we indicate how these modes are (partially) encoded in our system. The *rep* mode denotes a reference to a representation object that should not be leaked outside of the object. All ownership type systems encode *rep*; in ours, it is encoded as this $c\langle\sigma\rangle$. The *free* expression holds a reference that is uncaptured by any variable in the system. This is encoded as $\mathtt{unique}_p\, c\langle\sigma\rangle$, a unique type. Any l-value of that type in our system is (externally) free. The *var* mode denotes a mutable non-rep reference and is encoded as $p\, c\langle\sigma\rangle$, where this $\neq p$.

The *arg* mode is the most interesting of the modes. It denotes a reference to an external object with a guarantee that the underlying object will not be changed under foot: "that is, *arg* expressions only provide access to the immutable interface of the objects to which they refer. There are no restrictions upon the transfer or use of *arg* expressions around a program" [26]. We support *arg* modes in that we can parameterise a type by an immutable owner in any parameter. It is also possible for a class to declare all its owner parameters as immutable to prevent its instances from ever relying on a mutable argument object that could change under foot. On the other hand, we do not support passing *arg* objects around freely—the program must still respect owners-as-dominators.

The final mode, *val*, is like *arg*, but it is attached to references with value semantics. These are similar to our immutable classes.

5   Related Work

Boyland et al.'s Capabilities for sharing [8] generalise the concepts of uniqueness and immutability through capabilities. Their outstanding feature is the exclusive rights which allow the revocation of rights of other references. Boyland et al.'s system can model uniqueness with the ownership capability but exclusive rights make the system difficult to check statically.

Table 1. Brief overview of related work. OT=ownership types, OP=owner polymorphic, OAM=owners as modifiers, EO=Effective Ownership. [1]) not as powerful as there is no owner nesting; two non sibling lists cannot share *mutable* data elements; [2]) mutable fields can be used to store a reference to this and break read-only; [3]) see Section 4.2; [4]) no modes on owners, and hence no immutable parts of objects; [5]) none of the systems deal with value semantics for complex objects; [6]) if all methods of a class are read-only the class is effectively immutable; [7]) limited notion of contexts via this-mutability; [8]) allows breaking of owners-as-dominators with inner classes and it is unclear how this interplays with immutables.

Feature	Joe₃	SafeJava	Universes	Jimuva	Javari	IGJ	ModeJava	JAC	EO	Feature	Joe₃	SafeJava	Universes	Jimuva	Javari	IGJ	ModeJava	JAC	EO
Expressiveness										*Immutability*									
Staged const.	√	√	×	×	×	×	×	×	×	Class	√	×	×	√	√	√	×[6]	×[6]	×
Fract. perm.	√	×	×	×	×	×	×	×	×	Object	√	√	×	√	×	√	×	×	×
Non-rep fields	√	√[1]	√[1]	√[1]	×[2]	×[2]	×	×	×	Context-based	√	×	√	×	×[7]	×[7]	×[7]	×	×
										Read-only ref.	√	×	√	×	√	√	√	√	√
Flexible Alias Protection Modes										*Confinement and Alias Control*									
arg	√[3]	×[4]	×	×[4]	×[4]	×[4]	×[4]	×	×	OT	√	√	√	√	×	×	×	×	√
rep	√	√	√	√	×	×	×	×	√	OP meths	√	√	√	√	×	×	×	×	×
free	√	√	√	×	×	×	×	×	×	OAM	×	×[8]	√	×	×	×	×	×	√
val [5]	×	×	×	×	×	×	×	×	×	Unique	√	√	√	×	×	×	×	×	×
var	√	√	√	√	√	√	√	√	√										

Table 1 summarises several proposals and their supported features. The systems included in the table represent the state of the art of read-only and immutable. Except Joe₃, the table includes (in order) SafeJava [4], Universes [24,15,14,25], Jimuva [17], Javari [29], IGJ [32], JAC [19], ModeJava [27] and Effective Ownership [21]. We now discuss the different features in the table.

Expressiveness. Joe₃ and SafeJava support staged construction of immutables.

Figure 3 shows how we can encode fractional permissions [6]. Boyland suggests that copying rights may lead to observational exposure and proposes that the rights instead be split. Only the one with a complete set of rights may modify an object. SafeJava does not support borrowing to immutables and hence cannot model fractional permissions. It is unclear how allowing borrowing to immutables in SafeJava would affect the system, especially in the presence of back doors that break encapsulation.

To be able to retrieve writable objects from a read-only list, the elements in the list cannot be part of the list's representation. Joe₃, Universes, Jimuva and SafeJava can express this through ownership types. Only our system, thanks to owner nesting information, allow two non-sibling lists sharing mutable data elements. Javari and IGJ allow this through ad-hoc mutable fields which can circumvent read-only if an object stores a reference to itself in a mutable field.

Flexible Alias Protection Modes (also see Section 4.2). The *rep* mode denotes a reference belonging to an object's representation and so should not appear in its interface. A defensive interpretation of *arg* is that all systems that have object or class immutability partially support *arg*, but only our system support *parts* of an object being immutable. The *free* mode, interpreted as being equal to uniqueness, is supported by Joe$_3$ and SafeJava. No system handles *value* semantics except for primitive types. The *var* aliasing mode expresses non-*rep* references which may be aliased and changed freely as long as they do not interfere with the other modes, for example, in assignments.

Immutability. Immutability takes on three forms: *class immutability*, where no instance of a specific class can be mutable, *object immutability*, where no reference to a specific object can be mutable and *read-only* or *reference immutability*, where there may be both mutable and read-only aliases to a specific object. Explicit class immutability could easily be added to Joe$_3$ by introducing an immutable class annotation that would revoke owner and this.

Universes and Joe$_3$ provide what we call context-based immutability. Here it is possible to create a writable list with writable elements and pass it to some other context where the elements are read-only. This other context can add elements to the list which will be writable by the original creator of the list. The other systems in our table do not support this as they cannot allow *e.g.,* a list of writeables to be subsumed into a list of read-only references. In these systems, this practice could lead to standard covariance problems—adding a supertype to a list containing a subtype. Javari, IGJ and ModeJava all have a notion of this-mutable fields which inherit the mode of the accessing reference. This counts for some notion of context, albeit ad hoc and inflexible. In ModeJava a read-only list cannot return mutable elements. Javari and IGJ support this for elements are stored mutable fields, which opens the back door mentioned above.

Confinement and Alias Control. Joe$_3$, SafeJava, Universes and Jimuva all support ownership types. This is what gives Joe$_3$ and Universes its context-based immutability. SafeJava and Jimuva, despite having ownership types, do not have context-based immutability due to their lack of read-only references. Universes is the only system supporting the owners-as-mutators property, meaning that representation exposure is allowed for read-only references. Other approaches to confinement and alias control include Confined Types [3,31], which constrain access to objects to from within their *package*. Bierhoff and Aldrich recently proposed a modular protocol checking approach [2] based on typestates. They partly implement Boyland's fractional permissions [6] in their access permissions.

Object-Oriented Regions and Effects systems. Effect systems were first studied by Lucassen and Gifford [22] and Talpin and Jouvelot [28]. Leino [20], Greenhouse and Boyland [16] and (to some degree) Aldrich and Chambers [1] take a similar approach to dividing objects into regions, and using method annotations to specify which parts of an object may be modified by a specific method. Adding effects to ownership, à la Clarke and Drossopoulou's Joe$_1$ [10], gives a stronger notion of encapsulation and enables more accurate description of effects. The addition of scoped regions to our system (*cf.* §4.1), combines both of these approaches.

Effective Ownership. Lu and Potter's [21] work on Effective Ownership is similar in spirit to our work, especially wrt. effects on methods. Their goal is making ownership types more flexible, whereas we aim to express immutable and read-only idioms in an ownership types setting. Consequently, their system cannot express two objects owned by the same owner where only one is mutable nor context-based immutability, nor do they consider immutability or uniqueness.

6   Concluding Remarks

We have proposed Joe_3, an extension of Joe_1 and Joline with access modes on owners that can encode class, object and reference immutability, fractional permissions and context-based ownership with surprisingly little syntactical overhead. Future work will see a complete formalisation of the system, extended with inheritance and regions, including a dynamic semantics, and appropriate immutability invariants and soundness proofs.

References

1. Aldrich, J., Chambers, C.: Ownership domains: Separating aliasing policy from mechanism. In: Malenfant, J., Østvold, B.M. (eds.) ECOOP 2004. LNCS, vol. 3344. Springer, Heidelberg (2005)
2. Bierhoff, K., Aldrich, J.: Modular typestate checking of aliased objects. In: OOPSLA (2007)
3. Bokowski, B., Vitek, J.: Confined Types. In: OOPSLA (1999)
4. Boyapati, C.: SafeJava: A Unified Type System for Safe Programming. PhD thesis, Electrical Engineering and Computer Science. MIT (February 2004)
5. Boyland, J.: Alias burying: Unique variables without destructive reads. Software — Practice and Experience (2001)
6. Boyland, J.: Checking interference with fractional permissions. In: Static Analysis: 10th International Symposium (2003)
7. Boyland, J.: Why we should not add readonly to Java (yet). Journal of Object Technology (2006); Special issue: ECOOP 2005 Workshop FTfJP
8. Boyland, J., Noble, J., Retert, W.: Capabilities for Sharing: A Generalization of Uniqueness and Read-Only. In: Knudsen, J.L. (ed.) ECOOP 2001. LNCS, vol. 2072. Springer, Heidelberg (2001)
9. Clarke, D.: Object Ownership and Containment. PhD thesis, School of Computer Science and Engineering, University of New South Wales, Sydney, Australia (2001)
10. Clarke, D., Drossopoulou, S.: Ownership, encapsulation and the disjointness of type and effect. In: OOPSLA (2002)
11. Clarke, D., Potter, J., Noble, J.: Ownership types for flexible alias protection. In: OOPSLA (1998)
12. Clarke, D., Wrigstad, T.: External uniqueness. In: FOOL (2003)
13. Clarke, D., Wrigstad, T.: External uniqueness is unique enough. In: Cardelli, L. (ed.) ECOOP 2003. LNCS, vol. 2743. Springer, Heidelberg (2003)

14. Dietl, W., Drossopoulou, S., Müller, P.: Generic Universe Types. In: Ernst, E. (ed.) ECOOP 2007. LNCS, vol. 4609. Springer, Heidelberg (2007)
15. Dietl, W., Müller, P.: Universes: Lightweight Ownership for JML. Journal of Object Technology 4(8), 5–32 (2005)
16. Greenhouse, A., Boyland, J.: An object-oriented effects system. In: Guerraoui, R. (ed.) ECOOP 1999. LNCS, vol. 1628. Springer, Heidelberg (1999)
17. Haack, C., Poll, E., Schäfer, J., Schubert, A.: Immutable Objects for a Java-like Language. In: De Nicola, R. (ed.) ESOP 2007. LNCS, vol. 4421. Springer, Heidelberg (2007)
18. Hogg, J.: Islands: Aliasing protection in object-oriented languages. In: OOPSLA (November 1991)
19. Kniesel, G., Theisen, D.: JAC—access right based encapsulation for Java. Software — Practice and Experience (2001)
20. Leino, K.R.M.: Data Groups: Specifying the Modification of Extended State. In: OOPSLA (1998)
21. Lu, Y., Potter, J.: Protecting representation with effect encapsulation. In: POPL (2006)
22. Lucassen, J.M., Gifford, D.K.: Polymorphic effect systems. In: POPL (1988)
23. Müller, P.: Modular Specification and Verification of Object-Oriented Programs. PhD thesis, FernUniversität Hagen (2001)
24. Müller, P., Poetzsch-Heffter, A.: Universes: A type system for controlling representation exposure. Technical report, Fernuniversität Hagen (1999)
25. Müller, P., Rudich, A.: Ownership transfer in Universe Types. In: OOPSLA (2007)
26. Noble, J., Vitek, J., Potter, J.: Flexible alias protection. In: Jul, E. (ed.) ECOOP 1998. LNCS, vol. 1445. Springer, Heidelberg (1998)
27. Skoglund, M., Wrigstad, T.: Alias control with read-only references. In: Sixth Conference on Computer Science and Informatics (March 2002)
28. Talpin, J.-P., Jouvelot, P.: Polymorphic type, region and effect inference. Journal of Functional Programming (1992)
29. Tschantz, M.S., Ernst, M.D.: Javari: Adding reference immutability to Java. In: OOPSLA (2005)
30. Wrigstad, T.: Ownership-Based Alias Management. PhD thesis, Royal Institute of Technology, Kista, Stockholm (May 2006)
31. Zhao, T., Palsberg, J., Vitek, J.: Type-based confinement. Journal of Functional Programming 15(6) (2005)
32. Zibin, Y., Potanin, A., Artzi, S., Kieżun, A., Ernst, M.D.: Object and reference immutability using Java generics. Technical Report MIT-CSAIL-TR-2007-018, MITCSAIL (2007)

Object Incompleteness and Dynamic Composition in Java-Like Languages*

Lorenzo Bettini[1], Viviana Bono[1], and Betti Venneri[2]

[1] Dipartimento di Informatica, Università di Torino, bono@di.unito.it
[2] Dipartimento di Sistemi e Informatica, Università di Firenze,
{bettini,venneri}@dsi.unifi.it

Abstract. Object composition is often advocated as a more flexible alternative to standard class inheritance since it takes place at run-time, thus permitting the behavior of objects to be specialized dynamically. In this paper we present Incomplete Featherweight Java (IFJ), an extension of Featherweight Java with incomplete objects, i.e., objects that require some missing methods which can be provided at run-time by composition with another (complete) object. Incomplete object usage is disciplined by static typing, therefore the language enjoys type safety (which implies no "message-not-understood" run-time errors).

1 Introduction

Standard class-based object-oriented languages rely on class inheritance, method redefinition, and dynamic binding to achieve flexibility. However, these mechanisms may not suffice for representing the dynamic behavior of objects: all the possible scenarios may not be completely predictable in advance and they are likely to change after the software application has already been developed. With the aim of forecasting all the possible evolutions of the system entities, unfortunately classes are often designed with too many responsibilities, most of which are basically not used. Furthermore, the number of subclasses tends to grow dramatically when trying to compose different functionalities into single modules. In this respect, object composition is often advocated as an alternative to class inheritance, in that it is defined at run-time and it enables dynamic object code reuse by assembling existing components [19]. Furthermore, thanks to object composition, we can exploit a programming style that builds small software components (units of reuse), that can be composed in several ways to achieve software reuse (we refer to [26,15] and to the references therein for an insightful review of the limitations of inheritance).

On the other hand, object-based languages use object composition and *delegation*, a more flexible mechanism, to reuse code (see, e.g., the languages [27,20,12], and the calculi [18,1]). Every object has a list of *parent* objects: when an object cannot answer a message it forwards it to its parents until there is an instance that can process

---

* This work has been partially supported by the MIUR project EOS DUE and by EU Project Software Engineering for Service-Oriented Overlay Computers (SENSORIA, contract IST-3-016004-IP-09).

R.F. Paige and B. Meyer (Eds.): TOOLS EUROPE 2008, LNBIP 11, pp. 198–217, 2008.

the message. However, a drawback of delegation is that run-time type errors ("message-not-understood") can arise when no delegates are able to process the forwarded message [28]. In order to preserve the benefits of static type safety, several solutions have been proposed in the literature, such as design patterns [19] and language extensions integrating in class based languages more flexible mechanisms, such as, e.g., mixins [10], generic types [11], delegation (Kniesel [22] presents an overview of problems when combining delegation with static type discipline).

In this paper we present *Incomplete Featherweight Java* (IFJ), an extension of Featherweight Java [21,24] that combines the static type discipline of class-based languages with the flexibility of object-based ones. The programmer, besides standard classes, can define *incomplete* classes whose instances are *incomplete* objects that can be composed in an object-based fashion. Hence, in our calculus it is possible: (*i*) to instantiate standard classes, obtaining fully-fledged objects ready to be used; (*ii*) to instantiate incomplete classes, obtaining *incomplete objects* that can be composed (by *object composition*) with complete objects, thus yielding new complete objects at run-time. This provides a mechanism that is similar to a sort of dynamic inheritance since it implies both substitutivity (that is, a composed object can be used where a standard object is expected) and dynamic code reuse (since composition permits supplying at run-time the missing methods with those of other objects).

Therefore, we can model some features related to dynamic object evolution: while incomplete classes separate the object invariant behavior from the variant one at compile time, at run-time object composition customizes the unpredictable behavior based on dynamic conditions (for instance, the object state) in a type safe way. In particular, some behavior that was not foreseen when the class hierarchy was implemented might be supplied dynamically by making use of already existing objects, thus generating an unanticipated reuse of code and a sharing relationship of components.

Concerning the theory of incomplete objects, our main inspiration comes from [4]; however, while that calculus builds on top of the lambda calculus, here we aim at proving how object composition can fit within the basic principles of Java-like languages. This leads to some key design choices. Firstly, instead of employing structural subtyping as in [4], we keep the nominal subtyping mechanism that is typical of mainstream languages like Java and C++. This feature allows us to define an extension that is conservative with respect to the core Java, since it does not affect those parts of the programs that do not use incomplete objects. Furthermore, incomplete classes can rely on standard class inheritance to reuse code of parent classes (although this kind of inheritance does not imply subtyping). Thus incomplete objects provide two forms of code reuse: *vertical* (i.e., the code reuse achieved via standard class inheritance) and *horizontal* (i.e., the one achieved via object composition). Finally, in order to enhance run-time flexibility in composing objects we implicitly use structural subtyping during composition: an incomplete object can be composed with any object providing all the requested methods (the signatures must match) independently of the classes of these objects. Then the language extension we propose is not a simple automatic implementation of the object composition that one might implement manually. In fact, any object providing the required methods can be used in object completion, no matter what its class is. In case of a manual implementation, instead, the object should be stored in a class field thus forcing it to belong to a specific class hierarchy (see Section 2.2).

Concerning the semantics of method invocation on objects that are obtained by composition, our calculus implements *consultation* but not *delegation* (see Section 2.4), though in Section 5 we sketch an extension to delegation, the subject of future work. Let us note that, in the literature (e.g., [19]), the term *delegation*, originally introduced by Lieberman [23], is given different interpretations and it is often confused with the term *consultation* (sometimes simply called *forwarding*). In both cases an object *A* has a reference to an object *B*. However, when *A* forwards to *B* the execution of a message *m*, two different bindings of the implicit parameter this can be adopted for the execution of the body of *m*: with *delegation*, this is bound to the sender (*A*) thus, if in the body of the method *m* (defined in *B*) there is a call to a method *n*, then also this call will be executed binding this to *A*; with *consultation*, during the execution of the body the implicit parameter is always bound to the receiver *B*.

Our proposal also deals with possible additional methods (hidden by subsumption) that might rise the "width subtyping versus method addition" problem that is well known in the object-based setting (see, e.g., [18]). We solve this issue by representing objects as lists of subobjects in such a way that we can explicitly deal with the "scope" of a method invocation; we believe this solution is much more implementation oriented than the dictionaries of [25] and simpler than the one of [4].

Summarizing, our main intention is to have a language with a tradeoff between the dynamic flexibility that is typical of object-based languages and the static discipline of class-based languages. Objects are then still instances of classes (possibly incomplete classes) and they are still disciplined by the nominal subtyping, but they are also prototypes that can be used, via the object composition, to create new objects at run-time, while ensuring statically that the composition is type safe.

There are, in fact, settings in which it is important to exploit software units that are as simple as possible to facilitate reuse and, at the same time, flexible enough to enable dynamic reconfiguration and re-purposing. An example of such a scenario is the one of *learning objects* in the context of eLearning environments [9]. Standard learning objects are characterized by the lack of sufficient support for adaptive behavior. Therefore, a new view and implementation of adaptive learning objects may be obtained by exploiting incomplete objects that can be safely and independently used in different compositions. Foremost, these objects compositions are performed dynamically, i.e., at interaction time, since they can depend on information about the state or the history of the learner. Thus incomplete learning objects can satisfy basic software engineering principles, while providing the required pedagogical richness.

The calculus presented in this paper has a reduced set of features since we wanted to investigate the problem of safe and dynamic object composition in a core formal framework and to have a kernel language providing the basis for future enhancements and experiments with object compositions (some possible extensions are sketched in Section 5). We also wanted this core basis to be sound; in fact, our language enjoys the type safety property (see Section 3) which guarantees that in a well-typed program no "message-not-understood" can occur at run-time (this will also exclude possible run-time accesses to methods of an incomplete object).

$$\begin{array}{lll}
\text{L} ::= \text{class C extends C } \{\overline{\text{C}}\ \overline{\text{f}};\ \text{K};\ \overline{\text{M}}\} & & \text{classes} \\
\text{A} ::= \text{class C abstracts C } \{\overline{\text{C}}\ \overline{\text{f}};\ \text{K};\ \overline{\text{M}}\ \overline{\text{N}}\} & \text{incomplete classes} \\
\text{K} ::= \text{C}(\overline{\text{C}}\ \overline{\text{f}})\{\text{super}(\overline{\text{f}});\ \text{this.f}=\overline{\text{f}};\} & & \text{constructors} \\
\text{M} ::= \text{C m }(\overline{\text{C}}\ \overline{\text{x}})\{\text{return e};\} & & \text{methods} \\
\text{N} ::= \text{C m }(\overline{\text{C}}\ \overline{\text{x}}); & & \text{abstract methods} \\
\text{e} ::= \text{x} \mid \text{e.f} \mid \text{e.m}(\overline{\text{e}}) \mid \text{new C}(\overline{\text{e}}) \mid \text{e} \longleftarrow \text{e} & & \text{expressions} \\
\text{v} ::= \textbf{new C}(\overline{\textbf{v}}) :: \boldsymbol{\varepsilon} \mid \textbf{new C}(\overline{\textbf{v}}) :: \textbf{v} & & \text{values}
\end{array}$$

Fig. 1. IFJ syntax; run-time syntax appears shaded

2   Incomplete Featherweight Java

In this section we present syntax, typing and operational semantics of our proposal, the core language IFJ (*Incomplete Featherweight Java*), which is an extension of FJ (*Featherweight Java*) with incomplete objects. FJ [21,24] is a lightweight version of Java, which focuses on a few basic features: mutually recursive class definitions, inheritance, object creation, method invocation, method recursion through this, subtyping and field access[1]. Thus, the minimal syntax, typing and semantics make the type safety proof simple and compact, in such a way that FJ is a handy tool for studying the consequences of extensions and variations with respect to Java ("FJ's main application is modeling extensions of Java", [24], pag. 248). Although we assume the reader is familiar with FJ, we will briefly comment on the FJ part and then we will focus on the novel aspects introduced by IFJ.

The abstract syntax of IFJ constructs is given in Figure 1 and it is just the same as FJ extended with incomplete classes, abstract methods and object composition (and some run-time expressions that are not written by the programmer, but are produced by the semantics, that we will discuss later, Section 2.4). The metavariables B, C, D and E range over class names (both concrete and incomplete); M ranges over (standard) method definitions and N ranges over (abstract) method signatures; f and g range over attribute names; x ranges over method parameter names; e and d range over expressions and v and u range over values. As in FJ, we will use the overline notation for possibly empty sequences (e.g., "$\overline{\text{e}}$" is a shorthand for a possibly empty sequence "$\text{e}_1,\ldots,\text{e}_n$"). We abbreviate pair of sequences in a similar way, e.g., $\overline{\text{C}}\ \overline{\text{f}}$ stands for $\text{C}_1\ \text{f}_1,\ldots,\text{C}_n\ \text{f}_n$. The empty sequence is denoted by •. Following FJ, we assume that the set of variables includes the special variable this (implicitly bound in any method declaration), which cannot be used as the name of a method's formal parameter (this restriction is imposed by the typing rules). Note that since we treat this in method bodies as an ordinary variable, no special syntax for it is required.

A class declaration class C extends D $\{\overline{\text{C}}\ \overline{\text{f}};\ \text{K};\ \overline{\text{M}}\}$ consists of its name C, its superclass D (which must always be specified, even if it is Object), a list of field names $\overline{\text{C}}\ \overline{\text{f}}$ with their types, the constructor K, and a list of method definitions $\overline{\text{M}}$. The fields of C are added to the ones declared by D and its superclasses and are assumed to have distinct names. The constructor declaration shows how to initialize all these fields with

---

[1] FJ also includes up and down casts; however, since these features are completely orthogonal to our extension, they are omitted in IFJ.

the received values. A method definition M specifies the name, the signature and the body of a method; a body is a single return statement since FJ is a functional core of Java. In the following, we will write $m \notin \overline{M}$ to mean that the method definition of the name m is not included in $\overline{M}$. The same convention will be used for method signatures $\overline{N}$.

An incomplete class declaration class C abstracts D $\{\overline{C} \ \overline{f}; \ K; \ \overline{M} \ \overline{N}\}$ inherits from a standard (or incomplete) class and, apart from adding new fields and adding/overriding methods, it can declare some methods as "incomplete" (we will call these methods also "abstract" or "expected"). Note that, on the other hand, standard classes cannot inherit from incomplete classes (this is checked by typing, Section 2.3). The main idea of our language, is that an incomplete class can be instantiated, leading to *incomplete objects*. Method invocation and field selection cannot be performed on incomplete objects[2].

An incomplete object expression e_1 can be composed at run-time with a complete object expression e_2; this operation, denoted by $e_1 \leftrightarrow e_2$, is called *object composition*. The key idea is that e_1 can be composed with a complete object e_2 that provides all the requested methods, independently from the class of e_2 (of course, the method signatures must match). Then, in $e_1 \leftrightarrow e_2$, e_1 must be an incomplete object and e_2 must be a complete object expression (these requirements are checked by the type system); indeed, e_2 can be, in turn, the result of another object composition. The object expression $e_1 \leftrightarrow e_2$ represents a brand new (complete) object that consists of the sub-object expressions e_1 and e_2; in particular, the objects of these sub-expressions are not modified during the composition. In Section 4 we will get into more details about this point, and about how the language can be smoothly extended to the imperative setting. This also highlights the roles of incomplete and complete objects as re-usable building blocks for new objects at run-time, while retaining their identity and state. This is also another main difference with respect to [4], where incomplete objects are modified during the object composition (and thus they could not be re-used in further compositions).

We note that in this basic version of the language we do not allow object composition operations leading to incomplete objects, i.e., incomplete objects can only be fully completed. However, for instance, object compositions of the shape $(e_1 \leftrightarrow e_2) \leftrightarrow e_3$, where e_2 is incomplete in the methods provided by e_3, can be obtained as $e_1 \leftrightarrow (e_2 \leftrightarrow e_3)$ in IFJ. Furthermore, we prohibit the object composition between two complete objects: the semantics would not be clear and could lead to unexpected behaviors at run-time (for instance, a further composition of an object o with a complete object might lead to an accidental method overriding, because there might be a method in o with the same name and the same signature, but with a completely different semantics, of a method already present in the complete object). It is part of our main goal to keep the discipline that is typical of statically typed class based languages where some crucial intentions (e.g., when a method can be redefined) must be written explicitly by the programmer: during object composition, the requested methods must be explicitly declared in the incomplete classes.

Finally, values, denoted by v and u, are fully evaluated object creation terms. However, the object representation of IFJ is different from FJ in that fully evaluated objects

---

[2] Actually, field selection might be safely performed on incomplete objects but would make a little sense.

$$T <: T \qquad \frac{T_1 <: T_2 \qquad T_2 <: T_3}{T_1 <: T_3} \qquad \frac{\text{class C extends D } \{\ldots\}}{C <: D}$$

$$\frac{\text{class C abstracts D } \{\ldots\} \qquad \text{class D extends E } \{\ldots\}}{\langle C \rangle <: D}$$

$$\frac{\text{class C abstracts D } \{\ldots\} \qquad \text{class D abstracts E } \{\ldots\}}{\langle C \rangle <: \langle D \rangle}$$

Fig. 2. Subtyping rules

can be also compositions of many objects. Thus, objects are represented as lists of terms new $C(\overline{v})$ (i.e., expressions that are passed to the constructor are values too). For instance, new $C(\overline{v}) :: $ new $D(\overline{u}) :: \varepsilon$ represents the composition of the incomplete object of class C with a standard complete object of class D (ε denotes the empty list). This run-time representation of objects will be further explained in Section 2.4.

As in FJ, a class table CT is a mapping from class names to class declarations. Then a program is a pair (CT, e) of a class table (containing all the class definitions of the program) and an expression e (the program's main entry point). The class Object has no members and its declaration does not appear in CT. We assume that CT satisfies some usual sanity conditions: (*i*) $CT(C) = $ class C ... for every $C \in dom(CT)$ (*ii*) for every class name C (except Object) appearing anywhere in CT, we have $C \in dom(CT)$; (*iii*) there are no cycles in the transitive closure of the extends relation. Thus, in the following, instead of writing $CT(C) = $ class ... we will simply write class C ....

2.1 Subtyping

In the type system we will need to distinguish between the type of an incomplete object and the type of a composed object (i.e., an incomplete object that has been composed with a complete object). If C is the class name of an incomplete object, then $\langle C \rangle$ is the type of an incomplete object of class C that has been composed. To treat complete and incomplete objects uniformly, we will use T to refer both to C and $\langle C \rangle$. However, types of the shape $\langle C \rangle$ are only used by the type system for keeping track of objects that are created via object composition. Indeed the programmer cannot write $\langle C \rangle$ explicitly, i.e., T cannot be used in arrow types nor for declaring method parameters; this is consistent with Java-like languages' philosophy where the class names are the only types that can be mentioned in the program (apart from basic types).

The subtype relation $<:$ (defined for any class table CT) on classes (types) is induced by the standard subclass relation extended in order to relate incomplete objects (Figure 2). First of all, let us consider an incomplete class class C abstracts D $\{\ldots\}$; if D is a standard class, since C can make some methods of D incomplete, then it is obvious that an incomplete object of class C cannot be used in place of an object of class D. Thus, abstracts implements subclassing without subtyping. Instead, when the incomplete object is composed with a complete object (providing all the methods requested by C), then its type is $\langle C \rangle$, and it can be used in place of an object of class D (see third rule). Since, as said above, we do not permit object completion on a complete object, then a complete object can never be used in place of an incomplete one.

Introducing subtyping between incomplete objects would require checking that the sub-type does not have more incomplete methods than the supertype (contra-variance on requirements). To keep the presentation simple, however, in this first version we are not considering subtyping on incomplete objects (see Section 5). Instead, subtyping holds on their completed versions (last rule).

2.2 Programming Examples

In this section, we show how incomplete objects, and object composition, can be used to implement some recurrent programming scenarios. For simplicity, we will use here the full Java syntax (consider all methods as public) and we will denote object completion operation with <-.

We consider a scenario where it is useful to add some functionality to existing objects. Let us consider the development of an application that uses widgets such as graphical buttons, menus, and keyboard shortcuts. These widgets are usually associated to an event listener (e.g., a callback function), that is invoked when the user sends an event to that specific widget (e.g., one clicks the button with the mouse or chooses a menu item).

The design pattern *command* [19] is useful for implementing these scenarios, since it permits parametrization of widgets over the event handlers, and the same event handler can be reused for similar widgets (e.g., the handler for the event "save file" can be associated with a button, a menu item, or a keyboard shortcut). Thus, they delegate to this object the actual implementation of the action semantics, while the action widget itself abstracts from it. This decouples the action visual representation from the action controller implementation.

We can implement directly this scenario with incomplete objects, as shown in Listing 1: the class Action and SaveActionDelegate are standard Java classes (note that they're not related). The former is a generic implementation of an action, and the latter implements the code for saving a file. We then have three incomplete classes implementing a button, a menu item, and a keyboard accelerator; note that these classes inherit from Action and make the method run incomplete and override the method display. We also assume a class Frame representing an application frame where we can set keyboard accelerators, menu items, and toolbar buttons. An instance of class Button is an incomplete object (it requires the method run) and, as such, we cannot pass it to addToolbar, since Button $\not<:$ Action (subclassing without subtyping). However, once we composed such instance (through object completion operation, <-) with an instance of SaveActionDelegate, then we have a completed object (of type $\langle$Button$\rangle$) that can be passed to addToToolbar (since $\langle$Button$\rangle$ <: Action). Note that we compose Button with an instance of SaveActionDelegate which provides the requested method run, although SaveActionDelegate is not related to Action. Furthermore, we can use the same instance of SaveActionDelegate for the other incomplete objects.

We conclude this section by discussing some possible manual implementations in Java of this scenario, showing that our proposal is not simply syntactic sugar. With standard Java features, one could write the Button class with a field, say deleg, on which we call the method run. This approach requires deleg to be declared with a class or interface that provides such method, say Runnable. However, this solution

```
                        class Button abstracts Action {
 class Action {            void run(); // incomplete method    class SaveActionDelegate {
   void run() { }          void display() {                       void run() {
   void display() {}         // redefined to draw the button        // implementation
 }                        }                                       }
                       }                                       }


   class MenuItem abstracts Action {         class KeyboardAccel abstracts Action {
     void run(); // incomplete method          void run(); // incomplete method
     void display() {                          void display() {
       // redefined to show the item             // redefined to hook key combination
     }                                         }
   }                                         }


                                   SaveActionDelegate deleg =
                                     new SaveActionDelegate();
 class Frame {                   myFrame.addToMenu
   void addToMenu(Action a) {...}   (new MenuItem("save") <- deleg);
   void addToToolbar(Action a) {...}  myFrame.addToToolbar
   void setKeybAcc(Action a) {...}    (new Button("save") <- deleg);
 }                               myFrame.setKeybAcc
                                   (new KeyboardAccel("Ctrl+S") <- deleg);
```

Listing 1: The implementation of action and action delegates with incomplete objects and object completion

would not be as flexible as our incomplete objects, since one can then assign to `deleg` only objects belonging to the `Runnable` hierarchy.

On the other hand, if one wanted to keep the flexibility, he should declare `deleg` of type `Object`, and then call the method `run` by using Java Reflection APIs, (e.g., `getMethod`); however, this solution is not type safe, since exceptions can be thrown at run-time due to missing methods.

2.3 Typing

In order to define the typing rules and the lookup functions, we extend the sequence notation also to method definitions:

$$\overline{\texttt{C m}\,(\overline{\texttt{C}}\,\overline{\texttt{x}})\{\texttt{return e;}\}}$$

represents a sequence of method definitions:

$$\texttt{C}_1\,\texttt{m}_1\,(\overline{\texttt{C}}_1\,\overline{\texttt{x}})\{\texttt{return e}_1;\}\,\ldots\,\texttt{C}_n\,\texttt{m}_n\,(\overline{\texttt{C}}_n\,\overline{\texttt{x}})\{\texttt{return e}_n;\}$$

The signatures of the above method definitions will be denoted, in a compact form, by $\texttt{m}:\overline{\texttt{C}}\to\texttt{C}$. The same convention will be used for abstract method definitions (and their corresponding signatures). To lighten the notation, in the following, we will assume a fixed class table CT and then $<:$ is the subtype relation induced by CT. We will write $\overline{\texttt{C}}<:\overline{\texttt{D}}$ as a shorthand for $\texttt{C}_1<:\texttt{D}_1\wedge\ldots\wedge\texttt{C}_n<:\texttt{D}_n$.

We define auxiliary functions (see Figure 3) to lookup fields and method from CT; these functions are used in the typing rules and in the operational semantics.

A *signature set*, denoted by S is a set of method signatures of the shape $\mathtt{m} : \overline{\mathtt{C}} \to \mathtt{C}$. The *signature* of a class C, denoted by $sign(\mathtt{C})$, is a pair of signature sets $\langle S_1, S_2 \rangle$, where the

$$fields(\mathtt{Object}) = \bullet$$

$$\frac{\texttt{class C extends D } \{\overline{\mathtt{C}}\,\overline{\mathtt{f}};\ \mathtt{K};\ \overline{\mathtt{M}}\} \qquad fields(\mathtt{D}) = \overline{\mathtt{D}}\,\overline{\mathtt{g}}}{fields(\mathtt{C}) = \overline{\mathtt{D}}\,\overline{\mathtt{g}}, \overline{\mathtt{C}}\,\overline{\mathtt{f}}}$$

$$\frac{\texttt{class C abstracts D } \{\overline{\mathtt{C}}\,\overline{\mathtt{f}};\ \mathtt{K};\ \overline{\mathtt{M}}\,\overline{\mathtt{N}}\} \qquad fields(\mathtt{D}) = \overline{\mathtt{D}}\,\overline{\mathtt{g}}}{fields(\mathtt{C}) = \overline{\mathtt{D}}\,\overline{\mathtt{g}}, \overline{\mathtt{C}}\,\overline{\mathtt{f}}}$$

$$fields(\langle \mathtt{C} \rangle) = fields(\mathtt{C})$$

$$\frac{\begin{array}{c} \texttt{class C extends D } \{\overline{\mathtt{C}}\,\overline{\mathtt{f}};\ \mathtt{K};\ \overline{\mathtt{M}}\} \\ \overline{\mathtt{M}} = \mathtt{B}\,\mathtt{m}\,(\overline{\mathtt{B}}\,\overline{\mathtt{x}})\{\mathtt{return}\ \mathtt{e};\} \qquad sign(\mathtt{D}) = \langle \mathtt{S}, \emptyset \rangle \end{array}}{sign(\mathtt{C}) = \langle \{\mathtt{m} : \overline{\mathtt{B}} \to \mathtt{B}\} \cup \mathtt{S}, \emptyset \rangle}$$

$$\frac{\begin{array}{c} \texttt{class C abstracts D } \{\overline{\mathtt{C}}\,\overline{\mathtt{f}};\ \mathtt{K};\ \overline{\mathtt{M}}\,\overline{\mathtt{N}}\} \qquad sign(\mathtt{D}) = \langle \mathtt{S}_1, \mathtt{S}_2 \rangle \\ \overline{\mathtt{M}} = \mathtt{B}\,\mathtt{m}\,(\overline{\mathtt{B}}\,\overline{\mathtt{x}})\{\mathtt{return}\ \mathtt{e};\} \qquad \overline{\mathtt{N}} = \mathtt{E}\,\mathtt{n}\,(\overline{\mathtt{E}}\,\overline{\mathtt{x}}); \end{array}}{sign(\mathtt{C}) = \langle \{\mathtt{m} : \overline{\mathtt{B}} \to \mathtt{B}\} \cup (\mathtt{S}_1 - \{\mathtt{n} : \overline{\mathtt{E}} \to \mathtt{E}\}), \{\mathtt{n} : \overline{\mathtt{E}} \to \mathtt{E}\} \cup (\mathtt{S}_2 - \{\mathtt{m} : \overline{\mathtt{B}} \to \mathtt{B}\}) \rangle}$$

$$\frac{sign(\mathtt{C}) = \langle \mathtt{S}_1, \mathtt{S}_2 \rangle}{sign(\langle \mathtt{C} \rangle) = \langle \mathtt{S}_1 \cup \mathtt{S}_2, \emptyset \rangle}$$

$$\frac{sign(\mathtt{T}) = \langle \mathtt{S}_1, \mathtt{S}_2 \rangle \qquad \mathtt{m} : \overline{\mathtt{B}} \to \mathtt{B} \in \mathtt{S}_1 \cup \mathtt{S}_2}{mtype(\mathtt{m}, \mathtt{T}) = \overline{\mathtt{B}} \to \mathtt{B}}$$

$$\frac{\texttt{class C extends D } \{\overline{\mathtt{C}}\,\overline{\mathtt{f}};\ \mathtt{K};\ \overline{\mathtt{M}}\} \qquad \mathtt{B}\,\mathtt{m}\,(\overline{\mathtt{B}}\,\overline{\mathtt{x}})\{\mathtt{return}\ \mathtt{e};\} \in \overline{\mathtt{M}}}{mbody(\mathtt{m}, \mathtt{C}) = \overline{\mathtt{x}}.\mathtt{e}}$$

$$\frac{\texttt{class C extends D } \{\overline{\mathtt{C}}\,\overline{\mathtt{f}};\ \mathtt{K};\ \overline{\mathtt{M}}\} \qquad \mathtt{m} \notin \overline{\mathtt{M}}}{mbody(\mathtt{m}, \mathtt{C}) = mbody(\mathtt{m}, \mathtt{D})}$$

$$\frac{\texttt{class C abstracts D } \{\overline{\mathtt{C}}\,\overline{\mathtt{f}};\ \mathtt{K};\ \overline{\mathtt{M}}\,\overline{\mathtt{N}}\} \qquad \mathtt{B}\,\mathtt{m}\,(\overline{\mathtt{B}}\,\overline{\mathtt{x}})\{\mathtt{return}\ \mathtt{e};\} \in \overline{\mathtt{M}}}{mbody(\mathtt{m}, \mathtt{C}) = \overline{\mathtt{x}}.\mathtt{e}}$$

$$\frac{\texttt{class C abstracts D } \{\overline{\mathtt{C}}\,\overline{\mathtt{f}};\ \mathtt{K};\ \overline{\mathtt{M}}\,\overline{\mathtt{N}}\} \qquad \mathtt{m} \notin \overline{\mathtt{M}} \qquad \mathtt{m} \notin \overline{\mathtt{N}}}{mbody(\mathtt{m}, \mathtt{C}) = mbody(\mathtt{m}, \mathtt{D})}$$

$$\frac{\texttt{class C abstracts D } \{\overline{\mathtt{C}}\,\overline{\mathtt{f}};\ \mathtt{K};\ \overline{\mathtt{M}}\,\overline{\mathtt{N}}\} \qquad \mathtt{B}\,\mathtt{m}\,(\overline{\mathtt{B}}\,\overline{\mathtt{x}}); \in \overline{\mathtt{N}}}{mbody(\mathtt{m}, \mathtt{C}) = \bullet}$$

Fig. 3. Lookup functions

first set is the signature set of the defined methods and the second set is the signature set of the abstract methods. Of course, for standard classes, the second set will be empty.

The lookup function *fields*(C) returns the sequence of the field names, together with the corresponding types, for all the fields declared in C and in its superclasses. The *mtype*(m, C) lookup function (where m is the method name we are looking for, and C is the class where we are performing the lookup) differs from the one of FJ in that it relies on the new lookup function *sign*; the lookup function *sign* returns the signature of a class by inspecting the signature of its type. In particular, since the superclass D of an incomplete class C can be in turn an incomplete class, the methods that are complete are those defined in C and those defined in D that are not made incomplete by C (i.e., $\{\overline{m : \overline{B} \to B}\} \cup (S_1 - \{\overline{n : \overline{E} \to E}\}))$; conversely, the incomplete methods are the abstract methods of C and those of D that are not (re)defined in C (i.e., $\{\overline{n : \overline{E} \to E}\} \cup (S_2 - \{\overline{m : \overline{B} \to B}\}))$. Moreover, for a composed object of type $\langle C \rangle$ it returns a signature where the first element is the union of the signature sets of its class and the second element is made empty; this reflects the fact that now all the methods of the object are concrete. Since we introduced this lookup function, the definition of *mtype* is straightforward (w.r.t. the one of FJ [21]). The lookup function for method bodies, *mbody*, is basically the same definition of FJ extended to incomplete classes (note that it returns an empty element • for abstract methods).

A type judgment of the form $\Gamma \vdash e : T$ states that "e has type T in the type environment Γ". A type environment is a finite mapping from variables (including this) to types, written $\overline{x} : \overline{C}$. Again, we use the sequence notation for abbreviating $\Gamma \vdash e_1 : T_1, \ldots, \Gamma \vdash e_n : T_n$ to $\Gamma \vdash \overline{e} : \overline{T}$.

Typing rules (Figure 4) are adapted from those of FJ in order to handle incomplete objects and object composition. In particular, field selection and method selection are allowed only on objects of concrete types, where a *concrete* type is either a standard class C or $\langle C \rangle$. The key rule (T-COMP) for dealing with object composition is introduced. It checks that the left expression is actually an incomplete object ($S_2 \neq \emptyset$), and that the right one is a complete object that provides all the methods needed by the incomplete object. Note that the final type is the concrete type based on the original class of the incomplete object. This rule also shows that the typing of ←+ is structural, which is a key feature of the system, since it enhances the flexibility of object composition.

Also typing rules for methods and classes of FJ are adapted to deal with incomplete classes (note the use of the *override* predicate of [24] to check that the signature of a method is preserved by method overriding). Moreover, (T-CLASS) checks that a concrete class extends another concrete class and (T-ACLASS) checks that also the signatures of incomplete methods satisfy the *override* predicate. Typing rules for run-time expressions are in Figure 5; note that the type of a composed object is taken from the head of the list, consistently with the typing rule for object completion.

2.4 Operational Semantics

The operational semantics, shown in Figure 6, is defined by the reduction relation $e \longrightarrow e'$, read "e reduces to e' in one step". The standard reflexive and transitive closure of $\longrightarrow$ defines the reduction relation in many steps. We adopt a deterministic call-by-value semantics, analogous to the call-by-value strategy of FJ [24]. The congruence

concrete predicate

$$\frac{sign(\text{C}) = \langle \text{S}, \emptyset \rangle}{concrete(\text{C})} \qquad concrete(\langle \text{C} \rangle)$$

Expression typing

$$\Gamma \vdash \text{x} : \Gamma(\text{x}) \tag{T-VAR}$$

$$\frac{\Gamma \vdash \text{e} : \text{T} \qquad fields(\text{T}) = \overline{\text{C}}\,\overline{\text{f}} \qquad concrete(\text{T})}{\Gamma \vdash \text{e.f}_i : \text{C}_i} \tag{T-FIELD}$$

$$\frac{\Gamma \vdash \text{e} : \text{T} \quad \Gamma \vdash \overline{\text{e}} : \overline{\text{T}} \quad mtype(\text{m}, \text{T}) = \overline{\text{B}} \to \text{B} \quad \overline{\text{T}} <: \overline{\text{B}} \quad concrete(\text{T})}{\Gamma \vdash \text{e.m}(\overline{\text{e}}) : \text{B}} \tag{T-INVK}$$

$$\frac{fields(\text{C}) = \overline{\text{D}}\,\overline{\text{f}} \quad \Gamma \vdash \overline{\text{e}} : \overline{\text{T}} \quad \overline{\text{T}} <: \overline{\text{D}}}{\Gamma \vdash \text{new C}(\overline{\text{e}}) : \text{C}} \tag{T-NEW}$$

$$\frac{\begin{array}{ccc} \Gamma \vdash \text{e}_1 : \text{C} & sign(\text{C}) = \langle \text{S}_1, \text{S}_2 \rangle & \text{S}_2 \neq \emptyset \\ \Gamma \vdash \text{e}_2 : \text{T} & sign(\text{T}) = \langle \text{S}_1', \emptyset \rangle & \text{S}_2 \subseteq \text{S}_1' \end{array}}{\Gamma \vdash \text{e}_1 \longleftrightarrow \text{e}_2 : \langle \text{C} \rangle} \tag{T-COMP}$$

override predicate

$$\frac{mtype(\text{m}, \text{D}) = \overline{\text{C}} \to \text{C} \text{ implies } \overline{\text{C}} = \overline{\text{B}} \text{ and } \text{C} = \text{B}}{override(\text{m}, \text{D}, \overline{\text{B}} \to \text{B})}$$

Method and Class typing

$$\frac{\begin{array}{cc} \overline{\text{x}} : \overline{\text{B}}, \text{this} : \text{C} \vdash \text{e} : \text{T} & \text{T} <: \text{B} \\ \text{class C extends D } \{\overline{\text{C}}\,\overline{\text{f}}; \text{K}; \overline{\text{M}}\} & override(\text{m}, \text{D}, \overline{\text{B}} \to \text{B}) \end{array}}{\text{B m }(\overline{\text{B}}\,\overline{\text{x}})\{\text{return e;}\} \text{ OK IN C}} \tag{T-METHOD}$$

$$\frac{\begin{array}{cc} \overline{\text{x}} : \overline{\text{B}}, \text{this} : \text{C} \vdash \text{e} : \text{T} & \text{T} <: \text{B} \\ \text{class C abstracts D } \{\overline{\text{C}}\,\overline{\text{f}}; \text{K}; \overline{\text{M}}\,\overline{\text{N}}\} & override(\text{m}, \text{D}, \overline{\text{B}} \to \text{B}) \end{array}}{\text{B m }(\overline{\text{B}}\,\overline{\text{x}})\{\text{return e;}\} \text{ OK IN C}} \tag{T-METHODA}$$

$$\frac{\text{class C abstracts D } \{\overline{\text{C}}\,\overline{\text{f}}; \text{K}; \overline{\text{M}}\,\overline{\text{N}}\} \quad override(\text{m}, \text{D}, \overline{\text{B}} \to \text{B})}{\text{B m }(\overline{\text{B}}\,\overline{\text{x}}); \text{ OK IN C}} \tag{T-AMETHOD}$$

$$\frac{\begin{array}{c} \text{K} = \text{C}(\overline{\text{D}}\,\overline{\text{g}}, \overline{\text{C}}\,\overline{\text{f}})\{\text{super}(\overline{\text{g}}); \text{this}.\overline{\text{f}} = \overline{\text{f}};\} \\ fields(\text{D}) = \overline{\text{D}}\,\overline{\text{g}} \quad \overline{\text{M}} \text{ OK IN C} \quad concrete(\text{D}) \end{array}}{\text{class C extends D } \{\overline{\text{C}}\,\overline{\text{f}}; \text{K}; \overline{\text{M}}\} \text{ OK}} \tag{T-CLASS}$$

$$\frac{\begin{array}{c} \text{K} = \text{C}(\overline{\text{D}}\,\overline{\text{g}}, \overline{\text{C}}\,\overline{\text{f}})\{\text{super}(\overline{\text{g}}); \text{this}.\overline{\text{f}} = \overline{\text{f}};\} \\ fields(\text{D}) = \overline{\text{D}}\,\overline{\text{g}} \quad \overline{\text{M}} \text{ OK IN C} \quad \overline{\text{N}} \text{ OK IN C} \end{array}}{\text{class C abstracts D } \{\overline{\text{C}}\,\overline{\text{f}}; \text{K}; \overline{\text{M}}\,\overline{\text{N}}\} \text{ OK}} \tag{T-ACLASS}$$

Fig. 4. Typing rules

$$\frac{\Gamma \vdash \text{new } C(\overline{v}) : C}{\Gamma \vdash \text{new } C(\overline{v}) :: \varepsilon : C} \text{ (T-LISTH)} \qquad \frac{\Gamma \vdash \text{new } C(\overline{v}) : C \qquad \Gamma \vdash v : T}{\Gamma \vdash \text{new } C(\overline{v}) :: v : \langle C \rangle} \text{ (T-LIST)}$$

Fig. 5. Run-time expression typing

Reduction

$$\text{new } C(\overline{v}) \longrightarrow \text{new } C(\overline{v}) :: \varepsilon \qquad \text{(R-NEW)}$$

$$\text{new } C(\overline{v}) :: \varepsilon \longleftrightarrow v \longrightarrow \text{new } C(\overline{v}) :: v \qquad \text{(R-COMP)}$$

$$\frac{fields(C) = \overline{C}\,\overline{f}}{(\text{new } C(\overline{v}) :: v).f_i \longrightarrow v_i} \qquad \text{(R-FIELD)}$$

$$\frac{mbody(m, C) = (\overline{x}, e_0)}{(\text{new } C(\overline{v}) :: v).m(\overline{u}) \longrightarrow [\overline{x} \leftarrow \overline{u}, \text{this} \leftarrow \text{new } C(\overline{v}) :: v]e_0} \qquad \text{(R-INVK)}$$

$$\frac{mbody(m, C) = \bullet}{(\text{new } C(\overline{v}) :: v).m(\overline{u}) \longrightarrow v.m(\overline{u})} \qquad \text{(R-DINVK)}$$

Congruence rules

$$\frac{e \longrightarrow e'}{e.f \longrightarrow e'.f} \qquad\qquad \frac{e \longrightarrow e'}{e.m(\overline{e}) \longrightarrow e'.m(\overline{e})}$$

$$\frac{e_i \longrightarrow e_i'}{v_0.m(\overline{v}, e_i, \overline{e}) \longrightarrow v_0.m(\overline{v}, e_i', \overline{e})} \qquad \frac{e_i \longrightarrow e_i'}{\text{new } C(\overline{v}, e_i, \overline{e}) \longrightarrow \text{new } C(\overline{v}, e_i', \overline{e})}$$

$$\frac{e_2 \longrightarrow e_2'}{e_1 \longleftrightarrow e_2 \longrightarrow e_1 \longleftrightarrow e_2'} \qquad \frac{e_1 \longrightarrow e_1'}{e_1 \longleftrightarrow v \longrightarrow e_1' \longleftrightarrow v}$$

Fig. 6. Semantics of IFJ

rules formalize how operators (method invocation, object creation, object completion and field selection) are reduced only when all their subexpressions are reduced to values (call-by-value).

The expression $[\overline{x} \leftarrow \overline{u}, \text{this} \leftarrow \text{new } C(\overline{v}) :: v]e$ denotes the expression obtained from e by replacing x_1 with $v_1, \ldots, x_n$ with v_n and this with new $C(\overline{v}) :: v$. A run-time object is represented by a list of standard FJ objects, new $C(\overline{v})$; in order to treat composed objects and standard objects uniformly, we represent a standard object with a list of only one element, new $C(\overline{v}) :: \varepsilon$. The main idea of the semantics of method invocation is to search for the method definition in the (class of the) head of the list using the *mbody* lookup function. If this is found, rule (R-INVK), then the method body is executed; otherwise, rule (R-DINVK), the search continues on the next element of the list (of course, in a well-typed program, this search will succeed eventually).

Now the following question arises: What object do we substitute for this in the method body? This is a crucial issue in order to perform field selection and further method invocations correctly (and avoid the program getting stuck). Method and field selections in a method body expect to deal with an object of the class where the method (or field) is defined (or a subclass). Thus, it is sensible to substitute this with the sublist whose head new $C(\overline{v})$ is such that $mbody(m, C)$ is defined. This is also consistent with the concept of *consultation*. Thus, the list implements the scope of this inside a method body: the scope is restricted to the visibility provided by the class where the method is defined. Note that this solves also possible ambiguities due to name clashes, even for methods hidden by subsumption [25]. Suppose we have an incomplete class A that requires a method m and defines a method n; an instance of A can be completed with an object that provides m, say an object of class B that also defines a method n, possibly with a different signature. When we invoke m on the completed object, we actually execute the definition of m in B; if this method then invokes n, the definition of n in B will be executed, since the scope of this is actually restricted to B; this is consistent with the typing that has checked the invocation of n in $B.m$ using the signature of $B.n$.

3   Properties

The language IFJ enjoys the type safety property, thus no errors "message-not-understood" can occur at run-time. In this section, we sketch this proof by showing the main steps that are related to object composition. Namely, in the formal proofs, we explicitly deal with crucial points involving typing and semantics rules for incomplete objects, while we omit the parts that are similar or unchanged with respect to the corresponding proofs in FJ.

The following key lemmas state some crucial properties about the signatures of classes $C_1, \ldots, C_n$ when considering values of the shape

$$v = \text{new } C_1(\overline{v}_1) :: \ldots :: \text{new } C_n(\overline{v}_n) :: \varepsilon$$

Indeed, these properties are proved for the expression

$$e = \text{new } C_1(\overline{v}_1) \leftarrow\!\!+ \ldots \leftarrow\!\!+ \text{new } C_n(\overline{v}_n)$$

using typing and semantic rules. Then, the properties are inherited by v since v can only be obtained by applying rule (R-COMP) to e (Figure 6); it is clear that the application of (R-COMP) does not affect signatures of $C_1, \ldots, C_n$.

Lemma 1. *Let* $v = \text{new } C(\overline{v}) :: v'$ *such that* $v' \neq \varepsilon$ *and* $\Gamma \vdash v : T$ *where* $concrete(T)$. *Then*

1. $\Gamma \vdash v' : T'$ *for some* T' *such that* $concrete(T')$
2. *If* $sign(C) = \langle S_1, S_2 \rangle$, *for any* m *such that* $m : \overline{B} \to B \in S_2$ *then* $mtype(m, T_1) = \overline{B} \to B$

Proof.

1. By (T-LIST) and (T-COMP).
2. By (T-COMP).

Lemma 2. *If* $\Gamma \vdash \text{new } C_1(\overline{v}_1) :: \ldots :: \text{new } C_n(\overline{v}_n) :: \varepsilon : T$ *where* $concrete(T)$, *let* $sign(C_i) = \langle S_1^i, S_2^i \rangle$, $1 \leq i \leq n$, *then, for any method* m:

1. $mtype(\mathtt{m}, \mathtt{T}) = \overline{\mathtt{B}} \rightarrow \mathtt{B}$ *implies that there exists some* C_i, $1 \leq i \leq n$, *such that* $\mathtt{m} : \overline{\mathtt{B}} \rightarrow$
   $\mathtt{B} \in \mathtt{S}_1^i$
2. *For any* C_i, $1 \leq i \leq n$, $\mathtt{m} : \overline{\mathtt{B}} \rightarrow \mathtt{B} \in \mathtt{S}_1^i$ *implies* $mbody(\mathtt{m}, C_i) = \overline{\mathtt{x}}.\mathtt{e}$ *and* $\mathtt{this} : C_i, \overline{\mathtt{x}} :$
   $\overline{\mathtt{B}} \vdash \mathtt{e} : \mathtt{T}$ *for some* $\mathtt{T} <: \mathtt{B}$

Proof.

1. $mtype(\mathtt{m}, \mathtt{T}) = \overline{\mathtt{B}} \rightarrow \mathtt{B}$ implies that $\mathtt{m} : \overline{\mathtt{B}} \rightarrow \mathtt{B} \in \mathtt{S}_1 \cup \mathtt{S}_2$, where $sign(\mathtt{T}) = \langle \mathtt{S}_1, \mathtt{S}_2 \rangle$; then
   the proof follows by induction on n using (T-COMP).
2. By induction on the derivation of $mbody(\mathtt{m}, C_i)$.

The following substitution property is standard and it proceeds essentially as in FJ, since incomplete classes do not introduce crucial new subtyping relations.

Lemma 3 (Substitution Lemma).
If $\Gamma, \overline{\mathtt{x}} : \overline{\mathtt{B}} \vdash \mathtt{e} : \mathtt{T}$ *and* $\Gamma \vdash \overline{\mathtt{e}} : \overline{\mathtt{T}}$ *where* $\overline{\mathtt{T}} <: \overline{\mathtt{B}}$, *then* $\Gamma \vdash [\overline{\mathtt{x}} \leftarrow \overline{\mathtt{e}}]\mathtt{e} : \mathtt{T}'$ *for some* $\mathtt{T}' <: \mathtt{T}$.

Proof. Straightforward induction on the derivation of $\Gamma, \overline{\mathtt{x}} : \overline{\mathtt{B}} \vdash \mathtt{e} : \mathtt{T}$.

Theorem 1 (Type Preservation).
If $\Gamma \vdash \mathtt{e} : \mathtt{T}$ *and* $\mathtt{e} \longrightarrow \mathtt{e}'$ *then* $\Gamma \vdash \mathtt{e}' : \mathtt{T}'$ *for some* $\mathtt{T}' <: \mathtt{T}$.

Proof. By induction on a derivation of $\mathtt{e} \longrightarrow \mathtt{e}'$. The only interesting cases are:

- (R-COMP): By (T-COMP) and (T-LIST), the type is preserved after reduction.
- (R-INVK): By (T-INVK) and Lemma 2-2, using Substitution Lemma 3.
- (R-DINVK): By Lemma 1.

Theorem 2 (Progress). *Let* $\mathtt{e}$ *be a closed expression. If* $\vdash \mathtt{e} : \mathtt{T}$ *for some* $\mathtt{T}$, *then either* $\mathtt{e}$ *is a value or* $\mathtt{e} \longrightarrow \mathtt{e}'$ *for some* $\mathtt{e}'$.

Proof. By induction on $\vdash \mathtt{e} : \mathtt{T}$; the crucial case is:

- (T-INVK): the method invocation can be reduced either by (R-INVK) or by (R-DINVK); Lemma 2-1 is the key argument to guarantee that the search for the method body will eventually succeed (i.e., (R-INVK) will be applied after some applications of (R-DINVK)).

Theorems 1 and 2 show how type safety of FJ is preserved when adding incomplete objects with our approach, i.e., any well-typed IFJ program cannot get stuck.

4 Dealing with Imperative Features

Our language is based on FJ that abstracts the functional core of Java; then, also our approach has a functional flavor, i.e., it does not consider side effects and imperative features. Thus, it might not be clear what happens to the object state and identity during object composition, in an imperative setting.

In this section we want to show how the present approach can be adapted to an imperative version of FJ (e.g., using heaps and object identifiers similarly to [7]), based on our run-time representation of objects.

The key point is that, when objects are composed, the resulting object consists of a list of sub-objects; in particular these sub-objects are not modified. Thus, the states of the objects within an object composition never change and the object composition produces a brand new object.

Consider the (R-COMP) rule in Figure 6:

$$\text{new } C(\overline{v}) :: \varepsilon \leftarrow\!\!+ v \longrightarrow \text{new } C(\overline{v}) :: v$$

The new object contains the sub-objects without changing them (note that the removal of $:: \varepsilon$ from new $C(\overline{v}) :: \varepsilon$ is due only to our uniform representation for complete and incomplete objects and, obviously, has nothing to do with the state of the object itself).

Each object composition creates a brand new object and all the sub-objects are actually shared (for instance, in an imperative model each object composition gets a new object identifier); in particular, the code employing object composition in Listing 1 clarifies this point: the (same) complete object deleg is used for completing all the three incomplete objects. Actually we could have also written the code as follows:

```
SaveActionDelegate deleg = new SaveActionDelegate();
Action saveMenu = new MenuItem("save") <- deleg;
myFrame.addToMenu(saveMenu);
Action saveButton = new Button("save") <- deleg;
myFrame.addToToolbar(saveButton);
Action saveKeyb = new KeyboardAccel("Ctrl+S") <- deleg;
myFrame.setKeybAcc(saveKeyb);
```

Thus, modifying the internal state of deleg will assure that all the actions are updated too. For instance, if the SaveActionDelegate had logging features, we could enable them and disable them during the execution of our program, and all the actions resulting from the object compositions will use logging consistently.

This shows that objects are not only instances of classes (possibly incomplete classes), but they are also prototypes that can be used, via the object composition, to create new objects at run-time, while ensuring statically that the composition is type safe. We then can use incomplete and complete objects as our re-usable building blocks to assemble at run-time, on the fly, brand new objects.

Furthermore, this mechanism will assure that there will not be problems when an object is pointed to by references in different parts of the program. Actually, if we modified the objects directly during the object composition, what would happen to the existing references? Surely they would all refer to the modified objects, but we would create situations where a reference of an incomplete class type would point to a complete object. This would break our discipline of not composing already complete objects with other complete objects; but, most of all, it would undermine the type safety (recall that there is no subtyping between an incomplete class and a complete class).

Finally, not modifying incomplete objects directly also makes them more re-usable especially in cases when object composition may not have to be permanent: the behavior of an object may need to evolve many times during the execution of a program and

```
                      class Stream {
                        void write(byte[] b) { ... }
                        byte[] read() { ... }
                      }
class CompressStream abstracts Stream {          class BufferedStream abstracts Stream {
    redef void write(byte[] b) {                     Buffer buff;
      next.write(compress(b));                        redef void write(byte[] b) {
    }                                                    if (buff.isFull())
    redef byte[] read() {                                  next.write(b);
      return uncompress(next.read());                   else
    }                                                      buff.append(b);
    byte[] compress(byte[] b) {...}                    }
    byte[] uncompress(byte[] b) {...}                  redef byte[] read() { /* similar */ }
}                                                }
```

Listing 2: The implementation of streams using redefined methods

the missing methods provided during an object composition might need to be changed, e.g., because the state of the incomplete object has changed (we refer to the learning objects scenario in the Introduction). Since the original incomplete object is not modified, then it can be re-used smoothly in many object compositions during the evolution of a program.

5   Ongoing Extensions

The core language IFJ is rather compact and minimal, since we focus on proving how Java basic aspects and type safety are preserved when adding incomplete objects and object composition using our approach. In this section we sketch some further developments, that are quite interesting for enhancing programming flexibility, and we provide hints on how to deal with them (the full technical treatment of these further language constructs is the subject of future work).

A first extension could be permitting to redefine a method provided during object composition. In this case, the incomplete object can provide the implementation of a method m relying on the implementation of m that must be provided (at run-time) during object composition. This is similar to standard method overriding, but it takes place dynamically and at object level.

We then introduce another syntax for such redefined methods (in order to distinguish them by standard method overriding): redef C m $(\overline{C}\,\overline{x})${return e;}. In order to access the implementation of this method provided by the object used in object composition, we can use the keyword next from within a redef method (e.g., next.m()), in order to distinguish it from super[3]. Thus, with next, one can access the "next" object in the object list. Just like this, next is a variable that will be implicitly bound in redef methods.

---

[3] Actually in FJ super is not considered; however, if introduced, it could coexist with next.

With method redefinition we could easily implement a stream library, as sketched in Listing 2: the specific stream specializations rely on the methods provided during object completion (using `next`) and specialize them.

A further enhancement would be to provide *delegation*, instead of simple *consultation*. When implementing delegation, we need substitute for `this` the whole object (the whole list, not only the part that was scanned when searching for the method definition) and this will require representing an object as a pair of lists (the second one is used as a backup and represents the entire object, while the first one is the part examined when searching for the method definition).

It would also be quite useful to be able to compose two incomplete objects obtaining another incomplete object; this would permit having an incomplete object that can be completed in more than one step. For instance, consider the `CompressStream` in Listing 2: we could make the two `compress` and `uncompress` methods incomplete, so that we will be able to complete the `CompressStream` object with a stream object (providing the read and write functionalities that will be redefined) and a compressor object (implementing the actual compression algorithm). This way, a `CompressStream` can be reused independently from the stream and from the compression algorithm.

Finally, we could extend the subtyping relation also to incomplete classes (and thus incomplete objects); in particular, an incomplete object o_1 has a subtype of an incomplete object o_2 if o_1 has no more abstract methods than o_2 (thus, it has less requirements), while it must have exactly the same redefined methods (see also [6,5]).

6   Conclusions and Related Works

In this paper we presented *Incomplete Featherweight Java* (IFJ), an extension of Featherweight Java with incomplete objects, i.e., objects that require some missing methods which can be provided at run-time by composition with another (complete) object, combining the static type discipline class-based features with the flexibility of object-based ones. The language IFJ enjoys the type safety property, thus no error "message-not-understood" can occur at run-time. The implementation of incomplete objects in Java is currently under development.

Incomplete objects seem to be a useful language construct to deal with the problem of dynamic reconfiguration of mobile code [6], where incomplete software components can be sent over a network to be completed with local components. Furthermore, in the context of service oriented programming and web services, mechanisms enabling service composition and reconfiguration, based on types, could be implemented through incomplete objects. In this direction, we plan to investigate how our approach to object composition can be exploited in calculi that incorporate session types in an object-oriented framework, such as [14].

An explicit form of incomplete objects was introduced in [8], where an extension of Lambda Calculus of Objects of [17] is presented. In this work, "labelled" types are used to collect information on the mutual dependencies among methods, enabling a safe subtyping in width. Labels are also used to implement the notion of *completion* which permits adding methods in an arbitrary order allowing the typing of methods that refer to methods not yet present in the object, thus supporting a form of incomplete objects.

The context is the lambda calculus, while in this work we are interested in incorporating object composition into Java-like languages.

In [22] delegation is presented in the model of the language *Darwin*; however, this model requires some basic notions to be modified, such as method overriding. Our language, instead, proposes a conservative extension of a Java-like language (so that existing code needs not to be changed). Furthermore, in [22] the type of the *parent* object must be a declared class and this limits the flexibility of dynamic composition, while in our approach there is no implicit parent and missing methods can be provided by any complete object, independently from its class.

Incomplete objects can be seen as *wrappers* for the objects used in object composition. However, they differ from decorator-based solutions such as the language extension presented in [7]: incomplete objects provide a more general-purpose language construct and the wrappers of [7] could be actually implemented through incomplete objects.

Traits [15] are composable units containing only methods, and they were proposed as an add-on to traditional class-based inheritance in order to enhance decoupling and high cohesion of code in classes, therefore with the aim of allowing a higher degree of code reuse. Incomplete objects can be seen as a tool for rapid prototyping, that is, for adding methods on the fly to already existing objects. Traits and incomplete objects share an important feature, composition, which permits composing sets of methods "at the right level", for instance not too high in a hierarchy for traits, and "when needed" for incomplete objects. The main difference is that traits are a compile-time feature, while incomplete objects are composed at run-time. An issue to pursue as a further research may be the use of incomplete objects as an exploratory tool to design traits: experiments made at run-time without modifying a class hierarchy might give indications on where to put a method in a new version of the hierarchy.

There are some relations between aspects [13] and our incomplete objects. Both are used to combine features taken from different sources. In the aspect case, the main idea is to factorize into aspects some cross-cutting functions (such as logging services or concurrency primitives) that are needed globally by a library, instead of duplicating and scattering them into the business code. In our case, we consider objects as building blocks that can be used to combine features on the fly, in order to obtain and experiment with multi-function objects whenever it is desired. In a sense, the role of incomplete objects is orthogonal to the one of aspects, because the former play a local role, while the latter a more global one.

In [2], a general model (Method Driven Model) for languages supporting object composition is proposed: this is based on the design of classes in an aspect-oriented style. The authors do not formalize their model within a calculus, but it is possible to see that the main feature of a language based on this model would be to compose dynamically the overall behavior of an object from the multiple "aspects" that abstract the variant behavior, as discussed in [3]. The main difference between their proposal and ours is that for them the run-time behavior is codified in aspects, whereas we internalize it in Java by exploiting partial classes and object composition.

The language *gbeta* [16] supports a mechanism called "object metamorphosis", which is a mechanism to specialize dynamically an existing object, by applying to it a class as a constraint in such a way the object becomes an instance of that class. The main difference between the gbeta specializing objects and our incomplete objects is that the former maintain the object identity, while the latter are used to create dynamically new objects which are not instances of any classes present in the program. Both proposals are proved type-safe, but a more direct comparison is not straightforward, as the type system of gbeta exploits concepts such as virtual classes which are not present in a Java-like setting like ours. It is important to remark that one of our main design decision was that our extension must integrate seamlessly in a Java-like language as a conservative extension.

Acknowledgments. We thank the anonymous referees for comments which helped us to improve the paper.

References

1. Anderson, C., Barbanera, F., Dezani-Ciancaglini, M., Drossopoulou, S.: Can Addresses be Types (a case study: Objects with Delegation). In: WOOD 2003. ENTCS, vol. 82(8), pp. 1–22. Elsevier, Amsterdam (2003)
2. Babu, C., Janakiram, D.: Method Driven Model: A Unified Model for an Object Composition Language. ACM SIGPLAN Notices 39(8), 61–71 (2004)
3. Babu, C., Jaques, W., Janakiram, D.: DynOCoLa: Enabling Dynamic Composition of Object Behaviour. In: Proc. 2nd International Workshop on Reflection, AOP and Meta-Data for Software Evolution (RAM-SE) at ECOOP 2005 (2005)
4. Bettini, L., Bono, V., Likavec, S.: Safe and Flexible Objects with Subtyping. SAC 2005 10(4), 5–29 (2005); Special Issue: OOPS Track at SAC 2005
5. Bettini, L., Bono, V., Venneri, B.: Subtyping-Inheritance Conflicts: The Mobile Mixin Case. In: Proc. Third IFIP International Conference on Theoretical Computer Science (TCS 2004), Kluwer Academic Publishers (2004)
6. Bettini, L., Bono, V., Venneri, B.: MoMi: a calculus for mobile mixins. Acta Informatica 42(2-3), 143–190 (2005)
7. Bettini, L., Capecchi, S., Giachino, E.: Featherweight Wrap Java. In: Proc. of SAC 2007, Special Track on Object-Oriented Programming Languages and Systems (OOPS), pp. 1094–1100. ACM Press (2007)
8. Bono, V., Bugliesi, M., Dezani-Ciancaglini, M., Liquori, L.: A Subtyping for extensible, incomplete objects. Fundamenta Informaticae 38(4), 325–364 (1999)
9. Boyle, T.: Design principles for authoring dynamic, reusable learning objects. Australian Journal of Educational Technology 19(1), 46–58 (2003)
10. Bracha, G.: The Programming Language Jigsaw: Mixins, Modularity and Multiple Inheritance. PhD thesis, University of Utah (1992)
11. Bracha, G., Odersky, M., Stoutamire, D., Wadler, P.: Making the future safe for the past: Adding genericity to the Java programming language. In: OOPSLA 1998 Conference Proceedings. ACM SIGPLAN Notices, vol. 33(10), pp. 183–200 (October 1998)
12. Chambers, C.: Object-Oriented Multi-Methods in Cecil. In: Lehrmann Madsen, O. (ed.) ECOOP 1992. LNCS, vol. 615, pp. 33–56. Springer, Heidelberg (1992)
13. Crawford, D.: Communications of the ACM archive - Special Issue on Aspect-Oriented Programming, vol. 44. ACM, New York (2001)
14. Dezani-Ciancaglini, M., Mostrous, D., Yoshida, N., Drossopoulou, S.: Session Types for Object-Oriented Languages. In: Thomas, D. (ed.) ECOOP 2006. LNCS, vol. 4067, pp. 328–352. Springer, Heidelberg (2006)

15. Ducasse, S., Nierstrasz, O., Schärli, N., Wuyts, R., Black, A.: Traits: A mechanism for fine-grained reuse. ACM Transactions on Programming Languages and Systems 28(2), 331–388 (2006)
16. Ernst, E.: gbeta – a Language with Virtual Attributes, Block Structure, and Propagating, Dynamic Inheritance. PhD thesis, Department of Computer Science, University of Århus, Denmark (1999), http://www.daimi.au.dk/~eernst/gbeta/
17. Fisher, K., Honsell, F., Mitchell, J.C.: A lambda-calculus of objects and method specialization. Nordic J. of Computing 1(1), 3–37 (1994)
18. Fisher, K., Mitchell, J.C.: A Delegation-based Object Calculus with Subtyping. In: Reichel, H. (ed.) FCT 1995. LNCS, vol. 965, pp. 42–61. Springer, Heidelberg (1995)
19. Gamma, E., Helm, R., Johnson, R., Vlissides, J.: Design Patterns: Elements of Reusable Object-Oriented Software. Addison-Wesley (1995)
20. Goldberg, A., Robson, D.: Smalltalk 80: The Language. Addison-Wesley (1989)
21. Igarashi, A., Pierce, B., Wadler, P.: Featherweight Java: a minimal core calculus for Java and GJ. ACM Transactions on Programming Languages and Systems 23(3), 396–450 (2001)
22. Kniesel, G.: Type-Safe Delegation for Run-Time Component Adaptation. In: Guerraoui, R. (ed.) ECOOP 1999. LNCS, vol. 1628, pp. 351–366. Springer, Heidelberg (1999)
23. Lieberman, H.: Using prototypical objects to implement shared behavior in object oriented systems. ACM SIGPLAN Notices 21(11), 214–214 (1986)
24. Pierce, B.C.: Types and Programming Languages. The MIT Press, Cambridge (2002)
25. Riecke, J., Stone, C.: Privacy via Subsumption. Information and Computation 172, 2–28 (2002); 3rd special issue of Theory and Practice of Object-Oriented Systems (TAPOS)
26. Taivalsaari, A.: On the notion of inheritance. ACM Computing Surveys 28(3), 438–479 (1996)
27. Ungar, D., Smith, R.B.: Self: The power of simplicity. ACM SIGPLAN Notices 22(12), 227–242 (1987)
28. Viega, J., Tutt, B., Behrends, R.: Automated Delegation is a Viable Alternative to Multiple Inheritance in Class Based Languages. Technical Report CS-98-03, UVa Computer Science (1998)

The Meta in Meta-object Architectures

Marcus Denker[1], Mathieu Suen[2], and Stéphane Ducasse[2]

[1] Software Composition Group
University of Bern – Switzerland
[2] ADAM, INRIA Nord Europe – LIFL – CNRS UMR 8022 – France

Abstract. Behavioral reflection is crucial to support for example functional upgrades, on-the-fly debugging, or monitoring critical applications. However the use of reflective features can lead to severe problems due to infinite meta-call recursion even in simple cases. This is especially a problem when reflecting on core language features since there is a high chance that such features are used to implement the reflective behavior itself. In this paper we analyze the problem of infinite meta-object call recursion and solve it by providing a first class representation of meta-level execution: at any point in the execution of a system it can be determined if we are operating on a meta-level or base level so that we can prevent infinite recursion. We present how meta-level execution can be represented by a *meta-context* and how reflection becomes *context-aware*. Our solution makes it possible to freely apply behavioral reflection even on system classes: the meta-context brings stability to behavioral reflection. We validate the concept with a robust implementation and we present benchmarks.

1   Introduction

Reflection, a feature common to many modern programming languages, is the ability to query and change a system at runtime [20]. Reflection is a very desirable feature, particularly suited for the long-living and highly dynamic systems of today.

The original model of reflection as defined by Smith [25] is based on meta-level interpretation. The program is interpreted by an interpreter, such interpreter is interpreted by a metainterpreter leading to a tower of interpreters each defining the semantics of the program (the interpreter) it interprets.

However, a tower of interpreters is too slow in practice. To enable reflection in mainstream languages such as CLOS [20], Smalltalk [23, 13, 24] or Java [30], the tower of interpreters is replaced with a reflective architecture [22] where meta-objects control the different aspects of reflection offered by the language. Meta-objects define the new or modified behavior and describe where this new behavior is active. For example, in systems that use metaclasses like CLOS [20], Neoclasstalk [5], or MetaClassTalk [4], the metaclass of a class defines both the new behavior and which classes are affected by the new behavior. Recently, more elaborated schemes have been proposed (*e.g., partial behavioral reflection*

R.F. Paige and B. Meyer (Eds.): TOOLS EUROPE 2008, LNBIP 11, pp. 218–237, 2008.
© Springer-Verlag Berlin Heidelberg 2008

[30, 24]) that provide a more flexible and fine-grained way to specify both the location been reflected and the meta-object invoked.

In general, meta-objects provide the implementation of new behavior which is called at certain defined places from the base system. It is important to note that meta-objects are not special objects, the execution of code as part of a meta-object is not different to any execution occuring in the base level application. As both base and metacomputation are handled the same, we are free to call any part of the base-system in the meta-level code.

As a matter of fact, this means that meta-level code can actually trigger again the execution of meta-level functionality. There is nothing to prevent the meta-level code to request the same code to be executed again, leading to an endless loop resulting in a system crash. This is especially a problem when reflecting on core language features (*e.g.*, the implementation of Arrays or Numbers) since the chances are high that such features are used to implement reflective features themselves. These cases of spurious endless recursion of meta-object calls have been noted in the past in the context of CLOS [7].

The ability to reflect on system classes is especially important when using reflection for dynamic analysis. A tracing tool that is realized with reflection should be able to trace a complete run of the system, not only the application code. In addition to the problem of recursion, such a tracer has the problem of recording the execution of trace code itself.

If we go back to the infinite tower (the origin of meta-level architectures) we can see that here these problems do not exist by construction: *going meta* means jumping up to another interpreter. A reflective function is always specific to one interpreter. As a function that is reflective at a meta-level I_n is not necessarily reflective in I_{n+1}, the problem of infinite recursion does not happen.

An important question then is the difference between the meta-object and interpreter/infinite tower approach. The *metaness* in the case of the tower is defined by the interpreter used. The interpreter forms a context that defines if we are executing at the base level or at the meta-level. Calling reflective functionality (so called reification) is always specific to one interpreter. The meta-object approach now in contrast is lacking any mechanism to specify this contextual information: when executing a meta-level program, in a meta-object based reflective system, we lack the information that this program is executing at the meta-level. In addition, all reifications are globally active: we can not define to only trigger meta-object activation when executing base level code. The research question is then how can we incorporate the infinite tower property of explicitly representing the execution context into meta-object based architectures.

Our solution to this problem is to extend meta-object based reflective systems with a first class notion of meta-level execution and the possibility to query at any point in the execution whether we are executing at the meta-level or not. To model meta-level execution we propose the notion of a first class *context* and *context-aware reifications*.

This paper is organized as follows. First we present a simple example to illustrate our problem and elaborate on the system used for evaluating the solution. Section 3 discusses the problem in detail, the next section then provides an overview of *context* and *contextual reflection* which can solve the presented problem (Section 4). We present an implementation in Section 5 followed by an evaluation (Section 6). After an overview of related work (Section 7) we conclude with a discussion of future work in Section 8

2   Context and Example

For the rest of the paper, we discuss the problem of meta-object call recursion in the context of REFLECTIVITY, a reflective library implemented in Squeak [19]. We use REFLECTIVITY to validate our solution. The ideas we discuss in this paper are the outcome of a larger project whose goal is to provide better control of reflection. Thus we started with a model of behavioral reflection that already allows for fine-grained spatial and temporal control of reification [30, 24]. Nevertheless it should be noted that the problem presented in this paper represents a universal problem: we are not just fixing a bug in our REFLECTIVITY framework.

We first provide a short overview of partial behavioral reflection and discuss how to implement a simple example, which we use in the rest of the paper.

2.1   Partial Behavioral Reflection

With Reflex, Tanter introduced *partial behavioral reflection* [30] in the context of Java, the model was later applied to dynamic languages [24]. Here meta-objects are associated not per object (as in 3-KRS [22]) or per metaclass (as in CLOS [20]), but per instruction. The core idea of the Reflex model is to bind meta-objects to operations using a *link* (see Figure 1). One can think about the link as the jump to the meta-level reified as an object. A link thus conceptually invokes messages on a meta-object at occurrences of selected operations.

Link attributes enable further control of the exact message sent to the meta-object. For example, we can control if the meta-object is supposed to be invoked before, after or instead of the original operation, an *activation condition* link attribute controls if the link is really invoked.

For our experiment, we use an implementation of partial behavioral reflection for Smalltalk that uses an abstract syntax tree for selecting which instructions

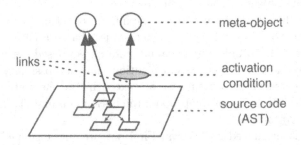

Fig. 1. Partial Behavioral Reflection

to reflected on. Before execution, the AST is compiled on demand to a low-level representation that is executable, in our case to byte-codes executable by the Squeak virtual machine. More in-depth information about this system and its implementation can be found in the paper on sub-method reflection [10].

Annotating a node of the AST with a link thus results in code that when executed will call the specified meta-object.

2.2 A Simple Example

The problem of meta-object call recursion is a known problem [7]. To show that it is relevant in practice, we have decided to keep our example as simple as possible. In Section 6.2 we discuss as more complex scenario how our solution is useful for dynamic analysis in general.

Imagine that we want to trace system activity: we want the system to beep when it executes a certain method. This audio based debugging is an interesting technique to determine if a certain piece of code is executed or not. In Squeak, there is a class Beeper that provides all the beeping functionality. When calling beep, the beep sound is played via the audio subsystem. The following example shows how to create a link that will invoke the message beep on the Beeper class.

```
beepLink := Link new metaObject: Beeper.
beepLink selector: #beep
```

Now we can install this beepLink on a method that is part of the system libraries. We take on purpose the method add: in OrderedCollection, a central class part of the collection libraries that is heavily used by the system. To set the link, we invoke the method link: on the AST-Node that stands for the whole method:

```
(OrderedCollection>>#add:) methodNode link: beepLink.
```

As result, a sound should be emited each time the method OrderedCollection»#add: is called. But as soon as we install this link, the system freezes. This clearly was not the intended outcome.

3 Infinite Meta-object Call Recursion

Let's analyze the cause for the problem presented above. After a discussion of some ad-hoc solutions, we show that the problem is caused by a missing model for the concept of the *meta-level execution*.

The Problem. To ensure that the problem is not caused by our framework, we modify the example to call a different method at the meta-object, the method beepPrimitive which directly executes functionality defined in the virtual machine.

```
beepLink := Link new metaObject: Beeper.
beepLink selector: #beepPrimitive.
```

When installing this link, we can see that it works as expected: we can hear a beep for all calls to the **add:** method, for example when typing characters in the Squeak IDE.

The problem thus lies in the code executed by the meta-object. The Squeak sound subsystem uses the method **add:** of OrderedCollection at some place to emit the beep sound. Thus, we call the same method **add:** from the meta-object that triggered the call to the meta in the first place. Therefore we end up calling the meta again and again as shown in Figure 2. This is clearly not a suitable semantics for behavioral reflection: it should be possible to use behavioral reflection even on system libraries that *are used to implement the meta object functionality themselves*.

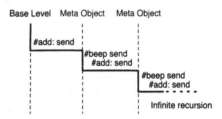

Fig. 2. Infinite recursive meta-object call

We present now two ad-hoc solutions.

Code Duplication. As the problem is caused by calling base level code from the meta-object, one solution would be to never call base level code from the meta-object, but instead provide a renamed copy for all classes and use these from the meta-level. Duplicating the complete system has, of course, all the standard problems of code duplication: space is wasted. In addition, the copy can easily become out of sync with the original. The problems could be minimized by just copying those methods that are really needed. In practice, it is not easy to identify these methods, especially in dynamic languages. In addition this would cause changes in the reflective layer to become fragile because any change would require the programmer to update the copied version of the base level. This is clearly not a good solution.

Adding Special Tests. Another solution could be to add special code to check if a recursion happens. The problem with this solution is that it is ad-hoc, the codebase becomes cluttered with checking instructions. It thus just patches the symptoms, the recursive call, and does not address the real problem.

The Real Problem: Modeling Meta-level Execution. The ad-hoc solutions are not satisfactory. The real problem exemplified by a recursive meta-call is that when going from infinite towers to meta-objects, the awareness that an execution occurs at the meta-level has been lost. Normally activation of a meta-object means a jump to the meta-level. The problem now is that this meta-level does not really exist in meta-object-based architectures: there is no way to query the system to know whether we are at the meta-level or not.

It should be noted again that the problem we have seen is not specific to a particular behavioral reflection framework. We observe the same problem when applying MethodWrappers [6] to system classes. Method wrappers wrap a method with before/after behavior. MethodWrappers are reflectively implemented in Smalltalk and thus use lots of system library code during the execution of the wrapped methods. The same problem was identified for CLOS [7] and is thus present in other meta-class based systems like for example MetaClassTalk [4].

4 Solution: A Metacontext

We have seen that the real cause for the problem of endless recursion lies in the absence of a model for *meta-level execution*: the fact that the system is executing meta-level code does not have a representation.

4.1 Modeling Context

At any point in the execution of some piece of code we should be able to query whether we are executing at the meta or at the base level. Such a property can be nicely modeled with the concept of *context*: the *meta-level* is a context that is active or inactive.

Such a context thus provides control-flow information: we want to know if we are in the control-flow of a call to a meta-object. But in addition, the context actually provides a reification: we have an object representing a specific control-flow, which in our case represents meta-level execution.

With a way to model meta-level execution, it is possible to solve the problem of recursive meta-object calls. A call to the meta-object can be scoped towards the base level: a meta-call should only occur when we are executing at the base level. If we are already at the meta-level, the calls should be ignored. This way, meta-object calls are only triggered by the base level computation, not the meta-level computation itself, thereby eliminating the recursion.

We will first describe a simplified model that only provides two levels of execution (base and meta) and does not allow any metameta-objects to be defined that are activated only from a meta-object execution. We describe later how to extend our model to support calls to these metameta-objects.

The Metacontext. To model the meta-level, we introduce a special *context*, the MetaContext. This context is inactive for a normal execution of a program. MetaContext will be activated when we enter in the meta-level computation and deactivate when we leave it (Figure 3). The meta-context thus models *meta-level execution*.

A simple model with just one meta-context is enough to distinguish the meta from the base level. We will see later that it makes sense to extend the meta-context to a possibly infinite tower of meta-contexts in Section 4.3.

Controlling meta-object activation. Just having a way to model meta-level execution via the meta-context is not enough to solve the problem of recursion,

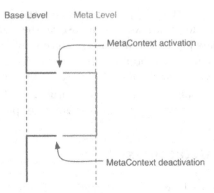

Fig. 3. The MetaContext activation

it is just the prerequisite to be able to detect it. We need to make sure that a call to the meta-object does not occur again if we are already executing at the meta-level. Thus, the call to the meta-level needs to be guarded so it is not executed if the execution is already occurring at the meta-level. In the context of behavioral partial reflection (*i.e.*, in the link-meta-object model that we used to show the problem), this means that the links are parameterized by the contexts in which they are active or not-active.

4.2   The Problem Revisited

With both the meta-context and the contextual controlled meta-object calls, we now can return to our example and see how our technique solves the problem of recursion. In our example, we defined the Beeper as a meta-object to be called when executing the add: method of OrderedCollection. The following steps occur (see Figure 4):

1. The add: method is executed from a base level program.
2. A call to the meta-object Beeper is requested:
    − We first check if we are at the meta-level. As we are not, we continue with the call.
    − We enable the MetaContext.
    − We call the meta-object.
3. Meta-object executes the beep method.
4. Meta-object calls the method add: method again
5. A Call to the meta-object is requested
    − We first check if we are at the meta-level. As we are executing meta-level code, the call is aborted.
6. Meta-object execution continues until it is finished.
7. On return to the base level, we deactivate the MetaContext.

Thus the recursive meta-call is aborted and the danger of recursion is eliminated. The model we described up to now with just one MetaContext is thus

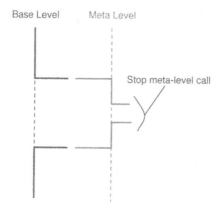

Fig. 4. Stopping infinite meta-call recursion

enough to solve the problem, but it not complete: it does not, for example, allow any calls to metameta-objects while already executing at the meta-level, which would make it impossible to observe or reason about metabehavior. In the next section, we therefore extend the model.

4.3   The Contextual Tower

As with the tower of interpreters, we can generalize the meta-context to form an infinite tower of meta-contexts. With the infinite tower of reflective interpreters, a reification is always bound to a specific interpreter. Normally, a jump from the base to the meta level means executing a reflective function that is defined as part of the interpreter I_1. But it is possible to define a reflective function one level up: this then is only triggered by the interpreter I_2 that interprets I_1, thus allowing to reflect on the interpreter I_1 itself. Figure 5 shows the reflective tower as visualized in the work of Smith [25].

Transposed to our contextual model, it follows that having just one context (the meta-context) is not enough. We need more contexts for meta-meta, meta-3 and so on. If we have this *contextual tower*, we can for example define a meta-meta object that is only called when we are executing at meta-1. Meta-object calls need thus not only be defined to be active for the base level, but they can optionally defined to be active for any of the meta-levels. This allows us to define meta*objects that reason about the system executing at any level, similar to the endless tower of interpreters.

As with all infinite structures, the most important question is how to realize it in practice. For the case of the infinite meta-context tower, there is an easy solution: contexts are objects, they can have state. We can parameterize the meta-context object with a number describing the meta-level that it encodes. Shifting to the meta-level means shifting from a context n to a context $n + 1$.

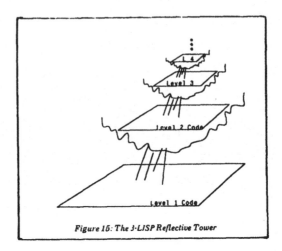

Fig. 5. The 3-Lisp reflective tower from [25]

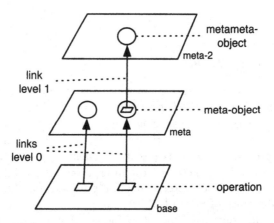

Fig. 6. The Contextual Tower up to the second level

Figure 6 shows an example. We have three contexts: the base level, the meta-level and meta-2. We see two links that are active at the base level. When called, they activate the meta-context with level 1. Then in the code of the meta-object (either the code of the meta-object itself or any library code executeted), we have a third link. This link is defined to be active only on meta-level 1, thus it will on execution enable meta-2. We show an example of such a level 1 link in Section 6.2.

An interesting and very nice property of the parameterized context is that the meta-contexts are only created on demand, they do not exist as an endless tower. This means, we have a form of partial reflection for providing a potential endless tower. If a meta-level is not needed, it does not cost anything.

4.4   The MetaContext Revised

The simple version of our idea with just one MetaContext is not enough to allow us to encode the Contextual Tower. We need a slightly modified model of MetaContext where the MetaContext is parameterized by the *level*. Such a parameterized MetaContext is not simply active or inactive, it is active for the level that it currently is set to. Thus when querying such a MetaContext, we give as a parameter a number denoting a meta-level. We will in the next section see how to realize such a context in practice.

5   Implementation

Now that we described the solution in general, we present an implementation of that model for REFLECTIVITY, our reflection framework. We first show how the context is implemented and then discuss contextual links.

5.1   Implementation of MetaContext

The MetaContext is a class that has one instance per thread (a thread-specific singleton). The instances are created on demand and are stored per thread. As threads are objects in Squeak, we extended them to be able to store additional state directly in an associated dictionary. This mechanism is then used to store the MetaContext instance.

Querying context. The MetaContext needs to model the meta-level. For that, it has one instance variable named level. We can increase the level by calling shiftLevelUp or decrease by shiftLevelDown. To test if the MetaContext is active for a certain level n we can call isActive: with a parameter denoting the level:

```
MetaLevel current isActive: 0
```

Sending current to the class MetaContext will retrieve the MetaContext singleton from the current process. If there is none yet, it will lazily create a Meta-Context with the level set to 0. Thus for a normal base level execution of code the expression above will return true.

Executing code in the MetaContext. To change the meta-level that code is executed at, we provide a way to run a block (an anonymous higher order function) one meta-level higher than the code outside the block. For example, to execute at meta-1, evaluate:

```
[ ... code executing on meta-1 ... ] valueWithMetaContext
```

If code is already executing at meta-1, calling valueWithMetaContext again will execute at meta-2:

```
[[ ... code executing on meta-2 ... ] valueWithMetaContext] valueWithMetaContext
```

The method valueWithMetaContext is implemented on the BlockClosure object, it will first shift the level of the current MetaContext up, then the block is executed. At the end the level of the context is shifted down to the previous value. We make sure that the downshift happens even in case of abnormal termination by evaluating the block using the exception handling mechanisms of Smalltalk:

```
valueWithMetaContext
    MetaContext current shiftLevelUp.
    ^ self ctxtEnsure: [MetaContext current shiftLevelDown]
```

To make sure that the execution of the context handling code itself does not result in endless loops, we do not call any code from the sytem libraries in this method. Instead, we carefully copy all methods executed by the context setup code. The copied methods reside in the classes of the system library, but they are prefixed with *ctxt* and edited to call only prefixed methods. One example is the call to ctxtEnsure: seen in the method above.

Concurrent meta-objects. As the MetaContext is represented by a thread-specific singleton, forking a new thread from the meta-level would mean that this thread has its own MetaContext object associated which is initialized to be at level 0. We have solved this problem by changing the implementation of threads to actually copy the meta-level information to the newly created thread. A thread created at the meta-level thus continues to run at the meta-level:

```
[ [ self assert: (MetaContext current isActive: 1) ]   fork ] valueWithMetaContext
```

As the context information is not shared with the parent thread, the meta-level of the new thread is independed, it can continue to run at the meta-level even when the parent thread already returned to the base level.

5.2   Realizing Contextual Links

Now that we have a suitable way to represent the meta context, we need to make the links and the code that is generated to call them *context-aware*. For that, we need to solve three problems:

1. the link needs to be defined to be specific to a certain meta level.
2. link activation should occur only when code is executing on the right meta-level.
3. link activation should increase the meta-level.

The first problem is solved by a simple extension of the Link class, whereas the other two are concerned with the code that our system generates for link activation. We will now show the required changes in detail.

Meta-level Specific Links. To allow the programmer to specify that a link is specific to a certain meta-level, we extend the link with a parameter called *level*. If *level* is not set, the link is globally active over all links (the standard behavior). The level can be set to any integer to define a link to only be active on that specific meta level. For our example, a link that is active only when executing base level code looks like this:

```
beepLink := Link new metaObject: Beeper.
beepLink selector: #beep;
beepLink level: 0.
```

Context-Aware Link Activation. To jump up one meta-level on link activation, we make sure that the code generated for a link is wrapped in a call to valueWithMetaContext. The resulting code will look like this:

```
[ ... code of the link  ... ] valueWithMetaContext
```

In addition to that, we need to make sure that the link is only called when we are on the correct meta level. This is done by checking if the current MetaContext is executing on the same level as the level that the link is defined to be active. Only if this is true, we activate the link and call the meta-object. The code we need to generate looks like this:

```
(MetaLevel current isActive: link level)  ifTrue: [
    [ ... code of the link  ... ] valueWithMetaContext
].
```

We will not go into the detail of how exactly the code is generated. The code can be found in the class GPTransformer of the REFLECTIVITY distribution[1].

6   Evaluation and Benchmarks

We first show that our solution solves the recursion problem, then we discuss how meta-context is useful for dynamic analysis. We describe *dynamic meta-level analysis* and realize an example. We present benchmarks to show the practicability of our approach.

6.1   The Problem Is Solved

We show that we can really solve the practical problem. For that, we define the link that activates the Beeper to be specific to level 0:

```
beepLink := Link new metaObject: Beeper.
beepLink selector: #beep;
beepLink level: 0.
```

Now we can install the link:

```
(OrderedCollection>>#add:) methodNode link: beepLink.
```

As soon as the link is installed, the next call to the **add:** method will trigger code-generation for that method. The code-generator will take the link into account and generate code as described earlier. Thus the recursive call to the **add:** method will not occur. We will thus hear a beep for every call to the **add:** method from the base level only.

[1] http://www.iam.unibe.ch/~scg/Research/Reflectivity

6.2 Benefits for Dynamic Analysis

Our initial reason for modeling meta-level execution was to solve the problem of meta-object call recursion, and thus making reflection easier to use. But the solution we presented, modeling meta-level execution with the help of a meta-context, is useful far beyond just solving the problem of recursion. In this section, we will discuss what it means for dynamic analysis. We show how it allows the programmer to analyze the code executed by meta-objects by enabling *dynamic meta-level analysis*.

Dynamic Analysis. One of the applications for behavioral reflection is dynamic analysis. For example, with reflection, it is fairly easy to introduce tracers or profilers into a running program [12] that normally require changes at the level of the virtual machine. One problem, though, with using reflection to introduce analysis code is that it is not clear which of the recorded events are resulting from the base level program execution and which from the code of the tracer itself. As long as we only trace application code, we can easily restrict the reflective tracer to the code of the application. But as soon as we want a complete system trace, we start to get into problems: recursion can occur easily (the problem we solved earlier), but even after working around recursion, we face another problem: how do we distinguish events that originated from the application from those that only occur due to the code executed by the tracer itself?

With our meta-level execution context, the problem described does not occur at all. The tracer (or any other tool performing dynamic analysis) is actually a meta-level program. A simple tracer would be the meta-object itself. More complex analysis tools would be called from a meta-object reifying the runtime event we are interested in. Thus, the code that performs the dynamic analysis is executing at the meta-level, while the links that trigger it are only active when executing a base level computation. This way we make sure that the infrastructure performing our analysis never affects the trace itself.

Dynamic Meta-level Analysis. An interesting challenge for dynamic analysis is that of analyzing the meta-level execution itself. Meta-level code should be lean and fast to not slow down the base computation more then really necessary. We thus are very interested in both tracing and profiling meta-level execution.

Our explicitly modeled meta-level execution makes this easy: we can define a link to be only active when executing at the meta-level. Therefore, we can install for example a trace-tool that exactly provides a trace of only those methods executed by a meta-object, even though the same methods are are called by the base level at the same time. We can thus as easily restrict the tracer towards meta-level execution as we restrict it to trace base level programs.

For our example, this means that we can use dynamic meta-level analysis to find the place in the sound-subsystem where the recursion problem happens when not using contextual links. In Section 3 we discuss that recursion happens, but we do not know where exactly the recursive call happens.

We define a link that is only active when we are executing code at level 1:

```
loggerLink := GPLink new metaObject: logger;
                selector: #log:;
                arguments: #(context);
                level: 1.
```

This link sends the message log: to the logger. The logger is an instance of class MyLogger:

```
logger := MyLogger new.
```

The method log: records the stack-frame that called the method where the link is installed on:

```
MyLogger>>log: aContext
        contexts add: aContext home sender copy
```

We install both a link calling the Beeper that is specific to level 0 and our link that is specific to level 1 on the method add:.

```
beepLink := Link new metaObject: Beeper.
beepLink selector: #beep;
beepLink level: 0.

(OrderedCollection>>#add:) methodNode link: beepLink.
(OrderedCollection>>#add:) reflectiveMethod methodNode link: loggerLink.
```

We can now inspect the logger object and see that it is recording the execution of SoundPlayer class»startPlayingImmediately: for every beep. Looking at this method, we find the code ActiveSounds add: aSound., which is the one spot in the sound system that calls the method add: of OrderedCollection. Thus we found with the help of dynamic meta-level analysis the exact call that causes the recursion problem as shown in Section 3.

6.3 Benchmarks

To assess if the system as presented is practically usable, we have carried out some benchmarks. Without the additional code for context activation, there is no overhead at all for calling a meta-object besides the call itself. The link specifies the meta-object and which method to call. The system generates from that information code that just calls the meta as specified. The problem now for analyzing the new context-enabled system is that the context code will, compared to the standard link activation, take a lot of time. In practice, though, meta-objects are usually there to do something: there is always code executed at the meta-level. So to make a practical comparison of the additional percentage of slowdown introduced by the context code, we need to compare the context-setup code not only to the link activation of an empty meta-object, but to a meta-object that actually executes code.

We will benchmark the slowdown of the context handling for the execution of different meta-objects. The variation between the meta-objects is the number of sends done at the meta-level. For the benchmark, we create a class Base with just one empty method bench. To play the role of a meta-object, we create a class Meta with one method in which we call an empty method in a loop. This method thus simulates a meta-object doing some work. We can easily change the amount of work done by changing the loop. To know how this simple benchmark compares to real code executed, we added a meta-object calling the Beeper and one converting a float to a string.

We install a link on the method in Base to call the method in Meta. We call the base method now in a loop and measure the time:

```
[100000 timesRepeat: [Base new bench ]] timeToRun
```

Table 1 shows the result when comparing both the original Geppetto and the context-enabled Geppetto for different meta-objects[2]:

Table 1. Slowdown of meta-object calls with context

meta-object	context (msecs)	standard (msecs)	slowdown
0 message sends	614	34	1'705.88%
10 message sends	723	165	338.18%
50 message sends	1040	470	121.28%
Beeper	1543	942	63.80%
100 message sends	1406	856	64.25%
200 message sends	2236	1621	37.94%
1234.345 printString	2534	1920	31.98%
500 message sends	4580	3907	17.23%
1000 message sends	8543	8029	6.40%

As expected, the slowdown in the case of an empty meta-object is substantial. But as soon as the meta-object itself executes code, the overhead starts to be acceptable. For calling the Beeper (from our running example), we have found an overhead of 63%. We are down to 17% on when executing 500 empty methods, and at 6.4% on 1000 methods.

It should be noted that this does not mean that the overhead observed for meta-object calls translate directly into a slowdown of a program using reflection. In a real program, the overall slowdown depends on how often meta-objects are called and how much time the program spends at the base level and meta-level compared to switching meta-levels.

---

[2] The benchmark was run on an Apple MacBook Pro, 2.4Ghz Intel Core 2 Duo with 2GB RAM on Squeak Version 3.9.

7   Related Work

Meta-object Architectures. There are many examples for meta-object based reflective systems. Examples are 3-KRS [22], the CLOS MOP [20] and other metaclass based systems like Neoclasstalk [5], or MetaClassTalk [4]. A more recent example is partial behavioral reflection for Java [30] and Smalltalk [24]. None of these systems provide a representation for meta-level execution.

One could even argue that all these systems are not really reflective (as they can not be used to reflect on the system itself) and it is debatable if the meta-objects in these systems are really *meta*. It has already noted by Ferber [14] that metaclasses are not meta in the computational sense, even though they are meta in the structural sense. For any computationally reflective system, we need to be able to decide if a computation is executing at the meta-level or not. Without this, there is no reason to talk about *meta-objects* at all.

Aspect Oriented Programming. There is an ongoing debate about the relationship of aspect oriented rogramming (AOP) [21] and reflection. Proponents of reflection claim that AOP is just a use-case for behavioral reflection, a pattern that can be easily implemented. The AOP community, though, would claim that reflection in turn is just the case of an aspect system where the domain is the language model itself, with the core-concepts (e.g. message sending) factored nicely into aspects and thus easily modifiable.

The ideas from this paper can contribute to this discussion. In AOP, a pointcut is globally visible: it matches even in the advice code itself by default. Conversely, we can say that the problem we noted in this paper is made an explicit and well known property in AOP, whereas it is a bug to be fixed in meta-object based reflection.

We claim that exactly here lies the difference between reflection and AOP: reflection needs the distinction between the base and the meta. Aspects, however, are a pure base level abstraction. Invoking an advice does not constitute a metacomputation, a level shift does not occur.

Contrary the notion that aspects are pure base level constructs, *Stratified Aspects* [3] define an extension that identify spurious recursion to be a problem and present the concept of metaadvice and metaaspects as a solution. This idea has some similarities to contextual reifications discussed in this paper, with the exception that meta-level execution is not modeled explicitly.

Context-Oriented Programming. ContextL [8,18] is a language to support *Context-Oriented Programming* (COP). The language provides a notion of *layers*, which package context-dependent behavioral variations. In practice, the variations consist of method definitions, mixins and *before* and *after* specifications. COP has no first-class notion of *context*, it is implicitly defined by the layers that are activated. The topic of reflection has been discussed for COP [9]. But the paper looks at reflective layer activation, not a reflective model of context nor the use of context to structure or control reflection itself.

Context-aware Aspects. The concept of context has seen some use in AOP [29]. As context specific behavior tends to crosscut base programs, it can advantageously be implemented as aspects. This leads to the notion of context-aware aspects, i.e., aspects whose behavior depends on context. The work has been continued in the direction of supporting reasoning on contexts and context history on the level of the pointcuts [16, 17].

Deployment strategies [28] provide full control over dynamic aspect deployment both related to the call stack and to created objects and functions. AspectBoxes [2] are another example where aspects are controlled via a form of a context, in this case defined by the classbox model [1]. A good overview and discussion on the many mechanisms for dynamically scoping crosscutting in general is described in the work of Tanter [27].

The MetaHelix. The problem of unwanted meta-level call recursion has been mentioned by Chiba and Kiczales [7]. The problem discussed is first the structural problem that *e.g.*, fields added by reflection to implement changed behavior show through to any user of introspection. The other problem mentioned is recursion, as any use of changed behavior can trigger a reification again. As a solution, the authors present the *MetaHelix*. All meta-objects have a field implemented-by that points to a version of the code that is not reflectively changed.

This approach is both more general and restrictive than our context based solution. It is more general, as it tries to solve the problem of the visibility of structural change. And it is more restrictive, as it does not model meta-level execution. The programmer has to call the right code explicitly, thus it can be seen as a controlled way to support the code copying solution presented in Section 3. The problem of structural changes is a very interesting one, as future work we plan to apply the ideas of the meta-context to structural reflection.

Subjective Programming. Us [26] is a system based on Self that supports subject-oriented programming [15]. Message lookup depends not only on the receiver of a message, but also on a second object, called the *perspective*. The perspective allows for layer activation similar to ContexL. The paper discusses the usefulness of subjectivity for controlling the access to reflection APIs, it does not go as far as using subjectivity for controlling behavioral reflection.

8   Conclusion and Future Work

In this paper we have analyzed the problem of the missing representation of meta-level execution in meta-object architectures. We have shown that the problem of infinite meta-object call recursion can be solved by introducing a representation for meta-level execution. We proposed to model the execution at the meta-level as a first class context and presented an implementation. Benchmarks show that the implementation can be realized in a practical manner.

For now, we have used the concept of *context* just to make the meta computation distinguishable from the base computation. We plan to extend the notion of contextual control of reification to other kinds of contexts then the meta-context.

We have experimented in the past with the idea of a first class model of change for programming languages [11]. We will explore the idea of context for structural reflection to model change. Virtual machine support for meta-contexts is interesting for two reasons. First, we hope to be able to improve performance by realizing all context setup code in the virtual machine. Second, as we explained in Section 5, the setup code executed when dealing with contexts has to be managed specially: we provide copies of all that code. We plan to move all this special code into the virtual machine.

An interesting question is how a context-aware reflective language kernel would look like and what the consequences for the language runtime and especially the reflective model would be. We plan to explore such a new reflective language kernel in the future.

Acknowledgments. We thank Eric Tanter, Robert Hirschfeld, Orla Greevy, Oscar Nierstrasz, Martin von Löwis, Toon Verwaest, Adrian Kuhn, Adrian Lienhard and Lukas Renggli for discussing various aspects of the concepts presented in this paper. We acknowledge the financial support of the Swiss National Science Foundation for the project "Analyzing, capturing and taming software change" (SNF Project No. 200020-113342, Oct. 2006 - Sept. 2008) and COOK (JC05 42872) funded by the french Agence Nationale de la Recherche.

References

1. Bergel, A., Ducasse, S., Nierstrasz, O., Wuyts, R.: Classboxes: Controlling visibility of class extensions. Journal of Computer Languages, Systems and Structures 31(3-4), 107–126 (2005)
2. Bergel, A., Hirschfeld, R., Clarke, S., Costanza, P.: Aspectboxes — controlling the visibility of aspects. In: Filipe, M.H.J., Shiskov, B. (eds.) Proceedings of the International Conference on Software and Data Technologies (ICSOFT 2006), pp. 29–38 (September 2006)
3. Bodden, E., Forster, F., Steimann, F.: Avoiding infinite recursion with stratified aspects. In: Hirschfeld, R., Polze, A., Kowalczyk, R. (eds.) GI-Edition Lecture Notes in Informatics NODe 2006 GSEM 2006, vol. P-88, pp. 49–64. Bonner Köllen Verlag, Gesellschaft für Informatik (2006)
4. Bouraqadi, N.: Un MOP Smalltalk pour l'étude de la composition et de la compatibilité des métaclasses. Application à la programmation par aspects (A Smalltalk MOP for the Study of Metaclass Composition and Compatibility. Application to Aspect-Oriented Programming. In: French). Thèse de doctorat, Université de Nantes, Nantes, France (July 1999)
5. Bouraqadi, N., Ledoux, T., Rivard, F.: Safe metaclass programming. In: Proceedings OOPSLA 1998, pp. 84–96 (1998)
6. Brant, J., Foote, B., Johnson, R., Roberts, D.: Wrappers to the rescue. In: Jul, E. (ed.) ECOOP 1998. LNCS, vol. 1445, pp. 396–417. Springer, Heidelberg (1998)
7. Chiba, S., Kiczales, G., Lamping, J.: Avoiding confusion in metacircularity: The meta-helix. In: Futatsugi, K., Matsuoka, S. (eds.) ISOTAS 1996. LNCS, vol. 1049, pp. 157–172. Springer, Heidelberg (1996)

8. Costanza, P., Hirschfeld, R.: Language constructs for context-oriented programming: An overview of ContextL. In: Proceedings of the Dynamic Languages Symposium (DLS) 2005, co-organized with OOPSLA 2005, pp. 1–10. ACM Press, New York (2005)

9. Costanza, P., Hirschfeld, R.: Reflective layer activation in ContextL. In: SAC 2007: Proceedings of the 2007 ACM Symposium on Applied Computing, pp. 1280–1285. ACM Press, New York (2007)

10. Denker, M., Ducasse, S., Lienhard, A., Marschall, P.: Sub-method reflection. Journal of Object Technology 6(9), 231–251 (2007)

11. Denker, M., Gîrba, T., Lienhard, A., Nierstrasz, O., Renggli, L., Zumkehr, P.: Encapsulating and exploiting change with Changeboxes. In: Proceedings of the 2007 International Conference on Dynamic Languages (ICDL 2007), pp. 25–49. ACM Digital Library (2007)

12. Denker, M., Greevy, O., Lanza, M.: Higher abstractions for dynamic analysis. In: 2nd International Workshop on Program Comprehension through Dynamic Analysis (PCODA 2006), pp. 32–38 (2006)

13. Ducasse, S.: Evaluating message passing control techniques in Smalltalk. Journal of Object-Oriented Programming (JOOP) 12(6), 39–44 (1999)

14. Ferber, J.: Computational reflection in class-based object-oriented languages. In: Proceedings OOPSLA 1989, ACM SIGPLAN Notices, oct 1989, vol. 24, pp. 317–326 (October 1989)

15. Harrison, W., Ossher, H.: Subject-oriented programming (a critique of pure objects). In: Proceedings OOPSLA 1993, ACM SIGPLAN Notices, vol. 28, pp. 411–428 (October 1993)

16. Herzeel, C., Gybels, K., Costanza, P.: A temporal logic language for context awareness in pointcuts. In: Proceeding of the Workshop on Revival of Dynamic Languages (2006)

17. Herzeel, C., Gybels, K., Costanza, P., D'Hondt, T.: Modularizing crosscuts in an e-commerce application in lisp using halo. In: Proceeding of the International Lisp Conference (ILC 2007) (2007)

18. Hirschfeld, R., Costanza, P., Nierstrasz, O.: Context-oriented programming. Journal of Object Technology 7(3) (March 2008)

19. Ingalls, D., Kaehler, T., Maloney, J., Wallace, S., Kay, A.: Back to the future: The story of Squeak, A practical Smalltalk written in itself. In: Proceedings OOPSLA 1997, ACM SIGPLAN Notices, pp. 318–326. ACM Press (November 1997)

20. Kiczales, G., Rivières, J.d., Bobrow, D.G.: The Art of the Metaobject Protocol. MIT Press (1991)

21. Kiczales, G., Lamping, J., Mendhekar, A., Maeda, C., Lopes, C., Loingtier, J.-M., Irwin, J.: Aspect-Oriented Programming. In: Aksit, M., Matsuoka, S. (eds.) ECOOP 1997. LNCS, vol. 1241, pp. 220–242. Springer, Heidelberg (1997)

22. Maes, P.: Concepts and experiments in computational reflection. In: Proceedings OOPSLA 1987, ACM SIGPLAN Notices, vol. 22, pp. 147–155 (December 1987)

23. Rivard, F.: Pour un lien d'instanciation dynamique dans les langages à classes. In: JFLA 1996. INRIA — collection didactique (January 1996)

24. Röthlisberger, D., Denker, M., Tanter, É.: Unanticipated partial behavioral reflection: Adapting applications at runtime. Journal of Computer Languages, Systems and Structures 34(2-3), 46–65 (2008)

25. Smith, B.C.: Reflection and semantics in a procedural language. Technical Report TR-272. MIT, Cambridge (1982)

26. Smith, R.B., Ungar, D.: A simple and unifying approach to subjective objects. TAPOS special issue on Subjectivity in Object-Oriented Systems 2(3), 161–178 (1996)
27. Tanter, É.: On dynamically-scoped crosscutting mechanisms. ACM SIGPLAN Notices 42(2), 27–33 (2007)
28. Tanter, É.: Expressive scoping of dynamically-deployed aspects. In: Proceedings of the 7th ACM International Conference on Aspect-Oriented Software Development (AOSD 2008), Brussels, Belgium, April 2008. ACM Press (to appear, 2008)
29. Tanter, É., Gybels, K., Denker, M., Bergel, A.: Context-aware aspects. In: Löwe, W., Südholt, M. (eds.) SC 2006. LNCS, vol. 4089, pp. 227–242. Springer, Heidelberg (2006)
30. Tanter, É., Noyé, J., Caromel, D., Cointe, P.: Partial behavioral reflection: Spatial and temporal selection of reification. In: Proceedings of OOPSLA 2003, ACM SIGPLAN Notices, pp. 27–46 (November 2003)

An AsmL Semantics for Dynamic Structures and Run Time Schedulability in UML-RT

Stefan Leue[1], Alin Ştefănescu[2,*], and Wei Wei[1]

[1] Department of Computer and Information Science
University of Konstanz
D-78457 Konstanz, Germany
{Stefan.Leue|Wei.Wei}@uni-konstanz.de
[2] SAP Research CEC Darmstadt
Bleichstr. 8, D-64283 Darmstadt, Germany
alin.stefanescu@sap.com

Abstract. Many real-time systems use runtime structural reconfiguration mechanisms based on dynamic creation and destruction of components. To support such features, UML-RT provides a set of modeling concepts including optional actor references and multiple containment. However, these concepts are not covered in any of the current formal semantics of UML-RT, thus impeding the testing and formal analysis of realistic models. We use AsmL to present an executable semantics covering dynamic structures and other important features like run time schedulability. The semantics is parametrized to capture UML-RT semantics variation points whose decision choices depend on the special implementation in a vendor CASE tool. We have built several different implementations of those variation points, including the one as implemented in the IBM Rational Rose RealTime (Rose-RT) tool. Finally, we illustrate how the proposed executable semantics can be used in the analysis of a Rose-RT model using the Spec Explorer tool.

Keywords: UML-RT, dynamic structures, formal semantics, AsmL, Rose-RT, Spec Explorer, model-based testing, model checking.

1 Introduction

UML-RT [28] was proposed as a UML dialect customized for the design of distributed embedded real-time systems [26]. UML-RT is based on the ROOM notation [27] which was originally developed at Bell Northern Research. Currently supported by the IBM Rational Rose RealTime (Rose-RT) tool [23], UML-RT finds applications in a broad range of domains including telecommunications [17], control systems [25,12], and automotive systems [11]. A UML-RT model consists of a set of concurrent autonomous objects, called actors, that exchange messages with one another through dedicated communication interfaces referred

---

* The work was done while this author was affiliated with the University of Konstanz.

R.F. Paige and B. Meyer (Eds.): TOOLS EUROPE 2008, LNBIP 11, pp. 238–257, 2008.

to as ports. A notable feature of UML-RT is the hierarchical and dynamic structure of an actor: An actor may contain a set of sub-actors in its inner structure, and a sub-actor can be dynamically constructed and destroyed at run time. Moreover, a sub-actor contained in one actor can be imported to the inner structure of another actor. This allows two actors to share a sub-actor serving as a messenger for its two containers. The dynamic structure feature of UML-RT is very useful since it reflects the architecture of many realistic distributed systems.

Software models play a central role throughout the whole life cycle of development processes following the model driven architecture paradigm [21]. Models are used for documentation, prototyping, code generation and testing. It is therefore of great importance that a software model is correctly designed. A promising way of increasing one's confidence in the correctness of a software model is the use of formal methods, in particular systematic state space exploration. This requires a formal operational semantics of the modeling language.

In this paper we report on the SURTA (Semantics of UML-RT in AsmL) project that proposes an executable semantics for UML-RT. The semantics is given in AsmL, a modeling language based on the theory of Abstract State Machines [2]. Developed by the Foundations of Software Engineering group at Microsoft Research, the AsmL language is supported by the Spec Explorer tool [29]. SpecExplorer enables the simulation, assertion checking, and test case generation of an AsmL model by exploring the generated finite state machine. AsmL is also tightly integrated into the Microsoft .NET framework. We use the .NET type system for describing meta-model level details of UML-RT. A further benefit of choosing AsmL is to exploit the verification and test case generation capabilities of Spec Explorer for Rose-RT models, for which the Rose-RT tool offers little support.

Compared to other existing semantics work for UML-RT, the main contributions of the SURTA project are as follows:

- We cover some important UML-RT features such as dynamic structures and run time schedulability. These include (1) actor incarnation/destruction, (2) actor importation/deportation, (3) dynamic port binding, (4) replications, (5) transition guards/actions, (6) controllers, and (7) other run time environment features.
- We implemented several variants of the UML-RT semantics. To accommodate the many ambiguities and semantic variation points in the semantics as described in [27], we give a parameterized semantics which can be extended for concrete CASE tool implementations. We define a most general semantics that can encompass all interpretations that are possible according to [27]. We also define a semantics that is in line with the Communicating Finite State Machines (CFSMs) [6] paradigm, and one that corresponds to the concrete semantics of UML-RT as implemented in the Rose-RT tool. Providing a semantics as implemented by a particular vendor tool will prove beneficial if this semantics entails a smaller state space than that allowed by the more general semantics. This allows those portions of the behavior to be disregarded that do not correspond to a behavior implemented by that

particular tool and hence by the deployed target system synthesized from the model. This would then result in a more efficient state space exploration.
- The architecture of SURTA has great extensibility for implementing and plugging in different concrete semantics. Additionally, SURTA allows a UML-RT model to be straightforwardly expressed in AsmL. The transformation of a model is no more complex than describing what syntactic elements are included in the model, and this can be fully automated.
- SURTA allows an easy encoding of system properties, which can be checked using the assertion checking feature of Spec Explorer.

Related work. [13] uses a notion of flow graphs into which a UML-RT model is transformed. However, there is no systematic transformation method available. It is also not obvious how such a transformation can improve the functional analysis of UML-RT models. An early approach to model checking RoseRT models is described in [24]. It aims at model checking the C++ code synthesized by RoseRT. This approach is rather inflexible, since it depends on the programming language chosen in the RoseRT models and on the particular code generator used. It also only supports a rather limited set of the syntactic features of RoseRT models. [30] uses labeled transition systems to formalize a subset of UML-RT mostly focusing on the behavior of state machines. [19] covers the timed aspects of UML-RT by translating a timed state machine into a timed automaton. However, it does not consider any other aspects of UML-RT. There are several approaches of formalizing UML-RT using process algebras [10,9,22,8,3]. Most of these works consider only synchronous communication. [9] considers asynchronous communication, but it allows only the use of *bounded* FIFO message buffers. While none of the above cited papers considers dynamic structures of UML-RT, [3] proposes a semantics for the so-called *unwired* ports using name passing in the π-calculus. The support of unwired ports enables changes in the communication topologies. However, the work described in [3] does not consider other kinds of dynamic structures that our work is addressing. Unlike our work, none of the existing work addresses the ambiguities and semantic variation points in the informal semantics of UML-RT, and most of them derive the operational semantics from the particular implementation in Rose-RT. [18] maps the modeling elements of UML to AsmL data structures, based on which a UML model can be transformed into an AsmL specification at the semantic level. This is different from our approach in which a UML-RT model is translated into AsmL purely syntactically. [5] compares the expressiveness of several formalisms for specifying dynamic system structures. SURTA supports almost all important dynamic structure operations that other formalisms provide, such as addition and removal of elements and connectors, iterative changes, and choice-based changes.

Outline. The paper is structured as follows. We give a brief introduction to UML-RT and AsmL in Sections 2 and 3, respectively. The architecture of SURTA is explained in Section 4. The executable semantics is then detailed in Section 5. We illustrate the usefulness of the given semantics in Section 6. We conclude the paper and suggest future work in Section 7.

2 UML-RT

Using an example model in Figure 1, we briefly introduce the set of UML-RT concepts for which we later define a semantics in Section 5. The model in Figure 1 has a number of clients that each requests a remote service. The request of a client prompts the client manager to send an unused service accessor object to the server. The server connection manager then imports the received object to both the coordination process (`serviceAccessorCoor`) and an available `serviceAccessorS` process. The coordination process informs the client side of a successfully established connection. The `serviceAccessorS` process then uses the imported accessor object to pass messages between the client and the service object assigned to the client.

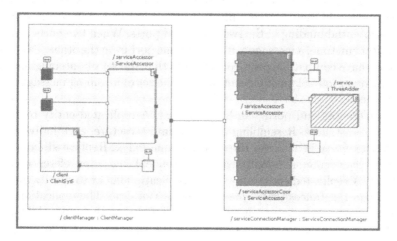

Fig. 1. A UML-RT model in which a number of clients request remote services. The model is taken from a collection of examples included in Rose-RT distributions, with slight modification to allow dynamic creation and destruction of **service** instances.

Static structure. The central structural concept in UML-RT is that of an *actor*, also called capsule in Rose-RT. An actor is an autonomously running object whose execution is influenced by other actors exclusively through message passing. Each actor is an instance of a certain *actor class*. An actor may hold a set of *actor references* (capsule role in Rose-RT), which are pointers to sub-actors. Figure 1 shows the internal structures of two actor classes: `ClientManager` and `ServiceConnectionManager`. Both actor classes contain sub-actor references like `client` and `serviceAccessorS`. A reference is *incarnated* when a new actor is created for the reference. An actor reference is *fixed* if its incarnation occurs when the enclosing actor is created. A reference is *optional* if its incarnation must be explicitly invoked by the enclosing actor. The sub-actor that an optional actor reference points to may be destroyed later by the container. An *imported* reference cannot be instantiated, and can only hold a pointer to an existing actor. In Figure 1, the reference `client` is fixed and the reference `service`, contained in `serviceConnectionManager`, is optional. Taking the graphic notations of Rose-RT, we denote an optional reference by a shadowed rectangle. Examples of imported references are `serviceAccessorS` and `serviceAccessorCoor`, represented by gray filled boxes.

The communication interface of an actor is a set of *ports* though which the actor sends and receives messages. Each port is associated with a *protocol* that determines which messages can be sent and received through the port. In Figure 1, ports are those small rectangles sitting either on actor reference boundaries or inside actor bodies. A port may be an *end port* through which its containing actor sends or receives messages. A port may also be a *relay port* that simply forwards messages from one side to another. A port may have a *conjugated* protocol, namely, the set of incoming messages and the set of outgoing messages defined in the original protocol are inverse. Ports with conjugated protocols are denoted by hollow rectangles. Ports in Figure 1 are connected with each other. Each connecting line defines a potential binding of the two connected ports. When two ports are actually *bound* at run time, a message can arrive at one port from the other. Two bound ports must have compatible protocols, namely that the set of outgoing messages allowed by one protocol must be contained in the set of incoming messages of the other protocol.

Actor references and ports can be replicated. A replicated entity represents a number of instances. Resembling an array data structure, each individual instance of the entity is accessed through a unique index. Replicated entities are graphically represented in a multilayered fashion, c. f. the actor reference `client` in Figure 1. A replicated entity may have a replication factor to specify the maximal number of instances that it may contain at run time. The replication factor of each replicated reference in our example is depicted as the upper-right corner number in its graphic notation. All ports in the example have also replication factors that are however not shown in the figure. Replication is used to obtain a more flexible and concise graphic representation of a model. However, replication also introduces ambiguities, e.g., when two replicated ports are connected, it is not clear which instance of one port should be bound to which instance of the other port at run time. We will discuss this problem in depth in Section 5.6.

Dynamic behavior. The behavior of an actor is expressed by an *extended hierarchical state machine*. In UML-RT, a transition is always triggered by the receiving of a message from one of the end ports of the corresponding actor. A transition may have a specified action to be executed when it is fired. Actions may alter local variables, send messages to other actors, or dynamically change the structure of the actor. States may also have entry actions and exit actions. The language used for specifying actions is not limited in UML-RT. For more information about state machines and their behavior, we refer readers to [20]. In this paper we consider only flat state machines, and leave the formalization of hierarchical state machines for future work. Currently, we must flatten the hierarchical state machines of a model before translating it into AsmL.

Controllers. At run time, each actor instance runs on a thread. Threads are executed independently in parallel. We abstract physical threads to the concept of *controllers*. A controller contains a set of actor instances, and schedules the executions of contained actors as well as the sending and receiving of messages.

Rose-RT. Widely used in industrial practices and academic research, Rose-RT is a powerful CASE tool for modeling distributed embedded systems using UML-RT formalism [23,14]. Rose-RT currently supports three programming languages, C, C++, and Java, for specifying transition actions in state machines.

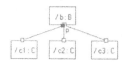

Fig. 2. A UML-RT model

Rose-RT is often taken as the main source of retrieving an operational semantics for UML-RT. This is problematic in two ways: First, the concrete Rose-RT semantics does not allow for non-determinism at all, and resolves non-determinism in a naive way: Consider the example in Figure 2. The replicated port p is connected to three ports that each belongs to a distinct reference below. Rose-RT decides that the instance of p indexed at 0 will be bound to the port of the first reference being added to the structure diagram when the model was built, say $c1$. This order fixing can be dangerous because a previously validated property may no longer holds for the system after, e.g., the reference $c1$ was deleted from the model and later added back. In this case, the instance indexed at 0 will no longer be bound to the port at $c1$, which may result in a violation of the property. Second, the Rose-RT semantics even has some inconsistencies with the informal UML-RT semantics suggested in [27].

3 AsmL

Space limitations do not permit us to provide a detailed description of the Abstract State Machine Language (AsmL in short), we refer the reader to [15] for more information. AsmL is an object-oriented software specification language. Its syntax resembles Java and C#, and it provides conventional object oriented programming features like encapsulation and inheritance. As a high-level specification language, AsmL also provides supports for non-determinism, parallel updates of variables, and assertion checking, as illustrated by the example in Figure 3. The program defines a class of integer intervals, which has two fields to specify the lower bound and the upper bound of an interval. The *shift* procedure shifts an interval by a specified offset. The *random* function returns an arbitrary integer number within the interval.

```
class Interval
  private var lower as Integer
  private var upper as Integer                    Main()
  public procedure shift(offset as Integer)         step
    step                                               let interval = new Interval(0, 5)
      lower := lower + offset                       step
      upper := upper + offset                         interval.shift(6)
  public function random() as Integer                 WriteLine(interval.random() > 5)
    return any number | number in {lower..upper}   step
  constraint wellformed:                              WriteLine(interval.random() > 5)
    lower <= upper
```

Fig. 3. An AsmL program working on integer intervals

Non-determinism. The returned value of the *random* function is picked non-deterministically from the interval by the run time environment of Spec Explorer, the specification analysis tool supporting AsmL. There are other program constructs in AsmL that allow non-deterministic choices, such as `choose i in S` which takes a random member from a set *S*.

Parallel updates of variables. The AsmL language has an important concept called `step`. Any update of a variable within one step does not take effect until the next step is executed. As an example, the second step in the *Main* procedure shifts an interval by 6, and checks if any value in the interval is now larger than 5. The checking occurs before the next step is executed, so the interval is still between 0 and 5 and the output of the checking is *false*.

Assertion checking. AsmL allows the use of class invariants, identified by the keyword `constraint`, as well as pre- and post-conditions for procedures and functions, denoted by the keywords `require` and `ensure`, respectively. The violation of any of these assertions will result in a runtime exception. Assertion checking does not only help revealing program errors, but also enables property verification by searching for assertion violations, as explained in Section 6.

Semantics of AsmL. The AsmL language is based on the Abstract State Machine formalism [4]. A formal semantics has been defined for the core of AsmL [15]. There are also other semantic definitions for AsmL [16]. Even if it does not possess a formal semantics for all of its syntactic features, AsmL with its support for non-determinism and its step semantics is nonetheless an ideal choice for defining an executable operational semantics for UML-RT, which is the main objective of our paper.

4   SURTA Architecture

The SURTA project defines an AsmL specification of the UML-RT semantics, including various realizations of semantic variation points. Our work is different from all other semantic work for UML-RT, e.g., [22,1,3], in that we do not aim at devising a semantic level translation procedure for individual models. The architecture of the SURTA semantics allows for the transformation of a UML-RT model to be entirely at the syntactic level: we need simply to describe what comprises the syntactic definition of a model in the AsmL specification. The execution of the model is then handled totally by the semantics of a chosen run time environment. This approach has at least the following advantages:

- The separation of syntax and run time behavior makes it highly flexible for implementing semantics variants: When a semantic variation point of UML-RT is differently realized, the syntactic level needs no or very little modification.
- Because a concrete UML-RT model is only syntactically transformed into AsmL, a change in the semantic level does not require the model to be re-transformed. In fact, how the semantic level of UML-RT is mapped can be completely transparent to users of the SURTA project.
- A straightforward syntactic translation of a UML-RT model into AsmL can be fully automated.

layer		core	concrete extension (e.g., Rose–RT)
syntactic levels	model description	UML–RT models	Rose–RT models
	meta–model level	actor classes, actor reference definitions port definitions, binding definitions variable definitions, message types state machine definitions, protocols	message priorties
semantic level	run time behavior	actor instances, actor references ports, port bindings, controllers actor incarnation/destruction actor importation/deportation buffers, message sending and receiving	Rose–RT port bindings pseudo FIFO buffers capsule incarnation

Fig. 4. The SURTA architecture

Figure 4 shows the architecture of the SURTA project. It has three levels: the syntactic *meta-model level*, the semantic *run-time behavior level*, and the *model description level*. Each level has a core that gives semantics for the unambiguous parts of the UML-RT language, which can be extended by different implementations for ambiguities and semantic variant points. The extensibility minimizes the effort for implementing a variant of some UML-RT semantics.

Meta-model level. This level mainly defines the syntactic composition of each UML-RT modeling concept. For instance, it defines what constitutes an actor class definition. On the other hand, it does not describe what an instance of an actor class is, and how instances of a class behave at run time. The concept of actor instances and its run time behavior are instead defined at the run time semantic level. The meta-model level links the other two levels, and provides indispensable information for actor reference incarnation and importation as will be explained in Section 5.6.

Run-time behavior level. This level defines run time entities that are instances of the modeling elements introduced in the meta-model level. As an example, actor instances are running entities when a UML-RT model is executed, and each running actor instance belongs to some actor class. This level defines the relationship between an actor instance and its defining class, the creation and destruction of an actor instance, port bindings, and many other actor instance related run time properties.

Model description level. This level defines concrete UML-RT models by creating the proper syntactic description of a model based on the relevant UML-RT modeling elements at the meta-model level. The model description level basically needs no knowledge of the run time behavior level. Exceptions are transition guards and actions in which some methods provided by a particular run time environment may be invoked, such as the incarnation of an actor reference, or the read/write of a variable (or, an attribute or a field) of an actor. However, in these cases we only need to know the signatures of the invoked methods while their implementations remain hidden.

Extensions. Each level in the SURTA architecture can be extended with different concrete semantic variation point realizations. Currently, we provide three different implementations: (1) a most general semantics in which each actor instance runs on a distinct thread, and messages are stored in bag-like data structures. This means that any message in a bag can be selected for triggering a transition; (2) a semantics based on Communicating Finite State Machines (CFSMs) [6], in which each actor instance runs on a distinct thread, and messages are stored in first-in-first-out (FIFO) queues such that only the head message can be received by a port; (3) a semantics based on the Rose-RT implementation the details of which will be presented in Section 5.

5   An Executable Semantics

In this section we present the AsmL specification of the UML-RT semantics in the SURTA project. Sections 5.1–5.3 explain how the syntactic definitions of UML-RT modeling elements are mapped. Sections 5.4–5.8 explain in detail the semantics of run time entities. Section 5.9 addresses model descriptions and gives the AsmL specification of the example in Figure 1. Due to space limitations we leave out a large part of implementation code of the definition of each UML-RT concept, and present only the part relevant to our discussion. Readers are referred to [20] for more details.

5.1   Actor Classes

The syntax of the central UML-RT concept of actor classes is defined to be a collection of actor reference definitions, port definitions, binding definitions, variable definitions, and a state machine description (see Section 5.2). This is reflected in the AsmL class *ActorClass* shown in Figure 5. Note that any object

```
class ActorClass
  private name as String
  private const subActorRefDefs as Set of SubActorRefDefinition
  private const portDefs as Set of PortDefinition
  private const bindingDefs as Set of BindingDefinition
  private const variableDefs as Set of VariableDefinition
  private const stateMachine as StateMachine
```

Fig. 5. The AsmL definition of actor classes

of the class *ActorClass* is a particular class of actors, but *not* an instance of an actor class. Actor instances are defined at the run time behavior level as explained in Section 5.6.

We omit the classes for actor reference definitions, port definitions, etc. The class of sub-actor reference definitions has (1) a field *myClass* to indicate the class of an actor reference; (2) a field *kind* to specify whether a reference is fixed, optional, or imported; and (3) a replication factor which is enforced to be a positive number in our specification. A port definition has one of three types: either an *external end port*, an *internal end port*, or a *relay ports*. An external end port is visible to the outside of the containing actor, and cannot be bound to any port inside the actor. An internal end port is visible only inside the actor, and cannot be connected to the outside world. A port definition has also a replication factor.

5.2   State Machines

As mentioned before, we formalize here only flat state machines. Hierarchical state machines are left for future work. The class of state machines consists of a set of states, transitions, and an initial state. A transition has a source state, a target state, one or more triggers, and an optional action. A trigger consists of a signal and a port. It may also contain a *guard* object so that the trigger is available only if the guard evaluates to true. Choice points are currently not mapped directly into SURTA. Instead, we integrate the Boolean condition of a choice point into transition guards. Note that a state machine is defined only once for a class of actor instances. The class *ActorInstance* does not contain state machine information except for a field to remember its current state. The state machine definition in an actor class guides actor instances to move from states to states.

Guards and actions. We define transition guards and actions as AsmL interfaces. A guard has a mandatory *evaluate* method to be implemented individually for each concrete transition guard. The evaluation of a guard depends on the current state of the respective actor instance and the content of the message used to trigger transitions. Unlike guards, the mandatory method *execute* of an action also takes a run time environment as one parameter. This is because the run time environment provides necessary information for the incarnation, destruction, importation, and deportation of actors, as well as for message sending and receiving.

5.3   Protocol

A protocol is defined to be a set of incoming message types and a set of outgoing message types. A protocol can be conjugated by reversing the two sets of message types. A message type is a pair of a string **signal** and a data type. A message contains a signal, a specified priority, and an optional data object. The signal of a message must be identical to the signal of its message type, and the data object in the message must have the type as specified in the message type.

Rose-RT message priorities. There are seven levels of message priorities defined in Rose-RT: *background, low, general, high, panic, system, synchronous*, from the lowest to the highest. Each priority corresponds to two message buffers in a controller in the Rose-RT run time environment, which we will discuss in Section 5.7.

So far we have been concerned with the meta-model level mappings. Starting with the next subsection we will discuss the run time behavior level that defines a semantics for run time UML-RT entities.

5.4   Actor References

Figure 6 defines the class of actor references. Note that it merely contains a reference to its definition and an instance mapping. As seen in the constructor method of the class, when an actor reference object is created, all fixed sub-actor references are incarnated.

```
class ActorReference
  private const myDef as SubActorRefDefinition
  private var instance as Map of Integer to ActorInstance
  ActorReference(aDef as SubActorRefDefinition)
    myDef = aDef
    match aDef.getKind()
      ActorReferenceKind.fixed:
        instance = {i -> new ActorInstance(aDef.getClass())
                    | i in {0..aDef.getReplicationFactor() - 1}}
      otherwise
        instance = {->} as Map of Integer to ActorInstance
```

Fig. 6. The AsmL definition of actor references

5.5   Ports

The class *Port* defines actual ports created at run time, as shown in Figure 7, extended by two sub-classes representing two types of ports: end ports and relay ports. A port object records the run time binding information of each of its indexed members. The only difference of the *EndPort* and *RelayPort* classes is that a relay port resides on the structural border of an actor and thus has two sides. One side connects to the outside world of the actor, the other to the inside world. Therefore, a relay port can be involved in more than one binding. We use a Boolean component in the *peer* field to indicate the side of connectivity.

```
class Port
   private const myDef as PortDefinition
class EndPort extends Port
   private var peer as Map of Integer to (Port, Integer) = {->}
class RelayPort extends Port
   private var peer as Map of (Integer, Boolean) to (Port, Integer) = {->}
```

Fig. 7. The AsmL definition of run time ports

5.6   Actor Instances

Figure 8 shows the fields of the class of actor instances: *myClass* indicates which actor class an actor instance belongs to, the internal structure (sub-actor references and ports), a valuation of the actor variables, and the current state of the actor instance.

```
class ActorInstance
   private const myClass as ActorClass
   private const subActorRefs as Set of ActorReference
   private const ports as Set of Port
   private var valuation as Map of VariableDefinition to Obj = {->}
   private var state as State
   ActorInstance(aClass as ActorClass)
      myClass = aClass
      state = aClass.getStateMachine().getInitialState()
      ports = {new EndPort(pDef) | pDef in aClass.getPortDefs() where pDef.isEndPort()} union
              {new RelayPort(pDef) | pDef in aClass.getPortDefs() where pDef.isRelayPort()}
      subActorRefs = {new ActorReference(rDef) | rDef in aClass.getSubActorRefDefs()}
      step while exists binding in getAllPossibleBindings() where binding.bothPartiesFree()
         choose binding in {b | b in getAllPossibleBindings() where b.bothPartiesFree()}
            binding.bind()
```

Fig. 8. The AsmL definition of actor instances

Constructor and port binding. Figure 8 also shows how an actor instance is constructed from an actor class definition: A run time port is constructed for each port definition of the class; a sub-actor reference is created for each reference definition of the class. The most intricate part of actor instance construction is how ports inside an actor should be bound, which is only vaguely described in [27]. This is especially relevant when binding replicated ports or ports of replicated actor references. As a solution, we leave the port binding problem as a semantic variation point. Figure 8 shows the most general binding strategy: when a port p can be bound to either p_1 or p_2, we non-deterministically choose one of p_1 and p_2 to be bound with p.

Rose-RT port binding. Rose-RT fixes the order of port bindings by giving priorities to actor references and ports according to the following rules: (1) For any two sub-actor references r_1 and r_2, if r_1 was added to the model earlier than r_2 was at model construction time, then the ports in the actor that r_1 points to are bound earlier. (2) For a replicated sub-actor reference, for any two indices $i_1 < i_2$, the ports of the reference member at i_1 are bound earlier than those of the member at i_2. (3) For any two ports p_1 and p_2 in a same actor, if p_1 was added to the model earlier than p_2, then p_1 will be bound earlier. (4) For a replicated port, the member of the port at a smaller index will be bound earlier.

```
public procedure importAt(actor as ActorInstance, aRef as ImportedActorReference,
                          index as Integer)
  require actor.getClass() = aRef.getClass() and aRef in subActorRefs
    and not aRef.isInstantiatedAt(index)
  step
    aRef.setInstanceAt(index, actor)
  step
    if (forall bDef in myClass.getBindingDefs holds getAllPossibleBindings(bDef) <> {})
      then step while exists binding in getAllPossibleBindings()
        where binding.bothPartiesFree()
        // bind port here.
    else
      WriteLine("No binding possible. Importation fails.")
      throw new Exception()
```

Fig. 9. The AsmL implementation of actor importation

The priority assignment based on indices is natural and easy to control at run-time. However, as discussed in the end of Section 2, priorities based on model element construction time can be dangerous when used during analysis. Therefore, we implement the order of port bindings only with respect to replicated entity indices, and leave other decision choices totally non-deterministic. Such an implementation deviates from the actual Rose RT semantics, and results in a super set of the model behavior that Rose-RT allows. Due to space limitations we omit the details of the implementation of Rose-RT port binding here, which can be found in [20].

Actor reference incarnation and destruction. The method *incarnateAt* of the class *ActorInstance* incarnates a sub-actor reference at a particular index. The method restricts the incarnated reference to be optional. After creating a new actor instance for the reference, the method checks whether there are now ports that need to be bound, and binds them using the most general strategy as described previously. The destruction of an actor reference unplugs all the ports in the actor that the reference at a particular index points to, and then removes the actor pointer from the reference at the index.

Actor importation and deportation. The informal UML-RT semantic regarding actor importation and deportation in [27] results in yet another substantial ambiguity. For an actor to be imported to a reference, it states that the actor must satisfy all the contracts that the reference has with its environment: If there is a binding defined for the reference, then the actor must have a free port that can be bound by this definition. Some confusion is again introduced through the concept of replication. As an example, when a replicated port of an imported reference needs to be bound during importation, it is not clear whether all members of the corresponding port in the imported actor must be free, or only some members of the port need to be free. Our solution, as shown in Figure 9, gives the most general semantics requiring that, for each binding definition that involves the imported actor reference, at least one actual binding can be established by this definition during importation.

Substitutability. The *importAt* method requires the imported actor be of the same class as the imported reference is. This is however unnecessary when substitutability is allowed. In this case, it is sufficient that the imported actor has a compatible set of ports to satisfy the binding contracts of the respective reference. However, the informally described communication interface compatibility gives rise to further ambiguities and confusions. We will address this issue in future work.

5.7 Controllers

We define controllers as an AsmL interface, which has the advantage that various concrete controllers can be implemented. We have implemented three controllers: (1) most general controllers using bag-like data structures for storing messages; (2) CFSM-based controllers using FIFO message queues; and (3) Rose-RT controllers that we discuss in detail in the following. The definitions for (1) and (2) can be found in [20].

Rose-RT controllers. A Rose-RT controller c can host multiple actor instances. It does not however offer a separate FIFO message queue for each end port of each hosted actor. Instead, it builds two queues, shared by all contained actors, for each kind of message priorities. One queue is to store internal messages, i.e., messages whose sender and receiver are both hosted by c. The other queue is for external messages whose sending actor resides in a different controller than c.

Scheduling executions of hosted actors. The *makeStep* method of the class *RoseRTController*, as shown in Figure 10, shows how a Rose RT controller schedules the executions of its hosted actors. The pre-condition of the method requires at least one actor to be executable, by checking whether there is a fireable transition. The principle of searching for fireable transitions is described as follows: It first appends the content of the highest-priority non-empty incoming message queue to the internal queue of the same priority. It then checks the head message of the internal queue of the highest priority. If the message cannot be used to trigger any transition, it checks the queue of the next lower priority. Whenever it finds a message that can be used to trigger (possibly multiple) transitions, the searching terminates and returns the set of fireable transitions triggered by that message. The *makeStep* chooses randomly a fireable transition to execute.

5.8 Run Time Environment

The role of a run time environment is to schedule controllers and to provide model designers with a set of operations such as actor incarnation and message sending. Figure 11 shows a part of the AsmL interface for run time environments. The last method *run* is used to execute a model. The other methods shown in the figure are functions that can be called in user-defined actions to incarnate/destroy actor references, import/deport actors, send messages, etc.

Rose-RT run time environment. Figure 12 shows the implementation of the *run* method in the class *RoseRTRunTimeEnvironment*. Controllers run on separate threads in the Rose-RT run time environment, and the order of controller executions is therefore non-deterministic. Note that every model has one unique

```
class RoseRTController implements Controller
  public procedure makeStep(re as RunTimeEnvironment)
    require executable()
    choose (actor, transition, buffer) in getFireableTransitions()
      step
        // Receive message here.
      step
        actor.getCurrentState().getExitAction().execute(actor, re)
      step
        transition.getAction().execute(actor, re)
      step
        actor.move(transition)
      step
        actor.getCurrentState().getEntryAction().execute(actor, re)
```

Fig. 10. The AsmL implementation of the Rose RT controller scheduling method

```
interface RunTimeEnvironment
  sendAt(actor as ActorInstance, portName as String, index as Integer, message as Message)
  incarnateAt(actor as ActorInstance, refName as String, index as Integer,
                controller as Controller)
  destroyAt(actor as ActorInstance, refName as String, index as Integer)
  importActorAt(actor as ActorInstance, inst as ActorInstance, refName as String,
                index as Integer)
  deportActorAt(actor as ActorInstance, refName as String, index as Integer)
  run(model as Model)
```

Fig. 11. The AsmL interface of run time environments

capsule class whose only instance at run time is used as the top container for all other capsules in the model. The model execution starts by creating an instance of the top capsule class. Afterwards, the executions of existing controllers interleave, along which new controllers may be created and destroyed. In each interleaving step, the run time environment checks whether there are any executable controllers from which a random one is picked for execution. If no executable controller exists, then the run time environment arbitrarily takes a non-empty message buffer in the system and removes the head message of that buffer. This makes sure that an unused message does not block the availability of other messages in the same queue.

5.9   Model Descriptions

The AsmL specification of a concrete UML-RT model is represented by a set of syntactic definitions of model elements based on the meta-model level data structures. A Rose-RT model in AsmL is composed of a set of capsule classes and the top capsule class. The set of protocols is not explicitly presented. As mentioned previously, the transformation of a Rose-RT model into its AsmL definition can be fully automated since it is a direct syntactic mapping. Exceptions are transition actions that can be written in a high level programming language like Java. Due to the different expressiveness and semantics of Java and AsmL, we cannot map the whole Java language into AsmL. However, a large part of Java features and statements can still be straightforwardly and automatically

```
class RoseRTRunTimeEnvironment implements RunTimeEnvironment
  private var controllers as Set of RoseRTController
  public procedure run(model as Model)
    step
      let topActorInst = new ActorInstance(model.getTopActorClass())
      let topController = new RoseRTController()
    step
      topController.addActor(topActorInst)
      add topController to controllers
    step while (exists controller in controllers where (controller.executable()
                    or controller.containsNonEmptyBuffer()))
      if (exists controller in controllers where controller.executable()) then
        let executables = {controller | controller in controllers where controller.executable()}
        choose controller in executables
          controller.makeStep(me)
      else
        choose controller in controllers where controller.containsNonEmptyBuffer()
          controller.removeSomeHeadMessage()
```

Fig. 12. The AsmL implementation of the Rose-RT run time environment

```
class SCMSRAction implements Action
  public procedure execute(actor as ActorInstance, re as RunTimeEnvironment) as Boolean
    var theClient as ActorInstance = re.getLastReceivedMessage(actor).getData()
                                     as ActorInstance
    step
      re.importActor(actor, theClient, "serviceAccessorCoor")
    step
      re.importActor(actor, theClient, "serviceAccessorS")
    step
      let srMessage = new Message("serviceReady", RoseRTMessagePriority.general)
      re.send(actor, "connectionSetup", srMessage)
    step
      re.deportActor(actor, "serviceAccessorCoor")
// ... ...
// Define the ServiceConnectionManager class
let serviceAPort = new ExternalWiredEndPortDefinition("serviceAccess",
                                                serviceAccessProt, true)
let service = new FixedCapsuleRoleDefinition("service", threeAdderClass, 8)
let SCMActive = new State("Active")
let sCMSRTGuard = new SCMSRTGuard()
let SCMSRTTrigger = new Trigger("serviceRequest", serviceAPort, sCMSRTGuard)
let sCMSRAction = new SCMSRAction()
let SCMSRTTran = new Transition("serviceRequest1", SCMActive, SCMActive, {SCMSRTTrigger},
                                sCMSRAction)
let SCMStateMachine = new StateMachine({SCMInit, SCMActive, SCMFull}, SCMInit,
      {SCMInitTran, SCMSRTTran, SCMSRFTran, SCMRSRTran, SCMDeportTran1, SCMDeportTran2})
let activeVar = new VariableDefinition("active", type of Integer)
let serviceConnectionManagerClass = new CapsuleClass(
    "ServiceConnectionManager", {service, serviceAccessorS, serviceAccessorCoor},
    {serviceAPort, connectionTPort, connectionSPort}, {SCMConn1, SCMConn2, SCMConn3},
    {activeVar}, SCMStateMachine)
let System5Class = new CapsuleClass("System5", {clientManager, serviceConnectionManager},
                    {}, {System5Conn}, {})
let capsuleClasses = {System5Class, serviceAccessorClass, clientSys5Class,
                        clientManagerClass, threeAdderClass,
                    serviceConnectionManagerClass}
let model = new RoseRTModel("System5", capsuleClasses, System5Class)
```

Fig. 13. The AsmL specification of the model in Figure 1

translated to AsmL equivalents. Figure 13 gives partly the AsmL specification
of the model in Figure 1.

6 Validating Models with SURTA

With the support of Spec Explorer, we intend to use the UML-RT semantics defined in SURTA to accomplish the following tasks: (1) model checking UML-RT models; (2) simulating UML-RT models for checking potential property violations; and (3) test case generation for model-based testing [7]. Model-based testing is out of the scope of this paper, and we will investigate this in future work. Model checking is impeded by the fact that the currently publicly available version of SpecExplorer is not completely exploring the state space, in particular if the AsmL model includes nondeterminisic choices, as is the case in SURTA code. We hence illustrate how the random walk simulation feature of SpecExplorer can be used to reveal property violations for Rose-RT models.

```
class MuTexVerification implements Verification
  var hadAccess as Set of CapsuleInstance = {}
  public function multipleAccess(rte as RunTimeEnvironment) as Boolean
    return exists client1 in rte.getCapsuleInstances("client"),
      client2 in rte.getCapsuleInstances("client") where client1 <> client2
      and client1.getCurrentState().getName = "operation"
      and client2.getCurrentState().getName = "operation"
  public function allHadAccess(rte as RunTimeEnvironment) as Boolean
    initially result as Boolean = true
    step
      if (forall controller in rte.getControllers() holds
        (not controller.executable()) and
        (not controller.containsNonEmptyBuffer())) then
        result := forall client in rte.getCapsuleInstances("client")
                    holds client in hadAccess
      else
        step foreach client in rte.getCapsuleInstances("client") where
              client.getCurrentState().getName() = "operation"
          add client to hadAccess
    step
      return result
  public procedure check(rte as RunTimeEnvironment)
    require (not multipleAccess(rte)) and allHadAccess(rte)
    skip
class RoseRTRunTimeEnvironment implements RunTimeEnvironment
  public procedure run(model as Model)
    step while (exists controller in controllers where (controller.executable()
                or controller.containsNonEmptyBuffer()))
      // Select an executable controller to execute.
      step
        try
          verification.check(me)
        catch
          e as Exception: WriteLine("Property violated.")
      step
        try // This additional check is for liveness properties.
          verification.check(me)
        catch
          e as Exception: WriteLine("Property violated.")
```

Fig. 14. A verification method to check mutual exclusion

Consider a simple model of a resource sharing system in which a central server grants exclusive access to a shared object to multiple clients. In the model, a client is possessing the object access when it is in the operation state. An important safety property, sometimes referred to as mutual exclusion, is that no more than one client is allowed to have access at any given point in time, i.e., only one client can be at the operation state. In SURTA, we encode the negation of the property into the function *multipleAccess* in a *MuTexVerification* class, as shown in Figure 14. This function is checked by the *check* method of the class. The *run* method of the *RoseRTRunTimeEnvironment* is modified to invoke the *check* method after each interleaving step. In this way, the property is checked automatically in every step of the model simulation.

An example for the checking of the violation of a liveness property is the fairness constraint that each client will eventually be granted access to the object. This property is encoded in the *allHadAccess* method in Figure 14. The method always returns true during the simulation, and in the meantime adds a client to the set *hadAccess* when the client reaches the state operation. When the simulation terminates, it checks whether all clients were added to the set. When this is not the case, the liveness property is violated. We checked the two above properties for the above described ressource sharing system using SURTA and SpecExplorer. The simulation revealed that the above mentioned liveness property was violated. To support debugging, we have SURTA report the state of the Rose-RT model after each interleaving step of the model execution, which results in an error trail when the property is violated. In our example, the output error trail suggests that the fairness property is violated because some client requests were removed when they occupied the head of the respective queue and could not be used at the moment. For more detail see [20].

7   Conclusion

We have presented an operational, executable semantics for a large portion of the syntactic features of the modeling language UML-RT. One of the benefits of the given semantics is that it allows for a straightforward, syntactic translation of a UML-RT model into an AsmL representation. We use a layered architecture for the semantics definition, which interprets the syntactic representation using an AsmL-defined run-time layer. The separation of syntactic representation and semantic interpretation greatly facilitates different implementations of semantic variation points. We illustrate how to use the random walk simulation capability of SpecExplorer in order to show the violation of safety and liveness properties.

Future work includes an automatic translation of UML-RT models into the AsmL representation. We also work on providing a semantics for the syntactic features of UML-RT that we do not currently handle, a task that is facilitated by the flexible structure of our semantics definition. We will develop a methodology for model based testing based on SURTA. We also plan to generalize the simulation based property validation approach sketched in this paper, in particular by extending it to handle more general LTL properties. Finally, we expect a complete state space exploration for AsmL to become available, which would avail our semantics to complete model checking.

Acknowledgment. We thank Daniel Butnaru for his assistance in implementing the SURTA project. We are grateful to anonymous referees for their valuable comments and suggestions.

References

1. Akhlaki, K.B., Tuñón, M.I.C., Terriza, J.A.H.: Design of real-time systems by systematic transformation of UML/RT models into simple timed process algebra system specifications. In: Proc. ICEIS (3), pp. 290–297 (2006)
2. AsmL – Abstract State Machine Language (Microsoft), http://research.microsoft.com/fse/asml
3. Bezerra, J., Hirata, C.M.: A semantics for UML-RT using π-calculus. In: Proc. RSP 2007, pp. 75–82 (2007)
4. Börger, E., Stärk, R.: Abstract State Machines: A Method for High-Level System Design and Analysis. Springer (2003)
5. Bradbury, J.S., Cordy, J.R., Dingel, J., Wermelinger, M.: A survey of self-management in dynamic software architecture specifications. In: Proc. WOSS, pp. 28–33. ACM (2004)
6. Brand, D., Zafiropulo, P.: On communicating finite-state machines. Journal of the ACM 30(2), 323–342 (1983)
7. Campbell, C., Grieskamp, W., Nachmanson, L., Schulte, W., Tillmann, N., Veanes, M.: Model-based testing of object-oriented reactive systems with Spec Explorer. Technical Report MST-TR-2005-59, Microsoft Research (2005)
8. Capel, M.I., Morales, L.E.M., Akhlaki, K.B., Terriza, J.A.H.: A semantic formalization of UML-RT models with CSP+T processes applicable to real-time systems verification. In: Proc. JISBD, pp. 283–292 (2006)
9. Engels, G., Küster, J.M., Heckel, R., Groenewegen, L.: A methodology for specifying and analyzing consistency of object-oriented behavioral models. In: ESEC / SIGSOFT FSE, pp. 186–195. ACM Press (2001)
10. Fischer, C., Olderog, E.-R., Wehrheim, H.: A CSP view on UML-RT structure diagrams. In: Hussmann, H. (ed.) FASE 2001. LNCS, vol. 2029. Springer, Heidelberg (2001)
11. Fuchs, M., Nazareth, D., Daniel, D., Rumpe, B.: BMW-ROOM: An object-oriented method for ASCET. In: SAE 1998, Society of Automotive Engineers (1998)
12. Gao, Q., Brown, L.J., Capretz, L.F.: Extending UML-RT for control system modeling. American Journal of Applied Sciences 1(4), 338–347 (2004)
13. Grosu, R., Broy, M., Selic, B., Stefanescu, G.: Towards a calculus for UML-RT specifications. In: Proc. OOPSLA (1998)
14. Gullekson, G.: Designing for concurrency and distribution with Rational Rose RealTime, Rational Software White Paper (2003), http://www.ibm.com/developerworks/rational/library/269.html
15. Gurevich, Y., Rossman, B., Schulte, W.: Semantic essence of AsmL. Theor. Comput. Sci. 343(3), 370–412 (2005)
16. Habibi, A., Tahar, S.: AsmL semantics in fixpoint. In: Proc. ASM, pp. 233–246 (2005)
17. Herzberg, D.: UML-RT as a candidate for modeling embedded real-time systems in the telecommunication domain. In: France, R.B., Rumpe, B. (eds.) UML 1999. LNCS, vol. 1723, pp. 330–338. Springer, Heidelberg (1999)

18. Kardoš, M.: Automated formal verification for UML-based model driven design of embedded systems. PhD thesis, Slovak University of Technology (2006)
19. Knapp, A., Merz, S., Rauh, C.: Model checking timed UML state machines and collaborations. In: Damm, W., Olderog, E.-R. (eds.) FTRTFT 2002. LNCS, vol. 2469, pp. 395–416. Springer, Heidelberg (2002)
20. Leue, S., Ştefănescu, A., Wei, W.: An AsmL semantics for dynamic structures and run time schedulability in UML-RT. Technical Report soft-08-02, University of Konstanz (2008), http://www.inf.uni-konstanz.de/soft/publications_en.php
21. OMG Model Driven Architecture (MDA), http://www.omg.org/mda
22. Ramos, R., Sampaio, A., Mota, A.: A semantics for UML-RT active classes via mapping into Circus. In: Steffen, M., Zavattaro, G. (eds.) FMOODS 2005. LNCS, vol. 3535, pp. 99–114. Springer, Heidelberg (2005)
23. Rational Rose RealTime tool. Shipped within Rational Rose Technical Developer, http://www.ibm.com/software/awdtools/developer/technical
24. Saaltink, M.: Generating and analysing Promela from RoseRT models. Technical Report TR-99-5537-02, ORA Canada, 1208 One Nicholas Street, Ottawa Ontario, K1N 7B7, Canada (1999)
25. Saksena, M., Freedman, P., Rodzewicz, P.: Guidelines for automated implementation of executable object oriented models for real-time embedded control systems. In: Proc. of the IEEE Real-Time Systems Symposium, pp. 240–245. IEEE Computer Society (1997)
26. Selic, B.: Turning clockwise: using UML in the real-time domain. Comm. of the ACM 42(10), 46–54 (1999)
27. Selic, B., Gullekson, G., Ward, P.T.: Real-Time Object-Oriented Modeling. John Wiley & Sons, Inc. (1994)
28. Selic, B., Rumbaugh, J.: Using UML for modeling complex real-time systems (March 1998), http://www.ibm.com/developerworks/rational/library/139.html
29. Spec Explorer tool, http://research.microsoft.com/SpecExplorer
30. von der Beeck, M.: A formal semantics of UML-RT. In: Nierstrasz, O., Whittle, J., Harel, D., Reggio, G. (eds.) MoDELS 2006. LNCS, vol. 4199, pp. 768–782. Springer, Heidelberg (2006)

Component Reassembling and State Transfer in MaDcAr-Based Self-adaptive Software

Guillaume Grondin[1], Noury Bouraqadi[1], and Laurent Vercouter[2]

[1] Déptartement IA, École des Mines de Douai
941 rue Charles Bourseul – B.P. 10838, 59508 Douai Cedex, France
grondin, bouraqadi@ensm-douai.fr
http://vst.ensm-douai.fr/noury
[2] Centre G2I, École des Mines de Saint-tienne
158 cours Fauriel, 42023 Saint-Étienne Cedex 02, France
vercouter@emse.fr
http://www.emse.fr/~vercouter

Abstract. In this paper, we introduce MaDcAr, a model of engines for dynamic and automatic (re)assembling of component-based software. In MaDcAr, an application description consists of the definition of some valid configurations and the state transfer rules to apply during adaptations. This description is uncoupled from any implementation and can therefore be reused with other components. Given an application description, a MaDcAr engine builds a constraint solving problem that makes it possible to choose an appropriate configuration and the components to assemble. This choice takes into account the cost of the target configuration with respect to the available resources. To ensure the application consistency, the engine relies on the state transfer rules to initialize the component attributes of the target assembly using the component attributes of the source assembly.

Keywords: Automatic Adaptation, Dynamic Adaptation, State Transfer, Uncoupling Components, Configurations.

1 Introduction

Adaptation is the process of modifying a software in order to take into account some change [KBC02], either in the execution context or in the software design. It is a three steps process: (i) *triggering* the adaptation process when required, (ii) *deciding* the most appropriate adaptations to perform given a context, and last (iii) actually *realizing* the adaptations. Adaptation is said to be *dynamic* if this process is performed at run-time, i.e. without stopping the whole application while modifying it. This dynamicity is required in different domains (Medical, Finance, Telecommunication, Product lines,...) where a stop may be financially very expensive or even dangerous from the human or the ecological point of view. It is also mandatory to build autonomous software that are able to adapt themselves.

R.F. Paige and B. Meyer (Eds.): TOOLS EUROPE 2008, LNBIP 11, pp. 258–277, 2008.
© Springer-Verlag Berlin Heidelberg 2008

In this paper, we focus on decision and realization steps of dynamic adaptation of component-based software [Szy02]. In this context, realizing an adaptation translates into a *reconfiguration*[1] of the components assembly that setup the adapted software. Such reconfiguration consists in adding, deleting or replacing components or connections that link them. The reconfiguration of such a software also includes changes of the components attribute values, and then the state transfer between components is part of the adaptation process.

In this article, we describe MADCAR [2] a model for engines dedicated to the dynamic and automatic adaptation of component-based software. Based on a constraint solver, this model provides a unified solution allowing not only the construction of software applications through automatic assembling but also their dynamic adaptation. Indeed, MADCAR relies on specifications that denote the set of valid assemblies and rules for switching from one assembly to the other (i.e. when to switch and how to deal with state transfer). These specifications are both global to the application and uncoupled from components. Therefore, MADCAR's approach avoids inconsistency issues encountered in approaches where each component adapts itself independently from the other components of the assembly [DL03, PBJ98]. Besides, specifications of assembling and adaptation can be reused with different sets of components. Last, our approach is generic since it makes only a few assumptions about the component model. MADCAR requires that components should provide contracts on components resource consumption (CPU, memory, energy) and some extra-functional interfaces allowing to manage the state and the activity of the components.

The use of hardware requirements for component selection during assembling and adaptation is a first evolution as compared to the first description of MADCAR [GBV06]. Another important evolution of MADCAR introduced since [GBV08] is the management of state transfer. The work presented in this paper permits to show how we use MADCAR to build self-adaptive software, for operating mobile bots. Moreover, we propose an early evalutation our framework.

The remaining of the this paper is organized as following. Section 2 introduce the concept of assembling engine and identifies some criteria to evaluate such adaptation infrastructure. Section 3 describes MADCAR. Next, section 4 focuses on state transfer during dynamic reassembling. Section 5 describes work related to component-based software adaptation and provides some preliminary evaluations of our work. Last, section 6 sums up our approach and sketches some perspectives.

2   Requirements for Assembling Engines

The automation of the assembling task requires an *assembling engine* which can behave on behalf of humans. This engine has to automatically build applications

---

[1] We use also "(re)assembling" to denote both the construction of an assembly and its reconfiguration.

[2] Model for Automatic and Dynamic Component Assembly Reconfiguration.

by assembling components. Moreover, dynamic adaptation requires the assembling of an application to be performed at run-time.

In this section, we introduce the concept of assembling engine. Then, we propose some criteria to measure the ability of an assembling engine (or similar adaptation infrastructures) to cope with the requirements of automation and dynamicity.

2.1 Definition of an Assembling Engine

The concept of assembling engine relies on existing definitions of automatic assembling [SMBV03, IT02]: *given a set of components and an application description, an* assembling engine *allows assembling available components in order to build an application that meets the provided description*. An abstract model of assembling engine is illustrated in Fig. 1. An abstract assembling engine requires four inputs:

- An arbitrary set of *components* can be used to build a new assembly. The assembled components can comply with different component models, to keep the property of generality. However, in this study, we make the assumption that all components comply with the same model.
- *Application description* refers to a specification of application's functionalities and its non functional properties. As for the component input, the application description which can be handled by an assembling engine is supposed to be domain-dependent. This description may possibly be empty. If so, the assembling engine is free to realize an arbitrary assembly based on the self-contained informations of the components and on the assembling policy.
- An *assembling policy* is a (partial) description of the engine's behavior. This input is the consequence of the property of openness and refers to customizations that allow directing the reassembling process (possibly according to the execution context).
- The *execution context* refers to various information [CCDG05] (e.g. CPU consumption, memory availability) which values must be considered to make the proper assembling decisions, and which changes may trigger a reassembling of an application. At run-time, the triggering and the decision steps of the assembling process are partially based on the execution context of the application. For instance, if the amount of available memory decreases then the assembling engine may decide to rebuild the assembly using lightweight components.

2.2 Evaluation Criteria

In order to evaluate and compare assembling engines we define the next criteria.

1. Degree of openness: refers to the customizability of the assembling strategy of the engine.

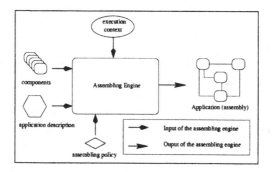

Fig. 1. Description of the inputs and the output of an assembling engine

2. Degree of consistency: it refers to the ability of the assembling engine to limit the unintentional introduction of functioning errors into the application because of the (re)assembling process.
3. Degree of availability: it refers to the ability of the assembling engine to ensure that certain services of the application can still be used during the (re)assembling process.
4. Degree of performance: it refers to the ability of the assembling engine to prevent the decrease of the performance of the application during a (re)assembling. Performance of the application is guaranteed when the application does not lack resources for running its services. Then, we evaluate the ability of the assembling engine to ensure that the resource consumption of the assembling process is low enough to guarantee that the application will not lack resources during a (re)assembling.
5. Degree of automation: it refers to the automation of the assembling process, i.e. the minimization of the number of tasks which need a human intervention. Those tasks may concern any of the three steps of the assembling process: triggering, decision and realization.

The criteria 1 directly refers to the (re)usability of an assembling engine. The criteria 2, 3, 4 represent various requirements that the assembling engine have to enforce in order to reassemble a running application without a dramatic loss on its quality of service.

3   The MaDcAr Model

MaDcAr is a model of engines for automatic assembling and adaptation of component-based software. Targeted adaptations range from a simple change of a component's attribute value to the replacement of a whole component assembly.

3.1   Requirements and Restrictions

MaDcAr uncouples application specifications from their implementations as promoted by Model Driven Architecture[3] [BJRV04]. It allows specifying an

---

[3] This is why the three letters M, D and A are highlighted in the MaDcAr acronym.

application without committing to a particular component model and without prior knowledge on the components that will be actually assembled as opposite to specialized approaches such as [CC07]. Therefore, MADCAR's assembly specifications can be reused with multiple sets of components possibly compliant with different component models.

To achieve this separation, components have to satisfy a few requirements. They should be homogeneous, self-documented and provide some extra-functional interfaces to manage their state and activity. By homogeneous we mean that components should conform with the same component model. Self-documentation refers to contracts. Components should own contracts describing their attributes, provided and required interfaces, and required hardware resources for their functioning (e.g. CPU, memory, energy)[4]. In addition, extra-functional interfaces are required for state management purpose (save/restore) and for activity management purpose (activate/deactivate).

Note that the current status of MADCAR still makes two restrictions. First, all the components of an application are located on a single device. We do not deal with the adaptation of assemblies of distributed components. Besides, we only study the horizontal composition of components, and we do not deal with hierarchical composition. MADCAR handles composites as black boxes and hence do not allow neither building new composites nor adapting existing ones.

3.2   The Assembling Engine

As shown on Fig. 2, a MADCAR **assembling engine** has four inputs: a *set of components* to assemble, an *application description* which is the specification of functional and extra-functional properties of valid assemblies, an *assembling policy* which drives adaptation decisions, and a *context* that refers to both information on hardware resources (CPU consumption, network bandwidth, etc.) and the application state (i.e. attribute values of assembled components).

The components, the application description and the engine can be reused for building different applications. A MADCAR assembling engine should be built as a framework that is specialized to deal with a given component model. Basically, this specialization requires implementing a small set of operations to handle components: the connection/disconnection of two components, the activation/deactivation of a component, and the import/export of a component state.

An application description is composed of a set of alternative configurations and a state transfer specification. The application description and the assembling policy are specified in terms of constraints. That is, an application reassembling consists in a Constraint Satisfaction Problem [Kum92]. Therefore, MADCAR assembling engines include a constraint solver to compute automatically appropriate assembling decisions.

---

[4] Note that we assume that the contracts are relevant with regard to the application and their trustworthiness is out of scope. Moreover, MADCAR can deal with components that do not provide contracts on resource consumptions by performing component selection only based on the application functional requirements.

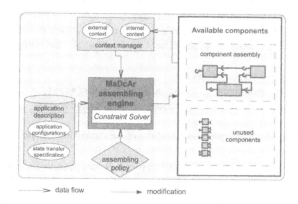

Fig. 2. MADCAR's inputs and Outputs

3.3   The Context Manager

Usually, the definition of an *execution context* consists in specifying a set of software sensors which can provide some "relevant values", i.e. values which must be used during an assembling process. In fact, *"Context is not simply the state of a predefined environment with a fixed set of interaction resources. It's part of a process of interacting with an ever-changing environment composed of reconfigurable, migratory, distributed, and multiscale resources."* [CCDG05].

Consequently, the first input of a MADCAR assembling engine is a **context manager** which models the evolution of an execution context. The context manager must define a set of sensors used by an assembling engine not only to affect adaptation decisions but also to trigger adaptations. In addition, it allows to define how often the contextual values are updated and if necessary how much of the previous values are memorized for each sensor.

Context manager's sensors may concern both external and internal aspects of the application. The *external context* of an application includes information about hardware resources (e.g. CPU, memory), available networks (e.g. current bandwidth, maximal bandwidth) and geophysical data (e.g. location, temperature). The *internal context* of an application consists in information about the available components: which of the components are unused, how are the components connected with each other and what is the application's current state (attributes' values of the component assembly).

In the examples presented in this paper, the sensors must provide at least the current levels of available CPU, free memory and available energy (e.g. battery) of the infrastructure where the components are deployed.

For illustration purpose, Fig. 3 shows sample sensor specifications. The net-workAvailability sensor periodically tests whether or not the Wi-Fi network is available by evaluating a function #isAvailable. This sensor feeds the external context of the application. The cacheSize sensor periodically fetches the current size of a cache attribute from the state of the application (see subsection 4.1). In this example, each observed resource has a separate update period.

```
networkAvailabilitySensor := Sensor new.
networkAvailabilitySensor resource: 'external/hardware/network/wifi'.
networkAvailabilitySensor operation: #isAvailable updatePeriod: 500.
...
bufferSizeSensor := Sensor new.
bufferSizeSensor resource: 'internal/stateTransferNet/cacheNode'.
bufferSizeSensor operation: #getSize updatePeriod: 200.
```

Fig. 3. A sample specification of an execution context

Designing a context manager raises typical performance issues, for instance when there are many sensors which often need to be updated. These issues go beyond the scope of this paper. In the following, we suppose that the values provided by the context manager are continuously up to date when they are accessed by the assembling engine. The few previous settlements concerning context management are sufficient to illustrate our automatic reassembling process. For further details on context modelization, one may refer to [CRS07, DL05, DSA01] which describe several generic context frameworks.

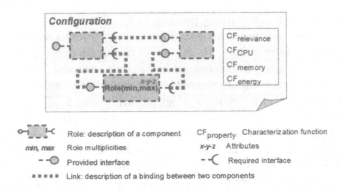

Fig. 4. A MADCAR configuration

3.4 Specification of Valid Assemblies

An application description in MADCAR defines the set of valid assemblies in the form of a set of alternative configurations. Each MADCAR **configuration** describes a *family of assemblies* that are similar because they share the same structural constraints. Direct references to the application's components are forbidden. Indeed, each configuration consists in a graph of roles and a set of characterization functions, as showed in Fig. 4. A **role** is a component description composed of a set of *contracts* [Mey92, BJPW99]. Those contracts must at least specify (a) a set of interfaces (required or provided) which symbolizes possible interactions with other roles, (b) a set of attributes which values allow to initialize components[5] and (c) two *multiplicities*. A role's multiplicities define the

---

[5] Each attribute is coupled with an initialization function (see subsection 4.1).

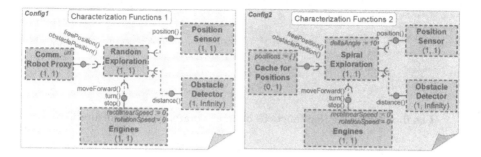

Fig. 5. Two configurations of an exploratory bot: *Config1* and *Config2*

minimal (*min*) and the maximal (*max*) numbers of components which can fulfill this role simultaneously[6].

Each configuration can be characterized through extra-functional properties. Configuration designers should provide at least one property which is the configuration's relevance for a given context (**relevance** for short). Other properties can be useful such as those providing costs of the configuration. Throughout the rest of this paper, we use examples of three properties: the CPU cost of a configuration (**CPU** for short), the memory cost of a configuration (**memory** for short) and the energy cost of a configuration (**energy** for short).

Extra-functional properties are used by the assembling engine to choose a configuration and several components for a future assembly. For each of property P, the configuration designer must implement a characterization function CF_P which measures P. $CF_{relevance}$ measures **relevance** according to a contextual situation, that is both sensors' values (external context) and application's state (internal context). CF_{CPU}, CF_{memory}, CF_{energy} measure three kinds of costs for a configuration given a set of components, assuming that available components are described by provided contracts about CPU, memory and energy requirements. To make the four configuration properties comparable with each other, a configuration designer must define characterization functions that are normalized. The results of a characterization function can range from 0 to 100.

To illustrate the concepts of MADCAR, we use an applicative scenario in the context of robotic rescue. We are designing different behaviors for exploratory bots[7]. For example, Fig. 5 shows two of an exploratory bot' set of configurations. *Config1* allows the bot to randomly explore the area and to transmit to a router its "observations" (free positions and obstacles' positions). *Config2* allows the bot to perform a more structured exploration and to store up its observations. Some characterization functions for *Config1*'s properties and *Config2*'s properties are given in Fig. 6. For instance, the relevance of these configurations depends on the neighborhood of the bot (i.e. nearby bots) and also on some internal parameters, like the cache of the bot's observations.

---

[6] When necessary, we will note a role $R(min, max)$, where $min \geq 1$ and $max \geq min$.

[7] We use robots equipped with a rotative camera, odometers, IR sensors and a WiFi enabled communication device [WB].

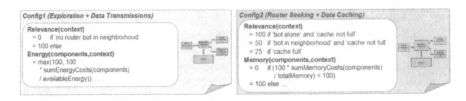

Fig. 6. Characterization functions of an exploratory bot's configurations

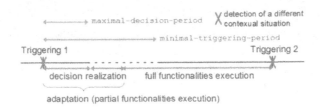

Fig. 7. Adaptation vs. execution in MADCAR

3.5   The Assembling Policy

An assembling policy permits to drive (re)assembling. It consists in specifying when (i.e. for which context) and how assembling must be done. In MADCAR, the **assembling policy** is decomposed into two different parts respectively used to: (1) the detection of the contextual situations that may require (re)assembling, and (2) the rules that guide the choices of the engine during (re)assemblings.

The first part of the assembling policy deals with required conditions for *adaptation triggering*. It consists in the specification of (1.a) a disjunction of several contextual situations and (1.b) the minimal period of time between two evaluations of the given contextual situations (called `minimal-triggering-period`). Formally, a contextual situation is a conjunction of conditions on some contextual values. An adaptation may occur each time the current context is matching one of the provided contextual situations. For example, the context $\{\,availableCPU = 2200;\ avaiblableMemory = 1024;\ availableEnergy = 60\}$ satisfies the contextual situation $(availableCPU > 1000)\&(availableMemory \geq 512)$, but it does not satisfy the contextual situation $(avaibleCPU > 1500)\&(availableEnergy \leq 10)$. The value of `minimal-triggering-period` not only limits the use of hardware resources by the assembling engine but also ensures that each successive assemblies of an application will be used during a significant period of time, as shown by Fig. 7. It is the responsibility of the application designer to specify a value big enough according to the application size and the underlying hardware capabilities. A too small value may lead to triggering too many adaptations (if the context evolves quickly), which in turn leads to freezing the application functionalities.

The second part of the assembling policy consists in the specification of (2.a) a selecting function SF_{bcc} that relies on the configurations' extra-functionnal properties in order to determine how they impact the decision process for the involved application, and (2.b) the maximal period of time allocated to the decision process (called `maximal-decision-period`[8]).

Selecting the best configuration and the best component set *bcc* consists in maximizing a selecting function SF_{bcc} provided by the application designer. This maximization that takes into account the current context is performed during a duration bounded by `maximal-decision-period`. An example of assembling policy is given by Fig. 8. This policy shows a selecting function defined by a simple additive function based on an addition with weight factors for the configuration's properties. But, the designer may specify a more complex function provided that the input parameters are a configuration, the set of components and the current context.

```
'---------- Triggering ----------'
minimal-triggering-period := 2000.
contextualSituations := {
    (availableEnergy ≤ 20) & (nbNeighbors ≥ 1).
    (nbAppearedNeighbors ≥ 1) & (nbPreviousNeighbors == 0).
    }.
'---------- Decision ----------'
maximal-decision-period := 1000.
```
$$SF_{bcc}(config, components, context) := 40 * config.CF_{relevance}(context)$$
$$-20 * config.CF_{energy}(components, context)$$
$$-10 * config.CF_{memory}(components, context)$$
$$-10 * config.CF_{CPU}(components, context).$$

Fig. 8. A sample specification of assembling policy for an exploratory bot

3.6   The (Re)Assembling Process

MADCAR can be used both to automatically build assemblies from unconnected components, and to automatically adapt (i.e. reassemble) existing component assemblies at run-time. The (re)assembling process consists in three successive steps: triggering, decision and realization.

1. *Triggering:* The assembling engine periodically checks if the current context matches one of the contextual situations defined in the assembling policy.
2. *Computation of a relevant component assembly:* The assembling engine selects the configuration and the component set which maximize the selecting function SF_{bcc} specified in the assembling policy. This maximization is a constraint satisfaction problem (CSP) with:
   - a variable $V_{GoodConfig}$ which domain is the set of available configurations;
   - a set of variables V_{R_i}, one for each role $R_i(min_i, max_i)$, which domain is the set of available components and which type is a collection of a size ranging from min_i to max_i;

---

[8] We require that `maximal-decision-period` < `minimal-triggering-period`.

- the constraints on each V_{R_i}, that is the contracts of the role R_i, extended with a constraint stating that all components selected for the configuration's roles must be different ;
- the objective function SF_{bcc} to be maximized according to the assembling policy.

A single CSP allows the MADCAR engine to select one of the configurations and to select the components to be used. The engine choose the configuration which best satifies the designer's preferences among the configurations that are eligible and relevant for the context. A configuration is said to be *eligible* when each of its role can be fulfilled by a at least n of components, where n is greater than or equal to the role's minimal multiplicity. A configuration is said to be *relevant* to a given context if its `relevance` property is not null.

3. *(Re)assembling:* Active components (i.e. threaded) belonging to the current assembly are deactivated[9]. Then, the newly selected components are assembled and initialized according to the chosen configuration. Last, assembled components are activated. During this step, the application's state is maintained through a state transfer mechanism.

4   State Transfer During Adaptations

"One-the-fly" reconfiguration raises the classic but tricky problem of *state transfer* [SF93]. Indeed, the application's state must be kept consistent when replacing components. We introduce here a formalism that allows the application designer to describe the application's state and to specify state transfer rules in an abstract manner, independently of the software components. One issue we have to face here is that the state cannot be stored into the components. Due to the uncoupling between configurations and components, each component may be used to alternatively fulfill different roles in the course of the reassemblings.

4.1   State of an Application

An application's state in MADCAR is based on the two kinds of role's attributes (see subsection 3.4). We distinguish two kinds of attributes in a role: fixed attributes and variable attributes. A role's *fixed attribute* suits to a data that is used only to initialize a component which has been selected to fulfill this role. The component does not modify the attribute's value. For instance, the maximal value of a circular counter is a fixed attribute. On the other hand, a *variable attribute* corresponds to a data that can be modified by a component. For example, the current value of a counter is a variable attribute.

In the MADCAR model, we define an **application's state** as the set encompassing values of all variable attributes of all roles in all configurations. The

---

[9] This assumes that they have an extra-functionnal interface allowing to control their activity. Deactivation/reactivation of a set of components is taken over from existing work [KM90].

current values of those attributes correspond to the current state of the application. When a component fulfilling a role R is removed from an assembly, component attributes tagged as variables in R must be saved. These data are restored afterwards to any other component which is chosen to fulfill R. Notice that, in the case of the attributes of a role which has a maximal multiplicity greater than one, it is a vector of values which is saved to memorize each attribute value for the components that fulfill this role. A vector of size n can initialize at most n components, and if there are still uninitialized components, then an initialization function specified in each role is used.

4.2   State Transfer Net

An application designer must not only specify role's attributes, but also links between attributes. Two attributes are said to be *linked* if a change in one attribute should impact the other in order to keep consistent the application state. Such links are related to the application semantics and the designer intention, and hence they cannot be deduced automatically. So, the designer has to make them explicit by specifying the state transfer in the form of a **state transfer net**. The nodes of this net are the application variable attributes. Links connect only attributes belonging to different configurations because the challenge is to perform state transfer when the application switches from one configuration to another. The state transfer net allows deducing a valid sequence of transfer and conversions in order to update the attribute values. That is a sequence of that keeps the application state consistent by avoiding information loss.

According to [VB03], there are at least two approaches to represent the state of a component-based application: one is based on an *abstract state*, and the other is *implementation based state*. The first approach relies on a "pivot" entity that mediates state transfer between interchangeable components. In the second approach, the import of a component state relies on the implementation of the state export of the replaced component. Our proposal in MADCAR can be viewed as a generalization of the first approach. Roles act as pivots for components. Moreover, the state transfer net allows specifying rules for changing the pivot and hence performing the state transfer between components that are different though semantically related. Besides, our work deals with the state transfer of a full application even in case of deep architecture change and not only for the replacement of a single component.

4.3   State Transfer Links

In a state transfer net, transfer rules are expressed by means of *transfer functions*. Every link carries transfer functions allowing to compute the values of an attribute from other attributes. Thus, given two nodes a and b connected by a link, the designer must provide two transfer functions: (1) $Transfer_{a-b}$ permitting to compute the value of b from a and (2) $Transfer_{b-a}$ permitting to compute the value of a from b.

Links are oriented denoting potential data loss. Consider as an example a link oriented from a to b (noted $a \triangleright b$). This orientation shows that a is *less rich than* b, that is, there can be a loss of information when transferring value of a to b. To avoid this loss, the transfer function $Transfer_{a-b}$ can use the old value of b (together with the current value of a) to compute the new value of b.

When there is a link $a \triangleright b$, we say that b is master of a and that a is slave of b. This hierarchy is transitive. Thus, if c is master of b, then it is an indirect master of a. Hence, the value of a can be computed from c through b and vice versa. We call this the *propagation* of state values. A master attribute which has no master itself is called an absolute master. The state of an application can be restricted to only the set of its absolute master attributes, because all the other attribute's values can be deduced - by propagation - from the absolute master attributes.

As for illustration, consider two configurations where the first contains a role with a variable attribute *uri* which allow to locate a server and the second configuration includes a variable attribute *port*, as well as a fixed attribute *server*. In this example, *uri* is a string composed of two parts, a server name and a server port, which are separated by a ':' character. An illustration of state transfer net is shown in Fig. 9. The transfer functions are the following:

$Transfer_{port-uri}$: `uri = uri.cutBeforeLast(':') + ':' + port.toString()`.
$Transfer_{uri-port}$: `port = uri.cutAfterLast(':').toInteger()`.

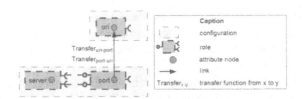

Fig. 9. Simple state transfer net in MADCAR

A state transfer net can have "multiple links" because data stored in a single attribute within a configuration can be distributed over multiple attributes within another configuration. We define two kinds of multiple links: a *join link* which connects a group of nodes to a single node, and a *fork link* which connects a single node to a group of nodes. As for the single links, multiple links carry transfer functions. For example, a link between one node a and a group of nodes $G_B = \{b_1, ..., b_j\}(j > 1)$ must be tagged by two transfer functions: (1) $Transfer_{a-b_1, b_2, ..., b_j}$ permitting to compute the values of G_B's nodes from a and (2) $Transfer_{b_1, b_2, ..., b_j-a}$ which computes the value of a from G_B.

In addition, multiple links are also oriented. The set of sink nodes of a join link is called a *master group*, and the set of source nodes of a fork link is called a *slave group*.

4.4   Consistency Rules

To ensure consistency during state transfers, state transfer nets must match the following rules:

- Each attribute should have at most one direct master: either a simple master attribute or a master group of attributes.
- Each attribute should have at most one direct slave: either a simple slave attribute or a slave group of attributes.
- The connection between two groups of nodes must be indirect. It should go through a *virtual node*, that is a node which does not correspond to any role's attribute in the configurations.
- Cycles are forbidden, i.e. any path within a net should never include twice the same node.
- If a set of attributes $\{a_1, ..., a_j\}(j > 1)$ that do not have a master are related and if none of them is richer than the others, then a virtual node v should be added into the net such as $\{a_1, ..., a_j\} \triangleright v$ (i.e. join link from group $\{a_1, ..., a_j\}$ to its master v).

These rules ensure that it is always possible to define a set of absolute master nodes. Moreover, they ensure that the transfer path between two attributes - if any - is unique because from any node, only one transfer function can be used to propagate (up or down) a value to other nodes.

4.5   State Transfer Process

The state transfer occurs during a reassembling process. It is performed in four successive stages:

1. read from the components of the current assembly the variable attribute values of each role within the current configuration,
2. propagate the variable attribute values toward absolute master attributes of the application based on the state transfer net,
3. propagate the variable attribute values from the absolute master attributes to all attributes (including those of the new configuration) based on the state transfer net,
4. initialize the attributes of the components that have been selected for the new configuration: the values of variable attributes for the configuration come from the state transfer net whereas the values of fixed attributes come directly from attribute specifications in the roles.

The previously described process takes place when switching from a configuration to another one. A specific case is the first execution of the application because no value is available for the fixed and variable attributes of the first configuration. Consequently, we use some initialization functions. Not only each role contains an initialization function for its fixed and variable attributes (see subsection 4.1), but also virtual nodes have their own initialization functions when they are absolute masters.

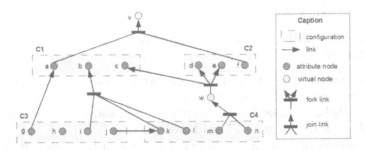

Fig. 10. Sample state transfer net in MADCAR (configurations' roles and transfer functions are not shown)

A sample state transfer net is shown in Fig. 10. The absolute master attributes are v (which is a virtual node), b, c, d, e and h. Let us consider the initialization of the application and let $C3$ be the chosen configuration. The initialization runs in three steps. First, the values of the absolute masters are computed from the initialization functions. Second, these values are propagated towards all the other attributes of the state transfer net. Third, the initialization of $C3$ must be completed. For each variable attribute of $C3$'s roles which have a maximal multiplicity strictly greater than one, the initialization function of the corresponding role is used to make a value vector for this attribute of the same size than the number of components that are selected to fulfill this role. At the end of the initialization, all fixed and variable attributes have a value.

Let us consider an adaptation from configuration $C3$ to configuration $C4$. The **first stage** of the state transfer consists in reading the values of g, h, i and j from the components which fulfill the roles of $C3$. In the **second stage**, the attribute values of $C3$ are successively propagated up to their absolute master attributes, in an arbitrary order (let it be g, h, i, j). The value of g is propagated toward attribute a of $C1$, then the value of a is propagated toward the absolute master attribute v thanks to the join link "$\{a, f\} \triangleright v$", using the temporary value of f and applying $Transfer_{a,f-v}$. Attribute h is an absolute master and does not need any propagation. The value of i is propagated toward b applying $Transfer_{i,k,l-b}$, the value of j is propagated toward attribute k of $C4$, and then the value of k is propagated to b applying $Transfer_{i,k,l-b}$ for the second time[10]. The **third stage**, which occurs at the end of the new assembly's building, consists in propagating the values of absolute master attributes up to the attributes of all configurations. For example, the value of b is propagated down to compute the values of i, k and l. In the **fourth stage**, each value of configuration $C4$'s attributes is used to initialize the components of the new assembly.

---

[10] The first time the function $Transfer_{i,k,l-b}$ is applied, b is computed from the new value of i and from the unmodified values of k and l. The second time, the new values of i and k are both used to recompute b. As l has not been modified, the computation of b is finished.

5   Discussion

5.1   Related Work

There exist many works related to adaptive and self-adaptative component-based software. We present a selection of the most representative ones[11].

SAFRAN [DL03] is an extension of the Fractal component model [12] that aims to support the development of self-adaptive components. SAFRAN relies on a reflective extension of Fractal allowing to modify a component behavior according to its execution context. The adaptation of each component is driven using an individual reactive policy based on ECA rules (Event–Condition–Action). This approach may lead to inconsistencies since each component has its own set of rules and adapts independently from the other components. Such application inconsistencies are detected afterwards at run-time. Running adaptations are cancelled and the application is brought back to its state preceding the adaptation. The management of such inconsistencies may be too costly, especially in resource constrained systems.

SOFA is a platform that aims at defining distributed component-based software [PBJ98]. In SOFA, an application is viewed as a component hierarchy. Each component has a fixed part that is in charge of its life-cycle (mainly updates), and a replaceable part (functional code or sub-components). But, to enable these (partial) replacements, developers should systematically implement some component extra-functional interfaces. This task is even more complex when it comes to building dynamically adaptive components and to deal with related consistency issues. Besides, a new version of a component should provide the same interfaces as the old version.

SOFA 2.0 [BHP06] has been introduced in order to better control architectural adaptations of applications thanks to three reconfiguration patterns. Patterns *nested factory*, *component removal*, and *utility interface* manage respectively component additions, component removals, and inter-component connections regardless their locations in the application hierarchy. Last, the SOFA components fixed part can be reconfigured in SOFA 2.0 thanks to a micro-components based approach.

CASA [MG05] is a framework allowing dynamic adaptation using different mechanisms. Every mechanism is dedicated to a particular adaptation target. Dynamic adaptation in low-level services (such as data transmission and compression) uses reflective technics. Dynamic aspect weaving and unweaving is used for transverse adaptations (such as changing security or persistency behaviors), and rely on PROSE [PGA02]. Dynamic changes in application attributes rely on *callback* methods. Last, dynamic component recomposition is dedicated to adaptations involving components addition, removal, and replacement. In CASA, each

---

[11] OSGi [All] is an industrial component model that handles an event mechanism for dynamic component addition. However, as there is no up-to-date representation of the component assembly, it is tricky to perform deep reassembling.

[12] http://fractal.objectweb.org

adaptation may use one or more of the above mechanisms according to the adaptation policy. Authors of CASA use their own component model and propose an original mechanism for dynamic component replacement. A component is an instance of a class, and can be dynamically replaced by another instance of the same class or of an alternative class fixed at design-time. A lazy component replacement strategy allows to strongly limit inconsistency issues. An adaptation policy directly links a context to an appropriate configuration. According to CASA authors, an adaptation policy can be dynamically changed since it is stored in an XML file separated from the application.

5.2   Comparison and Evaluation of MaDcAr

We can compare the previous works to MaDcAr following the qualitative criteria defined in section 2.

First, most of the described adaptation infrastructures - including MaDcAr-are open, as application designers can control adaptations using policies or some reconfiguration pattern. Concerning consistency, we can note that the adaptation specifications are local to components and connectors for SAFRAN and SOFA, which may result into inconsistencies. SAFRAN addresses such inconsistencies by *a posteriori* corrections that may negatively impact application performance. Such inconsistencies never occur with MaDcAr as well as with CASA, because adaptations are by essence consistent since their specifications are global to applications. Regarding the state transfer, MaDcAr shares with CASA an approach based on a pivot (see subsection 4.2), while SAFRAN and SOFA have an ad hoc approach based on the implementation. Last, but not least only MaDcAr does enable the reuse of adaptation specifications. Such specifications can not only be reused with different component sets, but they also can be reused with different component models.

As part of our experimentations for designing self-adaptive software operating on mobile robots, we have been able to measure the performance of component assembling. For example, we have triggered thousands of time the reassembling process of an exploratory bot composed of 2 configurations, about 12 components and a simple assembling policy. The average time for a reassembling was 48 ms when switching from one configuration to the other was necessary, but the measured values ranged from 29 ms to 182 ms. These values are acceptable because we do not expect the bot's context to change often within a second. However, we need to evaluate the tests on a scenario which involve several communicating bots that perform tricky tasks (e.g. video capture). Research is ongoing to benchmark our assembling engine independently of a specific application, in order to compare with other adaptation infrastructures like CASA [Gyg04].

6   Conclusion and Future Work

We described in this article MaDcAr, an engine model to assemble and to adapt component-based software, dynamically and automatically. Such an engine has four inputs: a set of components to assemble, an application description (i.e. a specification of functional and extra-functional properties of valid assemblies), an assembly policy (drives adaptation decisions), and a context (provides information such as application state, available CPU or network bandwidth). On application startup, MADCAR selects a configuration and assembles available components accordingly. When the context changes, the engine selects again the most appropriate configuration and reassembles available components accordingly while dealing with state transfer issues. Thus, the same mechanism for automatic assembling is used both for applications construction and adaptations.

A major characteristic of MADCAR is that it allows designers build generic specifications. The specification of an application architecture and its adaptations are totally uncoupled from the assembled components. No direct reference to components is allowed. In addition, the assembling policy is separated from the application description. Hence, MADCAR encourages separation of concerns. Besides, MADCAR supports unanticipated adaptations since both application descriptions and components can be replaced at run-time. Another benefit of MADCAR's approach is due to the fact that the adaptation specification is both global to the application and uncoupled from components. Therefore, MADCAR avoids adaptation consistency issues encountered in approaches where each components can adapt independently from the others. Morover, adaptation specifications can be reused with different components. Last, because MADCAR is independent of any component model, adaptation specifications including state transfer rules are generic and reusable with multiple component models.

We have implemented a generic MADCAR framework and we have specialized it for the Fractal component model [BCS02]. This specialization is named *AutoFractal*[13] and is dedicated to our Smalltalk implementation of the Fractal model *FracTalk*[14].

Regarding our future work, we aim at working on optimizing the assembling engine. So far, application designers can control adaptation temporal complexity by bounding the duration of adaptation decisions. We would like to go further and reduce the costs of decisions and state transfer in order to fit embedded software resource constraints. Another interesting research direction is to study an evolution of MADCAR that deals with the adaptation of distributed software.

References

[All]   OSGi Alliance, http://www.osgi.org/

[BCS02]   Bruneton, E., Coupaye, T., Stefani, J.: Recursive and dynamic software composition with sharing. In: Proceedings of the 7th ECOOP International Workshop on Component-Oriented Programming (WCOP 2002), Malaga, Spain (June 2002)

---

[13] http://vst.ensm-douai.fr/AutoFractal
[14] http://vst.ensm-douai.fr/FracTalk

[BHP06]   Bures, T., Hnetynka, P., Plasil, F.: Sofa 2.0: Balancing advanced features in a hierarchical component model. In: Proceedings of the 4th International Conference on Software Engineering Research, Management and Applications (SERA 2006), Washington, DC, USA, pp. 40–48. IEEE Computer Society (2006)

[BJPW99]   Beugnard, A., Jezequel, J.-M., Plouzeau, N., Watkins, D.: Making components contract aware. Computer 32(7), 38–45 (1999)

[BJRV04]   Bézivin, J., Jouault, F., Rosenthal, P., Valduriez, P.: Modeling in the large and modeling in the small. In: Aßmann, U., Aksit, M., Rensink, A. (eds.) MDAFA 2003. LNCS, vol. 3599, pp. 33–46. Springer, Heidelberg (2005)

[CC07]   Chang, H., Collet, P.: Compositional Patterns of Non-Functional Properties for Contract Negotiation. Journal of Software (JSW) 2(2), 12 (2007)

[CCDG05]   Coutaz, J., Crowley, J.L., Dobson, S., Garlan, D.: Context is key. Commununication of the ACM 48(3), 49–53 (2005)

[CRS07]   Conan, D., Rouvoy, R., Seinturier, L.: Scalable processing of context information with cosmos. In: Indulska, J., Raymond, K. (eds.) DAIS 2007. LNCS, vol. 4531, pp. 210–224. Springer, Heidelberg (2007)

[DL03]   David, P.-C., Ledoux, T.: Towards a framework for self-adaptive component-based applications. In: Stefani, J.-B., Demeure, I., Hagimont, D. (eds.) DAIS 2003. LNCS, vol. 2893, pp. 1–14. Springer, Heidelberg (2003)

[DL05]   David, P.-C., Ledoux, T.: WildCAT: a generic framework for context-aware applications. In: Proceeding of th 3rd International Workshop on Middleware for Pervasive and Ad-Hoc Computing (MPAC 2005), Grenoble, France (November 2005)

[DSA01]   Dey, A., Salber, D., Abowd, G.: A conceptual framework and a toolkit for supporting the rapid prototyping of context-aware applications. Special issue on context-aware computing in the Human-Computer Interaction Journal 16(2–4), 97–166 (2001)

[GBV06]   Grondin, G., Bouraqadi, N., Vercouter, L.: MADCAR: an Abstract Model for Dynamic and Automatic (Re-)Assembling of Component-Based Applications. In: Gorton, I., Heineman, G.T., Crnković, I., Schmidt, H.W., Stafford, J.A., Szyperski, C.A., Wallnau, K. (eds.) CBSE 2006. LNCS, vol. 4063, pp. 360–367. Springer, Heidelberg (2006)

[GBV08]   Grondin, G., Bouraqadi, N., Vercouter, L.: Assemblage automatique et adaptation d'applications à base de composants. In: Proceedings of the French-speaking Conference on Object Languages and Models (LMO 2008), pp. 21–37, Montréal, Canada, RNTI, Cépaduès Editions (2008)

[Gyg04]   Gygax, A.: Studying the effect of size and complexity of components on the performance of CASA. Intership report, Department of Informatics, University of Zurich (2004)

[IT02]   Inverardi, P., Tivoli, M.: Correct and automatic assembly of COTS components: an architectural approach. In: Proceedings of the 5th ICSE Workshop on Component-Based Software Engineering (CBSE5): Benchmarks for Predictable Assembly (2002)

[KBC02]   Ketfi, A., Belkhatir, N., Cunin, P.-Y.: Adapting applications on the fly. In: Proceedings of the 17th IEEE International Conference on Automated Software Engineering, Washington (ASE 2002), DC, USA, p. 313. IEEE Computer Society (2002)

[KM90]   Kramer, J., Magee, J.: The evolving philosophers problem: Dynamic
            change management. IEEE Transaction on Software Engineering 16(11),
            1293–1306 (1990)
[Kum92]   Kumar, V.: Algorithms for constraint satisfaction problems: A survey. AI
            Magazine 13(1), 32–44 (1992)
[Mey92]   Meyer, B.: Applying "design by contract". Computer 25(10), 40–51
            (1992)
[MG05]   Mukhija, A., Glinz, M.: Runtime adaptation of applications through dy-
            namic recomposition of components. In: Beigl, M., Lukowicz, P. (eds.)
            ARCS 2005. LNCS, vol. 3432, pp. 124–138. Springer, Heidelberg (2005)
[PBJ98]   Plasil, F., Balek, D., Janecek, R.: SOFA/DCUP: Architecture for com-
            ponent trading and dynamic update. In: Proceedings of the 4th IEEE
            International Conference on Configurable Distributed Systems (ICCDS
            1998), pp. 35–42 (May 1998)
[PGA02]   Popovici, A., Gross, T., Alonso, G.: Dynamic weaving for aspect-oriented
            programming. In: Proceedings of the 1st international conference on
            Aspect-oriented software development (AOSD 2002), pp. 141–147. ACM
            Press, New York (2002)
[SF93]   Segal, M.E., Frieder, O.: On-the-fly program modification: Systems for
            dynamic updating. IEEE Software 10(2), 53–65 (1993)
[SMBV03]   Sora, I., Matthijs, F., Berbers, Y., Verbaeten, P.: Automatic composition
            of systems from components with anonymous dependencies specified by
            semantic-unaware properties. Technology of Object-Oriented Languages,
            Systems & Architectures 732, 154–179 (2003)
[Szy02]   Szyperski, C.: Component Software: Beyond Object-Oriented Program-
            ming. Addison-Wesley Longman Publishing Co., Inc., Boston (2002)
[VB03]   Vandewoude, Y., Berbers, Y.: Meta model driven state transfer in com-
            ponent oriented systems. In: Proceedings of The Second International
            Workshop On Unanticipated Software Evolution, Warshau, Poland, pp.
            3–8 (April 2003)
[WB]   Wifibot, http://www.wifibot.com

A Comparison of State-Based Modelling Tools for Model Validation

Emine G. Aydal[1], Mark Utting[2], and Jim Woodcock[1]

[1] University of York, UK
[2] University of Waikato, New Zealand

Abstract. In model-based testing, one of the biggest decisions taken before modelling is the modelling language and the model analysis tool to be used to model the system under investigation. UML, Alloy and Z are examples of popular state-based modelling languages. In the literature, there has been research about the similarities and the differences between modelling languages. However, we believe that, in addition to recognising the expressive power of modelling languages, it is crucial to detect the capabilities and the weaknesses of analysis tools that parse and analyse models written in these languages. In order to explore this area, we have chosen four model analysis tools: USE, Alloy Analyzer, ZLive and ProZ and observed how modelling and validation stages of MBT are handled by these tools for the same system. Through this experiment, we not only concretise the tasks that form the modelling and validation stages of MBT process, but also reveal how efficiently these tasks are carried out in different tools.

1   Introduction

A model is a schematic description of a system, theory or phenomenon that accounts for its known properties, and may be used for further study of its characteristics. It translates the description of the features of the tested system into a precise presentation of the expected behaviour [13].

Model-Based Testing (MBT) is a new and evolving technique for generating a suite of test cases from requirements [10]. It helps to ensure a repeatable and scientific basis for product testing, gives good coverage of all the behaviour of the product and allows tests to be linked directly to requirements [11]. MBT is also defined as the automation of the design of black-box tests [12,11].

In the MBT context, a model serves two main purposes: it forms the basis for test-case generation and it acts as an oracle for the System Under Test (SUT). In order to fulfil these purposes, it is crucial that the modelling language in which the model is described is capable of expressing the properties expected from that model. These properties are studied under the title *specification paradigm* in [1]. Depending on the paradigm chosen, the characterisation of the specification differs, i.e., each paradigm describes the system by focusing on different aspects of the system. History-based specifications specify a system by characterising its

R.F. Paige and B. Meyer (Eds.): TOOLS EUROPE 2008, LNBIP 11, pp. 278–296, 2008.

maximal set of admissible histories whilst state-based specifications use admissible system states at some arbitrary snapshots. Transition-based specifications focus on the transitions from one state to another and functional specifications describe the system as a set of structured collection of mathematical functions [1]. In MBT, the *Model Paradigm* can be described as the combination of a *specification paradigm* and a modelling language. The specification paradigm chosen determines the set of modelling languages that are able to express the properties required for that paradigm. Having said that, it is still open to discussion how successful these languages are in expressing these properties and how well the current tools fulfil our expectations in analysing the models written in these languages.

In this study, we address this issue by modelling the same system in three modelling languages that use the state-based specification paradigm and by analysing these models with four different model analysis tools. Through this study, we explore the impact of the selection of a modelling language and a tool in the modelling and validation processes. In order to achieve this, we focus on the creation of an abstract model of the SUT from informal requirements, and the validation of the model via animation, e.g., snapshot generation. The term *snapshot* means a valid, restricted, arbitrary instance of the model. Validity is checked in accordance with the system invariants. Restrictions may be introduced in order to reduce the search space and to concentrate on the area of interest. The degree of arbitrariness changes from one modelling language/tool to another, but the idea is to be able to generate an instance of the model or to animate the operation with a minimum degree of user interaction.

The next section explains the contribution of this study in further detail. Section 2 provides background information about the modelling languages and the tools used in this study. The basic version of the case study is presented in Section 3. Section 4 gives the extended version of the case study, explains the expectations from the tools, and the results obtained. Finally, the experiment is summarised in Section 5.

1.1   Contribution

The modelling languages covered in this study are UML enriched with OCL, Alloy and Z. All of these languages are classified under the state-based specification paradigm. They all model the system as a collection of variables, declare the invariants that the system must satisfy and define the operations of the system by its pre- and post-conditions [8]. Although they seem to have similar, if not the same, targets, these languages differ a great deal in terms of their syntax and analysis. In the literature, there has been research stating the differences between UML and Alloy [6,7] and between UML, Z and Alloy [5]. However, these studies mainly focus on the languages and not the tools that parse and analyse these languages.

In this experiment, we model a Course Assignment System in all these three languages by using analysis tools that support these languages. The motivation behind this experiment can be summarised as follows:

- We use this experiment as a magnifying glass on the modelling and validation stages of model-based testing. Through this study, we clarify the tasks carried out during these stages for different modelling languages.
- By concretising the tasks during modelling and validation phases, we also reveal the expectations and the capabilities of the tools that analyse the models.
- In addition to these, in traditional MBT, the general tendency whilst validating an operation is to start from an input state and expect the tool to generate an output state. The drawback of this approach is that the tester is responsible for finding the initial valid state in order to carry out the rest of the process. In this paper, we demonstrate an extension of this approach, where possible, by generating both the input and the output state that represent the operation's execution.
- Furthermore, all the languages studied in this experiment have different degrees of formalism and they are generally being used by different groups of people in modelling, validating, and testing different systems. However, these communities may not be aware of the capabilities of the languages/tools that are used by other communities and they may not follow the improvements that occur in one another. The lack of such knowledge may have several impacts. For instance, the members of one community may not be able to see the benefits and the power of other modelling languages or analysis tools. Therefore the usage of tools may not be efficient and the perspective necessary to develop better testing tools may be limited.

  Within this context, we take an example system and use all these different tools to model and validate this system. Thus, this study not only concretises the tasks to be done, but also reports the difficulties and the advantages of modelling and validation by using the tools such as Alloy Analyzer, ProZ, ZLive and USE. By doing so, we contribute in bridging the gap between formal, semi-formal and perhaps non-formal environments.

2   Background

In this section, we give a brief overview of the modelling languages and the tools used in this study.

UML. Unified Modeling Language, OMG's most-used specification, offers a rich set of notations to model application structure and architecture as well as business processes and data structures [2]. When used together with the Object Constraint Language (OCL), it also provides a means to describe model behaviour and metamodel constraints. There have been many studies that use UML and OCL in different stages of MBT, ranging from model validation to test case generation [3,4]. After the popularity of UML/OCL is raised, many tool developers produced tools with different capabilities. Some examples to these tools are the OCL Compiler from the University of Dresden (OCLCUD), **UML Specification Environment (USE)** by Mark Richters in the University of Bremen, the OCL Compiler, produced by Cybernetic Intelligence GMBH and KeY by the University of Karlsruhe. After careful consideration, we decided to use the USE tool [17,18] in this study, especially due to its capabilities in generating automatic snapshots of the system and in validating pre-/post-conditions through scenarios in addition to its ability to verify the system invariants.

Z is a formal specification language used for describing and modelling computing systems [14]. It is based on the standard mathematical notation used in axiomatic set theory, first-order predicate logic and lambda calculus. We used two analysis tools in this experiment to parse and analyse the Z model of our case study: ProZ and ZLive. The **ZLive** animator is part of the CZT project, which provides a framework for building formal methods tools, especially for the Z specification language [19]. It provides a simple textual user interface that handles Z in LaTeX and Unicode markup. **ProZ** is an extension of the ProB animator and model checker to support Z specifications. It uses the *Fuzz* type checker by Mike Spivey for extracting the formal specification from a LaTeXfile [9].

Alloy is a simple structural modelling language based on first-order logic [15,16]. Alloy is similar to OCL, the Object Language of UML, but it has a more conventional syntax and a simpler semantics, and is designed for automatic analysis. Alloy is a fully declarative language, whereas OCL mixes declarative and operational elements. Z was a major influence on Alloy, but unlike Z, Alloy is first order. **The Alloy Analyzer** is a tool developed by the Software Design Group at MIT, for analyzing models written in Alloy [15]. It allows the user to generate instances of invariants, animate the execution of operations and check user-specified properties.

3 Case Study: Course Assignment System

The system modeled in this experiment is a simple Course Assignment System, where the students and lecturers are assigned to certain courses. The initial requirements and restrictions of the system are listed in Table 1. This section provides the details of how the system is modeled in UML, Alloy and Z as well as the expectations from the tools at this stage. The case study is extended further in Section 4 to specify the pre/postconditions of several operations.

3.1 Modelling the Static Structure of the System

In this phase of the experiment, we create the *basic model* for the Course Assignment Software, i.e., the static structure and the invariants of the system. The expectation from the tool at this stage is to parse the model written by the user and to create a valid, arbitrary instance of the model –an object diagram that satisfies all the system invariants– in a reasonable amount of time. The existence of such an instance increases confidence in the model by guaranteeing that there are no conflicting invariants.

Table 1. Requirements of Course Assignment Software

Req. No.	Requirement Description
R0	The system consists of courses, students and lecturers.
R1	Each course must be subscribed by at least one student.
R2	Each course can only be subscribed by students from certain years of their degree and this information is associated to each course.
R3	The total number of students for a course cannot exceed 7.
R4	Only one lecturer must be assigned to each course.
R5	Course ID must be unique.
R6	The lecturer assigned to a course must have at least 3 years of experience.
R7	A student must subscribe to at least 1 course.
R8	A student cannot subscribe to more than 6 courses.
R9	In his/her 4th year, the student cannot subscribe to more than 4 courses.
R10	The age of the students taking a course must be less than the age of the lecturer assigned to that course.
R11	A lecturer can be assigned to 3 courses at most.

During this phase, we observed analysis tools in terms of their ability to:

- create and visualise a valid instance of the model
- run with less user interaction
- perform in a reasonable amount of time
- return adequate information about the execution of the model

3.2   Modelling in UML and OCL with USE

The USE tool allows users to specify system models, invariants, and pre- and postconditions textually, and allows assertions to be checked [18]. The tool provides a multi-level platform where the model is defined in a .use file, the generation of an instance of the model is managed by an .assl file, the extra optional invariants are imposed in a .invs file and all these files as well as other USE-related commands are executed by calling .cmd files in command prompt of the tool. The class diagram of the system, as shown in Figure 1, consists of 4 classes: Course, Lecturer, Student and Person. Lecturer and Student classes are subclasses of the abstract class Person. For each requirement listed in Table 1, an invariant is written in OCL. The generation of snapshots is mainly driven by the user through the .assl file. Following is the shortened version of the .assl file used in this study.

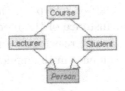

Fig. 1. Class Diagram derived in USE

```
procedure AssignCourses(countCourse:Integer, countStudent:Integer,
       countLecturer:Integer)
var theConstants:SystemConstants, theCourses:Sequence(Course),
theStudents:Sequence(Student), theLecturers:Sequence(Lecturer),aCourse:Course ;
begin
    theConstants := Create(SystemConstants);
    ...    ---values of the constants are assigned
    theCourses := CreateN(Course,[countCourse]);
    for c:Course in [theCourses]
    begin
        [c].cID := Try([Sequence{1..10}
            ->reject(cID1| Course.allInstances.cID->exists(cID2|cID1=cID2))]);
    ... end;
    theStudents := CreateN(Student,[countStudent]);
    for s:Student in [theStudents]
    begin
        [s].year := Try([Sequence{1..4}]);
        ... -- Assignment of other attributes
        aCourse := Try([Course.allInstances->asSequence
            ->select(c1| Course.allInstances
            ->forAll(c2|c1.attendees->size()<=c2.attendees->size()) )]);
        Insert(Assignment,[aCourse],[s]); --link creation
    end;
    theLecturers := CreateN(Lecturer,[countLecturer]);
    for l:Lecturer in [theLecturers]
    begin
        [l].expYear := Try([Sequence{1..40}])
        ... -- Attribute assignment and Link creation with a Course Object
    end;
end;
```

The order of objects generated by USE and the order of attribute assignment
is explicitly stated in the file. In the above case, it is set as SystemConstant
object, Course objects, Student objects and then Lecturer Objects. There are
both advantages and disadvantages of this approach. The obvious advantage is
that it is possible to give realistic values to the attributes. This ensures that the
snapshot generated is practical. In addition to this, the user can also control the
values assigned through *reject* and *if-then-else* expressions. However, there are
several drawbacks of this approach as explained below.

Finding the right order of objects: It is not straightforward to determine which
order produces the test cases more efficiently. To explore this more, we changed
the order of the object creation and ran the generator to find a valid snapshot of
the system. Table 2 shows the distinct orders associated to *variation numbers*,
the number of objects in the snapshot, the number of snapshots checked before
finding the valid snapshot and the number of seconds spent.

The field *Order* uses the letters S, L and C to represent Student, Lecturer and
Course objects respectively. The field *Number of Objects* shows the parameters
given to *AssignCourses*, i.e., number of Courses, the number of Student objects
and the number of Lecturer objects in the snapshot to be generated. Note that

Table 2. Effects of changes in order of object creation

Variation No	Order	Number of Objects	Snapshots checked	Estimated time spent(s)
1	C-S-L	(1,1,1)	5	1s
2	C-L-S	(1,1,1)	129	2s
3	L-S-C	(1,1,1)	30721	312s
4	S-C-L	(1,1,1)	5	1s
1	C-S-L	(2,2,2)	677	4s
4	S-C-L	(2,2,2)	2698	22s
5	S-C-L (*)	(2,2,2)	677	4s
1	C-S-L	(2,3,2)	677	4s
5	S-C-L (*)	(2,3,2)	Stopped after 92105	943s

the *Estimated time spent* is not an output of the tool, but is calculated by the user. It is clear from the first four rows of Table 2 that the order of object creation specified in the .assl file affects the valid snapshot generation process.

Finding the right order of links: We also implemented another version of variation-4, which has the same object creation, but different link creation order. Instead of generating the instances of the associations between the objects on-the-go, in variation-5, we created all the links at the end and realised that this improved the time spent.

Invariant check: In finding the valid snapshot, USE performs a *Depth-first* search and this is why the order of object creation request becomes an issue to be considered in writing the .assl file. It checks for invariant-conformance after all the objects and links are created. We are aware that some of the invariants can actually be embedded into the .assl file in creating objects by using *reject* and *if-then-else* statements. This may shorten the time to find a valid snapshot by restricting the values assigned to attributes of these objects, but it is, in fact, a repetition of constraints that already exist in the model. We believe that an on-the-fly invariant-check would improve the performance of USE a great deal.

3.3   Modelling in Alloy with Alloy Analyzer

In our first attempt to implement the system in Alloy, we used signatures for each class in UML and defined the associations as attributes of the Course class. For instance, *cAttendees* represented the set of Students in Course class. The problem with this definition of *Course* was that Alloy is unable to analyse the invariants that require a higher-order quantification. An example of these invariants is given below where it states that a student cannot subscribe to more than 4 courses in his/her 4th year.

```
fact LastYearLimit
{all s:Student, cSet : set Course {all c:cSet |
        s in c.cAttendees and s.sYear = 4 => #cSet <= 4}}
```

In our second attempt, we created another signature called *Department* and defined the associations as relations between the classes.

```
some sig Course
{   cID: Int, cAllowedYears: set Int}
one sig Department
{   CourseAssignment : Student some -> some Course ,
    TeachingAssignment : Course -> some Lecturer}
```

After this change, the invariant above could be written in first-order logic as:

```
fact LastYearLimit
{all d:Department, s:Student {s.sYear = 4 => # d.CourseAssignment[s] <= 4}}
```

Moreover, as shown in the definition of *Department*, Alloy also supports the multiplicity concept in relations. The *CourseAssignment* relation imposes that the students should subscribe to at least one course and that the courses should have at least one attendee.

In Alloy, the *run* command generates a valid instance of a given model. One of the first observations we made whilst executing this command is that the bitwidth for integer values is set to 4 by default, i.e., the range of values that an integer attribute can take is limited to [-8,7]. When there is a comparison of an integer and a value that is higher than 7, the value is rounded to this range and the comparison is made without any notification of an error or a warning. For instance, when there are 8 student objects in the system and we request the cardinality of the student objects, the result reads -8. As a workaround, we set the bitwidth for integer to 6 in the *run* command, but we believe that rounding without any notification may cause unforeseen problems in the system.

We also noticed that there is no *string* or *character* datatype. One way of implementing strings is to define a *string* signature and define it as a set of characters, which must also be declared as a signature. In order to simplify our model, we performed a data abstraction for the attributes of type string.

In terms of snapshot generation, Alloy Analyzer is found to be very powerful. Table 3 gives the results for several snapshots generated by using several SAT solvers and different numbers of objects.

Table 3. Snapshot generation with Alloy Analyzer

No. of objects	No. of vars	No. of primary vars	No. of clauses	SAT Solver	Time spent(ms)
(1,1,1)	6625	643	19609	berkmin	1047+407ms
				sat4j	844+109ms
(2,2,4)	13639	1294	37838	berkmin	2922+625ms
				sat4j	3000+94ms
(2,4,10)	26828	2336	73231	berkmin	11797+1859ms
				sat4j	12125+343ms

The numbers of objects are represented in the form of (Course, Lecturer, Student). The time spent, the number of variables, primary variables and clauses checked are given by the tool after finding the snapshot. The field *time spent* is given as an addition of two terms of which the first one represents the time whilst the tool is generating the Canonical Normal Form (CNF) of the model and the second is the duration of finding the snapshot that satisfies the invariants. As shown in Table 3, SAT Solvers have an impact on the time spent, but the fact that the user does not have to have any knowledge about the implementation of these SAT Solvers other than selecting them, makes the process easy.

Another advantage of this tool is that the user's role in the snapshot generation process is minimal. The user is not responsible for creating an extra file to manage the object or link creation. The invariant check is managed by SAT Solvers, so there is no concern as to where and when invariants are checked.

3.4   Modelling in Z with ZLive and ProZ

The Z specification of the course assignment is very similar to that of Alloy in that the Z version has the similar classes in *schema* form. The invariants of the system are embedded into the *Department* schema.

$$
\begin{array}{|l}
\hline
\;\textit{Department} \underline{\hspace{7cm}} \\
\quad studentSet : \mathbb{P}\; Student \\
\quad lecturerSet : \mathbb{P}\; Lecturer \\
\quad courseSet : \mathbb{P}\; Course \\
\quad CourseAssignment : Student \leftrightarrow Course \\
\quad TeachingAssignment : Course \nrightarrow Lecturer \\
\hline
\quad \operatorname{dom} CourseAssignment \subseteq studentSet \wedge \operatorname{ran} CourseAssignment \subseteq courseSet \\
\quad \operatorname{dom} TeachingAssignment \subseteq courseSet \wedge \operatorname{ran} TeachingAssignment \subseteq lecturerSet \\
\quad \forall\, s : studentSet \bullet \#(\{s\} \lhd CourseAssignment) \leq cMaxCourseSubscription \\
\quad \forall\, s : studentSet;\; listOfCourses : \mathbb{P}\; courseSet \mid \\
\qquad listOfCourses = CourseAssignment(\!|\, \{s\} \,|\!) \\
\qquad \wedge\; s.sYear = cExceptionalYear \bullet \#listOfCourses \leq 4 \\
\quad \forall\, s : studentSet;\; c : courseSet \mid s \mapsto c \in CourseAssignment \bullet \\
\qquad s.sYear \in c.cAllowedYears \\
\quad \forall\, s : studentSet;\; c : courseSet;\; lec : lecturerSet \mid s \mapsto c \in CourseAssignment \\
\qquad \wedge\; c \mapsto lec \in TeachingAssignment \bullet s.age < lec.age \\
\quad \forall\, c : courseSet \bullet (\#(CourseAssignment \rhd \{c\}) \leq cMaxAttendees) \\
\quad \forall\, lec : lecturerSet \bullet lec \in \operatorname{ran} TeachingAssignment \Rightarrow lec.lExpYear \geq cMinExpYear \\
\quad \forall\, lec : lecturerSet \bullet (\#(TeachingAssignment \rhd \{lec\}) \leq cMaxLecturerAssignment) \\
\hline
\end{array}
$$

As expected, the Z version of *Department* schema is more mathematical in terms of syntax than the other two versions. This mathematical form certainly brings formalism to Z, however it also makes comprehension more difficult for non-mathematicians. Therefore, one of the main expectations from the tools that analyse models written in LaTeXor some other markup version of a formal language like Z is to compensate this by providing more guidance to the user.

In this respect, the tools we used, ZLive and ProZ behave differently. ZLive allows the user to communicate with the tool via a set of commands, whereas ProZ provides a menu from which the user can choose what to do next. In terms of information given for syntactical errors, ZLive returns more explanatory information than ProZ.

In the modelling phase, we could parse and initialise the model. However, it is not possible to generate an arbitrary instance of the model other than the initial model. Note that in Z, the developer is responsible for writing a valid instance of the model to initialise the model, whereas the tools that analyse Alloy and UML could generate a valid snapshot without the user having to write the value of each attribute that needs to have a value to satisfy the system invariants.

3.5   Remarks

Table 4 outlines the factors that have an effect on the search for a valid snapshot for Alloy Analyzer and USE. Z tools are not considered here since we were only able to initialise the model with the Init schema written by the user.

Table 4. Factors affecting valid snapshot generation process

Factor	USE	Alloy Analyzer
Order of Object Creation	Relevant	N/A
Order of Attribute Value Assignment	Relevant	N/A
Selection of objects before linking to another object (criteria considered at this stage)	Relevant	N/A
Loop structure of object creation	Relevant	N/A
The point in which the invariants are analysed	Relevant	N/A
The range of variables	Relevant	Relevant
Constraint Solver embedded	N/A	Relevant
The number of objects to be created	Relevant	Relevant
Limitations on formulas in higher order logic	N/A	Relevant
Default Limitations on data types	Not observable	Relevant

In terms of general tool usage, Table 5 summarises our observations.

Table 5. Observations about the tool usage

Criteria	USE	Alloy An.	ZLive	ProZ
Create and visualise a valid instance of the model	Yes	Yes	No	No
Generation of snapshot without extra effort	No	Yes	N/A	N/A
Perform in a reasonable amount of time	No	Yes	N/A	N/A
Return information about the model execution	Partial	Yes	N/A	N/A
Provide adequate information about the errors that occur during the modelling and execution	Yes	Yes	Yes	No

4 Course Assignment - Extended Version

In the second phase of the experiment, we defined operations such as *Subscribe()*, *Unsubscribe()*, *Assign()*, *Deallocate()* through their pre- and post-conditions. We also created query operations to check the current status of the system. The main aim in the second phase was to ensure that the pre- and post-conditions associated to the operations are *realistic*. The word *realistic* implicitly contains the following statements:

- There is no pre-condition that is false for all possible instances of the system.
- There is at least one post-state that satisfies all postconditions and system invariants when the associated pre-state satisfies all pre-conditions and the system invariants.

One of the indirect objectives of this activity in the validation step of MBT is to find too strong/too weak system invariants, pre- and post-conditions.

In traditional MBT, it is generally the case that a pre-state is given as input to the tool and the tool is expected to find the associated post-state by animating the operation execution. This sort of animation is also called *forward animation* and it is certainly one way of checking the aforementioned objectives related to assertions and system invariants. Opposite of this, *backward animation* needs a post-state as input and generates a pre-state. In our approach, we followed a *non-directed* animation, where possible. Thus, the main expectation from the modelling tool at this stage was to generate a snapshot with two instances of the system where first one (pre-state) is the initial, valid instance of the model and the second one (post-state) presents the system after the execution of the operation under investigation. The advantage of this approach is that the user does not have to bring the system to the initial state by executing other operations, yet it is still possible to impose restrictions on the pre- or post-state.

In addition to this, we also analysed the modelling tools in terms of their capability in animating the operations with less user interaction, generating pre/post states of the operations and returning useful information about the execution.

4.1 Validation in UML and OCL with USE

The implementation of this phase with USE consists of the steps given in the first column of Table 6. The second, third and fourth columns show whether or not the tasks carried out by the user includes any *intellectual* or *procedural* work. *Intellectual* work stands for the tasks where the user has to understand the semantics of the operation and perform an action accordingly. *Procedural* work represents the administrational tasks such as writing the output of the tool into a new file, moving a file to a different location, etc.

Task-1 in Table 6 is explained in Section 3.2. Once the valid snapshot is generated, this is recorded and executed to actually bring the system into the state described by the snapshot. In the third step, the system is brought into another valid state where all the preconditions of the operation under investigation are satisfied. It is possible to combine Task-1 and Task-3 to generate a valid snapshot

Table 6. Validation of operations in USE

Task	Command Execution	Procedural Work	Intellectual Work
1. Generate a valid initial snapshot of the system	Yes	Yes	Yes
2. Record and execute the snapshot	Yes	Yes	No
3. Prepare the snapshot for the operation to be executed (Precondition adjustment)	Yes	Yes	Yes
4. Enter the operation	Yes	No	No
5. Animate the execution of the operation	Yes	Yes	Yes
6. Exit the operation	Yes	No	No

that already satisfies preconditions. For some operations, Task-3 may be void if the operation can run at any valid state of the system. We can analyse these steps further in the following .cmd file for the Course Assignment example:

```
open c:/<root>/CourseAssignment.use
gen start -b c:/<root>/CourseAssignment1.assl  AssignCourses(2,2,2)
gen result
read c:/<root>/snapshot.cmd
read c:/<root>/precond_Unsubscribe.cmd
!openter Student1 Unsubscribe(Student1,Course1)
read c:/<root>/Unsubscribe.cmd
!opexit true
```

The first three lines form Task-1 in Table 6. Before executing the next command, the output of the tool is written into the file *snapshot.cmd*. At this point, we have a system where there are 2 course objects, 2 student objects and 2 lecturer objects linked in accordance with the system invariants. The assertions of the *Unsubscribe* function as written in USE is given below:

```
context Student::Unsubscribe(s: Student, c: Course) : Boolean
    pre UnsubscribePre1:   s.courses->select(cID = c.cID)->size() = 1
    pre UnsubscribePre2:   s.courses->size() >= 1
    post UnsubscribePost1: s.courses->select(cID = c.cID)->isEmpty()
    post UnsubscribePost2: s.courses->size() = s.courses@pre->size() - 1
```

The commands written in *precond_Unsubscribe.cmd* file ensures that the preconditions of *Unsubscribe* function are satisfied when *!openter* command is executed. The *Unsubscribe.cmd* file animates the operation and finally the postconditions of the function are verified after the *opexit* command.

To conclude, the tool provides a platform where the user can animate the execution of an operation, but it is user's responsibility to create the .assl file that generates the initial, valid instance of the model and to make sure that the preconditions are satisfied. Given the tasks are carried out, the tool animates the operation execution. The main drawback of this technique is its dependability on the user. If the assertions of the system are not satisfied on Task-6, that does not mean that there is no state that this operation is run successfully. It may well be that the user could not bring the system in the right state to execute the operation or did not implement the operation correctly.

4.2 Validation in Alloy with Alloy Analyzer

In Alloy, the operations are written as *predicates*. The implementation of *Unsubscribe* function in Alloy is given below. The preconditions ensure that there is a student assigned to a course and that the course has more than 1 attendee. Postconditions state that the student is no longer an attendee of the course, the number of attendees in that course is decremented by one and that no change is made in the *TeachingAssignment* relation that represents the assignment of lecturers to courses.

```
pred Unsubscribe(d, d': DepartmentState)  {
    some s: Student,  c: Course {
    c in d.CourseAssignment[s]                              //pre1
    # c.~(d.CourseAssignment) >= 1                          //pre2
    d'.CourseAssignment = d.CourseAssignment - s->c        //post1
    # d'.CourseAssignment[s] = #d.CourseAssignment[s] - 1  //post2
    d'.TeachingAssignment = d.TeachingAssignment}}         //extra
```

In the search of pre- and post-states of the system before and after the execution of this operation, we use the following assertion:

```
assert CheckUnsubscribe{all d,d':DepartmentState| not Unsubscribe[d , d']}
```

In this assertion, we claim that the animation of *Unsubscribe* operation is not possible and expect the tool to find a counter example. The existence of counter example would mean that there is at least one state that allows the operation to run and another state that represents the system after the execution of the operation. Note that in both states, all the system invariants must be satisfied.

In Alloy, the call for assertions is managed by *check* command. In executing this command, it is possible to fix the number of objects we would like to see in the snapshot. If we do not specify this information explicitly, then the tool finds the snapshots that have less number of objects.

In the validation process with Alloy Analyzer, we observed that less amount of intellectual work is needed provided that the operation under investigation is defined correctly. There is no concept of entering or exiting an operation. Having said that, the user can still add further criteria to the *assert* statement to narrow down the search space.

4.3 Validation in Z with ZLive

ZLive provides a *command-prompt*-like platform where the user can interact with the tool by using commands that may have Z structure.

In order to facilitate the job of the user, we added *Add_ClassType_* operations into the Z specifications such as AddStudent, AddLecturer, etc. Thus, the creation of objects are done by calling such operations. For instance, to add a student into the student list, we can call the AddStudent schema with:

1.no constraint: *do AddStudent* which creates an arbitrary instance of the Student schema

2.some constraints: *do [AddStudent | sYear = 4]* which creates a Student object whose sYear value is set to 4.

3.specific values: *do[AddStudent | s? = ⟨sYear == 4, age == 21, name == 1000⟩]* which assigns all the attributes of the student object

This variety gives the user the flexibility to try different channels if the desired instance cannot be produced. Especially when the search space is too large, the tool may not be able to handle a call with no restriction, thus, imposing extra constraints on the schema by using the second and third approach may reduce the search space.

In addition to *do* operator, there is also semicolon -;- operator that can be used in the same context. The difference between *do* operator and *;* operator is that the latter takes the current state as pre-state, and produces a post-state by animating the execution of the operation. This approach is similar to ProZ as explained in Section 4.4. The *do* operator, on the other hand, does not take the current state into consideration, and, analogous to Alloy, generates a pre- and a post-state that represents the states before and after the execution of the operation under investigation. In fact, it is also possible to request the tool to find the pre-state by specifying an explicit post-state.

When an operation cannot be run for a particular pre-state, the tool returns *no solution*. An advantageous feature of the tool for such situations is the *why* command which gives more insight about why no solution could be found. However, the information given is very low level and assumes a certain level of subject-related knowledge from the user.

Another implicit benefit of the tool is that it introduces only a limited number of keywords and mainly uses Z syntax, thus, a Z-literate user would not have any difficulty interacting with the tool after having a rough look at the keywords.

4.4   Validation in Z with ProZ

ProZ identifies a schema as an operation if all variables of the state and their primed counterpart are declared in the operation, and no other schema in the specification refers to the operation [9].

An advantage of using ProZ is that it provides the user with a Graphical User Interface (GUI) where it is possible to observe the current values of the attributes, the history of the operations that are animated and the list of enabled operations at a given time, i.e., the operations whose preconditions are satisfied. When the tool parses the system model, the first and the only operation available is the *Init* operation. Init operation creates an empty set of student list, course list and lecturer list. In order to facilitate the job of the user in creating objects, we also added operations such as AddStudent, AddLecturer, etc.

The drawback of the GUI is that the tool actually attempts to list all the possible calls with the parameters in the accepted range as enabled operations. Since the number of such calls is high and both a timeout value and an animation setting limit the number of calls listed, the user is given only some of the enabled operations with a set of parameters. We noticed that the *timeout* button helps to retrieve the commands that are not visible in the Enabled Operation section by bypassing the timeout value, however this sometimes causes the application to get into a non-responsive mode which cannot be interrupted (other than by killing the application).

Although the idea of guiding the user by showing the enabled operations is sensible, this actually takes the freedom of choosing the parameters of the function from the user. It also makes it impossible to start from an arbitrary, valid state other than the *Init* state. For instance, in order to test the behaviour of *Subscribe* function when there are n Students, m Courses in the system, we need to call the *AddStudent* operation n times and *AddCourses* operation m times. In other words, it is not possible to create a valid, initial snapshot with n Students and m Courses with one command. This means that the user would not know whether it is possible to have a valid instance of the system with that many objects without actually going through the process of creating these objects. This is an obvious restriction especially if the tool is to be used in test-case generation.

5   Conclusion

In this paper, we focused on the modelling and validation steps of MBT. The tasks included in these steps are analysed in the scope of different model analysis tools. We modeled a Course Assignment system by using three state-based modelling languages, namely Z, Alloy and UML, and analysed the models by using four different tools: USE, Alloy Analyzer, ProZ and ZLive.

Table 7 provides a quick summary of our observations. Further explanations about our observations are given under the following titles.

Table 7. Observations about the tool usage

Criteria	USE	Alloy An.	ZLive	ProZ
Animation with less user interaction	Partial	Yes	Yes	Yes
Generation of pre- and post-states	No	Yes	Yes	No
Information about the execution	Yes	Yes	No	Partial
Requires expertise in one modelling language only	No	Yes	Yes	Yes

Animation in both directions: Alloy and ZLive recognise the pre- and post-states of the system and they are both capable of performing a non-directed, forward and backward animation of an operation. ProZ is able to simulate a forward animation and undo it, but it cannot discover a pre-state from a post-state. USE is able to carry out forward animation only.

Reduction in the search space (Introducing further constraints): ZLive, USE and Alloy have different ways of reducing the search space in generating snapshots. USE takes advantage of .ins files by introducing extra invariants to the system, Alloy allows the user to write such invariants within *assert* statements and ZLive uses the schema form as explained in Section 4.3. As far as we know, ProZ does not provide such flexibility to the user.

Search mechanisms: Due to the SAT Solvers embedded in ProZ and Alloy Analyzer, these tools treat the model as a set of constraints and thus they perform the search requests faster compared to ZLive and USE. The Alloy Analyzer is essentially a compiler that translates the problem to be analyzed into a huge boolean formula. After the formula is handed to a SAT solver, the solution is translated back by the Alloy Analyzer into the language of the model. All problems are solved within a user-specified scope that bounds the size of the domains, and thus makes the problem finite and reducable to a boolean formula [15]. Technically, the Alloy Analyzer is a model finder, not a model checker since given a logical formula, it finds a model of the formula. ZLive and USE, on the other hand, make use of depth-first search algorithms to find the requested snapshot, i.e., some valid state(s) of the system. In USE, as briefly described in Section 3.2, the order of objects to be generated is explicitly written in .assl file and this order certainly affects the search time. ZLive determines the order of object creation on the fly based on an optimisation algorithm.

Speaking the language of the tool: In USE, the user has to learn how to write .cmd, .assl and .use files in addition to OCL in which the assertions of the operations and invariants are specified. Alloy Analyzer requires the user to learn Alloy and to know the subtle differences between its constructs such as fact, predicate, assert, etc. ProZ and ZLive both require the user to be able to write the model in Z. With the command prompt ZLive provides, the user can also interact with the tool by using several other keywords and Z schemas. In ProZ, the user can only use the features provided in Graphical User Interface. This may be an advantage in that the user does not have to learn extra keywords/syntax, however, this also restricts the advanced user from being able to carry out complicated yet insightful queries about the model.

In addition to above observations, we also examined the validation techniques in close detail. Each tool has a different way of handling the tasks required to accomplish a certain type of validation and in some cases, tools were not able to realise certain tasks due to their inherent limitations. Table 8 provides a detailed overview of the tasks performed during validation and the tool's capabilities.

The tasks in Table 8 are divided into three categories: Valid State Generation, Operation Animation and Sequencing. Valid State Generation includes the tasks that involve in generating one state only. The first task in this group can be done by all the tools, whereas the the task 1.2 can be achieved only by USE and Alloy Analyzer. USE, however, needs intellectual input from the user in order to accomplish this task. The definition of *intellectual input* and further details about the task are given in Section 4.1. In ZLive and ProZ, the user has to start the validation process with the *init* schema and it is mostly the case that this schema initialises the system with no objects and therefore it would be fair to put a *No* to these fields in the table. However, it is technically possible, though

Table 8. Validation techniques and the state-based modelling tools

Task No.	Task	USE	Alloy An.	ZLive	ProZ
1	**Valid State Generation**				
1.1	Initialise the system with no objects	Yes	Yes	Yes	Yes
1.2	Automatically generate a valid non-empty state	Yes (intellect.)	Yes	Yes (intellect.)	Yes (intellect.)
1.3	Generate a valid non-empty state by using system operations	Yes (intellect.)	No	Yes	Yes
1.4	Generate a valid state with constraints	Yes (intellect.)	Yes	Yes	No
2	**Operation Animation**				
2.1	Forward Animation with input values supplied by the user	Yes	Yes	Yes	No
2.2	Forward Animation with no input values given	Yes (lim.)	Yes	Yes (lim.)	Yes (lim.)
2.3	Backward Animation with output values supplied by the user	No	Yes	Yes	No
2.4	Backward Animation with no output values given	No	Yes	Yes (lim.)	No
2.5	Non-directed animation	No	Yes	Yes (lim.)	No
2.6	Non-directed animation with constraints	No	Yes	Yes (lim.)	No
3	**Sequencing**				
3.1	Update the current state after the animation of an operation	Yes	No	Yes	Yes
3.2	Animate a user supplied sequence of operations	Yes (lim.)	No	Yes	Yes
3.3	Automatically explore all sequences of operations*	No	No	No	Yes

not practical, to write an *init* schema that creates objects. Having said that, this would require the user to put intellectual work in writing the schema in order to make sure that what is created in *init* schema does not conflict with system invariants. In addition, it is not possible to represent the creation of m number of objects in the *init* schema without explicitly defining each of them.

The difference between the tasks 1.2 and 1.3 is that 1.2 outputs a non-empty state, e.g. m number of objects of type x and n number of objects of type y, in one step with no user interaction. The task 1.3, on the other hand, may need $m + n$ steps in order to reach the same state.

The task 1.4 is useful especially when the user would like to start from a state that has certain characteristics, e.g., a field is assigned to a particular value, the range of some input is limited, etc. The only tool that is unable to perform this task is ProZ since the GUI of the tool does not allow the user to enter such inputs.

In terms of valid state generation, Alloy Analyzer is found to be the most powerful tool except when a valid non-empty state is to be generated by using system operations. The reason for this exception is related to the tasks in the third category explained later in this section.

The second category in Table 8 is concerned with Operation Animation, i.e., finding the pre- and/or post-states of a given operation. The reason for marking USE as *limited* in Task 2.2 is that without the limitations in the range of variables and maximum number of objects to be created, USE is not always capable of finding an input state. The limitation of ProZ in performing the same task (forward animation with no input values given) -strangely- comes from one of its strengths. The tool is able to list the enabled operations with possible parameter values. However, the list contains only a certain number of operations, thus a user cannot execute the operation with certain parameter values unless it is listed in the list. The section 4.4 gives further details about this issue.

In performing the tasks included in the second category, both Alloy and ZLive are proved to be competent. In terms of efficiency, ALLOY performs better since ZLive struggles to find a solution when the search space is too big.

In the final category -Sequencing-, the tasks focus mainly on animating a sequence of operations. The only tool that is not capable of realising the tasks 3.1 and 3.2 is Alloy Analyzer. The reason for this is that Alloy Analyzer does not keep track of state changes after an animation, i.e., it does not change the current state to the post-state. Thus, according to our observations, it is superb in performing one request at a time, but does not have the concept of carrying out a sequence of related actions one after the other.

The task 3.3 (essentially model checking) is not directly related to the main targets of this study, yet the tools' capabilities in performing the task could be observed. Other tasks that have not been explored in this study, but can be classified under this category include, but are not limited to, deadlock detection, feasibility check, etc.

It is our belief that the experiences reported in this paper shed light for potential users as well as for the developers of such tools in understanding the modelling and validation steps of MBT and the expectations in using model analysis tools.

References

1. Van Lamsweerde, A.: Formal Specification; a Roadmap: The Future of Software Engineering. In: Finkelstein, A. (ed.), ACM Press (2000) ISBN 1-58113-253-0
2. UML Resource Page (2007), http://www.uml.org/
3. Bertolino, A., Marchetti, E., Muccini, H.: Introducing a reasonably complete and coherent approach for MBT. Electr. Notes Theor. Comput. Sci. 116, 85–97 (2005)
4. Cavarra, A., Crichton, C., Davies, J., Hartman, A., Jeron, T., Maunier, L.: Using UML for automatic test case generation. In: Katoen, J.-P., Stevens, P. (eds.) TACAS 2002. LNCS, vol. 2280. Springer, Heidelberg (2002)
5. Jackson, D.: A Comparison of Object Modelling Notations: Alloy, UML and Z, MIT Lab for Computer Science (1999)
6. He, Y.: Comparison of the Modelling Languages Alloy and UML (2006), http://ww1.ucmss.com/books/LFS/CSREA2006/SER4949.pdf

7. Georg, G., Bieman, J., France, R.: Using Alloy and UML/OCL to Specify Run-Time Configuration Management: A Case Study. In: Workshop of the pUML-Group held together with the UML. LNI, vol. 17 (2001)

8. Utting, M., Pretschner, A., Legeard, B.: A taxonomy of model-based testing, Working paper series, University of Waikato, Department of Computer Science, 04/2006

9. Using ProZ for Animation and Model Checking of Z Specifications, http://asap0.cs.uni-duesseldorf.de/trac/prob/wiki/Using%20Z%20with%20ProB

10. Dalal, S.R., Jain, A., Karunanithi, N., Leaton, J.M., Lott, C.M., Patton, G.C., Horowitz, B.M.: Model-based testing in practice. In: Proceedings of International Conference of Software Engineering ICSE (1999)

11. Utting, M.: Position paper: Model-based testing, Verified Software: Theories, Tools, Experiments(VSTTE) (2006)

12. Utting, M., Legeard, B.: Practical Model-Based Testing. Morgan Kauffman (2007)

13. Bernard, E., Bouquet, F., Charbonnier, A., Legeard, B., Peureux, F., Utting, M., Torreborre, E.: Model-based Testing from UML Models. Lecture Notes in Informatics, pp. 223–230 (2006)

14. Z Notation, http://en.wikipedia.org/wiki/Z_notation

15. The Alloy Analyzer, http://alloy.mit.edu/

16. Jackson, D.: Software Abstractions: Logic, Language, and Analysis. MIT Press (2006)

17. UML Specifications Environment,
http://www.db.informatik.uni-bremen.de/projects/USE/

18. Gogolla, M., Buettner, F., Richters, M.: USE: A UML-based specification environment for validating UML and OCL. Sci. Comput. Program 69(1-3), 27–34 (2007)

19. CZT ZLive, http://czt.sourceforge.net/zlive/index.html

MontiCore: Modular Development of Textual Domain Specific Languages

Holger Krahn, Bernhard Rumpe, and Steven Völkel

Institute for Software Systems Engineering
Technische Universität Braunschweig, Braunschweig, Germany
http://www.sse-tubs.de

Abstract. Reuse is a key technique for a more efficient development and ensures the quality of the results. In object technology explicit encapsulation, interfaces, and inheritance are well-known principles for independent development that enable combination and reuse of developed artifacts. In this paper we apply modularity concepts for domain specific languages (DSLs) and discuss how they help to design new languages by extending existing ones and composing fragments to new DSLs. We use an extended grammar format with appropriate tool support that avoids redefinition of existing functionalities by introducing language inheritance and embedding as first class artifacts in a DSL definition. Language embedding and inheritance is not only assisted by the parser, but also by the editor, and algorithms based on tree traversal like context checkers, pretty printers, and code generators. We demonstrate that compositional engineering of new languages becomes a useful concept when starting to define project-individual DSLs using appropriate tool support.

1 Introduction

Reuse of developed artifacts is a key technique for more efficient development and high quality of the results. This is especially the case for object oriented programming: existing well-tested code is packed into libraries in order to reuse the developed components in new projects. However, these principles are not consequently applied when designing languages in general and domain specific languages (DSLs) in particular. Those languages are often built from scratch without explicit and systematic reuse of existing languages or fragments beyond some knowledge on language design in the heads of designers.

The idea of a DSLs is to assist the tasks of developing software through efficient development of models. Based on DSL models, property analysis, metrics, and smells as well as code generation help the developers to become more efficient and to deliver higher quality systems. Today, when applying DSL-based software development it takes too long to create all these tools, because they are implemented from scratch too often. Thus, we explain an infrastructure that allows reuse, extension, and composition of existing languages and their tools.

R.F. Paige and B. Meyer (Eds.): TOOLS EUROPE 2008, LNBIP 11, pp. 297–315, 2008.
© Springer-Verlag Berlin Heidelberg 2008

Our experience in some projects where we helped developers designing a language specific for their domain shows that the creation of high-quality languages is a labor intensive task. Hence, once a language is developed, the reuse in other contexts is highly desirable. This idea was discussed in [1] in form of design patterns for the development of DSLs. Different strategies such as language extension, language specialization, or piggypack (language combination) are introduced and preferred to a standalone realization. However, most of today's DSL frameworks do not support these patterns and so methodological assistance in this respect is poor.

In this paper we present work on appropriate tooling based on the MontiCore framework [2,3,4], which allows defining a DSL by an integrated specification of abstract and concrete syntax in a concise grammar-based format. It supports rule inheritance, introduction of interfaces, and associations directly in the grammar which results in an abstract syntax that outbalances the common tree structure and is comparable to current metamodeling standards. Because modularity and existing composition techniques are core requirements for reuse, we explore two mechanisms for modularizing grammars. We apply *language inheritance* that can be used in order to extend existing languages by redefining productions or adding alternatives in conjunction with the introduction of interfaces in a language definition. In addition, *language embedding* can be used to define explicit nonterminals in a grammar which can be filled by a fragment of another language (e.g., expressions or statements). Most importantly, this can be done at configuration time, and thus allows a modular independent development and compilation of tools that deal with language fragments. Because both, guest and host languages have separate lexers and parsers, they can be developed independently and do not interfere with each other. This technical separation allows a component based composition of grammars and their tools. Thus we are able to set up libraries of quality assured languages which can be reused in other contexts.

Both modularity mechanisms are implemented in MontiCore. In this paper we explain how these mechanisms are integrated in generation of language recognition artifacts such as parsers and lexers as well as the abstract syntax in the form of a strongly typed abstract syntax tree (AST). Furthermore, language specific editors with several comfort functionalities such as syntax highlighting or outlines can be generated as Eclipse plugins in a modular fashion to support an efficient use of the language under design [5].

The rest of this paper is structured as follows: Section 2 explains existing approaches from compiler design and metamodeling to design language based tools in a modular fashion. Section 3 describes the basic syntax of the MontiCore grammar format. In Section 4 two different concepts for defining abstract and concrete syntax in a modular way are explained. Section 5 describes how this modular language definition permits other functionalities like tree traversal and editor generation to be specified in a modular fashion. Section 6 concludes the paper.

2   Related Work

Modularity and composing complex systems from modules [6] is an important concept in computer science because it enables multiple developers to work concurrently on the same project. It allows them to understand the system part under design without requiring them to understand the whole system.

In [1] different design patterns are introduced. Especially *language extension* and *piggyback* describe two modularization mechanisms. *Language extension* describes the extensions of a host language (often an existing GPL) by elements that are domain specific. This approach for specifying domain specific languages (DSL) is often named *embedded* DSLs. *Piggyback* describes the extension of a DSL by extracts of other languages, for example, GPL statements in a DSL for describing context free grammars. This combination is often used as an input language for parser generators.

In the context of grammar based software (for short: grammarware [7]) the modular development of parsers is an important goal. The class of context free grammars is closed under composition in the sense that the composition of two context free languages is again a context free language. The main problem is that this property does not hold true for the subsets that are usually used for parsing like LL(k) or LR(k). To solve this problem, more sophisticated parsing algorithms like Generalized-LR [8] and Early parsers [9] have been created. Packrat parsing [10,11] uses parsing expression grammars which are closed under composition, intersection, and complement.

A particularly difficult problem is the composition on the lexical level. In [12] possible solutions are discussed. The concrete solution proposed for this problem is scannerless parsing where no separate lexer exists, which might in turn impose runtime difficulties depending on the composed languages. In the following we show that the control of the lexer state from the parser, that was not favored by the authors of [12] for technical reasons, can be seamlessly integrated in a DSL framework.

The focus of language libraries discussed in [12] is to realize embedded DSLs where the guest language is assimilated to the host language in order to design the extension in a modular way. MetaBorg [13,14] uses a GPL as a host language. The DSL is assimilated to the GPL functionality by mapping the DSL code to library code that provides the desired functionality. In contrast, our approach does not specifically aim at embedded DSLs but at the combination of separately developed DSLs that are all mapped to a GPL by separate but cooperating code generations. For this kind of problem the assimilation phase does not apply because due to their restrictive expressiveness usually different DSLs cannot be assimilated to each other. Embedded DSLs can also be realized with Attribute Grammars that focus on how distinct attributes can be realized in a modular way (e.g., using Forwarding [15]).

Even though the above mentioned parsing algorithms can achieve compositionality, an intrinsic problem of language composition is to avoid ambiguities in the composed language. Although GLR and Early can, depending on the implementation, return a set of all ASTs instead of a single one, further development steps like semantic analysis and code generation usually require the choice of exactly one tree. Packrat parsing does return at most one tree, as ambiguities are avoided by design. The alternatives are prioritized and limited backtracking functionality is possible by using predicates. Therefore, the developer has to pay close attention to the order of alternatives when designing a language. In general for any given parsing algorithm, ambiguities must be avoided and therefore, good language composition shall help the user to detect ambiguities and help him to circumvent them.

In the field of attribute grammars, modularity is a highly researched topic. Multiple language inheritance [16,17] helps to extend existing language and attribute definitions. Some approaches use generic patterns to create reusable grammar chucks (e.g., [18]). A few compiler frameworks, e.g., JastAdd [19], focus on modular extensible language definitions and compiler construction.

The focus of compiler design and DSL frameworks is a bit different. Compiler frameworks and related tools usually aim at programming languages and their modular extensions. An important property is that two extensions of a base language can be developed independently of each other and be integrated seamlessly. In this way, embedded DSLs are realized. The frameworks target at a single form of code generation usually towards the host language or bytecode. On the contrary, DSL frameworks focus on the creation of modeling languages that are not necessary executable. The DSLs are used for a variety of purposes like product and test code generation, documentation, and model-to-model transformations.

DSL frameworks (e.g., [20,21]) often rely on a graphical concrete syntax and do not support the user with a modular language definition. Other tools like [22] allow defining textual DSLs but do not provide modularity concepts either. DSL frameworks like OpenArchitectureWare [23] based on EMOF or Ecore and Moflon [24] based on CMOF use package imports and merges to allow a compositional definition of the abstract syntax of a language. The definition of the concrete syntax using tools like TCS [25] or xText [23] are usually not compositional.

3   Language Definition Using MontiCore

MontiCore uses an enriched context-free grammar as input format which is similar to the input format of Antlr [26] that is also used for parser generation. Figure 1 contains an illustrative example of a DSL describing a bookstore.

The grammar body consists of regular lexer and context-free parser rules. Lexer rules are marked by the keyword ident and defined by regular expressions. To simplify the development of new languages, we use predefined rules for IDENT and STRING to recognize names and strings. A language may declare its own lexer rules as shown in line 7. In addition, a mapping to a Java type can be defined. In our case, ID is mapped to the built-in type int. More complex mappings can be specified using Java directly [3].

Parser rules have a name and a right-hand-side (RHS) which describes the syntactical structure recognized by the generated parser as well as the structure of the abstract syntax. A RHS consists of references to other lexer or parser

─────────────────────── MontiCore-Grammar ───────────────────────

```
1  package mc.examples.bookstore;
2
3  grammar Bookstore {
4
5    // Create a token "ID" which is reflected
6    // as int in the abstract syntax
7    ident ID ('0'..'9')+ : int;
8
9    Bookstore = "bookstore" name:IDENT "{" ( Book | Journal )* "}" ;
10
11   Book = "book" id:ID title:STRING "by"
12           authors:Person ("," authors:Person)* ";" ;
13
14   Journal = "journal" id:ID title:STRING ";" ;
15
16   Person = forename:IDENT lastname:IDENT ;
17
18 }
```

Fig. 1. Bookstore example

rules, alternatives that are separated by "|", and blocks which are surrounded by brackets (e.g., line 9). Furthermore, optional elements can be expressed by a question mark, a Kleene star denotes unbounded repetitions, and a plus denotes a cardinality of at least one. In addition, we use a package mechanism similar to Java: grammars have a name (Bookstore in line 3) and an optional package (line 1) which determines the fully qualified name and the desired location in the file system.

MontiCore automatically derives an abstract syntax from this grammar format as follows. Each production forms a class having the same name as the production. Each reference to a lexer rule on the RHS forms an attribute of this class. References to parser rules are reflected as composition relationships with automatically determined cardinalities. In addition, the references can explicitly be named (e.g., line 12: authors:Person) in order to define the name of the attributes and compositions. Figure 2 shows the abstract syntax derived for our bookstore-example. Note that the abstract syntax is automatically mapped to Java classes in the same package as the grammar. Get- and set-methods for attributes as well as for compositions, tree traversal support, clone-methods, and equal-methods are automatically generated to simplify the use of the abstract syntax.

The abstract syntax is not limited to trees but additional associations between classes of the abstract syntax can be specified in the language definition. The linking of the objects is established after parsing the tree structure. The algorithms responsible for linking can either be specified in a declarative manner or can be hand-programmed depending on the suitability of standard mechanisms

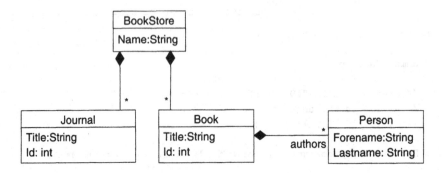

Fig. 2. Abstract syntax for the bookstore example defined in Figure 1

for references within a DSL. For deeper discussions on the grammar format as well as on the derivation of the abstract syntax and especially on the associations we refer to [3].

Typically counter-arguments exist against the decision of specifying abstract and concrete syntax in one format. We think that the most important pro argument is that no inconsistencies can occur between both artifacts which simplifies the development of a DSL. This cost reduction is of high importance as the initial investment for defining a DSLs has often to be proven worth by overall reduced project costs and quality improvements.

We are aware of tool infrastructure that can keep both artifacts consistent (like [27]) but think that the unified format also helps the user to keep both artifacts aligned with each other quite closely. The advantage is that the structure of the language (and based on that, its semantics) is aligned with the user perception of it (= the concrete syntax).

More technically, the most common counter-arguments are: First, there is a demand for multiple concrete syntaxes for a single abstract syntax. We doubt that this is the case for DSLs where the concrete syntax usually emerges from the domain. Often this argument targets at the reuse of development artifacts like code generation, but as model-to-model transformation facilities have emerged in the last years to a mature state, more explicit and flexible ways to reuse code generations for multiple languages than using a common concrete to abstract syntax mapper exist. Second, the abstract syntax is then not abstract enough, as syntactic sugar, associativity, and priorities of operators are still presented in the abstract syntax. This is not the case in MontiCore, as we extended the grammar format in such a way that multiple rules can refer to the same class in the abstract syntax. However, we will not discuss this feature in detail here.

MontiCore generates parsers that are based on Antlr 2.74. Therefore, the used parsing algorithm is LL(k) with semantic and syntactic predicates which is sufficient to parse a large variety of languages. We extended the parser genera-tor by adding the generation of heterogeneously and strongly typed AST-classes including inheritance and associations. The main criteria for choosing Antlr in re-spect to other parser generators mentioned in Section 2 was the relatively concise EBNF based syntax that makes it attractive to inexperienced language engineers.

The resulting parsers perform well and also due to the classical lexer/parser distinction standard algorithms for error messages and recovery strategies are well understood. The recursive descent structure of generated parsers makes it easy to debug the parsers and feasible for us to integrate the modularity concepts and the building of our abstract syntax as explained in this paper. In addition, every production can be used as a starting production which helps to reuse fragments in other composed languages.

4   Concepts of Modularity

In software engineering, the most commonly used modeling language is UML which is often combined with OCL for expressing constraints or actions. Taking this combination as an example for our language modularization mechanisms, we can make three main observations. First, a core which contains elements that are used in most of the UML sublanguages (e.g., classes or stereotypes) can be identified. It would be reasonable to extract these elements into a core language and to reuse it in other sublanguages like the UML suggests with its modular definition in different packages. Second, one could imagine using another constraint or action language than OCL for UML. Third, OCL could be combined with other languages when there is a demand for a constraint sublanguage. To summarize, a tight coupling between UML and OCL is not desirable when designing such a modeling language.

The reuse of parts of a language in a different context and a loosely coupled combination of languages are supported by MontiCore by its modularity concepts: *language inheritance* and *language embedding*. The former can be used to define a grammar by extending one or more supergrammars whereas *language embedding* permits to define explicit nonterminals in grammars which can be filled at configuration time by an appropriate embedded language. Both mechanisms are introduced in the following; we will discuss their effects especially on the abstract syntax and the advantages for defining new languages.

4.1   Language Inheritance

Language inheritance can be used when an existing DSL shall be extended by defining new productions or existing nonterminals shall be overridden without modification of the supergrammar. Therefore, the extending grammar defines only the differences between the existing language and the new one. We use the concept of multiple language inheritance as introduced in [16] for attribute grammars. It can be seen as a method to achieve *Language extension* or *Language specialization* as discussed in [1]. *Language extension* is typically the case when the subgrammar adds new alternatives to an existing rule by overriding it. A well-known example for language extension is LINQ [28] where SQL-statements can be used as an expression inside an existing general purpose language. *Language specialization* occurs, e.g., by adding additional context constraints. It is often used to remove "unsafe" features of a language to gain safe sublanguages. In both cases, the definition of new languages is not desirable. Instead, a reuse should be preferred.

The MontiCore grammar format allows developers to define language inheritance by using the keyword **extends** followed by a list of fully qualified grammar names in the header of a grammar. From the concrete syntax point of view, the nonterminals and terminals of all supergrammars are visible in the current grammar and can therefore be reused. Furthermore, MontiCore enables to override existing productions by specifying a production with the same name. In contrast to [16] we use an ordered inheritance approach where in the case of name collisions, i.e. two supergrammars use a common production name, the production from the first supergrammar is used. For example if both grammars A and B share a production name X and grammar C inherits from both A and B, the production from A is used. As an extension to the current implementation we plan to integrate a more sophisticated mechanism than the order of supergrammars to resolve conflicts. A simple example is shown in Figure 3 where the nonterminal Journal is redefined by adding editor information.

―――――――――――――――――――――― MontiCore-Grammar ――――――――――――――――

```
1 package mc.examples.bookstore2;
2
3 grammar ExtendedBookstore extends mc.examples.bookstore.Bookstore {
4
5    Journal = "journal" id:ID title:STRING "editors"
6             editors:Person ("," editors:Person)* ";" ;
7
8 }
```

Fig. 3. Definition of Language Inheritance in MontiCore

The inheritance on the grammar basis leads to a modification of the abstract syntax of the language that is comparable to a package merge [29]. For each overridden production a new class is created that inherits from all classes that are associated with the productions with the same name in the supergrammars. The key difference is that all unmerged classes remain unchanged and are not directly present in the merged package which is the package of the subgrammar. We found this approach appealing because algorithms such as transformations, code generators, or even symbol tables written for the original language still work for the extended languages (maybe with minor modifications for overridden productions).

The resulting abstract syntax for our running example is outlined in Figure 4. The new class Journal inherits from the version of its supergrammar. Please note that the new generated parser produces instances which conform to the new grammar, i.e., there will be only instances of mc.examples.bookstore.Book, mc.examples.bookstore2.Journal, mc.examples.bookstore.BookStore, and

`mc.examples.bookstore.Person`. Objects of `mc.examples.bookstore.Journal`
will be not be created.

Language inheritance can lead to multiple inheritance of classes in the abstract syntax which is a problem in the current MontiCore implementation. The upcoming generation of AST-classes will map the classes of the abstract syntax to Java interfaces and create implementations like other metamodeling tools [30,24] to avoid such problems.

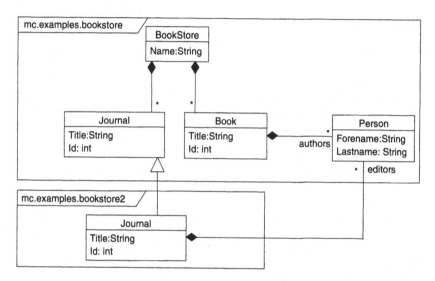

Fig. 4. Abstract syntax for the bookstore of Figure 3

This technique of overriding rules is typically used when the designer of the supergrammar does not foresee changes which are made in a subgrammar. However, there are scenarios where such modifications are predictable. In the case of our simple bookstore the developer may foresee that there will be subgrammars which introduce new items such as audio books. For these scenarios, MontiCore enables to define interfaces as possible extension point for subgrammars. Figure 5 shows a modified version of the basic grammar and the resulting abstract syntax.

Line 1 introduces a new interface `Item`, which is implemented by both `Book` and `Journal` (line 9 and 14 respectively). This definition leads to the generation of a Java-interface and the implements-relationship between the involved classes/interfaces. Note that we do not compute the attributes of interfaces automatically as the interfaces should serve as an extension point for new sublanguages which add new productions implementing this interface.

There are two main advantages of this version. First, a subgrammar can add new `Items` without changing or overriding the `Bookstore`. Therefore, a new production in the subgrammar simply implements the interface as described above. Second, the designer of the supergrammars can define attributes which have to be implemented by using the **ast** keyword that is used in order to modify

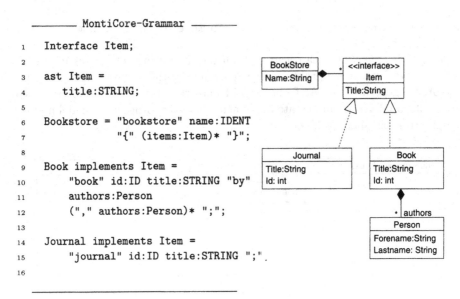

```
———————— MontiCore-Grammar ————————
1    Interface Item;
2
3    ast Item =
4       title:STRING;
5
6    Bookstore = "bookstore" name:IDENT
7                "{" (items:Item)* "}";
8
9    Book implements Item =
10      "book" id:ID title:STRING "by"
11      authors:Person
12      ("," authors:Person)* ";";
13
14   Journal implements Item =
15      "journal" id:ID title:STRING ";".
16
```

Fig. 5. Definition of bookstores using interfaces

the abstract syntax. Line 4 states that all implementing classes of the interface Item provide at least a title.

Using this approach the designer of a sublanguage is able to add new kinds of items by extending our basic grammar and defining these new items as subtypes of the item interface as shown in Figure 6.

```
————————————————— MontiCore-Grammar —————————————
1  package mc.examples.bookstore3;
2
3  grammar ExtendedBookstore extends mc.examples.bookstore.Bookstore {
4
5    AudioBook implements Item = "audiobook" id:ID title:STRING ";";
6
7  }
```

Fig. 6. Adding new items to the bookstore

In this simple example both grammars are not really decoupled from each other as the subgrammar directly inherits from the supergrammar. This might be a problem especially when only a few nonterminals of the subgrammar should be reused in other settings. In our example one can imagine that AudioBooks should be reused as items for a record shop. Using the former approach we had to change the subgrammar. Then, AudioBooks would implement another interface defined in the record shop grammar. However, this is often not desirable as the new grammar would be able to parse both book stores and record shops. In order to avoid this strong coupling MontiCore allows multiple grammar inheritance. This technique allows us to design both grammars separately by removing the inheritance between the grammars and the implements-relationship between `AudioBook` and `Item` and finally to define a third grammar which combines both supergrammars. Figure 7 shows an example. Please note that the grammar `mc.examples.audio.Audio` where the class `AudioBook` is defined is omitted here for space reasons because it is identical to the definition in Figure 6 except for the language and nonterminal inheritance.

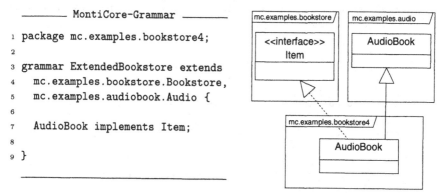

```
────────  MontiCore-Grammar  ────────

1  package mc.examples.bookstore4;

2

3  grammar ExtendedBookstore extends

4    mc.examples.bookstore.Bookstore,

5    mc.examples.audiobook.Audio {

6

7    AudioBook implements Item;

8

9  }
```

Fig. 7. Multiple grammar inheritance

Language inheritance is typically used when the sublanguage is very similar to the superlanguage because otherwise problems in the lexical analysis may occur. The lexer rules of the subgrammar are a combination of the lexer rules of all supergrammars. They can be overridden in the same way like parser rules. The keywords of the language are a union of all keywords of the supergrammar plus the newly defined keywords of the subgrammar. A prominent example for the consequences can be seen in the introduction of the `assert` keyword in Java - legacy code using `assert` as identifier had to be adapted in order to conform to the new language. However, this problem can be avoided using language embedding where the recognition of the involved languages is strictly decoupled from each other because separate parsers and lexers are used.

4.2   Language Embedding

Domain specific languages are usually designed for a specific task; therefore it is often necessary to combine several languages to be able to define all properties of the desired software system precisely. A typical example for this approach is OCL which is used to define additional constraints on a model that cannot be expressed in the host language (e.g., class diagrams).

For convenience and for the sake of clarity it is desirable to write an OCL statement nearby the artifact it is constraining in the same file. Using standard approaches and parsing technologies would result in a monolithic and huge grammar combining both host language and OCL. This is even more problematic when combinations of more than two languages are used. Therefore, an independent development of all involved languages and a flexible combination mechanism is highly desirable.

MontiCore provides external nonterminals in grammars which means that their derivation is determined at configuration time by another appropriate language. We modify the bookstore example to be combined with an appropriate bibliography format (e.g., bibtex) as shown in Figure 8. In this example, line 1 introduces the external nonterminal **Bookentry** which is used on the RHS of **Book** (line 8). Note that there is no further information about the language to be embedded; hence the combination with a language that provides an arbitrary definition for BookEntry is valid.

──────────────────── MontiCore-Grammar ────────────────────

```
1    external Bookentry;
2    external Journalentry / example.IJournalEntry;
3
4    Bookstore = "bookstore" name:IDENT "{" (Book | Journal)* "}" ;
5
6    Book = "book" id:ID title:STRING
7            "by" authors:Person ("," authors:Person)*
8            Bookentry ";" ;
9
10   Journal = "journal" id:ID title:STRING Journalentry ";" ;
11
12   Person = forename:IDENT lastname:IDENT ;
```

Fig. 8. Expressing constraints for the embedded language by interfaces

The usage of external nonterminals leads to a composition relationship to **ASTNode** which is the base interface of all AST classes in MontiCore. However, it is sometimes desirable to define constraints for an embedded language in form of interfaces which must be implemented by the top level node of the embedded grammar. Therefore, MontiCore allows declaring the name of the interface to be implemented next to the definition of the external nonterminal as shown in line 2 of Figure 8. This version introduces an external nonterminal **Journalentry** that restrict the top level node of the embedded grammar to classes that implement **example.IJournalEntry**. The slash marks these interfaces as handwritten, therefore it is possible to access properties of the embedded language in form of methods from the host language. Furthermore, in this version the composition relationship is more reasonable since it is typed with **examples.IJournalEntry** instead of **ASTNode**. In addition, this example shows that the combination of languages is not restricted to two grammars.

In order to enable an independent development MontiCore derives parsers and AST classes separately and combines these components at configuration time as shown in Figure 9. For each grammar we generate a lexer and for each production of that grammar an adapter to the parser generated by Antlr without considering a concrete language combination. Therefore, each production can be used as a start production which is an important property to combine language fragments. This method enables us to reuse these artifacts without recompilation. Then, we combine the parsers/lexers-combinations to a superordinated parser which is able to switch between the different grammars. Every time a concrete parser finds an external nonterminal the control is passed to the superordinated parser which invokes the parser/lexer-combination of the embedded language.

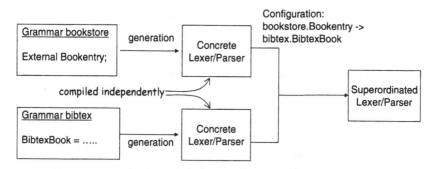

Fig. 9. Language embedding

Doing so, the bookstore parser ensures correct behavior by invoking the superordinated parser and thus, the bibtex parser (and lexer). Then, the rest of the text will be recognized according to that grammar. Thus, both languages are really independent from each other in their lexical and syntactic structure, and more important, the combination cannot be ambiguous as lexer and parsers are exchanged when switching the language. In order to allow compositional development beyond syntax, algorithms can be developed independently of each other as described in Section 5.

From a technical point of view a language combination consists of two pieces of information. The first one declares the grammar to be used when starting to recognize a text. The second piece of information in turn indicates which external nonterminal in a grammar should be replaced by which nonterminal of another grammar. Both can be expressed using a simple DSL as shown in Figure 10 or by combining the parsers/lexer by handwritten Java-code.

To realize the exchange of parsers and lexers in the desired fashion, we modified Antlr. First, all parsers/lexers use a shared queue which contains the input stream. Every time a parser consumes a token of length n, the first n characters are removed from the queue. It is important that this removal is not carried out when the lexer creates a token because it might be that the current lexer is not the right one for the currently considered part of the file. The main reason for this fact is that the position of the lexer is in front of the position of the parser in the file, especially when the parser uses its lookahead as this shifts the position

---
──────────────────────── MontiCore-Grammar ────────────────────────

```
1 // define rule Bookstore of the grammar mc.examples.bookstore.Bookstore
2 // to be used when starting to parse the text
3 mc.examples.bookstore.Bookstore.Bookstore bst <<start>>;
4
5 // embed bibtex rule for books as Bookentry
6 mc.examples.bibtex.Bibtex.BibtexBook bibBook in bst.Bookentry;
7
8 // embed bibtex rule for journals as Journalentry
9 mc.examples.bibtex.Bibtex.BibtexJournal bibJrn in bst.Journalentry;
```

Fig. 10. Combining languages using a special DSL

of the lexer forward without shifting the current position of the syntactical analysis forward in the same ratio. Whenever the parser invokes the superordinated parser in order to recognize an embedded language, the queue is reset to the end of the last token the host parser consumed. From this point onward, the embedded lexer starts to re-process the next characters. By this strategy we ensure the correct behavior of the embedded parser as no following token was typified by the host lexer. This strategy leads to repetitive lexing but does not impose great overhead as the maximal length of the re-typified character string is limited by the chosen lookhead or the considered length of syntactic or semantic predicates.

MontiCore grammars are a form of *grammar fragments* as defined in [31]. Grammar fragments do not have a defined start production and referred nonterminals may be undefined. In the MontiCore context every grammar could be understood as a grammar fragment, because every production can be used as start production. This behavior is especially useful if parts of a language shall be reused as it was the case when we embedded a rule for **Bookentry** and another rule of the same grammar for **Journalentry**.

The example shown so far enables a language developer to embed different languages to different external nonterminals. Different sublanguages can be used but the decision is bound at configuration time and only a single language can be used for one external nonterminal. In Figure 11 we developed our running example further such that the developer can embed multiple languages for a single external nonterminal.

The different languages are registered under a unique name. Then, we assign string values to variables like shown in line 5 where we parse **booktype** and assign this value to the global variable **bt** (**astscript {set(bt,booktype);}**). In line 10 we refer to this variable in order to decide which language is used for **Bookentry**. In line 13 a different approach is taken in the sense that we call an embedded language depending on the value of a variable of the current rule instead of a global variable. Using this way a bookstore grammar can be developed that allows multiple formats for defining journals and books and the user of the resulting language can choose the one to use.

```
                          ────── MontiCore-Grammar ──────
 1    external Bookentry;
 2    external Journalentry / example.IJournalEntry;
 3
 4    Bookstore = "bookstore" name:IDENT
 5                booktype:IDENT astscript { set(bt,booktype); }
 6                "{" (Book | Journal)* "}" ;
 7
 8    Book = "book" id:ID title:STRING
 9          "by" authors:Person ("," authors:Person)*
10          Bookentry<global bt> ";" ;
11
12    Journal = "journal" id:ID title:STRING
13               jt:IDENT Journalentry<jt> ";" ;
14
15    Person = forename:IDENT lastname:IDENT ;
```

Fig. 11. Using different parsers for a single nonterminal

5 Modular Development of Domain Specific Tools

The development of domain specific modeling languages consists not only of defining an abstract and a concrete syntax. Furthermore, there are several other steps necessary, e.g., code generation, syntactic checks, or the implementation of language specific tools. In the following we give two examples of how the further processing of modular languages is supported by MontiCore.

Modular visitors. Visitor-like algorithms simplify programming a code generator because each language construct can independently be translated as long as the tree structure of the AST is similar to the structure of the generated code. The main advantage of this design pattern is that the algorithm does not contain traversal code.

To increase the usability of the modular facilities within the MontiCore framework we complemented the modular language definition with a modular tree traversal. Without this facility a user would still program visitors for combinations of languages which are not reusable. Using our modular visitor concept, a user can program visitors independently for different fragments that handle the classes defined within a grammar. These classes can then be combined to a visitor without recompilation which invokes the different methods automatically. Thus, we use the same approach for combining visitors as for combining lexers and parsers in the case of language embedding.

For language inheritance the different visitors can be subtyped to change the behavior for the newly added or overwritten productions. Where subtyping is not feasible due to the single-supertype restriction Java imposes, delegation can be used.

Modular tool generation. Comfortable and usable tool support is an important success criterion for new domain specific modeling languages. However, the development of language specific tools such as editors is a time-consuming task, which gets even more complicated when we take the modularity concepts into account. Language embedding for example, requires not only an independent generation of parsers and lexers and a possibility to combine them at configuration time. The same approach should be reflected in tooling: independent development/generation of editors and afterwards, combination at configuration time. Doing so, it is possible to develop one editor for OCL separately and to combine it with other editors (e.g., for class diagrams, statecharts, or sequence diagrams) instead of implementing an editor for class diagrams with OCL, statecharts with OCL, and so on.

MontiCore grammars can be complemented by additional information which is used in order to generate language specific editors as Eclipse plugins. Generated editors offer different comfort functionalities such as syntax highlighting, an outline, foldable code regions, or error messages. We will only briefly introduce editor generation in this paper. For deeper discussion on editor generation we refer to [5].

The editor generation of MontiCore is fully integrated with the modularity concepts we discussed in this paper. For each grammar (which possibly has external nonterminals) we generate visitors as described in the beginning of this section. These visitors evaluate those parts of the abstract syntax which are defined in the current grammar. Among other things, they are able to provide an outline page with items, or to advise the document which code regions can be folded. Then, we are able to combine the visitors without recompilation in order to gain an editor which supports the current language combination (e.g., class diagrams and OCL). Furthermore, when handling grammar inheritance, we simply use object oriented inheritance between the generated editors. This allows us to override (or to complement) the behavior of the supereditor, and even more important, to further develop the supereditor without a need to recompile every subeditor, and thus, every sublanguage.

6   Conclusion and Outlook

In this paper we explained how the DSL framework MontiCore and especially how the defining grammar format has been extended to support two different kinds of modularity mechanisms. The modular development as well as the combination and extension techniques simplify the integration of DSLs and their according tools in software development projects.

Language inheritance can be used to extend existing languages by new nonterminals or to override existing nonterminals of the supergrammar. The effects on the abstract syntax are similar to those of UML package merge as only the delta is used to generate new abstract syntax classes. In the case of overriding, these new classes directly inherit from the old ones. Therefore, existing artifacts such as symbol tables, context constraint checkers, or code generation can be reused with minor modifications. *Language embedding* on the other hand is useful to explicitly add points of variation in modeling languages to include fragments of other languages. The strong decoupling of the languages by separate lexers/parsers minimizes interferences and permits a component based composition of grammars.

In addition, MontiCore supports the development of modular domain specific modeling languages beyond syntax. For this purpose, we explained how a language definition is complemented with further concepts like editor generation and tree traversal. Both concepts reflect the modular approaches for defining the abstract and the concrete syntax of a language.

MontiCore has been used to define several small DSLs as well as some complex languages. We realized a subset of UML [32,33] including statecharts, class, sequence, and object diagrams. Furthermore, we developed a grammar for OCL and Java 5 and helped industrial partners to implement a DSL for a part of an AUTOSAR specification [34]. In addition, we evaluated view based modeling of logical automotive architectures [35] with MontiCore. In addition, MontiCore itself is realized using a bootstrapping approach. Currently about 75% of the code is generated from several DSLs.

We currently elaborate on a possible connection of the MontiCore framework with EMF [30] as well as MOFLON [24] to simplify the interoperability of DSLs defined with MontiCore and metamodeling techniques. This will allow us to gain further support for model transformations and code generation from a variety of tools. Furthermore, we will explore composition of languages beyond syntax. This includes compositional context constraints and symbol tables as this plays an important role especially in the case of language embedding.

Acknowledgment. The work presented in this paper is undertaken as a part of the MODELPLEX project. MODELPLEX is a project co-funded by the European Commission under the "Information Society Technologies" Sixth Framework Programme (2002-2006). Information included in this document reflects only the authors' views. The European Community is not liable for any use that may be made of the information contained herein.

References

1. Spinellis, D.: Notable Design Patterns for Domain Specific Languages. Journal of Systems and Software 56(1), 91–99 (2001)
2. Grönniger, H., Krahn, H., Rumpe, B., Schindler, M., Völkel, S.: MontiCore 1.0 - Ein Framework zur Erstellung und Verarbeitung domänenspezifischer Sprachen. Technical Report Informatik-Bericht 2006-04, Software Systems Engineering Institute, Braunschweig University of Technology (2006)
3. Krahn, H., Rumpe, B., Völkel, S.: Integrated Definition of Abstract and Concrete Syntax for Textual Languages. In: Proceedings of Models 2007 (2007)
4. MontiCore Website, http://www.monticore.de
5. Krahn, H., Rumpe, B., Völkel, S.: Efficient Editor Generation for Compositional DSLs in Eclipse. In: Proceedings of the 7th OOPSLA Workshop on Domain-Specific Modeling 2007 (2007)

6. Parnas, D.L.: On the criteria to be used in decomposing systems into modules. Commun. ACM 15(12), 1053–1058 (1972)
7. Klint, P., Lämmel, R., Verhoef, C.: Toward an engineering discipline for grammarware. ACM Transactions on Software Engineering Methodology 14(3), 331–380 (2005)
8. Tomita, M.: Efficient Parsing for Natural Languages. A Fast Algorithm for Practical Systems. Kluwer Academic Publishers (1985)
9. Earley, J.: An efficient context-free parsing algorithm. Communications of the Association for Computing Machinery 13(2), 94–102 (1970)
10. Ford, B.: Packrat parsing: Simple, powerful, lazy, linear time. In: Proceedings of the 2002 International Conference on Functional Programming (2002)
11. Grimm, R.: Better extensibility through modular syntax. In: PLDI 2006: Proceedings of the 2006 ACM SIGPLAN conference on Programming language design and implementation, pp. 38–51. ACM, New York (2006)
12. Bravenboer, M., Visser, E.: Designing Syntax Embeddings and Assimilations for Language Libraries. In: 4th International Workshop on Software Language Engineering (2007)
13. Bravenboer, M., Visser, E.: Concrete syntax for objects: domain-specific language embedding and assimilation without restrictions. In: Proceedings of the 19th Annual ACM SIGPLAN Conference on Object-Oriented Programming, Systems, Languages, and Applications, OOPSLA 2004, Vancouver, BC, Canada, October 24-28, 2004, pp. 365–383 (2004)
14. Bravenboer, M., de Groot, R., Visser, E.: Metaborg in action: Examples of domain-specific language embedding and assimilation using stratego/xt. In: Lämmel, R., Saraiva, J., Visser, J. (eds.) GTTSE 2005. LNCS, vol. 4143. Springer, Heidelberg (2006)
15. Wyk, E., Moor, O., Backhouse, K., Kwiatkowski, P.: Forwarding in Attribute Grammars for Modular Language Design. In: Horspool, R.N. (ed.) CC 2002. LNCS, vol. 2304, pp. 128–142. Springer, Heidelberg (2002)
16. Mernik, M., Žumer, V., Lenič, M., Avdičaušević, E.: Implementation of multiple attribute grammar inheritance in the tool LISA. SIGPLAN Not. 34(6), 68–75 (1999)
17. Mernik, M., Lenič, M., Avdičaušević, E., Žumer, V.: Multiple Attribute Grammar Inheritance. In: Parigot, D., Mernik, M. (eds.) Second Workshop on Attribute Grammars and their Applications, WAGA 1999, Amsterdam, The Netherlands, pp. 57–76. INRIA Rocquencourt (1999)
18. Adams, S.R.: Modular Grammars for Programming Language Prototyping. PhD thesis, University of Southampton (1991)
19. Ekman, T., Hedin, G.: The jastadd system - modular extensible compiler construction. Sci. Comput. Program. 69(1-3), 14–26 (2007)
20. Ledeczi, A., Maroti, M., Bakay, A., Karsai, G., Garrett, J., Thomason, C.: The Generic Modeling Environment. In: International Workshop on Intelligent Signal Processing (WISP), IEEE (2001)
21. MetaCase Website, http://www.metacase.com
22. Meta Programming System Website, http://www.jetbrains.com/mps/
23. OpenArchitectureWare Website, http://www.openarchitectureware.com/
24. Amelunxen, C., Königs, A., Rötschke, T., Schürr, A.: MOFLON: A Standard-Compliant Metamodeling Framework with Graph Transformations. In: Rensink, A., Warmer, J. (eds.) ECMDA-FA 2006. LNCS, vol. 4066, pp. 361–375. Springer, Heidelberg (2006)

25. Jouault, F., Bezivin, J., Kurtev, I.: TCS: a DSL for the Specification of Textual Concrete Syntaxes in Model Engineering. In: Proceedings of the fifth international conference on Generative programming and Component Engineering (2006)
26. Parr, T., Quong, R.: ANTLR: A Predicated-LL(k) Parser Generator. Journal of Software Practice and Experience 25(7), 789–810 (1995)
27. Kadhim, B.M., Waite, W.M.: Maptool - Supporting Modular Syntax Development. In: Gyimóthy, T. (ed.) CC 1996. LNCS, vol. 1060, pp. 268–280. Springer, Heidelberg (1996)
28. Meijer, E., Beckman, B., Bierman, G.: Linq: reconciling object, relations and xml in the.net framework. In: SIGMOD 2006: Proceedings of the 2006 ACM SIGMOD international conference on Management of data, pp. 706–706. ACM, New York (2006)
29. Object Management Group: Unified Modeling Language: Superstructure Version 2.0 (05-07-04) (August (2005), http://www.omg.org/docs/formal/05-07-04.pdf
30. Budinsky, F., Steinberg, D., Merks, E., Ellersick, R., Grose, T.J.: Eclipse Modeling Framework. Addison-Wesley (2003)
31. Lämmel, R.: Grammar Adaptation. In: Oliveira, J.N., Zave, P. (eds.) FME 2001. LNCS, vol. 2021, pp. 550–570. Springer, Heidelberg (2001)
32. Rumpe, B.: Modellierung mit UML. Springer, Berlin (2004)
33. Rumpe, B.: Agile Modellierung mit UML: Codegenerierung, Testfälle, Refactoring. Springer, Berlin (2004)
34. Höwing, F.: Effiziente entwicklung von autosar-komponenten mit domänenspezifischen programmiersprachen. In: Proceedings of 5th Workshop Automotive Software Engineering, Bremen, Germany. LNI, p. 110 (2007)
35. Grönniger, H., Hartmann, J., Krahn, H., Kriebel, S., Rothhardt, L., Rumpe, B.: Modelling automotive function nets with views for features, variants, and modes. In: Proceedings of ERTS 2008 (2008)

Proof-Transforming Compilation of Eiffel Programs

Martin Nordio[1], Peter Müller[2], and Bertrand Meyer[1]

[1] ETH Zurich, Switzerland
{martin.nordio,bertrand.meyer}@inf.ethz.ch
[2] Microsoft Research, USA
mueller@microsoft.com

Abstract. In modern development schemes the processing of programs often involves an intermediate step of translation to some intermediate bytecode, complicating the verification task. Expanding on the ideas of Proof-Carrying Code (PCC), we have built a proof-transforming compiler which translates a contract-equipped program and its proof into bytecode representing both the program and the proof; before execution starts, the program will be run through a proof checker. The proofs address not only security properties, as in the original PCC work, but full functional correctness as expressed by the original contracts. The task of the proof-transforming compiler is made particularly challenging by the impedance mismatch between the source language, Eiffel, and the target code, .NET CIL, which does not directly support such important Eiffel mechanisms as multiple inheritance and contract-based exceptions. We present the overall proof-transforming compilation architecture, the issues encountered, and the solutions that have been devised to bridge the impedance mismatch.

Keywords: Software verification, program proofs, Proof-Carrying Code, proof-transforming compiler, Eiffel, CIL.

1 Introduction

The problem of software verification, hard enough in a traditional context, takes on new twists as advances in computing, designed to bring convenience and flexibility to users, also bring further headaches to verifiers. The work reported here addresses one such situation: verifying mobile code and other programs deployed through intermediate formats such as bytecode.

The problem arises because of the increased sophistication of our computing architectures. Along with new modes of computing arising from the role of the Internet, new modes of software deployment have emerged. Once we have written a program in a high-level language, instead of compiling it once and for all into machine code for execution on a given machine, we may generate intermediate code, often called "bytecode" (CIL on .NET, or JVM bytecode) and distribute it to numerous users who will execute it through either interpretation or a second phase of compilation known as "jitting". What then can and should we verify?

R.F. Paige and B. Meyer (Eds.): TOOLS EUROPE 2008, LNBIP 11, pp. 316–335, 2008.

If we trust the interpreter or the jitter, the verification effort could apply to the bytecode; but this is a difficult proposition because typical bytecodes (CIL, JVM) discard some of the high-level information, in particular about types and control flow, that was present in the original and can be essential for a proof. In addition, proofs in the current state of the art can seldom be discharged in an entirely automatic fashion (for example by compilers, as a byproduct of the compilation process): they require interactive help from programmers. But then the target of the proof should be the program as written, not generated code which means nothing to the programmer. This suggests sticking to the traditional goal of proving correctness at the source level.

The problem now becomes to derive from a proof of the source code a guarantee of correctness of the generated bytecode. Unlike the interpreter or jitter, the compiler is often outside of the operating system; even if it is trusted, there is no guarantee against a third party tampering with the intermediate code. The notion of Proof-Carrying Code (PCC) [8] was developed to address this issue, with an original focus on safety properties: with PCC, a program producer develops code together with a formal proof (a certificate) that it possesses certain desirable properties. The program consumer checks the proof before executing the code or, in the above scheme, before interpreting or jitting it.

The original PCC work uses a certifying compiler [12] to prove simple safety properties automatically during the compilation process. The present work addresses the entire issue of functional correctness by introducing a proof-transforming compiler (PTC). The development scheme with this approach involves the following steps:

- Verify the source program, taking advantage of proof technology at the programming language level. This step can involve interaction with the programmer or verification expert.
- Translate both the source program and the proof into intermediate code, using the PTC. This step is automatic.
- Before a user runs the code (through interpretation or jitting), check the proof. This checking is again an automatic task; it can be performed by a simple proof-checking tool.

Our proof-transforming compiler consists of two modules: (1) a *specification translator* that translates Eiffel contracts to CIL contracts; and (2) a *proof translator* that translates Eiffel proofs to CIL proofs. The specification translator takes an Eiffel contract (based on Eiffel expressions) and generates a CIL contract (based on first order logic). The proof translator takes a proof in a Hoare-style logic and generates a CIL bytecode proof.

Proof-transforming compilation can be fairly straightforward if the source and the target language are very similar. For example, PTCs have been developed from Java to bytecode [1,3,14]. The translation is more complex when the subset is extended with **finally** and **break** statements [11]. But the difficulty of the problem grows with the conceptual distance between the semantic models of the source and target languages. In the present work, the source language is

Eiffel, whose object model and type system differ significantly from the assumptions behind CIL, the target language. In particular, Eiffel supports multiple inheritance and a specific form of exception handling. This has required, in the implementation of Eiffel for .NET (which goes through CIL code), the design of original compilation techniques. In particular [5], the compilation of each Eiffel class produces two CIL types: an interface, and an implementation class which implements it. If either the source proof or the source specification expresses properties about the type structure of the Eiffel program, the same property has to be generated for the bytecode.

The translation of these properties raises challenges illustrated by the following example (interface only, implementation omitted) involving a reflective capability: the feature *type*, which gives the type of an object.

```
1 merge (other: LINKED_LIST [G]):LINKED_LIST [G]
          -- Merge other into current structure returning a new LINKED_LIST
3    require
             is_linked_list : other. type. conforms_to (LINKED_LIST [G].type)
5            same_type: Current.type.is_equal(other. type)
     ensure
7        result_type : Result.type. is_equal(LINKED_LIST [G].type)
```

The function *merge* is defined in the class *LINKED_LIST*. The precondition of *merge* expresses that the type of *other* is a subtype of *LINKED_LIST* and the types of *Current* and *other* are equal. The postcondition expresses that the type of *Result* is equal to *LINKED_LIST*.

The compilation of the class *LINKED_LIST* produces the CIL interface *LINKED_LIST_INTERF* and the implementation class *LINKED_LIST_IMP*. A correct PTC has to map the type *LINKED_LIST* in the clause *is_linked_list* (line 4) to the CIL interface *LINKED_LIST_INTERF* because in the target model decedents of the Eiffel class *LINKED_LIST* inherit from the interface *LINKED_LIST_INTERF* in CIL and not from *LINKED_LIST_IMP*. To translate the postcondition, we use the implementation class *LINKED_LIST_IMP* because this property expresses that the type of *Result* is equal to *LINKED_LIST*. Thus, the PTC has to map Eiffel classes to CIL interfaces or Eiffel classes to CIL classes depending of the function used to express the source property.

This example illustrates that the proof-transforming compiler cannot always treat Eiffel in the same way: while in most circumstances it will map them to CIL interfaces, in some cases (such as this one, involving reflection) it must use a CIL class.

The main problems addressed in this paper are the definition of contract translation functions and proof translation functions from Eiffel to CIL. These translations are complex because CIL does not directly support important Eiffel mechanisms such as multiple inheritance and exceptions with rescue blocks. To be able to translate both contracts and proofs, we use deeply-embedded Eiffel expressions in the contracts and the source proof. The main contributions of this paper are: (1) a contract translation function from Eiffel to CIL which handles the lack of multiple inheritance in CIL; (2) a proof translation function from Eiffel to CIL which maps rescue blocks into CIL instructions.

The rest of this paper explores the translation of programs and associated proofs: issues such as the above example, and the solutions that we have adopted.

Section 2 surveys the semantics of the source language, Eiffel, by presenting a Hoare-style logic; section 3 does the same for the target language, CIL. Section 4 presents the specification translator. Section 5 defines the proof transformation process. Section 6 illustrates this transformation through an example. Section 7 introduces a soundness theorem. Section 8 discusses related work, and Section 9 summarizes the result and describes future developments.

2   Source Language and Logic

In this section, we present the Eiffel subset used in this paper and summarize the logic that is used for the verification of Eiffel programs.

2.1   Basics

The source language is a subset of Eiffel [8] with the following syntax:

```
exp      ::= literal | var | exp op exp
instr    ::= x := exp | instr; instr
         |  from instr until exp loop instr end
         |  if exp then instr else instr end
routine ::= name (var : Type) :  Type is
              require boolExp
              [ local var : Type, ... ]
              do                     .
                instr
              [ rescue
                instr ]
              ensure boolExp
            end
```

Once routines are not included. Exceptions are, but expression evaluation cannot cause an exception.

Since exceptions raise some of the most interesting translation problems, the following reminder of Eiffel exception semantics is in order. The ideas behind exception handling in Eiffel (see [6]) are based on Design by Contract principles. A routine execution either succeeds - meaning it achieves its contract - or fails, triggering an exception. An exception is, more generally, an abnormal event during that execution, due for example in turn to the failure of a routine that it has called. The exception causes execution of the routine's **rescue** clause (either explicit or default). If at the end of the clause the variable **Retry** has value true, the normal routine body (do clause) is executed again, in a new attempt to satisfy the contract. If not, the routine execution failed, triggering an exception that can be handled through the **rescue** clause of the caller. This scheme implies a clear separation of roles between the do and rescue clauses: only the former is charged with achieving the routine's contract, as stated by the postcondition. The rescue clause only concerns itself with trying to correct the situation that led to the exception; in addition, it must, if it cannot Retry, re-establish the class invariant so as to leave the object in a consistent state for future calls.

Note that this specification slightly departs from the current Eiffel standard, where Retry is an instruction, not a variable. The change was suggested by our semantic work [7] and will be adopted by a future revision of the language standard. Assignments to Retry can appear in either a do clause or a rescue clause; if its value is true at the end of exception processing the routine re-executes its body, otherwise it fails, triggering a new exception.

2.2   Routine and Instruction Specifications

This paper focuses on the aspects of the translation framework that are most interesting for the translation of proofs. A technical report [13] gives the details for such other object-oriented mechanisms as object creation, attribute access, and routine call.

The logic for the source language is based on the programming logic introduced in [10,16], adapted for Eiffel and extended with new rules for the rescue/Retry exception mechanism.

Poetzsch-Heffter et al. [17] use a special variable χ to capture the status of the program, with values such as normal and exceptional. This variable is not necessary in the bytecode proof since non-linear control flow is implemented via jumps. To eliminate the variable, we use Hoare triples with two postconditions: one for normal termination, the other for exceptions. This simplifies both the translation and the presentation.

The specification of a routine, or more generally an instruction S, is a Hoare triple of the form $\{ P \}\ S\ \{ Q_n\ ,\ Q_e \}$, where P, Q_n, Q_e are deeply-embedded Eiffel expressions extended with universal and existential quantifiers, and S is a routine or an instruction. The third component of the triple consists of a normal postcondition (Q_n) and an exceptional postcondition (Q_e). We call such a triple *routine* or *instruction specification* depending on whether S is a routine or instruction.

To make proof translation feasible in the presence of changes to the type structure, it is essential that both preconditions and postconditions of the Hoare triples be deeply-embedded Eiffel expressions. A deep embedding preserves the syntactic structure of the expression, which we exploit during the translation of Eiffel types to CIL types.

A specification $\{ P \}\ S\ \{ Q_n\ ,\ Q_e \}$ defines the following refined partial correctness property [15]: if S's execution starts in a state satisfying P, then one of the following holds: (1) S terminates normally in a state where Q_n holds, or S triggers an exception and Q_e holds, or (2) S aborts due to errors or actions that are beyond the semantics of the programming language, for instance, memory allocation problems, or (3) S runs forever.

Compound   **Rescue clause**

$$\frac{\left\{P\right\}\; s_1\; \left\{Q_n\,,\,R_e\right\} \quad \left\{Q_n\right\}\; s_2\; \left\{R_n\,,\,R_e\right\}}{\left\{P\right\}\; s_1;s_2\; \left\{R_n\,,\,R_e\right\}}$$

$$\frac{P \Rightarrow I_r \quad \left\{I_r\right\}\; s_1\; \left\{Q_n\,,\,Q_e\right\} \quad \left\{Q_e\right\}\; s_2\; \left\{Retry \Rightarrow I_r \,\wedge\, \neg Retry \Rightarrow R_e\,,\,R_e\right\}}{\left\{P\right\}\; \text{do } s_1 \text{ rescue } s_2\; \left\{Q_n\,,\,R_e\right\}}$$

Loop

$$\frac{\left\{P\right\}\; s_1\; \left\{I\,,\,R_e\right\} \quad \left\{\neg e \,\wedge\, I\right\}\; s_2\; \left\{I\,,\,R_e\right\}}{\left\{P\right\}\; \text{from } s_1 \text{ until } e \text{ loop } s_2 \text{ end}\; \left\{(I \,\wedge\, e)\,,\,R_e\right\}}$$

Fig. 1. Rules for compound, rescue clause, and loop

2.3 Axiomatic Semantics

The axiomatic semantics consists of the axioms and rules for instructions and routines, as well as several language-independent rules such as the rule of consequence, allowing the strengthening of preconditions and weakening of postconditions. Figure 1 shows the rules for compound instructions, loops and **rescue** clauses. The compound and loop rules are standard. The rescue rule is one of the contributions of this paper.

In a compound, s_1 executes first; then s_2 executes if and only if s1 has terminated normally. In a loop, s_1 executes. If s_1 causes an exception then the postcondition of the loop is the postcondition of s_1 (R_e). If s_1 terminates normally and the condition e does not hold, then the body of the loop (s_2) executes. If s_2 terminates normally then the invariant I holds. If s_2 triggers an exception, R_e holds.

The **rescue** rule applies to any routine with a **rescue** clause. The following informal reminder of the Eiffel exception mechanism: if s_1 terminates normally then the **rescue** block is not executed and the postcondition is Q_n. If s_1 triggers an exception, the **rescue** block executes. If the instruction s_2 terminates normally and the **Retry** variable is true then control flow transfers back to the beginning of the routine and I_r holds. If s_2 terminates normally and **Retry** is false, the routine triggers the "routine failure" exception and R_e holds. If both s_1 and s_2 trigger an exception, the last one takes precedence, and R_e holds.

This rule interprets a **rescue** clause as a loop that iterates from s_1 loop s_2; s_1 until s_1 causes no exception or **Retry** is set to false. Note that the loop body is executed only if s_1 triggers an exception. The invariant I_r is the loop invariant, called retry invariant in this context.

3 Bytecode Language and Logic

The bytecode language consists of interfaces and classes. Each class consists of methods and fields. Methods are a sequence of labeled bytecode instructions, which operate on the operand stack, local variables, arguments, and the heap.

3.1 Bytecode Basics

The bytecode language we use is a slight variant of CIL. We treat local variables and routine arguments using the same instructions. Instead of using an array of local variables like in CIL, we use the name of the source variable. Furthermore, to simplify the translation, we assume the bytecode language has a type boolean. The bytecode instructions and their informal description are the following:

- ldc v: pushes constant v onto the stack
- ldloc x: pushes the value of a variable x onto the stack
- stloc x: pops the topmost element off the stack and assigns it to the local variable x
- bin_{op}: removes the two topmost values from the stack and pushes the result of applying bin_{op} to these values
- br l: transfers control to the point l
- brfalse l: transfers control to the point l if the topmost element of the stack is false and unconditionally pops it
- rethrow: takes the topmost value from the stack, assumed to be an exception, and rethrows it
- leave l: exit from the try or catch block to the point l

3.2 Method and Instruction Specifications

The bytecode logic we use is the logic developed by Bannwart and Müller [1]. It is a Hoare-style program logic, which is similar in its structure to the source logic. In particular, both logics treat methods in the same way, contain the same language-independent rules, and triples have a similar meaning. These similarities make proof transformation feasible.

Properties of methods are expressed by method specifications of the form $\{P\}$ $T.mp$ $\{Q_n, Q_e\}$ where Q_n is the postcondition after normal termination and Q_e is the exceptional postcondition. Properties of method bodies are expressed by Hoare triples of the form $\{P\}$ $comp$ $\{Q\}$, where P, Q are first-order formulas and $comp$ is a method body. The triple $\{P\}$ $comp$ $\{Q\}$ expresses the following refined partial correctness property: if the execution of $comp$ starts in a state satisfying P, then (1) $comp$ terminates in a state where Q holds, or (2) $comp$ aborts due to errors or actions that are beyond the semantics of the programming language, or (3) $comp$ runs forever.

Each instruction is treated individually in the logic since the unstructured control flow of bytecode programs makes it difficult to handle instruction sequences. Each individual instruction I_l in a method body p has a precondition E_l. An instruction with its precondition is called an *instruction specification*, written as $\{E_l\}$ $l : I_l$.

The meaning of an instruction specification cannot be defined in isolation. The instruction specification $\{E_l\}$ $l : I_l$ expresses that if the precondition E_l holds when the program counter is at position l, then the precondition of I_l's successor instruction holds after normal termination of I_l.

3.3   Rules

Assertions refer to the current stack, arguments, local variables, and the heap. The current stack is referred to as s and its elements are denoted by non-negative integers: element 0 is the topmost element, etc. The interpretation $[E_l]$: $State \times Stack \to Value$ for s is defined as follows: $[s(0)]\langle S, (\sigma, v)\rangle = v$ and $[s(i+1)]\langle S, (\sigma, v)\rangle = [s(i)]\langle S, \sigma\rangle$.

The functions $shift$ and $unshift$ define the substitutions that occur when values are pushed onto and popped from the stack, respectively. Their definitions are the following: $shift(E) = E[s(i+1)/s(i)$ for all $i \in \mathbb{N}]$ and $unshift = shift^{-1}$.

The rules for instructions have the following form:

$$\frac{E_l \Rightarrow wp(I_l)}{A \vdash \{E_l\}\ l : I_l}$$

where $wp(I_l)$ denotes the *local weakest precondition* of instruction I_l. The rule specifies that E_l (the precondition of I_l) has to imply the weakest precondition of I_l with respect to all possible successor instructions of I_l. The precondition E_l denotes the precondition of the instruction I_l. The precondition E_{l+1} denotes the precondition of I_l's successor instruction. Table 1 shows the definition of wp.

Table 1. Definition of function wp

I_l	$wp(I_l)$
ldc v	$unshift(E_{l+1}[v/s(0)])$
ldloc x	$unshift(E_{l+1}[x/s(0)])$
stloc x	$(shift(E_{l+1}))[s(0)/x]$
bin_{op}	$(shift(E_{l+1}))[s(1)\ op\ s(0)/s(1)]$
br l'	$E_{l'}$
brfalse l'	$(s(0) \Rightarrow shift(E_{l+1})) \wedge (\neg s(0) \Rightarrow shift(E_{l'}))$
leave l'	$E_{l'}$

4   Specification Translator

The specification translator translates Eiffel contracts into first order logic (FOL). The challenging problem in the specification translator is produced by the impedance mismatch between Eiffel and CIL. Due to CIL does not directly support multiple inheritance, Eiffel classes are mapped to interfaces or implementation classes. To be able to translate contracts, we use deeply-embedded Eiffel expressions.

4.1   Translation Basics

In Hoare triples, pre- and postconditions may refer to the structure of the Eiffel program. Therefore, in our logic, pre- and postconditions are deeply-embedded Eiffel expressions, extended with universal and existential quantifiers. The proof translation proceeds in two steps: first, translation of pre-and postconditions into FOL using the translation function presented in this section; then, translation of the proof using the functions presented in Section 5.

We have defined a deep embedding of the Eiffel expressions used in the contract language. Then, we have defined translation functions to FOL. The datatype definitions, the translation functions and their soundness proof are formalized in Isabelle. In this section, we present the most interesting definitions and formalizations, for a complete definition see [13].

4.2   Datatype Definitions

Eiffel contracts are based on boolean expressions, extended (for postconditions) with the old notation. They can be constructed using the logical operators ¬ and ∨, equality, and the type functions *ConformsTo* or *IsEqual*. Expressions are constants, local variables and arguments, attributes, routine calls, creation expressions, old expressions, boolean expressions, and *Void*. Arguments are treated as local variables using the sort *RefVar* to minimize the datatype definition. Furthermore, boolean variables are not introduced in the definition *boolExp*. They are treated as local variables using the sort *RefVar*. We assume routines have exactly one argument.

datatype *EiffelContract* = **Require** *boolExpr*
                      | **Ensure** *boolExpr*
datatype *boolExpr* = **Const** *bool*
                      | **Neg** *boolExpr*
                      | **Or** *boolExpr boolExpr*
                      | **Eq**   *expr expr*
                      | **Type** *typeFunc*

datatype *typeFunc* = **ConformsTo** *typeExpr typeExpr*
                      | **IsEqual** *typeExpr typeExpr*
datatype *typeExpr* = **EType** *EiffelType*
                      | **Type** *expr*
datatype *expr* = **ConstInt** *int*
                      | **RefVar** *var*
                      | **Att** *objID attrib*
                      | **CallR** *callRoutine*
                      | **Create** *EiffelType routine argument*
                      | **Old** *expr*
                      | **Bool** *boolExpr*
                      | **Void**
datatype *callRoutine* = **Call** *expr routine argument*
datatype *argument* =   **Argument** *expr*

EiffelTypes are *Boolean*, *Integer*, classes with a class identifier, or *None*. The notation (*cID* : *classID*) means, given an Eiffel class c, cID(c) returns its *classID*.

datatype *EiffelType* = **Boolean**
                        | **Integer**
                        | **EClass** (*cID* : *classID*)
                        | **None**

Variables, attributes and routines are defined as follows:

datatype *var*   = **Var** *vID EiffelType*
                        | **Result** *EiffelType*
                        | **Current** *EiffelType*
datatype *attrib*   = **Attr** (*aID* : *attribID*) *EiffelType*
datatype *routine* = **Routine** *routineID EiffelType EiffelType*

4.3   Object Store and Values

An object store is modeled by an abstract data type *store*. We use the object store presented by Poetzsch-Heffter [15]. The Eiffel object store and the CIL object store are the same. The following operations apply to the object store: *accessC*(*os*, *l*) denotes reading the location *l* in store *os*; *alive*(*o*, *os*) yields true if and only if object *o* is allocated in *os*; *new*(*os*, *C*) returns a reference to a new object in the store *os* of type *C*; *alloc*(*os*, *C*) denotes the store after allocating the object store *new*(*os*, *C*); *update*(*os*, *l*, *v*) updates the object store *os* at the location *l* with the value *v*:

accessC :: *store* → *location* → *value*
alive ::   *value* → *store* → *bool*
alloc ::   *store* → *classID* → *store*
new ::   *store* → *classID* → *value*
update ::   *store* → *location* → *value* → *store*

The axiomatization of these functions is presented by Poetzsch-Heffter [15].

A value is a boolean, an integer, the void value, or an object reference. An object is characterized by its class and an identifier of infinite sort *objID*.

datatype *value* = **BoolV** *bool*
                      | **IntV** *int*
                      | **ObjV** *classID objID*
                      | **VoidV**

4.4   Mapping Eiffel Types to CIL

To define the translation from Eiffel contracts to *FOL*, it is useful first to define CIL types and mapping functions that map Eiffel types to the CIL types: boolean, integer, interfaces, classes and the null type.

datatype *CilType* = **CilBoolean**
                        | **CilInteger**
                        | **Interface** *classID*
                        | **CilClass** *classID*
                        | **NullT**

The translation then uses two functions that map Eiffel types to CIL: (1) $\nabla_{interface}$ maps an Eiffel type to a CIL interface; (2) ∇_{class} maps the type to a CIL implementation class. These functions are defined as follows:

$$\nabla_{interface} :: EiffelType \rightarrow CilType \qquad \nabla_{class} :: EiffelType \rightarrow CilType$$
$$\nabla_{interface}(\textbf{Boolean}) = \textbf{CilBoolean} \qquad \nabla_{class}(\textbf{Boolean}) = \textbf{CilBoolean}$$
$$\nabla_{interface}(\textbf{Integer}) = \textbf{CilInteger} \qquad \nabla_{class}(\textbf{Integer}) = \textbf{CilInteger}$$
$$\nabla_{interface}(\textbf{EClass } n) = \textbf{Interface } n \qquad \nabla_{class}(\textbf{EClass } n) = \textbf{CilClass } n$$
$$\nabla_{interface}(\textbf{None}) = \textbf{NullT} \qquad \nabla_{class}(\textbf{None}) = \textbf{NullT}$$

The translation of routine calls needs method signatures in CIL and a translation function that maps Eiffel routines to CIL methods. The function $\nabla_{interface}$ serves to map types t_1 and t_2 to CIL types.

datatype $CilMethod = $ **Method** $methodID$ $CilType$ $CilType$
$\nabla_r ::$ $routine \rightarrow CilMethod$
$\nabla_r(\textbf{Routine } n\ t1\ t2) = (\textbf{Method}\ \ n\ \ (\nabla_{interface}\ t1)\ (\nabla_{interface}\ t2))$

4.5   Contract Translation

The translation of the specification relies on five translation functions: (1) ∇_b takes a boolean expression and returns a function that takes two stores and a state an returns a value; (2) ∇_{exp} translates expressions; (3) ∇_t translates type functions (conforms to and is equal); (4) ∇_{call} translates a routine call; and (5) ∇_{arg} translates arguments. These functions use two object stores, the second one is used to evaluate old expressions. *state* is a mapping from variables to values ($var \rightarrow value$). The signatures of these functions are the following:

$$\nabla_b :: boolExpr \rightarrow (store \rightarrow store \rightarrow state \rightarrow value)$$
$$\nabla_{exp} :: expr \rightarrow (store \rightarrow store \rightarrow state \rightarrow value)$$
$$\nabla_t :: typeFunc \rightarrow (store \rightarrow store \rightarrow state \rightarrow value)$$
$$\nabla_{call} :: callRoutine \rightarrow (store \rightarrow store \rightarrow state \rightarrow value)$$
$$\nabla_{arg} :: argument \rightarrow (store \rightarrow store \rightarrow state \rightarrow value)$$

The definition of the function ∇_b is the following:
$\nabla_b(\textbf{Const } b) = \lambda\ (h_1, h_2 :: store)\ (s :: state) : (BoolV\ b)$
$\nabla_b(\textbf{Neg } b)\ \ = \lambda\ (h_1, h_2 :: store)\ (s :: state) :$
$\qquad\qquad\qquad (BoolV\ \neg(aB(\nabla_b\ b\ h_1\ h_2\ s)))$
$\nabla_b(\textbf{Or } b_1\ b_2) = \lambda\ (h_1, h_2 :: store)\ (s :: state) :$
$\qquad\qquad\qquad (BoolV\ (aB(\nabla_b\ b_1\ h_1\ h_2\ s)) \vee (aB(\nabla_b\ b_2\ h_1\ h_2\ s)))$
$\nabla_b(\textbf{Eq } e_1\ e_2) = \lambda\ (h_1, h_2 :: store)\ (s :: state) :$
$\qquad\qquad\qquad (BoolV\ (aI(\nabla_{exp}\ e_1\ h_1\ h_2\ s)) = (aI(\nabla_{exp}\ e_2\ h_1\ h_2\ s)))$
$\nabla_b(\textbf{Type } e) = \lambda\ (h_1, h_2 :: store)\ (s :: state) : (\nabla_t\ e\ h_1\ h_2\ s))$

The function ∇_t maps the Eiffel types to CIL. The Eiffel function *ConformsTo* is mapped to the function $\preceq_c$ (subtyping in CIL). Its types are translated to interfaces using the function $\nabla_{interface}$. The function *IsEqual* is translated using the function $=$ (types equality in CIL). Its types are translated to CIL classes using the function ∇_{class}. The function ∇_t is defined as follows:

$\nabla_t(\textbf{ConformsTo } t_1 \ t_2) = \lambda \ (h_1, h_2 :: store)(s :: state) :$
$$(BoolV (\nabla_{interface}(\nabla_{type} t_1)) \preceq_c (\nabla_{interface}(\nabla_{type} t_2)))$$
$\nabla_t(\textbf{IsEqual } t_1 \ t_2) \quad = \lambda \ (h_1, h_2 :: store)(s :: state) :$
$$(BoolV (\nabla_{class}(\nabla_{type} t_1)) = (\nabla_{class}(\nabla_{type} t_2)))$$

The function ∇_{type} given a type expression returns its Eiffel type:

$\nabla_{type} :: \ typeExp \rightarrow \ EiffelType$
$\quad \nabla_{type}(\textbf{EType } t) \qquad = t$
$\quad \nabla_{type}(\textbf{Expression } e) = (typeOf \ e)$

The function ∇_{exp} translates local variables using the *state s*. Creation instructions are translated using the functions *new* and *alloc*. The translation of old expressions uses the second *store* to map the expression e to CIL. The definition is:

$\nabla_{exp}(\textbf{ConstInt } i) \quad = \lambda \ (h_1, h_2 :: store)(s :: state) : (IntV \ i)$
$\nabla_{exp}(\textbf{RefVar } v) \quad = \lambda \ (h_1, h_2 :: store)(s :: state) : (s(v))$
$\nabla_{exp}(\textbf{Att } ob \ a) \quad = \lambda \ (h_1, h_2 :: store)(s :: state) :$
$$(accessC \ h_1 \ (Loc \ (aID \ a) \ ob))$$
$\nabla_{exp}(\textbf{CallR } crt) \quad = \lambda \ (h_1, h_2 :: store)(s :: state) :$
$$(\nabla_{call} \ crt \ h_1 \ h2 \ s)$$
$\nabla_{exp}(\textbf{Create } t \ rt \ p) = \lambda \ (h_1, h_2 :: store)(s :: state) :$
$$(new \ (alloc \ h_1 \ (cID \ t)) \ (cID \ t))$$
$\nabla_{exp}(\textbf{Old } e) \quad = \lambda \ (h_1, h_2 :: store)(s :: state) :$
$$(\nabla_{exp} \ e \ h_2 \ h_2 \ s)$$
$\nabla_{exp}(\textbf{Bool } b) \quad = \lambda \ (h_1, h_2 :: store)(s :: state) :$
$$(\nabla_b \ b \ h_1 \ h_2 \ s)$$
$\nabla_{exp}(\textbf{Void}) \quad = \lambda \ (h_1, h_2 :: store)(s :: state) : (VoidV)$

The function ∇_{call} is defined as follows:

$\nabla_{call}(\textbf{Call } e_1 \ rt \ p) = \lambda \ (h_1, h_2 :: store)(s :: state) :$
$$(\textbf{CilInvokeVal } h_1 \ (\nabla_r \ rt) \ (\nabla_{exp} \ e_1 \ h_1 \ h_2 \ s)(\nabla_{arg} \ p \ h_1 \ h_2 \ s))$$

The function *CilInvokeVal* takes a CIL method m and two values (its argument p and invoker e_1) and returns the value of the result of invoking the method m with the invoker e_1 and argument p.

The definition of the function ∇_{arg} is the following:

$$\nabla_{arg}(\textbf{Argument } e) = \lambda \ (h_1, h_2 :: store)(s :: state) : (\nabla_{exp} \ e \ h_1 \ h_2 \ s)$$

4.6   Example Translation

To be able to translate contracts, first we embed the contracts in Isabelle using the above data type definitions. Then, we apply the translation function ∇_b which produces the contracts in FOL. Following, we present the embedding of the contracts of the function *merge* presented in Section 1. Its precondition is embedded as follows:

Type (**ConformsTo** (Type (**RefVar** *other*)) (EType *LINKED_LIST[G]*))
Type (**IsEqual** (Type (**RefVar** *Current*)) (Type (**RefVar** *other*)))

The deep embedding of *merge*'s postcondition is as follows:

Type (**IsEqual** (Type (**RefVar** *Current*)) (EType *LINKED_LIST[G]*))

The application of the function ∇_b to the precondition produces the following expression:

λ ($h_1, h_2 :: store$)($s :: state$) :
   $BoolV$(*typeOf other*) $\preceq_c$ (**interface** *LINKED_LIST[G]*)
λ ($h_1, h_2 :: store$)($s :: state$) : $BoolV$(*typeOf Current*) = (*typeOf other*)

The result of the application of the function ∇_b to the deep embedding of *merge*'s postcondition is the following:

λ ($h_1, h_2 :: store$)($s :: state$) :
   $BoolV$(*typeOf Current*) = (**CilClass** *LINKED_LIST[G]*)

In the precondition, the type *LINKED_LIST[G]* is translated to the interface *LINKED_LIST[G]* because the precondition uses the function *ConformsTo*. However, in the postcondition, the type *LINKED_LIST[G]* is translated to the class *LINKED_LIST[G]* because it uses the function *IsEqual*. The PTC can translates these types because it takes deeply-embedded Eiffel expressions as input.

5   Proof Translation

Our proof translator is based on two transformation functions, ∇_S and ∇_E, for instructions and expressions, respectively. Each yields a sequence of bytecode instructions and their specifications.

5.1   Transformation Function Basics

The function ∇_E generates a bytecode proof from a source expression and a precondition for its evaluation. The function ∇_S generates a bytecode proof from a source proof. These functions are defined as a composition of the translations of the proof's sub-trees. They have the signatures:

∇_E : *Precondition* × *Expression* × *Postcondition* × *Label* → *Bytecode_Proof*
∇_S : *Proof_Tree* × *Label* × *Label* × *Label* → *Bytecode_Proof*

In ∇_E the label is used as the starting label of the translation. *Proof_Tree* is a derivation in the source logic. In ∇_S, the three labels are: (1) *start* for the first label of the resulting bytecode; (2) *next* for the label after the resulting bytecode; this is for instance used in the translation of an **else** branch to determine where to jump at the end; (3) *exc* for the jump target when an exception is thrown. The *Bytecode_Proof* type is defined as a list of instruction specifications.

The proof translation will now be presented for the compound instruction, loops, and **rescue** clauses. The definition of ∇_E is simple, it translates expressions to CIL proofs. Due to space limitations, this definition is not presented here (see our technical report [13]). Furthermore, in this technical report, the translation also includes object-oriented features such as object creation and routine invocation.

5.2 Compound Instruction

Compound instructions are the simplest instructions to translate. The translation of s_2 is added after the translation of s_1 where the starting label is updated to l_b. Let T_{S_1} and T_{S_2} be the following proof trees:

$$T_{S_1} \equiv \frac{Tree_1}{\{\,P\,\} \quad s_1 \quad \{\,Q_n\,,\ R_e\,\}} \qquad T_{S_2} \equiv \frac{Tree_2}{\{\,Q_n\,\} \quad s_2 \quad \{\,R_n\,,\ R_e\,\}}$$

The definition of the translation is the following:

$$\nabla_S \left(\frac{T_{S_1} \qquad T_{S_2}}{\{\,P\,\} \quad s_1;s_2 \quad \{\,R_n\,,\ R_e\,\}}, \ l_{start}, l_{next}, l_{exc} \right) = \\ \nabla_S \left(T_{S_1}, \ l_{start}, l_b, l_{exc} \right) \\ \nabla_S \left(T_{S_2}, \ l_b, l_{next}, l_{exc} \right)$$

The bytecode for s_1 establishes Q_n, which is the precondition of the first instruction of the bytecode for s_2. Therefore, the concatenation of the bytecode as the result of the translation of s_1 and s_2, produces a sequence of valid instruction specifications. Section 7 will discuss soundness.

5.3 Loop Instruction

Let T_{S_1} and T_{S_2} be the following proof trees:

$$T_{S_1} \equiv \frac{Tree_1}{\{\,P\,\} \quad s_1 \quad \{\,I\,,\ R_e\,\}} \qquad T_{S_2} \equiv \frac{Tree_2}{\{\,\neg e \wedge I\,\} \quad s_2 \quad \{\,I\,,\ R_e\,\}}$$

The first step of translating the loop is to translate s_1 using ∇_S. Then, control is transferred to l_d where the loop expression is evaluated. The body of the loop is translated with l_c. The loop invariant holds at the begging of the loop expression evaluation (at l_d). The definition is:

$$\nabla_S \left(\frac{T_{S_1} \qquad T_{S_2}}{\{\,P\,\} \quad \begin{array}{l} \text{from } s_1 \text{ until } e \\ \text{loop } s_2 \text{ end} \end{array} \quad \{\,(I \wedge e)\,,\ R_e\,\}}, \ l_{start}, l_{next}, l_{exc} \right) =$$

$$\{I\} \qquad \begin{array}{l} \nabla_S (\ T_{S_1}, \ l_{start}, l_b, l_{exc} \ ) \\ l_b : \text{br } l_d \\ \nabla_S (\ T_{S_2}, \ l_c, l_d, l_{exc} \ ) \\ \nabla_E (\ I, \ e, \ \{shift(I) \wedge s(0) = e\}, \ l_d \ ) \end{array}$$
$$\{shift(I) \wedge s(0) = e\} \ l_e : \text{brfalse } l_c$$

5.4 Rescue Clause

The translation of rescue clauses to CIL is one of the most interesting translations. Since rescue clauses do not exist in CIL, this translation maps rescue clauses to .try and catch CIL instructions. Let T_{S_1} and T_{S_2} be the following proof trees:

$$T_{S_1} \equiv \frac{Tree_1}{\{\, I_r \,\} \quad s_1 \quad \{\, Q_n \,,\, Q_e \,\}} \qquad T_{S_2} \equiv \frac{Tree_2}{\{\, Q_e \,\} \quad s_2 \quad \left\{ \begin{matrix} Retry \Rightarrow I_r \,\wedge \\ \neg Retry \Rightarrow R_e \end{matrix} \,,\, R_e \right\}}$$

First, the instruction s_1 is translated to a .try block. The exception label is updated to l_c because if an exception occurs in s_1, control will be transferred to the catch block at l_c. Then, the instruction s_2 is translated into a catch block. For this, the exception object is first stored in a temporary variable and then s_2 is translated. In this translation, the Retry label is updated to l_{start} (the beginning of the routine). Finally, between labels l_e and l_i, control is transferred to l_{start} if Retry is true; otherwise, the exception is pushed on top of the stack and re-thrown. The definition is:

$$\nabla_S \left(\frac{T_{S_1} \qquad T_{S_2}}{\{\, P \,\} \quad \text{do } s_1 \text{ rescue } s_2 \quad \{\, Q_n \,,\, R_e \,\}} \,,\, l_{start}, l_{next}, l_{exc} \right) =$$

```
                                    .try{
                                        ∇_S (T_{S_1}, l_{start}, l_b, l_{retry}, l_c)
{Q_n}                                   l_b : leave l_{next}
                                    }
                                    catch System.Exception {
{Q_e ∧ excV ≠ null ∧ s(0) = excV}       l_c : stloc last_exception
{Q_e}                                   ∇_S (T_{S_2}, l_d, l_e, l_a, l_{exc})
{Retry ⇒ I_r ∧ ¬Retry ⇒ R_e}            l_e : ldloc Retry
{Retry ⇒ I_r ∧ ¬Retry ⇒ R_e ∧ s(0) = Retry}  l_f : brfalse l_h
{I_r}                                   l_g : br l_{start}
{R_e}                                   l_h : ldloc last_exception
{R_e ∧ s(0) = last_exception}           l_i : rethrow
                                    }
```

6 Example

The PTC processes a list of Eiffel classes. Every class consists of a sequence of routines. Every routine consists of its pre- and postcondition and the source proof. The PTC generates two CIL types per Eiffel class: the interface and the implementation class. Then, for each routine, it translates the pre- and postcondition using the functions defined in Section 4. Finally it translates the source proof using the functions defined in Section 5.

```
 1  safe_division  (x,y: INTEGER): INTEGER
    local
 3      z: INTEGER
    do
 5      { z=0 or z=1 }
        Result := x // (y+z)
 7      { zero and not_zero , z = 0 }
    ensure
 9      zero: y = 0 implies Result = x
        not_zero: y /= 0 implies Result = x // y
11  rescue
        { z=0 }
13      z := 1
        { z=1 , false }
15      Retry := true
        { Retry implies z=1 and not Retry implies false, false }
17  end
```

Fig. 2. Example of an Eiffel source proof

Figure 2 and 3 illustrates the translation. Figure 2 presents the source proof. The example function implements an integer division, which always terminates normally. If the second operand is zero, it returns the first operand; otherwise the result is equal to the integer division $x//y$. Line 7 uses *zero* and *not_zero* to denote the properties expressed by the postcondition labeled with these names ($y = 0$ *implies Result* $= x$ *and* $y/ = 0$ *implies Result* $= x//y$). The bytecode proof uses the same convention. The exceptional postcondition of the last instruction of the **rescue** block and the exceptional postcondition of the routine are both false because the routine always terminates normally.

Figure 3 presents the bytecode proof. The generated bytecode for the body of the routine is enclosed in a try block (lines 01 to 07). Since the routine always terminates normally, the precondition of the instructions at labels 17 and 18 is false.

7 Soundness Theorems

To be able to execute mobile code in a safe way, a soundness proof is required only for components of the trusted code base. Although PTCs are not part of the trusted code base, from the point of view of the code producer, the PTC should always generates valid proofs to avoid that the produced bytecode is rejected by the proof checker.

It is thus desirable to prove the soundness of both the proof translator and the specification translator. For the proof translator, soundness informally means that the translation produces valid bytecode proofs. It is not enough, however, to produce a valid proof, because the compiler could generate bytecode proofs where every precondition is false. The theorem states that if (1) we have a valid source proof for the instruction s_1, and (2) we have a proof translation from the source proof that produces the instructions $I_{l_{start}}...I_{l_{end}}$, and their respective preconditions $E_{l_{start}}...E_{l_{end}}$, and (3) the normal postcondition in the source

$\{z = 0 \lor z = 1\}$
$\{(z = 0 \lor z = 1) \land s(0) = x\}$
$\{(z = 0 \lor z = 1) \land s(1) = x \land s(0) = y\}$
$\{(z = 0 \lor z = 1) \land s(1) = x \land s(1) = y \land s(0) = z\}$
$\{(z = 0 \lor z = 1) \land s(1) = x \land s(0) = y + z\}$
$\{(z = 0 \lor z = 1) \land s(0) = x//(y + z)\}$
$\{zero\ and\ not\_zero\}$

$\{z = 0 \land excV \neq null \land s(0) = excV\}$
$\{z = 0\}$
$\{z = 0 \land s(0) = 1\}$
$\{z = 1\}$
$\{z = 1 \land s(0) = true\}$
$\{\neg Retry \Rightarrow false \land Retry \Rightarrow (z = 1 \lor z = 0)\}$
$\{\neg Retry \Rightarrow false \land$
$Retry \Rightarrow (z = 1 \lor z = 0) \land s(0) = Retry\}$
$\{z = 1 \lor z = 0\}$
$\{false\}$
$\{false \land s(0) = last\_exception\}$

$\{zero\ and\ not\_zero\}$
$\{zero\ and\ not\_zero \land s(0) = Result\}$

```
try {
  01 : ldloc x
  02 : ldloc y
  03 : ldloc z
  04 : binop+
  05 : binop//
  06 : stloc Result
  07 : leave 19
}
catch System.Exception {
  09 : stloc last_exception
  10 : ldc 1
  11 : stloc z
  12 : ldc true
  13 : stloc Retry
  14 : ldloc Retry

  15 : brfalse 17
  16 : br 01
  17 : ldloc last_exception
  18 : rethrow
}
19 : ldloc Result
20 : ret
```

Fig. 3. Bytecode proof generated by the PTC

logic implies the next precondition of the last generated instruction (if the last generated instruction is the last instruction of the method, we use the normal postcondition in the source logic), and (4) the exceptional postcondition in the source logic implies the precondition at the target label l_{exc} but considering the value stored in the stack of the bytecode, then every bytecode specification holds ($\vdash \{E_l\}\ I_l$). The theorem is the following:

Theorem 1

$$\vdash \dfrac{Tree_1}{\{P\}\ s_1\ \{Q_n\ ,\ Q_e\}} \land$$

$$(I_{l_{start}}...I_{l_{end}}) = \nabla s \left(\dfrac{Tree_1}{\{P\}\ s_1\ \{Q_n\ ,\ Q_e\}},\ l_{start}, l_{end+1}, l_{exc}\right) \land$$

$$(Q_n \Rightarrow E_{l_{end+1}}) \land$$

$$((Q_e \land excV \neq null \land s(0) = excV) \Rightarrow E_{l_{exc}}) \land$$

$$\Rightarrow$$

$$\forall l \in l_{start} ... l_{end} : \vdash \{E_l\}\ I_l$$

The soundness proof of the specification translator has been formalized and proved in Isabelle. First, we have defined evaluation functions from Eiffel expressions to values. $value_b$, $value_t$, $value_{exp}$, $value_{call}$ and $value_{arg}$ evaluate boolean expressions, Eiffel types, expressions, routine calls and arguments respectively. The theorem expresses: given two heaps and a state, if the expression e is well-formed then the value of the translation of the expression e is equal to the value returned by the evaluation of e. The theorem is the following:

Theorem 2

$$\forall b : boolExp, \ t : typeFunc, \ e : expr, \ c : CallRoutine, \ p : argument :$$
$$(wellF_b \ b) \Rightarrow (value_b \ b \ h_1 \ h_2 \ s) = ((\nabla_b \ b) \ h_1 \ h_2 \ s) \ \ and$$
$$(wellF_t \ t) \Rightarrow (value_t \ t \ h_1 \ h_2 \ s) = ((\nabla_t \ t) \ h_1 \ h_2 \ s) \ \ and$$
$$(wellF_{exp} \ e) \Rightarrow (value_{exp} \ e \ h_1 \ h_2 \ s) = ((\nabla_{exp} \ e) \ h_1 \ h_2 \ s) \ \ and$$
$$(wellF_{call} \ c) \Rightarrow (value_{call} \ c \ h_1 \ h_2 \ s) = ((\nabla_{call} \ c) \ h_1 \ h_2 \ s) \ \ and$$
$$(wellF_{arg} \ p) \Rightarrow (value_{arg} \ p \ h_1 \ h_2 \ s) = ((\nabla_{arg} \ p) \ h_1 \ h_2 \ s)$$

The full proofs can be found in our technical report [13]. The proof of theorem 1 runs by induction on the structure of the derivation tree for $\{P\}s_1\{Q_n, Q_e\}$. The proof of theorem 2 runs by induction on the syntactic structure of the expression and it is done in Isabelle.

8   Related Work

Necula and Lee [12] have developed certifying compilers, which produce proofs for basic safety properties such as type safety. The approach developed here supports interactive verification of source programs and as a result can handle more complex properties such as functional correctness.

Foundational Proof-Carrying Code has been extended by the open verifier framework for foundational verifiers [4]. It supports verification of untrusted code using custom verifiers. As in certifying compilers, the open verifier framework can prove basic safety properties.

Barthe *et al.* [3] show that proof obligations are preserved by compilation (for a non-optimizing compiler). They prove the equivalence between the verification condition (VC) generated over the source code and the bytecode. The translation in their case is less difficult because the source and the target languages are closer. This work does not address the translation of specifications.

Another development by the same group [2] translates certificates for optimizing compilers from a simple interactive language to an intermediate RTL language (Register Transfer Language). The translation is done in two steps: first, translate the source program into RTL; then, perform optimizations to build the appropriate certificate. This work involves a language that is simpler than ours and, like in the previously cited development, much closer to the target language than Eiffel is to CIL. We will investigate optimizing compilers as part of future work.

The Mobius project develops proof-transforming compilers [9]. They translate JML specifications and proof of Java source programs to Java Bytecode. The translation is simpler because the source and the target language are closer.

This work is based on our earlier effort [11] on proof-transforming compilation from Java to bytecode. In that earlier project, the translation of method bodies is more complex due to the generated exception tables in Java bytecode. However, the source and the target langues are more similar than the languages used in this paper. Furthermore, our earlier work did not translate specifications.

9   Conclusion

We have defined a proof-transforming compiler from a subset of Eiffel to CIL. The PTC allows us to develop certificates by interactively verifying source programs, and then translating the result to a bytecode proof. Since Eiffel supports multiple inheritance and CIL does not, we focused on the translation of contracts that refer to type information. We showed that our translation is sound, that is, it produces valid bytecode proofs. This translation can be adapted to other bytecode languages such as JVML. The main difference to CIL is the use of an exception table instead of .try and catch instructions as show in our previous work [11].

To show the feasibility of our approach, we implemented a PTC for a subset of Eiffel. The compiler takes a proof in an XML format and produces the bytecode proof. The compiler is integrated into EiffelStudio, the standard Eiffel development environment.

As future work, we plan to develop a proof checker that tests the bytecode proof. Moreover, we plan to analyze how proofs can be translated using an optimizing compiler.

References

1. Bannwart, F.Y., Müller, P.: A Logic for Bytecode. In: Spoto, F. (ed.) Bytecode Semantics, Verification, Analysis and Transformation (BYTECODE). ENTCS, vol. 141(1), pp. 255–273. Elsevier (2005)
2. Barthe, G., Grégoire, B., Kunz, C., Rezk, T.: Certificate Translation for Optimizing Compilers. In: Yi, K. (ed.) SAS 2006. LNCS, vol. 4134. Springer, Heidelberg (2006)
3. Barthe, G., Rezk, T., Saabas, A.: Proof obligations preserving compilation. In: Third International Workshop on Formal Aspects in Security and Trust, Newcastle, UK, pp. 112–126 (2005)
4. Chang, B., Chlipala, A., Necula, G., Schneck, R.: The Open Verifier Framework for Foundational Verifiers. In: ACM SIGPLAN Workshop on Types in Language Design and Implementation (TLDI 2005) (2005)
5. Meyer, B.: Multi-language programming: how .net does it. In: 3-part article in Software Development. May, June and July 2002, especially Part 2, http://www.ddj.com/architect/184414864?
6. Meyer, B.: Object-Oriented Software Construction, 2nd edn. Prentice Hall, Englewood Cliffs (1997)

7. Meyer, B., Müller, P., Nordio, M.: A Hoare logic for a subset of Eiffel. Technical Report 559, ETH Zurich (2007)
8. Meyer, B.: ISO/ECMA Eiffel standard (Standard ECMA-367: Eiffel: Analysis, Design and Programming Language) (June 2006), http://www.ecma-international.org/publications/standards/Ecma-367.htm
9. MOBIUS Consortium. Deliverable 4.3: Intermediate report on proof-transforming compiler (2007), http://mobius.inria.fr
10. Müller, P. (ed.): Modular Specification and Verification of Object-Oriented Programs. LNCS, vol. 2262. Springer, Heidelberg (2002)
11. Müller, P., Nordio, M.: Proof-transforming compilation of programs with abrupt termination. In: Sixth International Workshop on Specification and Verification of Component-Based Systems (SAVCBS 2007), pp. 39–46 (2007)
12. Necula, G., Lee, P.: The Design and Implementation of a Certifying Compiler. In: Programming Language Design and Implementation (PLDI), pp. 333–344. ACM Press (1998)
13. Nordio, M., Müller, P., Meyer, B.: Formalizing Proof-Transforming Compilation of Eiffel programs. Technical Report 587, ETH Zurich (2008)
14. Pavlova, M.: Java Bytecode verification and its applications. PhD thesis, University of Nice Sophia-Antipolis (2007)
15. Poetzsch-Heffter, A.: Specification and verification of object-oriented programs. Habilitation thesis, Technical University of Munich (1997)
16. Poetzsch-Heffter, A., Müller, P.: A Programming Logic for Sequential Java. In: Swierstra, S.D. (ed.) ESOP 1999. LNCS, vol. 1576, pp. 162–176. Springer, Heidelberg (1999)
17. Poetzsch-Heffter, A., Rauch, N.: Soundness and Relative Completeness of a Programming Logic for a Sequential Java Subset. Technical report, Technische Universität Kaiserslautern (2004)

Engineering Associations: From Models to Code and Back through Semantics

Zinovy Diskin[1], Steve Easterbrook[1], and Juergen Dingel[2]

[1] University of Toronto, Canada
zdiskin,sme@cs.toronto.edu
[2] Queen's University, Kingston, Canada
dingel@cs.queensu.ca

Abstract. Association between classes is a central construct in OO modeling. However, precise semantics of associations has not been defined, and only the most basic types are implemented in modern forward and reverse engineering tools. In this paper, we present a novel mathematical framework and build a precise semantics for several association constructs, whose implementation has been considered problematic. We also identify a number of patterns for using associations in practical applications, which cannot be modeled (reverse engineered) in UML.

1 Introduction

Modeling is a classical engineering instrument to manage complexity of system design. Its evolution in many branches of mechanical and electrical engineering, and practically everywhere in hardware engineering, has led to automated production. We do not see significant reasons to think that evolution of software engineering (SE) will be essentially different. The recent rapid advance of model-driven development (MDD) in many areas of SE shows potential of the process (cf.[21,13]). Particularly, there has been a real explosion in the market of forward, reverse and roundtrip engineering tools (MDD-tools).

1.1 The Problem

Among modeling notations used in OO analysis and design, Class Diagrams play a central role.[1] A basic type of class diagram is a graph whose nodes are classes and edges are associations between them. The latter present relationships between classes and can bear various adornments expressing properties of these relationships; Fig. 1 shows a few examples. The meaning of diagrams (a,b,d) should be clear from semantics of names. Diagram (c1) says that a pair of objects (c:Company, p:Position) determines zero or one Person object, and similarly (c2) says that a pair (p:Person, c:Company) determines zero or two Positions.

---

[1] A survey reported in [10] claims that *all* experts participating in the study evaluated Class Diagrams as the most important and the most useful of the UML notations.

R.F. Paige and B. Meyer (Eds.): TOOLS EUROPE 2008, LNBIP 11, pp. 336–355, 2008.

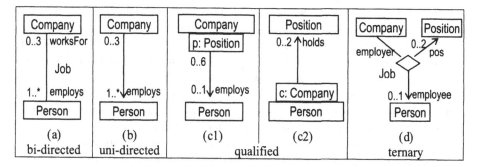

Fig. 1. A few sample associations

Note that if association ends are considered as directed mappings between classes then we name them by verbs to emphasize asymmetry (diagrams a,b,c). We use nouns when the ends are regarded as roles of the association considered as a symmetric relationship between classes (diagram d).

Implementation of these semantics is not quite straightforward, but everything looks manageable and an ordinary MDD-tool should accurately implement these constructs. However, the situation one finds in practice is in sharp contrast with these expectations. For example, the survey reported in [1] says that among ten major UML-based MDD-tools, none have implemented n-ary associations; only two – qualified associations; and only three – bidirectional associations (including those unidirectional, which have multiplicity constraints at both ends like, e.g., in Fig. 1b). In fact, the only (!) association construct well understood and implemented today is unidirectional binary association without multiplicity constraints at the source end (Fig. 1(b) with multiplicity 0..3 removed).

1.2   The Causes

The root of the problems with associations is that their simple and compact syntax hides an integrated *system* of concepts, mutually related and dependant of each other. For example, implementation of a bidirectional association in Fig. 1(a) may seem to be as simple as declaring attributes *employs* of type Collection⟨Person⟩ in class *Company* and *worksFor* of type Collection⟨Company⟩ in class *Person*. However, these two attributes are not independent and represent the two ends of the *same* association: updating one of them means updating the entire association, which implies a corresponding update for the other end. Hence, the mutator methods (setters) for the attributes belonging to different classes must be synchronized. The problem is essentially complicated by the possibility to combine several properties for one end and several other properties for the other end. For example, UML does not prevent declaring one end to be bag-valued, qualified and read-only while the other end is set-valued, also qualified and writable. In [1], several such complex cases of feature interaction are identified.

Another big issue is the two-facet nature of associations, which are both extensional and navigational concepts. A common understanding of multi-ary associations sees them as sets of links (tuples) or relations. This view is basic for databases, but software modeling is more concerned with traversing relations in different directions; UML calls this aspect *navigation*. In the navigational view, relations re-appear as extensions (graphs) of the mappings involved, and thus are always implicitly on the stage. Implementation needs a clear and precise specification of the relationship between the two views but the issue is rarely discussed in the literature. Indirectly and informally it is addressed in the UML Standard but its specification in the metamodel is seriously flawed [5]. Since modern MDD-tools are based on metamodeling, an inconsistent metamodel of a modeling construct makes its implementation practically impossible.

Thus, the concept of association encompasses an integral system of navigational and extensional modeling constructs. Its straightforward implementation in modern OO languages necessarily leads to assigning these constructs to different classes. The integrity of the concept is thus corrupted and needs to be recovered by an additional implementation of "synchronization" services. In other words, the concept of association cannot be implemented directly in languages like Java or C++, and needs special *design patterns*. Creating the latter is an issue and may be non-trivial as demonstrated in [1,16,14]. In addition, these works differ in their understanding of what associations and their properties are, and how to implement them. A part of this diversity is just normal: the same specification can be implemented in different ways. Yet another part is caused by the absence of precise semantics for the constructs and their subsequent different interpretations by the implementers. This latter part is substantial.

1.3   The Approach and Results

The problems above show the necessity of unambiguous and transparent semantics for associations formulated in independent mathematical terms. A step in this direction was made in [5] with emphasis on formal definitions and metamodeling for the general case of n-ary associations. In the present paper we continue this work towards practical applications and implementation rather then metamodeling, and focus on binary associations, which are most often appear in practice. Our basic assumption is that precise semantics of a modeling construct, if it is formulated in clear and understandable terms close to programming concepts, makes implementation a technical issue that can be delegated to practitioners. We formulate the following requirements for a mathematical framework to be useful for the task: (i) be expressive enough to capture all aspects of semantics of associations needed in applications; (ii) be abstract enough to avoid the danger of offering only "pictures of code" but simultaneously be understandable and transparent; (iii) be aligned/coordinated with the modeling concepts to facilitate continuity and cross-references between the models and the formalism; (iv) be aligned/coordinated with the programming concepts to facilitate continuity and cross-references between the formalism and the code.

In section 3 we present a formal framework, which we believe is sufficiently satisfactory w.r.t. these requirements, and in sections 4,5 we apply it to formalizing basic types of UML associations. The results of this work are collected in Tables 1,2 and Fig. 4. The left columns of the tables present UML constructs, and middle and right ones show their formal semantics; Fig. 4 is structured similarly. Since our formalism is graph-based and our formal specifications are also diagrams, comparison of formal and modeling constructs is transparent and comprehensible (requirement iii). On the other hand, the main building blocks of our formalism are sets and mappings, which are naturally expressible in terms of, say, generic interfaces of the Java Utility Package [4]; hence, requirement (iv) is satisfied. Conditions (i,ii) will be addressed in section 3.

Some rows of the Tables have their UML cell blank, which means that the corresponding real world situation (formally described in the middle and right cells) cannot be modeled in UML. Owing to computational completeness of programming languages, such situations can be coded but their adequate reverse engineering into UML is problematic. Moreover, as seen from the tables, these situations are quite natural for practical applications. The impossibility to model them adequately in UML contributes to the infamous phenomenon of *domain semantics hidden in the application code*. We propose a light modification of the UML toolbox for modeling associations, which nevertheless allows one to manage the issue. The new notational constructs are marked in the Tables by "Not UML!" tag. Thus, question or exclamation marks in our Tables mean problems of forward engineering – when they are in the middle or right columns, or reverse engineering – when they are in the left column. Forward and reverse engineering of qualified associations is thoroughly discussed in section 5; we also show that n-ary associations can be reduced to qualified ones.

2   Background and Relation to Other Works

Semantics for the concepts of relationship and aggregation and their database implementation is a well-known research issue that can be traced back to the pioneering works on data semantics by Abrial, Brodie, Chen and others in the 70s and early 80s (see [15] for a survey). Object-oriented modeling flourished a bit later and focused on navigation across relations, mainly binary ones; the corresponding construct was called association and had been widely used in OMT and other practical OOAD techniques [20]. The most significant of these practices were later catalogued, abstracted and standardized by OMG in the MOF/UML/OCL group of standards. The most essential contribution was made by UML2, in which a large system of constructs related to associations was defined [19, sect.7.3.44]. In addition to the main functionality of navigating between the classes, it comprises a lot of concepts like multiplicities and types of collections at the ends, ends' qualification and ownership, redefinition, subsetting, and more. These concepts may capture important aspects of semantics of the business/domain to be modeled, and in that case must be reflected in the design model and then accurately implemented. Accuracy in modeling and implementation of associations may be a critical issue, e.g., in designing real time or embedded systems, where using models is becoming increasingly popular [13,1]. Unfortunately, the standards provided neither a precise semantics nor even a consistent metamodel for the constructs [5,6].

In this paper we will use notation and terminology standardized by UML2, and when we write "the Standard", we mean the UML 2.1.1 Superstructure [19]. In UML2, ontological aspects of associations are specified by a special attribute "aggregationKind" and denoted by either a white diamond (proper aggregation) or a black diamond (composition). A detailed discussion can be found in [2]. These aspects of associations are beyond the goals of the present paper.

It has been noted and argued in [22,12] that actually two different notions of association, *static* and *dynamic*, are used in OOAD. The former is used for modeling structural relationships between classes, which are expressed by instance variables (attributes). The latter are channels over which messages can be sent; in UML2 they are specified in collaboration diagrams and do not influence the Association part of the metamodel. In this paper, we focus only on the static associations and their basic properties as they are defined in UML.

Semantics of associations in UML1.* and their usage had been discussed in [11]; a few works had focused on implementation in the context of forward [14] or reverse [16] engineering. These works became outdated after the acceptance of UML2, in which the technical aspects of the construct are essentially reworked. So far, the analysis of associations in UML2 has not gained much attention in the literature. The metamodel is analyzed in [5]. Paper [17] addresses the problem of heterogeneous collections at different association ends; our formal semantics allows us to build a transparent model of the issue and discover a useful implementation pattern that cannot be reverse engineered into UML. A recent paper [1] presents a detailed and careful discussion of how UML2 associations can be implemented in Java. However, they do not consider the extensional aspects of the concept, which we will show are crucial for its proper understanding and implementation. Particularly, we propose an entirely different semantics for qualified associations. We also propose a new semantics for unidirectional association with a multiplicity constraint at the opposite end.

3   Formal Semantics Framework

In this section we build our semantic framework. We begin with class diagrams and their semantics in terms of run-time instances. Then we abstract this description in mathematical terms and derive from it our formal framework for semantic interpretation.

3.1   Class Diagrams, Informally

Figure 2(a) presents a simple class diagram with a bi-directional association between classes *Company* and *Person*. The diagram says that run-time *Person*-objects have references *works* to (collections of) *Company*-objects, and the latter have references *employs* to (collections of) the former. Adornments near the association edge ends specify these collections in more detail. They say that, if C is a *Company* object, then the collection $C.employs$ is a non-empty bag; and for a *Person*-object P, $P.works$ is an arbitrary bag.

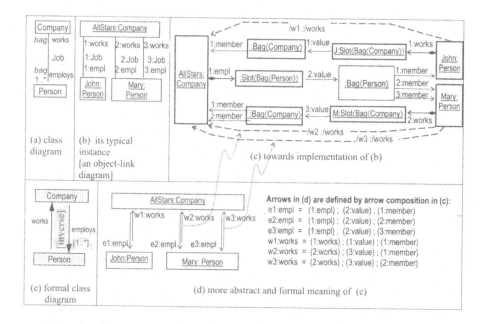

Fig. 2. Formal semantics for class diagrams: to be read consecutively (a)...(e)

Although collections are a technical issue, it is important for associations, and we need to consider briefly some details. For specifying types of collections, UML uses two Boolean attributes for association ends, *isUnique* and *isOrdered*. They provide four possible combinations of Boolean values: 11,10,01,00, which specify the following types of collections: *ordered set, set, list* and *bag* respectively (cf. [19, p.128]). To ease readability, we will directly write *bag* or *set* in our diagrams. Since the default values for *isUnique* is True and for *isOrdered* is False, UML considers an association end to be set-valued by default while a bag-valued end needs an explicit declaration *isUnique*=False. In the formal semantics framework developed below, the situation is inverted: being a bag-valued is a default assumption while being set-valued is a constraint. Indeed, a set is a particular case of bag, not the other way round. In this sense, UML's convention is a special *concrete syntax* for specifying the constraint of being a set.

The situation with ordering is more complicated. In fact, declaring an association end to be list-valued means that we implicitly deal with a qualified association (discussed later in section 5). An ordered set can be treated as a list without repeated elements, i.e., satisfying the *constraint* of Uniqueness.

3.2   Instances

A simple abstraction of a run-time configuration conforming to the model is presented in Fig. 2(b), where three objects are interrelated by three undirected edges or *links* (we write *empl* to save space). Objects are named "naturally" and typed by class names, ends of the links are named by numbers and typed by association end names. In the UML jargon, typing is often called *classifying* and classes and association ends are, respectively, *classifiers*; entities that are typed/classified are called *instances* of the respective classifiers.

In terms of information modeling, the diagram says that the company *AllStars* employs *John* and *Mary* with *Mary* counted twice (e.g., *Mary* can be employed at two different positions in the company). Correspondingly, *Mary* works for the company *AllStars* "two times". In a more implementation-oriented view, graph (b) shows objects holding references, but an object cannot hold multiple values in an instance variable slot. Rather, it holds a reference to a collection of values as shown by graph (c). For example, expression *AllStars.*(1:*empl*) refers to a memory cell, where a reference to a bag of *Person*-objects can be stored. In UML terms, *AllStars.*(1:*empl*) is a *slot*, whose contents is given by its *value*-attribute. Then expression *AllStars.*(1:*empl*).(2:*value*) denotes a bag of *Persons*. The latter can be implemented with Java generic collections [4]. Then setting a cursor (or Iterator, in Java terms) for this collection would list its three members with *Mary* counted twice. Similarly, attribute *works* of class *Person* is implemented by assigning slots of type *Bag⟨Company⟩* to *Person*-objects, for example, *J* and *M* in diagram (c). Slot assignment is done at compile time and does not change afterwards, and slots are not shared between objects, hence the black-diamond arrows. Value assignment is dynamic: a reasonable implementation is to consider that the same collection is changing its state.

Diagram (c) is built according to UML2 metamodel [19, Sect.7.2, Fig.7.8]. As is stressed by UML, it provides an abstract specification of the actual run-time configuration rather than its "mirror". For example, real addresses of slots depend on the order in which instance variables are defined inside classes (pointer arithmetic). Setting Iterator is also more complicated than it is shown in diagram (c). The latter thus presents a sufficiently abstract design model. However, for our further work it is useful to make it even more abstract and eliminate explicit presence of Collection objects in the model. To do this, we sequentially compose arrows in graph (c): (/w1:/works) = (1:works) ; (1:value) ; (1:member), (/w2:/works) = (2:works) ; (3:value) ; (1:member), and so on, where semicolon denotes composition and names of derived elements are prefixed by slash (UML's convention). That is, /w1,/w2,/w3 are derived directed links and /works is their common classifier – a virtual association end. What we really need for our further work is these derived links while the more detailed model and the way they are derived can be suppressed. The result is the graph in Fig. 2(d). It does not contain implementation details but it can be mapped to the implementation-oriented graph (c) augmented with derived elements: some elements of this map are shown in Fig. 2 by dotted "curly" lines (brown with a color display). We will term this and similar cases below by saying that model (d) is a *view* to model (c).

3.3   Formal Class Diagrams, I: Nodes, Arrows and Their Extension

Our next step is to collect the type/classifier names used in the instance graph (d) and organize them into a separate *type* graph as shown in Fig. 2(e) (ignore the label [**inverse**] for a moment). Nodes of this graph classify objects, and arrows classify directed links from the instance graph. Node rectangles are filled with dots to suggest that classes are populated with objects.

It is useful to invert our last passage from (d) to (e) and read it in the reverse direction from (e) to (d). We notice that each element E in graph (e) has an *extension* set $[\![E]\!]$: $[\![Company]\!] = \{AllStars\}$, $[\![Person]\!] = \{Mary, John\}$, $[\![works]\!] = \{w1,w2,w3\}$ and $[\![employs]\!] = \{e1,e2,e3\}$. Extensions of nodes are sets of objects, and extensions of arrows are sets of *labeled* directed pairs of objects. Labeling allows multiple occurrences of the same pair, i.e., extension of an arrow is a bag rather than a set of directed pairs. A collection of directed pairs is nothing but a (mathematical) *mapping* between the corresponding sets; more accurately, a *partially-defined multi-valued* mapping. We will designate such mappings with a black triangle head $f: X \blacktriangleright Y$, and keep the ordinary arrow head for a single-valued mapping $f: X \rightarrow Y$. By default, a multi-valued mappings is bag-valued because it corresponds to arbitrary instance graphs with multiple edges between the same nodes. Declaring a mapping to be set-valued is a constraint prohibiting duplication of edges in the instance graph. [2]

We will call graphs like (e) *formal class diagram* because their nodes correspond to classes and arrows to association ends, and at the same time have a formal meaning: nodes are sets and arrows are mappings. It can be specified by an *extension* (meta)map $[\![*]\!] : G \rightsquigarrow U$ with G the graph representing our formal diagram and U the graph specifying our semantic universe: its nodes are sets and arrows are partially-defined multi-valued mappings between them.

3.4   Formal Class Diagrams, II: Diagram Predicates

An important feature of the run-time instance graph (d) is that collections $[\![employs]\!]$ and $[\![works]\!]$ are isomorphic: they present the same set of object pairs traversed in the opposite directions. In this case we will say that the mappings are *co-extensional* or *inverse* (to each other). This feature is not a peculiarity of the particular instance (d) and must hold for *any* intended instance of the class diagram (e) as mappings *employs* and *works* present two opposite ends of the same association. Hence, we must add to our formal class diagram (e) a requirement that the arrows *employs* and *works* must have inverse extensions at any state of the system. In this case we call the arrows *inverse*.

Syntactically, we add to the graph (e) a formal expression, or *predicate declaration*, [inv](*employs*, *works*), where [inv] is a predicate name (abbreviating 'inverse') and *employs*,*works* are arguments. The semantics for this declaration is that we consider to be legal only those extension maps $[\![*]\!]$ of graph (e), which make mappings $[\![employs]\!]$ and $[\![works]\!]$ inverse. To respect this constraint at

---

[2] In the Java Utility Package, what we call a mapping $X \blacktriangleright Y$ would be specified by a generic interface `Map<X,Collection<Y>>`, where objects of the class `X` are called *keys* and respective collections are their *values*. The values are accessed by the method `get(X key)` of the return type `Collection<Y>` [4]. Note that Java uses the term "mapping" for an individual pair $[x, f.get(x)]$ rather than for the set of all such pairs when x ranges over $[\![X]\!]$ like we do.

any run-time moment, mutator methods (setters) must be synchronized and implemented with care, see [1] for details. Thus, the predicate declaration is an important part of the specification.

An important feature of predicates like [**inv**] is that their arguments must satisfy certain structural restrictions, e.g. for [**inv**], the two argument arrows must go between the same nodes in the opposite directions. In the paper we will see other such predicates and call them *diagram predicates*. For example, association end's multiplicity is also a diagram predicate, whose arity shape consists of a single arrow. A bit more formally, we begin with a signature Σ of diagram predicates, each is assigned with its *arity shape* graph. Then we may form Σ-*graphs*, i.e., graphs in which some diagrams are marked with predicates symbols from Σ so that the shape of the marked diagram matches the arity shape of the predicate (see [7, Appendix] and [9] for details). If Σ is clear from the context, we call Σ-graph merely *dp-graphs* with "dp" standing for "diagram predicate".

It is mathematically proven that formal set theories can be interpreted in the language of dp-graphs and, hence, any specification possessing a formal semantics can be modeled by dp-graphs [3]. It has an important consequence that not only associations but many modeling constructs can be formalized in the same uniform way [8,7].

4   Problems of Binary Associations

In this section we analyze semantics and propose implementation guidelines for the main use cases of binary associations. Results are presented in Table 1 for pure navigation and Table 2 for cases where extension is crucial. In both Tables, the left column presents typical UML class diagrams, the middle column shows their semantics in the framework of section 3 and the rightmost column presents typical instances of the diagrams. We will consecutively consider the rows in the tables.

4.1   Navigation: Is It That Simple? (Table 1)

Row 0: The baseline. The top row of Table 1 presents a very simple case: an unconstrained bi-directional association which we call the *baseline*. The class diagram shows the name Job of the association. Its counterpart in the formal diagram is an element "Job" framed with an oval. Formally, it is a name for the triple (*employs, works,* **inv**) and hence deletion of "Job" from the model implies deletion of its three components too. In UML jargon, "Job" is an object owning the elements of the triple and we use black-diamond ends of the corresponding meta-associations. Note that "Job" is not a classifier: its runtime "instances" are pairs of links, that is, a concept or a meta-construct rather than something really existing at run-time, see Fig. 2.

As discussed in the introduction, implementation of the baseline case requires accuracy to ensure synchronization of the ends' updates. It can be done in two different ways. One is to implement synchronized mutator methods for the attributes as suggested in [1]; care must be taken to avoid looping with mutual

Table 1. Back and forth between UML class diagrams and their semantics, I. (Color display would ease readability but a black-white version works too)

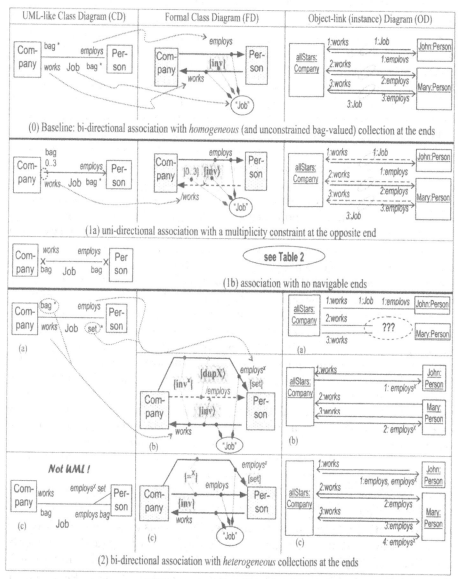

Legend for Formal Diagrams. **Classifiers:** Nodes are rectangles filled-in with dots. Arrows are a bit thicker than link-arrows. **Diagram predicates:** Names are [,]-bracketed (shaded by dark red). The arguments are shown by thin dotted lines. **Diagram operations:** Names are asymmetrically bracketed by [,⟩ (shaded by blue). The direction from the input to the output is shown by a dotted (blue) arrow. **Tuples (Object-containers):** Oval frame without filling and "quoted" names. The contents is shown by edges with black diamonds (composition); some of these edges are not shown to avoid clutter.

  Cross references between UML and formal diagrams are shown with dotted "curly" (brown) lines. Elements in UML diagrams modifying these mappings are circled.

synchronization. Another way is to implement an object "Job", which will manage access and updates of the mappings via communication with classes. We will call this approach to implementation *objectifying the association*.

Row 1a: Unidirectional association with a multiplicity constraint at the opposite end. Unexpectedly, implementation of this case is problematic. Respecting the multiplicity at the *works*-end seems to require that the end should be implemented as an invisible attribute of class *Person*. It means that class *Person* knows about class *Company*, which destroys decoupling between classes – one of the main goals of having unidirectional associations. In [1, pp.21-23], the problem is discussed in detail but seemingly without a good solution.

Let us consider semantics of the case. The Standard [19, Sect.7.3.3,p.42] says that for a given association, the set of its association ends is partitioned into *navigable* and *non-navigable* ends. The former are navigated efficiently while the latter are non-efficient or not navigable at all. This consideration is close to a well-known distinction between basic and derived data in databases. The former are stored in the database and hence are directly accessible; accessing the latter requires querying and hence computation. Some types of queries can be executed efficiently while others are not, yet data to be queried are not specified in the database schema and conceptually are quite distinct from basic data. The latter are immediately stored in the database and their access is always efficient. Thus, the distinction between navigable and non-navigable ends in UML is similar to the distinction between basic and derived data in SQL.

Formalization of this idea is shown in the middle diagram. By inverting the mapping *employs* (i.e., formally, by applying to it the operation **invert**), we come to a new derived mapping /*works* = [**inv**](*employs*) with [**inv**] standing for [**invert**]. Note asymmetry in the brackets to distinguish operations from predicates. Since mapping /*works* is derived from *employs*, the multiplicity constraint declared for it is, in fact, a constraint for the mapping *employs*.[3] Thus, what we need to do is to implement a specific constraint to mapping *employs*, which, in general, has nothing to do with attributes of class *Person*. The most immediate way to do this is to objectify the association by implementing an object "Job" that owns the mapping *employs*, computes its inverse and checks the multiplicity constraint. Class *Person* may know nothing about this, and the class coupling problem is thus resolved.

Row 1b: Both ends are non-navigable. This seems to be a meaningless idea (we are not aware of its discussion in the literature), yet the Standard explicitly allows such associations [19, Sect.7.3.3]. We analyze this case below in Sect. 4.2.

Row 2: Bi-directional association with heterogeneous collections at the ends. Suppose that one of the association ends, say, *employs*, is declared to be set-valued (*isUnique*=True in UML terms) while the opposite end is kept bag-valued, see UML diagram (a). It implies that in our UML-style instance diagram (a) (the upper rightmost in the row), we need to glue together the

---

[3] As a simple analogy, consider the following situation. Let X be a set of natural numbers and $S(X)$ denotes the sum of all members of X. When we say that $S(X)$ must be less than 100, it is a constraint to X rather than to $S(X)$.

duplicate ends 2:*employs* and 3:*employs*, but keep their opposite ends 2:*works* and 3:*works* separate. It cannot be done without destroying the structure of the graph (binary links cannot have three ends).

The problem generated a whole discussion in the UML community [18], which did not come to a certain conclusion. One solution is to consider associations with heterogenous collections at the ends illegal. However, it would prevent modeling many situations appearing in practice, see [17] for a detailed discussion. It appears that the problem is not in the heterogenous associations themselves but rather in an accurate formalization of their instance semantics.

A solution is again provided by considering operations and derived elements. The formal class diagram (b) shows three mappings: *works* and *employs* as before and, in addition, the duplicate eliminated version *employs*$^\times$ of mapping *employs* (the superscript reminds about duplicates crossed-out). This mapping is derived by applying operation **dupX** to *employs*. Now the inconsistent instance diagram (a) can be fixed as shown in diagram (b) below it. Mappings *works* and *employs*$^\times$ need not be co-extensional and the problem disappears.[4] We thus interpret the UML class diagram (a) as asserting that mapping *employs*$^\times$ rather than *employs* is to be implemented efficiently, and interpret the end *employs* by the formal mapping *employs*$^\times$. In other words, UML class diagram (a) amounts to a partial view to its fuller formal counterpart (b). This view is shown by "curly" dotted lines.

Note that in practical application we may need both mappings, *employs* and *employs*$^\times$, to be implemented efficiently. The corresponding formal diagram is shown in cell (c), where the predicate $=^\times$ declares mappings *employs* and *employs*$^\times$ to be equal up to duplicates. This situation (and code implementing it) cannot be modeled (reverse engineered) with UML. However, a slight addition to UML notation shown in the rightmost cell (c) fixes the problem.

4.2   Navigation and Extension (Table 2)

Table 2 presents our study of cases that involve extensional aspects of associations. These aspects are especially important for n-ary associations with $n \geq 3$ [6]. However, for binary associations too, there are several semantic phenomena missed from the literature and mistakenly treated in the Standard. The top row of Table 2 repeats the baseline case to ease references.

Rows 1,2: Association classes and non-navigable associations. UML class diagram in Row (1) presents a major association construct called Association Class. The Standard says [19, Sect.7.3.4 p.49]: "*An association may be refined to have its own set of features;[...]. The semantics of an association class is a combination of the semantics of an ordinary association and a class. [...]* the attributes of the association class and the ends of the association connected to the association class must all have distinct names. [...]. *It should be noted that in an instance of an association class, there is only one instance of the*

---

[4] Yet these mappings are still mutually inverse, hence label **inv**$^\times$ in the formal diagram.

Table 2. Back and forth between UML class diagrams and their semantics, II

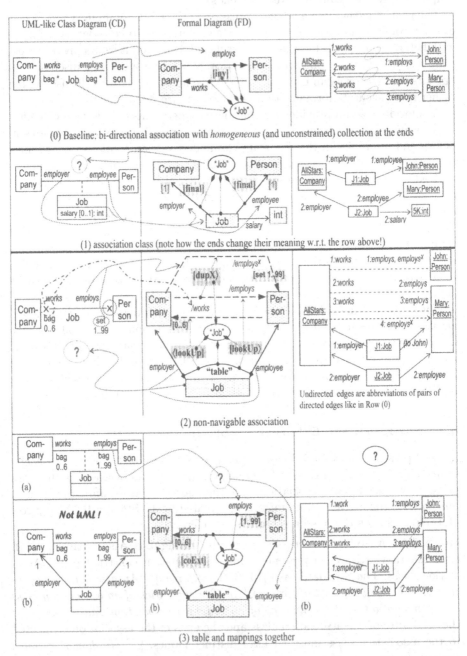

The legend is the same as in Table 1. The only new element is Semi-oval over class Job, which denotes the standard **"table"** container

associated classifiers at each end, i.e., from the instance viewpoint, the multi-plicity of the association ends are '1'. " For our case in Row 1, the non-italicized sentence in the quote says that the ends *employer* and *employee* are to be like attributes of class *Job*, which explains why duplication of names is prohibited. The next sentence says that a *Job*-instance is, in fact, a pair of instances, one from class *Company* and the other from class *Person*. Combination of these two requirements provides the formal diagram in the middle cell: class *Job* has two single-valued references *employer* and *employee* to classes *Company* and *Person*.

An important feature of the case is that defining attributes of the association class are immutable: if we have initialized object *J:Job* with values *J.employer = AllStars, J.employee = Mary* and *J.salary = 50K*, then only the value of *salary* can be changed later; changing *J.employee* from *Mary* to, say, *John* is impossible because it would change the link and hence the very object! Hence, we add to our formal diagram two more diagram predicate declarations **final**(*employer*) and **final**(*employee*) asserting immutability of the mappings.What we finally specified is a table *Job* with three columns (called also *projection mappings*), amongst which the pair (*employer, employee*) is considered as an immutable identifier. If an additional condition of disallowing duplicate values for pairs (*J.employer, J.employee*) holds, then the pair (*employer, employee*) would be exactly what is called the *primary key* to relation in the database theory.[5] Formally, we call a triple *T* = (*Job, employer, employee*) an *(association) table* if mappings *employer* and *employee* are totally defined, single-valued and immutable. From now on, we will designate such tables in our diagrams by a semi-oval with label "**table**".

Comparing Rows 0 and 1 shows that declaring an association to be a class changes the meaning of association ends. Making an association a class (in UML terms, *reifying* it) actually reifies its extension as a table and makes association ends projection mappings (columns) of this table rather than navigation mappings. However, interpreting association ends by projections does not mean that the old navigational mappings entirely vanished. By looking up the extension table in the two opposite directions, we can reconstruct the old mappings as it is shown by formal diagram in Row 2. Two labels [**lookUp**) denote two applications of the operation [**lookUp**) to the table, which produce mappings /*works* and /*employs*/ (we remind that slash-prefix denotes derived elements).Thus, our old association ends have reappeared but now as *derived* rather than *basic* elements. By our discussion of quote (Q1) p.11, it means that the old mappings are non-navigable as shown by UML diagram in Row 2. Now the multiplicity and collection-type constraints for non-navigable ends can be readily explained. For example, if a non-navigable end is declared to be set-valued (see UML diagram in Row 2), it means that we need to augment our formal diagram with one more derived element: the duplicate-eliminated version *employs*$^\times$ of the mapping *employs*. Thus, the UML diagram in Row 2 specifies a few constraints to a table, but the very table is not anyhow presented in the diagram! Besides conceptual

---

[5] In the earlier UML versions, this condition had indeed been assumed.

ambiguity, this notation does not define the names for the columns of the table and thus hinders cross-references between design and code.

Row 3: Navigation and extension together. The UML diagram (a) entirely conforms to the UML metamodel because any association can be declared to be a class. However, reifying an association as a class converts association ends into projection mappings (see Row 1) while having multiplicity constraint for the ends forces to interpret them navigationally. Semantics of the situation is clear and shown in formal and instance diagrams (b). However, mapping of the UML diagram (a) into the formal diagram (b) is ambiguous because we have two names for four mapppings.

On the other hand, it is an ordinary situation when both the extensional and the navigational components of association are required to be implemented efficiently, hence, be basic elements as specified by the formal diagram. We have a lot of redundancy in data representation, and the label **coExt** asserts that the following three sets must be equal: $\{(p,c) \mid p \in Person, c \in p.works\}$, $\{(p,c) \mid c \in Company, p \in c.employs\}$ and $\{(j.employee, j.employer) \mid j \in Job\}$. In other words, *Job* is the common graph of mappings *works* and *employs*. Though such situations are quite possible in practical applications and hence may be hidden in the application code, their reverse engineering into UML is problematic. To fix the gap, we propose the notational construct shown in row (3b) left. More generally, Figure 3 presents a modification of UML notation to manage the navigation-vs-extension issue.

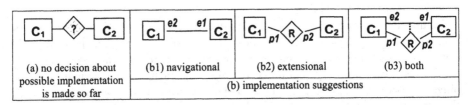

Fig. 3. Notational proposal

5   Qualified and *N*-ary Associations

Qualified associations are considered to be one of the most controversial constructs in the UML associations "package" [1]. Even simple unidirectional cases are rarely implemented in MDD-tools, let alone the bidirectional ones. The cause of the problems is that semantics of qualified associations is often misunderstood and their metamodel is essentially flawed [5,6]. The latter is due mainly to misunderstanding that a qualified association is merely a particular traversal of the corresponding ternary association and conversely, any ternary association determines a collection of mutually inverse qualified associations. The example shown in Fig. 1(c1,c2,d) is quite generic in this sense. Precise formal definitions (including the general case of *n*-ary association and its qualified counterparts with $(n-2)$-qualifiers) and the metamodel can be found in [5]. In the present paper we are interested in semantics and design patterns rather than in metamodeling.

The Standard distinguishes two cases of using the construct: the *general* and the *common* [19, Sect.7.3.44,p.129], which we will consecutively consider.

5.1 The General Case

A typical situation is shown in Fig. 1(c2), which says that a person at a given company can hold not more than two positions. That is, class *Person* has a getter method *holds* with a parameter *c* of type *Company*. What makes the case general (rather than *common* to be considered below) is that invocation *p.holds(c)* for an object *p:Person* returns a collection rather than a single *Position*-object. We can present the case as a binary multi-valued mapping *holds** : *Person* × *Company*→*Position*. The passages from *holds** to *holds* and conversely are well known in type theory and functional programming by names of *Currying* and *unCurrying* respectively. In its turn, the extension (graph) of mapping *holds** is a ternary relation over the participating classes. By choosing suitable names for the roles of this relation, we come to diagram (d) in Fig. 1. Note that according to Standard [19, p.42], multiplicities at the ends are, by definition, exactly those specified in qualified association diagrams Fig. 1(c1),(c2).

The ternary relation in Fig. 1(d) can be traversed in six different ways grouped in three pairs. For example, methods *holds:Person* → [*Company*→*Position*] at class *Person* Fig. 1(c2) and its counterpart *holds':Company* → [*Person*→*Position*] at class *Company*, give one such pair of traversals. Methods *employs: Company* → [*Position*→*Person*] Fig. 1(c1) and its counterpart *employs': Position* → [*Company*→*Person*] give another pair. With JavaGenerics, implementation of these qualified mappings is not more complicated than in cases considered above. Our analysis of binary associations above can be immediately generalized for multi-ary ($n \geq 3$) associations with qualified instead of ordinary ends.

5.2 The *Common* Case

This is the case when the multiplicity at the target end is 0..1 like in diagram (c1) in Fig. 1; it is repeated below in (1a) Fig. 4. If we collect all those pairs (*c:Company, p:Position*), for which *c.employs(p)* returns a single *Person*-value, into a set $X \subset$ *Company* × *Position*, then we will have a *totally defined single-valued* mapping **employs**: $X \to$ *Person*. Usually it means that the set X has a certain semantic significance and it makes sense to model it as a special new class. In our situation, such pairs can be considered as jobs, and we come to a formal class diagram (1b) in Fig. 4 (ignore the dashed derived arrows for a while). Predicate **key** in this diagram states that *Job*-objects are uniquely determined by pairs of values (*J.empler, J.pos*) ([7] provides formal details). Note that association end *employs* specified in the class diagram (1a) is nothing but a Curried version of mapping *emplee* in diagram (1b).[6]

Introducing a new class into the model for the common case of qualified associations makes sense for many practical situations where semantics is to be

---

[6] The multiplicity changes from [1] to [0..1] because not any pair (c, p) determines a job.

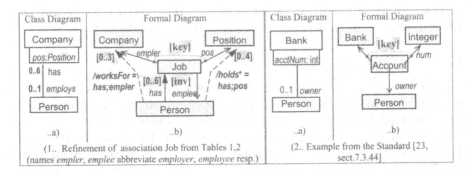

Fig. 4. The *common* case of using qualified associations. Non-shown multiplicities are exactly [1] by default.

explicated; diagrams (2a,b) in Fig. 4(2) present one more typical example. In fact, the issue is well-known in database design: in the relational language, a qualified association with multiplicity 1 is nothing but a so called *functional dependency*: $(empler, pos) \rightarrow emplee$ for the relation *Job*. Then remodeling diagram (1a) into diagram (1b) appears as a typical case of normalizing relational schemas according to functional dependencies. Thus, the common case of qualified associations actually encourages to model associations in a non-normalized way and to hide a semantically important class. It is not necessarily a "bad' design but the modeler should be aware of possible problems and recognize that diagram (1a) is only a partial view of semantics (1b).

5.3   Precise Modeling with Diagram Predicates and Operations

Formal diagrams like (1b,2b) in Fig. 4 not only accurately specify the mappings to which multiplicities in class diagram (1a,2a) refer, but allow specifying other important details of the situation. For example, to specify multiplicity of the end *worksFor* from diagram (a) in Fig. 1, we compose mappings *has* and *empler* and obtain a derived mapping $/worksFor(p.worksFor \stackrel{\text{def}}{=} \{J.empler \mid J \in p.has\}$ for a *Person*-object p), for which the required multiplicity can be declared. In addition, by inverting mapping */worksFor* we can augment our formal diagram with another derived mapping */employs*: *Company*→*Person*, and then map the entire diagram Fig. 1(a) to the augmented formal diagram. In this way **all** class diagrams in Fig. 1 can be presented as views to the formal diagram Fig. 4(1b) suitably augmented with derived elements (including Curried versions of binary mappings *emplee* and *pos*). This observation is crucial if we need to merge a few class diagrams without redundancy. None of the major MDD-tools addresses the issue.

Moreover, the same formal diagram can be used for specifying requirements beyond the class diagrams in Fig. 1. Suppose that despite the possibility of working for up to three companies, and of holding up to two positions at a company, a person is not allowed to have more than four positions in total. This multiplicity cannot be declared in either of diagrams in Fig. 1 yet it can be easily done with our formal diagram. To wit, by composing mappings *has* and *pos* we derive mapping */holds⁺* and declare it to be [0..4]-valued. Thus, our formal diagrams appear as a very flexible means of modeling associations and precise specifying their semantics as well.

6 Discussion and Conclusions

Ownership, Reification and Objectification. Cases presented in Tables 1,2 show that an ordinary binary association comprises six mappings: two projections (see p.349) and two navigable versions of each of the ends (bag-valued and set-valued). The UML2 metamodel calls mappings *properties*, and says that a binary association has two properties called its *ends*. Thus, the metamodel provides two names for six objects and hence a controversy is inevitable. For qualified associations, the situation is even worse.

An important aspect of this controversy is related to the infamous issue of association end *ownership*. In the earlier versions of the Standard, including UML 2.0, navigable ends have been considered to be owned by the classes implementing them while non-navigable ends were owned by the very association. This treatment confuses ownership with interpretation of association ends (either by navigation mappings between the classes or by projection mappings of the extension table). This confusion has not been identified in the literature and the issue has been repeatedly debated in the community. The latest version of the Standard, UML 2.1.1, has changed the formulation of ownership once again. Now ownership and navigability are declared to be entirely orthogonal concepts [19, sect. 7.3.3]. Because the extension table of an association is still neither specified in the metamodel nor explicated in the semantics sections of the Standard, the new treatment did not clarify the issue. Rather, it made it even worse by increasing the number of possible yet meaningless combinations of ownership and navigability.

The problem disappears in our semantic framework. Association ends are always owned by the association itself: if it is deleted from the model, the ends are also deleted even though they are implemented as members of the corresponding classes. In our formal diagrams, this is denoted by black-diamond meta-associations coming from the oval "Job"; the latter can be thought of as an object containing the ends. If the association is reified by the class *Job*, then the container object "Job" will contain the class *Job*! (see formal diagram in Table 2 Row 1). A part of UML's controversy around association is caused by confusing these two distinct concepts: the class *Job reifying* the association and the object "Job" *objectifying* it.

OO Programming vs. OO Modeling. Another side of the problem is a conceptual mismatch between OO modeling languages and OO programming languages. The former are usually diagrammatic and this is not just a syntactic sugar. Rather, the diagrammatic syntax of modeling languages follows their *diagrammatic logic* in the sense that a basic modeling unit, e.g., an association, is often an integral system of modeling elements, which consists of several nodes and edges; details and formal definitions of diagrammatic logic constructs can be found in [8,7,9]. Implementation of diagrammatic modeling constructs in a

OO framework requires their distribution over distinct classes. This causes synchronization problems, and the ownership controversy. We propose the following uniform and universal way of managing the issue. Irrespectively of the type of association, it can always be implemented by a special object, which (i) keeps track of all the components residing in distinct classes, (ii) manages their access and updates by communicating with the classes hosting (but not owning!) the components, and (iii) ensures synchronization and consistency w.r.t. the constraints declared in the model.

More technically, we propose to implement a generic (meta)class Association$\langle n \rangle$ with n the arity parameter. The members of this class are (i) mappings between the participating classes, (ii) the common extension table of these mappings (which is a class whose instance variables are projection mappings) and (iii) methods executing (diagram) operations discussed in the paper. Particularly, Association$\langle n \rangle$'s interface must include methods for Currying and unCurrying, projecting n-ary association to its m-ary, $m < n$, components and checking and maintaining the constraints. Implementation of this class as an Eclipse plug-in is planned for a future work.

Summary. Associations between classes are a major modeling concept in OOAD. Their essential feature is integrity: an association comprises a system of interrelated modeling elements. In contrast, implementation of associations in modern OO languages requires their elements to be distributed over distinct classes, which breaks the system into pieces. The integrity must then be recovered by implementing special synchronization means, which complicates the code. Implementation becomes even more intricate because of the interplay between basic (navigable) and derived (non-navigable) elements of associations.

A necessary prerequisite for addressing the problem is to have a clear semantic picture of what associations and their properties are. We have proposed a graph-based yet formal framework where these semantics can be built, and shown how naturally UML diagrams can be mapped into formal diagrams. This is the main contribution of the paper. It allowed us to explain semantics and implementation of a few controversial association constructs, e.g., unidirectional associations with multiplicities at the both ends, association without navigable ends, qualified associations. In addition, we have identified a number of patterns for using associations in practical applications, for which reverse engineering into UML is problematic. We have also suggested a universal pattern for implementing associations via their *objectification* and sketched the interface of the corresponding metaclass.

Acknowledgement. Thanks go to Bran Selic for many stimulating discussions of associations in general and their specification in UML2 in particular, and to anonymous referees for helpful suggestions. Financial support was provided by Bell Canada through the Bell University Labs, NSERC, and the Ontario Centres of Excellence.

References

1. Akehurst, D., Howells, G., Mcdonald-Maier, K.: Implementing associations: UML 2.0 to Java 5. Software and Systems Modeling 6, 3–35 (2007)
2. Barbier, F., Henderson-Sellers, B., Le Parc, A., Bruel, J.: Formalization of the whole-part relationship in UML. IEEE Trans. Software Eng. 29(5), 459–470 (2003)
3. Barr, M., Wells, C.: Category theory for computing science. PrenticeHall (1995)
4. Bracha, G.: Generics in Java programming language. Sun (2004), http://java.sun.com/j2se/1.5
5. Diskin, Z., Dingel, J.: Mappings, maps and tables: Towards formal semantics for associations in UML2. In: Nierstrasz, O., Whittle, J., Harel, D., Reggio, G. (eds.) MoDELS 2006. LNCS, vol. 4199. Springer, Heidelberg (2006)
6. Diskin, Z., Dingel, J.: Mappings, maps, atlases and tables: A formal semantics for associations in UML2. Technical Report CSRG-566, University of Toronto (2007), ftp://ftp.cs.toronto.edu/pub/reports/csri/566
7. Diskin, Z., Kadish, B.: Variable set semantics for keyed generalized sketches: Formal semantics for object identity and abstract syntax for conceptual modeling. Data & Knowledge Engineering 47, 1–59 (2003)
8. Diskin, Z., Kadish, B., Piessens, F., Johnson, M.: Universal arrow foundations for visual modeling. In: Anderson, M., Cheng, P., Haarslev, V. (eds.) Diagrams 2000. LNCS (LNAI), vol. 1889. Springer, Heidelberg (2000)
9. Diskin, Z., Wolter, U.: A diagrammatic logic for object-oriented visual modeling. ENTCS (to appear, 2008)
10. Erickson, J., Siau, K.: Theoretical and practical complexity of modeling methods. Communications of the ACM 50, 46–51 (2007)
11. France, R.: A problem-orineted analysis of basic UML static modeling concepts. In: ACM/SIGPLAN Conf. on Object-Oriented Programming, Systems, Languages, and Applications, ACM Press (1999)
12. Génova, G., Llorens, J., Fuentes, J.: UML associations: A structural and contextual view. J. of Object Technology 3(7) (2004)
13. Graf, S., Haugen, Ø., Ober, I., Selic, B.: Specification and validation of real time systems in UML. J.on Software Tools for Technology Transfer 8(2) (2006)
14. Guéhéneuc, Y., Albin-Amiot, H.: Recovering binary class relationships: Putting icing on the UML cake. In: ACM/SIGPLAN Conf.on Object-Oriented Programming, Systems, Languages, and Applications, ACM Press (2004)
15. Hull, R., King, R.: Semantic database modeling: Survey, applications and research issues. ACM Computing Surveys 19(3), 201–260 (1987)
16. Jackson, D., Waingold, A.: Lightweight extraction of object models from bytecode. IEEE Trans. Software Eng. 27(2), 156–169 (2001)
17. Milicev, D.: On the semantics of associations and association ends in uml. IEEE Trans. Software Eng. 33(4), 238–251 (2007)
18. OMG, E-Conference on UML2 Superstructure. Issue #5977 (2003), http://www.uml2-superstructure-ftpomg.org
19. OMG, Unified Modeling Language: Superstructure. Version 2.1.1 Formal/2007-02-03 (2007), http://www.omg.org/docs/formal
20. Rumbaugh, J., Blaha, M., Premerlani, W., Eddy, F., Lorensen, W.: Object-oriented modeling and design. Prentice-Hall (1991)
21. Selic, B.: Model-driven development: Its essence and opportunities. In: 9th IEEE Int. Symposium on Object-Oriented Real-Time Distributed Computing (2006)
22. Stevens, P.: On the interpretation of binary associations in the unified modeling language. Software and Systems Modeling 1(1) (2002)

On the Efficiency of Design Patterns Implemented in C# 3.0

Judith Bishop[1] and R. Nigel Horspool[2]

[1] Department of Computer Science, University of Pretoria, Pretoria, South Africa
jbishop@cs.up.ac.za
http://www.cs.up.ac.za/~jbishop
[2] Department of Computer Science, University of Victoria, Victoria, BC, Canada
nigelh@cs.uvic.ca
http://www.cs.uvic.ca/~nigelh

Abstract. From the very inception of design patterns, there was the anticipation that some of them would be superceded by new language features. Yet published implementations of classic patterns do not generally live up to this promise. The occurrence of generics, delegates, nested classes, reflection and built-in iteration is confined to a few patterns in a few published compendiums in a few languages. In this paper we trace the interplay between languages and patterns over the past decade and investigate how relevant language features really are for pattern implementation. We back our conclusions with a detailed look at the visitor pattern, examining the impact of C# developed in the past few years. We conclude that efficiency should play a large role in the choice of design pattern implementation, since some new features still bring with them runtime overheads.

Keywords: design patterns, efficiency, C# 3.0, visitor pattern, reflection, dynamic dispatch, delegates.

1 Introduction

Design patterns represent a layer of abstraction above that of programming language features. They are rapidly becoming a unit of discourse among software developers, and have transformed the way in which software is designed and discussed. The distance between design patterns and programming language features is, however, by no means constant. It varies between different languages, and more particularly within the same language as new features are introduced. Over the years, language design has evolved so that some patterns can be implemented almost directly. For example, the interface mechanism common in Java and C# almost dissolves the Template Method pattern. Not all patterns have benefited equally. Most implementations of the Visitor pattern still follow a complex structure of class and method interactions, made easier but not completely transparent, by advanced features such as generics and reflection.

These tensions are summarized in the diagram in Figure 1. We start with the full set of 23 patterns [11]. If a new language feature is included in an implementation of a pattern, it might have an effect on efficiency — for better or worse.

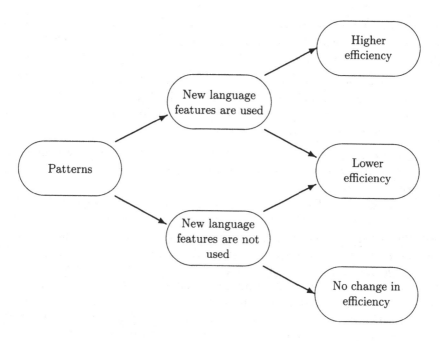

Fig. 1. The effect of language evolution on design pattern efficiency

It is this drop in efficiency that we wish to explore and quantify. An exhaustive study of all the patterns is underway: this paper is a starting point. It surveys and brings up to date the research on this issue over the past decade; it highlights certain patterns that are known to be responsive to language changes, and presents the results of experiments for one of the most complex patterns, the Visitor. An important contribution of the paper is the survey of methodologies used so far to match language features to patterns, thus enabling those in the higher efficiency group to be identified.

2   Relationship between Patterns and Languages

The abstraction level of languages rises constantly [4], having an inevitable effect on the way in which patterns are implemented. There is a movement towards leveraging the value of patterns by componentizing them in libraries. The background to these two movements, and their convergence, is now discussed.

2.1   Replacing Patterns by Features

Design patterns provide a high-level language of discourse for programmers to describe their systems and to discuss common problems and solutions. This language comprises the names of recognizable patterns and their elements. The proper and intelligent use of patterns guides developers into designing systems that conform to well-established prior practices, without stifling innovation.

The original group of patterns was implemented in the era of C++, with some tempering by Smalltalk [11] and reflected the capabilities of those languages, for good and bad. Indeed, Gamma states that

> If we assumed procedural languages, we might have included design patterns called "inheritance", "Encapsulation", and "Polymorphism". Similarly, some of our patterns are supported directly by less common object-oriented languages.

It was certainly not an aim of design patterns to force a certain way of coding, thus deprecating the value of new language features that could make design patterns significantly easier to express.

The debate over which language features these would be began a decade ago [3,12,1,6,7]. Java and more notably C# have added significant language features over the last decade. For example, C# 2.0, which was developed between 2002 and 2005, added generics, anonymous methods, iterators, partial and nullable types. C# 3.0, finalized in 2007, focuses on features that would bring the language closer to the data that pours out of databases, enabling its structure to be described and checked more accurately. These features included: implicit typing of local variables and arrays, anonymous types, object and array initializers, extension methods, lambda expressions and query expressions (LINQ).

Two studies that have looked at how to identify the patterns that would benefit from new language features, and thus would fall in the upper right part of Figure 1. Agerbo and Cornils [1] list reasons why it is important to divide patterns into the following classes:

- Language Dependent Design Patterns (LDDPs)
- Related Design Patterns (RDPs)
- Fundamental Design Patterns (FDPs)
- Library Design Patterns (LPDs)

The first category consists of patterns that are covered by a feature in one language, but not yet all. For example, the Factory Method aims to create objects whose exact classes are unknown until runtime. Using interfaces, which are common these days, the creator class can be bound at runtime. Similarly, the Chain of Responsibility pattern can make use of the delegate feature in languages such as C# and VB. Agerbo envisages that once the features supporting a pattern in the LDDP group become widely available across languages, the pattern essentially loses its status. It can then be removed from the pattern language of discourse. An advantage of this approach is that the number of patterns will stay within manageable proportions. The first column of Table 1 lists the patterns that Agerbo regarded as LDDPs.

RDPs are those that can be implemented using another pattern. The example quoted is the Observer pattern that can be implemented using the Mediator. Another common relationship is the Interpreter pattern which uses the Visitor [5]. The patterns that remain are then the fundamental ones, and according to this study they comprise the 11 shown in Table 2. Of course, we can immediately see that the list is dated, because Iterator and Memento, for example,

Table 1. Patterns supported by language features, the LDDPs of Agerbo and Cornils [1] and the cliches/idioms of Gil and Lorenz [12]

	LDDPs	*Cliches and idioms*
Chain of Responsibility	Delegates	
Command	Procedure classes	classes
Faade	Nested classes	encapsulation
Factory Method	Virtual classes	
Memento		persistence
Prototype	Pattern variables	Deep copy
Singleton	Singular objects	module
Template method	Complete block structure	overriding
Visitor	Multiple dispatch	Multi-methods

have been covered by advances in both Java and C# (iterators and serializable respectively). Nevertheless, the classification is a useful one because it can be applied to the burgeoning group of new patterns, not just to the original 23. We come back to Agerbo's LDPs under the Componentization section.

Gil and Lorenz [12] earlier attempted a similar classification. Their cliches and idioms could mimic features found in languages, whereas cadets are still

Table 2. Fundamental patterns identified as FDPs by Agerbo and Cornils [1] and as cadets by Gil and Lorenz [12]

	FDPs	*cadets*
Bridge	X	X
Builder	X	X
Composite	X	X
Decorator	X	X
Mediator	X	X
Proxy	X	X
State	X	X
Adapter		X
Chain of Responsibility		X
Interpreter		X
Observer		X
Strategy		X
Visitor		X
Abstract factory	X	
Flyweight	X	
Iterator	X	
Memento	X	
Total	11	13

candidates for language support. Their standpoint was that patterns, once identified as such, could and indeed should grow into language features. This group is shown in the second column of Table 1. At the time, the ones they identified as still requiring support are shown in Table 2.

Assessment. Both papers put forward the belief that the ultimate goal is that the patterns left in Table 2 should eventually develop into single language features or programming language paradigms. We do not fully agree with this standpoint for these reasons:

1. A feature is much more broadly applicable than just for one pattern. Delegates, for example, are used in Adapters, Mediators and Observers. We would be losing information if all these solutions were subverted under the term "delegate".
2. A pattern needs more than one prominent feature. The Visitor is an example here: the complexity of its design cannot be replaced by one single feature.
3. Patterns can have valid alternative implementations. The choice would be based on non-functional properties such as maintainability, traceability and most of all efficiency. One might be easier to understand, the other more efficient.

Thus every great programming idea cannot be turned into a realistic language feature, otherwise languages would explode. There will always be a place for design patterns.

Other work. In an in-depth but unpublished report that predates the above two, Baumgartner, Laüfer and Russo [3] make a call for features that will contribute to the implementation of design patterns, including (in modern parlance) interfaces, singleton variables, generics, metaclass objects, and multiple dispatch. In the ensuing years, language design has either realized the suggestions or has moved in other directions.

Bosch's work [6] concentrates on the reasons why languages should mimic design patterns, and gives several detailed examples in the context of a layered object model. His four point check list — traceability, the self problem, reusability and implementation overhead — is still valid today, but the contribution of his solutions is dimmed by being couched in terms of an object modeling language LayOM. The solutions presented address the first three points, but little mention is made of improvements in implementation overhead.

Subsequently, Chambers [7] examined the influence of the experimental languages of the day (Cecil, Dylan and Self) and looked ahead to first-class generic functions, multiple dispatching and a flexible polymorphic type system, all of which are once again in mainstream languages now.

2.2 Libraries of Design Patterns

The traceability problem mentioned by [6] can be addressed by implementing patterns as library components. When using such an LDP [1] it will be possible to trace from which design pattern the implementation ideas come. Arnout and Meyer [15] are keener on the benefits to be reaped by reuse of pattern implementations. Having analyzed the standard patterns, they conclude that fully two-thirds admit of a componentized replacement, enabling developers to rely on an API from a pattern library rather than re-implementing the pattern. However, achieving this level of re-use relies on some high level language features present in Eiffel, including genericity, agents, tuples, design by contract and multiple inheritance. Agerbo [1] reports being able to make library routines for 10 of the 23 patterns (43%) using, in particular, generics, virtual classes and nested classes.

There is some disagreement over the efficiency of this approach. Very early on, Frick *et al.* [9] highlighted the tension that exists between flexibility of a robust library and the efficient implementation of a class or method. Agerbo [1] reports that applying a design pattern from a library reduces the implementation overhead, whereas Arnout and Meyer present mixed results: the Abstract Factory pattern is report as having no overhead in the library implementation [2] but the Visitor pattern suffers a 40% degradation [15]. However, the Visitor pattern has long been known as sensitive to tinkering [17] and the library orientation might not be the only cause for the drop in performance. (We return to this theme later.) Another study [10] looks at a library version of the Strategy pattern, specifically aimed at embedded code. The concern is that virtual method calls that are key to this pattern really slow down execution. The solution proposed is to generate compile-time generated and optimized code, and the results show an improvement in both code size and speed.

The major effort in library support has now switched to the use of aspects with design patterns. Hannemann and Kiczales [14] were able to make routines for 12 patterns (52%). The paper presents results for the locality, reusability, composition transparency and (un) pluggability of the AspectJ versions of patterns. The benefits of localising patterns as aspects are the inherent code comprehensibility, better documentation and the potential for composability. It is worthwhile noting that these are very much the same benefits that are claimed for using higher-level language features.

3   The Impact of C# 3.0

The reader will have noticed that the majority of references in the previous section are to studies done in the late nineties (the exception being the work of Arnout and Meyer with Eiffel [2]), when C++, Java and the usual host of experimental languages were the prime contenders for pattern implementation. We choose to examine the impact of features in C# 3.0, a commercial object-oriented language, 10 years on.

3.1   Features in C#

C# 1.0, announced with the first .NET release in 2000 made significant advances over Java, shown in Table 3. C# 2.0 added five important features in 2005, especially generics, which had been available in some implementations for two years.

Table 3. The development of C#

C# 1.0 (2002)	C# 2.0 (2005)	C# 3.0 (2007)
structs properties foreach loops autoboxing delegates and events indexers operator overloading enumerated types with IO in, out and ref parameters formatted output	generics anonymous methods iterators partial types nullable types generic delegates	implicit typing anonymous types object and array initializers extension methods lambda expressions query expressions (LINQ)
API Serializable Reflection	standard generic delegates	

C# 3.0, finalized in 2006, focused on features that would bring the language closer to the needs of databases and has a distinct functional feel about it [16].

It is still open territory as to whether, and how, these new language features should be used in implementing design patterns. In books and writings on web sites the pull of custom is very strong. Because implementations of the patterns were originally given in C++ and Smalltalk, which have their own particular object-oriented styles, the translations into other languages have not always been completely satisfactory. It is a challenge to make the most of a language, while at the same time retaining the link with the design pattern and its terminology. Although design patterns do not force a certain way of coding, a look at the expository examples in most Java or C# books will show little deviation from the C++ style of the 1990s. It would seem that the promise of language features making patterns easier to implement has been slow to realize. The features are there now, and it is a question of showing how they can be used, and in assessing their efficiency. Not all the features listed in Table 3 are directly relevant for patterns, but a surprising number are.

3.2   Pattern Implementation in C#

We now present the results of two complete implementations of the patterns, from DoFactory [8] and Bishop [5].

DoFactory is a commercial organization that sells frameworks of patterns in C# and Visual Basic. They are widely consulted. Each pattern comes in three versions, known as Structural (not to be confused with structural as a pattern group), RealWorld and NETOptimized. The first version usually follows a direct implementation of the classic UML diagrams from Gamma *et al.* [11]. The RealWorld version expands the Structural implementation into a longer example where the names of classes reflect an actual scenario. Both these versions use

Table 4. Advanced C# features in design patterns: x indicates DoFactory's NETOptimized implementations, y indicates Bishop's set

	delegate/event	generics	iterator	nested class	Serializable	Reflection	extension methods	query expressions
Adapter	y							
Command	y							
Mediator	y							
Chain	x	x						
Observer	x y	x						
Abstract Factory		y						
Composite		x y						
Iterator			x y					y
Proxy				x y				
Singleton				x y				
Memento					x y			
Prototype					x y			
Visitor						x		
Bridge							y	

very little in the way of new language features, sticking to inheritance and interfaces for expressing the relationships between classes — essentially representing object-orientation at the Java or C++ level. Where it is very difficult to implement a pattern at this level in a short example (for example, deep copy in the Prototype pattern), the functionality is left out. A NETOptimized solution is a rework of the RealWorld version, using as many C# 2.0 features as are fitting. Since the programs have not been updated since 2006, they do not include any features new to C# 3.0.

The implementations in Bishop [5] had the specific aim of exploring new language features. They also come in two versions, known as the Theory code and Example code. The Theory code is similar in length and intent to the Structural versions from DoFactory, and presents a minimalist version of each pattern, in which the essential elements can be seen in stark relief. The Examples add flesh to the pattern, and in many cases use more or slightly different features as a result.

Table 4 itemizes those pattern implementations in DoFactory's NETOptimized and Bishop's Example sets that use advanced C# features. The patterns are sorted according to features used, from the left. Those patterns that are omitted — Builder, Decorator, Factory Method, State, Strategy, Interpreter, Faade, Template Method, Flyweight — did not use any of the mentioned features in either implementation.

All of the pattern implementations (both those mentioned in Table 4 and the rest) make use of normal OOPS features such as inheritance, overriding, composition, access modifiers and namespaces, as well as other C# features such as properties, indexers, structs and (in the case of the Bishop set) object and array initializers. Consider now what Table 4 reveals.

1. Delegates, generics, iterators and nested classes are the language features that are exercised by 10 of the patterns.
2. The .NET features of Serializable and Reflection are used by three patterns.
3. The C# 3.0 features of extension methods and query expressions make an appearance in two patterns.

¿From this list, we can extract various pattern-feature pairs for investigation in terms of efficiency. In particular, those patterns that are already using a feature in one set of implementations, but not the other, are excellent candidates. For example, we can consider delegates in the Adapter pattern or query expressions (LINQ) in the Iterator pattern. The next section presents several implementations of the Visitor patern taken from these sources and others, and compares them for efficiency.

4   Experimenting with the Visitor Pattern

The Visitor pattern defines and performs new operations on all the elements of an existing structure, without altering its classes. The pattern has two distinct parts: there are the classes that make up an object structure, and then there are the operations that will be applied to the objects in the structure. The complexity of the Visitor is enhanced by the fact that the object structure is usually assumed to have a variety of classes (often hierarchical) and different visit operations will be applicable for each type. There can also be different visitors, potentially traversing around the structure at the same time. Thus the language features required for its implementation revolve around type matching at runtime to find the correct Visit method.

There have been numerous studies of the Visitor pattern over the years, some of which are mentioned in Section 2.2 [17] [15]. What we present here is a fresh look at the pattern with four implementations, two of which make use of the features in Table 4 and two of which stick to ordinary OOP features.

While our prime aim is to reveal the efficiency of implementations that make use of different language features, we need to balance these results against the other non-functional requirements mentioned in Section 2: readability, writeability, maintainability and traceability. We introduce these, as we describe the four implementations.

4.1   Double Dispatch

The classic technique for implementing the Visitor pattern follows three steps. Each data type is made visitor-ready by adding an identical Accept method:

```
public override void Accept(IVisitor visitor) {
    visitor.Visit(this);
}
```

Then there is an interface that lists a version of `Visit` for every possible data type. When a data type is added, the interface has to be amended.

```
interface IVisitor {
    void Visit (Element element);
    void Visit (ElementWithLink element);
}
```

The content of the visiting code is in methods all called `Visit`, defined for each data type in the structure. The content of the methods is part of the application, not the pattern.

Once that is all in place, the method that traverses the data structure can call `Accept` on objects of structure and dynamic binding will ensure that the correct `Accept` and the correct `Visit` method is invoked. This is the double dispatch mechanism. A simple program would be:

```
public void CountElements(Element element) {
    element.Accept(this);
    if (element.Link!=null) CountElements(element.Link);
    if (element.Next!=null) CountElements(element.Next);
}
```

The effort required to set up this scaffolding for double dispatch is quite daunting, and works against all the goals of traceability, readability, writability and maintainability [6]. The type matching is done at runtime, but directly through the virtual method tables kept for each object. Its advantage therefore is that there is very little hidden overhead.

4.2   Reflection

A completely different implementation is to let the runtime system search for the type, using the metadata available through reflection. The Visitor includes the following standard dictionary and method:

```
static Dictionary<Type, MethodInfo> methods =
                new Dictionary<Type, MethodInfo>();

public override void Visit(Element x) {
    Type type = x.GetType();
    if (!methods.ContainsKey(type)) {
        Type[] types = { type };
        methods[type] = this.GetType().GetMethod("Visit", types);
    }
}
```

```
if (methods[type] != null)
    methods[type].Invoke(this, new object[] { x });
else
    throw new Exception("no Visit method found");
}
```

This **Visit** method takes it upon itself to find out which of the actual **Visit** methods need to be called. It searches through the metadata available regarding the signatures of the methods called **Visit**. This version is an improvement over than in the Dofactory, in that it caches the method reference once found, and will not go through the look up process again. The cache is a generic Dictionary indexed by the type of x.

The reflection implementation is non-invasive to both the data structure and the Visitor. However, reflection is expensive and the approach suffers from a severe speed overhead.

The use of reflection to implement the Visitor pattern was previously investigated by Palsberg and Jay [18], among others. Their solution encapsulated the reflection inside a library class which they called the Walkabout. A recent advance over the Walkabout by Grothoff [13] is the Runabout class. It generates bytecode at run-time to make the execution much faster — only about 2 to 10 times slower than double-dispatch once the overhead of creating the bytecode has been incurred.

4.3   Type Testing

A variation on double-dispatch which avoids invading the data structure is type testing (also called an extrinsic visitor [17]). The choice of the correct **Visit** method is done by a sequence of if statements in the application itself. Using the same program as before, the application's method will be:

```
public void CountElements(Element element) {
    if (element is ElementWithLink)
        Visit(element as ElementWithLink); else
    if (element is Element)
        Visit(element as Element);
    if (element.Link!=null) CountElements(element.Link);
    if (element.Next!=null) CountElements(element.Next);
}
```

Here it is the application that is polluted with details pertaining to the data structure. If the number of data types is large, and if the data structure is to be visited from more than one place in the application, this type testing can become tedious to write and maintain. A variation of this approach is to go back into the data types and have them maintain a class ID that can be used in a switch statement, somewhat faster than cascading if statements [17].

4.4   Delegates

Finally, we investigated the place of delegates in this pattern. Using a delegate, we don't have to pass the Visitor instance as a parameter into the data objects — the delegate contains a binding to both the Visitor instance and the method inside that instance. Then we replace a virtual dispatch v.Visit with a delegate call.

In each type in the data structure we add the following delegate and property:

```
public static VisitorDelegate vd;
public override VisitorDelegate VD { get {return vd;}}
```

Unfortunately, we cannot use the neat automatic property of C# 3.0 (where the get and set actions are generated by the compiler) because the property is overriding the property in the base type, and also giving access to a static field. The two unfortunately don't mix.

At the start of the Visitor, the delegates are set up, as in:

```
Element.vd = TallyFunction;
ElementWithLink.vd = delegate (Elements e) {
    Console.WriteLine("not counted");
};
```

where TallyFunction is a method of the Visitor class which visits an instance of type Element.

The advantage of the delegate method in terms of writeability is that the Visit methods can have different names, i.e. they do not all have to be called Visit, and also trivial visit functionality does not need a method at all: it can be expressed as an anonymous function. The above example shows both options. Thus, when using delegates, one can tailor one's code more to the real visiting, and not make it so stylised.

4.5   Results

We evaluate the Visitor implementations in two ways: for efficiency and for the non-functional properties.

In our experiments, the data structure being visited is a tree where there are N choices of the data type for a non-leaf node and L choices for the data type of a leaf node. All non-leaf nodes have two children. The tree was generated as a balanced tree of depth 10 in every case (so the tree contains 1023 nodes in total), where the data types of the nodes were selected randomly from the possible choices.

All times in Table 5 are reported as ticks per visited node, where one tick is equal to 100 nanoseconds. The times are measured over 100 traversals of the tree on an Intel Core 2 Duo running at 2.67GHz. Each visit method performs minimal work — just incrementing a counter. If visit methods did some real work (or performed I/O) then the timing differences would be obscured. In order to eliminate JIT effects from the timings, the test program performs one traversal

Table 5. Visitor pattern timings

Tree Classes			Visitor Implementation			
N	L	N+L	DD	TT	DE	RC
1	1	2	10	19	11	3791
2	1	3	10	23	12	3782
2	2	4	10	24	11	3809
3	2	5	11	30	13	3748
4	2	6	12	36	13	3852
4	3	7	14	39	16	3832
5	3	8	15	43	16	3784

N = Number of non-leaf classes
L = Number of leaf classes
DD = Double-dispatch implementation of visitor
TT = Sequence of type-tests to select visitor method
DE = Delegates to select visitor method
RC = Reflection with a cache to select visitor method

Times measured as ticks per node; 1 tick = 100 ns

of the data structure before starting the clock. All invoked methods are therefore JIT'ed in advance.

Both the double-dispatch and the delegate approach perform well. As long as the number of classes in the data structure is reasonable (say in the tens or twenties), the sequence of type-tests approach is probably good enough. (It should be noted that the is test is not necessarily fast.) However the implementation of reflection is comparatively so expensive that it should probably not be advocated either for large structures or for time critical applications.

The non-functional properties are a combination of the factors listed in Table 6.

In terms of non-functional properties, the reflection cached approach is a clear winner as it can add a visitor framework onto existing code. However, if building from scratch, the delegate version has much to recommend it, in that it is sensitive to the real code of the Visitor, in terms of naming and structure. The double-dispatch version, on the other hand, imposes a regimen of Accept and Visit methods, including the names.

We can also extend the Delegate implementation to handle multiple kinds of Visitor. Add a static list of delegates in each data structure class. Then each Visitor, when constructed, takes the next slot in each visitee class's array to fill in the delegate reference and remembers the index of that slot. The VD property in each data structure class becomes:

```
public static List <VisitorDelegate> vd;
public override VisitorDelegate VD (int slot)
   {get {return vd[slot];}}
```

Table 6. Visitor method implementation comparison

	Double Dispatch	Type Test	Delegates	Reflection Cached
Invasive of the data structure	Yes — add a standard method	No	Yes — add a delegate and property	No
Invasive of the Visitor	Interface listing a `Visit` method for each type	Only the type tests, embedded in the Visitor code	Delegate initialization in the constructor	Single standard `Visit` method containing a reflective test
Constraining the visitor	A `Visit` method must exist for each type	No — visit methods can have any name and be omitted	No — Visit methods can have any name and be omitted	All methods must be called `Visit`, but can be omitted
Main Disadvantage	Unnecessary empty `Visit` methods	Type tests might need to be repeated in the Visitor code	Cannot easily have two Visitors running together	Significant hidden overhead due to use of reflection
Main Advantage	No hidden overhead	Integrated with Visitor code	Works with the Visitor code to be efficient	Almost transparent to Visitor and data structure

There will be a small performance hit with the generalized approach because of the cost of passing the extra parameter and of indexing the delegates list. However, the changes are standard throughout the methods.

5   Conclusions and Future Work

This is the first time that a comparative study of patterns aimed at non-functional attributes has been made, and it brings up to date the work that was started more a decade ago. We have surveyed the various approaches to identifying the patterns that are amenable to new language features, and then tested how this is progressing in 2008 by using two sets of available pattern implementations. Homing in on one of the complex patterns, the Visitor, we conclude that new features such as delegates, generics and properties, when used together, can make for a readable implementation which has an acceptable efficiency overhead (the DE or delegates implementation).

In work ongoing we are examining the other patterns in the same way, and producing a bank of results. One problem we face is in isolating a testbed for a pattern, since some of them simply do not work well unless there is a real world harness in place. We shall therefore look at how patterns are used and position our experiments both in an image of the real world, and in an abstract environment.

Acknowledgements. Our thanks to Pierre-Henri Kuaté who ran the programs to obtain the results, and to him, Rhodes Brown and Stefan Gruner for helpful discussions. This work was supported by grants from the National Research Foundation of South Africa and the Natural Sciences and Engineering Research Council of Canada.

References

1. Agerbo, E., Cornils, A.: How to Preserve the Benefits of Design Patterns. In: Proc. OOPLSA, pp. 134–143 (1998)
2. Arnout, K., Meyer, B.: Pattern Componentization: the Factory Example. Innovations in Systems and Software Technology: A NASA Journal 2(2), 65–79 (2006)
3. Baumgartner, G., Läufer, K., Russo, V.F.: On the interaction of object-oriented design patterns and programming languages. Technical Report CSR-TR-96-020, Purdue University (1996)
4. Bishop, J.: Language features meet design patterns: raising the abstraction bar. In: Workshop on the Role of Abstraction in Software Engineering (ROA 2008), co-located with ICSE (to appear, 2008)
5. Bishop, J.: C# 3.0 Design Patterns. O'Reilly Media, Sebastapol (2008)
6. Bosch, J.: Design Patterns as Language Constructs. Journal of Object-Oriented Programming 11(2), 18–32 (1998)
7. Chambers, C., Harrison, W., Vlissides, J.: A Debate on Language and Tool Support for Design Patterns. In: Proc. 27th ACM SIGPLAN-SIGACT Symposium on Principles of Programming Languages, pp. 277–289 (2000)
8. Data and Object Factory, Design Pattern Framework: C# Edition (2006), http://www.dofactory.com/Default.aspx
9. Frick, A., Zimmer, W., Zimmermann, W.: On the Design of Reliable Libraries. In: Proc. of TOOLS 17, pp. 13–23 (1995)
10. Friedrich, M., Papajewski, H., Schröder-Preikschat, W., Spinczyk, O., Spinczyk, U.: Efficient Object-Oriented Software with Design Patterns. In: Czarnecki, K., Eisenecker, U.W. (eds.) GCSE 1999. LNCS, vol. 1799, pp. 79–90. Springer, Heidelberg (2000)
11. Gamma, E., Helm, R., Johnson, R., Vlissides, J.: Design Patterns: Elements of Reusable Object-Oriented Software. Addison-Wesley, Boston (1995)
12. Gil, J., Lorenz, D.: Design Patterns vs Language Design. In: Proc. of Workshop on Language Support for Design Patterns and Object-Oriented Frameworks (LSDF), pp. 108–111 (1997)

13. Grothoff, A.: The Runabout. Software: Practice and Experience (to appear, 2008)
14. Hannemann, J., Kiczales, G.: Design Pattern Implementation in Java and AspectJ. In: Proc. of OOPSLA, pp. 161–173 (2002)
15. Meyer, B., Arnout, K.: Componentization: the Visitor Example. Computer 39(7), 23–30 (2006)
16. Microsoft Corporation: C# 3.0 Reference Documentation, http://msdn2.microsoft.com/vcsharp
17. Nordberg III, M.E.: Variations on the Visitor Pattern. In: Proc. of Workshop on Pattern Languages of Programming (PLoP) (1996)
18. Palsberg, J., Jay, C.B.: The essence of the Visitor Pattern. In: Proc. 22nd IEEE Int. Computer Software and Applications Conf (COMPSAC), pp. 9–15 (1998)

A Framework for Model Transformation By-Example: Concepts and Tool Support*

Michael Strommer and Manuel Wimmer

Business Informatics Group
Institute for Software and Interactive Systems
Vienna University of Technology, Austria
{strommer,wimmer}@big.tuwien.ac.at

Abstract. Model-Driven Engineering is on its way to become the new software development paradigm, where model transformations are considered as a key technology to close the gap between specification and implementation. Several model transformation approaches and corresponding languages have been developed in the past years. Most of these approaches are metamodel-based, thus require knowledge of implementation details of modeling languages, which in contrast is not necessary for defining domain models in their concrete syntax. Therefore, Model Transformation By-Example (MTBE) approaches have been proposed for defining mappings between domain models from which model transformations are derived. However, until today no tool support for MTBE has been developed.

The contribution of this paper is the presentation of MTBE concepts necessary for deriving general model transformations based on metamodels from user-defined mappings between example models. More specifically, we describe a model mapping language and a metamodel mapping language, as well as reasoning algorithms to infer metamodel mappings from model mappings. Furthermore, we report on how MTBE concepts have been integrated into existing state-of-the-art graphical modeling and model transformation frameworks and give a critical discussion based on a case study.

Keywords: model transformation, mapping language, GMF, concrete syntax.

1 Introduction

As Model-Driven Engineering (MDE) gains importance in the process of software engineering, more advanced techniques for the management of modeling artifacts are required. A key technique for automatic management of modeling artifacts are model transformations [11]. Several model transformation approaches and languages [3] have been proposed in the past six years. Recently,

---

* This work has been partly funded by the Austrian Federal Ministry of Transport, Innovation and Technology (BMVIT) and FFG under grant FIT-IT-810806.0.

R.F. Paige and B. Meyer (Eds.): TOOLS EUROPE 2008, LNBIP 11, pp. 372–391, 2008.

two example-based approaches for developing model transformations have been proposed [14,16], which are called *Model Transformation By-Example* (MTBE), and are based on previous by-example approaches such as programming by-example [12] and query by-example [17]. Both MTBE approaches make use of user-defined mappings between example models to derive general model transformations based on metamodels. Hence, both approaches try to lift the difficult and complex task of developing model transformations on a more user friendly level. However, the two proposed approaches differ in that our approach [16] allows the user to define mappings between example models shown in their graphical notation which he/she is familiar with. This allows us to take into account the already defined mapping between abstract syntax (AS) and concrete syntax (CS) of the modeling language. Such a mapping may include constraints how elements from the abstract syntax (defined in the metamodel) are related to the concrete syntax, which can be reused in model transformations.

The first proposals for MTBE have outlined a by-example generation process of model transformations using simple *one-to-one* correspondences for mappings between example models, only. Furthermore, there is no prototypical implementation available to evaluate whether current MTBE approaches provide enough concepts for deriving more complex model transformations. In particular, when MTBE is applied in practice, model mappings going beyond simple *one-to-one* correspondences are necessary to derive complex model transformations. Hence, the creation and refinement of concepts is needed for defining more expressive mappings between models and between metamodels, as well as for deriving general metamodel mappings from specific model mappings. Finally, they have to be implemented in existing graphical modeling environments and model transformation frameworks in order to be evaluated.

In this work, we elaborate on necessary concepts for applying MTBE in practice. More specifically, first, we present a language for defining mappings between models shown in their concrete syntax going beyond simple one-to-one correspondences. Second, we provide a language for describing full equivalence and conditional equivalence mappings between metamodels. Third, we propose reasoning algorithms, which take mappings between example models as input and generate mappings between metamodels as output, i.e., algorithms for inferring general cases from specific cases. Finally, we present how these concepts have been incorporated into existing graphical modeling environments and transformation frameworks available in the Eclipse platform.

The benefit of this work is threefold. First, an implementation of MTBE concepts allows the validation and evaluation of current MTBE techniques. Second, an extendable prototype implementation allows experimentation with mapping languages and reasoning algorithms. Third, by integrating MTBE in state-of-the-art technologies, users can stay in their familiar modeling environments. This means that users can at least apply MTBE in a first step to generate an initial model transformation, which can be completed with techniques the user is familiar with.

2   MTBE at a Glance

This section discusses first the motivation for MTBE is presented and subsequently an overview of our proposed process for generating model transformations by-example is given. For an in-depth discussion of MTBE we kindly refer the interested reader to [16].

2.1   Motivation

Our MTBE approach is primarily motivated by shortcomings of current model transformation approaches. Most of these approaches lack a user-friendly and intuitive definition of model transformations. To ease the way for a more user-friendly procedure, we identified two main issues. The first issue is the gap between the way a user recognizes models and the way a computer processes models. When a user reasons about models, he/she usually does so in terms of CS elements. The computer on the other hand needs a model to be represented in AS. When it comes down to define model transformations, current transformation languages allow only the definition of model transformations based on the AS. This controversy is illustrated in Figure 1.

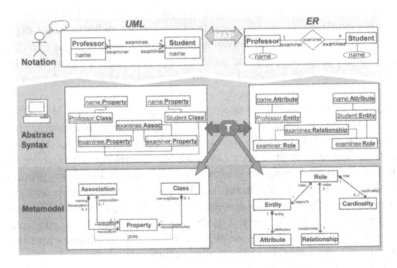

Fig. 1. Motivating MTBE

The second issue deals with the problem that in metamodels not necessarily all modeling concepts are represented as first-class citizens. Instead, concepts are frequently hidden in attributes, association ends or enumerations. We call this phenomenon concept hiding, which we introduced in [9]. As an example for concept hiding consider an instance of the class *Property* of the UML metamodel shown in Figure 1, that can either be an *attribute* or a *role* regarding to the setting of values and links. However, in the CS, the concepts *attribute* and *role* have a distinct representation. Thus, sometimes it is easier for the user to define model transformations on the model layer than on the metamodel layer.

2.2 MTBE Process

This subsection explains our model transformation generation process, which now consists of five steps in contrast to the three steps proposed in our previous work [16].

- **Step 1.** The initial step is the definition of models of the same problem domain in both modeling languages. The requirements on the models are twofold. First, concerning correctness, the models certainly have to conform to their metamodels. Second, concerning completeness, all available modeling concepts of the modeling languages should be covered by the models. The second issue is closely related to the question of what appropriate test cases for model transformations are, which is e.g. discussed in [7].
- **Step 2.** The second step in the process is that the user has to align the domain models (M1) by defining semantic correspondences in terms of mappings between model elements of the models. In previous work, we assumed only full equivalence mappings. In this work, we extend the model mapping language with additional mapping operators.
- **Step 3.** As soon as the model mapping task is finished, an analyzer component reasons about the user defined model mappings and produces mappings between metamodel elements in the third step. The output of this step is mapping model between the two given metamodels, which offers enough information for generating the model transformations.
- **Step 4.** Based on these metamodel mappings, a code generator has to produce executable model transformations, which are based on metamodel elements. The resulting model transformations are capable of transforming any source model conforming to the source metamodel, into a target model conforming to the target metamodel. It has to be noted that the code generator is capable of creating transformations for both directions, namely from the source metamodel to the target metamodel and back again.
- **Step 5.** Finally, the generated model transformations may need some user refinement for resolving ambiguities in the model mappings, arising from structural and semantical heterogeneities between the modeling languages. At this stage, it is possible to test the generated model transformations and check whether its execution leads to the desired output models. If not, either refinements of model mappings or of generated model transformations itself are required.

3 MTBE Concepts Revisited

The idea and basic concepts of MTBE have been already discussed in several papers [13,14,15,16]. During implementation, theoretical study, and realizing case studies, requirements for MTBE have changed over time leading to adjustments of existing and the creation of additional concepts in our approach. In the following three subsections, first, we discuss the notion of a model mapping language vital for the task of model alignment described in Step 2 in Subsection 2.2. Second, we describe the way how we do reasoning on the user defined model mappings, and third, we present a way to store the reasoning output in terms of metamodel mappings. The last two subsections are related to Step 3 of the MTBE process presented in Subsection 2.2.

3.1   Model Mapping Language

In this subsection, we present a refined version of our model mapping language by first introducing its AS and subsequently its CS.

Abstract Syntax. The metamodel for the model mapping language defines all mapping concepts that can be applied by the user to accomplish the task of bridging two modeling languages by means of mapping example models shown in their concrete syntax. The abstract root class *ViewElement*, depicted in Figure 2, is in fact only for implementation convenience and to visualize that inheriting classes have an associated element on the view. The central class is the abstract class *Mapping*, that serves as basis for all kinds of connections relating two graphical model elements of source and target languages. The design of mapping ends in the metamodel (cf. references *lhs* and reference *rhs*) allows for all kinds of mappings, i.e., *one-to-one*, *one-to-many*, and *many-to-many*. Elements of the languages to be integrated must have the corresponding abstract class *LeftViewElement* or *RightViewElement* as superclasses. How these requirements are realized within our MTBE approach is discussed in Subsection 4.1.

Actually, the remaining concrete classes form the bases for the concrete syntax of the mapping language, for which we defined a notation. However, the specification provided in Figure 2 is not sufficient to completely determine the

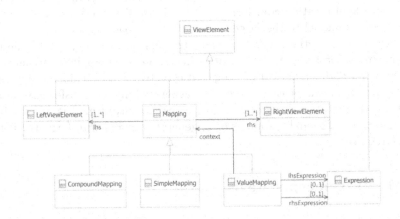

Fig. 2. Metamodel of the Model Mapping Language

abstract syntax of our mapping language. There exist further well-formedness rules for model which have to be defined with the Object Constraint Language (OCL) for each concrete subclass of class *Mapping*.

Simple Mapping. The concept that allows the user to draw simple *one-to-one* mappings between any two concrete syntax elements is represented by the *SimpleMapping* class. Additionally, to restrict on 1..1 multiplicities, the following constraint is necessary.

```
context SimpleMapping
inv: self.lhs -> size() = 1 and self.rhs -> size() = 1
```

Compound Mapping. To allow for *one-to-many* and *many-to-many* mappings, we introduced the *CompoundMapping* class. In order to complete the syntax specification the following constraint must hold for compound mappings.

```
context CompoundMapping
inv: self.lhs -> size() > 1 or self.rhs -> size() > 1
```

Value Mapping. The classes *ValueMapping* and *Expression* constitute what was introduced as string manipulation operator [13]. Whenever attribute values represented by labels are part of a mapping, it would be nice to have some sort of functions that can be applied to modify the participating attribute values appropriately. The container, which encapsulates the actual value mappings is the *ValueMapping* class, able to manage two lists whose elements point to a label. For each of these two lists, a function can be applied to. This function is stored within instances of *Expression* that supports e.g. the concatenation of values by accessing list elements through their index. A *ValueMapping* is however not self-dependent and thus must have a *context* specified, which can be either of type *SimpleMapping* or *CompoundMapping*.

Concrete Syntax. Above we have described the AS of our model mapping language. Now we briefly present what the corresponding CS of the model mapping language looks like. Figure 3 depicts the notation tables for our mapping language. Each concrete class of our mapping language has a distinct CS element for defining model mappings. How these elements may be used in real world examples has been already presented in our previous work [13] for business process models. In this work, see Section 5, we present a concrete application of the model mapping language for bridging structural modeling languages.

3.2   Reasoning Based on Pattern Matching

This subsection covers the conceptual step number three outlined in Subsection 2.2. Model transformations operate on the model level but need to be defined having knowledge how metamodel elements semantically correspond to each other. This is why we have to perform a movement from model mappings defined by the user up to metamodel mappings. Unfortunately, user mappings

Meta Element	Concrete Syntax Element	Meta Element	Concrete Syntax Element
SimpleMapping	- - - - - - - - - -	lhs, rhs (of ValueMapping)	■ {label}
CompoundMapping		Expression	{Value@Pos1}...{Value@Pos2}
ValueMapping			

Fig. 3. Notation tables of the Model Mapping Language

are in general not as accurate as metamodel mappings have to be in order to be used as input for the generation of model transformations. Model mappings usually consist of ambiguities mainly because of various structural and semantical heterogeneities occurring between different modeling languages and due to the user-friendly model mapping language.

To cope with the shift in "mapping space", we propose reasoning based on pattern matching. By applying any kind of predefined or custom-defined model pattern, we aim to create metamodel mappings from model mappings on an automatic basis. These metamodel mappings can be made persistent in a so-called mapping model, which allows to relate all kinds of metamodel elements. In the following, we present six core patterns that are illustrated in Figure 4. The first three patterns operate on the model level (cf. $M \Leftrightarrow M'$ in Figure 4) and produce an initial mapping model, whereas the last three patterns are based on the metamodel level (cf. $MM \Leftrightarrow MM'$ in Figure 4) and aim at the refinement of the initial mapping model.

Initializer Pattern. The first pattern matches if classes, attributes, and references in metamodels are identical resulting in full equivalence mappings between metamodel elements. The basis for this pattern represents simple mappings between model elements and reasoning capabilities to check whether mapped objects (e.g., instance of class A and instance of class B in Figure 4) have equivalent attribute values and links. With the help of this pattern, all simple equivalence mappings between two metamodels can be found. However, with this pattern it is not possible to resolve structural or semantical heterogeneities between modeling languages. For resolving such problems, we propose the following five patterns.

Pathway Pattern. The second pattern poses a challenge as alternate paths have to be found if someone wants to set the link from an instance of A to an instance of B when transforming from M' to M. Analysis of the metamodel alone would not be sufficient, because metamodels might be nearly identical but the reference semantics are different. An analysis of both models represented in AS has to be performed to check for the existence of an equivalent path in M' between an instance of C and an instance of D.

Split/Merge Pattern. The third pattern illustrates the case, where two concepts are represented as two classes explicitly in one language, whereas these two concepts are nested within one class in the other language. As an example consider the UML class *Property*, that specifies the concept multiplicity as attributes, whereas in the ER metamodel the concept multiplicity is expressed explicitly as a class. This means, in transformations there is either a merge of objects and values or a split into separate objects. In principal, there is no restriction on the number of classes that need to be merged or splitted as long as they are somehow related and connected through references. Note that a merge of classes leads to concept hiding whereas a split makes concepts explicit.

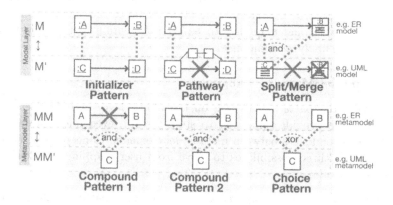

Fig. 4. Core Analyzer Patterns

Compound Pattern 1 – no structural connection. This pattern reasons about metamodel mappings which have been produced from compound mappings of the model level. In case no structural connection between instances of class *A* and class *B* can be found in the example model, then we simply define two independent classes *A* and *B* to be equivalent with one class *C*. This is the most trivial form of *one-to-many* mappings and leads to transformation rules which simply create two unrelated instances from one instance of class *C*.

Compound Pattern 2 – structural connection. This pattern also reasons about metamodel mappings produced for compound mappings of the model level and represents the opposite case of *Compound Pattern 1* in the sense that a structural connection between instances of class *A* and class *B* can be found in the example model. Consequently, this pattern produces metamodel mappings which lead to transformation rules for creating two linked instances from one instance of class *C*.

Choice Pattern. We encountered the case in which two distinct classes, such as class *A* and class *B*, are mapped to the one class *C*. This kind of metamodel mappings is produced for simple model mappings pointing from instances of one class to instances of several classes. Whenever this pattern is matched, further reasoning on the model represented in AS in combination with the CS definition is needed trying to distinguish between the concepts which are hidden. Again, consider our simple UML to ER integration scenario of Figure 1. Instances of class *Property* represent on the one hand attributes when no link to an association instance is set and on the other hand roles when a link is set. This distinction is also represented in the CS of UML, thus the constraints can be reused to build the xor constraint between the metamodel mappings. If the feature comparison in combination with the CS definition does not yield any result, the user has to decide and adjust the metamodel mappings or transformation code manually.

The application of these core patterns is vital for the generation and refinement of the metamodel mapping model. The metamodel mapping language, see Figure 5, allows at the moment only for full or conditional equivalence mappings. However, for model transformation generation purposes this metamodel can be extended with additional mappings to be able to contain further information generated by the analyzer component.

3.3   Metamodel Mapping Language

After applying the pattern matching on the model layer and the metamodel layer, we have to provide some way to store the retrieved information about semantic correspondences between metamodel elements. Conceptually, we have however spotted three possibilities to move from user mappings to executable transformation code:

1. Generate model transformation code in the course of pattern matching using a *template* based approach as supported by code generation frameworks.
2. Apply a *Higher Order Transformation (HOT)* [6] containing the pattern matching capabilities for analyzing the model mappings and generate a transformation model.
3. Run the pattern matching on model mappings and produce an intermediate *mapping model* upon a HOT is executed for producing a transformation model.

We believe that an intermediate mapping model capturing the derived correspondences between metamodel elements is well suitable for MTBE due to the following reasons.

- Existing implementations using mapping models between metamodels (e.g., HOTs and graphical editors) can be reused.
- Using a HOT ensures that we do not leave the *"modeling technical space"*.
- A mapping model between metamodels allows to keep track of the actual model transformation code generation. Thus, debugging is made easier.
- Complexity is reduced by separation of concerns by splitting the task moving from model mappings to model transformation code into two separate tasks.
- Customized HOTs can be easily applied leading to extensibility.

Figure 5 shows our basic mapping language for metamodels. The central concepts in this metamodel are represented by the classes *ConditionalEquivalence* and *FullEquivalence* used to distinguish between conditional equivalence mappings and full equivalence mappings. Equivalence mappings can additionally contain other mappings for specifying which reference mappings and attribute mappings belong to a certain class mapping. Note, that we do not categorize the mappings according to the types they reference. The task to interpret and act properly according to the types the mappings reference, is carried out by the HOT in a subsequent step.

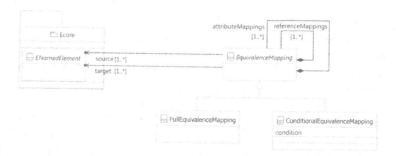

Fig. 5. Metamodel Mapping Language

Furthermore, the metamodel for metamodel mappings is quite different in its structure compared to the model mapping metamodel shown in Figure 2. The metamodel mapping language needs not to incorporate any usability and user-friendliness issues and can therefore contain any relevant information concerning the transformation model generation. For example, complex OCL conditions are also contained in the metamodel mapping model, cf. attribute *condition* in Figure 5.

In fact, one has to make sure that no information reasoned during the pattern matching process is lost. The metamodel in Figure 5 is to be seen as a core mapping language specification open for extension if necessary. This can be simply achieved by introducing additional subclasses of the abstract class *EquivalenceMapping*.

4 An Eclipse Based Implementation for MTBE

Our MTBE framework comprises several components. As can be seen in Figure 6(1), our implementation heavily relies on major Eclipse projects, providing essential functionalities our components are based upon. These components are the Eclipse Modeling Framework (EMF) [1], the Graphical Modeling Framework (GMF) and Eclipse serving as IDE. The components within Figure 6(2) comprise the user front-end and match with conceptual *Step 2* of the MTBE process. In Figure 6(3) all components facilitating the task of metamodel mapping modeled in *Step 3* are depicted. Figure 6(4) components correspond to *Step 4*, i.e., the code generation. Note that we omitted dependencies and interfaces among non-MTBE components to preserve readability. In what follows we will give a short description on each of the modules and will focus on the user front-end in subsequent sections.

Model Mapping Language. The *MappingLanguage* component provides a specification of several alignment operators in terms of an Ecore based metamodel, cf. *ML MM* in Figure 6. The implementation of this component allows the user to map different kinds of visual model elements as described in Subsection 3.1. The definition of this mapping language is central to the MTBE framework as it is directly or indirectly used by other components.

Merge Components. To be able to define mappings between model elements in a graphical way certain artifacts have to be available a priori in one or the other way. Therefore, it is assumed that at least a language definition in terms of a metamodel, a graphical definition of the concrete syntax, and a mapping between these two exist for every modeling language. To allow for mapping two metamodels within the Eclipse environment we decided to merge existing artifacts and build a single editor for both languages. This merging procedure is described in Subsection 4.1. The *MapMerger* component also takes care of the *MTBE Mapping Editor* component generation with the help of *GMF Tooling*.

MTBE Mapping Editor. Our graphical editor prototype uses the *GMF Runtime* and is built solely from *GMF Tooling* at the moment.

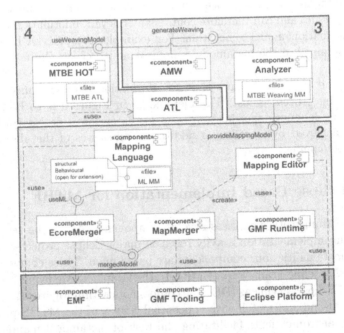

Fig. 6. Framework architecture. 1. Underlying frameworks. 2. User front-end. 3. Pattern matching and creation of weavings. 4. Transformation model generation.

Analyzer Component. The Analyzer takes the output model of the GMF editor, i.e., the user defined model mappings, as well as the corresponding meta-models and tries to match various kinds of patterns as presented in Subsection 3.2. The user can decide which of the available patterns shall be applied in order to translate the manual mappings into an AMW [5] weaving model conforming to the MTBE weaving metamodel, which basically captures the concepts presented in Subsection 3.3. This module will be designed in such a way to allow for several pattern extensions.

MTBE HOT Component. On top of our framework lies the *MTBE HOT* component. This component takes the generated weaving model as input and produces an ATL model conforming to the ATL 2006 metamodel [8]. The built in ATL transformation model can be used to generate transformations in both directions. After generation of the transformation models the AM3 extractor can be run to get the user readable ATL code. The advantage of this approach stems from the fact that all artifacts used in the code generation are models. No hand-coded templates or Java programs are involved to produce the ATL code. The output of the Analyzer module shall serve as input for several kinds of transformation code generators, depending on the use case, so we are not limited to ATL.

4.1   Integration of GMF

Our MTBE approach poses a novel idea as it moves the task of developing model transformation away from the complex structures of AS to the well-known notation elements of modeling languages. To achieve this increased usability for model engineers we decided to integrate the Graphical Modeling Framework (GMF) to be able to generate a graphical editor. The advantage of this decision is that we can use the capabilities of an emerging framework, supported by a large community. In order to apply GMF to create an editor out of a simple generation model we have to provide for model merging components in our MTBE framework. In the following we describe the merging process in more detail and explain how the generated editor can be used to define (appropriate) mappings between notation elements. In the context of MTBE we assume that a graphical editor for some modeling language can be fully generated from GMF (and EMF models). We do not cope with any editor-specific changes made to the generated code. Therefore, we rely on the declarative power of GMF models and their limitations.

Ecore File Sharing. The GMF mapping definition model, which constitutes the mapping from AS to CS, relies on an Ecore-based metamodel besides a graphical as well as a tooling definition model. The latter two we do not have to cope with in our merging process as they represent highly reusable elements. But for the Ecore model our MTBE framework needs a merging component which we call *EcoreMerger*, as shown in Figure 6. This component takes two Ecore models, representing different modeling languages, as input and generates a single Ecore file. Each language is represented by its own package, which is a child of a common root package. The root package itself has to contain a single class that owns all required containment references to classes from the original metamodels. These required references can easily be extracted from the two Ecore files, as these also have to consist of a single class acting as a container, which is a specialty of EMF. We introduced another type of class in the root package, because of GMF limitations, the *GMFElement{language name}*. This class serves as a supertype from which all classes of a modeling language have to inherit. Our EcoreMerger therefore has to modify all classes in these language packages accordingly. However, this design decision then allows us to have mappings defined between every two classes in the two modeling languages. To define these mappings in our graphical editor we also have to add mapping meta classes to our merged Ecore metamodel. This is done in the *mapping* package, that includes the *SimpleMapping* class with source and target references of type of the superclass *GMFElement{language name}*. After the work of the EcoreMerger is completed, the created Ecore file can be used to generate the EMF generation model as well as the EMF model and edit code, that are prerequisites for the GMF diagram code.

Mapping Definitions Merging. Similar to the joint Ecore file we have to provide a component that merges the two mapping definition models (GMFMap models) to a single model, the GMF generation part can handle the creation of diagram code. The algorithm for solving this task simply copies the different kinds of mapping elements from both mapping models into a single one and adjusts the XPath expressions for domain model elements to point to the newly created Ecore file. XPath expressions for tooling and graphics can be reused. After execution of our *MapMerger* (cf. Figure 6) tool the GMF generation model is produced from the merged mapping model to facilitate diagram code generation.

5   A Tour on the MTBE Framework

In this section, the functionality of our prototype is demonstrated by a small case study. The aim is to be able to transform UML models into Entity Relationship (ER) diagrams and vice versa. Note, that these two modeling languages have already been used in [16] to exemplify our MTBE approach. However, we had no implementation at hand to underpin our conceptual findings. With our prototype we are now in the position to demonstrate general MTBE concepts in practice. The MTBE plug-in as well as various artifacts and examples can be downloaded from our ModelCVS project site[1].

5.1   Integration Problem: ER2UML

Figure 7 illustrates two simplified metamodels of the ER diagram and UML class diagram, respectively. Generally speaking, both languages are semantically

---

[1] http://modelcvs.org/prototypes/mtbe.html

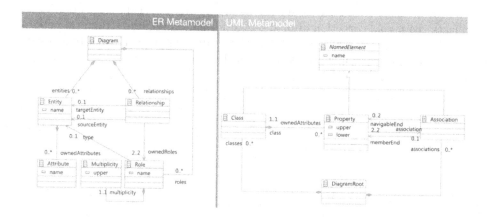

Fig. 7. Simplified ER and UML metamodels

nearly equivalent and thus the corresponding metamodels cover the same modeling concepts. Note that the metamodels for the two languages are designed such that their concrete syntax can be fully specified by declarative GMF components. Most important to us is that we can define the notation by means of the GMFMap model.

ER. The ER metamodel covers the basic concepts of *Entity, Relationship, Attribute, Role*, and *Multiplicity. Diagram* acts as the basic root element and is an implementation-specific of EMF. *Entities* are connected via *Relationships* through their *sourceEntity* and *targetEntity* references. *Entities* can further contain an arbitrary number of *Attributes. Relationships* can be assigned two distinct *Roles* through their *ownedRoles* reference. *Roles* are not contained in their corresponding *Relationship* but in the root element itself. Furthermore, a *Role* must be assigned to a certain *Entity*, which is done through the *type* reference. *Roles* are further enforced to contain a *Multiplicity* that consists of a single attribute called *upper* specifying the upper bound multiplicity of a role.

UML. The UML metamodel in turn consists of *Classes, Properties* and *Associations*. The abstract class *NamedElement* is for convenience only. The root element *DiagramRoot* is equivalent to *Diagram* in the ER metamodel. We introduced concept hiding in the UML metamodel by representing attributes and roles by the same class, namely by the class *Property*. One can only distinguish between these two concepts by the optional reference *association*, whose inverse reference is *memberEnd*. More specifically, an instance of class *Property* represents a role when the reference *association* is set. In case the reference *association* is not set by an instance of class *Property*, it represents an attribute. The class *Property* also comprises the attributes *lower* and *upper* in order to cover the concept multiplicity. Relationships between classes are achieved via roles and the *memberEnd* feature of *Association*. The feature *navigableEnd* of *Association* indicates whether a role is navigable or not.

Mostly all concepts presented in the ER metamodel are also covered in the UML metamodel. Although, the two metamodels can be considered semantically equivalent, there exist structural heterogeneities between them, that would complicate the manual creation of model transformations. These structural heterogeneities entail further reasoning upon the model mappings in order to generate a semantically richer mapping model, which is the basis for the model transformation generation.

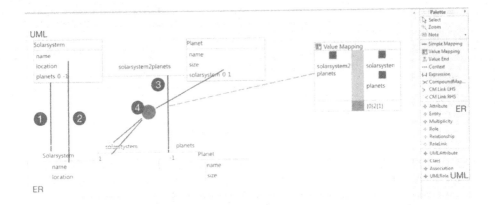

Fig. 8. Model mappings between ER and UML example models

5.2   User Defined Model Mappings

Figure 8 depicts the mappings between the ER example model and the UML example model established by the user. Each GMF tool provided in the palette, see right side of Figure 8, has been used and therefore all concepts are covered by the models. Table 1 summarizes the mappings specified by the user. In particular, we have mostly used simple mappings, however, for mapping roles in combination with multiplicities of ER models to properties of UML models, we employ a compound mapping. Furthermore, we need to attach a value mapping to the simple mapping between relationship and association in order to set the name of an association (note that in our ER metamodel the relationship itself does not have a name).

Table 1. Summary of model mappings.

Mappings	UML Model Elements	Mapping Kind	ER Model Elements
(1)	Solarsystem: Class	Simple Mapping	Solarsystem: Entity
(2)	name: Property	Simple Mapping	name: Attribute
(3)	solarsystem2planets: Association	Simple Mapping (+Value Mapping)	: Relationship
(4)	solarsystem: Property	Compound Mapping	solarsystem: Role 1: Multiplicity

Table 2. Summary of metamodel mappings.

MAP	UML MM Elements	ER MM Elements	Mapping	Comment	Pattern	Model MAP
C1	DiagramRoot	Diagram	*Full Equiv.*	Reasoned via GMF properties	X	X
C2	Class	Entity	*Full Equiv.*		Pattern 1	(1)
C3	Association	Relationship	*Full Equiv.*		Pattern 1	(3)
C4	Property	Role ⋈ Multiplicity	*Cond. Equiv.*	Property.association == null	Pattern 3 + Pattern 6	(4)
C5	Property	Attribute	*Cond. Equiv.*	Property.association != null	Pattern 6	(2)
A1	Class.name	Entity.name	*Full Equiv.*			
A2	Property.name	Attribute.name	*Full Equiv.*			
A3	Property.name	Role.name	*Full Equiv.*			
A4	Association.name	*Function*	*Full Equiv.*	Exp Annotation		(3)
A5	Property.upper	Role.multiplicty.upper	*Full Equiv.*			
A6	Property.lower	X	X	Default Value: 0		
R1	Class.ownedAttributes	Entity.ownedAttributes + User Interaction	*Cond. Equiv.*	Roles have to be collected (cf. C4, C5)		
R2	Association.navigableEnd	Relationship.ownedRoles	*Full Equiv.*	Convention		
R3	Association.memberEnd	Relationship.ownedRoles	*Full Equiv.*			
R4	DiagramRoot.associations	Diagram.relationships	*Full Equiv.*			
R5	DiagramRoot.classes	Diagram.entities	*Full Equiv.*			

5.3   Reasoning and Metamodel Mappings

Based on the model mappings, the Analyzer generates a mapping model capturing as many metamodel mappings as possible. Concerning our core patterns presented in Section 3.2, the Analyzer component can apply pattern 1, 3, and 6 shown in Figure 4 for finding equivalent classes as is summarized in Table 2. Pattern 1 generates the mappings *C2* and *C3*, while mapping *C1* has been additionally reasoned from GMF configurations to find the equivalent root classes which represent the modeling canvas. Pattern 3 is used to reason about the compound mapping (cf. model mapping (4)) which results in mapping *C4* from *Property* to the join of *Role* and *Multiplicity*. Furthermore, pattern 6 is able to generate the conditions for splitting properties into attributes and roles. From these class mappings, most of the attribute and reference mappings can be derived which are necessary for the model transformation. Due to brevity reasons, we only show the reference mappings necessary for transforming ER models into UML models. As one can see in Table 2, only one user interaction is necessary for completing the model transformations, namely the *Class.ownedAttributes* reference must be split in two subsets, one can be reasoned, however, the other has to be defined by the user.

5.4   ATL Code Generation

Based on the metamodel mappings, we show how our HOT produces valid ATL model transformations. The ATL code for transforming ER models into UML models depicted in Listing 1.1 comprises both, the automatically generated code by our HOT implementation and some user refined code fragments.

Listing 1.1. ER2UML transformation including user refined code

```
1  --- @atlcompiler atl2006
2  module ER2UML; --- Module Template
3  create OUT : UML from IN : ER;
4
5  rule diagram2diagramRoot{
6      from d : ER!Diagram
7      to dr : UML!DiagramRoot(
8          classes <- d.entities,
9          associations <- d.relationships
10     )
11 }
12
13 rule entity2class{
14     from e : ER!Entity
15     to c : UML!Class(
16         name <- e.name,
17         ownedAttributes <- e.ownedAttributes
18     )
19 }
20
21 rule attribute2property{
22     from a : ER!Attribute
23     to p : UML!Property(
24         name <- a.name
25     )
26 }
27
28 rule relationship2association{
29     from rel : ER!Relationship
30     to a : UML!Association(
31         name <- rel.ownedRoles.first().name+'_2_'+rel.ownedRoles.last().name,
32         memberEnd <- rel.ownedRoles -> collect( t |
33             thisModule.resolveTemp(Tuple{r = t, m = t.multiplicity}, 'p')
34         ),
35         navigableEnd <- rel.ownedRoles
36     )
37 }
38
39 rule role_multiplicity2property{
40     from
41         r : ER!Role,
42         m : ER!Multiplicity (
43             r.multiplicity = m
44         )
45     to p : UML!Property(
46         name <- r.name,
47         class <- ER!Relationship.allInstances()
48             -> select(x|x.ownedRoles -> collect(y|y.type)-> includes(r.type))
49             -> collect(y|y.ownedRoles).flatten()
50             -> select(y|y.type <> r.type).first().type,
51         upper <- m.upper
52     )
53 }
```

In general, the generation of transformation code dealing with object and value creation is rather simple. What complicates our automatic transformation model generation are links between the objects, especially when the metamodels have different structures due to structural heterogeneities. The first three ATL rules shown in Listing 1.1 can be derived fully automatically. Rule *relationship2association* comprises a tricky part in lines 32 to 34. Because we deal with multiple source pattern matching in rule *role_multiplicity2property*, we have to use the *resolveTemp* construct to query produced properties. Therefore, this reference assignment looks complicated in ATL, but may be generated out of the metamodel mappings. An issue we have to deal with manually is depicted in lines 47 to 50 of the last rule. As for *roles* in ER, we also have to set the container for the corresponding *properties* in UML. However, the concept of a role is mirrored among ER and UML and therefore it was not possible to automatically produce a metamodel mapping which is also depicted in Table 2 mapping *R1*. Therefore, a rather complicated query has to be defined by the user, which assigns *properties* to *classes*.

5.5   Lessons Learned

During our case study and experimenting with our prototype we discovered some limitations of our implementation.

GMF. For every two modeling languages a user wants to define model transformations, a unique editor with its own domain, graphics, tooling and mapping models has to be generated. There is no possibility to reuse already generated code. Before one can begin to define mappings on the concrete syntax, the merging and generation components of the MTBE framework have to be executed. In order to reduce the cost of time we have provided for an implementation that can do things nearly without user interaction. Another drawback of the current approach is that we are not able to cope with custom code in an available editor, which limits our design possibilities. For example UML roles are contained in a *Class* and not directly shown at an *Association* in our simple UML GMF editor.

HOT. Our basic Higher Order Transformation works well and produces model transformations in both directions. There are however some metamodel weavings that we do not fully support in our HOT, i.e., weavings that contain an OCL expression originating either from the notation or from some analyzer pattern. The problem is that OCL conditions are stored in weaving models as strings. But in the HOT we have to compute the equivalent abstract syntax trees for producing the ATL transformation model. As an alternative we consider a template based approach producing ATL code out of weaving models, where we could use plain OCL strings and need not handle abstract syntax trees.

6   Related Work

To our best knowledge, there exists no tool support for MTBE approaches so far. However, our idea of MTBE is related to common by-example approaches and to approaches that allow the definition of semantic correspondences between two (meta)models.

By-example approaches have a long history in computer science and can be traced back to Zloofs *Query-By-Example* (QBE) approach from 1975 [17] for querying relational databases. A more related by-example approach come from Lechner et al. [10]. By extending Zloofs QBE approach in order to enable the definition of schema transformers for web application models defined with WebML [2]. One of the novelties of their work is that they introduce a generation part using template definitions in addition to the query part.

Parallel to our MTBE approach, Dániel Varró proposed in [14] a similar approach. The overall aim of Varró's approach is comparable to ours, but the concrete realizations differ from each other. While we propose to define the model mappings between model shown in their concrete syntax, Varró's approach uses the abstract syntax to define the mappings between models, only. To transform one model into the other, Varró propose the use of graph transformations [4], while we are using transformations expressed in ATL. Despite their differences, both approaches have in common that they generate model transformations semi-automatically leading to an interactive and iterative process.

The mapping of model elements, as described in this paper, can also be compared with the weaving of (meta)models within the ATLAS Model Weaver (AMW) [5]. The model transformation generation process of the AMW currently focuses on using mappings between metamodels to derive ATL code [8]. Thus, AMW considers only the metamodel level, while our approach aims at generating model transformation code primarily from model mappings.

7   Conclusion and Future Work

In this paper, we have introduced refined and extended concepts for MTBE, which have been implemented in a prototype. This prototype allows for defining semantic correspondences between domain models shown in their concrete notation, from which model transformations can be generated. Our framework is based on emerging technologies which are based on Eclipse. Our prototype has shown that it is possible to realize a framework for MTBE based on the current versions of the underlying technologies. However, one important drawback of the proposed framework must be mentioned, namely the strong dependency on the success and the usability of the underlying technologies.

Concerning future work, the main concern is the improvement of the current prototype to cover the complete MTBE process, because only proper tool support enables full elaboration of the so far gained insights of our approach by studying the application on real world examples. Besides the prototype improvements, further directions are (1) extension of the model mapping language, (2) creation of reference examples, and (3) finding new reasoning algorithms for exploring more complex model transformations automatically.

Acknowledgments

We thank Gerald Müller and Abraham Müller for their support during implementation of the MTBE prototype and the anonymous referees for their helpful comments.

References

1. Budinsky, F., Steinberg, D., Raymond, E.M., Timothy, E., Grose, J.: Eclipse Modeling Framework. Addison Wesley (August 2003)
2. Ceri, S., Fraternalia, P., Bongio, A., Bramilla, M., Comai, S., Matera, M.: Designing Data-Intensive Web Applications. Morgan-Kaufmann (2003)
3. Czarnecki, K., Helsen, S.: Feature-based survey of model transformation approaches. IBM Syst. J. 45(3), 621–645 (2006)
4. Ehring, H., Engels, G., Kreowsky, H.-J., Rozenberg, G.: Handbook on Graph Grammars and Computing by Graph Transformation. World Scientific (1999)
5. Fabro, M.D.D., Bézivin, J., Jouault, F., Breton, E., Gueltas, G.: AMW: A Generic Model Weaver. In: Proc. of the 1re Journe sur l'Ingnierie Dirige par les Modles (IDM 2005) (2005)

6. Fabro, M.D.D., Valduriez, P.: Semi-automatic Model Integration using Matching Transformations and Weaving Models. In: Proc. of the ACM Symposium on Applied Computing (SAC 2007), Seoul, Korea (2007)
7. Fleurey, F., Baudry, B., Muller, P.-A., Traon, Y.L.: Qualifying input test data for model transformations. Software and Systems Modeling (2007)
8. Jouault, F., Kurtev, I.: On the Architectural Alignment of ATL and QVT. In: Proc. of ACM Symposium on Applied Computing (SAC 2006), Bourgogne, France (2006)
9. Kappel, G., Kapsammer, E., Kargl, H., Kramler, G., Reiter, T., Retschitzegger, W., Schwinger, W., Wimmer, M.: Lifting Metamodels to Ontologies - A Step to the Semantic Integration of Modeling Languages. In: Proc. of the ACM/IEEE 9th Int. Conf. on Model Driven Engineering Languages and Systems (MoDELS/UML 2006), Genova, Italy (2006)
10. Lechner, S.: Web-scheme Transformers By-Example. PhD thesis, Johannes Kepler University Linz (2004)
11. Mens, T., Gorp, P.V.: A Taxonomy of Model Transformation. Electr. Notes Theor. Comput. Sci. 152, 125–142 (2006)
12. Repenning, A., Perrone, C.: Programming By Example: Programming by Analogous Examples. Commun. ACM 43(3), 90–97 (2000)
13. Strommer, M., Murzek, M., Wimmer, M.: Applying Model Transformation By-Example on Business Process Modeling Languages. In: Proc. of ER 2007 Workshops, Auckland, New Zealand (2007)
14. Varró, D.: Model Transformation By Example. In: Proc. of the ACM/IEEE 9th Int. Conf. on Model Driven Engineering Languages and Systems (MoDELS/UML 2006), Genova, Italy (October 2006)
15. Varró, D., Balogh, Z.: Automating Model Transformation by Example Using Inductive Logic Programming. In: Proc. of ACM Symposium on Applied Computing (SAC 2007), Seoul, Korea (2007)
16. Wimmer, M., Strommer, M., Kargl, H., Kramler, G.: Towards Model Transformation Generation By-Example. In: Proc. of the 40th Hawaii Int. Conf. on Systems Science (HICSS 2007), Big Island, USA (2007)
17. Zloof, M.M.: Query By Example. In: Proc. of National Compute Conference (NCC 1975) (1975)

Web Applications Design and Development with WebML and WebRatio 5.0

Roberto Acerbis[1], Aldo Bongio[1], Marco Brambilla[2],
Stefano Butti[1], Stefano Ceri[2], and Piero Fraternali[2]

[1] WebModels S.r.l.
Piazzale Gerbetto, 6. I22100 Como, Italy
{roberto.acerbis,aldo.bongio,stefano.butti}@webratio.com
[2] Dipartimento di Elettronica e Informazione, Politecnico di Milano
Piazza L. Da Vinci, 32. I20133 Milano, Italy
{mbrambil,fraternal,ceri}@elet.polimi.it

Abstract. This paper presents WebRatio 5.0, a design tool that supports WebML (Web Modelling Language). WebML is a domain specific language (DSL) for designing complex, distributed, multi-actor, and adaptive applications deployed on the Web and on Service Oriented Architectures using Web Services. WebRatio 5.0 provides visual design facilities based on the WebML notation and code generation engines for J2EE Web applications. The tool is developed as a set of Eclipse plug-ins and takes advantage of all the features of this IDE framework. It also provides support of customized extensions to the models, project documentation, and requirements specifications. The overall approach moves towards a full coverage of the specification, design, verification, and implementation of Web applications.

1 Introduction

Although new paradigms of Web applications are arising, data-intensive Web applications still constitute the most diffused class of applications found on the Web. Since their size and complexity are typically high, the ideal software development process for this kind of applications should meet two goals: (i) incorporate requirements and model driven design in the development lifecycle; (ii) delivering a software architecture that meets the non-functional requirements of performance, security, scalability, availability, maintainability, usability, and high visual quality. Such process should also be amenable to automation, to let developers concentrate on functional requirements and optimization, and delegate the repetitive tasks (such as code implementation) to software tools.

The model-driven design of this kind of Web applications should start from well established requirement specifications and involves the definition of a data model (to specify the data used by the application), a hypertext model (to describe the organization of the front-end interface) and a presentation model (to personalize the graphical aspect of the interface). Afterwards, model verification and model transformations (e.g., for generating the running code) should be provided to complete the development process.

R.F. Paige and B. Meyer (Eds.): TOOLS EUROPE 2008, LNBIP 11, pp. 392–411, 2008.
© Springer-Verlag Berlin Heidelberg 2008

This paper presents the innovative features of the new release of the tool WebRatio 5.0 [1], currently fully deployed as an Eclipse plugin. Thanks to this evolution, the new version fully exploits the power of the Eclipse IDE that is integrated with its native modeling capabilities. Therefore, WebRatio 5 represents a new generation of model driven design (MDD) and engineering (MDE) tools for Web applications. It fully supports the WebML language and methodology, and exploits the implementation experience of previous versions of the software for providing user-friendly application design paradigms and reliable transformation engines. Besides taking advantage of the Eclipse features, WebRatio provides new capabilities in terms of support of model extensions, project documentation, and coverage of new phases of the development lifecycle. The WebML language and methodology adopted by WebRatio is a high-level notation for data-, service-, and process- centric Web applications. It allows specifying the data model of a Web application and one or more hypertext models, that can be based on business process specifications and can exploit Web service invocation, custom backend logic, and rich Web interfaces.

The main advantages WebRatio are the following:

- It provides a full-fledged MDE (Model Driven Engineering) approach to the development of Web applications, thanks to DSL support and model transformations that lead to automatic code generation;
- All the design and development activities are performed through a common interface, that includes the visual modeling of the Web application, the definition of the visual identity, and the development of new business components;
- All the design items (models, components, documentation, and so on) are stored into a common area (the so-called Eclipse workspace) and can be easily versioned into a versioning system, such as CVS;
- All the existing Eclipse plugins can be reused and integrated in the toolsuite;
- New and existing editors for model and code design can be easily integrated.

The paper is structured as follows: Section 2 and Section 3 provide a description of the WebML methodology and language respectively; Section 4 outlines the main features and describes the overall philosophy of the WebRatio toolsuite; and Section 5 concludes.

2   The WebML Methodology

As reported in Figure 1, the WebML approach to the development of Web applications consists of different phases. Inspired by Boehm's spiral model [2] and in line with modern methods for Web and software applications development [3] [4] [5], the WebML process is applied in an iterative and incremental manner, in which the various phases are repeated and refined until results meet the application requirements. The product lifecycle therefore undergoes several cycles, each producing a prototype or a partial version of the application. At each iteration, the current version of the application is tested and evaluated and then extended or modified to cope with the newly emerged requirements.

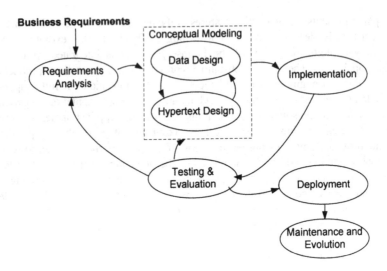

Fig. 1. Phases in the WebML development process

Requirements analysis focuses on collecting information about the application domain and the expected functions, and on specifying them through easy-to-understand descriptions. The main results of this phase are: the identification of the groups of users addressed by the application; the specification of functional requirements that address the functions to be provided to users; the identification of core information objects to be accessed, exchanged, and/or manipulated by users; and the decomposition of the Web application into site views, i.e., different hypertexts designed to meet a well-defined set of functional and user requirements.

Conceptual modeling consists of defining conceptual schemas, which express the organization of the application at a high level of abstraction, independently from implementation details. According to the WebML approach, conceptual modeling consists of data design and hypertext design.

- Data design corresponds to organizing core information objects previously identified during requirements analysis into a comprehensive and coherent data schema, possibly enriched through derived objects.
- Hypertext design then produces site view schemas on top of the data schema previously defined. Site views express the composition of the content and services within hypertext pages, as well as the navigation and the interconnection of components. In the case of applications where different user groups perform multiple activities, or in case of multi-channel applications, in which users can adopt different access devices, hypertext design requires the definition of multiple site views, addressing the user groups involved and their access requirements.

The models provided by the WebML language for data and hypertext design are briefly described in Section 3. A broader illustration of the language and its formal definition can be found in [6] and at [7].

The phases following conceptual modelling consist of implementing, testing and evaluating, deploying on top of a selected architecture, and maintaining/evolving the application.

WebRatio largely facilitates the implementation phase, because visual WebML specifications are stored as XML documents and these are the inputs for the WebML code generator, which then produces the data and hypertext implementation.

The testing phase is improved too [8], because the focus shifts from verifying individual Web applications to assessing the correctness of the code generator (that can be done once and for all). Then testing Web applications would reduce to validating the conceptual schema.

Quality assessment can benefit of new techniques as well. Existing frameworks [9] support the static (i.e., compile-time) analysis of conceptual schemas, and the dynamic (i.e., run-time) collection of Web usage data to be automatically analyzed and compared with the navigation dictated by the conceptual schema.

Finally, maintenance and evolution also benefit from the existence of a conceptual model. Requests for changes can in fact be turned into changes at the conceptual level, either to the data model or to the hypertext model, and then are propagated to the implementation. This approach smoothly incorporates change management into the mainstream production lifecycle.

3   The WebML Language

WebML is a domain specific language (DSL) for the design of data-intensive, service-intensive, and process-intensive Web applications. This section summarizes the basic WebML concepts, with particular attention to data model and hypertext model.

3.1   WebML Data Model

For the specification of the underlying data of the Web application, WebML does not propose yet another data modeling language; rather, it exploits the existing Entity-Relationship data model, or the equivalent subset of UML class diagram primitives. The fundamental elements of the WebML data model are therefore entities, defined as containers of data elements, and relationships, defined as semantic connections between entities. Entities have named properties, called attributes, with an associated type. Entities can be organized in generalization hierarchies and relationships can be restricted by means of cardinality constraints.

The data model can also include the specification of calculated data. Calculated attributes, entities, and relationships are called *derived* and can be denoted by adding a slash character '/' in front of their name and their computation rule can be specified as a logical expression written using declarative languages like OQL or OCL and added to the declaration of the attribute or relationship.

3.2   WebML Hypertext Model

The hypertext model enables the definition of the front-end interface, which is shown to a user in the browser. It enables the definition of pages and their internal organization in terms of components (called content units) for displaying content. It also supports the definition of links between pages and content units that support information location and browsing. Components can also specify operations, such as content management or user's login/logout procedures (called operation units).

The modular structure of an application front-end is defined in terms of site views, areas, pages and content units. A *site view* is a particular hypertext, designed to address a specific set of requirements. It consists of *areas*, which are the main sections of the hypertext and comprises recursively other sub-areas or pages. *Pages* are the actual containers of information delivered to the user. Several site views can be defined on top of the same data schema, for serving different user roles or devices.

Pages and areas are characterized by some relevance properties, which highlight their "importance" in the Web site. In particular, pages inside an area or site view can be of three types: the home page (denoted with a small "H") is the default address of the site view; the default page (denoted with a small "D") is the one presented by default when its enclosing area is accessed; a landmark page (denoted with a small "L") is reachable from all the other pages or areas within its enclosing module.

Pages are composed of *content units*, which are the elementary pieces of information, possibly extracted from data sources, published within pages. Units represent one or more instances of entities of the structural schema, typically selected by means of queries over the entity attributes or over relationships. In particular, *data units* represent some of the attributes of a given entity instance; *multidata units* represent some of the attributes of a set of entity instances; *index units* present a list of descriptive keys of a set of entity instances and enable the selection of one of them; *scroller units* enable the browsing of an ordered set of objects. Some variants are then available. For example the *multichoice, hierarchical, multisort* indexes allow one to choose multiple objects, organize a list of index entries defined over multiple entities hierarchically, and allow dynamic sorting of the contents respectively. Finally, *entry units* allow to publish forms for collecting input values from the user.

Units are characterized by a *source* (the entity from which the unit's content is retrieved) and a *selector* (a restriction predicate on the result set of the contents).

Units and pages are interconnected by *links*, thus forming a hypertext. Links between units are called *contextual*, because they carry some information from the *source unit* to the *destination unit*. In contrast, links between pages are called *non-contextual*. In contextual links, the binding between the source unit and the destination unit of the link is formally represented by link parameters, associated with the link, and by parametric selectors, defined in the destination unit.

In some applications, it may be necessary to differentiate specific link behaviours: an *automatic link*, graphically represented by putting a label "A" over the link, is "navigated" in the absence of a user's interaction when the page that contains the source unit of the link is accessed. A *transport link*, graphically represented as a dashed arrow, is used only for passing context information from one unit to another and thus is not rendered as an anchor.

As an example of page composition and unit linking, Figure 2 reports a simple hypertext, containing two pages of the **Movies** Area. Page **Recent Movies List** contains an index unit defined over the Movie entity, which shows the list of movies of the last month, and a data unit also defined over the Movie entity, which displays the details of the movie selected from the index. Two selectors (**[Year=system.**

`year()]`, `[Month=system.month()]`) are defined to restrict the selection only to the movies of the current month and year. The arrow between the two units is a contextual link, carrying the parameter `CurrMovie`, containing the object identifier (OID) of the selected item. The data unit includes a parametric selector (`[OID=CurrMovie]`), which uses the input OID parameter to retrieve the data of the specific movie.

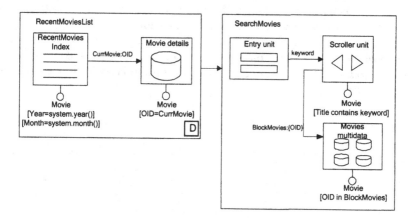

Fig. 2. Example of contextual and non-contextual navigation

OIDs of the objects displayed or chosen from the source unit are considered the default context associated with the link, thus they can be omitted and simply inferred from the diagram.

An example of non-contextual link is shown from the **Recent Movies List** page to the **Search Movies** page: this link does not carry any parameter, because the content of the destination page does not depend on the content of the source page.

Page **Search Movies** shows an interesting hypertext pattern; it contains three units: an entry unit denoting a form for inserting the keyword of the title to be searched, a scroller unit defined over the Movie entity and having a selector for retrieving only the movies containing that keyword in their titles (`[Title contains keyword]`), and a multidata unit displaying a scrollable block of search results. Through the scroller unit it is possible to move to the first, previous, next, and last block of results.

Parameters can be set as globally available to all the pages of the site view. This is possible through *global parameters*, which abstract the implementation-level notion of session-persistent data. Parameters can be set through the *Set unit* and consumed within a page through a *Get unit*.

WebML also supports the specification of content management, custom business logic, and service invocation. WebML offers additional primitives for expressing built-in update operations, such as creating, deleting or modifying an instance of an entity (represented through the *create*, *delete* and *modify* units, respectively), or adding or dropping a relationship between two instances (represented through the *connect* and *disconnect* unit, respectively). Other utility operations extend the previous set. For example, *login* and *logout* units are respectively used *(i)* for managing access control and verifying the identity of a user accessing the application site views and *(ii)* for closing the session of a logged user.

Operation units do not publish the content to be displayed to the user, but execute some processing as a side effect of the navigation of a link. Like content units, operations may have a source object (either an entity or a relationship) and selectors, and may have multiple incoming contextual links, which provide the parameters necessary for executing the operation. One of the incoming links is the activating link (the one followed by the user for triggering the operation).

Two or more operations can be linked to form a chain, which is activated by firing the first operation. Each operation can have two types of output links: one *OK link* and one *KO link*. The former is followed when the operation succeeds; the latter when the operation fails.

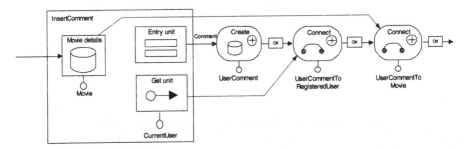

Fig. 3. Example of content management

The example in Figure 3 shows the content of the **Insert Comment** page in the **Movies** area. Through the entry unit the user can insert a comment for the movie currently displayed by the **Movie details** data unit. A get unit is defined to retrieve the data of the currently logged user, which have been stored in a global parameter after the login. When the user submits a comment, a chain of operations is triggered and executed: first a new comment instance is created in the **UserComment** entity, containing the text inserted by the user; then, the new comment is associated to the current user (by creating a new instance of the relationship **UserCommentTo RegisteredUser**) and to the current movie (relationship **UserCommentToMovie**). In the example, KO links are not explicitly drawn: by default they lead the user to the page from which the operation chain has been triggered.

3.5 Support of Web Services and Business Processes in WebML

The core concepts of WebML have been extended to enable the specification of complex applications, where Web services can be invoked and the navigation of the user is driven by process model specifications. In the next subsections we briefly present the extensions that have been integrated in the WebML model for designing service-enabled and process-enabled Web applications.

Service-Enabled Web Applications. To describe Web services interactions, WebML has been extended with a set of Web service units [10] implementing the WSDL classes of Web service operations.

WebML supports all the four categories of operations proposed in WSDL. *One-way* operations consist of a message sent by the client to the service; *Request-response* operations consist of one request message sent by the client and one response message built by the service and sent back to the client. *Notification operations* consist of messages sent to the service; *Solicit* and *response* operations are devised for receiving request messages sent to the service and providing messages as responses to the client. Operations initiated by the service as a means for *Web services publishing*. Appropriate *Service views* contain the definition of published services. The operations initiated by the client are instead integrated within the specification of the Web application.

Here we show an example of request-response operation. Assume that the request-response operation **SearchBooks** allows one to obtain a list of books meeting search criteria provided in input to the service (like, e.g., keywords contained in the title). The remote Web service responds with the list of books meeting the given search criteria. The request-response operation is modeled through the request-response unit, whose graphical notation is shown in Figure 4. This operation involves two messages: the message sent to service and the message received from the service.

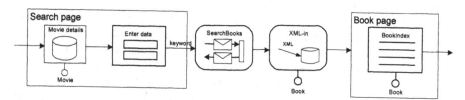

Fig. 4. Example of usage of the request-response operation

In the example of Figure 4, the user can browse to the **Search page**, where an entry unit permits the input of search criteria, preloaded from the currently selected movie. From this information, a request message is composed and sent to the **SearchBooks** operation of the Web service exposed by the service provider. The user then waits for the response message, containing a list of books satisfying the search criteria. Then, a set of instances of the **Book** entity are created through the XML-in operation unit (which receives in input XML data and transforms them into relational data), and displayed to the user by means of the **Book Index** unit; the user may continue browsing, e.g., by choosing one of the displayed books.

WebML supports also the *publication of Web services* that can be invoked by third party applications. The business logic of a Web service operation is described by a chain of WebML operations, specifying the actions to be performed as a consequence of the invocation of the service, and possibly building the response message to be sent back to the invoker. Each operation starts with a *solicit unit*, which triggers the service, and ends with the *response unit*, which sends back a response message.

Figure 5 shows an example of a service that provides the list of movies satisfying some search criteria. The WSDL operation is modeled through a chain of WebML operations starting with the solicit unit (**SearchSolicit**). The solicit unit receives the SOAP message of the requester and decodes the search keywords, passing them as parameters to the next WebML operation in the sequence. This is a so-called

XML-out operation unit, which extracts from the database the list of movies that correspond to the specified conditions and formats it as an XML document. After the XML-out operation, the composition of the response message is performed through the *response unit* (**SearchResponse**). Notice that the schema of Figure 5 can be seen as the dual specification of the SearchBooks service invocation pattern, represented in Figure 4.

In addition to the abovementioned examples, WebML supports also the exchange of asynchronous messages [11], and complex Web service conversations [10].

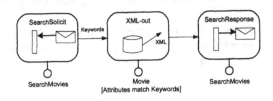

Fig. 5. Example of usage of the solicit-response operation

Process-Enabled Web Applications. Recent trends in Web applications are evolving from the support of online content browsing to the management of full-fledged collaborative workflow-based applications, spanning multiple individuals and organizations. WebML has been extended for supporting lightweight Web-enabled workflows [12][13], thus transferring the benefits of high-level conceptual modelling and automatic code generation also to this class of Web applications.

Integrating hypertexts with workflows means delivering Web interfaces that permit the execution of business activities and embody constraints that drive the navigation of users. The required extensions to the WebML language are the following:

- *Business process model:* a new design dimension is introduced in the methodology. It consists of a workflow diagram representing the business process to be executed, in terms of its activities, the precedence constraints, and the actors/roles in charge of executing each activity;
- *Data model:* the data model representing the domain information is extended with a set of objects (namely, entities and relationships) describing the meta-data necessary for tracking the execution of the business process, both for logging and for constraints evaluation purposes;
- *Hypertext model:* the hypertext model is extended by specifying the business activity boundaries and the workflow-dependent navigation links.

Besides the main models, the proposed extension affects the following aspects of the WebML methodology:

- *Development process:* some new phases are introduced to allow the specification of business processes. In particular, through a visual workflow editor, the analyst specifies the business process model, that is then processed by an automatic transformation that generates a set of hypertext skeletons implementing the specified behaviour. The produced skeletons can be modified by designers by means of CASE tools for conceptual Web application modeling; finally, the resulting models can be processed by WebRatio automatic code generators that produce the running Web application.

- *Design tools:* new visual editors shall be introduced for supporting the design of the workflow models within the WebML methodology;
- *Automatic generation tools:* a new transformer is needed for translating workflow diagrams into draft WebML specification of the Web applications implementing the process specification.

Many standard notations have been proposed to express the structure of business processes. For our purposes, we adopt the Business Process Management Notation (BPMN), which is compatible with Web service choreography languages (e.g., BPEL4WS) and standard business process specification languages (e.g., XPDL).

The extensions to the data model include some standard entities for recording activities instances and process cases, thus allowing one to store the state of the business process execution and enacting it accordingly. The adopted meta-model is very simple (see Figure 6): the **Case** entity stores the information about each instantiation of the process, while the **Activity** entity stores the status of each activity instance executed in the system. Each Activity belongs to a single Case. Connections to user and application data can be added, for the purpose of associating domain information to the process execution. Obviously, the designer can adopt more sophisticated meta-data schemas or even integrate with underlying workflow engines through appropriate APIs (e.g., Web services) for tracking and advancing the process instance.

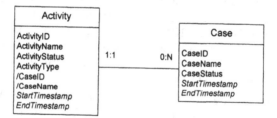

Derived attributes:
/CaseID {Self.Activity2Case.CaseID}
/CaseName {Self.Activity2Case.CaseName}

Fig. 6. Workflow meta-data added to the data model

Within the hypertext model, new primitives have been defined for specification of activity boundaries (namely *Activity areas* within the hypertext) and business process-dependent navigation (namely *workflow links*). Figure 7 shows some of these primitives: site areas marked as "Activity Areas" (A); special incoming links for checking the correctness of the status and starting an activity (i.e., Start and Resume links); special outgoing links for closing an activity (Complete and Suspend links). Notice that *if* and *switch* units can be used to express navigation conditions. *Distributed processes* and *SOA* can be obtained by combining the workflow primitives with Web services primitives [13].

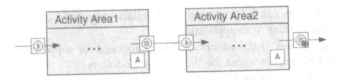

Fig. 7. Two activity areas and corresponding start and end links

A flexible transformation, depending on several tuning and style parameters, has been included in the methodology for automatically transforming workflow models into skeletons of WebML hypertext diagrams.

The produced WebML model consists of application data model, workflow metadata, and hypertext diagrams. The transformation supports all the main WfMC precedence constraints, which include sequences of activities, AND-, OR-, XOR-splits and joins, and basic loops.

Since no semantics is implied by the activity descriptions, the generated skeleton can only implement the empty structure of each activity, and the hypertext and data queries that are needed for enforcing the workflow constraints. The designer remains in charge of implementing the interface and business logic of each activity, by editing the generated hypertext within WebRatio.

4 WebRatio: A Tool for Designing WebML Models

WebRatio 5 has been implemented as a set of Eclipse [14] plug-ins. Eclipse is a framework for IDEs, in the sense that, besides being an IDE itself, it provides the infrastructure for defining new IDEs, i.e., new plug-ins for a particular programming language or model. For instance, plug-ins exist for Java, C/C++, Python, Perl, UML, and many others. Eclipse is an open source multi-platform framework, executable on Linux, Windows, and Mac OS X.

Design-time tool architecture. WebRatio 5 fully supports the WebML metamodel [1], including the most recent extensions for workflow-driven Web applications and Web services. The *design-time* part of WebRatio 5 is a GUI for application design comprising a set of editors, a set of transformers and model validators, and some workspace management components. Models are saved as XML documents. The design-time WebRatio GUI defines a special Eclipse perspective designed to better suit the needs of visual modelling. It comprises several panels, which include:

- *Model diagram editors* for the design of the WebML data model and hypertext models;
- *Advanced text editors* for the design of XML descriptors, Java components, and so on;
- *Form-based editors* for the specification of new components and for the properties of components instances;
- *Wizards* for the support of the most common design tasks (e.g., new projects);
- *Documentation editors* for refined and customized project documentation generation.

Diagram and text editors. WebML models can be specified visually thanks to proper diagram views in the WebRatio tool. *Diagram editors* for the design of the WebML data model and hypertext models represent the main design tools in WebRatio. The diagram editors are based on the GEF [15] framework and libraries. GEF is a very powerful framework for visually creating and editing models. Figure 8 (a) shows a snapshot of the data model editor, comprising the project tree, the main diagram editor, the component panel (bottom left), the property panel (center), and the error panel (bottom right). Figure 8 (b) shows a hypertext model editor view. The modeling views include also some wizards for specifying the details of the components, for specifying derivation rules in the data model, and so on.

In the implementation of the tool, we disregarded the choice of Eclipse Modeling projects such as ECore and EMF for performance reasons. Since the tool is being used in huge collaborative enterprise-wide projects, it is mandatory that the interface must be able to display and to manage large WebML models without performance flaws. Anyway, for the development of the core part of the tool, a proprietary meta-programming framework has been developed, that allowed to generate the first structure of the editors based on a proprietary meta-model of WebML.

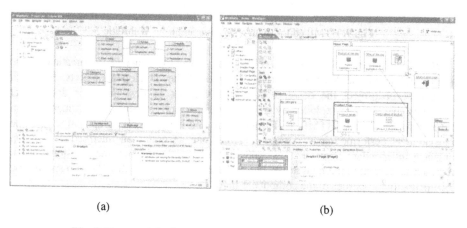

(a)   (b)

Fig. 8. Data model editor and hypertext model editor in WebRatio 5

Advanced text editors. Advanced editors are available within the tool for the design of XML descriptors, Java components, HTML structure of page templates and so on. The editors provide typical features like syntax highlighting, auto-completion, and so on. As an example, Figure 9 shows the HTML editor for page templates, with autocompletion and automatic inline help in action.

Model transformations and code generation. The WebML models are transformed with an MDE approach to increase the productivity of the development process. In particular, proper transformations are developed for automatic project documentation and code generation.

WebRatio code generators produce J2EE running Web applications starting from the WebML models. They are developed using the ANT, XSLT, and Groovy technologies. Groovy is an agile language using a Java-like syntax and fully integrated in the Java Platform, since it is actually translated to Java programs before being executed. It provides many features and facilities that are inspired by scripting languages, but also allows to exploit all the existing Java libraries. Further details on Groovy can be found at [16].

Fig. 9. HTML editor (with code completion) in WebRatio 5

With a similar technology, WebRatio is able to generate automatically the documentation of the WebML components and of the developed projects. For each component or project the designer can specify a set of descriptive or documental properties, that are then exploited by groovy transformations to generate documentation in different formats (PDF, HTML, RTF, and so on) and with different graphical styles. The translation is performed in two steps: the first one generates an intermediate markup language independent from the final outcome format; the second one transforms such intermediate format in the final result. Figure 10 shows the panels that allow to specify the documentation properties of the component Index Unit.

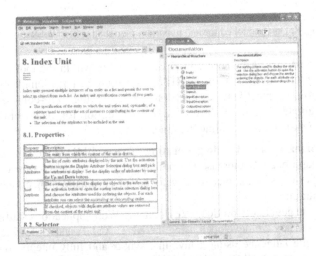

Fig. 10. Project documentation editor in WebRatio 5

Custom WebML components. Although existing WebML primitives and patterns should cover a large part of application requirements, the need of new functionalities and behaviours may arise. The WebRatio architecture is fully extensible, since it allows to specify new components (i.e., WebML units) and include them in the application design and code generation framework. A custom WebML unit consists of a component implemented by:

- a Java class that implements the service of the component; and
- a set of XML descriptors, defining the component interface in terms of inputs and outputs.

Appropriate *form-based editors* are available for the specification of new components. Thanks to these tools, the designer does not need to manually edit XML descriptors, because they are automatically generated by the tool upon completion of the properties within the forms. Figure 11 shows the editor of Index unit components;

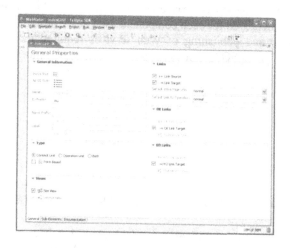

Fig. 11. Component definition editor in WebRatio 5

Script units. As mentioned before, WebRatio is fully extensible, allowing to define new WebML units at will. However, for simple needs, developing new units may not be needed, because a special generic WebML unit called *Script Unit* is available. This unit can be configured through an arbitrary Groovy script and can be immediately used in the models. Every time a script unit is placed in a Web project, the script source file must be specified. Writing a Groovy script is a simple and quick task, since it only requires basic knowledge of Java. The script that must be associated to the unit can include some peculiar aspects: the beginning of the script may contain comments that declare the inputs and outputs of the script unit, with a very straightforward syntax:

```
//inputs=INPUT1|INPUT2|...
//outputs=OUTPUT1|OUTPUT2|...
```

Inputs can be directly used as variables in the script code. The type of a input variable depends on which type of unit provides the input to the script unit, and therefore the script must be adapted to cope with different types of input variables (strings, array of strings, array of objects, objects, and so on). Outputs must be returned as a Java **map** object by the unit through the **return** instruction.

Runtime framework. The *run-time* WebRatio framework exploits a set of off-the-shelf object-oriented components for organizing the business tier:

- *Smart service creation:* services that implement units or business actions are created upon request, cached, and reused across multiple requesters;
- *Activity log:* a set of pre-built functions for logging each service is provided;
- *XML parsing and access:* access to the information stored in the XML unit descriptors is granted by standard parsing tools;
- *Connection pooling:* pre-built functions for dynamically managing a pool of database connection allow to optimize performance and reliability.

At runtime one single service class is deployed for each type of component (which is then instantiated with the smart service creation approach). Moreover, one runtime XML descriptor is deployed for each component used in the design (Figure 12).

The deployment and publishing of Web services required the extension of the WebRatio runtime with a SOAP listener able to accept SOAP requests.

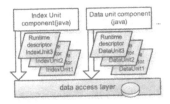

Fig. 12. Runtime view of Java components and XML descriptors for WebRatio units

Support of Rich Internet Applications. WebRatio 5 has been tailored to support also the new requirements imposed by Rich Internet Applications (RIAs), that are recognized to be one of the main innovations that lead to the Web 2.0 revolution. The advent of RIAs has allowed a much broader set of interaction possibilities within Web applications. Complex interactions such as drag and drop, dynamic resizing of visual components, and graphical editing of objects were once a prerogative of desktop applications, while now are available as standard patterns in Web applications too. These patterns clearly enable more flexible and usable interfaces, but at the same time require a more complicate application logics, both at client side and server side. Correspondingly, new runtime components and design patterns must be devised. This aspect has been heavily guided by industrial and end user requirements, provided by WebRatio customers. The tool covers the following aspects of RIAs:

- management of new hypertextual link behaviour, including partial page refresh, in-page popup windows, splash screens, dynamic tooltips, and waiting animations;
- interaction among page objects through drag and drop and dynamic dependencies;
- advanced data submission form specifications, including text autocompletion, on-event actions, and field dependencies.

Code generation and runtime support of these features have been developed by means of the best mix of opensource technologies, extensively exploiting the XMLhttpRequest method. The adopted runtime architectural solution consists of implementing each conceptual hypertext page with two dynamic pages that interact through XMLhttpRequest for providing the rich interface features: the first page is a back-end dynamic XML page that stores the data of interest for a specific navigation context; the second page is the front-end JSP page (including the required JavaScript needed for event management) that is shown to the user. The latter invokes extraction of pieces from the back-end XML page according to the user behaviour, and shows the results and the interface options to the user.

Collaborative work. WebRatio is integrated with CVS [17] for collaborative design and visual synchronization of project versions. WebRatio allows to compare a WebML project in the workspace with other versions or completely different projects. The compare operation can be performed in two different ways:

- Designers can compare two Web projects in the workspace, doing a local comparison. Different comparisons can be performed and the tools provides feedback on the two evaluated projects; or
- Designers can compare a Web project with the latest version committed on the CVS repository to which the project is connected. In this case, a synchronization operation is performed.

When a comparison is performed, comparison editors appear in the editor area. The differences between files are highlighted in the comparison editors, allowing to browse and copy changes between the compared resources. If the comparison is done on the entire Web project, the tool shows the Team Synchronizing Perspective, which lists all the changed resources. Then, it is possible to compare a single resource and to open the corresponding compare editor.

After a comparison is carried out, the WebRatio Compare Editor (Figure 13) opens in the editor area. The WebRatio Compare Editor allows to browse through all the differences and copy highlighted differences between the compared Web projects.

Fig. 13. Project comparison within WebRatio

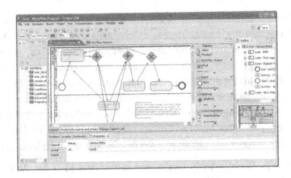

Fig. 14. The BPMN business process editor for Eclipse

Business Process Design. The long-term focus of the WebRatio 5 is oriented towards the full coverage of the development process. In this sense, some new *beta* pieces are being developed, for the coverage of new design steps. For instance, a new fully-integrated Business Process editor and WebML model generator [12] is now available (Figure 14 shows a sample snapshot). It generates skeletons of WebML models that comply with the BP specification and can be refined by the designer.

Industrial experience. Webratio has been widely used in real industrial scenarios for implementing big Web applications, for internet, intranet and extranet use. Typical WebRatio customers are large organizations that need to develop and maintain large and complex applications. Among the main success stories we can cite:

- The Acer EMEA and PanAmerica Marketing and Communication divisions, that have been using WebRatio since 2000, to develop all their B2C and B2B Web multilingual solutions. More than 60 complex Web applications are deployed in over 30 countries and are currently being maintained and evolved by only 5 developers working part-time on these projects (www.acer-euro.com).
- SIA (Società Interbancaria per l'Automazione), that is the leading Italian software integrator and solution provider in the banking sector and is using Webratio to develop complex Web front-ends for the customers, including the Italian bank association.
- Gemeaz (Accor Group), that has developed a large Web B2B application used by hundreds of Italian schools in order to manage the outsourced catering service.
- SIRMI, a leading Italian Marketing Research Company, that has developed an online Web application for integrating, managing and Web-deploying the databases of all the Italian IT companies; the B2C front-end supports powerful customizable Web queries and profile-based billing procedures.
- The Como Chamber of Commerce, that has commissioned the development of an innovative platform, based on web Services and Web front-ends for SMEs in homogeneous industrial districts; the platform supports corporate Web site publication, inter-company supply chain integration, product configuration, secure concurrent engineering, and technical documentation sharing.
- Politecnico di Milano, one of the largest European Technical Universities, that has developed with WebRatio the Web sites and CMS applications of the department of Electronics and Information and of the Department of Physics.

- Enel SpA, the main Italian electrical power supplier, that has been using WebRatio since 2005 for several intranet and extranet applications.
- Ikea Italia, that is now developing its new pieces of Web applications for internal and public use with WebRatio.

All these scenarios are characterized by high innovation, high complexity of the applications, and quick evolution of the requirements. The adopted MDE approach and the short development process, based on fast prototyping, greatly helps to fulfil the customers' requirements in a timely and effective manner. The new features of WebRatio 5 increase dramatically the productivity and the quality of the results.

Product and model comparison. Several models and languages have been developed for describing data-intensive Web applications; for a survey, see [18]. Among more recent projects, WebML is closer to those based on conceptual methodologies like W2000 [19] and OO-HMETHOD [20] (based on UML interaction diagrams), Araneus [21], Strudel [22] and OO-HDM [23].

Commercial vendors are proposing tools that claim to be oriented to Web development, however most of them have only adapted to Web environment from other fields. Among them, we can cite the following products: (i) Oracle JDeveloper 10g is heavily oriented to database design (http://www.oracle.com/tools), and provides UML-like data modeling and a very basic navigation model; (ii) Code Charge Studio (http://www.codecharge.com/studio), that provides a GUI for designing Web applications based on a set of predefined "page types", corresponding to database tables; (iii) Borland Enterprise Studio for Java (http://www.borland.com/estudiojava) is basically an advanced IDE tool, integrating some modeling features from TogetherJ and and basic WYSIWYG interfaces; (iv) Rational Rapid Developer (http://www.ibm.com/software/awdtools/rapiddeveloper) consists in a UML design tool, adapted to the Web environment, where automatic code generation is provided just for the business logic layers (model), while JSP (or analogous) pages must be coded by hand; (v) jABC (Java Application Building Center) is a project that offers a comprehensive modeling tool for complex Java applications, including Web applications but not limited to them. These tools either do not focus on the peculiar modeling needs of Web applications or work at a lower level with respect to WebRatio, providing a good development solution for the implementer, the Web designer or the programmer, but without really applying visual modeling and MDE approaches to Web application development. Moreover, none of them address with sufficient clarity the problems of application integration and business processes enactment.

Other tools, like ArgoUWE [25], are closer to WebRatio. ArgoUWE is a modeling tool that supports the UWE [26] methodology. Differently from WebML and WebRatio, UWE strictly adopts UML notations, MOF metamodeling, and MDA model transformation techniques, based on languages like QVT and ATL.

5 Conclusions

This paper illustrates the WebML language and methodology for designing Web applications, together with the WebRatio 5.0 tool based on the Eclipse framework that allows the model-driven specification of WebML models. The supported applications may include process management primitives, calls to Web services, and integration of heterogeneous data sources. WebML is a domain specific language (DSL) for specifying the design of complex, distributed, multi-actor, and adaptive applications deployed on the Web and on Service Oriented Architectures using Web Services. WebML was born in Academia but soon spun-off to the industrial field, where it faced the development of complex systems with requirements. This fruitful interplay of academic design and industrial experience made the language evolve from a closed notation for data-centric Web applications to an open and extensible framework for generalized component-based development. The core capability of WebML is expressing application interfaces as a network of collaborating components, which sit on top of the core business objects. WebML incorporates a number of built-in, off-the-shelf components for data-centric, process-centric, and Web Service-centric applications, and let developers define their own components, by wrapping existing software artifacts and reverse-engineering them. Thanks to the WebRatio tool, that eases the development of Web applications according to WebML methodology, application developers can concentrate only on the requirements of the application and on its high-level design, because code and project documentation are generated by the tool and correctness is automatically verified. The tool adopts the MDE approach to the design and development, carrying out a set of model transformations for producing additional design models, project documentation, and automatic code generation.

References

1. WebRatio (2008), http://www.webratio.com/
2. Boehm, B.: A Spiral Model of Software Development and Enhancement. IEEE Computer 21(5), 61–72 (1988)
3. Beck, K.: Embracing Change with Extreme Programming. IEEE Computer 32(10), 70–77 (1999)
4. Booch, G., Rumbaugh, J., Jacobson, I.: The Unified Modeling Language User Guide. Object Technology Series. Addison-Wesley, Reading (1999)
5. Conallen, J.: Building Web Applications with UML. Object Technology Series. Addison-Wesley, Reading (2000)
6. Ceri, S., Fraternali, P., Bongio, A., Brambilla, M., Comai, S., Matera, M.: Designing Data-Intensive Web Applications. Morgan Kaufmann, USA (2002)
7. WebML (2008), http://www.webml.org
8. Baresi, L., Fraternali, P., Tisi, M., Morasca, S.: Towards Model-Driven Testing of a Web Application Generator. In: Lowe, D.G., Gaedke, M. (eds.) ICWE 2005. LNCS, vol. 3579, pp. 75–86. Springer, Heidelberg (2005)
9. Fraternali, P., Lanzi, P.L., Matera, M., Maurino, A.: Model-Driven Web Usage Analysis for the Evaluation of Web Application Quality. Journal of Web Engineering 3(2), 124–152 (2004)
10. Manolescu, I., Brambilla, M., Ceri, S., Comai, S., Fraternali, P.: Model-Driven Design and Deployment of Service-Enabled Web Applications. ACM TOIT 5(3), 439–479 (2005)
11. Brambilla, M., Ceri, S., Passamani, M., Riccio, A.: Managing Asynchronous Web Services Interactions. In: Proc. of ICWS 2004, pp. 80–87 (2004)

12. Brambilla, M.: Generation of WebML Web Application Models from Business Process Specifications. In: Demo at ICWE 2006, pp. 85–86. ACM Press (2006)
13. Brambilla, M., Ceri, S., Fraternali, P., Manolescu, I.: Process Modeling in Web Applications. ACM TOSEM 15(4), 360–409 (2006)
14. Eclipse (2008), http://www.eclipse.org/
15. Eclipse GEF (2008), http://www.eclipse.org/gef/
16. Groovy (2008), http://groovy.codehaus.org/
17. CVS: Concurrent Versions System (2008), http://www.nongnu.org/cvs/
18. Fraternali, P.: Tools and Approaches for Developing Data-Intensive Web Applications: A Survey. ACM Computing Surveys 31(3), 227–263 (1999)
19. Baresi, L., Garzotto, F., Paolini, P.: From Web Sites to Web Applications: New Issues for Conceptual Modeling. In: Mayr, H.C., Liddle, S.W., Thalheim, B. (eds.) ER Workshops 2000. LNCS, vol. 1921, pp. 89–100. Springer, Heidelberg (2000)
20. Gómez, J., Cachero, C., Pastor, O.: Conceptual Modeling of Device-Independent Web Applications. IEEE MultiMedia 8(2), 26–39 (2001)
21. Merialdo, P., Atzeni, P., Mecca, G.: Design and development of data-intensive Websites: the Araneus approach. ACM TOIT 3(1), 49–92 (2003)
22. Fernandez, M.F., Florescu, D., Kang, J., Levy, A.Y., Suciu, D.: Catching the Boat with Strudel: Experiences with a Web-Site Management System. SIGMOD 1998, 414–425 (2000)
23. Rossi, L., Schmid, H., Lyardet, F.: Engineering Business Processes in Web Applications: Modeling and Navigation Issues. In: Third International Workshop on Web Oriented Software Technology, Oviedo, pp. 81–89 (2003)
24. Steffen, B., Margaria, T., Nagel, R., Jörges, S., Kubczak, C.: Model-Driven Development with the jABC. In: Bin, E., Ziv, A., Ur, S. (eds.) HVC 2006. LNCS, vol. 4383, pp. 92–108. Springer, Heidelberg (2007)
25. Knapp, A., Koch, N., Moser, F., Zhang, G.: ArgoUWE: A CASE Tool for Web Applications. In: EMSISE Workshop (2003)
26. Hennicker, R., Koch, N.: A UML-based Methodology for Hypermedia Design. In: Evans, A., Kent, S., Selic, B. (eds.) UML 2000. LNCS, vol. 1939, Springer, Heidelberg (2000)

Author Index

Acerbis, Roberto   392
Åkerblom, Beatrice   178
Apel, Sven   121
Artho, Cyrille   22
Aydal, Emine G.   278

Bettini, Lorenzo   198
Bishop, Judith   356
Bongio, Aldo   392
Bono, Viviana   198
Bouillon, Philipp   41
Bouraqadi, Noury   258
Brambilla, Marco   392
Brodie, Michael L.   1
Butti, Stefano   392

Ceri, Stefano   392
Clarke, Dave   178
Cohen, Tal   100

Denker, Marcus   218
Dingel, Juergen   336
Diskin, Zinovy   336
Ducasse, Stéphane   218

Easterbrook, Steve   336
Eichstädt-Engelen, Thomas   60
Ernst, Erik   161

Fraternali, Piero   392

Gil, Joseph (Yossi)   100
Grondin, Guillaume   258
Großkinsky, Eric   41

Hagiya, Masami   22
Horspool, R. Nigel   356

Krahn, Holger   297
Kuhlemann, Martin   121

Leue, Stefan   238
Leungwattanakit, Watcharin   22
Lopez-Herrejon, Roberto   121

Maman, Itay   100
Meyer, Bertrand   316
Müller, Peter   316

Nielsen, Anders Bach   161
Nordio, Martin   316

Östlund, Johan   178

Parizek, Pavel   2
Phink, Yuri   80
Plasil, Frantisek   2

Rivera, José E.   141
Rosenmüller, Marko   121
Rumpe, Bernhard   297

Schaaf, Martin   60
Ştefănescu, Alin   238
Steimann, Friedrich   41, 60
Strommer, Michael   372
Suen, Mathieu   218

Tanabe, Yoshinori   22

Utting, Mark   278

Vallecillo, Antonio   141
Venneri, Betti   198
Vercouter, Laurent   258
Völkel, Steven   297

Wei, Wei   238
Wimmer, Manuel   372
Woodcock, Jim   278
Wrigstad, Tobias   178

Yehudai, Amiram   80